HIGHER EDUCATION:
Handbook of Theory and Research

Volume VIII

Associate Editors

HIGHER EDUCATION:
Handbook of Theory and Research

Volume VIII

Edited by

John C. Smart
University of Illinois at Chicago

Published under the sponsorship of
The Association for Institutional Research (AIR)
and
The Association for the Study of Higher Education (ASHE)

AGATHON PRESS
New York

© 1992 Agathon Press
5648 Riverdale Avenue
Bronx, NY 10471-2106

ISBN: 0-87586-099-0
ISSN: 0882-4126

Library of Congress Catalog Card Number: 86-642109

Printed in the United States

Contents

The Contributors

JAMES T. AUSTIN is an assistant professor of psychology at The Ohio State University. He received his Ph.D. in 1987 from Virginia Polytechnic Institute and State University in industrial and organizational psychology. His research on goal-setting, criterion measurement, and structural equation modeling has appeared in industrial-organizational pyschology and quantitative journals

JAMES BESS is Professor of Higher Education at New York University, where he specializes in organizational theory, leadership theory, governance, institutional assessment, and comparative higher education. He received his Ph.D. from the University of California at Berkeley in 1971 and has degrees from Harvard (M.B.A.), New York University (M.A.) and Cornell (B.A.). The author or editor of five books and many articles and book chapters, Professor Bess was the recipient of a Fulbright and other research grants to Japan, where he spent a sabbatical year in 1986-87. He has served as a consultant to a number of colleges and universities. Professor Bess is a member of the Academy of Management, the Association for the Study of Higher Education, the American Educational Research Association, and the Association for Institutional Research.

JOHN M. BUDD is an associate professor with the School of Library and Information Science at Louisiana State University. He has published papers on the application of bibliometrics in the *Journal of Higher Education*, *College and Research Libraries*, and *Scientometrics*. His other research interests include extensions of communication theory to the library environment. His book *The Library and Its Users: The Communication Process* (Greenwood Press) was published in the summer of 1992.

DARRELL A. CLOWES teaches community college/higher education and educational foundation courses at Virginia Polytechnic Institute and State University. The focus of his research is curriculum issues in postsecondary education. He has published in such journals as *Community College Review*, *Journal of College Student Personnel*, *Journal of Higher Education*, and *Journal of Developmental Education*. He is editor of the *Community Services Catalyst*, and has been or currently is on the editorial boards of *Review of Higher Education*, *Community/Junior College Research Quarterly*, and *Journal of Developmental Education*. He is an active member of AERA, ASHE, and CUC.

CLIFTON F. CONRAD is Professor of Higher Education in the Department of Educational Administration, University of Wisconsin-Madison. Dr. Conrad's research has focused on curriculum in higher education: liberal and general education, academic change, and program quality. He has published 10 books and monographs and many articles, among them *The Undergraduate Curriculum* (1978), and *Curriculum in Transition: Perspectives on the Undergraduate Experience* (co-edited, 1990).

DAVID D. DILL is Professor of Education and Public Policy and Assistant to the Chancellor for Planning at The University of North Carolina, Chapel Hill. He is currently president of the Society for College and University Planning. His research and writings have focused on the organizational design and management of academic and R&D organizations. His current research examines academic standards and public policy.

MICHAEL J. DUNKIN is founding Professor of Teacher Education at the University of New South Wales—St. George Campus in Sydney, Australia. He was formerly Director of the Centre for Teaching and Learning at the University of Sydney. He is best known for his writings and research on teaching and teacher education and was the author, with Bruce J. Biddle, of *The Study of Teaching*. More recently he wrote the chapter on research on teaching in higher education for the third edition of *The Handbook of Research on Teaching* and edited *The International Encyclopedia of Teaching and Teacher Education*. He currently edits the journal *Teaching and Teacher Education: An International of Research and Studies*. His recent research has focused on orientations to teaching of newly appointed and award-winning university teachers. He has also published research in the area of determinants of academic career advancement of Australian academics.

DENNIS E. HINKLE is Dean of Education at Butler University. His research interests include the development and application of quantitative techniques to issues in higher education. He is coauthor of the textbook *Applied Statistics for the Behavioral Sciences* (2nd ed.) with W. Wiersma and S. Jurs.

HERBERT W. MARSH is Professor of Education (Research) at the University of Western Sydney (Macarthur) in Australia. His current research interests are students' evaluations of teaching effectiveness, self-concept, school effectiveness, and covariance structural modeling. He has published extensively in these areas in a wide variety of educational and psychological research journals. He is the author of the set of three self-concept instruments, the Self Description Questionnaire (SDQ) I, II, and III, and the student evaluation instrument Students' Evaluations of Educational Quality (SEEQ).

JOHN H. MILAM, JR. is Institutional Research Coordinator at George Mason University. He has held other institutional research positions at West Virginia University and the University of Houston. He received his Ph.D. in higher education from the University of Virginia and his M.A. and B.A. degrees from Goddard College. His research interests include alternative paradigms, organizational theory, executive information systems, microcomputer applications, adult development theory, and nontraditional learning.

GARY RHOADES is a faculty member at the University of Arizona's Center for the Study of Higher Education. His research interests include educational change, reform, and policy making, with a particular emphasis on the actions and beliefs of educational professionals and the impact these have on educational organizations and systems. Currently, he is studying the commercialization of science and the renegotiation of the terms of professional labor, connecting changes in the academy to conditions in the political economy of higher education, including the various apparatuses of "the state."

PATRICIA A. SCOTT is a Ph.D. student in the Department of Educational Administration, University of Wisconsin-Madison. Her research interests include the desegregation of higher education and college student learning and development.

DAVID S. WEBSTER is Associate Professor of Educational Administration and Higher Education at Oklahoma State University. He is the author of *Academic Quality Rankings of American Colleges and Universities* (Springfield, IL: Charles C Thomas, 1986) and has published articles on academic quality rankings in *Change, Higher Education, History of Education Quarterly, History of Higher Education Annual, Journal of the History of the Behavioral Sciences, Research in Higher Education, Review of Higher Education,* and other journals.

ROBERT A. YAFFEE is a statistical consultant at the Academic Computing Facility, Courant Institute of Mathematical Sciences, New York University. He received his Ph.D. from the Graduate Faculty of Political and Social Science of the New School for Social Research. He has lectured on logistic regression and ordinal logit models and has also applied these techniques to research on addiction severity among pathological gamblers for the Maryland Task Force on Gambling Addiction.

Collegiality: Toward a Clarification of Meaning and Function

James L. Bess
New York University

INTRODUCTION

Most academics fervently wish they could work in a campus environment that is infused with collegiality. From beginning days at graduate school, would-be scholars are told that the spirit of collegiality is the *sine qua non* of both an effective and salubrious college or university work environment. Without it, according to current belief, the ideals of good teaching and collaborative working relationships can too easily be replaced with the pettiness of bureaucratic squabbling, or worse. Early in the faculty career, however, the discovery is usually made that the ideal of collegiality seems both unrealistic and unachievable, except for very occasional pleasant aberrations from the status quo. Indeed, despite some tacit appreciation, most working academics do not even know what collegiality is. They do claim that it is usually not present on their own campuses—but they wish it were.

There are at least two reasons for attempting to provide some clarification of the meanings of collegiality. First, it behooves us to understand more fully so ubiquitous a concept in higher education, both as it is purveyed conceptually and as it is invoked in daily practical matters. If collegiality is highly honored in theory but widely breached in practice, then change is in order and understanding its first prerequisite. Second, current literature on successful leadership in industry suggests that the management of corporate ''culture'' may be important to the improvement of organizational effectiveness. Collegiality appears to be related to culture, but the connections need clarification. It also appears to connote something about decision-making patterns, as well as how people, particularly faculty, behave in colleges and universities. Again, there is some considerable ambiguity about these kinds of organizational patterns and activities

The author wishes to express his gratitude to several people who commented on preliminary drafts of this article: Oscar Chase, Floyd Hammack, James Hoyt, Gabriel Moran, Theodore Marchese, and the student members of a governance seminar at New York University. They may or may not agree with its ultimate content as presented here. Some of these ideas in less developed form have appeared previously in a book (Bess, 1988).

1

(Thompson and Tuden, 1959; Waters, 1989). This chapter, then, is an extended exploration of some conceptualizations and frameworks for thinking about a complex and important notion in higher education. The closer agreement can be reached about what constitutes collegiality, the better able its elements can be controlled in ways that are beneficial to the educational enterprise.

The chapter falls into several parts, dealing respectively with the *meaning* of collegiality, its *origins* or *sources*, its *functions* or *uses*, and with *needed research*. Since the initial aim is to clarify the "meaning" of a term—collegiality—it is necessary at the outset to indicate very briefly some philosophical assumptions that underlie the discussion. In the first part, therefore, three approaches to clarifying the meaning of collegiality are introduced: an ordinary language perspective, a value premise analysis, and a functionalist conceptualization. Following this methodologic propaedeutic, the paper continues with a more substantive discussion within the three formats. The first and longest section is divided into the three distinct commonplace domains of meaning in higher education in which the term collegiality is embedded: academic "culture," organizational "structure," and social "behavior." The relationships of the meanings within and across each context are discussed in this section. As will be seen, the argument is made that a disaggregation of the assumed singularity of the meaning of collegiality across the domains is necessary to appreciate its complexity and the uses to which people claim it is put. In this section also is a lengthy discussion of the meaning of the structure supporting the governance process when it operates in an allegedly collegial mode.

The second section looks to the core beliefs and values that underlie the essence of the meaning of collegiality in the three domains. The section considers the meaning of collegiality as it embodies such terms as "order," "rationality," and "trust." All organizations undergo periodic departures from behaviors that manifest these values, often for good reason. As Max Weber noted some time ago (1946, p. 238):

> Collegiate administration disappears when from the point of view of the ruler's interests a strictly unified administrative leadership appears to be more important than thoroughness in the preparation of administrative decisions.

Similar departures take place in allegedly collegial organizations. Blankenship (1977) asks:

> What happens in collegial organizations when a single member acts to force a change in the symbolic order or in systems of joint activity, as perhaps by administrative fiat? The answer lies in the conduciveness of the situation to collective negotiation. *A form of collective behavior may be signaled as a control mechanism.* (Emphasis added.)

That is, in some, but not all situations, when administrative fiat is seen as a violation of the "sense of community" or of shared governance, the autocratic perpetrator will be accused of violating the norms of the culture and will be dealt with accordingly. As will be seen below, such controls by the collectivity, surprisingly, may take place more when collegiality is *absent* than when it is present. In any case, understanding the nature of these seeming departures from reason and of the organizational reactions to them allows a more definitive characterization of the meaning of collegiality and its potential force in colleges and universities.

The third section of the chapter further clarifies the meaning of collegiality by revealing its functions in institutions of higher education. Borrowing heavily from Parsonian theory, the discussion focuses on latent social and organizational functions served by collegiality, as these may bring to light the meanings attached to the concept. A summary section follows that integrates the various meanings that have been considered in the three sections. The chapter concludes with some suggestions for future research.

PART I. METHODS OF SEEKING THE "MEANING" OF COLLEGIALITY

The search for an understanding of what things mean has long occupied philosophers. Various philosophic tools to aid in the search have been developed. While it is beyond the scope of this paper to engage in a philosophic discourse on how "meaning" itself may be understood and used (cf. Ogden and Richards, 1923), it is important to state some of the philosophic premises of the examination of the meaning of collegiality so that the aims of this paper can be better understood. Below, three common modes of establishing meaning are delineated to show their relevance for examining the meaning of collegiality.

The first mode seeks meaning in the clarification of the objective referents for a term. In one of the early writings of Ludwig Wittgenstein (1961) one finds a reasonably close approximation to this perspective. He notes:

> In everyday language it very frequently happens that the same word has different modes of signification—and so belongs to different symbols—or that two words that have different modes of signification are employed in propositions in what is superficially the same way.
>
> In order to avoid such errors we must make use of a sign-language that excludes them by not using the same sign for different symbols and by not using in a superficially similar way signs that have different modes of signification . . . (Wittgenstein, 1971, p. 29)

It is important, in other words, for purposes of clarity that there be unambiguous referents for a term. As Barrett (1978, p. 169) explains:

> One cardinal point in Wittgenstein's treatment of language is the identification, or at least close linking, of meaning with use. If you want to know the meaning of a word, he tells us, look to its use.

This is not to claim in this discussion that our present use of the term "collegiality" is meaningless as, perhaps, an analytic philosophic framework might suggest. Rather, the approach here is one of "ordinary language."

In this context, the definition of collegiality is "nominal" rather than real. The word "collegiality" on some occasions means the same thing to people discussing it, but different things at other times. It has no intrinsic, objective nature. Modern social science methods reflect a more pragmatic recognition of the Wittgenstein assertion. An investigator usually begins with only a vague notion of the phenomenon of interest. He or she then assembles a variety of ascriptions that people give to the concept and operationalizes these in some kind of test instrument, which is then administered to various samples. The empirically established relationships among the concepts are then calculated. Over time and use, the meaning of the concept comes to be understood as comprising one or more of the ascriptions. One form of the validity of a concept is thus established through an analysis of the relationships among the parts contributed by empirically determined interpretations. In the matter of this paper, collegiality, therefore, can be given meaning through an analysis of the ways in which commonsensical descriptions of its existence are seemingly correlated with one another (leaving to others, perhaps, the task of preparing more quantifiably exact tests and doing the statistical measurements to satisfy positivist social science requirements).

One further point of procedural clarification must be introduced in this section. In order to comprehend the meanings of collegiality using a validation approach, the domains in which the term is found must be circumscribed. It would not do, for example, to explicate the meaning of the word "pass" without knowing whether the context is education, football, a bridge card game, or a mountain range. Indeed, if the contexts overlap, the meanings may be contingently related. The domain of interest here is institutions of higher education, with the geographically bounded campus as the unit of analysis. Limits of space preclude discussion of collegiality as a phenomenon of the academic profession as a whole, since it is a subject of some considerable complexity with a quite different set of issues (cf. Clark, 1983; Fox, 1985).

Meaning established through validation can also be understood in terms of "measurement" theory. As Dubin (1969, p. 206) notes, the "validity" of a term is indicated by a consensus that a concept can be measured through the use of some means of assessing empirically its value across different situations. In the case at hand, the value of collegiality on a college campus might be determined by some test that informed social scientists agree measures it. Lacking such a test, the consensus of occupants of the culture where the concept is used can be substituted. That is, it can be assumed that informal and unobtrusive measures of the degree of collegiality can be obtained by knowledgeable persons in the field.

As will be seen, however, what is suggested in this chapter is that consensus about collegiality has not been reached; hence, the informal assessments used to measure it yield confusing, if not conflicting, information about its meaning and value. As Dubin continues, consensus breaks down when an investigator "raises questions about the empirical indicator based upon evidence that is independent of the circumstances of its employment." Dubin offers as an illustration the "deconstruction" by Allison Davis of the standard intelligence test into intelligence and cultural experience. So also, in this paper, the term collegiality will be decomposed into its constituent parts. The resulting clarification of meaning may not yield one and only one definition of collegiality, but will reveal its many extant meanings and functions, even if they may seem contradictory. Indeed, as will be seen, how one defines collegiality may depend in part on whether one works in an institution where it exists (cf. Argyris and Schon, 1974) or even one's gender (Glazer, 1990).

There is, perhaps, a misleading simplicity in this method, however. As Argyris and Schön (1982) note, some kinds of knowledge are "tacit" (cf. Polanyi, 1967) and do not lend themselves to deconstruction. Indeed, careful analytic scrutiny may do a disservice to the pragmatic functions being served by the knowledge. On the other hand, say Argyris and Schon of "theories in use," if the persons using the knowledge (or concept, in this case) are ineffective, the exposition of the tacit meaning given will allow its misuse to be corrected. In short, once more using Argyris and Schon, a gap between "espoused theories" and "theories in use" calls for an inquiry into meaning. This chapter then, explores the possibility and meaning of such a gap.

A second approach to assessing the meaning of collegiality is to look to the "values" that drive its use. So, for example, we may gain some understanding of what the term "America" stands for by examining the essential values that are claimed for it. Values in this case refer to basic assumptions and beliefs about individual motivation and social conditions that are said to be quintessentially fundamental and human, even as the strength of those assumptions and beliefs may vary in different cultures or situations (cf. Hofstede, 1980). Collegiality, in a similar way, may be understood by exploring the values that informed people might claim undergird its presence.

The third and last avenue to understanding the meaning of collegiality is through the functions it performs. Just as, for example, on a mundane level, we understand what "teeth" are by noting their function in mastication, or, we come to know what "organizational strategy" means by looking to the outcomes of systems where it is or is not employed, so also we may understand collegiality by explicating its functions in a college or university.

In sum, three approaches to the clarification of meaning—validation, valuation, and functional analysis—will be used in this essay.

PART II. COLLEGIALITY AS CULTURE,
STRUCTURE AND BEHAVIOR

It is necessary at the outset to distinguish among meanings of the term collegiality as an "organizational" phenomenon. In the current literature on organizational behavior, one of the knowledge domains seemingly relevant to collegiality, three distinguishable levels or foci of attention are commonly suggested: (1) "culture"; (2) "structure", and (3) "behavior." In examining the notion of collegiality in these terms, some of the various interpretations usually posed may become clearer, particularly if the connections across the three levels are revealed. What follows is a characterization of collegiality in each of these three focal areas. In each case a general understanding of the levels themselves precedes the discussion of the ways that collegiality is manifested in them.

The Meanings of Culture

Culture in the current professional lexicon generally refers to the folkways, mores, ethos, or values found in a circumscribed social system. It is manifested at various levels in social systems. As Parsons and Platt (1973, p. 36) note:

> Institutionalization gives rise to a zone of interpenetration between the cultural and the social systems, the two components of which, through composed parts of both systems, crosscut one another and constitute one subsystem.

At the grandest level of human society at large, values found to be cross-culturally imbedded in the human condition have an impact on behavior. Other forms of culture exist at the national, community, and institutional level. In working groups, culture is translated into norms that guide individual behavior toward or away from organizational objectives. For the system of concern here, organizations, culture connotes the normative framework which informally and subtlely influences and is influenced by the forms of decision making (or governance) in institutions and the behavior of the people making those decisions.

The ways in which organizational culture in general affects organizations is a currently salient topic, with copious writing about the profit-making sector (e.g., Deal and Kennedy, 1982; Allaire, 1984; Schein, 1985), about higher education (e.g., Dill, 1982; Kuh and Whitt, 1988; Chaffee and Tierney, 1988), and about new management approaches in Japan (e.g., Pascale and Athos, 1981). Schein suggests that organizational culture represents the accumulation of basic assumptions and beliefs that organizational participants have developed and share widely as they learn to adapt to outside environments and to manage internal conflicts. These values and beliefs are taken for granted. That is, most organizational participants, as they interact with one another, are not conscious of them in the normal routine of decision making. This is not necessarily to say that people do not "know" what counts or what is important; it is only to say that most actions, especially in strong, tightly coupled structures, are taken without constant recourse to the underlying value framework. Both recruitment and socialization reinforce the value commonality.

The management of culture has long been recognized as critical to organizational effectiveness (Selznick, 1957; Simon, 1957; Barnard, 1966). Some writers (e.g., Kerr and Jermier, 1978) have suggested further that culture (among other things) may act as a "substitute for leadership"—an incorporeal supervisor, ever present to help make sure that things get done "in the company way", and, importantly, in a fashion that removes some of the stigma of asymmetrical power in hierarchical interpersonal interactions. Culture is thus Weberian charismatic authority where that authority resides in the corpus as a whole, rather than in any one individual. Others—e.g., critical theorists—have suggested that the management of culture constitutes self-serving manipulation of the organization by those in power. Finally, from outside of the organization, professional norms and occupational norms enter at all levels, fuse with member values and often have an interactive effect on behavior (Clark, 1983).

There are, then, various sources of influence on organizational behavior that find their basis in culture. It is important to note that culture not only has a direct impact on behavior but that it generates structures that support values. These latter, in turn, profoundly influence behavior. Thus, in a college or university, one finds behavior influenced by the values of the organization and by its organizational structure which in turn, in Marxian manner, both reflect and reinforce the cultural influences.

One final point before discussing collegiality as a cultural phenomenon. It is necessary to stress that culture in an organization is partly a representation of the individuals who comprise the organization. Since organizations, particularly colleges and universities, may be complex and loosely coupled (i.e., many decentralized departments, often with few or no connections; separations of faculty and administrations in terms both of organizational and spatial boundaries), "culture" may not be homogeneous, and even in its heterogeneity may be inconsistent or/and ambiguous. While at the level of the academic department, there may be a fairly well agreed upon set of norms, there may be conflicts between these norms and those at the institutional, professional, or national levels. As will be seen below, these conflicts have a profound impact on the degree of institutionalization of collegiality and on the perceived and enacted roles and behavior of the faculty member.

Collegiality as Culture

Collegiality as culture (here labeled "c-collegiality" to differentiate it from some other forms of collegiality discussed below) is simultaneously part of the culture of an institution and part of the larger, generic academic culture, endemic to the profession as a whole (Clark, 1983). Present in varying degrees on different campuses, it is also a "feeder" culture, in Meryl Reis Louis' terms (Louis, 1985), one which is introduced into most academic organizations by virtue of the prior professionalization, socialization and work experience of their primary work force, the faculty.

Collegial Culture As Political Value

To be more precise about the cultural meaning of c-collegiality, however, we must ask what are its underlying assumptions and values. Since meaning at the cultural level has its referents in the reality of action, or practice, there are at least two common interpretations, one essentially political, the second, social or interpersonal. In the first place, the political connotation of c-collegiality refers to a set of values and beliefs surrounding the activity of "participatory democracy," particularly the idea that "stakeholders" (cf. Mitroff, 1983; Keeton, 1971) must be heard, and in certain instances, enfranchised to vote. (Note that this discussion of the political character of c-collegiality should not be confused with the later discussion of the structural character of collegiality. Here, the concern is with beliefs and ideologies.)

C-collegiality, however, differs from the pure political ideology of democracy partly because of its setting in an organization, rather than a polity, and partly because a collegiate organization is made up, in prominent part, of professionals. C-collegiality thus conveys the notion that members of the organization agree to *give up* some civic/political rights of participation on the assumption that "professional" values are sufficiently suffused in the organization as to protect individual rights from infringement by a contrary, indifferent, or uncaring majority or from a capricious organizational authority. As March and Simon (1958) report, when there is an assumption of consensus on basic values and goals (e.g., professionalism), disagreements are adjudicated through "analytic" modes. This recourse thus mitigates the need to resort to the zero-sum, sub-optimizing, political bargaining that appears to be antithetical to the idea of collegiality.

For example, on a campus dominated by c-collegiality, a faculty member's right to teach idiosyncratically need *not* be protected by either direct or representative democracy, since there is a strong belief among the faculty in the power and ubiquity of the value of academic freedom among academics as professionals. It is important to note, however, that in the absence of c-collegiality, professional values alone will not ensure the preservation of individual freedom, nor will they necessarily contribute to the enhancement of felicitous interpersonal relations. Professionalism provides a base set of internalized directives (as, for example, through the "norms of science"—see Merton, 1973), but is not the same as collegiality, either in a political or interactional sense. As will be explored later in the section on s-collegiality, collegiality seems to connote a decision-making structure with rights of participation to preserve some aspects of professionalism which, oddly, do not need protection in the presence of collegiality. A first understanding of the meaning of c-collegiality, then, is as a rather anomalous idea of a participatory right that may not need to be exercised in an organization of professionals. That is, given c-collegiality, a formal participatory governance structure designed to protect professional values is virtually unnecessary. Absent c-collegiality, however, members of the system seek some form of participation as a means of protecting their professional prerogatives. Anomalously, then, when allegedly "collegial" governance structures seem to be hard at work, it may reflect the absence of collegiality at the cultural level!

Collegial Culture as Modified Reciprocity Norms

The second interpretation of c-collegiality as a set of norms and values encompasses the idea of reciprocity—the felt obligation incurred by one party in a social setting in response to an interaction involving an uneven transfer of goods or services by the other. As one of the most fundamental of norms in all social settings (Levi-Strauss, 1949; Gouldner, 1960; Blau, 1964, p. 92ff), reciprocity as an ideal is especially strongly espoused in colleges and universities that are called collegial. The strength of the norm of reciprocity stems from "psychic bonding" in a social system—"psychic enhancements of conjugal or collaborative ties" (Kubiak, 1988; cf. Batson, 1990). When faculty or others identify with the college or its members, they feel an obligation to those members when they receive benefits from them.

Collegiality, however, seems to go beyond reciprocity—indeed, perhaps even to abrogate it. The norm of reciprocity refers to a belief in the necessity to restore the balance of favors among two or more persons, whereas collegiality means more. It is usually taken to mean the obligation not only to settle social debts to others and the community at large, but to go further than simple equity. It connotes a cultural value supporting the giving of favors altruistically without concern for a dyadic *quid pro quo* repayment. Sahlins (1965) calls this "generalized reciprocity" (though see Clark and Mills, 1979). Given c-collegiality, faculty do not consciously seek to become social creditors in their interactions with colleagues. Collegiality seems to mitigate the calculus of one-on-one social accounting on college campuses, replacing it with a more generalized, if subconscious, faith that the benevolence of the system as a whole will redound ultimately to individual benefit. As will be seen below, this willingness to renounce the need for immediate reciprocation has its base in a trust in the long range beneficence of the system (cf. Gamson, 1968; Befu, 1989; Dahl, 1984, pp. 55–57), a central tenet of collegial value.

In sum, c-collegiality actually embraces two essential ideals that seem contrary to the commonsensical view—the notion of *limited* political protection in the presence of professionalism; and the suspension of the expectation for reciprocity in interpersonal behavior.

Collegiality as Structure

At the second level of meaning noted above, another conception of collegiality emerges. It is grounded in our assumptions about and understanding of an organization's "structure"—usually decision-making structure. In discussing collegiality as structure, it is identified here as "s-collegiality," in contrast to c-collegiality above. It is not uncommon to hear statements in academic circles that decisions are made through a "collegial structure." Hence, it is important to understand more fully what such a structure for collegial decision making is, then relate it to the notion of c-collegiality sketched above.

One of the most common of terms found in the organizational theory literature, *structure* is also variously defined (Huber and McDaniel, 1986). In general, it is conceived as a pattern or design for the division of labor in an organization, the flow of work across units, the accountability and authority system within and across the disparate parts, as a "rational" system for parsimonious decision making within each part, and as a mode for integrating the disparate parts. S-collegiality usually is concerned primarily with the latter two. It typically connotes, on the one hand, the configuration of authority for making decisions within and between organizational units in a college or university (horizontally and vertically), and, on the other, the mode for adjudicating among competing claims by those units (be they organizational units or faculty members). It seems to be associated more with ongoing and regular conditions of governance rather than with the initial organization or subsequent reorganization of faculty into specialized curricular or research units. Since these macro-organizational issues usually arise infrequently, a "collegial structure" is more likely to convey a meaning having to do with mechanisms of cross-unit coordination/collaboration in the more routine matters of academic decision making (such as in curricular decisions) and the college or university-wide checks and balances against variations in unit quality in personnel decisions.

A brief explanatory digression is needed here. In crisis conditions calling for non-routine actions or in unstable periods of rapid organizational change, the idea of collegiality is *not* usually invoked. It is not that decisions of constitutional dimensions involving massive overhaul of a system are not often made through a collegial structure. It is just that the fluidity and ambiguity of the structure of governance and conflict adjudication as the organization undergoes significant change makes labeling the system as collegial problematic. The mere appearance of democratic governance even in unusual or crisis conditions does not ensure that collegiality is at work. The commonplace notion of collegiality is not usually employed to describe the organizational structure of a college campus undergoing major change. Stucture, and thus the term "collegial structure," is reserved for more long-term, static conditions of academic organizational life.

Colleges and universities are complex organizations of professionals and non-professionals, operating under diverse and often ambiguous authority systems.

Decisions made in these institutions fall into the usual array of organizational categories: resource acquisition and allocation (including personnel), product or service design, goal and image formation and promulgation, establishment of cross-unit linkages, and motivation and commitment enhancement (cf. Parsons, 1960; Helsabeck, 1973). The dual track system of administration and faculty decision making yields an amorphous authority structure that at different times takes on the characteristics of any of the six Aristotelian classes of political systems (monarchy, aristocracy, polity, tyranny, oligarchy, or democracy) or in contemporary terms a bureaucracy (Baldridge et al., 1978), a "professional bureaucracy" (Mintzberg, 1983, or an anarchy (Cohen and March, 1974). The exact placement depends on a number of contingencies including the type of institution (university, college, community college), its size and other characteristics (Blau, 1973; its structural characteristics: e.g., bureaucracy (Baldridge et al., 1978), "professional bureaucracy" (Mintzberg, 1983, anarchy (Cohen and March, 1974); and the nature of the particular decision (Childers, 1981; Hackman, 1985). The decisions in the categories above are assigned to various members of the organization with authority sometimes vested directly and finally in the line decision makers (faculty), sometimes in the bureaucracy, sometimes in both, and sometimes in neither. As will be seen, s-collegiality is not necessarily synonymous with political democracy.

C-collegiality in the common usage seems to refer to the institutionalization of the rights of stakeholders in decisions to participate in the decisions affecting them. It refers also to the recourse that participants have both to adjudicate conflicts as well as to redress grievances through expert rather than organizational authority. (See Bacharach and Lawler, 1980, for a fuller discussion of "bases" of authority).

The ambiguity of the meaning of collegiality lies at least in part in the lack of clarity about the structures for decision making that are appropriate for each of the decisions noted above (again, for example, resource allocation versus product—i.e., curriculum—design decisions). Certain structures do seem to conform unequivocally in the minds of all constituents to the criteria of stakeholder and/or expert authority involvement. That is, for certain decisions the extant structure allows either experts or stakeholders to participate, and there is little disagreement over ultimate jurisdiction. For other kinds of decisions, there is either ambiguity or disagreement about the desired or in-place structure. Thus, to determine whether a structure for decision making is viewed as collegial requires an examination of the degree to which it does not meet standards of expertise and stakeholder rights for particular kinds of decisions. Note that the question of *why* a structure is or is not collegial is not addressed here. There are, in fact, several theories of organizational participation in decision making that identify independent variables (such as expertise and stake) that normatively need to be addressed in order for "effective" decisions to be made (see, for example, Vroom and

Yetton, 1973; Vroom and Jago, 1988; Hoy and Miskel, 1987). These theories are more concerned with vertical dyad linkages (e.g., leader to followers), however, than with the structures themselves. They deal rather grossly with process issues rather than longer standing structural conditions for decision making.

Alternative Structures for Decision Making
Bearing in mind the expert and stakeholder criteria, let us now consider in greater depth some alternative structures for decision making that some might allege exist under the common-sense conception of a collegial system. Because workers in organizations need to coordinate their activities, and because it is important to organizational effectiveness for them to feel part of a single larger entity (instead of optimizing only a part of it), organizations must develop ways for linking individuals and departments with one another and for creating environments and incentives for people to collaborate. Many possibilities exist. Which ones are used depends on many contingencies, as noted above. Colleges obviously differ from manufacturing plants (and from one another) in terms of control, educational objectives, diversity of disciplinary approaches to teaching and research, degrees of professionalism, and numbers of students and faculty. They differ also accordingly in structure. Furthermore, in colleges and universities, in contrast to some profit-making organizations, the "technology" (of teaching and research)—i.e., the unpredictability of raw material inputs and the unavailability of ready behavior repertories suitable to processing the inputs (cf. Perrow, 1970)—makes it necessary for decision-making structures to incorporate non-programmed or programmable decision makers (i.e., human beings) as part of the structure itself.

Collegiality as structure, then, refers to a particular controlling and integrating mode of organizational design, with authority for required activities distributed in a unique way—usually involving the allocation of rights of participation for organizational members (modified, as noted earlier, by the values of c-collegiality). This definition of s-collegiality—as control and integration—may seem at first somewhat narrow and restrictive. Nonetheless, it seems to cover the vast majority of activities that most academics would ascribe to collegial structures. Recall that formalized cross-departmental decision making is a mode of ensuring that organizations maximize the organizational goals of the *organization as a whole*, rather than those of any one sub-unit. This dedication to the common, rather than to suboptimized subsets of the common, often is alluded to in discussions of collegial structures in academia. Members of college communities frequently invoke "old ivy," the institution in its entirety, as a rationale for decisions. Hence, it is important to see which kinds of the many forms of linking/coordinating structures in higher education used to advance the common cause can be properly labeled as collegial. (This is the Wittgensteinian approach noted at the outset of this chapter.)

As will be seen, different structures for control and integration have associated with them different forms of sanctions for ensuring that the coordination is carried out. Both the structures and the sanctions must be considered to determine their compliance with the conception of collegiality.

In the discussion that follows, several forms of coordinating structure found in practice will be compared with what is likely to be the common view of collegiality. To anticipate the argument somewhat, what will be seen is that certain structural configurations are clearly *not* what most academics would call collegial, while others may or may not be collegial, depending on the cultural context in which they are embedded or on the uses to which they are put.

While the organizational literature abounds with theory and research on structure and organizational design, what was needed for the purposes herein was a comprehensive, exhaustive set of alternatives. Among many writers, Mintzberg (1979; 1983; cf., Stoelwinder and Charns, 1981) satisfies this need. Mintzberg suggests five alternative coordinating modes for organizations in general: (1) standardization of work processes, (2) standardization of work outputs, (3) standardization of worker skills (4) direct supervision, and (5) mutual adjustment. Each of these calls for an organizational structure with varying kinds and degrees of participant decision-making related through formal authority relationships. Some of these coordinating modes are non-existent or rare in academia and for a variety of reasons would not be called collegial by most observers. One, the "professional bureaucracy," as Mintzberg notes, conforms to his understanding of how colleges and universities operate, though it remains to be seen whether it is "collegial." It will be helpful first, however, to eliminate structures that fall into the *inappropriate* category.

Bureaucratic and Hierarchical Coordinating Modes
The first three structural modes of coordination in the list above will be seen to be essentially bureaucratic and hierarchical. For example, standardization of work processes refers to the bureaucratic specification of rules and procedures for performing a role. Manifestly, if all workers are told what to do through formal, written instructions, there is little need for either bi-lateral or superordinate coordination, the necessary linkages across the individual task assignments having been predetermined and delineated as part of the task requirements of each job or role. If one unit in a manufacturing department specifies the dimension tolerances that they will abide from a unit sending them a part, the sending unit need only standardize the necessary transformation processes in its domain to avoid the need for coordination. What remains as a function of the organizational structure is not coordination but enforcement of conformity to the specifications. (To be sure, occupants of roles in this structure in some sense *do* make coordinating decisions by moderating behaviors that fall outside the rules.

However, a structure dominated by these conformity enhancing decisions and decision makers would seem more evaluative/punitive than coordinating.)

Standardization of work processes, then, implies the possibility that tasks can be almost totally prescribed. It also includes the threat of negative sanctions applied impersonally and universalistically by the organization and its hierarchical representatives in cases of failure to conform. This mode of control and coordination is not likely to be found in colleges since it violates many of the values and practices of professionals (Parsons and Platt, 1968; Baldridge, 1971; Blau, 1973). While Weberian bureaucracy presumes superior expertise in superordinates, in work organizations composed of professionals, expertise of both a task and managerial character is assumed to be widely dispersed, thus requiring rights of participation by organizational members who are not necessarily formally at high levels in the bureaucracy. As Weber (1946) recognized,

> With great regularity, the collegiate principal has been transferred from the central authority to the most varied lower authorities. (p. 238)

If, then, decision-making authority is exclusively hierarchical and supervisory, s-collegiality cannot be said to exist.

Or, if it is, it is not likely to be labeled as collegial. Such a structure will be seen as maladaptive to the organizational requirements of teaching and research. There are considerable and desirable differences among faculty in their teaching and research techniques. There also exists a strong tradition of academic freedom on most campuses (varying in strength, of course, across institutional (Carnegie) types). In view of these conditions, standardization of work processes (again, specification of rules and procedures for role performance) would appear to most as unworkable as it is undesirable. To repeat, the label of collegial probably would not be applied to college campuses where work processes are standardized and authority used to ensure conformity to singular organizational standards.

Let us now consider Mintzberg's second category of coordination—a structure for the standardization of work *output*. The usual meaning of "standardization of outputs" is the establishment by central organizational authorities of a quality criterion (e.g., zero defects) against which all outputs are measured prior to release from the organization. The procedure is usually followed in situations where quantification of standards is possible. Standardization of outputs demands that the final product be examined for its adherence to specifications acceptable to the organization. In organizations where final products are the result of sequential or reciprocal interdependence among units contributing to the final output (Thompson, 1967), standardization of output encourages collaboration among those units, with the structure for adjudication of conflict varying among different constituencies (cf., Lawrence and Lorsch, 1969). Structures for standardizing work output are often found in organizations with little input variance and with known, easily accessible, transformation procedures (see Perrow, 1970) or/and with few products and a well-defined, narrow constituency.

However, in an organization which is highly diversified (i.e., many different products and services) and where outputs are the result of pooled interdependence (i.e., workers are largely disconnected from one another), work output quality must be assured to some degree through a decision-making framework where output standards are *decentralized* to the producing units. In a college or university, both entering students and current knowledge are transformed (i.e., educated and made more sophisticated respectively) through the actions of largely autonomous faculty members and departments who, within loose limits, set their own performance criteria.

With regard to control of the outputs of teaching, "standards" for grading students are usually informally determined at the departmental level and are intentionally so nebulous as to allow widely varying levels of student performance to be accorded either high or low grades (the result being little uniformity across departments). With regard to sequencing of courses, there is often some requirement for standardization within the department, but there is rarely any direct specification of final output quality by a central administration[1] (though some specification of prerequisites across departments may occasionally exist).

Concerning research, where raw knowledge inputs are transformed into more informed output "packages," again, just as with "raw" students, there are widely varying beginning and end points which render centralized standardization of outputs most problematic. For example, some disciplines have established paradigms, while others are still relatively unexplored, resulting in outputs of substantially different natures. Moreover, the usual practice is for faculty to submit work externally for publication without prior screening for acceptability to the organization.

In sum, this well-remarked (if not revered) diversity and ambiguity in both teaching and research outcomes calls for a decentralized openness to outcomes of many kinds as legitimate organizational outputs. Not to permit it (let alone protect it in the name of academic freedom) might induce a restriction of the possibilities for the growth of students and the expansion of knowledge and might further limit faculty growth and development. Hence, a structure for decision making in which output standards are centrally determined is neither common in colleges and universities nor collegial.

An important question, then, is whether the opposite—a loosely coupled, decentralized structure for setting standards—is what is meant by "s-collegiality?" Two points are important to note here. First, standardization of work outputs is rarely centralized in higher education (though recent trends toward

---

[1]Except, perhaps, for remedial or professional education where licencing or credentialing actions at a still higher level of centralization set quality—or at least minimal performance standards.

statewide value-added assessments may change this). While the rarity of existence does not itself constitute evidence of non-collegiality, given the universal apotheosis of academic freedom in higher education, it would be hard to imagine a consensus that a campus that requires uniform outputs should be labeled collegial. Second, decentralization itself does not constitute an accurate meaning of s-collegiality. Let us consider each of these points in some detail.

It is not at all clear that mere decentralization of output standard setting is what is commonly meant by the structural component of collegiality (cf. Beyer and Lodahl, 1976). Indeed, an organizational *structure* that allows the setting of standards at the local departmental level does not appear to be part of the concept of collegiality at all. There are several reasons for this. First, as noted above, standards for output in publications are not usually determined by departmental faculty, except when colleagues are being reviewed for promotion and tenure. (More on this below.) Usually, external professional standards for publishability are the models for departmental publications (even though the quality of those standards may be different for institutions of different attributed national ranking or Carnegie classification). And standards for teaching are usually *assumed* to be high with little or no monitoring of student performance against organizational standards.

Thus, it would seem that even a decentralized "structure" for decision making with respect to standardization of outputs rarely exists in higher education. The "market" domination of line operations (cf. Ouchi, 1980) makes standardization hazardous, if not impossible. Hence, at this point, it could be concluded that mere decentralized control over work outputs is also not what we mean by the structure of collegiality. This is not to say, however, that decentralization of other functions besides output control does not connote some feature of s-collegiality. It is only to suggest that standardization of outputs either centrally or decentrally is not a mode of coordination that would normally be labeled collegial.

Coordination Through Skill Standardization
There is still another way in which faculty differences might be coordinated in academia. (Recall that s-collegiality is here being examined as a mode of coordination of faculty efforts.) The reference is to the third of Mintzberg's list of coordinating mechanisms—"standardization of worker skills." (Mintzberg, 1983, pp. 206–207; cf. Hardy et al., 1984). This mode of "coordination" removes the need for constant direct supervision because if standard worker competency (and goal commitment) can be assured (partly, perhaps, through c-collegiality), acceptable worker behavior and productivity will follow without the supervision. Since the absence of such immediate oversight is translated into the considerable worker autonomy experienced by faculty in higher education, perhaps the essence of collegiality can be traced to this form of coordinating

structure. The argument in this case seems to be reasonably valid. Centralized recruitment and employment policies for faculty, in point of fact, do standardize worker skills. Collegiality (s-collegiality) in higher education does in part mean standardization of faculty skills. Some extended discussion is called for to explain why.

For a variety of reasons, most institutions attempt to recruit faculty who are quite similar in background, training, intellectual dispositions and attitudes to those tenured faculty already employed at the institution. Through the experiences of graduate-level education, academic neophytes are, in fact, "standardized" at least insofar as work procedures and professional ethics are concerned, thus assuring at least a general set of professional dispositions and skills (primarily in the area of research—the neglect of training in teaching being both widespread and well-documented). Anticipatory socialization (Bess, 1978) and institutional socialization complete the local skill standardization process. Thus, when we refer to a collegial coordinating structure of an institution of higher education, one meaning is the decision-making structure by which faculty are selected to be members of the institution. Although this is not a definition of collegiality that would be readily offered by most academics, in point of fact, the procedures of recruiting and choosing new workers through a structure designed to ensure standardization of worker skills and attitudes is an essential part of collegiality. They give confidence to faculty that the culture of collegiality will be sustained and that decision-making processes will be carried out in a manner consistent with what is assumed to be academic tradition.

In many ways, of course, finding like-minded colleagues is not unique to higher education, since in virtually any organization, there is a desire for new employees to "fit" into the existing culture. (An extreme case of this occurs in most Japanese organizations.) In contrast to hiring methods in hierarchical, bureaucratic organizations, however, the authority structure for selecting new academic personnel is at least partially vested (both *de jure* and *de facto*), in line workers—the faculty. Importantly, within limits, how much is vested turns out not to be as critical to the appellation of collegiality as some other conditions, which will be discussed later. But it does appear that *peer involvement in colleague selection for the purpose of ensuring standardization of skills* is strongly associated with the meaning of s-collegiality. The technology of research and teaching that requires extraordinary faculty work autonomy demands that extra attention be paid to skill standardization and that peers be the judges of the degree of conformity of potential new recruits. The meaning of s-collegiality, then, is also at least partially tied to the decision-making structure associated with the standardization of skills through peer control of recruitment. (Whether these recruitment skills are themselves standardized is a subject taken up below.) More simply, we almost always mean by s-collegiality faculty dominance in the decision-making structures for recruitment and employment of faculty.

Coordination Through Direct and Indirect Supervision

Thus far, several structures for decision making in higher education have been considered. Two have been rejected or partially rejected as not typifying s-collegiality, while a third seems to reflect it. For example, it was suggested that "standardization of work processes" as a mode of control is antithetical to the conceptualization of the faculty member as professional. Also rejected was "standardization of work outputs" as not collegial, since any such structure in higher education would ignore the diversity of outputs of students and knowledge and the necessity to be responsive to them. Mintzberg's third structural mechanism discussed here was "standardization of worker skills." In this case, there was some reason to believe that the structure that most academics label as collegial has to do at least in part with assuring that new academic personnel have the skills and values desired by the institution and that institutions which vest at least part of the responsibility for this process in faculty are properly called collegial.

We turn now to "direct supervision," Mintzberg's fourth suggested mode of coordination and ask whether institutions with this mode can also be labeled collegial. At face value, it is not likely. First of all, rarely, if ever, is authority exercised through real time oversight, with one faculty member or department chair observing and ordering a correction of another faculty member's behavior in a "vertical dyad relationship" (cf. Dansereau, Graen and Haga, 1975.) If it were, it would be viewed as a short-term aberration, certainly inconsistent with the common understanding of the nature of academic interpersonal relationships. There are, of course, constructive (if infrequent) classroom visits among faculty, and faculty in the same institution do occasionally read one another's papers prior to publication; but these are usually peer interactions, not the "supervisory" ones that carry the authority of negative organizational sanctions to which Mintzberg refers.[2] As a structure of coordination, then, direct supervision is clearly not collegial in nature.

Supervision, of course, carries with it the image of "line" oversight drawn from typical factory/production terminology. While as noted, this seems not to refer to collegiality, there is an aspect of the structure of the coordinating apparatus at upper levels in the administrative hierarchy in college and university organizations that does appear to resemble direct supervision. It lies at the structural confluence of the bureaucratic and faculty decision-making processes.

For example, the typical administrative authority structures on college campuses incorporate a decision review process for curricular and especially personnel decisions initiated by the faculty. The review, however, is indirect and

---

[2]Lack of space here prohibits a discussion of collegiality and untenured faculty. The indefiniteness of the outcomes of the probationary period and the class-biased bifurcation of the faculty into tenured and untenured ranks inhibits the extension of c-collegiality across ranks. It may exist within the untenured ranks in small departments, but competition restricts it in large departments.

post hoc, rather than "supervisory"—statutory authority for both domains having been allocated to faculty. The question is whether this administrative review structure itself is an aspect of s-collegiality (though on face appearance, it would not seem likely). The answer depends on some other conditions involving the decisions which are usually considered through the structure. Let us consider, then, the structures for the two most typical academic decisions—promotion and tenure and curriculum.

Indirect supervision or control is the common structure for academic review of promotion and tenure decisions. The dual track nature of the review process— the simultaneous consideration by both faculty and administration of the performance of the faculty member—is a second part of what is most often meant in allusions to collegiality as structure in higher education. Because of the expectation, or at least possibility, of extremely long periods of employment (e.g., a lifetime) at one institution, and due to the high levels of autonomy in academic work, personnel decisions are given special attention. Some degree of uniformity of belief and attitude *across* separated units in the institution is necessary, since at least in the teaching area, students are shared, and there must be some measure of agreement about how they are to be treated and exchanged. Just as with hiring decisions, promotion and tenure decisions tend to make more uniform the collective predispositions of faculty in a department or even on an entire campus, thereby mitigating the need for more active and apparently intrusive coordination. This, then, is a combination of Mintzberg's supervision—interpreted here as indirect supervision—and standardization.

Perhaps surprisingly, what seems to be "collegial" about this coordination mode is the *sharing* of authority for the process across faculty and administrators. Most faculty identify more with their departments (and perhaps their school) rather than with their total institution. Whereas faculty often complain about allegedly unjust bureaucratic interference in specific promotion and tenure peer decisions in their own departments, they usually, but not always, will recognize the legitimacy of a check and balance system that can override parochial considerations and suboptimizing decisions at the more decentralized level of the department. Note, however, that the manifest logic of the system's design does not connote invariable agreement with the system's decisions, even in the presence of c-collegiality.

Others have argued, of course, that s-collegiality refers simply to the constitutionally established structures in the faculty governance alone which prevent the system from lapsing into self-serving and group-serving suboptimizations. These mechanisms typically call for elected representation on committees that review critical decisions. It is important, however, to distinguish here between structures serving the needs of a political democracy and those performing the function of collegiality. They may, but do not necessarily coincide.

The origins of the structure of political democracy hark back to Enlightenment assumptions about individuality and freedom in a social system comprising people with legitimately heterogeneous goals and behaviors. Protection of the rights of all, especially from a powerful and potentially hostile and/or self-serving government, demands the vigorous and continuous participation of citizens. But "organizations" are not only polities (some being almost completely apolitical). They are also enterprises with rather narrowly articulated goals (however ambiguously defined) embracing workers with a more restricted range of cognitive and affective predilections than in pure polities (cf. Tonnies, 1957). Moreover, participation in organizations joins personal and organizational goal seeking, though the overlap may be imperfect, if not accidental. That is, the assumption is made that in most organizations, there is some considerable agreement about goals both between and within hierarchical levels. Throughout the higher education system, there is (usually) a consensus that the personal strivings and achievements of faculty closely mirror or are identical with the aims of the institution (the dangers of both ecological and anthropomorphic fallacies notwithstanding). A social unit that recruits, selects and dismisses members (i.e., an organization) is more homogeneous in composition than one that enfranchises all over a certain age (a polity). This condition and its acceptance by members of the organization make legitimate the *joint* participation of organizational/administrative or hierarchical leadership and organizational citizenry in decision making (cf. Clark, 1970). It allows "total" political democracy to be modified by the introduction of structured administrative influence.

Let us return to the question of the legitimacy of Mintzberg's fourth mode of coordination (direct supervision) as descriptive of collegiality. Earlier it was argued that direct supervision at the departmental level is not collegial. What has been asserted just above is that supervision is likely to be viewed as collegial in its indirect mode when the mechanism of dual authority shared among organizational role occupants (the administration) and political system role occupants (faculty) is operative. S-collegiality as indirect supervision, then, consists of an organizational framework that actually permits involvement of "authorities" from both the polity and the hierarchy.

S-collegiality is not, in other words, simply academic review by peers, but the system of *joint* review by faculty and administration. Just as with the conclusions about c-collegiality, this one also appears to contest the common view. However, while this conclusion might not be drawn by some faculty who see s-collegiality as essentially the political structure for making decisions through democratic faculty participation, it is likely that empirical testing of "pure" versus "mixed" systems (cf. Lunsford, 1963) would result in more attributions of collegiality for the mixed structure (provided other c-collegiality conditions also exist).

It is important to point out that joint faculty–administration decision making is a *necessary* but not *sufficient* condition for s-collegiality. The label of collegial attached to a decision-making structure in a college or university depends on how the structure is used. Structure, in general, is, after all, an instrument for action, and the latter can differ depending on the intentions of the actor(s). A hammer, for example, can be either a bludgeon or a nail inserter. The instrument of structure in any organization follows in particular from the character and strength of the norms and values held by the users of the structure (cf. Argyris and Schon, 1974). In an organization such as a college or university, if the norms and values of c-collegiality prevail, the structure will be identified as embodying s-collegiality. The negative is also true. In the absence of c-collegiality, the same decision-making structure will be seen as not collegial—or, at least as failing to realize its potential collegiality. In sum, a collegial structure for tenure and promotion decisions may exist in form, but only through its use can it be appropriately so labeled. Even a carefully crafted constitution for joint decision making in some democratic or quasi-democratic format cannot alone be determined with certainty to be collegial. The skeleton will work only in a live body which self-consciously cares for its psychological self. *Mens sana in corporo sano.*

Let us now take up for illustrative purposes the second key domain of decision making for faculty—curriculum development—to determine whether the structure employed can be labeled collegial, using the modified definition of "indirect supervision" as an integrating mode. Here the reference is to the coordination of curriculum, largely through faculty or joint faculty-administration curriculum committees. The question is what distinguishes collegial from non-collegial forms of "supervision" over curricular matters.

Decisions about curriculum in higher education are essentially "technology" decisions, comparable in the profit making sector to decisions dealing with the methods to be used by manufacturing firms to transform raw material into finished products or by service firms to develop more satisfied clients. In the profit making domain, such decisions are often made through extended discussions among line and staff personnel, the patterns of discussion varying by industry (and country—as in Japan). It would not be unreasonable to believe that faculty would call the academic structures for addressing questions of technology "collegial," since they also seem to involve sharing of power. Here again, however, the structure alone does not justify the appelation. There is something different about the structure for curricular decisions in higher education that distinguishes it as "collegial" in contrast to comparable structures for technology decisions in the profit-making world—particularly in service industries where clients are involved. And again the distinction lies in the uses to which the structure is put.

As is fairly commonly acknowledged, in order to achieve desired organizational ends (from their point view), wise deans pick curriculum committee members whose predilections are in accord with the dean's. Further, faculty committee members are known to make decisions that are not infrequently biased in directions which favor themselves or their departments. The withholding or even distortion of information in committees of this sort in the interests of advancing personal or departmental aims at the expense of others' is not unusual. Thus, just as with mixed authority modes of decision making about personnel matters, so also in the area of curriculum, what distinguishes s-collegiality from the structure of simple peer or staff/line joint decision making are the assumptions about the uses to which knowledge shared will be put. A necessary but not sufficient condition for s-collegiality in the curriculum area is a set of norms supportive of openness and integrity in information exchange. To be labeled collegial, even a structure with shared authority must also embody sufficient trust in peers and authorities. This important notion of trust is taken up later (cf. Leslie, 1975).

The Senate as Indirect Supervisor/Coordinator
To this point, the typical committee structure in higher education has been considered to determine whether its character is what conveys the sense of collegiality in the light of Mintzberg's supervision mode of coordination. It is necessary to turn finally to a discussion of the quintessence of faculty participation in the governance processes—the academic or college/university senate structure. Perhaps it is this plenary body, in its reincarnation of Greek democracy, to which faculty refer when they discuss collegiality.

There are relatively few non-academic institutions *qua* organizations where participants have meaningful opportunities to influence decisions affecting them through some kind of formal democratic structural body. Some profit-making organizations, of course, have elaborate mechanisms, both formal and informal, to factor employee input into corporate decisions at all levels—e.g., the Japanese *nemawashi* and *ringei* system. These can also be legitimately characterized as embodying some aspects of s-collegiality.

However, it is important to note here still once more that the mere presence of this apparatus for decision making should not be taken, in and of itself, to mean that an institution is "collegial." Senates serve both manifest and latent functions in colleges and universities (Birnbaum, 1987). Their manifest function is to provide a forum for decision making about institution-wide matters of importance. This activity can be carried out in various ways. In one scenario, for example, the senate only occasionally engages in substantive discussions of matters critical to the institution's functioning. Planning, strategy formation, financial control, recruitment, marketing, and curriculum development are usually carried out by others in different settings. Conflicts arise and are largely resolved elsewhere. To be sure, there are times when matters vital to the total institution's well-being are brought to the senate for a vote. The argument can be made, however, that when the senate itself becomes a frequent forum for making decisions, it signifies its *failure* as a collegial structure.

In other words, when a senate becomes the locus of protracted resolution of conflict, it reflects a breakdown in the collegial mechanism of the system. It means that politics rather than trust and reciprocity have come to dominate the norms of interpersonal exchange in the system as a whole. As March and Simon (1958) and Pfeffer (1977) note, manifested substantive conflict over system matters occurs when a diversity of goals forces organizations away from consensus seeking to dissensus resolving systems. In sum, most academics will not see as collegial an institution whose senate business is constantly taken up with conflicted discussion of critical matters. On the other hand, in an alternative scenario, it is clear that when the senate considers *important* matters relatively infrequently, it will probably represent s-collegiality in the common view.[3] Metaphorically, if there is an active program of fire prevention in a building, the smoke alarm will not be necessary. But it is comforting to have it. When it goes off too frequently, the prevention program is clearly not effective. Thus, in a collegial system, the very existence of a senate to some extent obviates the necessity of its being used. The academic trivia that pass through the senate apparatus, then, could signal not a failing in the decision-making body, but a success. The mere presence of the plenary body called a senate does not alone contain sufficient evidence to judge the degree of structural collegiality at a college or university.

Coordination Through Mutual Adjustment
In this, the final part of this discussion of the structure of collegiality, we turn to the last of the Mintzberg categories—"mutual adjustment," or the process by which individuals or departments informally link their efforts through accommodation to one another. Certainly this appears to be collegial, but recall that in this analysis what is sought are *structures* that can be labeled as collegial. There are probably relatively few institutions that are formally organized to permit and depend on this informal kind of coordinating activity. The reason is that there is comparatively little apparent need for real time adjustments in activities among faculty—both teaching and research being quite insular. In a few scattered instances, enlightened academics see through the arbitrary circumscription of faculty roles and recognize the importance of ongoing collaboration. In these cases (e.g., a matrix organization at the University of California at Santa Cruz; a federated learning community structure at Evergreen State), structures for decision making that allow for mutual adjustment are established. So, while this mode is carried in the normative freight of c-collegiality, and would be labeled as collegial structure if found, it is presently the exception rather than the rule.

[3]Here the latent and manifest functions of the senate merge. Senates and their disaggregated committees serve as a medium for information exchange, especially on large campuses where decentralized production systems are geographically and intellectually remote from one another. They are also an important source of security for faculty, providing visible channels of recourse for potential grievances.

To summarize this section on s-collegiality, it would appear that its meaning is shrouded in ambiguities having to do with the uses to which the structures are put. What most academics on superficial inspection would ordinarily label as a collegial structure might not in fact reflect the meaning that a more profound conceptualization of the term suggests. The corollary is also true: what many might not call collegial (e.g., sharing of authority for promotion and tenure between faculty and administration) is indeed so. Thus, there is no structure *per se* that can unequivocally be called collegial. The manifest and latent functions of the structure, in point of fact, give guidance as to its collegiality, and these functions are determined externally from both the culture and from the behavior of the participants in the institutions. In turn, the structure affects both. Earlier the nature of the culture under the rubric of "c-collegiality" was considered. It was followed by the just completed discussion of "s-collegiality." It is necessary now to turn to the last of the three components of the meaning of collegiality, collegial behavior, or "b-collegiality."

Collegiality as Behavior

"B-collegiality" refers to the set of actions in which faculty and administrators engage as they fulfill the various institutional roles that are "shaped" by c-collegiality and s-collegiality. Hence, b-collegiality behaviors "emerge" out of the value and norm context of the culture and from the structure of collegiality. What collegial behavior most commonly means is altruistic or prosocial action. In Weberian terms (Weber, 1947), these behaviors are driven more by *zwert-rational* rather than *zweckrational* orientations—that is, by objectives centered beyond the individual's personal needs (though this may convey more of a cognitive explanation of the behavior than is justified). As Brief and Motowidlo (1986) define it, prosocial behavior is:

(a) performed by a member of an organization,
(b) directed toward an individual, group, or organization with whom he or she interacts while carrying out his or her organizational role, and
(c) performed with the intention of promoting the welfare of the individual, group, or organization toward which it is directed.

B-collegiality is different from the behaviors formally "required" by the organization's standard employment expectations in that they go beyond what is formally called for by the college (cf. Homans, 1950), and they are directed toward organizationally valued ends. Staw (1984) suggests that since prosocial behavior may stem from social and cultural norms, non-hedonistic behavior can become the institutional norm with intelligent management of the organizational culture, even in a university setting.

Without getting too deeply into philosophical meanings, however, it could be

said that such pro-social behavior is predicated on the assumption of a beneficence residing in the institution, particularly as personified by its leaders (cf.
Gamson, 1968). A somewhat cynical Hobbesian perspective, of course, would
call for an interpretation of prosocial behavior as ultimately self-serving (cf.
Clark and Mills, 1979). In the case of collegiality, however, there seems to be
no conscious expectation of reciprocation from the community as a whole, just
as reciprocity is not anticipated from an individual receiver. An ultimate return
is simply taken for granted in a non-cognitive sense.

Brief and Motowidlo list thirteen categories of prosocial behavior ranging
from providing job related or personal services, to engaging in citizenship activities, including whistle blowing (cf. Organ, 1988) to volunteering ideas and
effort. The prosocial behavior that might be called collegial, then, is largely
interpersonal in nature. And, it stems from beliefs about the personal motivation
and values that drive it—namely, that others can and should be treated as mature
adults, that the interactions must be non-exploitive, and that the results of the
interactions can be non-zero sum and integrative, rather than distributive (i.e.,
can expand the total goods and services available to the community as a whole).

At a college or university, b-collegiality would be said to exist in the common
view when the majority of faculty members engage in "organizationally valued"
prosocial behavior. This might include such activities as volunteering willingly
to take over another's class in an emergency, sending (unsolicited) bibliographic
references to a colleague, offering to give up a perquisite in recognition of the
need for equity in their distribution, and knowingly tolerating opposing points of
view. In sum, collegial behavior seems to connote a "giving" of one's self to
one's colleagues (individually or collectively *qua* "the institution"), often at
some personal sacrifice, though without much awareness of that sacrifice. Indeed, were it possible accurately to obtain (from faculty, for example) the behavioral norms of the collegiate culture, reports of such "expectations" might
not emerge. Thus, once again, collegiality (here, b-collegiality) appears anomalously as activities that are not normatively expected (or missed in their absence) and for which there are few, if any, negative sanctions for non-compli-
ance, but which constitute part of the meaning most academics would ascribe to
the term. As noted at the outset, the scarcity of collegiality on college campuses
may make it difficult to find community members who can report anything but
ideal rather than modal, observed behavior.

PART III

The several meanings normally attributed to collegiality, having been disass-
embled in Part II, the attempt in this section is to clarify the underlying bases
of the meanings *across* the three components and to explain, in part, its varying
strength on different campuses.

The Meanings of Collegiality

As has been noted, there are several meanings of collegiality that are apparent from commonsense understanding and several that depart from it. Moreover, "meaning" can be said to be derived in several ways—by ascription of those familiar with a phenomenon, by examining antecedent conditions, and by looking at consequences.

When it is operative, the idea of collegiality seems to "inhabit" the three levels of social system analysis—culture, structure, and behavior—and critically affects the modes of manifestation of each in any one institution. Two seminal collegial values and their corollaries undergird this process. Both values are concerned with the strength of faculty beliefs (held both cognitively and affectively) in the benignness of the resources on which organizational participants depend—the system itself and the participant's coworkers. That is, the meanings of collegiality rest essentially on (1) the belief in the propriety of order and rationality in the structure and process of deliberations concerning organizational decisions (cf. Weber, 1947); and (2) the belief in and commitment to the value of goodwill of colleagues (cf. Leslie, 1975). Observers from different disciplinary perspectives might trace these two dimensions back to the most basic human and social system needs for order and sustenance—or, perhaps, to a balance of reason and emotion, left brain/right brain equality, or any number of other philosophic explanations. It is not surprising that so profound a set of ideas comprises the essence of collegiality, since the latter is an expression of an ideal condition of working life for most academics. The realm of the ideal usually leads to considerations of profound meaning. The place of collegiality in academic life needs exploration at this deep level.

How strong a force collegiality is in all three levels of meaning (c-collegiality, s-collegiality, and b-collegiality) at any institution is a function of the magnitude and "shape" of the two beliefs. The two dimensions—belief in rationality and trust in colleagues—along with their corollaries, are noted below:

1. Belief in rationality and order—the extent to which problem solving is seen normatively as concerted decision making according to predetermined organizational repertories, unafflicted by *ad hoc* personal capriciousness.

   a. Superordinate goals—belief in the principle that effort toward the perceived common good is a rational means of personal self-advancement. (Note: this is different from the calculation of the probability of reciprocation.)

   b. Information sharing—belief in the necessity, viability, and likelihood of open exchange of information.

c. Evaluation and control—belief in the authority of expertise regardless of the formal organizational status of the holder of that expertise.

2. Belief in the goodness of others and the willingness to act on that belief—the extent to which collective others are seen as a source of succor in both good and bad times.
   a. Disposition to act on others' behalf without prior consideration of the probabilities of reciprocation.
   b. Faith in the probity and integrity of others in organizationally oriented interpersonal interactions.
   c. Disposition to discuss personal or organizational problems that may reveal weaknesses.

To consider each of these in depth is beyond the scope of this paper (see Bess, 1988, for further discussion). So also is the explanation of the modes of leadership and organizational development that give collegiality its strength and utility on a campus. What will be considered generally, however, are some of the potential sources of distortion to collegiality. A discussion of how and why collegiality varies across campuses should help further in revealing its complex, multiple meanings. That is, disaggregating the *sources* of the differences should contribute to the determination of whether collegiality has a universal or particularistic institutional meaning in the academic community.

Variations in Collegiality Across Institutions
Given the above-noted conceptual definitions, how can the variance in collegiality across different campuses be accounted for? The explanation lies in part in a consideration of the sources of influence on organizations in general. Although this kind of analysis is the subject of the entire academic field of organizational behavior and hence well beyond the confines of this paper, it is, nevertheless, possible to outline the primary forces using standard open systems theory. In this case, the influences on the beliefs and values of collegiality can be arrayed systemically as they depict the ways faculty roles are configured, interpreted, and played out. As with beliefs and values other than collegiality, at least six sources of role and role behavior exist in an organization's environment, culture, and structure. These sources of varying demand on role behavior can be graphically portrayed as a series of concentric circles, each of which separately exerts an influence. The sources are manifested first as "ambient" stimuli (Hackman, 1969) within the organization, broadly defining the role normatively for all members of the organization. In turn, this is translated both formally and informally into required and emergent sentiments (cf. Homans, 1950) that formally

and informally define role incumbent interactions and behavior. The permutations of varying role expectations emanating from the different rings are many, resulting in comparably varied institutional and individual interpretations. It is important to note, furthermore, that the sent roles may be weak or strong and ambiguous or clear. They may also be congruent or incongruent (different sources sending different messages).

These differences in behavioral expectation represented by the proximate or distant sources of influence result in various kinds of role ambiguity or/and role conflict for the incumbent. That is, different messages originating from different sources (rings) will result in varying compromises to the integrity and strength of the two dimensions of collegiality identified above—belief in rationality and trust in colleagues.

For example, the more cosmopolitan the faculty on a campus, the more influential will be the pressures from outside professional groups. In an employment context, however, where that pressure is not given high prominence (e.g., community colleges), the local sent role will represent a different set of expectations to the faculty. Where the sent roles involve the dimensions of collegiality, there may also be either conflict or ambiguity for the faculty member. The rings, then, constitute the discrete forces of collegiality both outside and inside an institution. They influence the strength and shape of collegiality at that institution, while simultaneously the force of collegiality mitigates the negative effects of the externally generated conflict and ambiguity on faculty behavior.

As noted in Exhibit 1, there are five somewhat interdependent sources: an idealized faculty role "transmitted" by (1) the *profession* (perhaps further differentiated by academic field); a generalized faculty role transmitted by (2) the *academic sector* in which the institution stands (e.g., in the Carnegie classification); (3) a formal, bureaucratic set of role expectations transmitted through the structure of the local *institution* and department; (4) an informal set of role expectations transmitted by the local *campus culture* and department; and (5) the self-directed role expectations of the *faculty member* transmitted by the faculty member himself or herself. Differences in the transmitted role expectations between the different rings results in either role ambiguity or role conflict. There are seven key "zones" of ambiguity or conflict stemming from conditions of (1) professionalization or socialization; (2) differences between institutions; (3) local sanctions; (4) collegiality; (5) guilt; (6) education and training; and (7) skill levels.

Using these symbols, it is possible to anticipate differences in special quality and strength of collegiality on any campus. It is also possible to identify more clearly some of the types of ambiguity and conflict that render collegiality so illusive a concept. As will be seen, there are many possible combinations of ring type and strength. Several will be discussed, although quite broadly, since research evidence is lacking as to how concretely the permutations and combina-

EXHIBIT 1. Behavior Collegiality and Role Clarity/Ambiguity*

Role Sources

P	An idealized faculty role transmitted by the profession—essentially, collegiality espoused or/and myths and wishes about the role.
C	A generalized faculty role transmitted by the academic community sector in which the institution stands (e.g., in the Carnegie classification)
I	The formal role expectations transmitted through the structure of the local institution and department.
N	The informal role expectations transmitted by the local campus culture and department.
S	The role expectations of the faculty member transmitted by him/herself.
B	Behavior of the faculty member

Zones of Ambiguity and/or Conflict

P−C	Professionalization/Socialization
C−I	Institutional Differentiation
I−N	Local Sanctions
P−I	Collegiality
P−B	Guilt
C−B	Education and Training
S−B	Skill Level

*Adapted from Bess (1988).

---

tions of role clarity, ambiguity, and conflict in the different zones manifest themselves in a parsimoniously small number of configurations that can be meaningfully labeled.

In this discussion of ambiguity and conflict, it is important to distinguish between those that are knowledge-based and others that are interpersonally based. As Parsons and Platt (1973) note, the academic system is grounded in cognitive rationality, and it is likely that (indeed organizationally healthy if) disputes arise in the "disorderly movement of the growth of knowledge" (paraphrasing Parsons' and Platt's quotation of Shils, p. vii). Moreover, in a system where role specification is diffuse, it is reasonable to expect that there will be frequent misunderstandings and/or overlaps of jurisdiction. It is, however, probable that where c-collegiality and s-collegiality on a campus are strong, ambiguity and conflict arising from the different messages from role senders will be short-lived and more tolerable for faculty role incumbents. Thus, as noted above, the differences across the sources of faculty roles affect both the strength and shape of collegiality, and the latter makes those differences more tolerable.

For example, it can be said that faculty on a campus are more likely to act collegially when both the institutional type faculty roles and the roles mandated by the specific campus (I and N) approximate the ideal of collegiality for the profession (P)—i.e., when P = I,N. This "PIN" convergence merges the three major professional and bureaucratic influences on the typical academic's motivation, thus lessening the ambiguity and conflict experienced. On the other hand, if there are differences across these sectors, the local campus may find the strength of its collegiality lessened.

Clearly, there are differences between the expectations of the faculty in research universities, comprehensive colleges, liberal arts colleges, and community colleges. Whether the *concept* of collegiality as well as its strengths and quality differ across these sectors is a researchable question. It may be, for example, that the technology of multi-functioned organizations like universities necessarily politicizes them (cf. Pfeffer, 1978), in which case collegiality may be an unrealizable goal. Indeed, it may be an unjustifiable source of anxiety and guilt among faculty who would like to believe that collegiality is possible under all academic circumstances.

Differences between P and I are labeled here arbitrarily as the ambiguity or conflict of "professionalization/socialization." In other words, the processes of imprinting behavioral expectations from different sources can result in a state of ambiguity or conflict for the faculty member. A similar kind of ambiguity or conflict (C–I) results when there is a difference between the institutional type expectations and the institution itself, as, for example, when a college is on the cusp of a shift to a different Carnegie status (e.g., comprehensive university to research university). This might be called the ambiguity or conflict of "institutional differentiation."

Yet other conflicts and ambiguities exist when there is a gap between formal and informal institutional expectations (I–N, or the conflict of local sanctions), between the ideal of the profession and the actual demands of the institution (P–I, or the conflict of collegiality), the ideal of the profession and the actual behavior of the faculty member (P–B, or the conflict of guilt), the results of the specialized education and training and the behavior that results (C–B, or the conflict of education and training), and, finally, between what the institution asks and the faculty member does (S–B, or the conflict of skill level).

If a college or university faculty adopts fully the beliefs and values of the profession, its faculty will experience little or no conflict with the ideals with which they have been impregnated in graduate school. Similarly, faculty behavior will be more collegial when the roles that a majority of faculty send themselves (S) are congruent with the idealized professional role (P)—i.e., when S = P. Usually when that happens, norms (N) will emerge to support role behavior which is ideally collegial (P)—i.e., N = P. To summarize, the transmission of the twin dimensions of collegiality may result in role conflict or ambiguity of a special nature that compromises the strength of that collegiality but is, in turn, mitigated by it. Again, the nuances of these relationships need to be investigated through careful research.

Functions of Collegiality

It is necessary to turn now to the third method of analyzing the meaning of collegiality—by considering the uses or functions it serves. While functional analysis may be said to be biased toward the static or stable aspects of social systems, such an analysis seems relevant to social institutions like colleges and universities that are largely conservative in nature. In their prime educational function of transmission of knowledge, colleges and universities change slowly. The external forces that may cause internal stress are most frequently attended to by changes that serve to retain the essential mission and character of these kinds of institutions, even though some of the methods for attending to the functions may shift to accommodate changing environmental circumstances or new technologies. This may suggest some teleological proclivity in the structure and functioning of a college or university, with the systems perspective of "equifinality" (the same outcome can result from different means) explaining the variations in current practice.

Collegiality plays various roles in sustaining and enhancing the conservationist character of colleges and universities. A functionalist approach not only serves to explain the place of institutions of higher education in the larger system in which it exists, but it also explains how the needs of the organization are met. In classic Parsonian terms (Parsons, 1951), all organizations must attend to four fundamental prerequisites in order to perform effectively both in terms of the system that supports them and the actors within the organizations. These functions are served by values and structures. While collegiality as it has been defined in this work clearly does not satisfy all of the prerequisites, it does contribute meaningfully and importantly to them. In Exhibit 2, on the left are listed the four functions which all social systems must satisfy, and on the right, the functions served by the culture and structure of collegiality in attending to those functions.

As will be noted, collegiality, through its cultural and structural components, would appear to provide a means of satisfying the important function of maintaining patterns and relieving tensions in a social system. In inducing members of the academic community to cooperate with one another, the need to satisfy the integrative needs of a system is met by collegiality. To the third functional need, to assure a continuous flow of resources and to distribute them efficiently, collegiality makes an important contribution. And last, collegiality functions to provide incentives to members to strive toward institutionally sanctioned goals and to provide consistent images to outside constituencies.

It would be foolish, of course, to suggest that collegiality is the sole ingredient in the formula for institutional effectiveness in higher education. Its functions, however, seem to be manifold. The "meaning" of collegiality as interpreted through the functions it serves thus reveals still more multidimensionality in the concept that must be sorted out through rational and empirical research.

EXHIBIT 2. Functions of Collegiality*

Organizational Needs	Functions of Collegiality
Latency—the need of all organizations to maintain patterns and reduce tensions.	C-collegiality provides means of socialization, norm establishment, standard setting and behavior control.
	S-collegiality gives stability and confidence in existing grievance recourse; opportunity for social interaction across subunit boundaries; satisfactions from participation.
Integration—the need to establish collaborative arrangements so that different parts of the system work together smoothly.	C-collegiality provides incentive to maximize satisfactions of inter-unit and interpersonal interaction.
	S-collegiality offers forum for conflict identification and resolution.
Adaptation—the need of the organization efficiently to secure resources from the outside and distribute them inside.	C-collegiality provides a sense of equity in distribution of resources.
	S-collegiality gives opportunity for efficient acquisition and internal distribution of resources, given decentralization.
Goal Attainment—the need of the organization to make salient the goals and objectives of the organization and to permit members the opportunity to find satisfaction in their achievement.	C-collegiality offers institutional continuity of image and purpose permitting efficient recruitment of students and faculty and placement of graduates.
	S-collegiality permits identification of and commitment of departments to specific environmental domains of concern; restricts overlap and permits satisfactions with achievement both of subunit and institution.

*Adapted from Bess (1988, p. 111).

SUMMARY

This essay was intended to provide some clarification of the meaning of collegiality. A concrete definition of the term, however, is difficult to offer, given the complications brought on by the differences between espousals of what collegiality is and the actual theories in use (especially given the fact that the same structure on different campuses may or may not be collegial). It is also complicated by the seductiveness of superficial obeisance to the cherished ideal for academics that has existed for some time. As has been shown, deeper analysis reveals alternatives that may seem opposite to what appear to be intuitively obvious current views (e.g., joint faculty/administration decision making).

The disaggregation of the idea of collegiality into its three separate components—the culture of collegiality, the structure of collegiality, and the behavior of collegiality—helps to unravel some of the meanings and to examine the core of the concept. Embedded in all three are two essential ideological and/or dispositional outlooks of faculty: rationality and trust in others. When these are lacking, the likelihood of finding collegiality on a campus is not high. Further, when the origins of collegiality are examined, it becomes evident that conflict and ambiguity resulting from transmissions across different external sectors render the manifestations of collegiality on any one campus idiosyncratic, hence difficult to classify. Finally, it can be seen that the functions served by collegiality indicate that it has several related components, the connections among which are yet to be sorted out.

Collegiality is probably a unique and complex organizational phenomenon that may "fit" institutions of higher education better than organizations in the profit-making sector (though it exists there in slightly different forms and by other names). It seems to serve necessary functions in the operation of a college or university. While other kinds of culture and other structures may also serve those functions, it would seem that collegiality may contribute importantly to the effectiveness and efficiency of these supremely complex institutions.

REFERENCES

Allaire, Y., and Firsirotu, M.E. (1984). Theories of organizational culture. *Organizational Studies* 5(3): 193–226.

Argyris, C., and Schön, D. A. (1982). *Theory in Practice, Increasing Professional Effectiveness.* San Francisco: Jossey-Bass Publishers.

Bacharach, S. B., and Edward J. Lawler, E. J. (1980). *Power and Politics in Organizations.* San Francisco: Jossey-Bass Publishers.

Baldridge, J. V., Curtis, D. V., Ecker, P., and Riley, G. L. (1978). *Policy Making and Effective Leadership.* San Francisco: Jossey-Bass.

Barnard, C. I. (1938). *The Functions of the Executive.* Cambridge, MA: Harvard University Press.

Barrett, W. (1977). *Irrational Man: A Study in Existential Philosophy.* Westport, CT: Greenwood Press, 1977.

Batson, C. D. (1990). How social an animal? The human capacity for caring. *American Psychologist* 45(3): 336–346.

Befu, H. (1989). A theory of social exchange as applied to Japan. In Y. Sugimoto and R. E. Mouer (eds.), *Constraints for Understanding Japan.* London: Kegan Paul International.

Bess, J. L. (1988). *Collegiality and Bureaucracy in the Modern University*. New York: Teachers College Press,

Birnbaum, R. (1987). The latent organizational functions of the academic senate: Why senates don't work but won't go away. Paper delivered at the Annual Meeting of the Association for the Study of Higher Education, San Diego, February.

Blankenship, R. H. (1977). *Colleagues in Organizations, The Social Construction of Professional Work*. New York: John Wiley and Sons.

Blau, P. M. (1964). *Exchange and Power in Social Life*. New York: John Wiley and Sons.

Blau, P. M. (1973). *The Organization of Academic Work*. New York: Wiley-Interscience.

Brief, A. P., and Motowidlo, S. J. (1986). Prosocial organizational behaviors. *The Academy of Management Review* 11(4): 710–725.

Cameron, K. S., and Eltington, D. R. (1988). The conceptual foundations of organizational culture. In J. C. Smart (ed.), *Higher Education: Handbook of Theory and Research*. Volume IV. New York: Agathon Press.

Chaffee, E. E. and Tierney, W. G. (1988). *Collegiate Culture and Leadership Strategies*. New York: American Council on Education and Macmillan Publishing Company.

Childers, M. E. (1981). What is political about bureaucratic-collegial decision-making? *Review of Higher Education* 5(1): 25–45.

Clark, B. R. (1983). *The Higher Education System*. Berkeley: The University of California Press.

Clark, B. R. (1970). *The Distinctive College: Antioch, Reed and Swarthmore*, Chicago: Aldine.

Clark, B. R. (1971). Belief and loyalty in college organization. *Journal of Higher Education* 42: 499–520.

Clark, B. R. (1972). The organizational saga in higher education. *Administrative Science Quarterly* 17: 178–184.

Clark, M. S. and Mills, J. (1979). Interpersonal attraction in exchange and communal relationships. *Journal of Personality and Social Psychology* 37: 12–24.

Cohen, M. D., and March, J. G. (1974). *Leadership and Ambiguity: The American College Presidency*. New York: McGraw Hill Book Company.

Dahl, R. A. (1984). *Modern Political Analysis*. Fourth Edition. Englewood Cliffs, NJ: Prentice-Hall.

Dansereau, F. R., Graen, G., and Haga, W. J. (1975). A vertical dyad linkage approach to leadership within formal organizations: a longitudinal investigation of the role making process. *Organizational Behavior and Human Performance* 13(1).

Deal, T. E., and Kennedy, A. A. (1982). *Corporate Cultures: The Rites and Rituals of Corporate Life*. Reading, MA: Addison-Wesley.

Dill, D. D. (1982). The management of academic culture: notes on the management and meaning of social integration. *Higher Education* 11: 303–320.

Dubin, R. (1969). *Theory Building*. New York: The Free Press.

Fox, M. F. (1985). Publication, performance, and reward in science and scholarship. In J. C. Smart (ed.), *Higher Education: Handbook of Theory and Research*. Volume 1. New York: Agathon Press.

Gamson, W. (1968). *Power and Discontent*. Homewood, IL: Dorsey Press.

Glazer, J. S. (1990). Feminism and professionalism: the case of education and business. Paper presented at the Annual Meeting of the Association for the Study of Higher Education, Portland, OR.

Gouldner, A. W. (1960). The norm of reciprocity. *American Sociological Review* 25(2): 161–179.

Hackman, J. D. (1985). Power and centrality in the allocation of resources in colleges and universities. *Administrative Science Quarterly* 30: 61–77.

Hackman, J. R. (1976). Group influences on individuals. In Marvin D. Dunnette (ed.), *Handbook of Industrial and Organizational Psychology*. Chicago: Rand McNally College Publishing Company.

Hardy, C., Langley, A., Mintzberg, H., and Rose, J. (1984). Strategy formation in the university setting. In James L. Bess (ed.), *College and University Organization: Insights from the Behavioral Sciences*. New York: New York University Press.

Helsabeck, R. E. (1973). *The Compound System, A Conceptual Framework for Effective Decisionmaking in Colleges*. Berkeley: Center for Research and Developent in Higher Education, University of California.

Hofstede, G. H. (1980). *Culture's Consequences, International Differences in Work-Related Values*. Beverly Hills, CA: Sage Publications.

Homans, G. C. (1950). *The Human Group*. New York: Harcourt, Brace and World.

Huber, G. P., and McDaniel, R. R. (1986). The decision-making paradigm of organizational design. *Management Design* 32(5): 572–589.

Kerr, S. and Jermier, J. M. (1978). Substitutes for leadership: their meaning and measurement. *Organizational Behavior and Human Peformance* 22: 375–403.

Kuh, G. D., and Whitt, E. J. (1988). *The Invisible Tapestry: Culture in American Colleges and Universities*. ASHE/ERIC Higher Education Report No. 1. Washington, DC: American Association for Higher Education.

Lawrence, P. R., and Lorsch, J. *Organization and Environment*. Boston: Harvard University Press, 1967.

Leslie, D. W. (1975). Legitimizing university governance: theory and practice. *Higher Education* 4(2): 233–246.

Levi-Strauss, C. (1949). Le principe de feciprocite. In *Les Structures Elementaires de la Parente*. Abridged and translated by R. L. Coser and G. Frazer. Paris: Presses Universitaires de France.

Louis, M. R. (1985). An investigator's guide to workplace culture. In P. Frost et al., *Organizational Culture*. Beverly Hills: Sage Publishing Company.

Lunsford, T. F. (1963). Authority and ideology in the administered university. In C. E. Kruytbosch and S. L. Messinger (eds.), *The State of the University*. Beverly Hills: Sage Publications.

March, J. G., and Simon H. A. (1958). *Organizations*. New York: John Wiley and Sons.

Merton, R. K. (1973). *The Sociology of Science*. Chicago: University of Chicago Press.

Mintzberg, H. (1979). *The Structure of Organizations*. Englewood Cliffs, NJ: Prentice-Hall.

Mintzberg, H. (1983). *Structure in Fives, Designing Effective Organizations*. Englewood Cliffs, NJ: Prentice-Hall.

Meyer, J. W., and Rowan, B. (1977). Institutionalized organizations: formal structure as myth and ceremony. *American Journal of Sociology* 83(2): 340–363.

Mitroff, I. I. (1983). *Stakeholders of the Organization Mind*. San Francisco: Jossey-Bass.

Organ, D. W. (1988). *Organizational Citizenship Behavior: The Good Soldier Syndrome*. Lexington, MA: Lexington Books, D.C. Heath and Company.

Ouchi, W. G. (1980). Markets, bureaucracies, and clans. *Administrative Science Quarterly* 25(1): 129–141.

Parsons, T. (1951). *The Social System*. Glencoe, IL: The Free Press.

Parsons, T., and Platt, G. M. (1973). *The American University*. Cambridge, MA: Harvard University Press.

Platt, G. M., and Parsons, T. (1968). Decision making in the academic system: influence and power exchange. In C. E. Kruytbosch and S. L. Messinger (eds.), *The State of the University*. Beverly Hills, CA: Sage.

Pascale, R. T., and Athos, A. G. (1981). *The Art of Japanese Management*. New York: Simon and Schuster.

Perrow, C. (1970). *Organizational Analysis: A Structural View*. Monterey, CA: Brooks/ Cole.

Pfeffer, J. (1977). Power and resource allocation in organizations. In B. M. Staw and G. R. Salancik (eds.), *New Directions in Organizational Behavior*. Chicago: St. Clair Press.

Pfeffer, J. (1978). *Organizational Design*. Arlington Heights, IL: Davidson, Harlan, Inc.

Polanyi, M. (1958). *Personal Knowledge: Towards Post-Critical Philosophy*. Chicago: University of Chicago Press.

Ronge, V. (1974). The politicization of administration in advanced capitalist societies. *Political Studies:* 22(1): 86–93.

Sahlins, M. D. (1965). On the sociology of primitive exchange. In Association of Social Anthropologists of the Commonwealth: *The Relevance of Models for Social Anthropology*. Monograph No. 1. New York: Praeger.

Schein, E. H. (1985). *Organizational Culture and Leadership*. San Francisco: Jossey-Bass Publishers, Inc.

Selznick, P. (1957). *Leadership in Administration*. New York: Harper and Row Publishers.

Simon, H. A. (1957). *Administrative Behavior*. 2nd Edition. New York: The Free Press.

Staw, B. M. (1984). Motivation research versus the art of faculty management. In J. L. Bess (ed.), *College and University Organization: Insights from the Behavioral Sciences*. New York: New York University Press.

Stoelwinder, J. U., and Charns, M. P. (1981). The task field model of organizational analysis and design. *Human Relations* 34(9): 743–762.

Thompson, J. D. (1967). *Organizations in Action*. New York: McGraw Hill Book Company.

Thompson, J. D., and Tuden, A. (1959). Strategies, structures and processes of organizational decision. In J. D. Thompson and A. Tuden, *Comparative Studies in Administration*. Pittsburgh: University of Pittsburgh Press.

Toennies, F. (1957). *Community and Society (Gemeinschaft und Gesellschaft)*. Translated by C.P. Loomis. East Lansing: Michigan State University Press.

Vroom, V. H., and Jago, A. G. (1988). *Managing Participation in Organizations*. Englewood Cliffs, NJ: Prentice-Hall.

Vroom, V. H., and Yetton, P. W. (1973).*Leadership and Decision-making*. Pittsburgh: University of Pittsburgh Press.

Waters, M. (1989). Collegiality, bureaucratization, and professionalization: a Weberian analysis. *American Journal of Sociology* 94(5): 945–1072.

Weber, M. (1947). *The Theory of Social and Economic Organization*. (T. Parsons, ed.; A. M. Henderson and T. Parsons, trans.). New York: Free Press.

Weber, M. (1946). *From Max Weber: Essays in Sociology*. Translated, edited and with an Introduction by H. H. Gerth and C. W. Mills. New York: Oxford University Press.

Wittgenstein, L. (1921). *Tractatus Logico-philosophicus*. The German text of Wittgenstein's *Logisch-Philosophische Abhandlung*. New edition of the translation by D. F. Pears and B. F. McGuinness. London: Routledge and Kegan Paul, 1971.

Quality by Design: Toward a Framework for Academic Quality Management

David D. Dill
University of North Carolina at Chapel Hill

The research university, the cathedral of learning, rather than interpreting and integrating the larger society, came more and more to mirror it. Far from becoming a new community that would bring coherence out of chaos, it became instead a congeries of faculty and students, each pursuing its own ends, integrated not by any shared vision, but only by the bureaucratic procedures of the administration.

(Bellah et al., 1991, p. 155)

When you're through improving, you're through!
Don Mattingly

INTRODUCTION

The environment of colleges and universities is undergoing a major change in the last decades of the twentieth century. In the wake of external criticism regarding the perceived confusion and increasing irrelevance of academic programs in the United States, particularly undergraduate curricula (Association of American Colleges, 1985; Bennett, 1984; National Commission on Higher Education Issues, 1982; Study Group on the Conditions of Excellence in American Higher Education, 1984), some state governments have imposed external academic standards on colleges and universities, and both the national and state governments are calling upon institutions to make their existing academic standards more manifest (Morgan and Mitchell, 1985). Quality, long considered an ineffable abstraction in academe, is now discussed as something that can be managed and improved (Astin, 1991; Bergquist and Armstrong, 1986; Loder, 1990; Mayhew et al., 1990; Seymour, 1992; Seymour and Collett, 1991; Wilson, 1987). More recently, academic institutions have begun exploring the adoption of busi-

I wish to express my appreciation to Paul Batalden, Burton Clark, Jack Evans, Don Hossler, William McGaghie, Curtis McLaughlin, Frank Stritter, Deborah Teeter, and Everett Wilson for their valuable comments on this manuscript. The fallacies that remain are mine alone.

ness and industry management innovations for quality improvement (Marchese, 1991).

In a context of external calls for reform, and internal advocacy of particular solutions, it is possible that the most significant means for improving quality in academic settings will remain unexplored. The major contribution that scholarship can make to such discussions, particularly during their early stages, is to articulate a framework around which existing information can be organized and directions for needed research defined (Anthony, 1988). In the spirit of improving quality in colleges and universities, the objective of this review is wholly pragmatic. To paraphrase Kurt Lewin's famous remark, there is nothing as practical as a good framework. A means of classifying the relevant topics in an area is of equal value to researchers who wish their findings to relate to a developing body of knowledge, to instructors seeking an orderly arrangement for conveying available information, to systems designers who seek to improve existing academic processes, and to academic managers who wish to understand how to act more effectively.

The focus of this review is on *academic* quality. Each of the traditional functions of academic institutions—teaching, research, and public service—can potentially benefit from an attention to quality management (Seymour, 1991). The provision of public service by colleges and universities—for example, the management of medical faculty practice plans or the management of continuing education programs—is not substantially different from the provision of services in the private sector. The administration of academic research projects—particularly in engineering, medicine, the basic sciences, and certain fields of the social sciences—bears many similarities to the conduct of research in non-academic settings. In both these cases there is a developing literature on quality management, and its application to academic institutions is fairly direct. In the core function of teaching, however, the application of the existing literature and research on quality management is less clear. In the language of total quality management as it is being currently applied, what are the academic "processes" that need to be improved? Who are the "customers"? How are "customer perceptions" of quality to be determined? Who has responsibility for academic quality? There is also need for a more creative synthesis of existing conceptions of quality management with knowledge about the organization and management of academic institutions (Chaffee, 1989). For example, although academic institutions in all countries have become large organizations with hundreds of faculty members and thousands of students engaged in the repetitive production of categorically defined products—a liberal arts student, an MBA graduate, a research biologist, a surgeon—the production processes of most academic institutions are still conceived largely in terms of individual students.

The intent of the analysis to follow, therefore, is to conceptualize academic quality management at a level consistent with the reality of contemporary colleges and universities, that is, the management of quality in academic programs. The following section will more fully investigate the use of the term quality in higher education, and will contrast it with that in contemporary industrial settings. The succeeding sections will: review the means by which academic organizations seek to minimize quality variation in their academic programs; present a brief history of mechanisms for managing academic quality in American colleges and universities; and explore the implications of the organization and values of academic institutions for the implementation of academic quality systems. The concluding sections will introduce a framework for academic quality management and employ it to suggest possible directions for future research in the area.

A PERSPECTIVE ON QUALITY

The word "quality" has been used as a term of art in higher education, a mental abstraction that varies depending upon the perspective of the user (Olscamp, 1978). When quality has been defined as a concept that can be observed, counted, and objectively specified, it has most often been through peer assessments of institutional or program reputation (Cameron, 1985). The very first academic quality rankings were conducted in the initial decade of the twentieth century by J. McKeen Cattell (1910), based upon the judgment of leading researchers in ten fields of the basic sciences and two of the social sciences. Since Cattell's study, hundreds of quality ratings utilizing peer assessments have been published, most of them for a single professional field or academic discipline. Reviewing the history of scholarly peer assessments, Webster (1983; 1985a,b; 1986) compiled nine major multi-disciplinary academic quality rankings that rated at least fifteen academic disciplines and/or professional fields:

Major multi-disciplinary academic quality rankings*

Compilers	Year Published	Numbers of Fields Rated
Hughes	1925	20
Hughes	1934	35
Keniston	1959	24
Cartter	1966	29
Roose and Anderson	1970	36
Margulies and Blau	1973	17
Blau and Margulies	1974–75	18
Ladd and Lipset	1978	19
Jones, Lindzey and Coggeshall	1982	32

*(adapted from Webster, 1985a, p. 68)

In addition, during the 1980s, annual quality rankings of institutions of higher education, also employing forms of peer assessment, have been published by national periodicals such as *U.S. News and World Report.*

Extensive research has been conducted on these institutional and program ratings to identify predictors of academic quality (Astin, 1985; Astin and Solmon, 1979; Astin and Solmon, 1981; Beyer and Snipper, 1974; Conrad and Blackburn, 1985a,b; Conrad and Blackburn, 1986; Drew and Karpf, 1981; Fairweather, 1988; Fairweather & Brown, 1991; Garvin, 1980; Hagstrom, 1971; King and Wolfle, 1987; Lawrence and Green, 1980; Webster, 1981; Young et al., 1989). These studies reveal that measures of faculty scholarship and research, student selectivity, unit size, and various indicators of resources such as institutional dollars per student, size of endowment, and student/faculty ratios, are highly correlated with quality ratings, although the combination of variables varies depending on the unit of analysis (i.e., undergraduate education, graduate programs, or institutions as a whole). In addition, all of these measures are highly intercorrelated. For example, graduate program quality rankings are highly related to respondents' familiarity with the institutions, and a halo effect exists in which a graduate or undergraduate program may receive a high quality rating because it is at an institution of perceived quality (Fairweather, 1988; Kuh, 1981).

Alternative conceptions of quality in undergraduate institutions have been suggested (Astin, 1985; Solmon, 1981; Webster, 1981) including measures of student outcomes (Astin, 1991; Ewell, 1988). Outcome measures that have previously been studied include the proportion of an institution's baccalaureate recipients who complete doctoral degrees, the proportion who receive graduate fellowships, the proportion who are listed in *Who's Who*, the persistence rate of an institution's undergraduates, the lifetime earnings of its alumni, and alumni's ratings of their undergraduate experience. As Astin (1985) suggests, while the term outcome is generally thought synonymous with institutional impact, outcome studies are extremely difficult to interpret because of the high intercorrelations between reputational measures, particularly student selectivity, and various outcome measures. Furthermore, Astin's analysis reveals that differences in student outcomes at the graduate level are largely attributable to differences in student inputs.

One major problem of the reputational and outcomes views of quality, as currently defined, is the temptation to improve reputation or outcomes through external efforts that enhance the visibility of the institution rather than through internal efforts that improve the quality of educational programs. Thus, institutional administrations may address their time and resources to public relations, student recruitment, and fundraising rather than the redesign of critical educational processes. Finally, the voluminous research on program and institutional reputation, based primarily on ex post facto analyses of secondary data, provides a very limited understanding of how the quality of education can be improved.

In contrast to this focus on assessing quality in higher education through various measures of reputation, Cameron (1985) points out that quality in business and industry is measured through "the absence of errors" (p. 2). High quality products are extremely reliable and work without requiring repair. Low quality products are those with faults and mistakes. It is this latter perspective on quality that is now beginning to appear in the literature of higher education under the term "total quality management" (Seymour, 1991; Sherr and Teeter, 1991). What are the distinguishing characteristics of the business perspective on quality?

Quality control as a systematic activity in manufacturing has existed in the United States for over 60 years following the pioneering work of Walter Shewhart (1931). Active application of quality control knowledge in American industry languished following World War II, because of rapidly expanding markets and limited international competition (Garvin, 1988). In contrast, the Japanese adopted the ideas of Shewhart disciples, such as W. Edwards Deming (1986), and creatively applied them in their industrial sector. Other major contributors to the field have included Juran (1951), Feigenbaum (1961), Crosby (1979), and, increasingly, Japanese writers such as Ishikawa (1985). During the 1980s, as the dynamics of international industrial competition changed dramatically, American manufacturers "rediscovered" the potential for quality control. Deming's work, under the broader rubric of "total quality management" (TQM), has generated renewed interest and is now influencing quality management thinking in American higher education. Deming's writings offer a comprehensive perspective for achieving continual improvement in quality through knowledge of variation, guidelines for management, and specific analytical tools and methods. Deming's (1986) managerial guidelines are simplistically summarized in his so-called "14 points" (below). There have been various efforts to translate these 14 points into terms more accessible to possible adopters (Gitlow and Gitlow, 1987; Scherkenback, 1988) including those in higher education (Cornesky et al., 1990; Miller, 1991).

Deming's 14 points*

1. Create constancy of purpose for improvement of product and service.
2. Adopt the new philosophy.
3. Cease dependence on mass inspection.
4. End the practice of awarding business on price tag alone.
5. Constantly and forever improve the system of production and service.
6. Institute modern methods of training on the job.
7. Institute modern methods of supervising.
8. Drive out fear.

9. Break down barriers between departments.
10. Eliminate numerical goals for the work force.
11. Eliminate work standards and numerical quotas.
12. Remove barriers that hinder the hourly workers.
13. Institute a vigorous program of education and training.
14. Create a structure in top management that will push everyday on the above 13 points.

*(adapted from Deming, 1986).

Many of the 14 points for implementing total quality management advocated by Deming (1986) and his followers may fairly be described as old management elixer in new containers. For example, the requirement of gaining top management support before implementing TQM (point 14) has been a standard tenet of planned change advocates for decades (Dill and Friedman, 1979). The emphases on developing high morale among workers, education and training of personnel, satisfaction derived from the work itself rather than external incentives, and encouraging worker participation in decision-making (points 6–8, 10, and 11) have all been central components of the "human relations school" of management (Perrow, 1986). Nonetheless, among Deming's 14 points are several ideas that make his perspective particularly significant and challenging for institutions of higher education. Further, his perspective is undergirded by a sophisticated and creative application of Shewhart's (1931) statistical process control, with an emphasis on reducing variation.

At its core, Deming's (1986) program advocates that organizations commit themselves to continuous improvement of products and services to meet customers' needs. The Deming perspective can be further clarified by factoring his 14 points into six foundational themes. First, the imperative of constant and continuous improvement of quality (points 1 and 5). This goal can be compared to Crosby's (1979) program of "zero defects," but to do so underestimates the adaptive potential of continuous improvement. Zero defects might feasibly be achieved, but a dedication to *continuous* quality improvement would ultimately challenge existing quality standards themselves and encourage breakthrough innovations in underlying processes and products. This goal of continuous improvement is quite compatible with the academic value of the continual discovery (improvement) of knowledge, and of the ongoing professional self-development of faculty members. However, the academic value of continuous improvement has not been systematically applied to the underlying processes of education in colleges and universities.

A second key point of the Deming approach (1986) is the emphasis on obtaining consistent quality in incoming resources through the careful management of suppliers (point 4). While many institutions of higher education have placed an emphasis on student testing and selection, the potential relationship between variation in student outcomes and variation in measures of incoming student abilities has been under-investigated (for a counter argument, see Astin, 1991). Furthermore, little attention has been given to the role of colleges and universities as "customers," and their potential to improve the quality of their "suppliers."

A third key element in Deming's program (1986) is the active participation of all members of an organization's productive workforce in the improvement of quality (points 12 and 13). Among contemporary writers on quality management, Deming is distinctive in his call for workforce training and involvement in quality management, and this approach is highly consistent with academic norms of collegial decision-making as well as faculty authority over and responsibility for the design of educational programs.

In addition to these three themes, which are broadly compatible with academic culture, Deming's program (1986) contains three additional elements that challenge academic norms. For example, Deming stresses the importance of meeting customer needs as the basis for improving products and services (point 1). The opposition of academics, particularly humanists and social scientists, to the demands of the real world, and to the value of "utility," played a critical role in the emergence of the American university (Veysey, 1965), and continues to be an important force in defining the precarious balance between academic integrity and social need (Bellah, et al., 1991). A second point of tension is Deming's focus on the need for cooperation and coordination as a means of improving quality: Deming calls for each function to cease optimizing its own activity, and work together as a team (points 3, 5 and 9). Academic organizations have been categorized as the most differentiated of organizations (Weick, 1983) with very limited mechanisms for the horizontal integration of functionally separate units, as well as a strong value system of individual and program autonomy. Deming's emphasis on coordination in the improvement of quality is therefore, paradoxically, likely to generate both high resistance and, if implemented, high benefit. Third, Deming emphasizes that the improvement of quality does not come from inspection, or what in education might be termed assessment, but from *design*— from the continuous improvement of the underlying processes of production.

The emphasis on the design and redesign of underlying processes is the central tone in the complex chord of quality improvement that Deming (1986) plays. The centrality of design is further clarified by Deming's analytical perspective, which is wholly directed at reducing variation. This orientation to reducing variation, quite recognizable to educational researchers, is a creative application of the analysis of variance derived from the work of Shewhart (1931). Deming reasoned that in a given production process, samples of the product at any point would reveal variations from stated specifications. Such variation was an inevitable part of organizational life. The critical issue was to distinguish variation due to chance from variation indicative of problems in the production process.

Probability rules could be used to identify random error, because random variation occurred within statistically determined limits. Variation occurring outside those pre-established limits, or readings that revealed a trend, or "run," suggested the production process was no longer in "control," and indicated a problem to be investigated. Deming termed these non-random sources of error "special causes," usually traceable to the activities of an individual employee, or a particular lot of material. Once corrected, the existing process could be brought back into "statistical control."

Useful as the foregoing perspective is, it is not Deming's (1986) major point. Rather, Deming distinguishes between "special causes" and "common causes" of variation. Simply because a process was in statistical control did not mean it was optimal. To move the quality average up or down (e.g., percentage of students graduating, average score on comprehensive exams, number of entering students requiring mathematics remediation, etc.), or to narrow the range of variation around the target point, required changing underlying processes shared by numerous operators, machines, or products. Common causes therefore included poor product design, incoming materials unsuited to their use, inefficient technologies, and ineffective supervision. Furthermore, Deming argued that while special causes may potentially be corrected by the actions of individuals, common causes, which supposedly account for 85 percent of all quality problems, can only be corrected by the actions of management or collectivities.

The distinction between special and common causes of variation reveals the potential power of Deming's perspective on quality improvement, and suggests both its possible significance for higher education, and why it will be difficult to implement. For example, Cross (1990), reflecting the prevailing academic norm of individual autonomy, argues that large scale academic improvement will come from the application of academic assessment techniques by individual faculty members in their own classrooms. From Deming's (1986) perspective, it is immediately clear that this will address special causes of quality variation in student learning, but that the substantial gains in academic quality possible by addressing the common causes of variation will continue to be ignored. To attack common causes of variation in what students learn would require systematically reducing the variability of knowledge possessed by incoming students, and continually redesigning academic programs and underlying educational processes based upon assessments of what students learn, as well as the expectations of those with whom graduates are placed. This effort would require a degree of coordination and collective participation among faculty members (i.e., the "management") in academic program design that clearly conflicts with prevailing academic norms of individual and program autonomy (Clark, 1963).

QUALITY MANAGEMENT IN HIGHER EDUCATION:
CLANS, BUREAUCRACIES, AND MARKETS

Examined superficially, the contemporary concern with quality management in higher education appears to introduce a wholly new perspective. A review of some of the classic histories of American higher education, for example, reveals no direct reference to the term "quality" (Bledstein, 1976; Brubacher and Rudy, 1976; Kimball, 1986; Rudolph, 1962; Veysey, 1965). But when quality management is redefined as the reduction of variation, and when this perspective is applied to understanding the nature of higher education processes, the means by which quality has been achieved historically in higher education come more clearly into focus.

Academic institutions, where the core processes are teaching, research, and scholarship, are intensely human organizations. Variation in organizational processes can be attributed primarily to differing patterns of human behavior, rather than to variability in machines, or mechanical processes. Every human organization confronts the challenge of reducing the variability, instability, and unpredictability of individual human actions in order to create the cooperative patterns of behavior necessary for an organization to function (Katz and Kahn, 1978). Allport (1933) drew attention to the difference between the normal distribution of individual behavior outside organizational settings, and the sharply reduced variation in individual behavior characteristic of those engaged in cooperative actions within organizations. Allport graphically represented the distribution of individual behavior in organizations with the "J" curve: the extreme cases are reduced in number, the "bell-shape" is sharpened to a peak, and the distribution becomes asymmetrical. For example, the distribution of class times across a 24 our period at a residential college would likely be quite different if the times reflected the normal predispositions of students rather than the production needs of the institution.

A major focus of the field of organizational theory, therefore, has been the development of models concerned with "control," that is, the mechanisms whereby organizations have attempted to reduce variation in human behavior (Ouchi, 1979). The primary focus of these models has been on shared values and enforced rules of conduct. For example, Ouchi (1980) has classified organizational control into three categories: clans, bureaucracies, and markets. By clans he means the reliance on normative mechanisms including shared values, traditions, and networks of socialization and communication. Thus, variability in the process of instruction may be reduced by shared beliefs about the knowledge to be taught, as well as common ethical standards regarding teaching, that are part of the faculty culture at the level of a department, school, or overall university (Dill, 1982). By bureaucracy, Ouchi (1980) means the reliance on hierarchical authority and rules as a means of achieving cooperation among organizational members. Thus, variability in professional teaching may be reduced by a certification examination mandated by a state-endorsed board of examiners. Less intuitively, Ouchi (1980) outlines *market* forms of organizational control that rely neither on shared norms among providers, nor on organizationally sanctioned rules and regulations, but rather on market forces to shape individual behavior. In this way, variability in the process of teaching may be reduced through consumer and supplier contractual arrangements in which competition and prices replace the normative beliefs of professionals or organizational regulations as a means of behavioral control.

The applicability of Ouchi's model (1980) is illustrated in a cross-national comparison of systems of higher education (Clark, 1983). The British university system was typified by a long tradition of clan or collegial control with very limited use of administrative hierarchy and bureaucratic rules and regulations: "There is no direct and comprehensive chain of command, and the notion of an order being issued from one person to another is generally felt to be alien to the way in which British universities should govern their affairs" (Moodie and Eustace, 1974, p. 21). The heavy reliance on tradition and a common professional culture was made possible by the maintenance of a small, elite higher education system and by the existence of only two universities—Oxford and Cambridge—until the middle of the nineteenth century. As late as 1970 almost one-third of all university teachers had received their education from Oxbridge (Van de Graaf, 1978). A common tradition regarding the nature of an academic program—the single-subject honors degree—was characteristic of university education. Variance was further reduced through the collegial mechanism of faculties, groupings of professors from related subjects who articulated common admissions standards, developed and regulated required examinations in all subject fields, and reviewed new courses and proposed programs (Moodie and Eustace, 1974).

A further and unique form of clan control in British universities was the use of external examiners to assure common academic standards across departments (Williams, 1979). Each external examiner was expected to approve drafts of the required examination papers in the designated department, assess a sample of completed examination papers, conduct, where appropriate, oral exams as a means of validating the examinations process, and participate with the department's internal board of examiners in the awarding of marks. The use of external examiners has been a tradition in the British university system for over a hundred years; characteristic of the reliance on shared norms rather than bureaucratic regulation, there was no formal codification of this process until 1989 (CVCP, 1989).

By contrast, on the continent, variation in academic behavior was reduced by means of national regulations regarding the demonstrated knowledge necessary for a student to gain admission to university, as well as the curricular content necessary for individual degrees and courses of study (Neave and Rhoades, 1987). Variation in academic programs was further reduced by the requirement that university students successfully complete nationally regulated examinations in order to receive academic credentials. In comparison with the clan model of control characteristic of the British system, the continental systems relied heavily on hierarchical authority and standardizing rules and regulations—the bureaucratic model of control.

The American system of higher education, has been characterized as relying primarily on market mechanisms as a means of control due to the system's size, diversity, and the historic absence of state and federal regulations on the content of education (Clark, 1983). The development of American higher education, however, suggests a continuing evolution in the mechanisms employed at the organizational level for reducing variation. The earliest American colleges exhibited clan procedures of control, which were gradually supplemented by institutionally-based hierarchy and rules, and have culminated in increasing reliance on market-based mechanisms.

THE REDUCTION OF ACADEMIC VARIANCE IN AMERICAN HIGHER EDUCATION: A BRIEF HISTORY

The earliest means of reducing variation, reflected in the organization of the colonial colleges, was through instruction in a common tradition of set texts and adherence to the recitation method of instruction (Kimball, 1986). For example, as late as 1819 five faculty members and two tutors instructed all 118 students at the University of North Carolina in a set program of studies required of all students (Powell, 1972). Variation in student knowledge at entrance was controlled by a carefully defined system of preparatory studies that required a student to demonstrate knowledge of specific subjects and books, including *Caesar's Commentaries* (7 books), as well as *St. John's Gospel*, and the *Acts of the Apostles*, both in Greek. Variation in instruction was reduced by an explicit listing of subjects and works—*Sallust*, the whole, Cicero's *Orations*—to be taught to all students at the appropriate class level: freshman, sophomore, junior, and senior. Variation was further reduced by standardizing the process of instruction. The entire freshman class was taught as a cohort, and the same faculty member taught each required subject to each class. Finally, the form of teaching was standardized through the use of the recitation method of instruction; individual students were required to memorize texts and then recite them in class.

Several critical points can be made about this early form of quality management. First, while the colonial colleges exhibited little of the collegial authority structure usually associated with clan control, the standardization of these colleges was more clearly a product of common norms and a shared tradition than mandated regulation. Kimball (1986), for example, has argued that, despite the obvious differences in language, political control, and religious authority among higher education institutions, the curricula and forms of instruction in the universities of western Europe and the colonial colleges of early America reflected a common cultural heritage up until the end of the eighteenth century. Second, while the colonial colleges possessed, from a modern perspective, a rigid curriculum and limited conception of education (Veysey, 1965), the colleges clearly illustrated the mechanisms whereby a clan form of academic quality control can produce a coherent educational design and common standards of instruction intended to reduce variation. A primary reliance on tradition as a form of control, including a fixed curriculum with set texts, and a common form of instruction (i.e., the Socratic seminar) is still employed by the St. John's Colleges of Annapolis, Maryland, and Santa Fe, New Mexico (Grant and Riesman, 1978). Shared norms and beliefs, in the form of faculty cultures and subcultures, continue as the principal form of variance reduction in the disciplines and professional fields (Becher, 1989). For example, the design of an academic program in an upper division major, graduate field, or professional school is primarily dependent upon collegial mechanisms and appeals to shared disciplinary norms. Standardization in instruction continues to rely upon disciplinary traditions: the case method of teaching in business schools; case analysis in law schools; rounds in medical schools; and the evocative lecture of the humanities.

The exclusive reliance on the clan model as the primary means of assuring quality control within American colleges and universities declined after the American revolution because of changes in the larger society as well as in the academic profession (Veysey, 1965). The enlightenment conception of freedom involved individualistic free choice, and it was this value that became ascendant in American culture following establishment of the new nation. Harvard President Charles W. Eliot, who argued against the required classical curriculum and for the elective principle, articulated these values clearly:

> "Free choice implies that there are no studies which are recognized as of supreme merit . . . the accumulated wisdom of the race cannot prescribe with certainty the studies which will best develop the human mind in general between the ages of eighteen and twenty-two" (Eliot, 1898, pp. 140–141).

This argument was pregnant with academic variation.

The political and legal framework of the emerging American nation did not offer the existing colleges and universities the luxury of monopoly status. Unlike European universities, American colleges and universities could be independent of the state; national regulations did not limit opportunities for institutional innovation or adaptation to new markets (Ben-David, 1972). In the early part of the nineteenth century enrollments in American colleges with classical curricula dropped substantially despite a rapidly growing population (Burke, 1982). It was only with the opening of new universities that adopted forms of the elective principle, and more importantly added programs in the sciences, modern languages, and applied professions, that enrollments rose again. This response to market forces also served the emerging faculty interest in specialization.

The introduction of flexibility in the curriculum for both students and faculty members as well as the rapid growth in enrollment of colleges and universities after the Civil War, required the adoption of more bureaucratic modes of variance reduction. During the nineteenth century the relatively low state of the American secondary schools, and the idiosyncratic requirements of the developing colleges produced substantial variation in background and ability among entering college freshmen, even within a particular institution. This in turn motivated various organizational innovations to standardize the knowledge of incoming college students (Brubacher and Rudy, 1976). In 1870 state institutions such as the University of Michigan adopted the German practice of certifying students based upon their high school diploma. Unlike the German practice, there were no state regulations and exams to assure uniformity of public high schools; hence the Michigan faculty visited and inspected local high schools at regular intervals. In 1878 the New York State Board of Regents adopted standardizing examinations for determining entrance to colleges. In 1880 the Regents published high school course syllabi to furnish guidance for schools preparing students for the Regents' examinations. These various approaches, however, did not address the issue of assessing students who crossed state lines. In the 1890s, under the leadership of Nicholas Murray Butler of Columbia University and Charles W. Eliot of Harvard, the forerunner of the College Entrance Examination Board was created to insure uniformity in college requirements and examinations. Following the success of psychological testing in the First World War, greater emphasis in admissions was placed upon tests that estimated potentiality and aptitude.

In addition to the mentioned changes in the process of admissions, the adoption of the elective curriculum had other implications for the management of colleges, including rules to govern student curricular choice, and record keeping on the choices made. Consistent with the demands of bureaucratic control, more administrators were needed to coordinate the intricate credit system required for student admissions and educational accounting (Duryea, 1973). One of the first of the administrative specializations, subordinate to the office of the president, was the office of registrar. The median period of greatest growth in registrar positions took place during the 1880s when the elective curriculum was on the rise and academic bookkeeping became much more complicated.

The elimination of the holistic design of the classical curriculum and the adoption of the elective curriculum also left unsettled the means by which the elective curriculum could be coordinated into an academic program for students.

Unlike Europe's standardizing regulations on curricula and exams, which were promulgated by national ministries of education, the United States' curricular rules were developed and imposed through the governance process of each institution:

> The scholars within each department took an internal view of their subject, which they pressed upon the faculty as a whole in the usual juggling and balancing operations of university politics. The result was to turn the curriculum into a congeries of departmental courses, each taught by a specialist and linked by a variety of schemes which combined elements of compulsion and free election, of concentration and distribution (Handlin and Handlin, 1970, pp. 76–77).

Thus the design of undergraduate programs, particularly in large universities, came to rely on negotiated rules and regulations governing student course selections. Developed by representative faculty committees, these regulations were interrupted by occasional experiments with more coherent designs such as the contemporary civilization program at Columbia University in 1919, the undergraduate college at the University of Chicago in the 1930s, and the program in general education at Harvard in 1945 (Ben-David, 1972). Brubacher and Rudy (1976) assert that the result has been a set of requirements in which individual courses were taught with little conscious attention to their interrelation, and the undergraduate educational program reflected an intellectual agnosticism about overall design.

In addition to attempting to reduce the variation in students' general education programs by rules on course selections, numerous colleges also adopted collegial forms of "inspection" (Smallwood, 1935). For example, after President Eliot was succeeded by A. Lawrence Lowell in 1909, Harvard initially experimented with, and eventually adopted, general examinations in each disciplinary field. These exams required students to synthesize and organize an entire subject as a means of distinguishing between normal and honors degrees. After the First World War, Swarthmore College President Frank Aydelotte, a former Rhodes Scholar, adapted the English external examiner system to the United States by inviting faculty members from other universities to set the examinations for honors students at the College. A third example of the influence of British quality control methods in the United States was implemented at Reed College just prior to World War I. Students entering the senior year of college were expected to pass a qualifying examination, following which they were required to complete a thesis, and pass an oral defense before graduation.

A final form of bureaucratic control unique to the American system was the effort to develop standards for institutions and programs of higher education. Following the Civil War the number of new institutions of higher education in the United States steadily increased, with limited governmental effort toward standardization and control (Brubacher and Rudy, 1976). New York State, through its Board of Regents, established minimum standards for colleges and universities. But New York was unusual; the majority of states passed no regulations to govern educational programs or degrees to be granted, nor did they exercise any supervision over institutions, once they had been incorporated. Continued efforts were made in the last half of the nineteenth century to encourage the United States Bureau of Education to assume a role in standardization, but these efforts failed. At the beginning of the twentieth century a cooperative of educational institutions called the North Central Association of Colleges and Secondary Schools developed criteria for the accreditation of colleges, and other comparable regional associations followed. Throughout the twentieth century the number and variety of accrediting agencies for both institutional and specialized programs have proliferated. While the American system of accreditation can be seen as a clan or collective form of control, it has been an ineffective guarantor of academic quality. Criticism of the process has been constant, because accreditation reviews do not inspect student performance directly, but rely primarily upon institutional indicators of quality (Astin, 1991). Recent calls for the recognition of student learning outcomes as an indicator of quality have had some effect on both institutional and program accreditation (Dinham and Evans, 1991; Thrash, 1988). Regulations issued in 1987 will require all federally approved accreditation organizations to collect outcomes information as part of the accreditation process (Ewell, 1991b).

The movement from the classical to the elective curriculum, as well as the spread and elaboration of colleges and universities, limited the effectiveness of the clan model of control as a means of reducing variation in American undergraduate higher education. Similar to the European pattern, bureaucratic forms of control evolved, relying primarily on rules and regulations addressing the processes of admissions, registration, college examinations, and standards for institutional accreditation. Unlike Europe, where bureaucratic forms of control developed in national ministries of education, thus standardizing the overall system of higher education, in the United States bureaucratic forms developed primarily within each institution. Therefore, bureaucratic forms of academic control in the United States have not led to the same degree of standardization in quality across institutions common to other developed countries.

The concept of a market form of control has been closely associated with American higher education because the absence of national government policies regulating higher education has led to an open competition among institutions for students, faculty members, and resources, and the consequent adaptiveness of institutions to new programs desired by the public (Ben-David, 1972; Clark, 1983). Between 1636, when Harvard was founded, and 1980 the open market system of higher education in the United States grew from 1 to 3,150 institutions of higher education (Clark, 1987). While many institutions failed, particularly during the depression periods of the 1830s, 1880s, and 1930s (Burke, 1982), the clear trend was toward institutional proliferation and diversity (Birnbaum, 1983). Market control at the national level caused an increase, rather than a decrease, in variation.

Ben-David (1972), however, suggests that, with occasional downturns, America has experienced a continual "boom economy" for higher education fueled by an expanding domestic economy, constantly growing population, and, unlike continental Europe and England, a near total absence of governmental policy on academic quality standards. There is substantial evidence, beginning in the 1970s, that this market became saturated, that critical resources such as government support, students, and the very credibility of the institutions themselves are now static or in decline, and that a truly competitive economy exists in American higher education for the first time in its history (Zammuto, 1986). Recent research (Cameron and Tschirhart, 1992) confirms the development of a "post-industrial environment" for colleges and universities in the United States, characterized by substantial turbulence including rising competition and increasingly scarce resources. For example, more money is now spent on postsecondary education outside colleges and universities than inside them, the percentage of postsecondary education provided by colleges and universities is in decline, and the failure rate for institutions of higher education recently exceeded that for either government or business organizations. Cameron and Tschirhart (1992) further discovered that colleges and universities that maintained their effectiveness in this new environment, did so by adopting new management strategies. Many academic institutions have, for instance, responded by systematically reducing the collection of programs that they offer (Dube and Brown, 1983; Heydinger, 1983; Shirley and Volkwein, 1978). These program evaluation procedures are modeled on the portfolio analysis schemes of investment managers—assessing each academic program based upon its potential for growth, stability, or decline. Intrinsic to these program assessments are judgments regarding each program's quality, usually based upon external peer assessments, as well as assessments of the program's capacity to attract students, and external financial support.

Market control as a substitute for collegial values or bureaucratic regulation is also evident in the adoption of "every-tub-on-its-own-bottom" or "profit center" approaches to university resource allocation (James, 1990). In this approach, a unit's worth is determined through internal competition, and is measured in part by its ability to generate revenues from tuition, gifts, and research grants. This latter example illustrates the critical components of market control: competition, outputs sufficiently explicit that they can be measured, and a resulting quantifiable value that reflects the unit's internal efficiency. The evolution toward market control as a means to reduce variation in quality has also become visible in state government efforts to improve higher education through outcomes assessment legislation (Astin, 1991; Ewell, 1991b; National Governors' Association, 1986; Newman, 1987). In the mid-1980s several national reform reports appeared that called for publicly available, institutionally comparable, student performance information that could inform consumer choice on which college to attend, and could guide state-level policy and resource allocation decisions:

> First, to be maximally credible, assessment techniques should be easily understood and should, if possible, result in quantitative indicators of institutional or program performance. Although academic improvement remains a goal, it is achieved primarily through the action of external market forces informed by assessment results and through the unilateral responses of institutions to incentives or sanctions applied through their appointed governing or regulatory bodies. Above all, the process should emphasize demonstrable return on investment in the form of aggregate student performance (Ewell, 1991b, p. 80).

The essential exchange relationship characteristic of market control is illustrated by state policies on incentives: "performance funding" as practiced in Tennessee, in which those institutions demonstrating the best assessment scores receive additional resources (Banta, 1986); or "directed investment" as practiced in Florida, New Jersey, and Virginia, in which marginal resources are directed to institutions whose assessments reveal problems and deficiencies (Berdahl and Studds, 1989). While at the beginning of the 1980s only 3 or 4 states had initiated outcomes assessment programs, by 1991, 27 states had implemented a program, and an additional dozen states are expected to enact programs in the next five years (Ewell, 1991b).

The detailed history of quality management in American higher education has yet to be written. This brief review begins to suggest the range of quality control mechanisms that have evolved in colleges and universities. Characteristic of the clan or collegial model, variation in quality has been reduced through consensually developed curricula, common instructional techniques, and collegial forms of student evaluation such as external examiners. Bureaucratic means of reducing variation, relying principally upon hierarchical authority and rules, have evolved in the United States primarily at the institutional level, in the form of admissions standards, and academic distribution requirements. Market forms of reducing variation, by contrast, place emphasis on competition, measurable outcomes, and a contractual relationship between program providers and customers or beneficiaries.

More significantly, this analysis also suggests an evolution in the means of controlling quality in American academic organizations from clan or collegial forms of quality control, to bureaucratic means of control, and more recently to various adaptations of market control mechanisms. These observed changes correspond with an emerging theory of organizations termed the "transactions costs" model (Williamson, 1985). Williamson has argued that the emergence of particular organizations, as well as aspects of their internal structure, can be understood in terms of the organization's efficiency in negotiating, enforcing, and adjusting transactions between parties. Both economic and organizational analyses (Lawrence and Lorsch, 1986; Williamson, 1985) suggest that as the market for an organization's products becomes more competitive, hierarchical or bureaucratic forms of control may become less efficient. In a hierarchical structure, insulated from market forces, managers have the incentive to pursue functional (i.e., sub-unit) goals beyond levels optimal for the effectiveness of the overall organization. Similar analyses of academic management have suggested that the inefficiencies of contemporary forms of bureaucratic decision-making and control are contributing to declining academic productivity (Massy, 1989).

The historical evolution of control mechanisms in American higher education, from clan, to a mixture of bureaucratic and clan, and to increasing institutional adoption and external imposition of market control mechanisms, suggests a decline in the efficiency of colleges and universities to organize transactions under competitive conditions. These developments seem to support Williamson's (1985) essential argument that market forms of control are the most efficient means of organizing transactions. Thus, as external demands for efficiency in higher education increase, market forms of control, such as requirements for academic outcomes assessments, may be imposed through public policy, as is now occurring in the states reported above. Similarly, university reforms currently being implemented in the United Kingdom and Europe are beginning to strip away the bureaucratic regulations that previously controlled universities, and are subjecting academic institutions to market forces (Dill, 1992).

These changes would suggest that the rise of market forms of control, and the decline of hierarchical or clan forms of control, are inevitable in higher education. Ironically, however, clan or collegial forms of control have been found, under certain circumstances, to be more efficient than market mechanisms as a means of organizing transactions under competitive conditions (Williamson, 1985). Research on Japanese organizations, for example, has consistently illustrated the competitive superiority of forms of control emphasizing collegial decision making, the development of employees, and a strong institutional culture (Ouchi, 1980). How is it that in a period when clan and collegial control mechanisms are being actively advocated in business and industry, they appear to be declining in academic institutions (Dill, 1982)? This anomaly calls for an analysis of academic values and academic structure.

ACADEMIC INTEGRATION AND ACADEMIC AUTONOMY: THE FUNDAMENTAL CONFLICT IN IMPROVING EDUCATIONAL QUALITY

The evolution of the American college and university system appears to have produced a structural form and value system within academic institutions largely inimical to contemporary concerns with quality improvement (Wilson, 1987). The relationship between organizational structure, academic values, and educational process requires further explication.

In a classic analysis of organizations, Lawrence and Lorsch (1986) argued that as organizations expand and confront more complex demands from their environments, they implement a more segmented division of labor. Academic organizations, for example, continuously subdivide into specialties, programs, and departments as they struggle to respond to the growing complexity of knowledge, and of societal demands for specialized education. Lawrence and Lorsch described this process as "differentiation," the organization's segmentation into different administrative and operational units. Differentiation, however, connotes both structural and behavioral differences. That is, academic departments are not only actively involved in different subject matters, but they also recruit specialists with differing prior educations and capabilities, and with distinctive habits of work, forms of organization, and values (Becher, 1989; Biglan, 1973). But, Lawrence and Lorsch argued, if organizations are to continue to survive the dynamic interactions with their environments, they must also seek unity of effort by linking together the differentiated segments. This process they described as "integration;" it involves various mechanisms designed to increase communication and decrease conflict among units with differing functions and orientations.

Academic institutions are among the most highly differentiated and least integrated of organizations (Alpert, 1985; Weick, 1983). Clark (1983) argues that because free inquiry and the autonomy of reason are necessary conditions for academic work, differentiation is intrinsic to the task of discovery and invention:

> The basic direction of change . . . is toward fragmentation and loose coupling. As the disciplines and professional fields become evermore specialized, they tend as aggregates, to be ever more disunited. The sources of change lie in the interests, ideas, and organization of these disparate areas. Each field has important dynamics of its own. Each is an autonomous career: for example that of physicist or economist or classicist. Each has organizational turf to maintain, define, and expand. Each has a bounded body of knowledge, analytical approaches, and methods it can claim as its own . . . (p. 206)

Similarly, Weick (1983) has articulated the tradeoff between academic cohesion and scholarly accuracy: actions that strengthen the community may weaken scholarship; actions that strengthen scholarship may weaken community. Because the validity of its knowledge is essential to the university's survival, social ties or collegial arrangements that may limit and bias scholarship are not valued.

The scarcity of lateral linkages is reinforced by the norm of academic freedom, and autonomy. As Clark (1963) suggests, over time the norms of academic freedom and authority have devolved from a protective shield for the academic profession as a whole, to protection for the rights of collective faculties, to protection for the autonomy of the separate disciplines, to now safeguarding the autonomy of the individual faculty members, even from the collective authority of her or his colleagues.

This extreme form of individualism in academic settings is illustrated by the manner in which necessary linkages are carried out. In other organizations linkages are managed by administrative units or by clearly established collective mechanisms. In academic organizations, linkages are accomplished by the activities, frequently informal, of individuals (Weick, 1983):

> A dean, the senior person in an area, the expert on a topic, the person who has least status, or the person with extra time are chosen for locally idiosyncratic reasons to represent larger interests, which themselves are not homogeneous. (p. 17)

The most difficult coordination, that which exists between the separable functions of teaching, research, and public service, is assumed to occur *within* a particular faculty member as she/he thinks through the impact of one activity or the other; an assumption unique to academic institutions (Bess, 1982; Weick, 1983). Even when integration involves cross-departmental, or cross-specialty, coordination within the single function of teaching, the bureaucratic or collegial mechanisms for coordination are weak (Bess, 1982). Again reliance for integration falls to the individual, in this case the individual student who is expected to make sense out of an academic program that may lack a coherent, integrated design. Kimball (1986) argues that the individualism of the contemporary university has turned the required classical curriculum of the early colleges on its head:

> Conversely, what is also not appreciated is that the individualism and free pursuit of truth . . . hazard self-indulgent and nihilistic education and culture, which can lead finally to anarchy. The chaotic liberal education of the late twentieth century stands, in fact, at the opposite pole from the dogmatic liberal arts of the early nineteenth century (p. 237).

The lack of consistent academic program design and reinforcing quality control has been revealed in studies of the extraordinary variation in the course selections of undergraduate students (Ratcliffe and Associates, 1990; Zemsky, 1989), and has led to charges that academic individualism is responsible for the observed anomie, confusion, and disinterest among many college students (Bellah et al., 1991). Less noted is the parallel between the dehumanizing, specialized, repetitive piece work of modern manufacturing, and the disconnected, specialized, repetitive course teaching characteristic of contemporary American undergraduate programs. If the former may contribute to a loss of meaning and commitment to craft among industrial workers, the latter may similarly contribute to faculty members' flights from undergraduate teaching. Instead, faculty members have increased their commitment to graduate and professional teaching, where a course *may* be part of a coherent program for each student, and to research and scholarship, where faculty members' efforts can lead to a complete, publicly acknowledged, and signed work of craftsmanship.

The decline of integrating mechanisms in academic institutions is due not only to the ascendancy of individual specialization and autonomy, but also to the ways in which we have come to view academic organizations. During the 1970s a highly influential collection of studies of academic institutions emerged that typified academic structure as "loosely coupled" (Cohen et al., 1972; Meyer and Rowan, 1978; Weick, 1976). Loosely coupled systems were described as highly differentiated, with limited and tentative responsiveness between elements (Weick, 1976). Within academic organizations, loose coupling was described as "organized anarchy" and was correlated with unclear technology, ambiguous goals and preferences, and fluid participation by members (Cohen et al., 1972). Within educational organizations more generally (Meyer and Rowan, 1978), loose coupling was associated with an observed lack of relationship between means and ends, as well as with an absence of inspection and evaluation of educational work. Educational structure was argued to consist largely of myth and ceremony, and the legitimacy and quality of educational organizations were dependent upon an unexamined "logic of confidence" (Meyer and Rowan, 1978). Loose coupling has become a dominant perspective for understanding academic structure (Birnbaum, 1988; Clark, 1983; Peterson, 1985), and, unsurprisingly, research and scholarship on organizational mechanisms for integration and lateral coordination in institutions of higher education has been limited (Bess, 1982; Dill, 1982).

There is a critical need for revisiting the perspective of loose coupling, particularly as it applies to academic organizations, because the perspective has been misrepresented and overgeneralized (Orton and Weick, 1990). Organizational models that stress the ambiguity and loose connections, the lack of relationship between means and ends, and the largely symbolic nature of academic organization, indirectly delegate increased authority and autonomy to individual faculty members, at the expense of collegial authority and collegial control. As Perrow (1986) has observed, organizational structure is a function not only of core technology and environment, but also of power. Similarly, Williamson (1985) has argued that one reason for the observed inefficiencies of organizational structures is the "opportunism" of organizational members who wish to pursue their own goals rather than those of their organization. Thus, there is a genuine potential for self-interested bias in academic models that present academic organizations as necessitating decoupled structures. Furthermore, the contingent nature of loosely coupled systems has generally been underestimated. These descriptive models were articulated immediately following the period of the largest expansion of higher education in American history (Ben-David, 1972).

Cohen et al.'s (1972) original research noted that the conditions of "organized anarchy" were partially a function of "organizational slack" understood as money and other resources provided by the organization's environment. Similarly, Weick (1976) argued that loosely coupled systems were related to slack times when there is an excessive amount of resources relative to demands, as well as to weak feedback linkages between outcomes and inputs. Weick explicitly suggested treating loose coupling as a dependent variable; he suggested identifying the environments or contexts, including different national contexts, that affect whether coupling is loose or tight. More recently Weick (Orton and Weick, 1990) emphasized that loose coupling was intended, and must be understood, as a dialectical concept, combining the contradictory concepts of autonomy and connection: "When loose coupling is portrayed as decoupling, the diminished emphasis on connectedness, responsiveness, and interdependence dissolves the dialectic." (p. 207)

Studies of R & D organizations—settings that share with academic organizations the norms of professional specialization, the technology of research and discovery, and the problems of structural segmentation—have led to a markedly different tradition of research on organizational structure, with an emphasis on the problems of organizational integration (Dill and Pearson, 1991). Research on reducing the cost and time of new product and process development, as well as increasing product and process quality, consistently reveals the importance of horizontal integrating mechanisms in research organizations, including informal "information networks," the integrating role of "product champions," innovation teams, cross-functional task forces, and various adaptations of matrix structures. Research on effective technology-based companies (Schoonhoven and Jelinek, 1990), suggests that these horizontal integrating mechanisms promote both individual and organizational learning whereby an organization re-designs itself. This "multi-learning"—learning across multiple levels, and across multiple functions—can lead to a strong culture of innovation in processes and products (Imai et al., 1985).

The tradition of individual faculty autonomy, and of a corresponding loosely coupled organizational structure, has had a substantial impact on the academic program of colleges and universities. It has led to a rich diversity of instruction providing greater student choice, and mitigated faculty value conflicts, particularly in the humanities and social sciences, through greater specialization. But it has also arguably eroded the collegial structures of academic quality control, substantially increased the costs of education while decreasing instructional productivity, and likely increased variation in student learning (Massy, 1989; Seymour, 1989). While the importance of academic autonomy, particularly in the selection and pursuit of scholarly and research topics, is essential to the academic enterprise (Clark, 1983), the extension of individual autonomy to the structure of the curriculum is much less easy to defend. Two recent national reports focusing on academic curricular content and structure have suggested that academic institutions are largely, and unhealthily, unaccountable to their primary constituents for their educational product (Bennett, 1984; Association of American Colleges, 1985). The previously discussed state and federal initiatives on market control and outcomes assessment have been a primary result of these criticisms. From the standpoint of the academic profession, a responsible reaction to these criticisms would be a more substantive program of research on the nature of collegial integrating mechanisms and means of quality control in institutions of higher education. As one concerned academic remarked:

> The principle of autonomy cannot be ditched; on the contrary, strong relevance and accountability measures . . . must be met with increased consciousness concerning the internalist mechanisms for quality control in the knowledge process (quoted in Becher, 1989, p. 169).

DEMING REVISITED

The opportunities and challenges for institutions of higher education provided by the Deming (1986) perspective on quality management, introduced earlier, can now be more clearly drawn. First, Deming's approach provides a framework to guide managerial action within organizations subject to market economic forces. One criticism of the emerging economic theory of the firm is the failure of the model to relate efficiencies in decision-making structure to efficiencies in production techniques, although both can be understood as essential contributors to organizational form (McGuinness, 1990). That is, transaction costs may be a function both of the design of organizational structure and of the underlying organizational technology. By focusing on reduction in the variance of products and processes, Deming's analysis could lead to continual improvement in both the basic production processes of an organization, and their supporting organizational structure, thus lessening the costs of transactions. The Deming perspective thereby provides an insight into the means by which the design of the production process provides longer term efficiencies critical to success in a competitive system. In addition, Deming's focus on quality as judged by the customer provides an internal organizational perspective compatible with the supposed perspective of a customer in the market transaction model. Again, to the extent that customer needs become the focus of organizational actions, the amount of opportunism, that is, self-interested activity by organizational participants (Williamson, 1985), and its contribution to inefficiency, are diminished.

With regard to the world of higher education, Deming provides a framework relevant to organizations confronting a competitive market and the threat of market control. First, the Deming perspective emphasizes the importance of precise measures of outcomes, understood as measurements of product quality, which is wholly consistent with the emerging public policy orientation towards academic outcomes assessment (Ewell, 1991a). However, Deming's orientation would emphasize sampling from these outcomes measures at every stage in the production process, to identify common and special causes of variation in processes and products and thereby improve academic quality. Thus, rather than using outcomes assessment measures and techniques to "certify" existing products, Deming's approach would be to study assessment data as a means of organizational learning, so as to improve an academic institution's future competitive position (cf. Ewell, 1984). Second, Deming's focus on those who benefit from a product would require colleges and universities to develop a base of external information on customer needs relevant to program design and development that could provide some objective information to the increasingly subjective debates over academic content among academic professionals. This would be a further, and from an institutional perspective, strategically constructive response to the current demands for external control of academic institutions. Third, Deming's emphasis on sub-unit coordination and development of the worker's individual and collective capacity to improve production processes would lead to an emphasis on an active effort to resuscitate collegial mechanisms for academic program design and quality control, as well as to the development of individual faculty expertise in the skills necessary to assess variation in educational quality (Cross and Angelo, 1988).

In sum, the strengths of Deming's perspective are precisely aligned with the weaknesses of American college and university educational organization. However, to improve academic quality, a simplistic, one-dimensional application of current conceptions of total quality management is unlikely to be effective (Garvin, 1988). Rather, a framework for quality management in higher education is needed, drawn from insights in Deming's approach, but grounded in the context of academic organizations.

A FRAMEWORK FOR QUALITY MANAGEMENT
IN HIGHER EDUCATION

In contrast to the earlier, largely implicit, clan and bureaucratic mechanisms for reducing variation in academic quality, the contemporary environment of market control has led to overt discussions of means of managing academic quality in higher education. The initial effort was the development of systematic efforts to assess educational outcomes (Astin, 1991; Ewell, 1988). A second phase is the direct application of TQM methods from business and industry to academic institutions (Coate, 1991). Each of these approaches has weaknesses, particularly when contrasted with Deming's (1986) perspective on quality management. A third perspective is needed, that conceives of education as an ongoing process and stresses the centrality of academic design.

Assessment, as it is currently practiced, focuses primarily on the detection of variation in the performance of students. Quality, insofar as it is an articulated concern, is regarded as a concept to be defined through the procedures of assessment. Astin (1991) has outlined an assessment program which parallels the total quality management perspective of Deming in its systemic orientation and its concern with improvement. First, Astin argues that equating academic quality with an institution's perceived reputation, or with its relative resources (e.g., the size of a university's endowment, its average faculty salary, or its average student admissions score), leads to a narcissism in which the institution's relationship to the larger society becomes not one of service, but one of exploitation. Instead, Astin defines quality in terms of an institution's capacity to develop the talents of its admitted students—what economists call value-added. Astin's assessment program therefore requires both measures of student inputs, and the student's educational environment, so that causal connections between educational practices and student development can be accurately estimated, and educational improvements that increase the talent development of students can be designed.

In one important respect, Astin's perspective is superior to that of Deming. Total quality management evolved in the industrial sector where the product is inanimate, and where improvements in the production process require independent assessments of product quality. Astin's framework evolved from evaluations of programs designed to develop human beings, where the individual being developed can provide direct testimony as to the effectiveness of the production process. Thus his model outlines an important role for students whose criticism of educational policy and practice can be influential in educational improvement efforts.

In several respects the two perspectives overlap, but with different emphases. For Astin the validity of educational outcomes is inevitably a value judgment derived from a subjective weighing of multiple perceptions: student, faculty, state, and employer. Deming in contrast, stresses the customer's perception of quality. Thus the application of Deming's perspective to academic institutions would accentuate the social legitimacy of academic programs and outcomes.

In other respects Astin's academic assessment model replicates the failures of earlier programs of quality control in American industry. For example, there is some evidence that early experiments in academic assessment have led to collegial discussion regarding sources of variation in academic program outcomes (Astin, 1991; Adelman, 1989; Fong, 1988) and thereby motivated some interest in academic program design among faculty members. Unfortunately, while Astin suggests that faculty ownership and involvement in assessment would be ideal, it is not absolutely essential to his program, and is left undiscussed. Rather, Astin places primary emphasis on instituting systematic programs of measurement, building comprehensive information systems, and developing the expertise necessary to conduct studies on the relationship between inputs, educational environments, and outputs. Deming's perspective in contrast places primary emphasis on relatively simple analyses, but emphasizes mechanisms for involving and developing those directly responsible for the production process. This weakness of Astin's assessment approach is similar to the weakness Garvin (1988) observed in low quality American manufacturing plants. That is, quality improvement became the responsibility of highly trained staff experts and sophisticated systems removed from the actual processes of production. Quality improvement was thus pursued through a focus on detection—"assessing in" quality—rather than through the prevention of errors. As Garvin (1988) suggests, the detection, or "policeman" approach to quality, can become a license to accept poor quality and to markedly increase costs, particularly if the focus becomes that of rework or remediation. Rather, to be maximally effective, Garvin argues that quality improvement must actively address means of improving program design, a perspective largely absent from the academic assessment literature. However, by encouraging the development of comprehensive assessment information systems, assessment programs are laying the groundwork for more systematic efforts at quality improvement.

Subsequent to, and largely separate from academic assessment efforts, a small number of colleges and universities have adapted the techniques of TQM from American business and industry to the management of higher education. Several surveys of these institutions have been conducted, employing samples of convenience, that have identified up to 25 colleges and universities known to be involved in TQM (Coate, 1991; Seymour and Collett, 1991). Over one-third of the early adopters of TQM have been community colleges or technical institutes where the academic structure is more centralized and hierarchical, and where industrial norms of management would be more readily accepted in both administration and educational programs (Clark, 1987). In both two-year and four-year institutions TQM has been applied most systematically in administrative areas similar to those in business and industry such as financial services, facilities planning, and facilities maintenance, as well as academic service areas such as registration, admissions, financial aid, student placement, and housing (Coates, 1991; Seymour and Collett, 1991; Seymour, 1991).

Seymour (1991) reported the following perceived benefits from these pioneering attempts to implement TQM in colleges and universities: providing people a voice in the improvement of their work environment; a shift from staff explaining, to staff listening to customers; improved cycle time in critical processes;

improved morale; growth in decision making based upon data; increased contact among people in different but related functions; the development of a common language; increased knowledge of what the institution is about; reduced rework and scrap; and both direct savings in ongoing expenses, and indirect savings in potential expenses. Seymour (1991) also reported perceived frustrations in the applications of TQM to colleges and universities: a high time investment due to personnel training and overly ambitious project selection; insufficient administrative commitment; resistance to change, particularly in cross-functional projects; the difficulty of moving from the superficial application of TQM tools, to the adoption of quality management as an operating philosophy; team leaders and members who have little experience in working as a team; and institutional concern that the results are not sufficiently tangible.

In addition to these initial perceptions of the benefits and frustrations of the TQM experience, a description of the process used to implement TQM is also beginning to emerge from these early adopters (Coate, 1991):

- Creation of a steering committee composed of individuals with interest and expertise in quality management
- Creation of quality management teams supported by a facilitator/trainer
- Identification of critical processes
- Training in the philosophy and tools of total quality management
- Identification and survey of customer needs
- Identification of problems, data gathering, and analysis
- Development and implementation of solutions

Several points can be made about these applications of TQM from business and industry. In contrast to the assessment movement, TQM places its emphasis on the improvement of critical processes through the reduction of variation. Quality is thus perceived not as a concept to be defined, but as a problem to be solved, principally through applications of statistical quality control methods implemented by teams of individuals engaged in the critical process. Within this framework, the role of professional staff is clearly that of support—training and troubleshooting. While responsibility for quality may be widely cast, actual responsibility focuses within the hierarchy of quality management projects, and particularly within each team. Quality is thus "controlled in."

There are a number of obvious problems to this approach to quality improvement. First, since the perspective is imported directly from the business world and applied primarily to business functions within colleges and universities, applications to the core processes of higher education—education and research—have been slow and superficial, although they are being initiated at major universities such as the University of Michigan (Whitaker and Associates, 1990). Second, this conceptual approach to quality management has been limiting because of a failure to see the potential relationships between quality management and extant, related functions such as academic asessment (Ewell, 1991a) and instructional development (Diamond, 1989). Finally, by focusing on the training and development of individuals and small groups in analytical techniques largely drawn from industrial organizations, the approach risks reductionism. The value of a more holistic and integrative approach to quality management and to the pivotal role of design may be ignored.

Figure 1 compares the two previous approaches, assessment and TQM (which in the figure is more accurately defined as "statistical quality control") with what Garvin (1988) terms "quality management." The latter approach, derived from research on leading American and Japanese businesses, has as its primary concern neither detection nor control, but "coordination." Quality is viewed as a problem to be solved, but rather than being addressed defensively in terms of identified variations in individual processes, it is attacked proactively and holistically through a concern with overall design. The emphasis is on the entire program chain, from the management of "sources", through customer research, and to the contribution of all functional groups to *preventing* quality failures. The methods therefore focus at a different level of analysis than has typified academic assessment, or academic applications of statistical quality control—on the means of designing and continually improving programs and systems. Quality professionals again perform the role of support personnel, but focus their efforts on quality assessment, quality planning, and program design. Academic quality in this conception becomes the responsibility of all academic programs, with strong leadership exercised collegially by the faculty as a whole. Quality in this approach is not "assessed in," not "controlled in," but "designed in."

Academic quality management, as outlined in Figure 2, conceives of quality in systemic terms. The notion of reducing variation in a system of production from sources to customers is fundamental to the Deming (1986) approach to quality management. As Garvin (1988) argues, this approach is particularly valuable in contexts in which technical or performance data can be gathered on products produced in large volumes. The approach is less valuable for low volume products or those, such as custom-made crafts, that are individually produced. With the development of assessment information systems, outcome or performance data on students are now becoming more broadly available. Furthermore, in most academic institutions and programs, particularly undergraduate and professional programs, students are educated collectively in relatively large numbers.

Figure 2 suggests that an educational program may be conceived as an interrelated system. Within the system various sources supply students who are educated through a designed program featuring specific educational processes (e.g., case study instruction) and then placed with various customers. The educational program is continually designed and redesigned based on customer

Identifying Characteristics	Assessment	Statistical Quality Control	Quality Management
primary concern	detection	control	coordination
view of quality	a concept to be defined	a problem to be solved	a problem to be solved but one that is attacked proactively
emphasis	program improvement	process improvement	the entire program chain, from source management to customer research, and the contribution of all functional groups to preventing quality failures
methods	educational assessment	statistical tools, analytical techniques, and project teams	program and system design
role of professional staff	conducting assessment studies and reviews	training, trouble-shooting	quality assessment, quality planning, and program design
who has responsibility for quality	academic department	quality team	all academic programs, with strong collegial faculty leadership
orientation and approach	"assesses in" quality	"controls in" quality	"designs in" quality

Adapted from Garvin (1988, p. 37).

FIGURE 1. A framework for academic quality management.

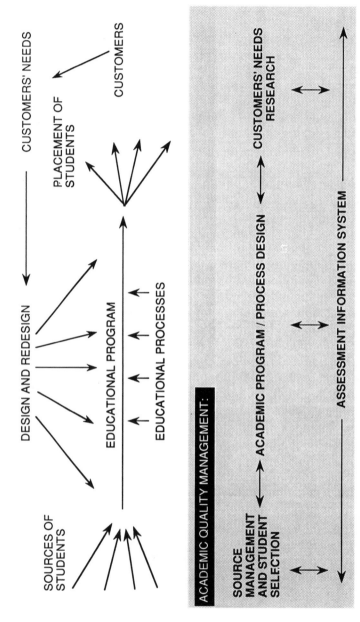

FIGURE 2. Stages of contemporary quality management in higher education.

needs as well as faculty knowledge and expertise. This framework can be potentially applied at any level of analysis, but will be examined here at the level of individual institutions of higher education.

Within this framework, the functions of assessment and statistical quality control can be placed. Assessment as currently practiced represents student performance measurements at various points in the educational program; statistical quality control represents the intensive study of particular educational processes contributing to the overall educational program. Academic quality management, as defined here, represents the management of the entire program chain from student sources to customer needs. In particular, as Figure 2 outlines, the core activities of academic quality management would address certain critical intersects in the chain: source management and student selection; program and process design; customer needs research; as well as the design and management of a supporting quality information system.

SOURCE MANAGEMENT AND STUDENT SELECTION

Competitive pressures for student recruitment have led to an increasing interest in enrollment management that includes systematic efforts to increase respectively, student applications, student acceptances, and student retention (Hossler et al., 1990). Intrinsic to this development is a concern with student quality and student success. Applications of this approach also have adopted the quality management emphasis on cross-functional teams and increased coordination of related processes including admissions, registration and housing, often under an integrating enrollment management officer.

An academic quality management approach, however, would place much greater emphasis on assuring the continual improvement and reliability of incoming student performance on measures of academic quality defined as critical by those involved in designing the academic program. This might entail not only assessing students for admission on critical measures, but also systematically sampling freshman students, not as a means of placement, but as a means of validating the preparation of the student body and the effectiveness of the admissions selection process in providing students with as little unwanted variation as possible on the essential criteria of academic quality. Source management would entail identifying and tracking individual high schools in terms of the quality of their student product over time. This might involve identifying the historical acceptance/rejection rates of their graduates at the focal institution, the number of incidents of remedial placements or advanced credits received by their admitted graduates, and the retention rate of their admitted graduates. In those cases where the focal institution has a measurable number of students from a particular source, the institution of higher education might not only provide information to the source about their students' performance, but might also take actions to actively encourage the improvement of the source's quality (cf. the role of the University of Michigan in the nineteenth century). Many of these activities are currently being conducted as part of existing enrollment management programs (Hossler et al. 1990). An academic quality management perspective would place greater emphasis on the relationship between student selection and long-term student success on academic tasks, as well as the integration and coordination of source management and student selection with the process of academic program design.

ACADEMIC PROGRAM/PROCESS DESIGN

While there has been an extensive investment by institutions of higher education in instructional and faculty development over the last several decades, these efforts have largely focused on the development of individual faculty members and courses (Weimer and Lenze, 1991). This stress on improving individual faculty skills in instruction, course planning, and student assessment has been the equivalent in quality improvement terms of what Deming calls "special causes" of variation. Only a few institutions and some professional programs such as medicine and business have experimented with more coordinated program designs sensitive to "common causes" of variation (Diamond, 1989). Predictably, experience in the implementation of such program design efforts stresses the importance of cross-functional design teams, including faculty members representing all critical specialties necessary for a program design, as well as individuals with experience in instructional design, educational assessment, and materials production (Diamond, 1989). Systematic research on design factors associated with quality products in manufacturing settings has suggested that the use of reliability or conservative engineering, product line breadth, manufacturing process flow and sequencing, and the degree of confusion and change in underlying processes are all associated with variation in quality (Garvin, 1988).

The application of these concepts to academic program design could be fruitful. For example, the amount of complexity in program components may also be an important contributor to variation in academic quality (Burstyn and Santa, 1977), and the early identification and pre-testing of vital academic program components could also contribute to reducing predictable variation. Educational program-line breadth may also contribute to increased quality variation in academic settings, particularly since academic organizations provide little coordinated support for program and process design, and academic resources often vary by subject fields. As Paul Batalden has observed (private communication), "students experience horizontally what academic departments have developed, assembled, and delivered vertically." As an example, separate Ph.D programs for each academic sub-field within a professional school therefore are likely to lead to greater variation in academic quality than a single Ph.D program with collegially defined standards, collegially designed common program components, and separable sub-components for each academic field. Academic program design advocates, similar to their industrial counterparts, also stress the importance of the sequencing of various academic program components to effective student learning (Diamond, 1987), and research on student undergraduate course selections suggests that an inattention to the flow and sequencing of academic program and process elements may contribute a substantial amount of variation to academic outcome measures (Ratcliffe and Associates, 1990; Zemsky, 1989).

Recent educational assessment research at Harvard University (Light, 1990; Light, 1992), based upon interviews with students as well as alumni, has reinforced the importance of certain underlying content (such as writing and quantitative analysis) to student success in their academic program, as well as their later career success. Although this content is taught within many academic fields, and although research suggests that there are means of reducing variation in these essential skills through the redesign of instructional processes (Light, 1992; McKeachie et al., 1987), the norms of program and individual autonomy have prevented academic institutions from pursuing these potential improvements in a proactive, coordinated manner.

The potential for collegial program and process design, however, is illustrated by the organization and management of the Harvard Business School (Christensen et al., 1991). The programmatic design of the school's MBA degree, including the content and sequencing of each course component, is collegially designed by the school faculty. This design also extends to educational process (Christensen, 1987). Faculty in the school are trained in the discussion-centered or case study method, which is the dominant instructional mode in the school, classrooms are designed to facilitate this instructional process (Christensen et al., 1991), and the school heavily invests in a case research and development unit supporting its educational program. The Harvard Business School's extraordinary investment in program and process design has provided a competitive advantage over competing business schools, and the school successfully markets both its education programs and the underlying case study educational technology. Other leading business schools are now aggressively implementing quality management techniques in their academic programs (Bateman and Roberts, 1992).

CUSTOMERS' NEEDS RESEARCH

One contribution of the educational assessment movement to academic quality management has been the increased research on college alumni, as well as on potential employers, regarding the relevance of academic skills and knowledge to post-academic success (Pace, 1979). Alumni surveys have been helpful in identifying the particular value in the workplace of general components of an undergraduate education, such as skills in writing and foreign languages (Light, 1992), or, through analyses of subsets of alumni, of the relevance of specific subject areas to success in various occupational categories (Diamond, 1989). In particular professional areas, such as the health professions, employer surveys have focused on the relative importance of specific subjects and skills to specific professional categories as one means of defining outcomes appropriate to professional education (Coleman et al., 1987; Ziv et al., 1990). Efforts to use external surveys of non-alumni have also been attempted as a means of providing information relevant to the design of general education programs (Adelman, 1989).

Research of this type approximates the use of market research in quality management, although as Garvin (1988) discovered, even the American plants with the best record on quality failed to systematically study what represented quality from the customer's point of view. Rather, market research in industry focused on means of reducing manufacturing costs and problem solving. The use of market field research in academic program and process design is still in its infancy, because of concern over its academic legitimacy as well as issues regarding the timeliness of data and the problems of defining valid market segments. However, colleges and universities are now developing extensive databases on alumni, generally because of fundraising activities, and these alumni surveys could be used to identify predictable and stable alumni placement sectors such as post-graduate and professional education, business, and teaching, as well as particular occupational clusters. Surveys of alumni regarding "field failures," that is, aspects of their own education that proved ineffective or inadequate, as well as the perceptions of alumni in various occupational sectors as to what constituted "quality" academic preparation, could provide institutions with potentially valuable customer research on quality. Furthermore, by concentrating on alumni data, the overhead costs of such research could be minimized, the response rate enhanced, and the institutional legitimacy of the information increased.

QUALITY INFORMATION SYSTEMS

Research on quality systems in industry reveals that the highest quality products were produced by companies with extensive quality information systems (Garvin, 1988). These systems included receiving inspection data on parts and supplies, sophisticated in-line testing equipment for collecting data on defects at every stage of production, quality audits in which a small number of completed products were extensively analyzed by members of the production team, extensive and timely reports on field failure rates, a substantial investment in the development of innovative, locally designed testing equipment, and carefully planned meetings in which critical production personnel reviewed quality information.

Early analyses of assessment information systems in higher education reveal some interesting parallels and sharp differences (Astin, 1991; Ewell, 1991b). For example, most academic institutions require standardized tests from students applying for admission and administer academic placement exams to entering students. Fewer institutions administer standardized exams or collectively developed comprehensive exams at the conclusion of academic programs, and very few systematically survey alumni on their post-program behavior and/or satisfaction. Most institutions regularly collect data on student graduation and drop out rates, and registration records offer a data archive with some potential for assessing student outcomes (Ratcliffe and Associates, 1991). Ewell (1991b) suggests increased evidence of investment at the institutional level in innovative forms of assessment, particularly the substitution of performance-based assessments for multiple-choice tests, and the transition to "embedded" assessment. The embedded feature incorporates the assessment of student outcomes into the academic expectations of a course or program, thus lessening the need to motivate student participation in special assessment activities.

While these assessment procedures parallel the structure, but not the thoroughness or consistency of industrial quality information systems, a more marked difference is in the form and use of the information collected. Because academic outcome assessment is usually a form of market control, emphasis is placed on certifying students through the assessment process; therefore, assessment information must be collected on each student, and the external validation of the assessment mechanism is critical to institutional legitimacy. By contrast, in the Deming (1986) perspective on quality management, validity is established through the use of market research in *product design and development*. While the validity and reliability of quality measures is an issue, they are established relative to the organization's design specifications for the original product. Consequently, quality information systems can be based upon the study of variations in samples throughout the production process, rather than upon measures of each unit. This simple but critical difference underscores the absence of a legitimate design process in academic organizations.

A number of elements already suggested would be critical components of an ideal academic quality information system necessary to support the management processes of student selection and source management, program/process design, and customer research. This information, necessarily defined by individuals from all stages of the academic process, could include measures of the performance of applying students, measures of the performance of accepted students, measures of the performance of students at key program subcomponents as well as at the completion of the overall program, measures of the performance of program graduates, and measures of alumni "customer" expectations for the performance of students in defined fields (Astin, 19921; Bare, 1980). Following the logic of quality control, many of these measures could be based on samples of students, utilizing assessments "embedded" in the education process itself. Furthermore, special in-depth "audits," or extended exit assessments of samples of graduating students might be conducted for additional information on academic quality (Seymour, 1992).

Much information is currently available, although consistent with the high differentiation of academic organizations, it resides in separate offices and supports different functions (Astin, 1991). Typically, information on entering student performance is collected and stored by the admissions office, placement exams are conducted by departments, program performance tests are either absent altogether (Ewell, 1991b) and/or vary substantially in standards and uses, and data regularly collected on alumni is generally reserved for public relations and fund-raising purposes. As Zemsky and Massy (1990) emphasize, many of the "back rooms," or analytical staffs of these functions essentially overlap. Creating an academic quality information system would require coordinating these data gathering efforts, developing common definitions and standards, and most importantly, integrating the quality information system with an active initiative in program and process design. This latter point underscores the unique role of leadership in a knowledge-driven organization such as a college or university. In these contexts, the challenge is to empower the collegial mechanisms of the knowledge professionals to improve academic quality and hold them responsible for deciding how quality will be measured, and how the resulting data will be continually used for quality improvement.

ACADEMIC QUALITY MANAGEMENT:
AN AGENDA FOR RESEARCH

Research on managers, including administrators in higher education (Dill, 1984), consistently suggests that a critical function of their role is to provide clarifying pictures to those within organizations on the opportunities, challenges and essential purposes of organizational life. Correspondingly, managers, like researchers, benefit most from new gestalts or frameworks that provide a fresh understanding of old realities, identify previously undetected levers (variables) for change (prediction/detection), and infuse new confidence to pursue the ambiguities of management (research). While the framework for academic quality management outlined above will require further development and elaboration, it provides an initial and necessary model for synthesizing existing knowledge, and suggesting valuable direction for related research.

An important initial step in research on academic quality will be further conceptual refinement. For example, within higher education the conception of "customer" is much more complex than in manufacturing or traditional service organizations. In part this is a function of the multiple consumers and supporters of colleges and universities as well as these customers' complex and multi-dimensional desires. In part it is a function of the unique role of students in the academic production process. Are students to be considered raw material, work in process until commencement? Or are they better conceived as both customers and co-producers, partners in the production process through their interactions with faculty members and with each other (Astin, 1991)? These questions have implications for the systematic definition of customers, and the collection, as well as interpretation, of customer perceptions of quality. The development of a taxonomy of critical customers by institutional level and type (Clark, 1987), could encourage broad-scale academic research on the nature and composition of customer perceptions of quality useful to the needs of academic institutions as well as policy makers. These questions also have significant implications for the means by which academic institutions empower their internal constituencies to improve academic quality. What role, for example, do students conceived as co-producers play in academic quality management?

A related question is how best to conceive of collegial mechanisms to support academic program and process design. Recent research (Cameron and Tschirhart, 1992; Dill and Helm, 1988) underscores the demands the new competitive environment places upon the decision-making processes of colleges and universities. Centralized, hierarchical decision structures do not have the capacity to gather information and effectively analyze it in order to make the critical design choices necessary for institutional effectiveness in competitive contexts. Collegial faculty structures for continuous learning, information sharing, and academic improvement are more adaptive, but these horizontal integrating mechanisms are as likely to be resisted by elements of the faculty itself as by elements of the administration. What collegial forms for academic quality improvement are viable in academic settings?

On this latter question, descriptive research that explores the collegial integrating mechanisms and organizational arrangements by which academic program and process design has been successfully implemented would be especially valuable. Comparative studies of the academic organization and program design process across schools and colleges could be an effective place to begin.

For example, a number of business schools have adopted variations of a matrix organizational structure for managing academic programs. How do these schools manage academic quality and how do their structure and procedures compare to the more decentralized, informal systems typical of colleges of arts and sciences? What integrating mechanisms—task forces, integrating individuals, administrative units—appear to be effective in coordinating academic program design and development, and does the form of these integrating mechanisms vary by disciplinary or professional field, and/or by institutional type (Clark, 1987)? How does the organization and management of the academic design process in corporate or for-profit degree-granting organizations compare with similar processes in traditional academic organizations (Betters-Read, 1986)? What forms of integrating mechanisms have proved effective in the academic design process in British universities, which traditionally have been governed by a clan form of control?

The tension between cross-functional integration and coordination, and both program and individual autonomy, are a fundamental issue in higher education, given its tradition of high differentiation. This same issue confronts other well known efforts at horizontal integration in complex universities, efforts such as the organization of fund-raising, the organization of information systems, the organization of libraries, and the provision of continuing education. Studies of these different functions that identify effective practices for coordinating subunits, for eliminating duplication in data-gathering, for defining common standards, and for dividing administrative responsibility may present useful models for integration in academic settings applicable to academic quality management.

Within business and industry, quality management is increasingly being embraced because of its dual potential for providing competitive advantage in products and lowering the costs of production. A number of writers have attempted to develop a framework for quality costs (i.e., the costs of poor quality) in business and industry (Feigenbaum, 1961; Groocock, 1986). Similarly, the total costs of academic quality might be categorized into assurance costs, prevention costs, internal failure costs, and external failure costs. Assurance costs would include expenses associated with student placement tests, student performance assessments, student exit interviews, and customer research, essentially the costs of maintaining an academic quality information system. Prevention costs would include the costs of faculty development programs, academic process modifications, and efforts to improve source quality—essentially the costs of improving quality. Internal failure costs would include the costs of academic remediation (''rework''), the costs associated with student dropouts (e.g., counseling, ''good will''), and the costs of replacing student attrition (e.g., the recruitment and admission of transfer students). Finally, external failure costs would include the costs—largely calculated now in terms of goodwill and institutional reputation—of graduated students who are judged inadequate (''defective'') in the marketplace. The development of a more systematic means for classifying and measuring these costs for different types of colleges and universities, and the analysis of these costs over time, could be an important effort, inasmuch as the real costs of quality variation in higher education are borne by tuition payers and tax payers. A means of estimating the costs in lost quality of various organizational arrangements could stimulate greater interest in alternative conceptions of academic program design.

For administrators the quality management process itself is a critical form of research, a means to learn about their own organization. A related form of action research is "benchmarking" (Hayes, et al, 1988), in which a company constantly seeks out other organizations whose core "processes" (e.g., purchasing, market research) represent the state of the art, and attempts to use these models as a basis for improving the quality of its own processes. This competitive, comparative search for benchmark processes can be usefully compared to the much more limited practice of peer-group analysis in higher education (Brinkman and Krakower, 1983), where the focus is on collecting comparative data on finances and enrollment from academic institutions in a similar market segment, but where little attention is given to identifying organizations with innovative and effective academic processes such as academic appointments and promotions, student recruitment, student placement, and academic program design.

More systematic research on the relationship between the policy environment of institutions of higher education and the improvement of academic quality will also be needed. As Garvin (1988) astutely observed, the techniques of quality management applied most successfully in Japanese organizations were known decades before in the United States. Their successful implementation in Japanese industry may be due in part to cultural factors, but can also be traced to the substantial degree of coordination provided at the national level, for example, in the propagation of national standards for manufacturing, in the development of national comparative data, and in government support for the training and development of professionals in quality control. In sharp contrast, the American tradition has been to rely primarily upon the independent actions of competing and uncoordinated business organizations to improve product quality; a recent exception being the Commerce Department's creation of the national Malcolm Baldrige Quality Award competition. The comparison of this policy environment of American business with the policy environment of American higher education, featuring regional accrediting organizations and a weak state and federal role in establishing academic standards, is instructive. Recent state initiatives in academic standards (Ewell, 1991a) and emerging federal initiatives in K–12 educational standards (Dill, 1988) suggest substantial opportunity for change in this policy context. Policy research at the state and federal level on means of supporting the improvement of academic quality will likely be of critical importance.

Research on academic quality management itself is essentially research on the organization and management of the educational process in higher education. Although traditional disciplinary research will make a contribution in critical areas such as the economics of quality, the reliability of various quality measures, and factors affecting the improvement of academic program and process design, at the outset, case studies and comparative research that can aid our understanding are most needed.

CONCLUSION

In 1908 Abraham Flexner wrote that colleges were increasing the number of their graduates rather than improving the quality. Flexner was concerned that the resources of colleges were being diverted to research and that teaching was suffering. He criticized the chaotic state of the elective curriculum, called for the renewal of some authority over pedagogy, and argued that enrollments should be limited to the number of students a college could adequately teach.

Three-quarters of a century later there is increasing public concern regarding the effectiveness and efficiency of academic programs. The traditional modes of academic quality control, clan and bureaucratic, have become less effective because of the constant fracturing of academic knowledge and the powerful norms of program and individual autonomy, as well as the complexity inherent in the size of contemporary colleges and universities.

Academic organizations, often very large ones, still organize their academic programs as if each student's education is crafted by an individual faculty member, rather than acknowledging the reality that each student's education is a product of the uncoordinated work of many teachers, as well as other influences. Such a system invites substantial variation in academic quality, and encourages the inefficient use of resources. Under these circumstances the incursions of market forms of control are predictable. The management of academic quality at the institutional level offers a potential alternative to externally mandated forms of accountability and will likely be pursued more vigorously by colleges and universities. At the heart of any such effort must be a collegial responsibility for academic design.

REFERENCES

Adelman, C. (1989). Introduction: Indicators and their discontents. In C. Adelman (ed.), *Signs and Traces*. Washington, DC: Office of Research, U.S. Department of Education.

Allport, F. (1933). *Institutional Behavior*. Chapel Hill: University of North Carolina Press.

Alpert, D. (1985). Performance and paralysis: The organizational context of the American research university. *Journal of Higher Education* 56(3): 241–281.

Anthony, R. (1988). *The Management Control Function*. Boston: Harvard Business School.

Association of American Colleges. (1985). *Integrity in the College Curriculum: A Report to the Academic Community*. Washington, DC: Association of American Colleges.

Astin, A. (1985). *Achieving Educational Excellence*. San Francisco: Jossey-Bass.

Astin, A. (1991). *Assessment for Excellence*. New York: American Council on Education/ MacMillan.

Astin, A., and Solmon, L. (1979). Measuring academic quality. *Change* 11(6): 48–51.

Astin, A., and Solmon, L. (1981). Are reputational ratings needed to measure quality? *Change* 13(7): 14–19.

Banta, T. (1986). *Performance Funding in Higher Education: A Critical Analysis of Tennessee's Experience*. Boulder, CO: National Center for Higher Education Management Systems.

Bare, A. (1980). The study of academic department performance. *Research in Higher Education* 12(1): 3–22.

Bateman, G. and Roberts, H. (1992). *What We Think We Are Learning from the Teaching Lab: Extended Discussion*. Chicago: Graduate School of Business, University of Chicago.

Becher, T. (1989). *Academic Tribes and Territories: Intellectual Enquiry and the Cultures of Discipline*. Milton Keynes: SRHE and Open University Press.

Bellah, R., Madsen, R., Sullivan, W., Swidler, A. and Tipton, S. (1991). *The Good Society*. New York: Alfred Knopf.

Ben-David, J. (1972). *American Higher Education*. New York: McGraw-Hill.

Bennett, W. (1984). *To Reclaim a Legacy: A Report on the Humanities in Higher Education*. Washington, DC: National Endowment for the Humanities.

Berdahl, R., and Studds, S. (1989). *The Tension of Excellence and Equity: The Florida Enhancement Programs*. College Park, MD: National Center for Postsecondary Governance and Finance, University of Maryland.

Bergquist, W., and Armstrong, J. (1986). *Planning Effectively for Educational Quality: An Outcomes-Based Approach for Colleges Committed to Excellence*. San Francisco: Jossey-Bass.

Bess, J. (1982). *University Organization: A Matrix Analysis of the Academic Profession*. New York: Human Services Press.

Betters-Reed, B. (1986). Search for integration of theory and practice: The early history and analysis of three innovative graduate institutions. Paper presented at the Association for the Study of Higher Education, San Antonio, Texas, February, 1986.

Beyer, J., and Snipper, R. (1974). Objective versus subjective indicators of quality in graduate education. *Sociology of Education* 47(4): 541–557.

Biglan, A. (1973). Relationships between subject matter characteristics and the structure and output of university departments. *Journal of Applied Psychology* 57(3): 204–213.

Birnbaum, R. (1983). *Maintaining Diversity in Higher Education*. San Francisco: Jossey-Bass.

Birnbaum, R. (1988). *How Colleges Work*. San Francisco: Jossey-Bass.

Blau, P., and Margulies, R. (1974–75). The reputations of American professional schools. *Change* 6(10): 42–47.

Bledstein, B. (1976). *The Culture of Professionalism*. New York: W.W. Norton.

Brinkman, P. and Krakower, J. (1983). *Comparative Data for Administrators in Higher Education*. Boulder, CO: National Center for Higher Education Management Systems.

Brubacher, J., and Rudy, W. (1976). *Higher Education in Transition*. New York: Harper & Row.

Burke, C. (1982). *American Collegiate Populations: A Test of the Traditional View*. New York: New York University Press.

Burstyn, J., and Santa, C. (1977). Complexity as an impediment to learning: A study of changes in selected college textbooks. *Journal of Higher Education* 48(5): 508–518.

Cameron, K. (1985). Institutional effectiveness in higher education: An introduction. *The Review of Higher Education* 9(1): 1–4.

Cameron, K., and Tschirhart, M. (1992). Postindustrial environments and organizational effectiveness in colleges and universities. *Journal of Higher Education* 63(1): 87–108.

Cartter, A. (1966). *An Assessment of Quality in Graduate Education*. Washington, DC: American Council on Education.

Cattell, J. (1910). A further statistical study of American men of science. *Science* 32(828): 672–688.

Chaffee, E. (1989). *Key Organizational Issues that Affect the Pursuit and Assessment of Quality*. College Park, MD: National Center for Postsecondary Governance and Finance, University of Maryland.

Christensen, C. (1987). *Teaching and the Case Method*. Boston: Harvard Business School.

Christensen, C.; Garvin, D.; and Sweet, A. (eds.), (1991). *Education for Judgment: The Artistry of Discussion Leadership*. Boston: Harvard Business School Press.

Clark, B. (1963). Faculty organization and authority. In T.F. Lunsford (ed.), *The Study of Campus Cultures*. Boulder, CO: Western Interstate Commission for Higher Education.

Clark, B. (1983). *The Higher Education System*. Berkeley: The University of California Press.

Clark, B. (1987). *The Academic Life: Small Worlds, Different Worlds*. Princeton: The Carnegie Foundation for the Advancement of Teaching.

Coate, L. (1991). Implementing total quality management in a university setting. In L.A. Sherr and D.J. Teeter (eds.), *Total Quality Management in Higher Education*. New Directions for Institutional Research No. 71. San Francisco: Jossey-Bass.

Cohen, M., March, J., and Olsen, J. (1972). A garbage can model of organizational choice. *Administrative Science Quarterly* 17(1): 1–25.

Coleman, M., Bruce, A., and Reilly, B. (1987). A perspective on the medical technology curricula: Results of a three-state survey. *Laboratory Medicine* 18(10): 615–617.

Conrad, C., and Blackburn, R. (1985a). Correlates of departmental quality in regional colleges and universities. *American Educational Research Journal* 22(2): 279–295.

Conrad, C., and Blackburn, R. (1985b). Program quality in higher education. In J.C. Smart (ed.), *Higher Education: Handbook for Theory and Research*, Vol. I. New York: Agathon Press.

Conrad, C., and Blackburn, R. (1986). Current views of departmental quality: An empirical examination. *Review of Higher Education* 9(3): 249–66.

Cornesky, R. et al. (1990). *W. Edwards Deming: Improving Colleges and Universities*. Madison: Magna Publications.

Crosby, P. (1979). *Quality Is Free*. New York: McGraw-Hill.

Cross, K., and Angelo, T. (1988). *Classroom Assessment Techniques: A Handbook for Faculty*. Ann Arbor: National Center for Research to Improve Postsecondary Teaching and Learning, University of Michigan.

Cross, K. (1990). Collaborative classroom assessment. Paper presented at the Fifth National Conference on Assessment in Higher Education, Washington, DC.

CVCP. (1989). *Academic Standards in Universities*. London: Committee of Vice Chancellors and Principals.

Deming, W. (1986). *Out of the Crisis*. Cambridge: Massachusetts Institute of Technology Center for Advanced Engineering Study.

Diamond, R. (1989). *Designing and Improving Courses and Curricula in Higher Education: A Systematic Approach*. San Francisco: Jossey-Bass.

Dill, D. (1982). The management of academic culture: Notes on the management of meaning and social integration. *Higher Education* 11(3): 303–320.

Dill, D. (1984). The nature of administrative behavior in higher education. *Education Administration Quarterly* 20(3): 69–99.

Dill, D. (1988). Toward a system of educational quality control: National achievement tests and the "theory of screening." In R. Haskins and D. MacRae (eds.), *Policies for America's Public Schools: Teachers, Equity, and Indicators.* Norwood, NJ: Ablex Publishing.

Dill, D. (1992). Academic administration. In B.R. Clark and G. Neave (eds), *The Encyclopedia of Higher Education.* Oxford: Pergamon Press.

Dill, D., and Friedman, C. (1979). An analysis of frameworks for research on innovation and change in higher education. *Review of Educational Research* 49(3): 411–435.

Dill, D. and Helm, K. (1988). Faculty participation in strategic policy-making. In J. Smart (ed.), *Higher Education: Handbook of Theory and Research,* Vol. IV. New York: Agathon Press.

Dill, D., and Pearson, A. (1991). The self designing organization: Structure, learning, and the management of technical professionals. Paper presented at the Portland International Conference on Management of Engineering and Technology, Portland, OR., October, 1991.

Dinham, S., and Evans, L. (1991). Assessment and accreditation in professional schools. *The Review of Higher Education* 14(2): 217–37.

Drew, D., and Karpf, R. (1981). Ranking academic departments: Empirical findings and a theoretical perspective. *Research in Higher Education* 14(4): 305–320.

Dube, C., and Brown, A. (1983). Strategic assessment: A rational response to university cutbacks. *Long Range Planning* 16(2): 105–113.

Duryea, E. (1973). Evolution of university organization. In J.A. Perkins (ed.), *The University as an Organization.* New York: McGraw-Hill.

Eliot, C. (1898). *Liberty in education.* In C.W. Eliot, Educational Reform: Essays and Addresses. New York: Century.

Ewell, P. (1984). *The Self-Regarding Institution: Information for Excellence.* Boulder, CO: National Center for Higher Education Management Systems, 1984.

Ewell, P. (1988). Outcomes, assessment, and academic improvement: In search of usable knowledge. In J.C. Smart (ed.), *Higher Education: Handbook of Theory and Research,* Vol. IV. New York: Agathon Press.

Ewell, P. (1991a). Assessment and TQM: In search of convergence. In L.A. Sherr and D.J. Teeter (eds.), *Total Quality Management in Higher Education.* New Directions for Institutional Research, No. 71. San Francisco: Jossey-Bass.

Ewell, P. (1991b). To capture the ineffable: New forms of assessment in higher education. In G. Grant (ed.), Review of Research in Higher Education. 17. Washington, DC: American Educational Research Association.

Fairweather, J. (1988). Reputational quality of academic programs: The institutional halo. Research in Higher Education 28(4): 345–56.

Fairweather, J., and Brown, D. (1991). Dimensions of academic program quality. *The Review of Higher Education* 14(2): 155–176.

Feigenbaum, A. (1961). *Total Quality control.* New York: McGraw-Hill.

Flexner, A. (1908). *The American College: A Criticism.* New York: The Century Co.

Fong, B. (1988). Old wineskins: The AAC external examiner project. *Liberal Education* 74(3): 12–16.

Garvin, D. (1988). *Managing Quality: The Strategic and Competitive Edge.* New York: Free Press.

Garvin, D. (1980). *The Economics of University Behavior.* New York: Academic Press.

Gitlow, H., and Gitlow, S. (1987). *The Deming Guide to Quality and Competitive Position*. Englewood Cliffs, NJ: Prentice-Hall.

Grant, G., and Riesman, D. (1978). *The Perpetual Dream: Reform and Experiment in the American College*. Chicago: University of Chicago Press.

Groocock, J. (1986). *The Chain of Quality*. New York: John Wiley.

Hagstrom, W. (1971). Inputs, outputs, and the prestige of university science departments. *Sociology of Education* 44(4): 375–397.

Handlin, O., and Handlin, M. (1970). *The American College and American Culture*. New York: McGraw-Hill.

Hayes, R; Wheelwright, S; and Clark, K. (1988). *Dynamic Manufacturing*. New York: The Free Press.

Heydinger, R. (1983). *Using Program Priorities to Make Retrenchment Decisions: The Case of the University of Minnesota*. Atlanta: Southern Regional Education Board.

Hossler, D., Bean, J., and Associates. (1990). *Strategic Enrollment Management*. San Francisco: Jossey-Bass.

Hughes, R. (1925). *A Study of the Graduate Schools of America*. Oxford, OH: Miami University Press.

Hughes, R. (1934). A report of the committee on graduate instruction. *Educational Record* 15(2): 192–234.

Imai, K; Nonaka, I; and Takeuchi, H. (1985). Managing the new product development process: How Japanese companies learn and unlearn. In K.B. Clark, R.H. Hayes, and C. Lorenz (eds.), *The Uneasy Alliances*. Boston: Harvard University Press.

Ishikawa, K. (1985). *What is Total Quality Control? The Japanese Way*. Englewood Cliffs, NJ: Prentice-Hall.

James, E. (1990). Decision processes and priorities in higher education. In S.A. Hoenack and E.L. Collins (eds.), *The Economics of Universities*. Albany, NY: SUNY Press.

Jones, L., Lindzey, G., and Coggeshall, A. (eds.). (1982). *An Assessment of Research-Doctoral Programs in the United States* (5 vols.) Washington, DC: National Academy Press.

Juran, J. (ed.), (1951). *Quality Control Handbook*. New York: McGraw-Hill.

Katz, D., and Kahn, R. (1978). *The Social Psychology of Organizations*. 2nd ed. New York: John Wiley & Sons.

Keniston, H. (1959). *Graduate Study and Research in the Arts and Sciences at the University of Pennsylvania*. Philadelphia: University of Pennsylvania Press.

Kimball, B. (1986). *Orators and Philosophers: A History of the Idea of Liberal Education*. New York: Teachers College Press.

King, S., and Wolfle, L. (1987). A latent-variable causal model of faculty representional ratings. *Research in Higher Education* 27(2): 99–106.

Kuh, G. (1981). *Indices of Quality in the Undergraduate Experience*. (AAHE/ERIC Higher Education Research Report No. 4.) Washington, DC: American Association of Higher Education.

Ladd, C., and Lipset, S. (1978). *1977 Survey of the American Professoriate: Technical Report*. Storrs, Conn.: Social Science Data Center, University of Connecticut.

Lawrence, J., and Green, K. (1980). *A Question of Quality: The Higher Education Ratings Game*. (AAHE/ERIC Higher Education Research Report No. 5.) Washington, DC: American Association for Higher Education.

Lawrence, P., and Lorsch, J. (1986). *Organization and Environments*. Boston: Harvard Business School Press.

Light, R. (1990). *The Harvard Assessment Seminars: Explorations with Students and*

Faculty about Teaching, Learning, and Student Life. (First Report) Cambridge, MA: Harvard Graduate School of Education and Kennedy School of Government.

Light, R. (1992). *The Harvard Assessment Seminars: Explorations with Students and Faculty about Teaching, Learning, and Student Life*. (Second Report) Cambridge, MA: Harvard Graduate School of Education and Kennedy School of Government.

Loder, C. (1990). *Quality Assurance and Accountability in Higher Education*. London: Kogan Page.

Marchese, T. (1991). TQM reaches the academy. *AAHE Bulletin* 44(3): 3–9.

Margulies, R., and Blau, P. (1973). The pecking order of the elite: America's leading professional schools. *Change* 5(9): 21–27.

Massy, W. (1989). A strategy for productivity improvement in college and university academic departments. Paper presented at the Forum for Postsecondary Governance, Santa Fe, New Mexico, October 1989.

Mayhew, L., Ford, P., and Hubbard, D. (1990). *The Quest for Quality: The Challenge for Undergraduate Education in the 1990s*. San Francisco: Jossey-Bass.

McGuinness, T. (1990). Markets and managerial hierarchies. In R. Clarke and T. McGuinness (eds.), *The Economics of the Firm*. Oxford: Basil Blackwell.

McKeachie, W; Pintrich, P; Lin, Y; and Smith, D. (1987). *Teaching and Learning in the College Classroom: A Review of the Research Literature*. Ann Arbor: National Center for Research to Improve Postsecondary Teaching and Learning, University of Michigan.

Meyer, J., and Rowan, B. (1978). The structure of educational organizations. In M. Meyer (ed.), *Environment and Organizations*. San Francisco: Jossey-Bass.

Miller, R. (ed). (1991). *Adapting the Deming Method to Higher Education*. Washington, D.C.: The College and University Personnel Association.

Moodie, G., and Eustace, E. (1974). *Power and Authority in British Universities*. Montreal: McGill-Queens' University Press.

Morgan, A., and Mitchell, B. (1985). The quest for excellence: Underlying policy issues. In J.C. Smart (ed.), *Higher Education: Handbook of Theory and Research*, Vol. I. New York: Agathon.

National Commission on Higher Education Issues. (1982). *To Strengthen Quality in Higher Education: Summary Recommendations of the National Commission on Higher Education Issues*. Washington, DC: American Council on Education.

National Governors' Association. (1986). *Time for Results: The Governor's 1991 Report on Education*. Washington, DC: National Governor's Association.

Neave, G., and Rhoades, G. (1987). The academic estate in western europe. In B. Clark (ed.), *The Academic Professions: National, Disciplinary, and Institutional Settings*. Berkeley: University of California Press.

Newman, F. (1987). *Choosing Quality: Reducing Conflict Between the State and the University*. Denver: Education Commission of the States.

Olscamp, P. (1978). Can program quality be quantified? *Journal of Higher Education* 49(5): 504–511.

Orton, J., and Weick, K. (1990). Loosely coupled systems: A reconceptualization. *The Academy of Management Review* 15(2): 203–223.

Ouchi, W. (1979). A conceptual framework for the design of organizational control mechanisms. *Management Science* 25(4): 833–48.

Ouchi, W. (1980). Markets, bureaucracies, and clans. *Administrative Science Quarterly* 25(1): 129–41.

Pace, C. (1979). *Measuring Outcomes of College: Fifty years of Findings and Recommendations for the Future*. San Francisco: Jossey-Bass.

Perrow, C. (1986). *Complex Organizations: A Critical Essay*. (3rd ed.) New York: Random House.

Peterson, M. (1985). Emerging developments in postsecondary organization theory and research: Fragmentation or integration. *Educational Researcher* 14(3): 5–12.

Powell, W. (1972). *The First State University*. Chapel Hill, NC: University of North Carolina Press.

Ratcliffe, J. and Associates. (1990). Determining the Effect of Different Coursework Patterns on the General Learned Abilities of Colllege Students. Working Paper OR 90–524. Ames, IA: Research Institute for Studies in Education at Iowa State University, and University Park Center for the Study of Higher Education at Pennsylvania State University.

Roose, K., and Andersen, C. (1970). *A Rating of Graduate Programs*. Washington, DC: American Council on Education.

Rudolph, F. (1962). *The American College and University*. New York: Vintage Books.

Scherkenback, W. (1988). *The Deming Route to Quality and Productivity: Road Maps and Road Blocks*. Rockville, MD: Mercury Press.

Schoonhoven, C., and Jelinek, M. (1990). Dynamic tension in innovative high technology firms: Managing rapid technological change through organizational structure. In M.A. Von Glinow, and S.A. Mohrman (eds.), *Managing Complexity in High Technology Organizations*. New York: Oxford University Press.

Seymour, D. (1989). Hodge podge: Or the unintended results from straying too far afield. *Planning for Higher Education* 17(4): 3–12.

Seymour, D. (1992). *On Q: Causing Quality in Higher Education*. New York: American Council on Education/Macmillan.

Seymour, D. (1991). TQM on campus: What the pioneers are finding. *AAHE Bulletin* 44(3): 10–13,18.

Seymour, D., and Collett, C. (1991). *TQM in Higher Education: A Critical Assessment*. Methuen, MA.: Goal/QPC.

Sherr, L., and Teeter, D. (eds.), (1991). *Total Quality Management in Higher Education*. New Directions for Institutional Research 71. San Francisco: Jossey-Bass.

Shewhart, W. (1931). *Economic Control of Quality of Manufactured Product*. New York: D. Van Nostrand Company.

Shirley, R., and Volkwein, J. (1978). Establishing academic program priorities. *Journal of Higher Education* 49(5): 472–488.

Smallwood, M. L. (1935). *An Historical Study of Examinations and Grading Systems in Early American Universities*. Cambridge: Harvard University Press.

Solmon, L. (1981) A multidimensional approach to quality. In Thomas Stauffer (ed.), *Quality—Higher Education's Principal Challenge*. Washington, DC: American Council on Education.

Study Group on the Conditions of Excellence in American Higher Education. (1984). *Involvement in Learning: Realizing the Promise of American Higher Education*. Washington, DC: National Institute of Education.

Thrash, P. (1988). Educational "outcomes" in the accrediting process. *Academe* 74(4): 16–18.

Van de Graaff, J. (1978). Great Britain. In J.H. Van de Graaff, B.R. Clark, D. Furth, D. Goldschmidt, and D.F. Wheeler, *Academic Power: Patterns of Authority in Seven National Systems of Higher Education*. New York: Praeger.

Veysey, L. (1965). *The Emergence of the American University*. Chicago: University of Chicago Press.

Webster, D. (1981). Advantages and disadvantages of methods of assessing quality. *Change* 13(7): 20–24.

Webster, D. (1983). America's highest ranked graduate schools, 1925–1982. *Change* 15(4): 14–24.

Webster, D. (1985a): Institutional effectiveness using scholarly peer assessments as major criteria. The Review of Higher Education 9(1): 67–82.

Webster, D. (1985b). James McKeen Cattell and the invention of academic quality rankings, 1903–1910. Review of Higher Education 8(2): 107–121.

Webster, D. (1986). *Academic Quality Rankings of American Colleges and Universities.* Springfield, Ill.: Charles C. Thomas Publishers.

Weick, K. (1976). Educational organizations as loosely coupled systems. *Administrative Science Quarterly* 21(1): 1–19.

Weick, K. (1983). Contradictions in a community of scholars: The cohesion-accuracy tradeoff. *The Review of Higher Education* 6(4): 253–267.

Weimer, M., and Lenze, L. (1991). Instructional interventions: A review of the literature on efforts to improve instruction. In J.C. Smart (ed.), *Higher Education: Handbook of Theory and Research*, Vol. VII. New York: Agathon Press.

Whitaker, G., and Associates. (1990). *Enhancing Quality in an Era of Resource Constraints: Report of the Task Force on Costs in Higher Education.* Ann Arbor: Office of the Provost, University of Michigan.

Williams, W. (1979). The role of the external examiner in first degrees. *Studies in Higher Education* 4(2): 161–168.

Williamson, D. (1985). *The Economic Institutions of Capitalism.* New York: Free Press.

Wilson, E. K. (1987). Department reviews for product improvement in higher education. In J.C. Smart (ed.), *Higher Education: Handbook of Theory and Research*, Vol. III. New York: Agathon Press.

Young, D., Blackburn, R., Conrad, C., and Cameron, K. (1989). Leadership, student effort, and departmental program quality: An exploration of quality across levels of analysis. *The Review of Higher Education* 12(3): 265–277.

Zammuto, R. (1986). Managing decline in American higher education. In J.C. Smart (ed.), *Higher Education: Handbook of Theory and Research*, Vol. II. New York: Agathon Press.

Zemsky, R. (1989). *Structure and Coherence: Measuring the Undergraduate Curriculum.* Washington, DC: Association of American Colleges.

Zemsky, R., and Massy, W. (1990). Cost containment: Committing to a new economic reality. *Change* 22(6): 16–22.

Ziv, L; Ehrenfeld, M; Kurtzman, C; and Hudani, P. (1990). Follow-up of Hadassah nursing school's first seven graduate classes. *Journal of Professional Nursing* 6(4): 229–234.

Beyond "the State": Interorganizational Relations and State Apparatuses in Post-secondary Education

Gary Rhoades
University of Arizona

What is "the state"? In the conversations and scholarship of higher education scholars there is repeated reference to something called "the state." Yet the field lacks a clearly articulated conceptualization or theory of the state, of what it is and what it does. I am intrigued by the fact that although we talk about the state a lot, we study it relatively little. And although the state is portrayed in our private dialogue in multifaceted ways, as an intricate set of agencies and organizations, it is presented in our scholarship in uncomplicated terms. In this chapter, I explore conceptions of the state found in the higher education literature. In an effort to enrich those understandings, I draw on recent work in political sociology that raises new questions about how we might think about and study the state.

The images that higher education practitioners and scholars have of the state are filtered through their images of themselves and of colleges and universities. In other words, our view of the state is shaped by our point of view. What we study, and the way we study it, are patterned by our sense of ourselves as professionals working in special, independent enterprises. We see and present ourselves in terms of meritocracy and expertise. As individuals and as a group we justify our professional status by virtue of having access to and producing knowledge, and of utilizing that knowledge in our clients' best interests (we claim to be governed more by considerations of quality and service than by self-interest). As professionals, we see ourselves and our institutions as different from other sorts of enterprises, and requiring special treatment in the form of greater autonomy vis-a-vis political and bureaucratic concerns, pressures, and organizations. This conception of autonomy is connected to a conception of ourselves as neutral (Slaughter, 1988). Our conception of ourselves and of academic enterprises assumes that we are or should be independent relative to major societal institutions and structures of power. We have an interest in presenting an image of the state that affords us a considerable measure of autonomy.

We are deeply engaged and implicated in the phenomena we claim to study objectively.

The disjunctures between our private discourse and our scholarship are related to our self-image and our self-interest. If the state figures prominently in our conversations, it is a topic that receives relatively little direct empirical consideration in our scholarship. The mainstream literature on the state is, in general, as much ideological as empirical. It is largely descriptive. And the descriptions it provides carry prescriptive and proscriptive connotations. The mainstream literature looks more to the possible effects of state activity, toward the end of influencing that activity, than it does to the actual interaction between state and campus actions and conditions, toward the end of analyzing that relationship. We talk a lot about the state because it has a profound influence on the academy. And the way we study it is oriented to influencing that state influence on the academy. Similarly, if in our conversations the state is characterized in variegated and complex ways, in our scholarship it is portrayed in relatively consistent and simple terms. The mainstream literature is marked more by easy stereotypes than by careful studies of the state, more by characterizing and categorizing the state for the purposes of autonomy and taxonomy than by analyzing the state to understand the nature of its operations and its interaction with higher education. Such treatment may be the result of efforts to achieve analytical parsimony. But the results consistently serve professional self-interest.

How, then, do we portray the state? In answering this question, it is important to note that most of the portrayals are indirect—the state is not the principal object of study. Whether in everyday usage or in scholarship, the state is always someone and/or something else. It is out there. It impinges on us, regulates us, constrains us. The state is distinct from, and in contraposition to, the academy. State practices contravene the codes and practices of the academy. The state is identified with formal authority, with formal governmental institutions. The state is inefficient. It is portrayed as bureaucratic and political rather than professional in terms of its members, its organization, and what drives its operation.

Embedded in such portrayals are silent but significant representations of academe. In posing the state as other, we are absolved of responsibility for state actions and our accountability as public servants is minimized (faculty in "private" institutions can be seen as public servants in two regards: their institutions are closely tied to the state and are in many ways accountable to the state, legally and financially; and a major element of the academic profession's image and ideology is that we serve and act in the interests of our immediate clients and of the general public). In presenting formal institutions of the state as the source of authority, we downplay the importance of other sources of authority and suggest that we lack formal authority. In characterizing the state as inefficient, we depict ourselves as productive, and imply that professional activities are undermined and threatened by the bureaucratic and political tendencies of the state.

In this chapter, several literatures in higher education are analyzed. First, I content analyze leading journals in higher education over the past five years. Second, I examine relevant chapters in the *Handbook*. Third, I review some major books in the higher education literature on the state, considering the conceptualizations found in some classics of the field.

After eliciting the prevailing portrayals of the state from these literatures, I provide three empirical examples of the limitations of these understandings of "the state." My aim is not to present research projects, although each of the examples is grounded in completed investigations. I simply wish to illustrate in different concrete contexts that prevailing conceptions of the state fail to capture important realities in the relations and interaction between postsecondary education institutions and the state.

Having raised some empirical problems, I turn to the theoretical underpinnings of prevailing understandings of the state in the higher education literature. I note the correspondence between these understandings and the basic assumptions of structural-functional and pluralist theory in political sociology. Such theoretical groundings are rarely discussed in the higher education literature. Perhaps such assumptions are so widely shared among higher education scholars that there is no need to explicate, consider, and reconsider them. But sociologists are a much less consensual lot. Structural-functional and pluralist theory have been under serious fire for decades, and have been challenged by alternative theories about political institutions and their relationship to other institutions and structures of power in society. Quite different views of the state have emerged, generally involving broader and more inclusive conceptions of the state that deal as much with governance as with government (Lagemann, 1989), and that connect state activity to structures of power in civil society. Prevailing conceptions of the state in the sociological literature relate patterns of state activity to patterns of power grounded in race, class, and gender.

The sociological debate surrounding the state has its own limitations, but it provides the analytical foundations for some recent work in higher education. Along these lines, I review Barrow's (1990) and Slaughter's (1990) books. I contrast their understanding of the state, and the substantive and analytical focuses that come out of that, with the prevailing understandings.

In closing the chapter, I rephrase my opening question, "What is the state?" and suggest that in Hughes' (1958) terms, this is a "false question," for the state is not simply something that can be objectively described, but is a designation that is subjectively ascribed. To ask, what is the state, is to pose a taxonomic question, as if the state is purely an objective entity that can easily be classified. If one sees the label, "the state," as a symbol that is socially defined and constructed, then one's questions become not taxonomic, but constructive, oriented to process and to efforts to establish and sustain power.[1] One might ask what the processes are by which groups and organizations define themselves as separate from the state. For most scholars in higher education, the state is studied in terms of how its policies impact on organizational autonomy, effectiveness, and quality. I offer an orientation that focuses on process and power. The driving question is, How does the state shape the construction of patterns of social relations (and power) in higher education, and how do patterns of relations (and power) in higher education and society shape our construction of the state?

THE STATE IN LEADING HIGHER EDUCATION JOURNALS

Academic journals are an important source for examining the conceptions embedded in higher education scholarship. The simple question of what is studied reveals what questions and knowledge are considered important. The types of problems being studied says a good deal about the orientation of the field, about who we are pursuing and producing knowledge for. For example, the most highly developed literature in higher education is about students (Silverman, 1987). What kinds of questions do we ask about students? Our questions are parental, and are oriented to the formal authorities in colleges and universities. They are socialization questions about student development and college effects. How can we better integrate students into our campus communities? How can we influence them in ways that ensure they take on "appropriate" values? The voices, concerns, and political activities of the students are not major subjects of study. Nor are the questions oriented to the down side of college and university life, to patterns of racism and sexism that are perpetuated by various dimensions of the collegiate experience in America. There is a big difference between seeing "the problem" as being students who for reasons of cultural background, ethnicity, etc. have a hard time adapting to and being integrated into collegiate life, versus seeing "the problem" as being racist and sexist collegiate cultures that promote the targeting and attacking of certain categories of students as other. To paraphrase a comment made by Thurgood Marshall in relating a story he was told, there is not a campus [versus a city] in the country where as a minority you have to hold your hand up in front of your face to know that you are a person of color. Why is that not a major topic of study in our literature? The types of "problems" that are studied say something about what is viewed by the field as problematic, and about whose viewpoint is being adopted.

    The state is a much less studied topic than students (Silverman, 1987). But I

---

[1]My thinking on these matters has been profoundly influenced by an ongoing dialogue over the years with a wide range of colleagues. Here I want to acknowledge in particular the ideas and influence of three of my closest intellectual colleagues, Patricia Gumport, Sheila Slaughter, and William Tierney. Of course, they bear no responsibility for the ideas I develop in this chapter, and for what I have made of our continuing exchanges.

pursue the same sort of analysis of how many and what kinds of studies of the state are presented in the leading higher education journals. Probing into the questions that are and are not asked regarding the state provides a sense of what is viewed as important and problematic in the field. Such a sense is also revealed in the particular language that is used to refer to the state, and to the nature and extent of the discussion that surrounds reference to the state. In other words, how do people talk about the state?

Journal articles provide a good sense of scholarly discourse because they are peer reviewed. They give the observer a sense of conventional usage in the language and conceptualizations of scholars. For example, if certain terminology and assumptions about the state are widely held, it is likely that these will receive little explication. If, on the other hand, the assumptions held by the author are contested, then presumably authors will be forced by reviewers to provide some explanation of what they mean by the terminology they are using. They will have to be more explicit about their conceptions and assumptions regarding the state.

In looking at leading journals in the higher education literature, my analysis is guided by the above sorts of questions. First, I review the titles, abstracts, introductions and conclusions of the articles, identifying those that concentrate specifically on some dimension of the state. This provides a sense of the extent to which the state is directly considered in the literature. It also yields a reading of the context in which the state is considered in the literature. In other words, in reviewing the titles, abstracts, introductions, and conclusions, I not only identify relevant articles, but attend to the kinds of questions they are posing about the state, or the way that the state figures into the questions they are posing. A second level of analysis that I undertake focuses more specifically on the conceptualization of the state that is embedded in the previously identified articles. I examine the terminology that is used to refer to the state and probe for the assumptions that are made and the characterizations that are provided of the state and its activities. The results are presented for each journal chronologically, with brief discussion of each entry.

Three core professional journals in the field were analyzed for the years 1986–1990: *Higher Education* (HE), *Journal of Higher Education* (JHE), and *Review of Higher Education* (RHE). The latter two can be characterized as generalist journals. The choice of JHE and RHE is justified by the fact that these are two of the most prestigious outlets for higher education scholars.[2] The choice of HE is justified by both its prominence in the field and by its comparative focus. Given that focus, I knew the journal would contain more articles dealing

---

[2]In gentle, but genuine, deference to John Smart, editor of the *Handbook*, and of *Research in Higher Education* (RHE), which is also one of the most prestigious and widely read higher education journals, I did not focus on RHE in large part because its focus is explicitly institutional, as is evidenced not just by this reader's familiarity with the journal but by the "Information for Authors" that is provided in the back of the journal for respective contributors.

with the state (see also Silverman, 1987). In a sense, I wanted to oversample. I also believe that a useful way of determining how higher education scholars view the state is to look at how they contrast our system with the higher education systems and states of other countries; that this would be one context in which basic assumptions about the state would be stated explicitly. I chose to focus on the last five years of issues for each of these journals for two reasons. First, I wanted to concentrate on a time period of several years in order to get a sufficient number of articles to analyze. At the same time, I was not interested in doing an historical analysis of changing conceptions over time—I see the *Handbook* as providing more a state-of-the art than an historical perspective on topics. Second, Silverman (1987) has analyzed articles in higher education journals prior to 1986, and his research offers some detail on research on the state.

Journal of Higher Education

In each of the five years sampled, few articles in *The Journal of Higher Education* deal explicitly with the state. Of the 29 articles in 1986, two deal with the state. Of the 30 articles in 1987, one deals with the state. Of the 27 articles in 1988, three deal with the state. Of the 31 articles in 1989, two deal with the state. Of the 29 articles in 1990, one deals with the state. These figures overstate an explicit focus on the state. Most of these papers' principal focus is the university. Although the state is mentioned, it is not studied. The questions that are being posed relate to institutional autonomy, to how state policies and laws impact on universities. The terminology varies, but the assumptions and characterizations are consistent: the state is external and is a threat, it consists of formal political bodies, it is inefficient and intrusive.

The first article in 1986 is "The University and Morality: A Revised Approach to University Autonomy and its Limits" (Alexander, 1986). The author is a sociologist, and is the leader of the neo-functionalist tradition, which builds on structural-functionalism. In asking, "What should the morality of the university be?," Alexander argues that the corporate institution of the university, as distinct from the body of the faculty, should "seek to insulate itself as thoroughly as possible from any social commitment." It must remain neutral. Autonomy is an important part of this neutrality. There is little discussion of what constitutes the state, but it is clearly a world of accountability, control, and political commitment that threatens the basic value and morality of academe, cognitive rationality.

The second article in 1986 is "Campus Autonomy and its Relationship to Measures of University Quality" (Volkwein, 1986a). Volkwein is one of the few people who has put some basic assumptions about the state to empirical test. His question is, To what extent is state regulation of public universities associated with campus quality? He "finds little evidence to support a relationship between freedom from state academic and financial constraints, on the one hand, and faculty and student quality and external funding success, on the other." (p. 521) The focus is on the effects of the state on universities, with a standard conception of the state in terms of the legislative, judicial, executive, and administrative branches of government that have formal authority and exercise control over public universities. The state is viewed as separate from public universities, as is evident in Volkwein's use of resource dependency theory—the state is part of the external environment.

The one article that deals with the state in 1987 is "Higher Education in a Consumer Society," by me (Rhoades, 1987a). Significantly, this is a comparative piece that contrasts four national systems of higher education in terms of their political institutions. The question that drives the research is, To what extent do political institutions enhance consumers' ability to politically influence higher education? The argument is that the nature of American political institutions affords lay groups multiple mechanisms and means by which to articulate their demands. Various terms are utilized in referring to the state—e.g., government, political institutions, state—and Rhoades focuses on various parts of the state—e.g., national ministries, legislative, executive, and judicial branches, federal and state levels. But they all refer to formal structures of government lying outside the academy. The state is an instrument that is subject to the efforts of external groups to shape governmental action. In contrast to prevailing portrayals, the state is presented as a positive force for innovation and responsiveness that ensures flexibility in the system.

Two other articles in 1987 deal with state institutions of higher education from an historical perspective. I do not include them in my "count" of articles focusing on the state because they are not directly concerned with the state. Johnson (1987) and Ratcliff (1987) examine the origins of the state university idea and of public junior colleges, although they do not focus on state involvement in shaping these new institutions. In both cases, the state is conceptualized as formal governmental institutions that are separate from and that fund and control postsecondary education institutions.

The first article in 1988, "State Legislatures and the Autonomy of Colleges and Universities: A Comparative Study of Legislation in Four States, 1900–1979" (Fisher, 1988), returns to the theme of autonomy. Fisher examines the extent to which the legislative stance toward autonomy has changed over time in four states—"Do state legislatures pose an increasing threat to the autonomy of colleges and universities?" She finds that "State legislatures and other state government bodies have always been involved in and to some extent have always intruded upon the affairs of higher education. There has been a continual feeling that, although intrusions by state legislatures have not yet gone too far, institutions might be on the brink of serious loss of autonomy." (p. 159) Fisher focuses on state legislatures and the major higher education acts they have passed. The state is seen as external to higher education, as having formal authority, and as constituting a serious threat to the autonomy of higher education institutions, which is defined as "the institution's power to conduct its affairs and use its resources as it determines, without interference or regulation by outside bodies." (p. 136)

The second article in 1988, "Academic Freedom and the State: Reflections on the Uses of Knowledge" (Slaughter, 1988) is the only article from 1986 to 1990 to utilize "the State" (in its general sense) in its title and to theorize explicitly about it. Slaughter's opening discussion of her conception of the state and education (no other JHE paper did so) is no doubt due to her neo-Marxian orientation, which because it lies outside the mainstream in the field of higher education, requires some explication. In reviewing the changing conditions in which academic freedom is defined, Slaughter does not juxtapose higher education to the state, but treats it as a sector of the state, with the expansion of the two being interconnected. The state is not treated as the principal source of authority, but is related to the capitalist production process. The state is an arena and a participant in conflict that shapes and is shaped by patterns of race, class, and gender. It is not portrayed as being inefficient, but is treated as the repository of important material and ideological resources to which various groups are trying to gain access.

The third article in 1988, "The Organizational Context for Affirmative Action for Women Faculty" (Hanna, 1988), touches on another major theme in the higher education literature. The case law literature focuses on the effects of rulings by federal agencies and the courts on campus activities. As the title of this paper suggests, the study is of the organization rather than of the state and its policies. The state is portrayed as an external regulator which threatens to distort the internal processes of the organization. What is interesting about treating the state as the repository of significant formal authority is that the state has rarely, if ever, retaliated against an institution by withdrawing funds because of affirmative action violations. Of course, individual court cases are another matter, but Hanna's focus, like that of many other scholars, is on cases of organizations, not individuals.

In 1989, an article by Volkwein (1989), "Changes in Quality among Public Universities," follows up on his earlier analysis of the relationship between state regulation and campus quality. Volkwein finds, "that campus autonomy has virtually no meaningful association with measures of quality. Instead, the sizes and resource bases of public universities appear to hold the keys to quality." (p. 148) Volkwein is interested in studying not the workings of the state itself, but the effects of the state on higher education organizations. The conceptual framework he utilizes is drawn from an organization theory that conceives of organizations as separate from their environments, and treats the state as part of that environment, even for public institutions.

The second article in 1989, "The Cooperative Research Laboratory: Policy

Implications for Higher Education'' (Emmert and Crow, 1989), deals with science and indirectly with science policy, topics that receive little attention in the higher education literature. Their question is, What organizational characteristics of university based R & D laboratories are most likely to stimulate commercializable products? They focus on policy implications both for universities and for the government, with the aim being to encourage the development of commercial products that will promote economic development. The state is operationalized as various funding agencies. It is cast in the role of external agent that should act to generate economic development by directing its funds to certain kinds of laboratories. It is a resource that should facilitate the productive activity of universities and businesses, an external partner that should take on the role of underwriter.

The one article in 1990, ''Adapting to Diversity: Organizational Influences on Student Achievement'' (Richardson and Skinner, 1990), returns to the common theme of the organizational effects of state policy. In this case, the focus is on how the state policy environment can encourage organizational adaptations that lead to improved participation and graduation rates for minority students. The state is defined in terms of formal bodies such as the legislature, the courts, and coordinating boards, which by virtue of their formal authority—e.g., court decisions, statutes, fiscal appropriations—set up incentive systems for the organizations they control. The state is part of the external environment. The authors are careful to reject a ''cookbook'' approach by state policy makers, emphasizing the importance of strategies that are ''institutionally appropriate'' and are sensitive to the unintended and harmful effects that state policies can have on universities. The importance of university autonomy, of the need for local actors to develop ''context-relevant'' and sensitive strategies, is underscored.

Review of Higher Education
The five year sample of *Review of Higher Education* issues, as with *The Journal of Higher Education*, offers a relatively small number of articles that deal explicitly with the state. Of the 29 articles in 1986, three deal with the state. Of the 19 articles in 1987, one deals with the state. Of the 24 articles in 1988, two deal with the state. Of the 20 articles in 1989, two deal with the state. None of the 23 articles in 1990 deals with the state. As with the JHE, the figures for the RHE overstate the explicit focus on the state. For the most part, the articles do not explore, either empirically or theoretically, the dimensions and operations of the state. Several of the RHE articles do focus on public policy. But the focus is on policies, policy choices, and policy effects, not on policy processes or the relationship among policy domains and state agencies and sectors. The general characterization of the state is much the same as in JHE articles. The state is external to higher education. It has formal authority over higher education. It is a threat to the internal integrity of higher education organizations.

The first article in 1986, "Academic Freedom for Universities" (Leslie, 1986), touches on the recurring theme of university autonomy. In dealing with the legal apparatus of the state, Leslie examines developments that have given academic freedom rights and privileges to the corporate university. The very formulation of the question treats the state as an external agent that has the formal authority to either control or accord considerable latitude to higher education institutions. Such latitude, freedom, and autonomy are posed as central values of the university and as being central to the integrity of the institution and to its serving the broader interests of society.

The second article in 1986, "State Financial Control of Public Universities and its Relationship to Campus Administrative Elaborateness and Cost: Results of a National Study" (Volkwein, 1986b) offers additional results obtained by Volkwein in exploring the effects of state regulation. As in his JHE contributions, Volkwein conceives of the state as an external regulatory body, part of the external environment. He explores the effects of this environment on the internal organizational structure and efficiency of universities. Volkwein finds "little evidence that freedom from the burdens of state control encourages individual campuses to reduce administrative overhead." (p. 282) However, he does find that "Those campuses which are encumbered by elaborate fiscal and personnel controls by their state officials are less likely to develop alternative sources of revenue, or do so less effectively." (p. 283) In other words, tight state controls are not cost effective in that they encourage too much dependence on state funding.

The third article in 1986, "Legislature and University Conflict: The Case of California" (Zusman, 1986), represents one of the few direct studies of the state in the JHE and RHE. Zusman explores the struggle for authority between the state legislature and the University of California, the autonomy of which is inscribed in the state constitution. Zusman is studying the interaction among different branches of government. In contrast to most other higher education researchers, Zusman treats the state's authority as unclear, problematic, and subject to negotiation. Her empirical analysis concentrates on that negotiation process, exploring the strategies utilized by different branches of government to assert their authority. Nevertheless, Zusman sees the state as separate from the university and as infringing (or attempting to do so) on the university's autonomy and basic academic functions to the detriment of the university. The struggle and negotiations are seen as problematic, with legislative efforts to assert authority characterized as encroachments on university territory.

The one article in 1987, "Higher Education Reform and Ad Hoc Committees: A Question of Legitimacy" (Mitchell, 1987), offers a direct conceptual treatment of the state. The legitimacy of higher education is linked to the legitimacy of the "modern democratic state." As with Zusman, Mitchell goes well beyond most higher education researchers by treating the formal authority of the state as problematic, as something that is in flux and requires study. He sees the fluctuations in state legitimacy as impacting on higher education. Mitchell's focus is on ad hoc committees, which he suggests have long been part of government policymaking. In casting these committees as "legitimation devices," Mitchell maintains that we need to move toward "authentic soul searching," suggesting that government bodies are more oriented to sustaining the standing of the state than they are to change, that their political nature and goals undermines their effectiveness for improving higher education.

In 1988, two articles focus on the effects of state policy on minority students. The first, "The Impact of Financial Aid on Ethnic Minorities" (Stampen and Fenske, 1988), considers the impact of different combinations of student aid on minority student access and persistence. The state itself is not considered, except in terms of its policies. The policies are treated as givens in the analysis, which centers on the effects of policies. The second article, "Minority Degree Achievement and the State Policy Environment" (Callan, 1988), examines the results of state initiatives to improve the educational opportunities of minority students and suggests the actions necessary for successful efforts. In focusing on formal state policy initiatives, Callan conceptualizes the state in standard terms: as consisting of governors, legislators, and state higher education board members; as separate from higher education institutions; as the source of formal authority; and as neither particularly effective nor efficient. He voices the conventional concern for campus autonomy, "State leaders should envision their role as stimulators, supporters, and evaluators; they should set challenging goals and insist on accountability, leaving the tailoring and management of specific programs to colleges and universities." (pp. 362–63)

In 1989, there are two articles that present agendas for policy research and in the process discuss the state. The first, "Policy Research for the University Research System" (Averch, 1989), examines science policy issues. Averch deals with the "university research system," and treats the state residually, as a source of financial input. His only direct references to the state have to do with whether the federal financing of research (via various federal agencies) should be more centralized, and whether the resources that are allocated should be more concentrated. The state is cast as being outside the university research system, as being the source of funds, and as needing to improve upon its efficiency and effectiveness. The second article in 1989, "A Policy Research Agenda for Postsecondary Student Aid" (Hansen, 1989), proposes a research agenda to assist in the selection of public policy choices in the area of student aid. Policymakers are clearly defined as other, as being more practically than theoretically oriented, as not being social scientists and not sharing their language. They are also defined as being inherently political, and in some sense as not efficient.

Higher Education

The numbers of articles dealing with the state in *Higher Education* are far greater than in the other two higher education journals. Of 41 articles in 1986, eight deal with the state. Of 42 articles in 1987, 10 deal with the state, with four of these coming in a special issue on "Planning for Diminishing Resources" edited by Sheila Slaughter. Of 36 articles in 1988, 13 deal with the state. Of 35 articles in 1989, seven deal with the state. And of 51 articles in 1990, 14 deal with the state. Due to these numbers, the presentation in this section will not be article by article, but will consist of a synthesis of how the state is treated in *Higher Education* articles. The focus, as in the previous sections, will be on the topical context in which the state is mentioned, and on the terminology, characterizations, and assumptions regarding the state.

As with the other higher education literature, the articles in *Higher Education* are largely descriptive and prescriptive. They do not provide explicit discussion of the theoretical framework that underlies their rendition and assessment of conditions in higher education. Nevertheless, they do give us more detail about the state than articles in the other two higher education journals. Moreover, what they focus on, describe, and prescribe has much to say about what these scholars ascribe to the state. Finally, they provide some insight into dimensions of state operations that are lacking in articles in the previous two journals.

The topical contexts in which the state is considered are much like those found in JHE and RHE articles. About one-quarter of the articles deal with finance policies, including resource allocations to higher education. Such work ranges from a focus on student loan schemes (Bray, 1986) to funding formulas (Darling et al., 1989) to the impact of state government reductions in higher education allocations (special issue, 16(2), 1987). Another quarter of the articles address coordinating structures and regulations in higher education. In some cases, this work describes organizational arrangements that affect different sectors of higher education (Geiger, 1988). In other cases, it focuses on planning arrangements at the system or national level (Maassen and Potman, 1990). The largest number of articles examine the impacts of policy. For example, a large number of articles on Australia describe the impact of governmental policies regarding matters such as institutional mergers (Harman, 1986) or research policy (Neumann and Lindsay, 1988). Other articles deal with the impact of new national framework laws (Pritchard, 1986) or various levels of state policies related to equal opportunity (Lindsay, 1988). Finally, some of the articles track recent trends and historical developments in the state's intervention in higher education (Harman, 1988; Marshall, 1990) or in the development of national systems of higher education (Altbach, 1989; Hayhoe, 1988).

In these contexts, the state is conceived of and talked about in much the same way as in the previously examined literature. The state is seen as external to higher education and as increasingly threatening the internal integrity of higher education systems. Perhaps the most common analytical focus is on autonomy, and on the ill effects of state actions. Titles such as, "Autonomy and Control: A University Funding Formula as an Instrument of Public Policy" (Darling et al., 1989), "Accountability in Higher Education: The Danger of Unintended Consequences" (Elton, 1988), and "End of an Era: The Collapse of the 'Buffer' Approach to the Governance of Australian Tertiary Education" (Marshall, 1990) convey a sense of the way the state and higher education are regarded.

For example, the economic rationality of the state is counterposed to the internal educational rationality of the universities. The state is portrayed as an external constraint that impinges on efficiency and rationality within the university, for example, by inhibiting the exercise of rational decision making regarding budget cuts (Hardy, 1988), or by undermining with its research policy the critical productive connection between research and teaching (Neumann and Lindsay, 1988).

For the most part, the state is conceived in terms of formal political institutions. But in a few cases, the comparative work in *Higher Education* moves conceptually beyond the scholarship in the other higher education journals by attending to the relations between different state sectors. For example, Pritchard (1986) examines a higher education law promulgated by the federal government in (then) West Germany. As she indicates, the states have two years to adjust their laws to come into compliance with the federal law, and the political party that dominates state government opposes the changes brought about by the newest amendment to the federal law. Similarly, Harman (1986) addresses the conflict among various parts of government that surround the federal government's efforts in Australia to restructure higher education. Although universities are established under state legislation, and are legally responsible to the state ministry, their funding is controlled by the federal government. Moreover, the coordinating body that oversees higher education, and mediates between it and the federal government— the Commonwealth Tertiary Education Commission—has come into conflict with the Prime Minister over the federal government's efforts. What emerges is a sense of the complexity of state operations and interactions in federal systems, even if one remains within the confines of formal governmental bodies. This is a picture that is obviously relevant for the federal system in the United States. As Lindsay (1988) suggests, the state is a complex nexus of governmental levels, branches, and policies—legislative, judicial, executive, and administrative:

> The interactive relations among federal policies, state policies, and institutional policies must constantly be taken into account. . . . Institutional plans are monitored and evaluated separately and as part of a statewide Adams mandate; state plans are monitored by federal agencies. The evaluation findings at the institutional level can be transmitted to state and federal agencies which can modify criteria in light of what is or is not successful. (pp. 575–76)

On a few occasions, articles in *Higher Education* also move beyond the current higher education literature by focusing on policy formation, on the relationship between higher education and other social welfare policies, and on the interrelationship between state and society, examining the way patterns of politics and power shape the academy. For example, Harman (1986) and Pritchard (1986) speak to the lobbying efforts of various interest groups—though they focus on faculty and institutional associations—surrounding national policy formation. Davis (1987) explores the competition between higher education and other social welfare areas that are funded by government. She analyzes the social (equality) and economic (return on investment) dimensions of the human capital (investment in people) arguments that are advanced by higher education leaders, noting that these arguments are now being challenged. Hayhoe (1988) examines the impact of three political reforms and movements on the "knowledge orientation" of Chinese universities, considering the interactive influence between these political developments and university students and intellectuals, and focusing particularly on the growth of various social science fields. Higher education is treated as being intricately connected with China's polity, defined in broad terms, including intellectuals involved in various forms of political/theoretical dialogue. Finally, Slaughter (1987) places the discussion of postsecondary spending policies in a broad political economic context that explains state actions in terms of corporate interests that are served by policies that redefine the role of higher education.

Such work represents important exceptions in the higher education literature. If these exceptions point to new possibilities in studying "the state," they also point to the rule of prevailing conceptualizations of the state in the higher education literature.

Review of Higher Education Journals: Conclusion
The conceptualization of the state is remarkably consistent and consistently tacit throughout the articles from 1986–1990 in *Higher Education, The Journal of Higher Education*, and the *Review of Higher Education*. Due to the comparative nature of the papers, there were far more articles in HE than the other two journals that dealt with the state. So much of comparative work focuses on the formal structures of national educational systems, and this generally involves describing the formal governmental arrangements that seem to be so different from those in the United States. For the most part, such treatment of the state is not grounded in any explicit theory of the state, though the detail that is provided sometimes takes scholars beyond the generally simple conception of "the state" to complex configurations of organizational arrangements. The descriptions of the state in each of the journals are presented in a manner that suggests we all know and agree to what constitutes the state. The state is separate from universities—it is an external, political influence on a system shaped by professional

values. It has formal authority with respect to higher education, and consists of those governmental bodies that have and exercise that authority in higher education. The exercise of that authority often compromises the internal integrity of higher education institutions, with state intervention being characterized not only as intrusion but as inefficient and ineffective.

Given this conceptualization, it makes sense to pose certain questions having to do with the state. The consistent conceptualization is connected to a consistency in the topics that are addressed, topics having to do with campus autonomy and the institutional effects of state policy. In looking at autonomy, articles take the formal authority of the state as given (not as problematic, open to negotiation, and a possible subject for investigation) and consider the legal or regulatory aspects of the state. In looking at the effects of state policy, articles take the policies as given (not as subjects for investigation) and address various impacts on institutions, such as the effect of student aid policies on participation and graduation rates, or the effect of regulation on administrative costs and organizational practices.

In his analysis of higher education journals, Silverman (1987) found some patterns that were similar to the ones described here. For example, he categorized types of articles according to their epistemological structure—the way they approach the subject matter. He found that only a handful of the articles on state/national issues were conceptually oriented. Most of the articles could be categorized as "conceptual humanist," as presenting and advocating a point of view about a particular issue or policy, as opposed to empirically studying it. Under the general category of state/national issues, Silverman included: national policy/general references; comparative national systems; state issues and planning; governance and coordination; finance; resource allocation and budgeting; productivity and cost-benefit analysis; educational opportunity; student financial assistance; and work and education. Silverman found that the largest number of articles was in the category of comparative national systems, just as I found that the largest number of articles consisted of comparative pieces in *Higher Education*. The next largest category in Silverman's analysis was national policy, with almost all of the articles being conceptual humanist—in other words, presenting a position about policy rather than studying it. The combined categories of productivity, student aid, and educational opportunity also represented a large number of articles. In some respects, then, the literature of the 1970s is consistent with that of the late 1980s in its treatment of the state.

Some authors offer somewhat different treatments of the state. Zusman (1986) and Mitchell (1987) treat the formal authority of the state as something that is contested and problematic rather than being clear and given. They study that contest, with Zusman empirically exploring the struggle between different sectors of the state over authority. Slaughter (1988), like Zusman and Mitchell, sees the state as an important ideological resource, but she takes a step beyond them in dealing with authority. She relates the authority of the state to external structures and bases of power such as class, and she sees this power as being in flux and as being contested. In her conceptualization, higher education is presented as a sector of the state.

Some authors, of course, write for higher education journals, *and* other kinds of journals.[3] It is possible that the articles they publish outside higher education are more conceptually explicit and developed than those they send to the journals I reviewed. Although I have not systematically reviewed such authors and publications, my sense as a reader and scholar in this area is that the general conceptualization of the state that marks peoples' work holds regardless of the journals in which it appears. Moreover, the state of the art reviews appearing in the *Handbook*, which are reviewed in the next section of this chapter, should pick up much the work that cuts across fields of study and various journals. Finally, if there is a substantial difference between the characterizations and treatment of the state presented in papers appearing in higher education versus other journals, this is an important piece of data about our field. It would say something about what scholars perceive to be acceptable and appropriate for higher education scholarship. And my concern, after all, is with the discourse that marks our field, not with discovering the real beliefs and conceptions of scholars in our field.

THE STATE OF THE ART AND THE STATE

One of the explicit purposes of the *Handbook* is to provide state-of-the-art literature reviews that synthesize the findings and set the future course of higher education research. The aim is to facilitate the development of cumulative knowledge, with considerable attention directed to the conceptual and methodological character of the literature. The *Handbook* offers reviews in 12 general areas of higher education research that are intended to achieve broad coverage. Each of the 12 areas has an Associate Editor, responsible for coordinating and monitoring the choice of topic and author.

In looking at the 12 categories in the first volume of the *Handbook*, although "the state" does not appear in any of them, there are several in which one might expect to find some discussion of the state. It happens that these categories correspond to the general topical areas I identified for journal articles that dealt with the state: comparative higher education, organizational theory and behavior, legal issues, finance and resource allocations, and governance and planning. The latter category is one in which you might expect to find direct empirical and

---

[3]For this point and many other thoughtful suggestions about the manuscript, I am much indebted to the careful reading and sensitive handling of the Associate Editor, James Hearn. Of course, Jim bears no responsibility for the way I have taken and used his remarks. But he can be held accountable for having asked me to write this chapter!

theoretical treatment of the state. But the associate editor in this area for the first several years was Kenneth Mortimer, best known for his writings on institutional governance. The current chapter is the first one in the eight years of the *Handbook* to deal specifically and conceptually with the state. By the sixth volume of the *Handbook*, the category of government and higher education had been added (governance and coordination was retained and legal issues was dropped).[4] The terminology of governance and coordination, and now government and higher education, suggest a focus, not unlike that found in journal articles, on the state as a separate entity, and on its formal institutions, its formal authority, and its formal functions. In this section, I review chapters that deal with the state in the first six volumes—1985–90—of the *Handbook*.

In the first volume of the *Handbook*, the one chapter dealing directly with the state, "Legal Parameters of the Faculty Employment Relationship" (Lee and Olswang, 1985), focuses on the courts and case law. The purpose of such research generally, and in this chapter, is to track trends in litigation and court decisions and determine their impact on universities and their implications for administrative practice. Lee and Olswang see the courts as a potential threat to the autonomy of universities and to academic norms, although they conclude that "the judiciary defers to academic autonomy when academe conducts its affairs responsibly and with integrity." (p. 246) None of the literature cited, and none of the recommendations for future research that are provided, involve empirical or theoretical treatment of how the courts operate, of the litigation and decision making processes or of the relationship of court activities to other branches of government and to structures of power outside government. Instead, the questions posed by Lee and Olswang address organizational processes within universities. They represent the point of view of organizations trying to cope with the courts.

In the second volume of the *Handbook*, there are two chapters that deal with the state. The first, "Affirmative Action Employment Discrimination: The Higher Education Fragment" (Clague, 1986), examines case law as it affects higher education. In closing the review, Clague offers a variation on the typical case law analysis by pointing to the interaction between the executive branch and the courts. She indicates that, "Although the executive branch cannot dictate to judges, it can influence the judiciary in three ways: it can bring reverse discrimination suits of its own or intervene as amicus curiae in support of private reverse discrimination plaintiffs; more important, it can influence the federal courts through new appointments." (p. 153) Treating other branches of government, and universities for that matter, as active agents contesting the formal authority

---

[4] Whether this and other changes are matters of conscious, policy-oriented decisions, or were simply personnel and logistical matters (though the two often overlap) of who was available is not really important for my purposes. I am more interested in the effect such categories have on the way the field is reviewed and constructed.

of another branch of government, and shaping the case law that affects higher education, provides a considerably broader and more sophisticated view of the state than has been considered in most legal analyses in higher education. If Clague does not offer such analysis herself, she at least points to the possibility in her closing remarks of enriching our understanding of the state.

The second chapter in 1986 is "Evaluation Research and Educational Decision-Making" (Shapiro, 1986). Apart from briefly mentioning the impetus for evaluation provided by the Higher Education Act of 1965 and by the fiscal crises of states in the 1970s, the state is left unconsidered. The references at the state level are primarily to state boards, which are seen as "external agencies that demand accountability in the administration of higher education academic programs." (p. 193) Shapiro's discussion of the press for accountability offers a view of the state as formal authority, and as political as opposed to rational. His focus is on what the organization can do and is forced to do in the face of this external pressure.

In the third volume of the *Handbook*, there are three chapters that deal with the state in the context of topical concerns that reflect the journal literature reviewed earlier. The first is by Volkwein (1987), "State Regulation and Campus Autonomy," and follows the thinking and analysis of his contributions to the periodical literature. Volkwein offers a discussion of the "deeply held convictions about autonomy and effectiveness" (p. 124) that are held by higher education scholars, noting that "Most of the literature on the topic is based on informed opinion [or, I would say, self-interest] rather than on empirical research" (p. 144). The strength of convictions about the benefits of autonomy is evident in Volkwein's closing discussion. After finding that autonomy is unrelated to campus effectiveness or administrative expenditures, Volkwein states that "These findings raise questions about the value of spending state resources and energy on centralized control practices." (p. 144) The research questions that he poses for further investigation similarly reflect the power of conventional beliefs, aiming, as they do, to identify benefits of reduced control and decentralized management.

The second chapter in the 1987 volume is, "An Analysis of Student Academic Rights" (Young and Braswell, 1987). Tracking the relevant case law, Young and Braswell consider the extent to which the judiciary continues to exercise restraint and protect academic autonomy and recognize academic freedom. In closing, the authors provide campus administrators with guidelines to protect institutional interests. Their final sentence conveys the sense of their enterprise, "Although some litigation is inevitable, only well informed administrators can deter necessary [I presume they meant *un*necessary litigation—was this a Freudian sic?] litigation." (p. 357)

The third chapter in the 1987 volume is a comparative study, "The Expansion of Higher Education Enrollments in Agrarian and Developing Areas of the Third

World'' (Maxwell, 1987). In reviewing theories regarding worldwide expansion of enrollments, Maxwell touches on political and state variables—e.g., political modernization, centralization—that have been linked to enrollment growth. In closing, he is critical of the loose or nonexistent theoretical and operational definition of various terms and concepts that are utilized as political variables. However, he does not focus specifically on the state, nor does he offer much in the way of rethinking such variables.

In the fourth volume of the *Handbook*, only one of the twelve chapters deals with the state, in a brief reference. The chapter, ''Strategy and Resources: Economic Issues in Strategic Planning and Management in Higher Education'' (Hearn, 1988), adopts an organizational point of view in talking about strategic planning. The brief reference to the state is of the ''political context'' that is part of the external environment which Hearn examines in terms of the interpenetration of ''external'' and ''internal'' environments. Hearn contrasts the flexibility and freedom available to for-profit organizations in acting strategically with respect to the marketplace, to the situation confronted by higher education institutions, whose freedom to act in the marketplace is limited by their ''societal charge.'' The state, which is not explicitly identified, is cast as the external influence that limits the applicability of the strategic metaphor and strategic practice.

In the fifth volume of the *Handbook*, three chapters deal with the state. The first chapter, ''Strategy and Effectiveness in Systems of Higher Education'' (Chaffee, 1989), takes the uncommon approach of considering strategy and effectiveness from the standpoint of state systems of higher education rather than of individual universities or colleges: ''Systems of higher education have grown in number and importance in recent years, yet the literature has given relatively little attention to them.'' (Chaffee, 1989, p. 1) Given Chaffee's position in the North Dakota State Board of Higher Education, perhaps her focus is not surprising. What is interesting is that Chaffee applies the literature on organizational effectiveness and strategy to systems of higher education, arguing that these systems are, in fact, organizations. Thus, the state is treated as something outside of the system, an external constituency (this point is displayed in a figure that delineates such constituents). The boundaries are clear, with the state conceptualized as being outside of higher education, and as consisting of the governor and state legislators.

The second chapter in the 1989 volume, ''Student Financial Aid and Institutional Behavior: How Institutions Use and Benefit from Student Aid'' (McPherson, Wagner, and Willie-Schiff, 1989), addresses the effects of federal financial policies from the perspective of the organization. Two questions that organize the chapter: ''1. How do institutions, in practice, set tuition and package institutionally awarded financial aid in response to demand? 2. How important is federal student aid as a source of budgetary support for colleges and universities?'' (p. 199) The state is dealt with in terms of federal policies, and the policies that are focused on deal specifically and exclusively with higher education—e.g., federally funded generally available student aid, specially directed aid programs, federal research spending. The focus is on policy choices, and on an economic analysis of the effects of such choices on colleges and universities.

The third chapter in the 1989 volume, "Managing Uncertainty: Environmental Analysis Forecasting in Academic Planning" (Morrison and Mecca, 1989), also adopts the organizational point of view. There are very few references to the state. To the extent that the state is considered, it is as part of the external environment that must be scanned. The particular references are to federal government requirements regarding recipients of federal student aid, and state regulations regarding articulation between two- and four-year colleges and universities. The state is other, and is the source of formal authority.

In the sixth volume of the *Handbook*, two chapters deal with the state. The first, "The American College History: A Survey of its Historiographic Schools and Analytical Approaches from the Mid-Nineteenth Century to the Present" (Goodchild and Huk, 1990), refers to the state in discussing "the policy school" of college historiography. The focus of such research is on the influence of external political forces on institutional development. As with most other policy research in higher education, the work that Goodchild and Huk cite takes the policies as given and examines their effects on colleges and universities. In some cases—particularly in dealing with financial policies—there is discussion of policy choices, in an effort to influence those choices.

The second chapter in the 1990 volume, "An Analysis of State Formula Budgeting in Higher Education" (Ahumada, 1990), also deals with the state in the context of policy analysis. In reviewing funding policies, Ahumada concerns himself with university resource requirements and autonomy in internally allocating resources: "The state should preserve the university's flexibility to determine its instructional resource needs and carry our needed internal allocation or reallocation of resources as dictated by funding realities and its long-range plans.'' (p. 492) The policy analysis is a review of choices and their effects from the point of view of the institutions.

Review of *Handbook* Chapters: Conclusion

The treatment the state receives in state-of-the-art literature reviews in the *Handbook* from 1985 to 1990 is very much like what was found in three core higher education journals, consistent and consistently tacit. In the six volumes of the *Handbook*, there are, respectively 1, 2, 3, 1, 3, and 2 chapters that specifically mention the state. If anything, there is less consideration of the state in the *Handbook* than in the journals. The only two times in six years the state appears in a chapter title is in reference to states, as in "State Regulation . . ." (Volkwein, 1987) and "State Formula Budgeting . . ." (Ahumada, 1990). And the references to the state were not generally found in the introductions and conclusions, as they were in the journal articles. As in the journals, the state is mentioned, but it is not directly studied. The principal focus is on colleges and universities. To the extent it was considered, the state was consistently portrayed as other, as the source of formal authority, and as intrusive and problematic.

The topical contexts in which the state was mentioned were also much like what was found in the journals, and were evident in the 12 categories that organize the review chapters. Five chapters dealt with the state in the context of public policy. The policy area ranged from program review to state and federal financial policies and regulations. Three chapters mentioned the state in discussing strategic planning from the organizational standpoint. Three chapters had a legal focus. And one chapter had a comparative focus.

The topical commonalities with the journal literature translate into the same kinds of questions being asked and the same sort of standpoint being adopted in looking at the state. For all of the *Handbook* chapters, the question underlying their consideration of the state was, How does it affect colleges and universities? Higher education scholars virtually all adopt the perspective of the organization trying to contend with the state. The state is seen as other, as threatening, as an external force.

There is an intriguing paradox here. On the one hand, the state is to a considerable extent regarded as an illegitimate intruder on higher education affairs. The state is driven by political and bureaucratic forces. These are counterposed to the professional forces that drive the academy, and are posed as being counterproductive to the work of the academy. On the other hand, the state is treated as the source of formal authority (and of considerable resources), and that authority is taken as given (and the resources are often treated as a matter of entitlement) rather than being questioned. In studying case law, state policies and regulations, scholars question the advisability of various policy choices by speaking to their possible effects, but they do not question the formal authority of state institutions. They do not treat that authority as problematic. They do not look within the state at the negotiation of power. The resolution of these seemingly contradictory positions taken in the literature is actually relatively simple, and is linked to the professional belief system (some would say ideology) of academe. Higher education scholars and practitioners are drawing on a classical distinction in organization theory between bureaucratic and professional authority. Bureaucratic authority, in this case the state, is positional authority, based on the position or office one holds in the formal chain of command. Professional authority, in this case higher education scholars and practitioners, is based on expertise. In the value schema of higher education, formal authority is recognized, but expertise is seen as more compelling, reasonable, and rational. In the higher education literature, the sanctioning authority of the state is recognized, but there is an effort to mitigate the ill effects of such sanctions through reason and persuasion and appeals to the authority and competence of experts. For example, in the policy literature the focus is more on policy choices and effects than on the processes by which policies are developed and implemented, and resisted. The literature, even in the ostensibly "objective" descriptions it provides, is as much policy advocacy as it is policy analysis. It is an effort by higher education scholars, who are subject to the state's formal authority, to influence policy in ways that preserve as much as possible their autonomy vis-a-vis the state (and their claim to its resources).

In one respect, it is hardly surprising that state-of-the-art literature reviews in the *Handbook* mirror the higher education journal literature. The chapters do, after all, synthesize the literature. In another respect, it is disappointing that *Handbook* chapters have failed thus far to identify gaps in the literature in terms of the conceptualization of the state. If one of the major purposes of *Handbook* chapters is to provide a map of past scholarship, of what is known, these chapters should also direct us to what is not known, and chart future paths for exploration.

The treatment of the state in the higher education literature is conceptually and empirically underdeveloped. The treatment is narrow even within the confines of the tacit conceptualization that is prevalent. For example, several of the *Handbook* chapters dealt with the influence of various types of financial policies on colleges and universities. The focus of this work is overwhelmingly on student aid policies at the federal level and on resource allocation and regulation at the state level. In fairness, these areas are where the most dollars are for most institutions. But for some institutions, considerable financial support comes from other areas, such as research and training grants, which receive very little treatment in the literature. Perhaps recent developments involving Stanford and other research elites will contribute to studies of the effects of the indirect cost recovery rates that are set by various federal agencies. There is even less attention devoted to more general economic policies—e.g., tax laws, economic development initiatives of the municipal, state, and federal government—that impact on higher education. This is unfortunate, because organizations (like individuals) are often driven as much or more by potential revenues that are on the margin than by the large, relatively stable funding (such as student aid and state allocations) that comes to them each year.[5] The actions of universities with regard to technology transfer illustrate this point.

My points about the *Handbook* chapters are twofold. First, scholarship in higher education on the state is characterized by a self-interested agenda of maintaining institutional autonomy, which has meant dealing with a relatively narrow set of questions. That political agenda (wrapped though it is in professional ideology) has impeded the development of an intellectual agenda that is

---

[5] I am indebted to Larry Leslie for this point, which he is developing in an analysis of student aid and commercial science in Australian higher education.

grounded in various perspectives on, questions about, and conceptions of, the state. A second point is that even within the confines of prevailing conceptions of and questions about the state, the literature is quite limited. As noted above, in adopting the vantage point and interests of the higher education institution, there are a wide range of state policies and activities that have yet to be fully considered in terms of their impact on colleges and universities. There are myriad state activities that have a profound impact on higher education and yet that do not specifically target the postsecondary education world. Higher education scholars have yet to get beyond state agencies, policies, and regulations that deal specifically and exclusively with higher education.

THE STATE IN HIGHER EDUCATION CLASSICS

Perhaps I can be forgiven the "great books" approach to higher education literature on the state. In reviewing periodicals and *Handbook* chapters, I have found virtually no direct conceptual or empirical treatments of the state. A prevailing and clear portrayal of the state has emerged, but it is a cursory, sketchy rendering of the subject that lies in the background of most scholarly compositions. By contrast, some books explicitly address the state, affording us the opportunity to explore how higher education scholars conceive of and represent the state when they provide a fuller treatment of the topic.

As always, the choice of great books is problematic. In its particulars, my list of "classics" may be different than that of many readers. But in selecting higher education books on the state, I have tried to include contributions that are prominent in our bibliographies and our syllabi. My sample is selective, not inclusive, but I believe it is representative in terms of how the state is treated in "the classics." In making the choices, I relied on my sense of the field, as one who has followed work in this area for over a decade, and on articles that have identified core readings in higher education generally (Budd, 1990; Weidman, Nelson, and Radzyminski, 1984), and in the politics of higher education (Dill, 1979). No doubt, some classics are not reviewed here, including many of my personal favorites. However, I am comfortable that the books I have selected as representative of the higher education canon qualify as such. No doubt, the books I have selected are mainstream higher education books, as opposed to those that are overtly more sociological, economically, or other discipline focused. However, my focus in this review is on the canon in higher education.

Given the limited nature of the literature on the state, some of the selections were relatively clear. Two major books on the federal government are Gladieux and Wolanin's *Congress and the Colleges* (1976), and Finn's *Scholars, Dollars, and Bureaucrats* (1978). Two major contributions on state level governance are studies of statewide governing boards by Berdahl, *Statewide Coordination* (1975), and Millett, *Conflict in Higher Education* (1984). One of the most prominent contributions to the policy literature is Breneman and Finn's *Public Policy and Private Higher Education* (1978). The definitive book on the state in comparative higher education is Clark's *The Higher Education System* (1983).

In addition to the "classics" on the state, I selected some more general "classics" to examine the extent to which and the manner in which they treated the state. Included were the following: Bowen's *Investment in Learning* (1977), because it is the major contribution in the area of economics, a discipline that has heavily influenced the way higher education scholars study public policy; Brubacher and Rudy's *Higher Education in Transition* (1976), because it is a central contribution in the area of history as well as generally, and it is more comprehensive in its treatment of higher education and history than are Rudolph (1962) and Veysey's (1965) books; the Carnegie Council's *Three Thousand Futures* (1980), because the Carnegie Commission and Council studies of the 1970s represent the single most powerful influence on the state and higher education literature; and Cohen and March's *Leadership and Ambiguity* (1974), because it is perhaps the central contribution in the area of administration and organization.

Gladieux and Wolanin's *Congress and the Colleges: The National Politics of Higher Education* (1976) remains the definitive study of Congressional activities regarding higher education. The focus of the rich narrative is the politicking surrounding the passage of The Education Amendments of 1972. For Gladieux and Wolanin, the state consists of legislative, executive, and administrative branches of government. But unlike most higher education scholars, they note the narrowness of their focus even in this regard:

> The federal impact on higher education is far flung, involving scores of agencies and stemming from a variety of national objectives like space exploration, foreign assistance, health care, and agriculture. This study does not address the totality of federal activity impinging directly or indirectly on colleges, universities, and students. . . . The focus, rather, is on the core of federal higher education programs and policies centered in the Department of HEW, and the legislation authorizing them. (1976, p. xii)

Unfortunately, later higher education scholars have not redressed such limitations by investigating a broader range of governmental bodies. Nor have they duplicated Gladieux and Wolanin's treatment of relations between branches of the state—in their case, between the legislative and executive branches.

Politics, for Gladieux and Wolanin means the lobbying and negotiations surrounding a governmental decision. Lobbying is conceived of in terms of various interest groups—e.g., the higher education associations—trying to influence the votes or choices of governmental officials. Later higher education scholars have not analyzed efforts by higher education organizations—whether by the Washington associations, by professional associations of faculty, or by individual institutions—to influence government policy. Gladieux and Wolanin's generalizations about policy making provide some propositions about how the state operates. Later scholars in higher education have not picked up on the latter point to develop a model of governmental policy making, to make the policy process the center of their analyses. Gladieux and Wolanin suggest that "there were multiple and diverse sources of policy options" (p. 259), identifying various governmental bodies, higher education associations, foundations, and scholars. They also suggest that "decision making was pluralistic," that there were multiple decision making points, many political actors who could influence the outcome, and a plurality of policy preferences among major actors. Finally, they identify an important pattern to federal policy making: "New policy choices were modifications and additions to existing policies, and where important departures occurred, current programs and arrangements frequently served as models." (p. 257) Politics are portrayed as being open, not being monopolized by any particular group, and policy making is portrayed as being incremental.

Finn's *Scholars, Dollars, and Bureaucrats* (1978) provides an overview of federal spending and regulatory activities related to higher education. Of particular interest is the detail that is provided regarding the executive and administrative branches of federal government. Finn indicates that federal policy toward higher education is piecemeal, "Programs for higher education overlap and are scattered among many multifunction agencies. Policymaking by agency officials and congressional leaders is fragmented, spasmodic, and issue specific." (p. 176) Money is channeled to higher education through hundreds of programs administered more than two dozen agencies.

In looking at dollars, Finn identifies three categories of financing mechanisms in the federal government. In addition to the typical categories of student aid and payments to institutions (for which he includes research and development funds), Finn includes "provisions in the tax laws that reduce federal revenues by affording private outlays for higher education favorable tax treatment." (p. 9) However, higher education scholars have not taken heed. Finn also details various executive branch agencies that administer significant higher education programs. Most such agencies have largely been overlooked in the higher education literature—e.g., The Defense and Labor Departments, the Veteran's Administration, the National Science Foundation.

Although Finn concentrates on federal agencies that fund and regulate higher education, he indicates that the actions of the agencies are actually reactions to constituent pressure.

> The bureaucrats are not to be blamed, except perhaps for occasional excess or whimsy in interpreting the law. It is the lawmakers who are responsible, but they acted in order to help or appease groups that sought changes. Hence anyone who seeks to mitigate the effects of government regulation on colleges and universities had best recognize at the outset that it is not a struggle between the academy and the bureaucracy, but between parts of the society that want change and parts that resist changing. (p. 141)

Unfortunately, higher education scholars continue to cast their discussions of autonomy and accountability in terms of the campus and the statehouse. They have not picked up on Finn's point and examined patterns and processes by which groups seek to impact the academy through influencing state action.

In discussing reforms and structures that are designed to improve the federal government's handling of education policy, Finn comments on the push to establish a Department of Education. He notes that the initiative for such a move came from the National Education Association, and questions how such a department will affect higher education policy. The point is critical at both the federal and state levels of government, but is unexplored in higher education policy analysis. What is the relationship between different sectors of education in governmental policymaking? More generally, how do the efforts of interest groups in one policy domain impact other policy domains?

Berdahl's *Statewide Coordination of Higher Education* (1971) is a classic treatment of statewide boards that has profoundly influenced the way we talk about these boards and the way we define university autonomy. The typology he provides of coordinating and governing boards persists in our discourse, as does his distinction between substantive and procedural autonomy. Berdahl seeks to reduce the friction between state governments and universities, arguing that a partnership can best be effected by a statewide agency that can serve as intermediary between higher education and state government.

In providing an overview of the state boards, Berdahl focuses on the functions of planning, budget review, and program approval. Berdahl's choice of areas of state decision making was guided by his interest in substantive versus procedural autonomy. A good deal of detail is provided regarding the membership and staffing of the state boards and their involvement in the three decision making areas. Only very brief passages are provided dealing with the relationship between these intermediaries and the legislative and executive branches of state government. For Berdahl, the state consists of the formal branches of government.

One of Berdahl's chapters is devoted to relationships between different state sectors and the impact this has on the statewide coordination of higher education. For example, Berdahl briefly examines the impact of federal programs on state activities. A series of significant questions are raised regarding the interaction between the actions of two different levels of government. Later higher education scholars have for the most part not picked up on Berdahl's observations. That is unfortunate, and somewhat surprising, given that in the last decade the federal government has in a variety of ways renegotiated its role relative to state governments, and that in a wide range of policy areas federal and state efforts overlap, overrun, and undercut each other. Another set of sectoral interactions that Berdahl discusses are the relations between higher education and the public schools. Here Berdahl foreshadows what has become a crucial issue in deliberations surrounding the state budget. In some states, the two educational sectors have banded together to improve both their shares of the state pie. In other states, the two sectors are competitors and seek to advance their interests over those of the other sector. Moreover, not only in budget matters, but in questions of educational reform, the policy deliberations in one sector are influenced by developments in the other sector (and this is not even factoring in the difference between the two- and four-year sectors in higher education). Thus far, higher education scholars have failed to examine such interactions, to consider the effects and effectiveness of different coalitional strategies, to address issues that are central to state education policy, policymakers, and institutional leaders. We lack an understanding of even the relations between state coordinating boards in higher education and state boards of education.

Millett's *Conflict in Higher Education: State Government Coordination Versus Institutional Independence* (1984) is a recent and comprehensive treatment of statewide coordinating structures that oversee public four-year institutions (some of these boards also oversee community colleges, but Millett does not deal with boards that are specific to community colleges). The title of Millett's book says something about his perspective, although his purpose is to reduce tension between state governments and institutions by reasonably acknowledging the justifiable concerns of each. The state is seen as an external threat to internal autonomy. But the book does not focus on the dynamics of conflict, or on state government, as the title suggests. Instead, the empirical work of the book is largely static and taxonomic, and is focused on state coordinating structures more than on state governments.

State governments are identified as the primary authorities in relation to higher education. But Millett offers little analysis of actual state operations. A short history of state universities and a discussion of the current concerns of members of state governments are provided, the latter based on a survey of governors, legislators (education and appropriations committee chairs), state budget officers, and state higher education agency heads. The sample of "policy leaders" that were surveyed says a good deal about the conception of state government that underlies the work of Millett and others—it consists of legislative, executive, and administrative branches of government (the judiciary does not figure in, although constitutional autonomy of some public universities is mentioned).

The empirical contribution of Millett is to provide a classification of types of statewide coordinating structures. If Millett explicitly notes that such organizational arrangements "are never static," and on occasion describes such changes, he does not analyze the political processes that drive changes in structures. Similarly, if Millett notes the importance of relations between the coordinating structures, and the governor and the legislature, and if he provides general statements about the patterns of such relations (e.g., governing boards tend to be seen by state government as advocates for the institutions, and advisory boards tend to rely on gubernatorial or legislative instruction), he does not analyze particular cases of relations among various bodies of the state government. The reader gets no sense, for example, of patterns of relations among the higher education coordinating agencies, state boards of education, and state boards overseeing community colleges. Yet Millett has provided scholars with a wide range of problems and propositions for investigation. Unfortunately, higher education scholars have not taken up the challenge to explore the dynamics of relations among different state organizations. Indeed, they have yet to systematically address, in even a static fashion, parts of state government that may in some realms exercise the greatest influence on higher education—e.g., executive departments that can influence financial and personnel management at the institutional level.

Breneman and Finn's *Public Policy and Private Higher Education* (1978) targets an issue of central concern in policy circles. In this edited volume, some of the authors already reviewed (e.g., Gladieux and Wolanin, Berdahl, and Finn) contribute chapters on various dimensions of the treatment of private colleges and universities in public policy. The juxtaposition of the state to private higher education underscores the prevailing view of the state as a threat to the normal operation of various markets in higher education. The concern throughout is that the state may disadvantage private institutions in its higher education policies. For example, in underwriting public higher education in various ways, the state gives public institutions an unfair advantage in the student marketplace.

The chapters in Breneman and Finn's volume provide the kind of detail, and raise the kinds of questions, that are lacking in much of the higher education literature. For example, in discussing federal politics, Gladieux and Wolanin note provisions in the Education Amendments of 1972 that protected the interests of privates. In earlier work (Wolanin and Gladieux, 1975), they identified a key element of the political culture of the higher education policy arena (or subgovernment) as the conviction that federal policy should be neutral and not advantage public over private institutions. Later higher education scholarship has paid too little attention to questions of educational beliefs that influence the actions of policymakers. A chapter by Berdahl examines the politics surrounding state aid to private higher education institutions, detailing the groups and coalitions that have shaped policy in several states. Given the current climate of privatization, and the increased valuation and consideration of private educational alternatives at all levels of education, it is surprising and unfortunate that higher education scholars have not undertaken studies similar to that of Berdahl. Finally, a chapter by Nelson on financial trends and issues indicates that the private sector is by no means independent of government, with nearly half the educational income of privates coming from public programs. Although Nelson does not make the point, one might suggest that the label of private is one that is politically advanced and maintained, but is financially questionable. Such a point brings us back to policymakers' beliefs about different sectors of higher education, how these shape public policy, and how higher education institutions shape and play on these beliefs.

Clark's *The Higher Education System: Academic Organization in Cross-National Perspective* (1983) sets forth a language for comparative study in higher education.

> My purpose is to improve the state of the art by detailing systematically how higher education is organized and governed. . . . to set forth the basic elements of the higher education system, as seen from an organizational perspective. (p. 2)

Perhaps in part because of this task, Clark deals more explicitly than any of the previous authors with his conception of the state. One of the three basic elements of higher education systems that Clark examines is "authority, the distribution of legitimate power throughout the system" (p. 7, the organization of work, and beliefs are the other two. He identifies different levels and forms of authority, ranging from the department to the nation and from guild to bureaucratic. Clark's focus on authority matches his focus on formal political institutions of government.

In discussing what holds national systems together, Clark places them on a continuum ranging from tight state coordination to market linkages. The state is juxtaposed to the market and to higher education institutions. The state is associated largely with administrative apparatuses that oversee higher education (e.g., Ministries). The larger the administrative bureaucracy, the tighter the control and the stronger the state. To some extent, the state is equated with bureaucracy. However, Clark also points to the coordinating efforts and powers of the professional oligarchy, which can essentially control the bureaucracy. The example he provides is of Italy, where the powers vested in chair holding professors have been parlayed into effective control of national bodies that oversee higher education. But he also notes that in the United States, systemwide academic oligarchy, weak though it is, can affect some higher education matters such as science policy. Higher education scholars might pick up on this point and explore the penetration of professional forms of authority into state activities.

One of the most significant and challenging observations Clark makes concerns corporatism, "a relation between government and supposedly 'outside' organized groups, in which the groups have formal rights to influence governmental decisions." (p. 171) In the context of corporatist arrangements, the boundaries between the state, higher education, and various interest groups become blurred. Clark suggests that such arrangements enable outside groups to coopt the government, as in the case of inside academic professionals who penetrate and coopt various governmental bodies. For the most part, higher education scholars have not pursued analyses of corporatist arrangements in the United States and their effects on state policy making. Clark raises the question of the extent to which professional authority has gained effective power over the formal, bureaucratic authority of the state.

The more general "classics," which constitute the general reading of higher education scholars and practitioners, provide much less detail on the state than the books discussed above. None places the state on center stage. Not surprisingly, the sketchy background treatment is consistent with the prevailing conceptualization of the state in the literature. In Bowen's *Investment in Learning: The Individual and Social Value of American Higher Education* (1977), there is virtually no mention of the state. The guiding question of the book is, "Are colleges and universities worth what they cost?" (p. xiii), and Bowen details a wide variety of outcomes of higher education, ranging from cognitive learning and moral development to monetary and nonmonetary rates of return on higher education. The entire project is framed in response to challenges to the value of higher education and calls for accountability, which Bowen traces in part to the increased skepticism of "the public." Bowen's answer constitutes a form of policy analysis that characterizes much higher education scholarship—considering a range of policy choices and their effects and providing policy recommendations, all without addressing policy apparatuses and processes. In this case, Bowen catalogues the great value of higher education, and calls for its further expansion.

In Brubacher and Rudy's *Higher Education in Transition: A History of American Colleges and Universities, 1636–1976* (1976), one chapter is devoted to "The Federal Government and Higher Education," and brief mention is made in two pages of state coordinating boards. The federal involvement that is discussed centers on legislative action regarding higher education—e.g., the Morrill Act and the Education Amendments of 1972. Some mention is also made of executive agencies that support higher education in various ways—e.g., service academies, military training, research and development. And some interesting thoughts are provided regarding "the impact of wars on American higher education." However, the treatment of the state is peripheral, just as Brubacher and Rudy suggest that "federal activity before 1965 always operated on the periphery, never at the heart, of higher learning." (p. 219)

The research studies sponsored by the Carnegie Council and the Carnegie Commission have had a tremendous impact on the higher education literature in a wide range of fields. Several of the books that came out of these series' focused specifically on state and federal government's relationships to higher education. However, two of the most influential volumes, *Three Thousand Futures: The Next Twenty Years for Higher Education* (Carnegie Council, 1981), and *Leadership and Ambiguity: The American College President* (Cohen and March, 1974), deal with the state only peripherally, if at all. The title of the Carnegie Council volume is revealing. It is as if each of the 3,000 colleges and universities were independent enterprises. Millett (1984) has suggested that a more apt title would have been "fifty futures," acknowledging the tremendous influence of state governments on higher education. If this, too, is an oversimplification, since there are diverse futures within state systems and there are diverse futures for different sectors of private institutions, the point nevertheless is well taken that colleges and universities are part of larger collectivities that profoundly shape their future. In the Carnegie volume, the state figures into the discussion of higher education's future briefly, in two respects, as a resource and as a threat. One section speaks to hopes and fears, in series of bullets. Another section advises the state and federal governments to follow particular courses of action, and cautions against others. Among the fears are the possibilities of reduced public resources for higher education and increased penetration into the internal life of colleges and universities by public authorities. At the state level:

> The other [fear] is that some educational and financial planners will see an opportunity to "rationalize," to seize control of systems of higher education, to make higher education an agency of state government. . . . Higher education performs as a largely autonomous segment of society so much better than it would as just another government bureau. (p. 120)

At the federal level, one of the fears is of zealous execution of federal regulations. The message is that higher education should be autonomous (and well funded), and that the intrusion of the external state into the affairs of higher education threatens the integrity of the enterprise.

Much like the Carnegie Council volume, Cohen and March's book (1974) treats colleges and universities as independent enterprises. So much so that remarkably, Cohen and March discuss the American college president with virtually no reference to the state. They focus on paths to and from the presidency, on leadership, decision choices, and the use of time. This is probably the most widely read book in the field on organization and administration, and it ignores one of the most salient dimensions of the worklives of higher education administrators. It separates leadership from relations with the external environment, and deals with management in terms of relations with local and internal constituents of the organization.

Review of the "Classics": Conclusion

If choosing "great books" is problematic, it is nevertheless useful to review what might qualify as "classics." The field's designation of classics is not simply an academic, esoteric term and exercise. It is a professional statement of what knowledge and perspectives are important. As such, it is also a political valuation and exercise that reflects what is regarded as important knowledge and influences what kinds of knowledge we pursue.

The treatment of the state in the general classics mirrors its treatment in the periodical literature and the *Handbook* chapters. The vantage point adopted is that of the individual higher education organization, with the state being seen as part of the external environment. The organization is the center of attention. The state is viewed with peripheral vision (and is often seen as operating on the periphery) and with suspicion. It represents formal authority. It consists of those formal governmental bodies that fund and regulate higher education. It is marked by bureaucratic and political characteristics, cultures, and motivations that are antithetical to the academy. To the extent that the state figures into the story it is not as a study in itself, but as a foil, a study of its effects on higher education.

The "classics" that speak specifically to the state do not move beyond the prevailing conceptualization of the state in the studies they conduct. However, they do offer directions for research that would enrich the prevailing view. They have pointed to the importance of: parts of the state—executive and adminis-trative branches of government—that do not deal exclusively with higher edu-cation but have a significant impact on it; relations among different parts and branches of the government; relations between higher education and the schools, the impact that different coalitional patterns and sectoral strategies have on state allocations;[6] the mechanisms through which higher education seeks to influence state policy; and patterns in the process by which public policy is constructed? Unfortunately, scholarship in the field has generally not followed up on these leads.

EMPIRICAL LIMITATIONS: CASES BEYOND "THE STATE"

How adequate is the prevailing conceptualization of the state in the higher education literature? The literature on the state is obviously thin. The "real world" of higher education and the state is obviously complex. To what extent does the prevailing conceptualization capture and help us understand the world we live and work in? In this section, I offer some discussion of three empirical worlds in exploring this question—commercial science, community college prison education programs in Arizona, and program review in two community colleges in Florida. The "real world" cases that are organized under these topics suggest that there are serious limitations to the prevailing conceptualization of the state. They should lead us to direct our scholarly inquiries beyond "the state," as it has been defined in higher education periodicals, *Handbook* chap-ters, and "classics."

My discussion is drawn from recent investigations in which I have been involved as researcher, consultant, and dissertation chair. The studies deal with phenomena that are common in the world of postsecondary education, and are relevant to a broad cross-section of colleges and universities. My aim is to informally discuss professional practices in higher education that involve the state, considering the general questions of the relationship between higher

---

[6]The focus might also be on relations with public sector institutions and policy domains other than the schools, such as corrections, which some might suggest is much the same as schools, only enrollments are up.

education and the state, and the nature of the state. The issues I discuss occupy a good deal of attention and time in the lives of many within and outside of higher education. They do not figure prominently in higher education scholars' conceptions and studies of the state.

Commercial Science and Economic Development

Recent years have seen an increased emphasis on the contribution higher education can make to local, state, regional and national economies. Economic development has become a buzzword in public policy and business circles. Most states and municipalities have created economic development corporations. In the past decade, partnerships between higher education institutions and private industry have proliferated. Research university arrangements with the private sector may involve undergraduate and graduate programs, as well as the commercialization of science. Their research role is to develop technologies that will enhance the economic vitality of the region and the nation. Various sorts of policies and organizational arrangements aim to facilitate the transfer of high technology to the marketplace. Such arrangements often involve state universities, agencies of the federal government, and private sector corporations.

Most of the impetus for forming a closer partnership between higher education and business has come from not-for-profit institutions. It is the presidents of higher education institutions who are scrambling to establish connections with the corporate world, not the other way around. It is changes in state statutes and federal laws that have enabled and encouraged universities to transfer technologies developed by faculty and to benefit financially from that transfer by holding title to the patents of faculty work. At the state and regental level, conflict of interest and competition with private sector restrictions have been relaxed so that universities can gain access to the proceeds of faculty endeavors in commercializing science. At the federal level, legislation in 1980 enabled universities to own the products and reap the rewards of faculty research funded by the federal government. Various arms of the state have shown much initiative in promoting the technology transfer activities of universities and faculty, and in encouraging connections between public and private universities, and private industry.

In promoting technology transfer activities, state agencies are encouraging the use of public monies to create products that will yield private profit. Consider a typical scenario. A faculty member in a public university comes up with a patentable product. S/he has developed that product while being paid a salary from the state, in labs that were created and sustained with monies from the state (channeled through departmental budgets) and from federal agencies (channeled through research grants). In addition to obtaining a patent through the university or a not-for-profit patenting organization such as Research Corporation, the professor sets up her or his own company to manufacture and market the product, using venture capital and other start-up assistance provided by the university (channeled through a foundation or corporation that is separate from the university on paper only).[7] That company is eventually bought out by a major corporation (a common occurrence in the area of biotechnology—see Kenney, 1986). For all its investment in the faculty member, lab facilities, legal, administrative, and advisory services, and in the company, the state gets only those royalties that come back to the university (in most cases, quite minimal). The major corporation saves the expense of paying a scientist, furnishing them with a lab, etc., and it gains the profits, the value, that was created by those public monies. Without passing judgment on whether the scenario described above is good or bad, right or wrong, it does *not* fit the image of a state that is greedy and parasitic, feeding (through taxation) off the economic value that is created elsewhere, but never producing anything of value itself. Some sectors of the state have given property rights and state property away to universities and to industry.

Recently, members of some sectors of the state have raised questions about the use of public monies by academics and universities. Whether in the conflict of interest regulations generated by the National Science Foundation and the National Institutes of Health, in the creation of an Office of Scientific Integrity in NIH, in the inquiries of members of Congress regarding big science and conflict of interest, or the actions of federal agencies regarding indirect cost rates, the bloom is off the rose of the courtship between the not-for-profit and for-profit sectors and the involvement of universities in commercially relevant science.

This is important stuff. Big money is involved, directly and indirectly. Disputes between governmental agencies and institutions such as Stanford over indirect cost rates and the use of the monies generated by these rates, are costing universities millions of dollars and are compromising their image, perhaps costing them philanthropic support in the future. Generally, millions of dollars are also involved in controversial agreements between universities and corporations to establish certain programs of study and research that will service the company involved.

Big policy issues are also at stake. Throughout the country, universities and boards of regents are redrafting conflict of interest and intellectual property policies, trying to re-establish the academy's credibility and preempt any efforts at the state and national level to establish greater restrictions on the activities of faculty and universities. Campuses are establishing new financial systems— e.g., accounting procedures—to restore faith in the academy's use of public monies. These matters are of much consequence for higher education, and of

---

[7]Many faculty in private universities also utilize public monies, in the form of federal research grants. They also benefit from the non-profit status of their private institutions and of patent organizations, which as a result enjoy certain tax benefits from the federal government.

much concern to administrators. But they are not the stuff of most higher education scholarship.

Much of my recent work has focused on questions surrounding the commercialization of science in the name of economic development. For several years, Sheila Slaughter and I have examined policy making and litigation regarding intellectual property and conflict of interest (Rhoades and Slaughter, 1990, 1991a,b; Slaughter and Rhoades, 1990a,b). Several points of interest regarding the state come out of this work.

The separation between the state and some branches of higher education is far from clear in the federal courts. In several cases, federal courts have defined a public university as an "arm of the state." Indeed, on some occasions, public universities use their status as part of the state as a basis for claiming 11th Amendment immunity in the federal courts. In intellectual property disputes and conflict of interest cases, courts have defined academics in public universities not as independent professionals or as relatively autonomous professional members of academic organizations, but as employees of their organizations and of the state.

The separation is also far from clear in state law. In California, despite the celebrated constitutional autonomy of the University of California, in matters of conflict of interest, UC faculty must follow regulations that apply to all state employees. In some other states, special legislation has been passed to relax conflict of interest regulations in relation to faculty in public universities. But they are still treated legally as state employees.

Moreover, some parts of the state are acting not as regulators and taxers of private property, but as direct organizers and producers of capital. States and state systems of higher education have legalized activities and arrangements surrounding commercial science that were previously illegal. In addition, a review of the court cases involving patent disputes offers a picture of public organizations not as ineffective, bureaucratic enterprises, but as effective competitors in the marketplace and the courtroom, enterprises that are moving assertively into high technology markets and are actively defending their patent rights and privileges.

The commercialization of science is a hotly contested area of activity, not just in the law, but in the minds, policies, and actions of various actors in the public domain. In the courts, this is an emergent area of law, marked by split decisions, reversals on appeal, and unclear patterns of precedent. At the state and federal levels of government, competing messages about property ownership and conflict of interest have been sent by different and sometimes the same agencies of government. Finally, in looking at various actors in the public domain, from faculty in public universities, to campus administrators, to systemwide officials, to state legislators, to state bureaucrats, one finds differential drafting of policies and statutes and different interpretations of the parameters these policies and statutes set. The observations described above raise some questions about the prevailing conceptualization of the state, and they pose some questions for future consideration. If the state is not clearly separate and *the* source of authority, then we might begin to think a little differently about policy and law. It would make sense, for example, to inquire into the process by which policies are developed and implemented, focusing particularly on the competing parties to the process, and on universities' initiative in the process. Many of the changes in state law that have relaxed regulations regarding conflict of interest and intellectual property have been fashioned by representatives of the academy. Similarly, instead of tracking case law to identify trends in what the courts are ruling, with the formal authority of the judiciary essentially being accepted as clear and given, we might begin to analyze case law in terms of patterns of contest and relations of power among members of the academy, among sectors of the state, and in the so-called private sector. Our research would begin to speak to relations of power in the state and to the social relations of the academy, to the reconfiguration of academic labor in relation to the corporate university and corporate capital. If, as a result, we begin to view the state as a productive enterprise, or at least as one that is involved in productive activity, then we might wish to conduct cost-benefit analyses of the investment of public resources in particular kinds of arrangements and enterprises designed to foster economic development.

Community College Outreach in Contracting Postsecondary Education

Community colleges are renowned not just for being open door institutions, but for stepping outside the door and inviting people in. These colleges have reached out in a variety of ways to a variety of clienteles. They have been innovative and entrepreneurial in identifying and servicing diverse constituencies. The responsiveness of community colleges to any and all student clienteles, and their willingness to treat everything and everyone as an opportunity, has led many to criticize them for trying to be all things to all people. But whatever the criticism, community colleges are the statues of liberty of higher education. They take in the poor, the outcast, the huddled masses, students from less fortunate and favored groups, and their student profiles are closer to the diversity of Ellis Island than any other postsecondary educational institution. One of the examples of the outreach efforts of colleges is their involvement in contracting out their services to correctional institutions to run postsecondary education programs for inmates.

Colleges' work with inmates plays into prominent educational themes of the nation and of community colleges. The ideas of education solving major social problems, of creating opportunities for people to become productive members of society, of providing such opportunities to everyone, and of giving people second, third, and fourth chances, all figure into the colleges' work with inmates. The hope and the promise are that providing inmates with education will reduce recidivism, change destructive attitudes and behaviors, and give inmates preparation for productive employment. The basic philosophy underlying the postsecondary education prison programs emphasizes human development, and is articulated in a focus on classroom processes, values clarification, consequential thinking and decision making, and interpersonal and coping skills. College administrators and faculty see and portray themselves as the "last chance" for these students.

My involvement with the prison education programs of community colleges came as a consultant to the Arizona Department of Corrections.[8] The project was to assess the quality of the educational programming being provided inmates at five different prison sites, and to offer suggestions regarding how to enhance the quality of that programming. However entrepreneurial and locally oriented they may be, community colleges are in a very real sense state enterprises. They rely heavily on state resources for their revenues, they are generally part of state systems, and their governance structure is often connected to the State Board of Education.[9] And as my consultancy suggests, they are subject to state review.

A point about student aid revenues that came up in my interviews with college and correctional personnel signifies the complex interconnections among different parts of "the state." It was clear that one of the incentives for conducting prison education programs, and one of the points of protracted negotiation for both parties, was Pell Grant monies. So the action of one branch of government, or arm of the law, to increase access to higher education by providing federal student aid, creates incentives for a different branch of government and a set of public institutions to compete for those federal monies in ways that shaped the nature and provision of postsecondary education programs to inmates.[10]

[8]That in itself raises some interesting questions about relations among state agencies. Concerns about the effectiveness and efficiency of state-funded programs had led legislators to designate a certain percentage of program monies to evaluation. The message and incentive for state agencies, then, was to conduct evaluations to please the legislature. So one branch of the state government (the legislature) encouraged another branch of the state government (the Department of Corrections) to evaluate the programming provided by still another branch of the state (the community colleges, whose contracts with the Department were intergovernmental agreements). The Department of Corrections then contracted with me (through another intergovernmental agreement), a state employee at the University of Arizona, to conduct the evaluation. Relations among public agencies are complex, to say the least.

[9]In the past, community colleges received most of their revenues from local government, largely through property taxes. In recent years, however, the largest share of their funding comes from the state (see Breneman and Nelson, 1981).

[10]Although it does not relate to inmate students, recent actions by the federal government regarding default rates on student loans provide a second case and another layer of complexity of interconnections among different parts of the state. The student aid programs legislated and funded by Congress are clearly designed to promote increased access to higher education, particularly for members of underrepresented groups. Now an administrative branch of the federal government—the Education Department—is threatening to sanction institutions with overly high default rates on student loans. Of course, the institutions that are most threatened tend to be those that serve the most underrepresented populations. Many of the institutions are trade schools. However, a number are also

The diversity of the organizations that make up the state became clear in talking with people in the colleges and the Department of Corrections. Virtually everyone who was interviewed commented on the distinct cultures and purposes of these enterprises. Security is the Department's primary concern, which gives rise to a characteristic culture, evident in the way Department personnel go about their work. Routine, order, and hierarchy are connected to the distance and distrust that mark relations with and attitudes toward the inmates. Education is the college's primary concern, which is associated with a distinctive culture, apparent in the way college personnel go about their work. Innovation, organized anarchy, and collegiality are connected to the informal, service orientation that marks interaction with the inmates. As one college administrator said, "They're closed, rigid, and structured, and we're open, flexible, and exploratory." The college people cast themselves as the professionals versus the bureaucrats. Although they recognized the need for and legitimacy of the legal and coercive power of the Department, they presented themselves as better able to meet the needs of the inmates by virtue of their professional expertise and orientation. They also presented themselves as entrepreneurial, as more innovative and in some sense market oriented. They cast the Department as the typical inefficient, irrational state bureaucracy, and constructed themselves, in a sense, as part of an independent, professional sector that survived by being responsive to its clientele and markets. Such casting ignored the realities of the colleges' public character. For example, individual colleges essentially operated (like public schools) within local catchment areas that were defined by the state system of colleges, so that each local college contracted with the respective local prison site. In this regard, there was virtually no competition for clients.

Close investigation revealed that the cultures of the colleges and the Department are not so different. Both organizations are engaged in intrusive surveillance and control. Of course, there are some differences in this regard. For the Department, such control is custodial, physical, and external in nature, oriented to managing the immediate behaviors of the inmates (managing their movements). For the college, such control is psychological and internal in nature (and thus more intrusive), oriented to changing the attitudes and future behaviors of inmates (managing their minds).

For me, the consulting project raises a couple of intriguing points about the state and higher education. At perhaps the most superficial level, it suggests the value and necessity of examining parts of the state that are completely ignored in the higher education literature. For example, although there is much research on the courts and case law, there is virtually none on law enforcement, despite widespread concern about various types of crime on campus. The project also

public community colleges, which are performing the central function, defined in their mission statements set by the state, of providing access to higher education. Yet another situation of conflicting and intricate relations among various bodies in the public domain.

points to the importance of considering the interaction among state agencies, for in considering such connections, certain commonalities may become evident. As professionals, we do not like to think of ourselves as exercising power over our clients, power that fundamentally shapes their possibilities and futures. It is hard to ignore that when the clients are inmates, whose parole, etc., may be contingent on whether they take certain courses and how they perform in them. But such power is always in the hands of educational professionals. For we are members of a state enterprise that labels, sorts, and certifies legal realities of and for our clients. A final point is the idea that some public institutions work hard to present themselves as entrepreneurial, as independent rather than state-controlled enterprises. As professionals, we construct not just the identities of others, but of ourselves. The process by which we construct ourselves as independent and as deserving of autonomy merits exploration.

Program Review and Economic Development

Among the principal formal governmental bodies mentioned in the higher education literature are the state boards that oversee public higher education. Most public colleges and universities are part of a state system, and are subject to the authority of a state board. The literature on state boards tends to be taxonomic, categorizing boards into typologies (Berdahl, 1971; Millett, 1984), or tracking changes in types of boards. The focus is more on the formal responsibilities of these bodies than on their actual interaction with other parts of state government and with higher education institutions.

One of the principal formal responsibilities of the state boards is in the area of program review. The nature of this responsibility varies from state to state. Program review has probably received more empirical attention than any other area of state board authority. In recent years, scholars have focused particularly on the role of financial considerations in guiding state-mandated program review (Green, 1981; Hines, 1988). For the most part, this policy literature is descriptive and/or prescriptive. It consists more of tracking trends and pointing to possible threats to the autonomy and integrity of colleges and universities, than of analyzing costs and benefits of the review process. The literature also focuses largely on public four-year institutions, overlooking state level program review responsibilities and activities that relate to community colleges (White, 1991).

My discussion of state level program review policy here is based on a dissertation recently completed under my directorship (White, 1991). The study involved analyzing the internal governance structures of two community colleges by tracking their implementation of state mandated program review policy. White selected a state (Florida) which had articulated a clear and strong program review policy. By studying the implementation of policy, White departed from conventional approaches to the state, treating the authority of the state in program review not as given, but as problematic, as something that is negotiated by the state board and the institutions. White was interested in the extent to which and the manner in which two different community colleges would respond to state policy. In the process, he would gain a sense of the internal governance structure of community colleges.

White's work was consistent with prevailing conceptualizations of the state in one regard, at least when he began his research. The state was conceived of as the State Board of Community Colleges, embodied in a formal political structure of government. White did not seek to explore—empirically or conceptually—the relationships among this state board, the state board overseeing four-year institutions, the state legislature, and the executive and other administrative branches of state government. However, in conducting and writing up his research, White began to raise some questions about the nature of the state, and about where authority in program review was centered.

In general, he found that in order to understand program review in Florida, one had to go beyond the state, as it is conventionally defined. At a very superficial level, the formal authority of the state board was evident in the colleges' compliance behavior. The proper paperwork was submitted. The rules and procedures established by the state were followed. Yet, paper compliance was decoupled from the organization's internal activities. The formalized activities surrounding state mandated program review were detached from the "actual" program review activities of the colleges. Formal compliance is externally directed, aimed at satisfying the state, and in this regard it is quite effective. At the same time, state policy is ineffective in shaping internal program review decisions. Forces and concerns that were not part of the state's program review policy, actually governed the review of programs within the college.

As White (1991, pp. 464–45) concludes: "It is clear that both these local community colleges are open and responsive to business and industry to a degree which, at least in program review, exceeds their responsiveness to the state." If the colleges filed the right reports to the state, in conformance with state rules and productivity measures, college decisions regarding programs were guided by needs and productivity measures defined by the local business community. Whether this is good or bad, it is important. For it takes us beyond prevailing conceptions of the state and/versus higher education, by revealing that in at least some matters of formal governance, authority lies outside formal governmental institutions.

Both of the colleges White studied were very much committed to economic development initiatives and to developing close connections with the business community. Both sought to influence state policy along these lines. In one case, the college lobbied the state board and legislature to explicitly extend the mission of community colleges to include economic development activities. In another case, the college lobbied to block the introduction of certain performance measures in program review, and called on private industrial partners to support their efforts. In other words, the colleges actively negotiated the terms of their work with the state board and legislature, reshaping state policy to fit their local interests. One public organization lobbied another branch of the state, in the service and with the support of private industry. Again, this takes us beyond the prevailing conceptualization of the state to a view of the state as a nexus of interconnected organizations that cut across formal public and private domains.

Empirical Limitations: Conclusion

Each of the empirical situations discussed above suggests that there are a range of questions about higher education and the state that are not being addressed. Together, the studies point to the limitations of focusing on what have conventionally been defined in the higher education literature as the formal political institutions of government. Together, they also challenge the prevailing view of the state as separate from higher education, as *the* source of authority, and as inefficient. They make the abstraction of the state concrete, and they reveal that the world of higher education and the state is complicated, blurred, and socially constructed.

THEORETICAL UNDERPINNINGS:
THE POLITICAL SOCIOLOGY OF THE STATE

Scholarship is always undergirded by a conceptual framework, whether or not the author is explicit about or even aware of it. In the higher education literature that touches on the state, conceptual frameworks are rarely mentioned, let alone discussed. Yet the consistent portrayal of the state that is evident in the literature reflects some of the basic assumptions of the general social theory known as structural-functionalism. And the content of the portrayal, as well as the context in which the state is mentioned, reflects the perspective of pluralist theory in political sociology. In this section, the theoretical underpinnings of higher education scholarship on the state are considered.

The first step in exploring the tacit conceptual framework of higher education scholars is to discuss the central elements of structural-functional and pluralist theory. In political sociology, these theories have been subjected to serious criticism for several decades. Indeed, they are so dated that they have been substantially revised and updated, reappearing now as neo-functionalism and neo-pluralism (Alexander and Colomy, 1990; Dunleavy and O'Leary, 1987). In addition to examining the concepts, assumptions, questions, and perspectives of the original theories, which are evident in the higher education literature, I briefly consider the critique of these theories. Such a discussion should highlight the limitations of higher education's treatment of the state and offer alternative paths for pursuing research on the state.

The second step is to consider the political sociology of the state. Three journals were content analyzed for the years 1986–1990. The *American Journal of Sociology* and the *American Sociological Review* are the two leading journals in sociology, and provide a good sense of how the state is treated in the general sociological literature. The *Sociology of Education* was also analyzed to examine the extent to which and the manner in which the state has figured into sociological studies of education. As with my review of the higher education journals, my interest is in the questions scholars ask about the state (or how the state factors into questions they ask—when is the state discussed) and the way they talk about the state. To what extent is the state a subject of study, and in what topical contexts? And what is the terminology that is used, and the assumptions and characterizations that underlie this usage? Rather than pursuing these questions article by article, they will be discussed in a synthesis of how the state is treated in each of the three journals, identifying patterns along each of the dimensions of the analysis and providing some examples to clarify these themes. My aim is not to detail all the sociological theories of the state, but to give readers a sense of the kinds of questions that get asked in sociology journals, and the kinds of portrayals of the state that are presented.

Structural-Functional and Pluralist Theory
The tacit and consistent conceptualization of the state that emerges from the higher education literature presents the state as separate from higher education, as the source of formal authority, and as intrusive, inefficient, and threatening to the internal integrity of higher education organizations. In each of these respects, the prevailing conception reflects the assumptions of structural-functionalism. The substantive contexts and the ways in which the state is studied, reflect the work of pluralist scholars.

For structural-functionalists, society is constituted of several subsystems that interpenetrate one another yet are analytically distinct. One of the central concepts is differentiation, the replacement of institutions that have multiple functions by more specialized institutions. Structural-functionalists order history according to a pattern of increased differentiation. Differentiation is seen as a process of evolution and modernization, with more complex, differentiated institutional arrangements viewed as more advanced and more effective. For example, the concept of political modernization is linked to the separation of church and state. Similarly, educational modernization is linked historically to the separation of education from religious and political institutions, with the development of a specialized, professionalized institutional arena. Generally, the intrusion of one subsystem on another is viewed as dysfunctional. The state's intervention in the sphere of education, then, is regarded as distorting the normal and effective functioning of that institutional system. The arena of politics is distinct from and threatening to the arena of learning and knowledge production. Given this conceptualization of different subsystems performing different functions, it makes sense to center one's consideration of politics in the political subsystem. Different sorts of activities and social processes are seen as centered in different spheres of action. Politics are equated with the formal political process. And the state consists of the formal political institutions of government. Moreover, the focus is on legitimate authority, for structural-functionalists see subsystems and society as a whole as being integrated by a prevailing value system and a commitment to existing institutional structures.

If the assumptions of higher education scholars are structural-functional, the types of questions that are asked and where they are pursued are pluralist. Pluralists study behavior surrounding formal political institutions—e.g., voting and decision making—rather than structures of power. The assumption is that the important political action takes place in formal governmental arenas. Moreover, pluralists conceptualize political action in terms of diverse interest groups, that shift depending on the issue in question. Higher educationists certainly do not pursue the study of political activity to the fullest extent of pluralist principles. With some important exceptions (Gladieux and Wolanin, 1976), scholars in higher education have focused on the effects of policy rather than on the lobbying surrounding its formulation. But to the extent that they have studied the state, higher educationists have concentrated on formal governmental bodies. And their conception of politics and political action mirrors pluralist views.

Structural-functional and pluralist theory have been subjected to serious critique since the late 1950s. Criticism of the former has centered on the failure to consider power and conflict, to examine mechanisms and social groups that shape differentiation, and on its assumption that highly differentiated systems are superior. Criticism of the latter centered on the failure to consider concentrations and different levels of power among groups, and structures that pattern state actions regardless of who holds office.

Critical scholars have called into question the basic assumptions of structural-functionalism and pluralism in ways that are evident in current sociological research on the state. For critical scholars, politics and power are an integral part of all social realms. They are not centered in a separate subsystem, in formal governmental institutions. Politics are as much a part of classroom interaction as they are of Congressional deliberation. Similarly, critical scholars do not assume that there are clear boundaries between the state and institutional sectors such as higher education. Indeed, they often adopt quite inclusive conceptions of the state, focusing on various types of ideological state apparatuses (Althusser, 1971) that shape prevailing systems of belief. The terms applied to these parts of the state may vary, but the idea is much the same, that various institutions are political, inextricably intertwined with the state, and connected to the reproduction of capitalist society (Miliband, 1969). Included among these institutions are the church, schools, family, and the media. Critical scholars, then, look beyond the state, as it appears in the higher education literature.

In looking at the state, critical scholars focus more on power than authority, and they do not see either power or legitimate authority as being grounded solely or even primarily in governmental institutions. Instead, they see power as deriving from the resources and structures of class. What this means, of course, is that not all groups are relatively equal, as in pluralism, and that political conflict is shaped by patterns of class relations rather than being diverse and issue specific. In looking at higher education, for example, this can mean looking at the interconnections between higher education groups and corporate capital and considering how these shape the missions and functioning of colleges and universities (Brint and Karabel, 1989; Scott, 1983; Slaughter, 1990). An examination of how higher education institutions are governed, then, takes critical scholars beyond the confines of government.

Finally, for many critical scholars, the governing of institutions goes beyond decision making and instrumental control of certain organizations. An important dimension of power is structural. In other words, regardless of who is making and influencing decisions, state actions are constrained by the logic of the capitalist economy and class relations, by various dimensions of economic and cultural power that shape political agendas, raise certain questions, and impact what choices seem necessary and reasonable or realistic (Lukes, 1978; O'Connor, 1973; Poulantzas, 1974). Such an approach to power moves critical scholars beyond identifying elites in answering the question of who rule, as important as those questions are (Domhoff, 1990; Mills, 1956).

In analyzing the state, the critical question for critical scholars has been the relationship between the state and civil society. The autonomy of the state is always considered "relative," mitigated by class structures and actors. This forms the foundation of later sociological literature that examines state/society interconnections rather than treating the two as separate spheres of activity.

Sociology of Education

In terms of numbers, the treatment of the state in the *Sociology of Education* is not so much unlike its treatment in higher education journals. Of 18 articles in 1986, none deal with the state. Of 20 articles in 1987, three deal with the state. Of 19 articles in 1988, two deal with the state. Of 20 articles in 1989, one deals with the state. And of 19 articles in 1990, one deals with the state. The state is not a central topic of study.

However, there are some interesting differences between the *Sociology of Education* and higher education journals in the context and the way in which the state is treated. The state figures more prominently in the *Sociology of Education* articles than in articles in higher education journals. The state is not a foil, but is a central explanatory variable or dimension of an explanatory framework. Interestingly, none of the *Sociology of Education* articles dealing with the state are on higher education (higher education is a topic of several articles dealing with other issues). Of the seven articles, four have to do with patterns of school-ing—the development, expansion, and demand for schooling. For example, as Benavot and Riddle (1988) indicate, there are several theories explaining the origins and spread of mass schooling: some point to the relationship between industrialization and/or urbanization and patterns of schooling; some point to the actions of and conflict among various status groups and classes; and still others point to the role of the state. Much comparative work on enrollment patterns stresses the state's compelling interest in constructing a national society through systems of mass schooling. The state is featured not as a bogeyman, but as part of theories, as part of explanatory frameworks about education.

In the *Sociology of Education*, the topical contexts in which the state is examined include studies (comparative and otherwise) of enrollment patterns, and studies of state policies (e.g., desegregation) that affect patterns of school-ing. On the one hand, such topical contexts conform in their general parameters (comparative work, policy research) to those evident in higher education schol-arship. But in the sociological research, the state is discussed in the context of theories about education, whereas in higher education research the state is men-tioned as an influence on colleges and universities, but it is not fit within systematic analytical frameworks or theories about the state and education.

The way the state is talked about in the *Sociology of Education* articles also differs from the conceptualization found in articles in higher education journals. First, in many cases, the state is not treated as something that is separate from education. Instead, education is seen as a state mechanism or instrument by which the state constructs a unified national polity (a society of citizens of the nation-state), and by which it competes in the global arena (Ramirez and Boli, 1987). Education is a component of state activity. Second, although the state is treated as a source of authority, there is much consideration of other sources of authority. In some cases, this means status groups and classes that press their interests on agents and agencies of the state. In other cases, it means professional groups that are in many ways part of the state, and that function in quasi-governmental bodies (Rhoades, 1987b). The sociological, literature, then, offers expanded views of the state and of authority. It also treats the state not as an inefficient intruder into the educational realm, but as a central creator and pro-vider of education, and as a contributor to the expansion of schooling.

American Journal of Sociology

In terms of numbers, the treatment of the state in the *American Journal of Sociology* is not unlike its treatment in higher education journals and in the *Sociology of Education*. Indeed, proportionately, the state receives less treatment in the *American Journal of Sociology*. Of 33 articles in 1986, two deal with the state. Of 36 articles in 1987, two deal with the state. Of 36 articles in 1988, two deal with the state. Of 33 articles in 1989, six deal with the state. And of 36 articles in 1990, three deal with the state.

If the state is not a central topic of study in this generalist sociology journal, it is nevertheless, as in the *Sociology of Education*, a subject that receives more direct and systematic empirical and theoretical treatment than it does in higher education journals. The state is also treated in a more diverse range of contexts than in either higher education journals or the *Sociology of Education*. There are articles on the state coming out of the sociology of education, sociology of deviance, sociology of the welfare state, and political sociology. In the sociology of education, one article tests the nation building and modernization theories of school expansion (Garnier, Hage, and Fuller, 1989). In the sociology of deviance, one article examines the effects of the states increased powers and exercise of surveillance on crime (Gillis, 1989). In the sociology of the welfare state, research sought to explain matters such as patterns of welfare spending (Pampel and Williamson, 1988) and policy making (Stryker, 1990). In political sociology, articles addressed questions such as the ability of corporate groups to shape state policy (Jacobs, 1988) and the conditions surrounding the development and collapse of democratic regimes (Stephens, 1989).

Given such diversity of contexts in which the state is considered, it is not surprising that the state is conceived and talked about in a variety of ways. In some of the examples noted above, the state is a variable. It is a "strong state," operationalized as the centralization of its administrative apparatus, or of its legal and coercive powers, and this strength is related to something else, such as the expansion of education or the incidence of different types of crime. The state can also be seen as an actor or a coercive agent, in either of the above cases or in studies of social welfare policy. In the latter cases, the research often studies and seeks to explain patterns of state activity. This can mean explaining state policies in terms of external society—for example, characteristics of industrialism, the extent of different classes' economic power, the nature of interest group politics. It can also mean looking at how professionals within and outside the state shape the thinking that underlies social welfare policies, and how they sometimes shape the policies themselves. Sometimes, then, the state is viewed as an instrument in the hands of powerful groups, such as corporate business.

The articles in the *American Journal of Sociology* offer expanded and complicated conceptions of the state. If the state is separate from society, it is nevertheless profoundly influenced by the nature of society. One of the central points of debate in political sociology is the relationship between the state and civil society, the degree of autonomy held by the state relative to status groups and social classes, the extent to which the state is an independent actor. In this context, it makes little sense to portray the state as *the* source of authority. The articles in the *American Journal of Sociology* point to realms and bases of authority—both within and "outside" the state—that are not considered in the higher education literature. For example, they examine the state's powers of coercion and surveillance. The state is presented as a "power container" that engages in "internal pacification" by generating and controlling information, defining normal (not just legal) behavior, and classifying people into various statuses (Giddens, 1987; Gillis, 1989). Such powers are exercised by arms of the state such as education (Foucault, 1977). Despite characterizations of the state as "relatively autonomous bureaucrats," some sociologists emphasize not the separation of the state from civil society, but instead stress and examine the link between "economic logics" (dynamics of the political economy) and state actions (Block, 1986; Hooks, 1990a). Therefore, the focus in sociology tends not to be on how the state intrudes on institutions such as education, but on the ways that external society and structures of power intrude on the state.

American Sociological Review

The extent to which the state is treated in *American Sociological Review* articles far exceeds that found in the other sociology and higher education journals. Of 53 articles in 1986, four deal with the state. Of 53 articles in 1987, three deal with the state. Of 55 articles in 1988, seven deal with the state. Of 61 articles in 1989, twelve deal with the state. And of the 58 articles in 1990, eleven deal with the state.

Most of the articles in the *American Sociological Review* deal with the relationship between the state and society. This analytical focus appears in a variety of substantive contexts. It may emerge in studies of state policies that reflect and impact on social relations in society—for example, immigration policies that are shaped by white working class and small business groups (Boswell, 1986), efforts by capitalist groups to inhibit through various arms of the government the organizing efforts of trade unions (Griffin, Wallace and Rubin, 1986), or state actions that restrict or facilitate competition among various professional segments seeking to monopolize a domain of work (Torres, 1988). The analytical focus on state/society interaction may emerge in studies of the influence powerful groups have on the state—for example, the relationship between political action committees of corporate capital and the involvement of businesses with different arms of government (Boies, 1989; Burris, 1987). It may surface in studies of the rise and fall of legitimacy of democratic regimes—for example, relating the stability of democratic regimes to consensually unified elites, regardless of other demographic and socioeconomic developments (Higley and Burton, 1989).

Much of the debate in political sociology surrounding the relationship between the state and civil society has been shaped by neo-Marxian challenges to pluralist theories in the 1960s and 1970s, as previously discussed. Such challenges to pluralism have focused on concentrations of economic and political power in society and on the need for states to attend to certain economic interests regardless of who is in power and who is making formal political decisions. In relating class structures to state structures and activities, neo-marxists also provided a broad conception of the state that encompassed a variety of institutions— e.g., education and the mass media—that had not previously been treated as part of the state.

More recently, research that focuses on the welfare state has generated state centered theories that incorporate much of the previous political sociological debate and yet accord considerable independence and initiative to agents and structures and patterns of the state in their explanations (Skocpol and Amenta, 1986). Such work points to the causal significance of autonomous state factors while at the same time connecting state actions to social contexts that are shaped by class and other social structures. For example, in examining the United States Department of Agriculture, Hooks (1990b) notes the decline of this agency's autonomy as it came to be "captured" and to serve the interests of elite farmers. Yet he attributes this capture in large part to "administrative decisions initiated by the state set in motion the decline of bureaucratic strongholds within the USDA." (p. 29) Class and state are closely intertwined, a point that Stryker (1989) stresses in his analysis of Congress' elimination of the National Labor Relations Board's Division of Economic Research. In looking at the influence of social scientists on state agencies, Stryker considers interconnections among "agency actors, state actors outside the agency, and class actors outside the state." (p. 341) The point is that in "Bringing the State Back In" (Evans, Rueschemeyer, and Skocpol, 1985), these sociologists have not taken class out.

In such "state centered work," the state is seen as a center of administrative and coercive power (Giddens, 1987). If class continues to be factored into such analyses, some sociologists have stressed the importance of other social structures. For example, Quadagno (1988, 1990) focuses on "gender and race in welfare state dynamics." (1990, p. 14) In her view, the social provisions of the welfare state in the United States are best understood as being organized around race and gender. As she indicates, "Feminist theorists argue that welfare programs constitute a mechanism furthering women's subordination in the way they link income security with family structure and dependency relations." (1990, p. 14) Other feminists have moved beyond an examination of the welfare state to consider the gendered nature of the state and of law (MacKinnon, 1989).

The empirical and theoretical work found in *American Sociological Review* articles challenges the prevailing conceptualization of the state in the higher education literature. As should be evident, the state is not seen as separate from, but as deeply enmeshed in the social dynamics of the "outside world." The driving analytical concern that comes out of sociology is, "Instead of assuming the separation of the state and social forces, we investigate how they interact to shape policy." (Gilbert and Howe, 1991, p. 204). The sociological research on the welfare state suggests "a blurring of boundaries between state and society."

(Quadagno, 1987, p. 119). It is obvious that although sociologists regard the state as a source of authority, they also consider it a source of coercion and they consider other sources of authority, power, and coercion in concert and connection with the state. Finally, the question of state efficiency, and its intervention into other institutional sectors, is generally reversed, with the focus being on how external social forces intrude on and shape/distort state activity. Some recent work suggests that the state is both a potentially effective competitor with private industry and an effective organizer of the economy through the manipulation of property rights, a point that is particularly relevant to the technology transfer activities of universities (Campbell and Lindberg, 1990).

Theoretical Underpinnings: Conclusion
The sociological literature on the state, then, has much to offer higher education scholars. At the very least, it raises serious questions about the assumptions and theoretical underpinnings of the prevailing conceptualization of the state in the higher education literature. At best, it offers new directions and models for research on the state, which is viewed in complex and inclusive ways. For example, in the *Sociology of Education*, articles treat the state as an explanatory variable that accounts for patterns of schooling and enrollment. Articles in the *American Journal of Sociology* add the dimension of treating the state as an independent actor, a powerful agent of coercion and surveillance. Articles in the *American Sociological Review* center on the question of state/society relations and connections and point to state centered logics and dynamics. To some extent, the heading of this section is misleading. It is not just theoretical work and underpinnings that we can draw from sociology. Perhaps what is most valuable is the extensive empirical work that shows the state as a concrete, complex reality worthy of systematic study from a variety of vantage points.

EXPANDING OUR CONCEPTION OF THE STATE

Two recent books in higher education offer examples of how we might expand our conception of the state (Barrow, 1990; Slaughter, 1990). Both are influenced by and speak to the sociological debate surrounding the state. Both are embedded in the concepts and analytical focus that come out of variations of neo-Marxian theory. A brief review and critique of them suggests the value of moving beyond the state as it is conceptualized in the higher education literature.

In *The Higher Learning and High Technology*, Slaughter (1990) explores the dynamics of higher education policy formation through a case study of the Business-Higher Education Forum. To get a sense of the distinctiveness of her approach, it is instructive to compare her opening sentence with that of Gladieux and Wolanin's (1976), who also examine higher education policy.

The central problem this book addresses is the national policy formation process in higher education. (Slaughter, 1990, p. 1)

This is a study of policy making by the federal government. (Gladieux and Wolanin, 1976, p. xi)

The analytical thrust of Slaughter's research is evident in her title, which plays on Veblen's (1918) critique of business' influence on higher education. Part of her premise and argument is that "Rather than the federal government, together with the scientific community and foundations, having the dominant voice [in the national higher education policy formation process], the corporate community, in partnership with leaders of research universities, has become more vocal and taken a more active position." (p. 3) Slaughter's empirical contributions are to trace the characteristics of and connections between corporate and university leaders, and to detail the ideology and interests that drive the corporate-university partnership and the policies the Forum promotes. Her theoretical contributions are to introduce the concept of "institutional class" and to challenge us to move beyond the false dichotomization of the state and civil society. The bases of class organization identified by Slaughter inhere not only in the ownership of the means of production, but in the relationship to and the ability to command the resources of major societal institutions such as higher education. The institutional class encompasses actors in public and private sectors who act in terms of principles and interests defined more by the class than by their institution. In other words, university presidents who are members of the institutional class act more in the interests of the institutional class Slaughter identifies than in the interests of higher education. In looking at the state, Slaughter focuses on the connection between class and the state, pushing us to consider how institutions construct themselves as "private," and how domination by the institutional class affects the autonomy of state apparatuses, such as different sectors of higher education.

In *Universities and the Capitalist State*, Barrow (1990) examines the reconstruction of American higher education in the early twentieth century according to a corporate ideal. That ideal was consistent with the imperatives of capitalist society and was organized around ideas of efficiency, functional division of labor, tangible returns on investment, and employer-employee relations. Barrow focuses on the efforts of the United States Bureau of Education, and details the colonization and control of its work by private foundations that worked the will of corporate capital. The aim was the creation of an ideological state apparatus. The reconstruction of American higher education was effected by the corporate class interested in the reproduction of capitalist society. Among Barrow's empirical contributions are a detailing of both the membership of particular elements of the corporate liberal elite on university boards, and of the relations between the Bureau of Education, foundation leaders, and university leaders in shaping the pattern of social relations within higher education (e.g., relations between faculty and administrators). Among his theoretical contributions are the connection of patterns of class with patterns of professionalism, and the treatment of the Bureau of Education, and of higher education, as ideological state apparatuses. Barrow's remarks in his introduction about conceptions of the state, makes for a useful summation in closing of where expanded conceptions of the state might take us.

> Conceptually the state and political power can no longer be identified merely with classical definitions of government. The state has become a social-industrial complex of overlapping public (and even nominally private) associations that formulate policy, exercise regulatory authority, and assist in social control from a variety of independent institutional centers. (p. 4)

In moving us beyond the state, these particular studies tell us very little about the operations of the state, traditionally conceived. As with much of the sociological literature on the state, Slaughter and Barrow have more to say about the political activities of institutional and social classes than they do about the workings of "the state." Yet, they point the way conceptually for pursuing the study of formal political institutions and activities. For they identify sources of power and patterns of struggle and action that should be considered in studying the formulation of formal governmental policy regarding higher education. Such policy making is complex, and the actions of different agencies and apparatuses, and the interpretations that different state actors apply to policies, are connected in significant ways with patterns of class and professional relations (Rhoades and Slaughter, 1990, 1991a,b; Slaughter and Rhoades, 1990a,b).

CONCLUSION: MOVING BEYOND "THE STATE"

In opening this chapter, I posed the question, What is the state? But in the higher education literature, the phrase is more an answer than a question, in the tradition of the game show "Jeopardy." What is separate from, alien, and a threat to, higher education? What has formal authority over higher education? What is bureaucratic, politicized, and inefficient? The answer to these clues, or cues, is, "what is the state." It is not a question in the higher education literature. The state is not something that is studied or theorized about. It is something about which we have tacit understandings. It is something about which we invoke easy truths in simple categories. We refer to the dangers of state control, to the increased press for accountability by state legislatures and coordinating bodies, to the burden of federal regulations and the intrusions of the courts. We chant these phrases, but we do not study these phenomena.

In the sociological literature, the state is studied, but not in the taxonomic terms of, "What is the state." Various strands of research address various parts of the state. In political sociology, sociologists study the relationship between the state and society, often providing a broad view of what constitutes the state. Research relates patterns of state activity to the power and actions of status groups and classes in society, and focuses on how various apparatuses of the state (e.g., ideological apparatuses such as public education) shape and are shaped by class relations and social dynamics of power. In the study of crime, and of social movements and revolutions, sociologists examine the state's exercise of its coercive powers, both psychological and physical. Research speaks to how the state, by virtue of its administrative and police powers, surveils and labels a wide range of behaviors, determining what is normal or legal, and what is deviant or illegal, and acting accordingly. In the study of the welfare state, sociologists examine patterns of state policymaking in the area of social welfare, relating these patterns to internal logics of the state, to external (often economic) logics, and to configurations and relations of social class. Research speaks to how and why the state operates as it does, adopting certain types of social welfare policies at certain points in time. In the study of education (almost entirely elementary and secondary), sociologists study the role of the state in shaping patterns of schooling. Research treats the state as a variable in explaining the development, expansion, and institutional configuration of schooling.

For the most part, sociological research on the state does not directly deal with higher education. Nevertheless, the lines of research discussed above have direct relevance for higher education scholarship dealing with the state. Higher education is a central societal institution, and some would suggest a central state institution. The questions addressed by political sociologists are quite applicable to higher education, calling our attention to higher education's state functions, to its interaction with and its embodiment of social structures of power. What is the relationship between this branch of the state and social patterns and relations of race, class, and gender? How are we shaped by these social structures, and how do we contribute to their perpetuation? In a time when we talk much (and do little) about diversity and yet find our campuses and classrooms marred by various forms of hateful speech and violence, such questions are critical.

The questions addressed by sociologists of deviance and of social movements are also meaningful for higher education scholars, directing our attention to dimensions of our activities and of state functions that we have largely ignored. What role does higher education play in defining what is "normal," in classifying and certifying people in particular social statuses? In what ways is the coercive power of the state exercised by us, administratively and physically— e.g., in student and academic affairs and policework, in administrative responses to political activities, and in personnel practices and actions? What is the relationship between higher education and major social movements—how are we shaped by them, and how do we foster or inhibit their development? In a time when campus crime is an important issue, when various parts of the academy are involved in shaping definitions of mental, emotional, and physical health, and when some such definitions are being challenged, such questions should be considered.

The questions posed by sociologists studying the welfare state are relevant to policy analysts in higher education, pointing to policy domains and analytical frames that would shed light on policy and practice in higher education. How is higher education policy influenced by other social welfare policies, and what state processes and interests shape such public policies? In a time when higher education finds itself in competition with the public schools and the prisons for state funding, and when criticisms of the quality of schooling have led to omnibus education bills, such questions are particularly meaningful. Finally, the questions asked by sociologists of education about the schools are relevant to higher education as well, reminding us of the state's influence on the size and nature of higher education. How are the curricular and organizational patterns of higher education related to characteristics and activities of the state? In a time when so many state systems are "downsizing," when states are so caught up in the push for economic development and are enlisting colleges and universities in this enterprise, such questions are painfully pertinent.

In opening this chapter, I not only asked, What is the state? I noted that our view of the state is shaped by our point of view. In addition, then, to asking new questions, coming out of sociological research, I now rephrase my opening question to read, What do we make of the state, and of ourselves? The original question is a "false question" (Hughes, 1958), in that it mistakes a matter of subjective valuation with a matter of objective classification. The notion of the state carries with it certain baggage. In the United States, that baggage is for the most part negative, akin to an albatross. The state is not seen as prestigious, it is not seen as rational, it is not seen as efficient, it is not seen as productive. In all these respects it is juxtaposed and contrasted to the private sector. Factor in the greater regulations and demands for accountability that are associated with state enterprises, and it is hardly surprising that institutions such as higher education try to distance themselves from the state, seek to avoid being regarded and treated simply as one of many state agencies. Consequently, colleges and universities emphasize their status as independent corporations, and seek to be treated as such.

If relations between the state and higher education lie on a continuum, beyond the Pearly Gates is a situation of minimal state control and maximal campus autonomy, in which the campus is a separate corporate entity and the state approaches it in laissez faire fashion. Beyond the Gates of Hell is the reverse situation, in which the campus is treated as a state agency and the state exerts direct control over all dimensions of support and services (Hines, 1988). Higher education scholars try to define "reality" as somewhere between, affording themselves as much autonomy as is realistically possible, or as they can negotiate.

There is much talk among higher education scholars these days of connecting our research to our stakeholders. I am suggesting that in research involving the state we are the principal stakeholders we serve. The voices we study and articulate, and the interests we serve, are our own. Our authorial position is shaped by our professional position.

Higher education scholarship that deals with the state is limited, conceptually and empirically. In this chapter, I have suggested that we move beyond "the state." We need to move beyond formal government to consider the broad range of apparatuses, status groups and classes that are involved in governance. We need to look within the state at interorganizational relations among various state sectors, branches, and agencies. We need to explore dimensions and parts of the state and of ourselves that we have ignored. We need to acknowledge that we are part of the state. Regardless of the sector of higher education we are in, we are closely linked to and in many ways are part of the state. We carry much responsibility for and in state action. We have much authority. We, too, are inefficient and must be held accountable in ways that will prod us to consider how productive we are and to whose benefit. As Pogo said, "we have met the enemy and they are us." In the matter of the state, I suggest that we move beyond tacit understandings to explore state processes and relations of power: processes by which the state acts, and by which higher education constructs itself as independent of the state and negotiates its autonomy; and power that is exercised by the state (and by us as part of the state), power that both shapes and is shaped by external patterns of social relations.

REFERENCES

Ahumada, Martin M. (1990). An analysis of state formula budgeting in higher education. In J. C. Smart (ed.), *Higher Education: Handbook of Theory and Research, Volume VI.* New York: Agathon.

Alexander, J. C. (1986). The university and morality: a revised approach to university autonomy and its limits. *Journal of Higher Education* 57(5): 463–76.

Alexander, J. C., and Colomy, P. (eds.). (1990). *Differentiation Theory and Social Change: Comparative and Historical Perspectives.* New York: Columbia University Press.

Altbach, P. G. (1989). Twisted roots: the Western impact on Asian higher education. *Higher Education* 18(1): 9–30.

Althusser, L. (1971). Ideology and ideological state apparatuses. In L. Althusser, *Lenin and Philosophy and Other Essays.* New York: Monthly Review Press.

Averch, H. A. (1989). Policy research for the university research system *The Review of Higher Education* 12(4): 329–38.

Barrow, C. W. (1990). *Universities and the Capitalist State: Corporate Liberalism and the Reconstruction of American Higher Education, 1894–1928.* Madison: The University of Wisconsin Press.

Benavot, A., and Riddle, P. (1988). The expansion of primary education, 1870–1940: trends and issues. *Sociology of Education* 61(3): 191–210.

Berdahl, R. O. (1971). *Statewide Coordination of Higher Education*. Washington, D.C.: American Council on Education.

Block, F. (1986). Political choice and the multiple "logics" of capital. *Theory and Society* 15: 175–91.

Boies, J. L. (1989). Money, business, and the state: material interests, Fortune 500 corporations, and the size of political action committees. *American Sociological Review* 54(5): 821–33.

Boswell, T. E. (1986). A split labor market analysis of discrimination against Chinese immigrants, 1850–82. *American Sociological Review* 51(3): 352–71.

Bowen, H. (1977). *Investment in Learning: The Individual and Social Value of American Higher Education*. San Francisco: Jossey-Bass.

Bray, M. (1986). Student loans for higher education. *Higher Education* 15(3–4): 343–54.

Breneman, D. W., and Finn, C. E. Jr. (1978). *Public Policy and Private Higher Education*. Washington, D.C.: The Brookings Institution.

Breneman, D. W., and Nelson, S. C. (1981). *Financing Community Colleges: An Economic Perspective*. Washington, D.C.: The Brookings Institution.

Brint, S., and Karabel, J. (1989). *The Diverted Dream*. New York: Oxford University Press.

Brubacher, J. S., and Rudy, W. (1976). *Higher Education in Transition: A History of American Colleges and Universities, 1636–1976*. New York: Harper and Row.

Budd, J. M. (1990). Higher education literature: characteristics of citation patterns. *Journal of Higher Education* 61(1): 84–97.

Burris, V. (1987). The political partnership of American business: a study of corporate political action committees. *American Sociological Review* 52(6): 732–44.

Callan, P. M. (1988). Minority degree achievement and the state policy environment. *The Review of Higher Education* 11(4): 355–64.

Campbell, J. L., and Lindberg, L. N. (1990). Property rights and the organization of economic activity by the state. *American Sociological Review* 55(5): 634–47.

Carnegie Council on Policy Studies in Higher Education. (1980). *Three Thousand Futures: The Next Twenty Years for Higher Education*. San Francisco: Jossey-Bass.

Chaffee, E. E. (1989). Strategy and effectiveness in systems of higher education. In J. C. Smart (ed.), *Higher Education: Handbook of Theory and Research, Volume V*. New York: Agathon.

Clague, M. W. (1986). Affirmative action employment discrimination. In J. C. Smart (ed.), *Higher Education: Handbook of Theory and Research, Volume II*. New York: Agathon.

Clark, B. R. (1983). *The Higher Education System: Academic Organization in Cross-National Perspective*. Los Angeles: University of California Press.

Cohen, M. D., and March, J. G. (1974). *Leadership and Ambiguity: The American College President*. New York: McGraw-Hill.

Darling, A. L., England, M. D., Lang, D. W., and Lopers-Sweetman, R. (1989). Autonomy and control: a university funding formula as an instrument of public policy. *Higher Education* 18(5): 559–84.

Davis, D. (1987). Educational funding and management under constraint with special reference to higher education in Australia. *Higher Education* 16(1): 63–73.

Dill, D. D. (1979). Teaching in the field of higher education: politics of higher education courses. *The Review of Higher Education* 2(2): 30–33.

Domhoff, G. W. (1990). *The Power Elite and the State: How Policy is Made in America*. New York: Aldine de Gruyter.

Dunleavy, P. and O'Leary, B. (1987). *Theories of the State: The Politics of Liberal Democracy*. New York: Meredith Press.

Elton, L. (1988). Accountability in higher education: the danger of unintended consequences. *Higher Education* 17(4): 377–90.

Emmert, M. A., and Crow, M. M. (1989). The cooperative university research laboratory: policy implications for higher education. *Journal of Higher Education* 60(4): 408–22.

Evans, P. B., Rueschemeyer, D., and Skocpol, T. (eds.). (1985). *Bringing the State Back In*. Cambridge: Cambridge University Press.

Finn, C. E. Jr. (1978). *Scholars, Dollars, and Bureaucrats*. Washington, D.C.: The Brookings Institution.

Fisher, L. (1988). State legislatures and the autonomy of colleges and universities: a comparative study of legislation in four states, 1900–1979. *Journal of Higher Education* 59(2): 163–89.

Foucault, M. (1977). *Discipline and Punish*. London: Allen Lane.

Garnier, M., Hage, J., and Fuller, B. (1989). The strong state, social class, and controlled school expansion in France, 1881–1975. *American Journal of Sociology* 95(2): 279–306.

Geiger, R. (1988). Public and private sectors in higher education: a comparison of international patterns. *Higher Education* 17(6): 699–712.

Giddens, A. (1987). *The Nation-State and Violence: Volume Two of a Contemporary Critique of Historical Materialism*. Berkeley: University of California Press.

Gilbert, J., and Howe, C. (1991). Beyond 'state vs. society': theories of the state and New Deal agricultural policies. *American Sociological Review* 56(2): 204–20.

Gillis, A. R. (1989). Crime and state surveillance in nineteenth century France. *American Journal of Sociology* 95(2): 307–41.

Gladieux, L. E., and Wolanin, T. R. (1976). *Congress and the Colleges: The National Politics of Higher Education*. Lexington, Massachusetts: Lexington Books, D.C. Heath and Company.

Goodchild, L. F., and Huk, I. P. (1990). The American college history: a survey of its historiographic schools and analytic approaches from the mid-nineteenth century to the present. In J. C. Smart (ed.), *Higher Education: Handbook of Theory and Research, Volume VI*. New York: Agathon.

Green, K. C. (1981). Program review and the state responsibility for higher education. *Journal of Higher Education* 52(1): 67–80.

Griffin, L. J., Wallace, M., E., and Rubin, B. A. (1986). Capitalist resistance to the organization of labor before the New Deal: why? how? success? *American Sociological Review* 51(2): 147–67.

Hanna, C. (1988). The organizational context for affirmative action for women faculty. *Journal of Higher Education* 59(4): 390–411.

Hansen, J. S. (1989). A policy research agenda for postsecondary student aid. *The Review of Higher Education* 12(4): 339–48.

Hardy, C. (1988). The rational approach to budget cuts: one university's experience. *Higher Education* 17(2):151–73.

Harman, G. (1986). Restructuring higher education systems through institutional mergers: Australian experience, 1981–3. *Higher Education* 15(6): 567–86.

Harman, G. (1988). Tertiary education and public policy: Australia's response to a changing environment. *Higher Education* 17(3): 251–66.

Hayhoe, R. (1988). China's intellectuals in the world community. *Higher Education* 17(2): 121–38.

Hearn, J. C. (1988). Strategy and resources: economic issues in strategic planning and management in higher education. In J. C. Smart (ed.), *Higher Education: Handbook of Theory and Research, Volume IV*. New York: Agathon.

Higley, J. and Burton, M. G. (1989). The elite variable in democratic transitions and breakdowns. *American Sociological Review* 54(1): 17–32.

Hines, E. W. (1988). *Higher Education and State Governments: Renewed Partnership, Cooperation, or Competition?* ASHE-ERIC Higher Education Report No.5. Washington, D.C.: Association for the Study of Higher Education.

Hooks, G. (1990a). The rise of the Pentagon and United States state building: the defense program as industrial policy. *American Journal of Sociology* 96(2): 358–405.

Hooks, G. (1990b). From an autonomous to a captured state agency: the decline of the new deal in agriculture. *American Sociological Review* 55(1): 29–43.

Hughes, E. C. (1958). *Men and Their Work*. Glencoe, Illinois: The Free Press.

Jacobs, D. (1988). Corporate economic power and the state: a longitudinal assessment of two explanations. *American Journal of Sociology* 93(4): 852–81.

Johnson, E. L. (1987). The "other Jeffersons" and the state university idea. *Journal of Higher Education* 58(2): 127–50.

Kenney, M. (1986). *Biotechnology: The University-Industrial Complex*. New Haven: Yale University Press.

Lagemann, E. C. (1989). *The Politics of Knowledge: The Carnegie Corporation, Philanthropy, and Public Policy*. Middletown, Connecticut: Wesleyan University Press.

Lee, B. A., and Olswang, S. G. (1985). Legal parameters of the faculty employment relationship. In J. C. Smart (ed.), *Higher Education: Handbook of Theory and Research, Volume I*. New York: Agathon.

Leslie, D. W. (1986). Academic freedom for universities. *The Review of Higher Education* 9(2): 135–58.

Lindsay, B. (1988). Public and higher education policies influencing African-American women. *Higher Education* 17(5): 563–80.

Lukes, S. (1978). *Power: A Radical View*. New York: The Macmillan Press.

Maassen, P. A. M., and Potman, H. P. (1990). Strategic decision making in higher education: an analysis of the new planning system in Dutch higher education. *Higher Education* 20(4): 393–410.

MacKinnon, C. A. (1989). *Toward a Feminist Theory of the State*. Cambridge: Harvard University Press.

Marshall, N. (1990). End of an era: the collapse of the 'buffer' approach to the governance of Australian tertiary education. *Higher Education* 19(2): 147–68.

Maxwell, W. E. (1987). The expansion of higher education enrollments in agrarian and developing areas of the third world. In J. C. Smart (ed.), *Higher Education: Handbook of Theory and Research, Volume III*. New York: Agathon.

McPherson, M. S., Wagner, A. P., and Willie-Schiff, N. (1989). Student financial aid and institutional behavior: how institutions use and benefit from student aid. In J. C. Smart (ed.), *Higher Education: Handbook of Theory and Research, Volume V*. New York: Agathon.

Miliband, R. (1969). *The State in Capitalist Society*. London: Winfield and Nicholson.

Millett, J. D. (1984). *Conflict in Higher Education: State Government Coordination Versus Institutional Independence*. San Francisco: Jossey-Bass.

Mills, C. W. (1956). *The Power Elite*. New York: Oxford University Press.

Mitchell, B. L. (1987). Higher education reform and ad hoc committees: a question of legitimacy. *The Review of Higher Education* 11(2): 117–36.

Morrison, J. L., and Mecca, T. V. (1989). Managing uncertainty: environmental analysis/

forecasting in academic planning. In J. C. Smart (ed.), *Higher Education: Handbook of Theory and Research, Volume V*. New York: Agathon.

Neumann, R. and Lindsay, A. (1988). Research policy and the changing nature of Australia's universities. *Higher Education* 17(3): 307–22.

O'Connor, J. (1973). *The Fiscal Crisis of the State*. New York: St. Martin's Press.

Pampel, F. C., and Williamson, J. B. (1988). Welfare spending in advanced industrial democracies, 1950–80. *American Journal of Sociology* 93(6): 1424–56.

Poulantzas, N. (1974). *Political Power and Social Classes*. London: New Left Books.

Pritchard, R. (1986). The third amendment to the higher education law of the German Federal Republic. *Higher Education* 15(6): 587–608.

Quadagno, J. (1987). Theories of the welfare state. *Annual Review of Sociology* 13: 109–28.

Quadagno, J. (1988). *The Transformation of Old Age Security: Class and Politics in the American Welfare State*. Chicago: University of Chicago Press.

Quadagno, J. (1990). Race, class, and gender in the U.S. welfare state: Nixon's failed family assistance plan. *American Sociological Review* 55(1): 11–28.

Ramirez, F. O., and Boli, J. (1987). The political construction of mass schooling: European origins and worldwide institutionalization. *Sociology of Education* 60(1): 2–17.

Ratcliff, J. L. (1987). "First" public junior colleges in an age of reform. *Journal of Higher Education* 58(2): 151–80.

Rhoades, G. (1987a). Higher education in a consumer society. *Journal of Higher Education* 58(1): 1–24.

Rhoades, G. (1987b). Folk norms and school reform: English secondary schools. *Sociology of Education* 60(1): 44–53.

Rhoades, G. and Slaughter, S. (1990). Re-Writing the codes: the reconstruction of policies affecting science. Presented at the Association for the Study of Higher Education meetings, Portland, November 1990.

Rhoades, Gary, and Slaughter, S. (1991a). The public interest and professional labor: research universities. In William G. Tierney (ed.), *Culture and Ideology in Higher Education: Advancing a Critical Agenda*. New York: Praeger.

Rhoades, G. and Slaughter, S. (1991b). Professors, administrators, and patents: the negotiation of technology transfer. *Sociology of Education* 64(2): 65–77.

Richardson, R. C., and Skinner, E. F. (1989). Adapting to diversity: organizational influences on student achievement. *Journal of Higher Education* 61(5): 485–511.

Rudolph, F. (1962). *The American College and University: A History*. New York: Vintage Press.

Scott, B. A. (1983). *Crisis Management in American Higher Education*. New York: Praeger.

Shapiro, J. Z. (1986). Evaluation research and educational decision making. In J. C. Smart (ed.), *Higher Education: Handbook of Theory and Research, Volume II*. New York: Agathon.

Silverman, R. J. (1987). How we know what we know: a study of higher education journal articles. *The Review of Higher Education* 11(1): 39–60.

Skocpol, T., and Amenta, E. (1986). States and social policies. *Annual Review of Sociology* 12: 131–57.

Slaughter, S. (1987). New York state and the politics of postsecondary spending. *Higher Education* 16(2): 173–98.

Slaughter, S. (1988). Academic freedom and the state: reflections on the uses of knowledge. *Journal of Higher Education* 59(3): 241–62.

Slaughter, S. (1990). *The Higher Learning and High Technology: Dynamics of Higher Education Policy Formation.* Albany: State University of New York Press.

Slaughter, S. and Rhoades, G. (1990a). Re-norming the social relations of science: technology transfer. *Educational Policy* 4(4): 341–61.

Slaughter, S. and Rhoades, G. (1990b). From lactobacillus acidophilus to hairy cell leukemia: litigation over copyright, patents, and trademarks in the university community. Presented at the Association for the Study of Higher Education meetings, Portland, November 1990.

Stampen, J. O., and Fenske, R. H. (1988). The impact of financial aid on ethnic minorities. *The Review of Higher Education* 11(4): 337–54.

Stephens, J. D. (1989). Democratic transition and breakdown in western Europe( )1870–1939: a test of the Moore thesis. *American Journal of Sociology* 94(5): 1019–77.

Stryker, R. (1989). Limits on technocratization of the law: the elimination of the National Labor Relations Board's division of economic research. *American Sociological Review* 54(3): 341–58.

Stryker, R. (1990). Science, class, and the welfare state: a class centered functional account. *American Journal of Sociology* 96(3): 684–726.

Torres, D. L. (1988). Professionalism, variation, and organizational survival. *American Sociological Review* 53(3): 380–94.

Veblen, T. (1918). *The Higher Learning in America: A Memorandum on the Conduct of Universities by Business Men.* New York: Viking Press.

Veysey, L. R. (1965). *The Emergence of the American University.* Chicago: University of Chicago Press.

Volkwein, J. F. (1986a). Campus autonomy and its relationship to measures of university quality. *Journal of Higher Education* 57(5): 510–28.

Volkwein, J. F. (1986b). State financial control of public universities and its relationship to campus administrative elaborateness and cost: results of a national study. *The Review of Higher Education* 9(3): 2667–86.

Volkwein, J. F. (1987). State regulation and campus autonomy. In J. C. Smart (ed.), *Higher Education: Handbook of Theory and Research, Volume III.* New York: Agathon.

Volkwein, J. F. (1989). Changes in quality among public universities. *Journal of Higher Education* 60(2): 136–51.

Weidman, J. C., Nelson, G. M., and Radzyminski, W. J. (1984). Books perceived to be basic reading for students of higher education. *The Review of Higher Education* 7(3): 279–87.

White, K. B. (1991). The implementation of state mandated program review: a case study of governance and decision making in community colleges. Doctoral dissertation, Center for the Study of Higher Education, University of Arizona.

Wolanin, T. and Gladieux, L. (1975). The Political culture of a policy arena: higher education. In Matthew Holden and Dennis Dresang (eds.), *What Government Does.* Beverly Hills: Sage Publications.

Young, D. Parker, and Braswell, M. C. (1987). An analysis of student academic rights. In J. C. Smart (ed.), *Higher Education: Handbook of Theory and Research, Volume III.* New York: Agathon.

Zusman, A. (1986). Legislature and university conflict: the case of California. *The Review of Higher Education* 9(4): 397–418.

Students' Evaluations of University Teaching: A Multidimensional Perspective

Herbert W. Marsh,

University of Western Sydney, Macarthur,

and

Michael J. Dunkin,

University of New South Wales

INTRODUCTION

The Purposes of Students' Evaluations of Teaching Effectiveness

The most widely noted purposes for collecting students' evaluations of teaching effectiveness (SETs) are variously to provide: (1) diagnostic feedback to faculty about the effectiveness of their teaching that will be useful for the improvement of teaching; (2) a measure of teaching effectiveness to be used in administrative decision making; (3) information for students to use in the selection of courses and instructors; and (4) an outcome or a process description for research on teaching. The first purpose is nearly universal, but the next three are not. At many universities systematic student input is required before faculty are even considered for promotion, while at others the inclusion of SETs is optional or not encouraged at all. Similarly, in some universities the results of SETs are sold to students in university bookstores as an aid to the selection of courses or instructors, whereas the results are considered to be strictly confidential at other universities.

The fourth purpose of SETs, their use in research on teaching, has not been systematically examined, and this is unfortunate. Research on teaching involves at least three major questions (Gage, 1963; Dunkin, 1986; also see Braskamp, Brandenburg and Ory, 1985; Doyle, 1975, 1983): How do teachers behave? Why do they behave as they do? and What are the effects of their behavior? Dunkin goes on to conceptualize this research in terms of: a) process variables (global teaching methods and specific teaching behaviors); b) presage variables

The authors would like to acknowledge the helpful comments from Philip Abrami, Kenneth Feldman, Dennis Hocevar, and Wilbert McKeachie on earlier versions of this chapter.

(characteristics of teachers and students); c) context variables (substantive, physical and institutional environments); and d) product variables (student academic/professional achievement, attitudes, and evaluations). McKeachie, Pintrich, Lin, Smith, and Sharma (1990) have blended this approach with a cognitive approach that includes student motivation, student cognition, and student involvement in self-regulated learning as well as student learning as important educational outcomes. SETs are important both as a process-description measure and as a product measure. This dual role played by SETs, as a process description and as a product of the process, is also inherent in their use as diagnostic feedback, as input for tenure promotion decisions, and as information for students to use in course selection. However, Dunkin's presage and context variables also have a substantial impact on both the process and the product, and herein lies a dilemma. SETs, as either a process or a product measure, should reflect the valid effects of presage and context measures. Nevertheless, since many presage and context variables may be beyond the control of the instructor, such influences may represent a source of unfairness in the evaluation of teaching effectiveness—particularly when SETs are used for personnel decisions (see subsequent discussion).

SETs are sometimes used to infer course quality. It is argued here, however, that responses to instruments such as SEEQ are probably not very useful for this purpose. Research indicates that the ratings are primarily a function of the instructor who teaches the course rather than the course that is being taught (see later discussion), and thus provide little information that is specific to the course. This conclusion should not be interpreted to mean that student input is not valuable for such purposes, but only that the student responses to instruments such as SEEQ are not appropriate as a source of student input into questions of course, as opposed to teacher, evaluations.

A Construct Validation Approach to the Study of Students' Evaluations

Particularly in the last 20 years, the study of SETs has been one of the most frequently emphasized areas in American educational research. Literally thousands of papers have been written and a comprehensive review is beyond the scope of this chapter. The reader is referred to reviews by Aleamoni (1981), Braskamp, Brandenburg, and Ory (1985), Cashin (1988) Centra (1979, 1989), Cohen (1980, 1981), Costin, Greenough and Menges (1971), de Wolf (1974), Doyle (1975, 1983), Feldman (1976a, 1976b, 1977, 1978, 1979, 1983, 1984, 1986, 1987, 1988, 1989a, 1989b), Kulik and McKeachie (1975), Marsh (1982b, 1984b, 1985, 1987), McKeachie (1963, 1973, 1979), Murray (1980), Overall and Marsh (1982), and Remmers (1958, 1963).

In the early 1970s there was a huge increase in the collection of SETs at North American universities that led to a concomitant increase in research. The ERIC system contains over 1,300 entries under the heading "student evaluation of teacher performance'' and Feldman (1990b) noted that his collection of books and articles contained about 2,000 items. In the 1970s, however, there were few well-established research paradigms and methodological guidelines to guide this early research, and insufficient attention was given to those that were available. Many studies conducted during this period were methodologically unsound, but their conclusions were nevertheless used as the basis of policy and subsequent research. Richard Schutz, editor of the *American Educational Research Journal* during the late 1970s, commented that the major educational research journals may have erred in accepting for publication so many SET studies of questionable quality during this period (personal communication, 1979). In the 1980s there were fewer articles published in major research journals than in the late 1970s, but they were typically of a better quality. Based on ERIC citations, however, the number of SET studies from all sources declined only moderately during this period, methodologically flawed studies continue to be reported, and the quality of papers presented at conferences and published in less prestigious journals is still quite varied. During the late 1970s, and particularly the 1980s, research paradigms and methodological standards evolved, but they are presented in a piecemeal fashion in journal articles. Hence, an important aim of this chapter is to present the research paradigms and methodological standards that have evolved in SET research.

Validating interpretations of SETs involves an ongoing interplay between construct interpretations, instrument development, data collection, and logic. Each interpretation must be considered a tentative hypothesis to be challenged in different contexts and with different approaches. This process corresponds to defining a nomological network (Cronbach, 1971) in which differentiable components of SETs are related to each other and to other constructs. Within-network studies attempt to ascertain whether SETs consist of distinct components and, if so, what these components are. This involves logical approaches such as content analysis and empirical approaches such as factor analysis and multitrait-multimethod (MTMM) analysis. Some clarification of within-network issues must logically precede between-network studies where SETs are related to external variables. Several perspectives about SET underlie this construct validity approach (see Marsh, 1987, for more detail): effective teaching and SETs designed to reflect teaching effectiveness are multidimensional; no single criterion of effective teaching is sufficient; and tentative interpretations of relations with validity criteria and with potential biases should be evaluated critically in different contexts and in relation to multiple criteria of effective teaching.

DIMENSIONALITY OF STUDENTS' EVALUATIONS

In this section we examine the multidimensionality of SETs and appropriate dimensions to be included, emphasizing in particular the SEEQ instrument.

Three overlapping approaches to this problem are considered: (1) an empirical approach emphasizing statistical techniques such as factor analysis and MTMM analysis; (2) a logical analysis of the content of effective teaching and the purposes the ratings are intended to serve, supplemented by reviews of previous research and feedback from students and instructors; and (3) a theory of teaching and learning. In practice, most instruments are based on the first two approaches—particularly the second—and the third approach seems not to have been used in the SET literature. Here, we offer support for the content of the SEEQ scales using all three approaches.

The Need for a Multidimensional Approach

Effective teaching is a multidimensional construct (e.g., a teacher may be organized but lack enthusiasm). Thus, it is not surprising that a considerable body of research has also shown that SETs are multidimensional (see Marsh, 1987). Information from SETs depends upon the content of the items. Poorly worded or inappropriate items will not provide useful information. If a survey instrument contains an ill-defined hodgepodge of different items and SETs are summarized by an average of these items, then there is no basis for knowing what is being measured. Particularly when the purpose of the ratings is formative, it is important that careful attention be given to the components of teaching effectiveness that are to be measured. Surveys should contain separate groups of related items that are derived from a logical analysis of the content of effective teaching and the purposes that the ratings are to serve, and that are supported on the basis of theory and previous research and by empirical procedures such as factor analysis and MTMM analysis.

Support for the claim that SETs are most appropriately considered a multidimensional construct must be evaluated—at least in part—in relation to the purposes that the ratings are to serve. As noted above, SETs are broadly recommended for four purposes. For personnel decisions, there is considerable controversy as to whether a multidimensional profile of scores or a single summary score is more useful (Abrami, 1989a, 1989b; Abrami and d'Apollonia, 1991; Marsh, 1987, 1991a). For feedback to teachers, for use in student course selection, and for use in research on teaching, however, there appears to be general agreement that a profile of distinct components of SET based on an appropriately constructed multidimensional instrument is more useful than a single summary score.

The Content of Factor Analytically Based SET Instruments

The SET literature contains examples of instruments that have a well defined factor structure and that provide measures of distinct components of teaching effectiveness. In addition to SEEQ, some of these instruments (the actual instruments are presented by Marsh, 1987) include: Frey's Endeavor instrument

(Frey, Leonard and Beatty, 1975; also see Marsh, 1981a, 1987); The Student Description of Teaching questionnaire developed by Hildebrand, Wilson and Dienst (1971); and the Michigan State SIRS instrument (Warrington, 1973). Factor analyses of responses to each of these instruments identified the factors that each was intended to measure, demonstrating that SETs do measure distinct components of teaching effectiveness. The systematic approach used in the development of these instruments, and the similarity of the factors that they measure, support their construct validity. The strongest support for the multidimensionality of SETs apparently comes from research using SEEQ.

The SEEQ Instrument
In the development of SEEQ: 1) a large item pool was obtained from a literature review, forms in current usage, and interviews with faculty and students about what they saw as effective teaching; 2)students and faculty were asked to rate the importance of items; 3) faculty were asked to judge the potential usefulness of the items as a basis for feedback; and 4) open-ended student comments were examined to determine if important aspects had been excluded. These criteria, along with psychometric properties, were used to select items and revise subsequent versions, thus supporting the content validity of SEEQ responses (the SEEQ scales and the items in each scale are presented in Table 1).

Factor Analysis of SEEQ Responses
Factor analytic support for the SEEQ scales is particularly strong. To date, more than 30 published factor analyses of SEEQ responses have identified the factors that SEEQ is designed to measure (e.g., Marsh, 1982b, 1983, 1984b, 1987, 1991b; Marsh and Hocevar, 1984, 1991a). Marsh and Hocevar (1991a) described the archive of SEEQ responses that contains ratings of 50,000 classes (representing responses to nearly 1 million SEEQ surveys). From this archive, 24,158 courses were selected and classified into one of 21 different subgroups varying in terms of teacher rank (teaching assistant or regular staff), level of instruction (undergraduate or graduate), and academic discipline. Twenty-two separate factor analyses of the total sample and each of the subsamples all identified the nine factors that SEEQ is designed to measure. For each of the 24,158 sets of ratings, two sets of factor scores were computed: one based on the factor analysis of responses to the particular subgroup to which the set belonged and one based on the factor analysis across the total group (across the 21 subgroups). Within all 21 subgroups correlations among the two sets of factor scores were very high and the median correlation was greater than $r = .99$. Because of large number and diversity of classes in this study, the results provided very strong support for the generality of the factor structure underlying SETs. When instructors evaluated their own teaching effectiveness on the same SEEQ form as completed by their students, factor analyses of SETs and instruc-

TABLE 1. Factor analyses of students' evaluations of teaching effectiveness (S) and the corresponding faculty self-evaluations of their own teaching (F) in 329 courses. (Reprinted from Marsh [1984b] by permission of the American Psychological Association.)

Evaluation items (paraphrased)	1 S	1 F	2 S	2 F	3 S	3 F	4 S	4 F	5 S	5 F	6 S	6 F	7 S	7 F	8 S	8 F	9 S	9 F
1. Learning/Value																		
Course challenging/stimulating	42	40	23	25	09	-10	04	04	00	-03	15	27	09	05	16	23	29	20
Learned something valuable	53	77	15	02	10	-02	04	04	01	-01	10	00	10	04	17	09	16	06
Increased subject interest	57	70	12	05	08	07	07	07	02	-03	18	08	13	-04	19	05	14	-02
Learned/understood subject matter	55	52	12	12	13	12	03	03	03	11	-01	-01	09	07	14	-04	-23	-11
Overall course rating	36	33	25	29	16	09	12	08	09	02	12	16	13	-08	14	27	08	16
2. Enthusiasm																		
Enthusiastic about teaching	15	29	55	42	16	00	07	02	21	15	10	00	05	16	01	09	05	06
Dynamic & energetic	08	03	60	70	15	-01	11	01	08	05	06	05	07	16	01	05	06	03
Enhanced presentations with humor	10	04	66	58	-04	06	05	01	13	08	12	02	14	07	02	-18	-07	-10
Teaching style held your interest	09	12	59	64	23	20	16	06	06	00	03	14	10	05	06	03	-02	-03
Overall instructor rating	12	27	40	54	23	09	14	08	23	02	11	16	10	-08	05	27	05	16
3. Organization																		
Instructor explanations clear	12	00	07	24	55	42	20	09	05	04	10	06	13	01	06	23	-08	-03
Course materials prepared & clear	06	06	03	-02	73	69	09	09	10	-02	04	04	03	03	10	03	01	12
Objectives stated & pursued	19	12	-05	-08	49	41	03	05	08	05	14	08	25	27	06	05	01	06
Lectures facilitated note taking	-03	02	20	09	58	53	-17	07	-02	05	14	04	15	06	08	01	-04	-05
4. Group Interaction																		
Encouraged class discussions	04	06	10	-02	01	03	84	86	03	00	00	00	06	00	06	-05	00	-03
Students shared ideas/knowledge	02	08	06	-07	-04	-01	85	88	05	13	05	01	06	-02	10	-10	01	01
Encouraged questions & answers	03	-04	06	09	14	06	62	69	16	09	15	03	07	11	08	21	00	01
Encouraged expression of ideas	07	01	02	06	01	-11	73	75	23	-09	11	07	12	12	08	09	00	-02
5. Individual Rapport																		
Friendly towards students	-04	10	17	06	00	-06	13	12	68	78	-01	-05	13	02	10	-05	-07	01
Welcomed seeking help/advice	04	-10	05	02	02	07	06	00	85	75	-04	04	12	06	05	20	03	-04
Interested in individual students	07	10	11	-09	00	07	14	01	69	77	-01	-09	14	03	08	-09	03	09
Accessible to individual students	02	-13	-11	-11	16	09	09	-02	62	43	20	25	13	13	00	14	04	07
6. Breadth of Coverage																		
Contrasted implications	-05	02	12	01	05	03	08	01	-03	01	72	84	08	-03	14	02	08	-06
Gave background of ideas/concepts	08	03	08	10	16	07	-03	-02	02	02	71	78	01	08	11	-01	03	03
Gave different points of view	04	-06	04	09	11	11	08	16	06	01	72	55	17	17	06	-06	08	08
Discussed current developments	23	29	08	-04	-04	-04	05	12	09	00	50	48	05	05	16	10	-01	-02
7. Examinations/Grading																		
Examination feedback valuable	-03	01	08	09	06	-11	09	05	08	12	-04	03	72	62	05	-03	09	03
Eval. methods fair/appropriate	06	02	00	-03	03	14	06	06	14	06	10	17	69	64	11	11	08	04
Tested emphasized course content	08	00	-01	04	11	21	07	01	06	00	11	-04	70	58	07	10	-02	-03
8. Assignments																		
Reading/texts valuable	-06	09	-03	-03	03	07	09	-06	03	03	07	-07	01	11	05	-08	02	04
Added to course understanding	12	01	-01	-12	01	04	09	21	01	17	-02	08	07	05	07	10	06	10
9. Workload/Difficulty																		
Course difficulty (Easy-Hard)	-06	00	06	-01	04	-05	02	02	-01	00	08	00	-04	08	10	04	85	74
Course workload (Light-Heavy)	14	-04	-09	-01	03	02	07	07	08	08	06	01	08	01	08	04	88	86
Course pace (Too Slow-Too Fast)	-20	07	12	00	04	18	-09	-09	06	02	-03	-07	04	-08	05	21	62	32
Hours/week outside of class	14	00	07	00	-11	00	07	02	00	02	03	-04	03	-08	05	21	73	46

Note. Factor loadings in boxes are the loadings for items designed to measure each factor. All loadings are presented without decimal points. Factor analyses of student ratings and instructor self-ratings consisted of a principal-components analysis, Kaiser normalization and rotation to a direct oblimin criterion. The analyses were tor self-evaluations each identified the same SEEQ factors (Marsh, 1982c; Marsh and Hocevar, 1983; Marsh, Overall and Kesler, 1979b). The results from the largest of these studies, based on evaluations of instructors in 329 courses, are presented in Table 1. These studies demonstrate that the SEEQ factors identified in factor analyses of SETs also generalize to instructor self-evaluations.

Higher-Order SEEQ Factors
Factor analytic studies demonstrate that SEEQ measures distinct dimensions of teaching effectiveness, but some researchers argue that SETs should be considered as a relatively unidimensional construct for some purposes. Abrami (1985; also see Abrami and d'Apollonia, 1991; Marsh, 1991a) proposed a compromise analogous to the intelligence hierarchy in which there are distinct first-order factors, but a single higher-order factor. Marsh (1987) suggested that Abrami's proposal could be tested using recent advances in the application of confirmatory factor analysis (CFA) and hierarchical CFA (HCFA) that are summarized below. Whereas no previous research had formally tested the higher-order structure of SETs, Marsh (1991b) reviewed studies by Abrami (1985, 1989a, 1989b), Frey (1978), Feldman (1976b), and others to derive higher-order models positing 1, 2, 3, and 4 higher-order factors that are summarized in Table 2 and Figure 1.

The model with one higher-order factor tests Abrami's suggestion that there is only one higher-order factor. The two higher-order factor model is based on Frey's (1978) claim that specific dimensions of his Endeavor instrument can be explained in terms of two global dimensions called Skill and Empathy (see Table 2). The three higher-order factor model follows from Feldman's (1976b) suggestion that his specific categories of effective teaching could be classified into three global categories (see Table 2) related to the instructor's role as a presenter (actor or communicator), facilitator (interactor or reciprocator), and manager (director or regulator). Comparison of the content of these global components (Table 2) suggests that Frey's Rapport and Feldman's facilitator represent similar constructs. The four higher-order factor model is based on the observation that Workload/Difficulty is relatively uncorrelated with any of the other SEEQ factors except, perhaps, Assignments.

It is important to emphasize that each of the higher-order models is predicated on the assumption that there is a well-defined set of first-order factors. Hence, Marsh (1991b) initially used CFA to test the first-order structure of SEEQ responses. Consistent with previous exploratory factor analyses, these results provided support for the 9 first-order factors that SEEQ is designed to measure. First-order models positing 1, 2, 3, or 4 first-order similar to the second-order factors were not able to fit the data.

The purpose of HCFA is to determine whether a smaller number of second-order factors can be used to explain relations among first-order factors (for further discussion of HCFA see Marsh, 1991b; Marsh and Hocevar, 1985).

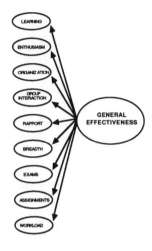

MODEL H1

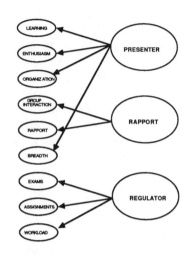

MODEL H3

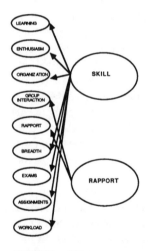

MODEL H2

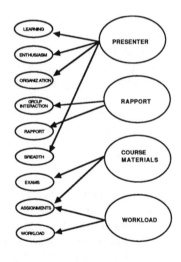

MODEL H4

FIGURE 1. Four a priori higher-order models of relations among first-order SEEQ factors. Each first-order factor is inferred from multiple indications (i.e., items). In order to avoid clutter, the multiple indicators of the first-order factors and correlations among the higher-order factors are not presented. (*Reprinted from Marsh (1991a) by permission of American Psychological Association.*)

TABLE 2. Categories of effective teaching adapted from Feldman (1976b, 1983, 1984) and the students' evaluations of educational quality (SEEQ) and endeavor factors most closely related to each category *(adapted from Marsh [1991a] by permisson of the American Psychological Association.)*

Feldman's Categories	SEEQ Factors	Endeavor Factors
1) Stimulation of interest (I)	Instructor Enthusiasm	None
2) Enthusiasm (I)	Instructor Enthusiasm	None
3) Subject knowledge (I)	Breadth of Coverage[a]	None
4) Intellectual expansiveness (I)	Breadth of Coverage	None
5) Preparation and organization (I)	Organization/Clarity	Organization/Planning (I)
6) Clarity and understandableness (I)	Organization/Clarity	Presentation Clarity (I/II)
7) Elocutionary skills (I)	None	None
8) Sensitivity to class progress (I/II)	None	None
9) Clarity of objectives (III)	Organization/Clarity	Organization/Planning (I)
10) Value of course materials (III)	Assignments/Readings	None
11) Supplementary materials (III)	Assignments/Readings	None
12) Perceived outcome/impact	Learning/Value	Student Accomplishments (I/II)
13) Fairness, impartiality (III)	Examinations/Grading	Grading/Exams (II/I)
14) Classroom management (III)	None	None[a]
15) Feedback to students (III)	Examinations/Grading	Grading/Exams (II/I)[a]
16) Class discussion (II)	Group Interaction	Class Discussion (II)
17) Intellectual challenge (II)	Learning/Value	Student Accomplishments (I/II)[a]
18) Respect for students (II)	Individual Rapport	Personal Attention (II/I)
19) Availability/helpfulness (II)	Individual Rapport	Personal Attention (II/I)
20) Difficulty/workload (III)	Workload/Difficulty	Workload (I)

Note. The actual categories used by Feldman in different studies (e.g., Feldman, 1976, 1983, 1984) varied somewhat. Categories 14 and 20 were included by Feldman (1976) but not in subsequent studies. Feldman (1976b) also proposed three higher-order clusters of categories that are identified by I (presentation), II (facilitation), and III (regulation) in parentheses following each category. Frey (1978) proposed two higher-order clusters of categories for factors from his Endeavor instrument that are identified by I (skill) and II (rapport) in parentheses following each Endeavor factor. When one of Feldman's categories or one of Frey's factors is associated with more than one higher-order cluster, the one that it is most strongly associated is presented first.

[a]Whereas these factors most closely match the corresponding categories, the match is apparently not particularly close.

Conceptually, it is like doing a second factor analysis based on correlations among the first-order factors. Comparing the ability of the four HCFA models to fit the data, the four higher-order factor model was found to be the best. For even this model with four higher-order factors, however, much of the true score variance in first-order factors was not explained by the higher-order factors. The results demonstrate that the SEEQ responses cannot be adequately explained by one or even a few summary scores. Furthermore, the results of the higher-order factor models need to be evaluated carefully. If the purpose of the HCFA is to examine relations among the first-order factors, then the results of this study are useful. If, however, the purpose of the HCFA is to justify the use of a smaller number of second-order factors to summarize SEEQ responses instead of the nine first-order factors, then the results are not particularly useful.

The Applicability Paradigm
SETs are commonly collected and frequently studied at North American universities, but not in most other parts of the world. Because of the extensive exposure of North American research, there is a danger that North American instruments will be used in new settings without first studying their applicability. In order to address this issue, Marsh (1981a) described a new paradigm for studying the applicability of two North American instruments (SEEQ and Endeavor; see Table 2) that was used with Australian students at the University of Sydney. This applicability paradigm was subsequently used in five other studies: Hayton (1983) with Australian students in Technical and Further Education schools; Marsh, Touron and Wheeler (1985) with students from the Universidad de Navarra in Spain; Clarkson (1984) with students from the Papua New Guinea University of Technology; Watkins, Marsh, and Young (1985) with students from the University of Canterbury in New Zealand, and Marsh and Roche (1991) with Australian students in the newly established University of Western Sydney.

In these studies students from a cross-section of disciplines selected "one of the best" and "one of the worst" lecturers they had experienced (or a "good," an "average," and a "poor" teacher in later studies), and rated each with the SEEQ and Endeavor items. As part of the study, students were asked to indicate "inappropriate" items, and to select up to five items that they "felt were most important in describing either positive or negative aspects of the overall learning experience in this instructional sequence" for each instructor they evaluated. Analyses included: a) a discrimination analysis of the ability of items and factors to differentiate between "best" and "worst" instructors; b) a summary of "not appropriate" responses; c) a summary of "most important item" responses; d) factor analyses of the SEEQ and Endeavor items; and e) a MTMM analysis of agreement between SEEQ and Endeavor scales that are posited to be matching (see Table 2). A detailed evaluation of this set of studies is beyond the scope of this chapter and the reader is referred to Marsh (1986, 1987). The results of these six studies—particularly the factor analyses and MTMM analyses—suggest that students from some different countries do differentiate among different components of teaching effectiveness, that the specific components do generalize across different nationalities, and that students differentiate among dimensions of effective teaching in a similar manner when responding to SEEQ and Endeavor. Across the studies the findings support the applicability and construct validity of the SEEQ and Endeavor when administered to university students in very different settings.

Feldman's Categories of Effective Teaching

Feldman (1976b; also see Feldman, 1983, 1984) derived the different components of effective teaching by categorizing the characteristics of the superior university teacher from the student's point of view. He reviewed research that either asked students to specify these characteristics or inferred them on the basis of correlations with global SETs. His list of categories (Table 2) provides the most extensive set of characteristics that are likely to underlie SETs. Nevertheless, Feldman used primarily a logical analysis based on his examination of the student evaluations literature, and his results do not imply that students can differentiate these categories. His categories, however, provide a useful basis for evaluating the comprehensiveness of SET factors on a given instrument.

Feldman (1976b) noted that factors identified by factor analysis typically corresponded to more than one of his categories. In Table 2 we have attempted to match Feldman's categories with the empirical factors identified in responses to the SEEQ and Endeavor instruments that are used in the present investigation. There is substantial overlap in the empirical factors from the two instruments (also see Marsh, 1986). Most of Feldman's categories are associated with empirical factors from the two instruments, although SEEQ factors represent Feldman's categories more comprehensively than do Endeavor factors. All of the factors in SEEQ and Endeavor represent at least one of Feldman's categories and most reflect two or more categories. In contrast, none of Feldman's categories reflects more than one of the empirical factors. This logical content analysis demonstrates that there is substantial overlap between Feldman's categories and the empirical factors but that Feldman's categories reflect more narrowly defined constructs than do the empirical factors.

Teaching-Learning Theories as a Basis of SEEQ Scales

SET instruments are typically not based on theories of teaching and learning. Furthermore, there is a surprising absence of evaluation of the content of SET scales in relation such theories. The instructional elements represented in the rating instruments should, however, be consistent with principles of effective teaching and learning established on the basis of accepted theory and research. It is important, therefore, that the factors underlying instruments such as SEEQ be inspected to see if they conform to principles of teaching and learning emerging from attempts to synthesize knowledge of teaching effectiveness.

For this analysis it is appropriate to focus upon theory and research in adult education, since SETs are most commonly obtained in post-secondary school situations. While Dubin and Okun (1973) were unable to find a single theory of learning that provided adequate guidance for teachers of adults, Mackie (1981) was satisfied that from the writings of behaviorists, cognitivists and personality theorists, 10 principles could be derived: (a) The learner must be motivated to learn; (b) The learning situation should take account of individual differences in learning capacities and learning style; (c) New learning should take into account the learner's present knowledge and attitudes; (d) What is to be learned should be reinforced; (e) The learning situation should give opportunities for practice; (f) The learner should be an active participant trying out new responses rather than just listening; (g) The material to be learned should be divided into learnable units and given in appropriately paced sequence; (h) Coaching or guidance should be given in the development of new responses; (i) What is learned should be capable of being successfully generalized from the learning situation; and (j) The material to be learned should be presented in a way that will emphasize the characteristics to be learned and do so in a way which is as meaningful as possible to the learner.

These principles were subsequently endorsed by Stephens (1985) and Brookfield (1989). Fincher (1985) engaged in a similar process of extracting "well-intended generalizations or working hypotheses" from the literature. He went on to trace the skepticism that developed regarding attempts to formulate such general principles but concluded that "most general principles of learning would not seem disconfirmed as much as they appear forgotten" and to express the belief "that efforts on the part of college instructors to adapt and to apply general principles of learning would be in the best interests of learners" (p. 92). Fincher's list was very similar to Mackie's, but included specific mention of the importance of the learner's experiences of success and failure. On the bases of the above, it seems appropriate to compare the content of the SEEQ factors with the general principles of teaching and learning put forward by Mackie and Fincher.

1. Learning/Value. In essence this factor denotes subjective feelings of success obtained through participation in a course and/or at the hands of a particular teacher. Students who are challenged and stimulated, who consider their learning through the course to have been worthwhile, whose interest in the subject was increased, who are conscious of having understood the subject-matter, and who generally rate the course highly are clearly expressing feelings of accomplishment on challenging learning tasks.

2. Instructor Enthusiasm. A minimal condition for learning is that attention be aroused. Stimulus salience, that is, the extent to which a stimulus stands out against a background, is known to be crucial in evoking interest and attention. It is to be expected, therefore, that teachers who impress students with their enthusiasm, dynamism, and energy and who make judicious use of humor will have students who are interested and attentive. Moreover, teacher enthusiasm can vicariously induce enthusiasm for the subject in students. Students who rate their teacher highly are more likely to model their behavior toward a subject based upon that teacher. Thus, the latter's enthusiasm can be acquired by students. Students whose interest in and enthusiasm for a subject are aroused are likely to have enhanced achievement in learning the subject. This factor is especially relevant to the principle that learners must be motivated to learn.

3. Organization/Clarity. The essential ingredients of this factor are structure and clarity. By cuing learners about the organization of subject matter, by providing advance organizers, by scheduling student exercises, and assignments appropriately and by inducing appropriate cognitive schemata, teachers assist students' memory retrieval and formation of linkages between new material and material previously learned. These principles of teaching and learning are time-honored and widely accepted elements of information processing theories of learning. While clarity is clearly an expected outcome of careful preparation and good organization, it can be important as a correlate of teacher knowledge of the subject, with teacher uncertainty producing vagueness which inhibits student understanding. Students who perceive instruction to be well organized and clear are, thus, likely to enjoy enhanced knowledge and understanding of course material. The Organization factor is pertinent to several accepted principles of teaching and learning.

4. Group Interaction. Learning in institutionalized educational contexts is a social phenomenon. That is, except in rare cases of individual tuition, instruction is given to groups of students ranging from small to very large in size. This factor refers to verbal interaction in classrooms in the form of questions and answers facilitating the expression and sharing of ideas and knowledge. Higher ratings on items comprising this factor suggest that the motivational potential of social interaction with others in learning contexts is being capitalized upon and also that the classroom context is being exploited as a venue for activity in practicing and testing ideas and obtaining feedback. As such the Group Interaction factor has a strong basis in principles of teaching and learning.

5. Individual Rapport. Opportunities to provide for individual differences in capacity and to take account of learners' present knowledge and attitudes in higher education depend heavily upon individual contacts with instructors. Furthermore, individual tuition and guidance are available to the extent that instructors are interested in and accessible to individual students. Students who feel welcome also have greater access to motivationally significant opportunities such as face-to-face reinforcement and encouragement. The Individual Rapport factor is consistent with several of Mackie's (1981) principles.

6. Breadth of Coverage. This factor reflects students' responses to items concerning the contrasting of implications of various theories, the provision of the backgrounds of ideas and concepts, the presentation of different points of view, and the discussion of current developments. These all have to do with substantive qualities of instruction. Each would seem to have the potential to increase student knowledge and understanding through facilitating generalization beyond the confines of the specific situation, to clarify the material to be learned and its meaningfulness to the learner. This factor relates closely to principles (i) and (j) above.

7. *Examinations/Grading*. The instructional value of examinations and grading lies in the quality of the feedback and in the stimulus to study they provide. The items comprising this factor apply specifically to feedback and less specifically to motivational issues. Students' perceptions of fairness and relevance of assessment procedures are probably associated with their motivation to learn. However, this factor's main basis in principles of learning is reinforcement in the form of knowledge of results and affective consequences of that knowledge.

8. *Assignments/Readings*. Student work in higher education especially is largely oriented to the completion of assignments, including required readings. Thus, positive SETs of the texts and supplementary readings and of other assignments probably indicate that activity in learning was found to be valuable and that the learning experiences involved were meaningful. Assignments provide students with opportunities to practice new knowledge and skills. Furthermore, learning tasks that constitute assignments are often presented in learnable units even if they are not always completed in an appropriately paced sequence. The Assignments factor, too, seems consistent with sound principles of learning.

9. *Workload/Difficulty*. Work that is seen by students to be too much or too difficult is almost by definition given without consideration of learners' capacities and prior learnings. Moreover, such work can not be appropriately paced or presented in desirably learnable units. Overloaded students find it difficult to experience subjective feelings of success and receive little or no reinforcement. They are likely to be forced into adopting learning strategies that minimize their ability to understand and generalize from the specific learning situation. On the other hand, students for whom success is too easily won lose motivation to succeed and are unlikely to value such learning highly. It would seem that student would value more highly achievement that involved them in overcoming substantial obstacles and that have necessitated relatively enduring commitments. This suggests the possibility of nonlinear relations between Workload/Difficulty and other indicators of teaching effectiveness such as student learning. There can be little or no doubt that the Workload factor is consistent with accepted principles of teaching and learning.

Summary of the Dimensionality of Students' Evaluations

In summary, many SET instruments are not developed using a theory of teaching and learning, a systematic logical approach that ensures content validity, or empirical techniques such as factor analysis. The evaluation instruments discussed above and particularly research based on SEEQ provide clear support for the multidimensionality of the SET construct. The debate about which specific components of teaching effectiveness can and should be measured has not been resolved, although there seems to be consistency in those that are identified in responses to the most carefully designed instruments such as SEEQ and Endeavor. Furthermore, the SEEQ factors are apparently applicable to a wide diversity of educational settings. SETs cannot be adequately understood if this multidimensionality is ignored. Many orderly, logical relationships are misinterpreted or cannot be consistently replicated because of this failure, and the substantiation of this claim will constitute a major focus of the remainder of this Chapter. SET instruments, particularly those used for research purposes, should be designed to measure separate components of teaching effectiveness, and support for both the content and the construct validity of the multiple dimensions should be evaluated.

RELIABILITY, STABILITY AND GENERALIZABILITY

Traditionally, reliability and validity are seen as opposite ends of a continuum of generalizability. Reliability refers to the generalizability of scores representing the same construct collected under maximally similar situations (e.g., internal consistency, alternative form correlations, and test-retest correlations), whereas validity refers to the generalizability of scores representing different constructs that are hypothesized to be related (e.g., SETs and student learning). As is obvious in this review, however, the separation is not so easy. The agreement between responses to matching SEEQ and Endeavor scales, for example, could be argued to reflect either reliability or validity. Short-term stability is typically interpreted to be an indication of reliability, but long-term stability could be argued to reflect either reliability or validity. Because of the limitations in the reliability/validity distinction, the broader term generalizability is useful. For present purposes we review studies of relations between two or more sets of SETs in this section on reliability and generalizability, and review relations between SETs and other constructs in the next section on validity.

Reliability
The reliability of SETs is commonly determined from the results of item analyses (i.e., correlations among responses to different items designed to measure the same component of effective teaching) and from studies of interrater agreement (i.e., agreement among ratings by different students in the same class). The internal consistency among responses to items designed to measure the same component of effective teaching is consistently high. However, such internal consistency estimates provide an inflated estimate of reliability since they ignore the substantial portion of error due to the lack of agreement among different students within the same course, and so they generally should not be used to measure the reliability of SETs (see Gilmore, Kane, and Naccarato, 1978, for further discussion).

The correlation between responses by any two students in the same class (i.e., the single rater reliability) is typically in the .20's but the reliability of the class-average response depends upon the number of students rating the class, as originally described by Remmers (1931; also see Feldman, 1977, for a review of methodological issues and empirical findings). For example, the estimated reliability for SEEQ factors is about .95 for the average response from 50 students, .90 from 25 students, .74 from 10 students, .60 from five students, and only .23 for one student. Given a sufficient number of students, the reliability of class-average SETs compares favorably with that of the best objective tests. In most applications, this reliability of the class-average response, based on agreement among all the different students within each class, is the appropriate method for assessing reliability. Recent applications of generalizability theory demonstrate how error due to differences between items and error due to differences between ratings of different students can both be incorporated into the same analysis, but the error due to differences between items appears to be quite small (Gilmore, Kane, and Naccarato, 1978).

Generalizability: The Perspective of Former Students
Some critics suggest that students cannot recognize effective teaching until after being called upon to apply their mastery in further coursework or after graduation. According to this argument, SETs completed by former students who evaluate courses with this added perspective will differ systematically from those by students who have just completed a course. Drucker and Remmers (1950) originally countered this contention with a cross-sectional study showing that responses by ten-year alumni agreed with those of current students. More recent cross-sectional studies (Centra, 1979; Howard, Conway and Maxwell, 1985; Marsh, 1977) have also shown good correlational agreement between the retrospective ratings of former students and those of currently enrolled students.

In a true longitudinal study (Marsh and Overall, 1979a; Overall and Marsh, 1980) the same students evaluated classes at the end of a course and again several years later, at least one year after graduation. End-of-class ratings in 100 courses correlated .83 with the retrospective ratings (a correlation approaching the reliability of the ratings), and the median rating at each time was nearly the same. Firth (1979) asked students to evaluate classes at the time of graduation from their university (rather than at the end of each class) and one year after graduation, and he also found good agreement between the two sets of ratings by the same students. These studies demonstrate that SETs are quite stable over time, and argue that added perspective does not alter the ratings given at the end of a course. Hence, these findings not only provide support for the long-term stability of SETs, but they also provide support for their construct validity.

In the same longitudinal study, Marsh and Overall (1979a) demonstrated that, consistent with previous research, the single-rater reliabilities were generally in the .20's for both end-of-course and retrospective ratings. (Interestingly, the single-rater reliabilities were somewhat higher for the retrospective ratings.) However, the median correlation between end-of-class and retrospective ratings, when based on responses by individual students instead of class-average responses, was .59. The explanation for this apparent paradox is the manner in which systematic unique variance, as opposed to random error variance, is handled in determining the single rater reliability estimate and the stability coefficient. Variance that is systematic, but unique to the responses of a particular student, is taken to be error variance in the computation of the single-rater reliability. However, if this systematic variance was stable over the several year period between the end-of-course and retrospective ratings for an individual student, a demanding criterion, then it is taken to be systematic variance rather than error variance in the computation of the stability coefficient. Hence, there is an enduring source of systematic variation in individual student SETs that is not captured by internal consistency measures. This also argues that while the process of averaging across the ratings produces a more reliable measure, it also masks much of the systematic variance in individual SETs, and that there may be systematic differences in ratings linked to specific subgroups of students within a class (also see Feldman, 1977; Centra, 1989). Various subgroups of students within the same class may view teaching effectiveness differently, and may be differentially affected by the instruction which they receive, but there has been surprisingly little systematic research to examine this possibility.

Generalizability—Teacher and Course Effects

Researchers have also asked how highly correlated SETs are in two different courses taught by the same instructor or in the same course taught by different teachers on two different occasions. This research examines the generality of SETs, and the relative importance of the effects of the instructor who teaches a class and the particular class being taught.

Marsh (1981b) arranged ratings of 1,364 courses into 341 sets such that each set contained ratings of: the same instructor teaching the same course on two occasions, the same instructor teaching two different courses, the same course taught by two different instructors, and two different courses taught by different instructors (Table 3). For the overall instructor rating, the correlation between ratings of different instructors teaching the same course (i.e., a course effect) was −.05, while correlations for the same instructor in different courses (.61) and in two different offerings of the same course (.72) were much larger (Table 3). While this pattern was observed in each of the SEEQ factors, the correlation between ratings of different instructors in the same course was slightly higher for some evaluation factors (e.g., Workload/Difficulty, Assignments, and Group Interaction) but had a mean of only .14 across all the factors. In marked contrast, correlations between background variables in different sets of courses (e.g., prior subject interest, class size, reason for taking the course) were higher for the same course taught by two different instructors than for two different courses taught by the same instructor (Table 3). Based on a path analysis of these results, Marsh argued that the effect of the teacher on SETs is much larger than is the effect of the course being taught, and that there is a small portion of reliable variance that is unique to a particular instructor in a particular course that generalizes across different offerings of the same course taught by the same instructor. SETs primarily reflect the effectiveness of the instructor rather than the influence of the course, and some teachers may be uniquely suited to teaching some specific courses. A systematic examination of the suggestion that some teachers are better suited for some specific courses, and that this can be identified from the results from a longitudinal archive of SETs, is an important area for further research.

These results provide support for the generality of SETs across different courses taught by the same instructor, but provide no support for the use of SETs to evaluate the course. Even SETs of the overall course were primarily a function of the instructor who taught the course, and not the particular course that was being evaluated. In fact, the predominance of the instructor effect over the course effect was virtually the same for both the overall instructor rating and the overall course rating. This finding probably reflects the autonomy that university instructors typically have in conducting the courses that they teach, and may not generalize to a setting in which instructors have little autonomy. Nevertheless, the findings provide no support for the validity of SETs based on instruments like SEEQ as a measure of the course that is independent of the instructor who teaches the course.

Marsh and Overall (1981) examined the effect of course and instructor in a setting where all students were required to take all the same courses, thus eliminating many of the problems of self-selection that plague most studies. The same students evaluated instructors at the end of each course and again one year after graduation from the program. For both end-of-course and follow-up ratings, the particular instructor teaching the course accounted for 5 to 10 times as much variance as the course. These findings again demonstrated that the instructor is the primary determinant of SETs rather than the course he or she teaches.

Murray, Rushton, and Paunonen (1990) used archive data to examine overall instructor ratings of 46 psychology instructors in as many as 6 different course types including 5 categories of undergraduate courses and a single category for graduate level courses. Because the graduate and undergraduate courses were evaluated on 7- and 5-point response scales respectively, ratings within each of the six course types were standardized separately. Included in the analysis were ratings of instructors teaching at least two courses within the same category. The number of teachers included in each category varied from 29 to 40. Correlations among mean ratings of the same teacher within the same course type over

TABLE 3. Teacher and course effects: Correlations among different sets of classes for student ratings and background characteristics. (*Reprinted from Marsh [1984b] by permission of the American Psychological Association.*)

Measure	Same teacher, same course	Same teacher, different course	Different teacher, same course	Different teacher, different course
Student rating				
Learning/Value	.696	.563	.232	.069
Enthusiasm	.734	.613	.011	.028
Organization/Clarity	.676	.540	−.023	−.063
Group interaction	.699	.540	.291	.224
Individual rapport	.726	.542	.180	.146
Breadth of coverage	.727	.481	.117	.067
Examinations/Grading	.633	.512	.066	−.004
Assignments	.681	.428	.332	.112
Workload/Difficulty	.733	.400	.392	.215
Overall course	.712	.591	−.011	−.065
Overall instructor	.719	.607	−.051	−.059
Mean coefficient	.707	.523	.140	.061
Background characteristic				
Prior subject interest	.635	.312	.563	.209
Reason for taking course (percent indicating general interest	.770	.448	.671	.383
Class average expected grade	.709	.405	.483	.356
Workload/Difficulty	.773	.400	.392	.215
Course enrollment	.846	.312	.593	.058
Percent attendance on day evaluations administered	.406	.164	.214	.045
Mean coefficient	.690	.340	.491	.211

different years (mean r = .86) was very high. The consistency in ratings of the same instructor across the five undergraduate course types (rs of .78 to .52, mean = .66) was also very high, but the consistency between the five undergraduate course types and graduate level courses was much lower (rs of .06 to .33, mean = .15). Because scores within each course type were standardized separately, mean differences in ratings of different course types could not be considered. These values—except for consistency across graduate and undergraduate courses—are higher than reported elsewhere (e.g., Marsh, 1981b) due in part to the fact that scores were aggregated across several courses within the same course type and because variance due to different course types was removed through standardization within course types. Except for the ratings of graduate level courses, these results are generally consistent with Marsh's (1981b) findings. The suggestion that SETs of the same instructor in undergraduate and graduate level courses are only modestly correlated is not consistent with SEEQ research, and may be idiosyncratic to Murray's study of teachers within a single psychology department and the different instruments used to assess undergraduate and graduate level classes.

Gilmore, Kane, and Naccarato (1978), applying generalizability theory to SETs, also found that the influence of the instructor who teaches the course is much larger than that of the course that is being taught. They suggested that ratings for a given instructor should be averaged across different courses to enhance generalizability. If it is likely that an instructor will teach many different classes during his or her subsequent career, then tenure decisions should be based upon as many different courses as possible—Gilmore, Kane, and Naccarato, suggest at least five. However, if it is likely that an instructor will continue to teach the same courses in which he or she has already been evaluated, then results from at least two different offerings of each of these courses was recommended. These recommendations require that a longitudinal archive of SETs be maintained for personnel decisions. These data would provide for more generalizable summaries, the assessment of changes over time, and the determination of which particular courses are best taught by a specific instructor. It is indeed unfortunate that some universities systematically collect SETs, but fail to keep a longitudinal archive of the results. Such an archive would help overcome some of the objections to SETs (e.g., idiosyncratic occurrences in one particular set of ratings), would enhance their usefulness, and would provide an important data base for further research.

Generalizability of Ratings Over Time

The two most common approaches to the study of stability and change refer to the stability of means over time (mean stability) and to the stability of individual differences over time (covariance stability). Research in the last section considered the generalizability of individual differences across different courses; the results indicated that teachers rated highly in one course tend to be rated highly in all the courses that they teach. Research described here focuses on the mean stability over time.

Most studies of the mean stability of teaching effectiveness are based on cross-sectional studies at the primary and secondary school level and have not used SETs as an indicator of teaching effectiveness. In an early review of this research, Ryans (1960) reported an overall negative relation between teaching experience and teaching effectiveness. He suggested, however, that there was an initial increase in effectiveness during the first few years, a leveling out period, and then a period of gradual decline. In her review of research since the early 1960s, Barnes (1985) reached a similar conclusion. She further reported that teaching experience beyond the first few years was associated with a tendency for teachers to reject innovations and changes in educational policy.

At the university level, Feldman (1983) reviewed studies relating overall and content-specific dimensions of SETs to teacher age, teaching experience, and academic rank. He reported that SETs were only weakly related to these three measures of seniority, but that distinct patterns were evident. Overall evaluations tended to be negatively correlated with age and—to a lesser extent—years of teaching experience, but tended to be positively correlated with academic rank. Thus, younger teachers, teachers with less teaching experience, and teachers with higher academic ranks tended to receive somewhat higher evaluations. Age and teaching experience showed reasonably similar patterns of correlations with overall and content-specific dimensions. Academic rank, however, had a more varied pattern of relations with the content-specific dimensions. Academic rank tended to be positively correlated with some characteristics such as subject knowledge, intellectual expansiveness, and value of course materials, but negatively correlated with other characteristics such as class discussion, respect for students, helpfulness and availability to students. Consistent with the reviews by Ryans (1960) and Barnes (1985), Feldman noted that in the few studies that specifically examined nonlinear relations, there was some suggestion of an inverted U-shaped relation in which ratings improved initially, peaked at some early point, and then declined slowly thereafter.

Most SET research has considered ratings collected in one specific course on a single occasion and there is surprisingly little research on the stability of mean ratings received by the same instructor over an extended period of time. Cross-sectional studies like those reviewed by Feldman (1983) provide a poor basis for inferring what ratings younger, less-experienced teachers will receive later in their careers or what ratings older, more-experienced teachers would have received if evaluated earlier in their careers. Clearly, there are important limitations in the use of cross-sectional data for evaluating how ratings of the same instructor varies over time. For this reason, Marsh and Hocevar (1991b) examined changes in ratings of a large number of teachers who had been evaluated continuously over a 13-year period with SEEQ.

Using the SEEQ archive consisting of evaluations of 50,000 courses collected over a 13-year period, Marsh and Hocevar (1991b) selected all teachers who were evaluated at least once during each of 10 different years between 1976 and 1988. This process identified 195 different teachers who had been evaluated in a total of 6,024 different courses (an average of 30.9 classes per teacher) from a total of 31 different academic departments. All SETs for the same instructor at the same level (graduate or undergraduate) offered in the same year were then averaged, resulting in 3,135 unique combinations of instructor, year, and course level. In order to evaluate the influence of the instructor the mean rating of each instructor over all undergraduate classes and over all graduate classes was computed. In the main regression models considered (Table 4), these instructor mean ratings were included along with the linear and nonlinear components of the year

TABLE 4. Changes in Multiple Dimensions of Students' Evaluations Over Time for Ratings of the Same Instructor: The Effects of Instructor, Year (1976–1988), Level (undergraduate and graduate), and Their Interaction (N = 3135). *(Reprinted from Marsh and Hocevar [1991] by permission of Pergamon Press.)*

Dimension	r for Instr	Standardized Beta Weights For:						
		Instr	Year	Year2	Level	YrxLev	YR2xlev	Mult R
Factor scores								
Learning/Value	.701**	.703**	.001	−.045**	−.023	.018	.025	.703**
Enthusiasm	.822**	.822**	−.016	−.019	−.003	.010	.006	.822**
Organization	.770**	.770**	−.048**	−.025	.000	.017	−.004	.772**
Group interact	.814**	.815**	−.012	−.020	−.009	−.013	.010	.815**
Indiv rapport	.747**	.746**	−.026	.016	.006	.006	−.009	.748**
Breadth	.735**	.735**	.005	−.011	.000	.009	−.007	.736**
Exams	.678**	.678**	−.028	−.017	.006	−.008	−.014	.678**
Assignments	.704**	.704**	−.004	−.024	−.008	.012	.006	.704**
Workload	.797**	.797**	−.020	−.009	.010	−.009	.007	.797**
Overall ratings								
Course	.725**	.725**	−.031	−.028	−.013	−.031	.019	.726**
Instructor	.756**	.755**	−.048**	−.020	−.010	.009	.015	.758**

$*p < .05$; $**p < .01$.

Note. The Instructor (instr) component was obtained by taking the mean of the instructor ratings for undergraduate classes and for graduate classes, and then including these means in the prediction of ratings. Because these means were computed separately for graduate and undergraduate level courses, it has the effect of eliminating variance due to course level.

(1976–1988), the course level (2 = graduate, 1 = undergraduate), and their interactions. Hence, the effects of the individual instructor were controlled in evaluating the effects of the other variables. As has been found previously, the individual instructor accounted for most of the variance in each of the different SEEQ scores. There were almost no systematic changes in ratings over time. Year accounted for no more than 1/4 of 1 percent in any of the evaluation scores, and—despite the large N and powerful design—only reached statistical significance for 2 of 11 scores (see Table 4).

The Marsh and Hocevar (1991b) study showed that the mean stability of SETs of the same teachers over a 13-year period of time was remarkably strong. The mean ratings for their cohort of 195 teachers showed almost no systematic changes over this period. Supplemental analyses suggested that the standards that students used apparently did not change over this period. The nonlinear effects suggested from cross-sectional studies were not observed for either the total sample, or subsamples of teachers with little, intermediate, or substantial amounts of teaching experience at the start of the 13-year longitudinal study. These results are important because this was apparently the only study to examine the mean stability of faculty ratings using a longitudinal design with a large and diverse group of teachers over such a long period of time.

Generalizability: Profile Analysis

Thus far, we have considered only the generalizability of individual SEEQ scales. Marsh (1987), however, noted the need to examine profiles of SEEQ scores as well as the individual scales that make up the profile. More specifically he suggested that each instructor has a distinguishable profile of SEEQ scales (e.g., high on organization and low on enthusiasm) that generalizes over different course offerings and is distinct from the profiles of other instructors. Marsh and Bailey (in press), because no other research known to them had evaluated SET profiles in this manner, conducted a profile analysis of ratings selected from the large SEEQ archive. They considered 3,079 sets of class-average responses for 123 instructors—an average of 25 classes per instructor—who had been evaluated regularly over a 13-year period. Because there were so many sets of ratings for each instructor, it was possible to determine a characteristic profile of SEEQ scores for each instructor by averaging across all his or her ratings. In profile analyses, it is important to distinguish between the level of scores (whether an instructor receives high or low ratings) and the shape of the profile (e.g., relatively higher on organization and relatively lower on enthusiasm). Although both are important considerations, the focus of the Marsh and Bailey study was on profile shape.

The profile of 9 SEEQ scales (e.g., Enthusiasm, Organization, Group Interaction) for each instructor was shown to be distinct from the profiles of other instructors, generalized across course offerings over the 13-year period, and generalized across undergraduate and graduate level courses. This support for the existence of a distinguishable profile that is specific to each instructor has important implications for the use of SETs as feedback and for the relation of SETs to other criteria such as student learning. Thus, for example, it may be that being organized and enthusiastic is very conducive to student learning, whereas being organized (but not enthusiastic) or enthusiastic (but not organized) has little effect on student learning. Although such possibilities were not specifically considered in the Marsh and Bailey (in press) study, this is an important direction for further research. The results also provide further support for the multidimensionality of SETs.

Student Written Comments—Generality Across Different Response Form
Braskamp and his colleagues (Braskamp, Brandenburg, and Ory, 1985; Braskamp, Ory, and Pieper, 1981; Ory, Braskamp, and Pieper, 1980) have examined the usefulness of students' written comments and their relation to

responses to rating items. Student comments were scored for overall favorability with reasonable reliability and these overall scores correlated with responses to the overall rating item ($r = .93$) close to the limits of the reliability of the two indicators (Ory, Braskamp, and Pieper, 1980). Braskamp, Ory, and Pieper (1981) sorted student comments into one of 22 content categories and evaluated comments in terms of favorability. The comment favorability was again highly correlated with the overall instructor rating (0.75). In a related study, Ory and Braskamp (1981) simulated results about a hypothetical instructor consisting of written comments in their original unedited form and rating items—both global and specific. The rating items were judged as easier to interpret and more comprehensive for both personnel decisions and self-improvement, but other aspects of the written comments were judged to be more useful for purposes of self-improvement. Speculating on these results, the authors suggested that "the nonstandardized, unique, personal written comments by students are perceived as too subjective for important personnel decisions. However, this highly idiosyncratic information about a particular course is viewed as useful diagnostic information for making course changes" (pp. 280–281). Murray (1987), however, reported on a survey at the University of Western Ontario in which faculty were asked to evaluate the usefulness of SETs as feedback; 54 percent, 65 percent, and 78 percent endorsed the usefulness of global SETs, student comments, and ratings of specific teaching behaviors respectively.

Lin, McKeachie and Tucker (1984) compared statistical summaries of SETs and written comments in promotion and salary decisions. Previous research had shown that teaching ability in general, and statistical summaries of SETs in particular, had little effect on promotion decisions compared to research productivity. Based on theories of influence developed in social psychology, they reasoned that more vivid and concrete presentations of SETs might increase their importance in promotion decisions. In their experimental design, simulated promotion dossiers were prepared in which evidence for teaching ability was presented as statistical summaries alone or as statistical summaries supplemented by direct quotations of student comments that were consistent with the statistical information. Staff in the dossiers were depicted to be of high or medium teaching ability. Their results showed that for the most able teachers, the effects of statistical summaries and comments were more positive than statistical summaries alone. For the less able teachers, the effects of statistical summaries and comments were more negative than statistical summaries alone. Thus, the student comments seemed to increase the credibility and enhance the impact—for good or for bad—of the statistical summaries. Because the researchers did not consider comments alone or comments that were inconsistent with the statistical summaries, there was no basis for comparing the relative impact of the two sources of information.

The research by Braskamp and his colleagues demonstrates that student comments, at least on a global basis, can be reliably scored and that these scores agree substantially with students' responses to overall rating items. This supports the generality of the ratings. Their findings supported the usefulness of student comments (in addition to rating items) for purposes of diagnostic feedback, but did not indicate the relative usefulness of the unedited, original comments as opposed to the results of detailed content analyses. Both the Murray survey results and the Lin, McKeachie and Tucker experimental study suggest that student comments may be more useful than global ratings, but Murray's study suggests that ratings on specific components may be even more useful. Perhaps, as may be implied by Ory and Braskamp (1981), the useful information from comments that cannot be obtained from rating items is idiosyncratic information that cannot easily be classified into generalizable categories, that is so specific that its value would be lost if it was sorted into broader categories, or that cannot be easily interpreted without knowledge of the particular context. From this perspective, the attempt to systematically analyze student comments may be counterproductive. If such analyses are to be pursued, then further research is needed to demonstrate that this lengthy and time consuming exercise will provide useful and reliable information that is not obtainable from the more cost effective rating items.

VALIDITY

The Construct Validation Approach to Validity

Abrami, d'Apollonia, and Cohen (1990) note that there are two disparate views on how to validate SETs. In one, students are seen as the consumers of teaching and SETs provide a measure of consumer satisfaction. From this perspective the ratings are valid so long as they accurately reflect student feelings. In the other view, SETs are valid if they accurately reflect teaching effectiveness. This second perspective is more controversial, is the focus of most validity research, and is the emphasis here.

SETs, as one measure of teaching effectiveness, are difficult to validate since no single criterion of effective teaching is sufficient. Historically, researchers have emphasized a narrow, criterion-related approach to validity in which student learning is viewed as the only criterion of effective teaching. Such a restrictive framework, however, inhibits a better understanding of what is being measured by SETs, of what can be inferred from SETs, and how findings from diverse studies can be understood within a common framework. Instead, Marsh (1984b, 1987) advocated a construct validation approach, in which SETs are posited be positively related to a wide variety of other indicators of effective teaching and specific rating factors are required to be most highly correlated with variables to which they are most logically and theoretically related. Within this framework, evidence for the long-term stability of SETs, the generalizability of ratings of the same instructor in different courses, the agreement of SETs and student written comments, and the agreement in matching scales from two different SET instruments can be interpreted as support for the validity of SETs. The most widely accepted criterion of effective teaching is student learning, but other criteria include changes in student behaviors, instructor self-evaluations, the evaluations of peers and/or administrators who actually attend class sessions, the frequency of occurrence of specific behaviors observed by trained observers, and the effects of experimental manipulations. A construct validity approach to the study of SETs now appears to be widely accepted (e.g., Cashin, 1988; Howard, Conway, and Maxwell, 1985).

In this section we examine empirical relations between SETs and other potential indicators of effective teaching. The intent is not specifically to evaluate the construct validity of these other criteria as indicators of effective teaching, but to some extent this is inevitable. One of the most difficult problems in validating interpretations of a measure is to obtain suitable criterion measures. To the extent that criterion measures are not reliably measured, or do not validly reflect effective teaching, then they will not be useful for testing the construct validity of SETs. More generally, criterion measures that lack reliability or validity should not be used as indicators of effective teaching for research, policy formation, feedback to faculty, or administrative decision making.

Student Learning—The Multisection Validity Study

Student learning, particularly if inferred from an objective, reliable, and valid test, is probably the most widely accepted criterion of effective teaching. Learning, however, is not generally appropriate as an indicator of effective teaching in universities. Examination scores cannot be compared across departments, across different courses within the same departments, or—except in special circumstances—even across offerings of the same course taught by different teachers. It may be reasonable to compare pretest and post-test scores as an indicator of learning, but it is not valid to compare the pretest-posttest changes in different courses. It may be useful to determine the percentage of students who successfully master behavioral objectives, but it is not valid to compare percentages obtained from different courses. In a very specialized, highly controlled setting it may be valid to compare teachers in terms of operationally defined learning, and this is the intent of multisection validity studies. Most university teaching, however, does not take place in such a setting. SETs are related to learning in such a limited setting on the assumption that such results will generalize to settings where learning is not an adequate basis for assessing effective teaching, and not to demonstrate the appropriateness of learning as a criterion of effective teaching in those other settings.

The multisection validity paradigm
In the ideal multisection validity study: a) there are many sections of a large multisection course; b) students are randomly assigned to sections, or at least enroll without any knowledge about the sections or who will teach them, so as to minimize initial differences between sections; c) there are pretest measures that correlate substantially with final course performance for individual students that are used as covariates; d) each section is taught completely by a separate instructor; e) each section has the same course outline, textbooks, course objectives, and final examination; f) the final examination is constructed to reflect the common objectives by some person who does not actually teach any of the sections, and, if there is a subjective component, it is graded by an external person; g) students in each section evaluate teaching effectiveness on a standardized evaluation instrument, preferably before they know their final course grade and without knowing how performances in their section compares with that of students in other sections; and h) section-average SETs are related to section-average examination performance, (see Yunker, 1983, for discussion on the unit-of-analysis issue) after controlling for pretest measures (for general discussion see Abrami, d'Apollonia, and Cohen, 1990; Benton, 1979; Cohen, 1981, 1987; Marsh, 1984b, 1987; Marsh and Overall, 1980; Yunker, 1983). Support for the validity of the SETs is demonstrated when the sections that evaluate the teaching as most effective near the end of the course are also the sections that perform best on standardized final examinations, and when plausible counter explanations are not viable.

Methodological Problems
Rodin and Rodin (1972) reported a negative correlation between section-average grade and section-average evaluations of graduate students teaching different quiz sections. Ironically, this highly publicized study did not constitute a multisection validity study as described above, and contained serious methodological problems (e.g., Cohen, 1987; Doyle, 1975; Frey, 1978; Marsh, 1987): the ratings were not of the instructor in charge of the course but of teaching assistants who played an ancillary role; a negative correlation might be expected since it would be the less able students who would have the most need for the supplemental services provided by the teaching assistants; the study was conducted during the third term of a year-long course and students were free to change teaching assistants between terms and were not even required always to attend sections led by the same teaching assistant during the third term; there was no adequate measure of end-of-course achievement in that performance was evaluated with problems given at the end of each segment of the course, and students could repeat each exam as many as six times without penalty; and these negative findings are generally inconsistent with the findings of subsequent research. In reviewing this study, Doyle (1975) stated that "to put the matter bluntly, the

attention received by the Rodin and Rodin study seems disproportionate to its rigor, and their data provide little if any guidance in the validation of student ratings.'' (p.59). In retrospect, the most interesting aspect of this study was that such a methodologically flawed study received so much attention.

Even when the design of multisection validity studies is more adequate, numerous methodological problems may still exist. First, the sample size in any given study is usually small—about 15 sections—and produces extremely large sampling errors. As noted by Abrami, d'Apollonia, and Cohen (1990), however, this problem can be overcome in part by meta-analyses of all such studies. Second, most variance in achievement scores at all levels of education is attributable to student presage variables and researchers are generally unable to find appreciable effects due to differences in teacher, school practice, or teaching method (Cooley and Lohnes, 1976; McKeachie, 1963). Thus it may be that instructors have only a limited effect on what students learn. In multisection validity studies, however, so many characteristics of the setting are held constant, that differences in student learning due to differences in teaching effectiveness are even further attenuated in relation to likely effects in more representative settings. Hence, although the design is defensible, it is also quite weak for obtaining instructor produced achievement differences that are used to validate SETs. Third, the comparison of findings across different multisection validity studies is problematic, given the lack of consistency in measures of course achievement and student rating instruments. Although it may be possible to code study-level differences so as to evaluate their impact, comprehensive schemes (Abrami, d'Apollonia, and Cohen, 1990) are so complicated that this problem may not be resolvable. Fourth, performance on objectively scored examinations that have been the focus of multisection validity studies may be an unduly limited criterion of effective teaching (Dowell and Neal, 1982; Marsh and Overall, 1980). Other criteria of teaching effectiveness besides student learning—defined largely by multiple choice tests that measure lower-level objectives such as memory of facts and definition—should be considered. For example, Marsh and Overall (1980) found that sections who rated their teacher most highly were more likely to pursue further coursework in the area and to join the local computer club (the course was an introduction to computer programming), and that these criteria of effective teaching were not significantly correlated with student learning. Fifth, presage variables such as initial student motivation and particularly ability level must be equated across sections for comparisons to be valid. Even random assignment becomes ineffective at accomplishing this when the number of sections is large and the number of students within each section is small, because chance alone will create differences among the sections. This paradigm does not constitute an experimental design in which students are randomly assigned to treatment groups that are varied systematically in terms of experimentally manipulated variables, and so the advantages of random assignment are not so clear as in a standard experimental design.[1] Furthermore, the assumption of truly random assignment of students to classes in large scale field studies is almost always compromised by time-scheduling problems, students dropping out of a course after the initial assignment, missing data, etc. For multisection validity studies the lack of initial equivalence is particularly critical, since initial presage variables are likely to be a primary determinant of end-of-course achievement. For this reason it is important to have effective pretest measures even when there is random assignment. In summary, the multisection validity design is inherently weak and there are many methodological complications in its actual application.

Meta-analyses

Cohen (1981) conducted what appears to have been the most influential meta-analysis of multisection validity studies. In his review he included all known studies, regardless of methodological problems such as found in the Rodin and Rodin study. Across 68 multisection courses, student achievement was consistently correlated with SETs of Skill (.50), Overall Course (.47), Structure (.47), Student Progress (.47), and Overall Instructor (.43). Only ratings of Workload/Difficulty were unrelated to achievement. (The relation between Difficulty and achievement may be nonlinear but this possibility was apparently not considered.) The correlations were higher when ratings were of full-time teachers, when students knew their final grade before rating instructors, and when achievement tests were evaluated by an external evaluator. Other study characteristics (e.g., random assignment, course content, availability of pretest data) were not significantly related to the results. Many of the criticisms of the multisection validity study are at least partially answered by this meta-analysis, particularly problems due to small sample sizes and, perhaps, the issue of the multiplicity of achievement measures and student rating instruments. These results provide strong support for the validity of SETs.

    Cohen updated this meta-analysis in 1986 and provided a critical analysis and reanalysis in 1987 (see Cohen, 1987). In his 1987 reanalysis, Cohen placed more emphasis on the multidimensional nature of the SETs. For example, he distinguished between summary ratings that were aggregates across specific components and global ratings, he more critically evaluated the classification of specific

---

[1]The value of random assignment is frequently misunderstood in student evaluation research, and particularly in the multisection validity study. Random assignment is not an end, but merely a means to control for initial differences in treatment groups that would otherwise complicate the interpretation of treatment effects. The effectiveness of random assignment is positively related to the number of cases in each treatment group, but negatively related to the number of different treatment groups. In the multisection validity study the instruction provided by each teacher is a separate treatment, his or her students are the treatment group, and there is usually no a priori basis for establishing which of the many treatments is more or less effective. Hence, even with random assignment it is likely that some sections will have students who are systematically more able (prepared, motivated, etc.) than others, and this is likely to bias the results (also see Yunker, 1983).

dimensions, and he distinguished between specific dimensions inferred from single items and from multi-item scales. The reanalysis suggested that achievement/SET correlations were higher for global rating items than aggregated summary scores and for multi-item scales representing specific dimensions than single-item ratings of specific dimensions (presumably because multi-item scales are more reliable; see Rushton, Brainerd, and Pressley, 1983). Cohen (1987) also presented results for a subset of 41 "well-designed" studies; correlations between achievement and different SET components were Structure (.55), Interaction (.52), Skill (.50), Overall Course (.49), Overall Instructor (.45), Learning (.39), Rapport (.32), Evaluation (.30), Feedback (.28), Interest/Motivation (.15), and Difficulty (-.04), in which all but the last two were statistically significant. For an even more restrictive set of 25 "high quality" studies, the validity coefficients were somewhat lower, but the small N (less than 10 for all but the overall instructor rating) made comparisons dubious. On the basis of his meta-analyses, Cohen (1987, p.12) concluded that "I am confident that global ratings of the instructor and course, and certain rating dimensions such as skill, rapport, structure, interaction, evaluation, and student's self-rating of their learning can be used effectively as an integral component of a teaching evaluation system."

Feldman (1989a), based in part on earlier work by d'Apollonia and Abrami (1987) and Abrami, Cohen, and d'Apollonia (1988; see Feldman, 1990a), extended Cohen's (1981, 1987) meta-analysis by increasing the number of specific dimensions from 9 to 28. Cohen's 9 dimensions were represented by 16 dimensions in Feldman's analysis. For example, Cohen's conglomerate "skill" category—which correlated .51 with achievement—was represented by 3 dimensions in Feldman's analysis that correlated with achievement .34 (instructor's knowledge of the subject), .56 (clarity and understandableness), and .30 (teacher sensitivity to class level and progress). Hence, the strong correlation between skill and achievement in Cohen's study was primarily due to instructor clarity and understandableness. Similarly, the high correlation between structure and achievement in Cohen's study (r = .55) is more a function of teacher preparation and organization of the course (r = .57) than clarity of course objectives (r = .35) in Feldman's (1989a) reanalysis. Feldman also considered specific dimensions that he indicated were not represented in any of Cohen's dimensions, and some of these were significantly correlated with achievement: pursued and met objectives (.38), elocutionary skills (.38), enthusiasm (.29), personality characteristics(.25),intellectual challenge (.25), classroom management (.24), pleasantness of classroom atmosphere (.24), and nature, quality and frequency of feedback (.23). Both Feldman's and Cohen's reviews were based on a mix of studies using single-item and multi-item scales, and in this sense they are comparable. It should be noted, however, that single-item scales are less reliable than multi-item scales and thus likely to be less correlated with achievement (as noted by Cohen, 1987). Hence, the results of both reviews probably underestimate relations that would be obtained with a carefully constructed set of multi-item scales. Curiously, Feldman (1989a) chose not to interpret his results as an attempt to validate the specific dimensions. He noted, for example, that the specific dimensions are not alternative indicators of student learning. Whereas this is an appropriate rationale if validity is narrowly defined to be criterion-related validity, it is not appropriate within the broader perspective of construct validation that is emphasized here.

Particularly the Cohen (1987) and Feldman (1989a) meta-analyses indicate that some specific dimensions of the ratings are more highly correlated with achievement than are overall instructor ratings, further supporting the contention that SETs cannot be adequately understood if their multidimensionality is ignored. It also follows, as a statistical necessity, that an optimally weighted combination of specific components and the global ratings would be even more highly correlated with achievement. An important limitation in these meta-analyses, however, was their inability to determine the size of this optimal correlation based on multiple scores or the optimal weights for each dimension and the global ratings. Because of the lack of a uniform set of evaluation components in SET research, this problem is unlikely to be resolved in further meta-analytic research.

Counter Explanations.

The grading satisfaction hypothesis. Marsh (1984b, 1987; Marsh, Fleiner and Thomas, 1975; Marsh and Overall, 1980; also see Palmer, Carliner, and Romer, 1978) identified an alternative explanation for positive results in multisection validity studies that he called the grading satisfaction hypothesis (or a grading leniency effect). When course grades (known or expected) and performance on the final exam are significantly correlated, then higher evaluations may be due to: a) more effective teaching that produces greater learning and higher evaluations by students; b) increased student satisfaction with higher grades which causes them to "reward" the instructor with higher ratings independent of more effective teaching or greater learning; or c) initial differences in student characteristics (e.g., prior subject interest, motivation, and ability) that affect both teaching effectiveness and performance. The first hypothesis argues for the validity of SETs as a measure of teaching effectiveness, the second represents an undesirable bias in the ratings, and the third is the effect of presage variables that may be accurately reflected by the SETs.

Even when there are no initial differences between sections (and there are always at least random differences), either of the first two explanations is viable. Cohen (1987), for example, found that validity correlations were substantially higher when students already knew their final course grade, and noted that "a potential source of bias—are good teachers receiving high ratings or are students rewarding teachers who give high grades?—was empirically demonstrated to affect the correlational effect size.'' Palmer, Carliner, and Romer (1978) made similar distinctions but their research has typically been discussed in relation to the potential biasing effect of expected grades (also see Howard and Maxwell, 1980, 1982) rather than multisection validity studies. Dowell and Neal (1982) also suggest such distinctions, but then apparently confound the effects of grading leniency and initial differences in section-average ability in their review of multisection validity studies.

Abrami, d'Apollonia, and Cohen (1990) specifically cite Marsh's (1987) discussion of the grading satisfaction hypothesis, but then dismiss it so long as ''section differences in students and instructor grading practices, including timing, are uniform across classes'' (p.221). Whereas these are desirable characteristics and prerequisites of a good multisection validity study, they do not rule out the grading satisfaction hypothesis. Typically, there is no way of unconfounding the teaching effectiveness that supposedly led to the (good or poor) grades and (high or low) satisfaction with the grades if the grades and satisfaction are correlated. Abrami, Cohen, and d'Apollonia argue that ''the alleged effect of grading satisfaction will operate consistently, if at all, in each section of a multisection course unless instructors first produce differences in student learning. Under these conditions, grading satisfaction cannot explain mean section differences in either student ratings or student achievement'' (p.221). There are, however, several problems in this reasoning. First, there is an implicit assumption that all section differences in criterion test performance—systematic and random—are instructor-produced effects. This assumption is completely unrealistic and cannot even be tested without assessing teaching effectiveness independent of student learning and SETs. If there are section-average differences in test performance that are not due to the instructor—even random effects—and the resulting higher or lower course grades affect satisfaction, then the grading satisfaction hypothesis is likely to inflate the validity coefficients. Second, even if all section differences in criterion test performance did reflect instructor effects, there still is no way to unconfound the influences of grades and satisfaction with grades. This may be a moot issue if teaching effectiveness and satisfaction with grades are perfectly correlated—another dubious assumption in the Abrami Cohen, and d'Apollonia argument—but this is unlikely even in a tightly controlled multisection validity study. So long as there are section-average differences in satisfaction with grades that are independent of teaching effectiveness, the grading satisfaction hypothesis is viable. Third, as noted by Abrami, d'Apollonia, and Cohen (1990), ''the problem is especially pronounced when one is studying multiple classes outside the multisection paradigm where there is more variability in grading practices'' (p.221). Thus, if the results from the multisection paradigm are to generalize, it is important to know how much of the grade/SET correlation is due to teaching effectiveness and to satisfaction with grades.

This can only be examined in a setting in which the effects of effective teaching and satisfaction with grades are established separately.

In the two SEEQ studies (Marsh, Fleiner and Thomas, 1975; Marsh and Overall, 1980), the grading satisfaction hypothesis was not a viable alternative to the validity hypothesis. The researchers reasoned that in order for satisfaction with higher grades to affect SETs at the section-average level, section-average expected grades must differ at the time the student evaluations are completed. In both these studies SETs were collected before the final examination, and student performance measures administered prior to the final examination were not standardized across sections. Hence, while each student knew approximately how his or her performance compared to other students within the same section, there was no basis for knowing how the section-average performance of any one section compared with that of other sections, and thus there was no basis for differences between the sections in their satisfaction with expected grades. Consistent with this suggestion, section-average expected grades indicated by students at the time the ratings were collected did not differ significantly from one section to the next, and were not significantly correlated with section-average performance on the final examination (even though individual expected grades within each section were substantially correlated with examination performance). Since section-average expected grades at the time the ratings were collected did not vary, they could not be the direct cause of higher SETs that were positively correlated with student performance, or the indirect cause of the higher ratings as a consequence of increased student satisfaction with higher grades. Marsh (1987) further noted that since the grading satisfaction hypothesis can only be explained in terms of expected grades the use of actual grades may be dubious unless students already know their final grades when the SETs are collected. In studies where section-average expected grades and section-average exam performance are positively correlated, the grading satisfaction hypothesis cannot be so easily countered.

Reliability of section-average achievement differences. Surprisingly, the reliability of section-average differences in achievement is a critical problem that is largely ignored in multisection validity studies. For example, in their critique of multisection validity studies, Abrami, d'Apollonia, and Cohen (1990) noted that only about one third of the studies reported the reliability of individual achievement test scores, but they apparently failed to recognize that the more critical concern is the reliability of section-average achievement scores. Even if individual achievement scores are perfectly reliable, the reliability of section-average achievement scores will be zero if the average achievement score is similar in each section.[2] Because much of the variance in individual achievement is due to

[2]The intra-class correlation can be used to assess the reliability of section-average achievement in the same way that it is used to assess the reliability of section-average student ratings (see earlier discussion; also see Feldman,1977). This can be accomplished with a one-way ANOVA that divides

individual student characteristics, most of the variance is probably attributable to within-section differences. Hence, section-average achievement scores are likely to be much less reliable than section-average SETs.

If section-average differences in achievement are small or unreliable, then a modest SET/achievement correlation is the best that can be expected. It is only when there are large and reliable section-average differences in achievement that a small achievement/SET correlation reflects negatively on the validity of the SETs. Thus, the size and reliability of section-average differences in learning place an upper limit on the size of SET/achievement correlations. A more realistic estimate of the true SET/achievement relation would be a correlation that is corrected for unreliability in the section-average achievement and, perhaps, the section-average SETs. Because this issue is largely unexplored in individual studies and meta-analyses, there is no way determine how much higher the true validity coefficients—appropriately corrected for unreliability—would be than those that have been reported. We suspect, however, that the differences are substantial in some studies and large enough to be substantively important in most studies. It is clear that existing research has underestimated—seriously we suspect—the true correlation between section-average SETs and section-average achievement.

Student Study Strategies and Learning Outcomes
Prosser and Trigwell (1990, 1991) discussed the multisection validity paradigm and proposed that SETs should be evaluated in relation to student study strategies (e.g., deep vs. surface) and the quality of learning outcomes (varying from simple and concrete understanding to complex and abstract understanding). In a study of 11 classes from different disciplines, Prosser and Trigwell (1990) reported significant and positive correlations between global SETs and students adopting deeper study strategies. In the second study (Prosser and Trigwell, 1991), students from 11 sections of a Communications course completed SETs, a common final examination, and standardized instruments assessing study strategies and learning outcomes. Global ratings were negatively related (nonsignificantly) to final exam performance but were significantly and positively related to study strategies and to the learning outcome measure. Characterizing the learning outcome measure as the quality of learning and the exam score as the quantity of learning, the authors noted that the two components of learning were

variability in individual student scores into within-section and between-section components. If section-average differences are no larger than expected by chance, then the reliability of section-average scores is—by definition—zero. Estimates of reliability for section-average scores are higher when there are larger differences between sections, smaller differences within sections, and larger numbers of students within each section. Whereas these reliability estimates are not typically reported, the reliability should be higher when the average number of students in each section is larger (all other factors being equal—always a worrisome assumption) and this relation could be tested in meta-analyses.

almost unrelated. The authors, noting limitations in these studies, indicate that the results should be interpreted cautiously. Nevertheless, the research is heuristic and demonstrates one direction for expanding the nature of outcome variables in multisection validity studies.

Implications for Further Research
Multisection validity studies should be designed according to the criteria discussed earlier. The interpretation of multisection validity studies may be substantially affected by section-average differences in pretest scores, the type of achievement tests used to infer student learning, the quality of SETs used to infer instructional effectiveness, the expected grades at the time students evaluate teaching effectiveness, and the reliability of section-average differences in student achievement. Hence it is important to test for the statistical significance of such differences and to provide some indication of effect size or variance explained. Pretest measures should be substantially related to final examination performance of individual students, and multiple regressions relating pretest scores to examination scores should be summarized. Nevertheless, if initial section-average differences are large, then the statistical correction for such initial differences may be problematic. Furthermore, if section-average expected grades are significantly correlated with section-average examination performance, and if the size of the validity coefficient is substantially reduced when the effects of expected grades are controlled, then grading satisfaction may be a viable alternative explanation of the results. Further research is needed to evaluate the potential confounding between teaching effectiveness, student learning, satisfaction with grades, and SETs. Finally, there is need to expand the range of outcome measures to include other criteria such as student learning at different levels in the Bloom taxonomy, quality of learning and study strategies, and affective outcomes.

The reliability of section-average achievement scores is a critical concern that has been largely ignored in multisection validity studies. This problem reflects a negative bias—one that makes SETs appear to be less valid—in all existing research and meta-analyses. Because these reliability estimates are not reported, the size of this negative bias cannot be accurately estimated and cannot be corrected in meta-analyses. Nevertheless, we suspect that the negative bias is substantial. This is an important concern that must be considered in future research or reanalyses of existing research.

Abrami, d'Apollonia, and Cohen (1990) summarized problems with the implementation of meta-analyses of multi-section validity studies and provided a set of 75 study features that may influence the results. Existing research, however, is not adequate to establish the effects of these features leading the authors to conclude that many more studies are needed that are more fully documented in relation to their coding scheme. Whereas we fully endorse this recommendation, it is relevant to point out that few multisection validity studies have been conducted in the last decade. Hence, whereas problems identified by Abrami, Cohen, and d'Apollonia may not be inherent weaknesses in the multisection validity design, it may be a very long time before there is a sufficient body of research to resolve the problems. From a practical perspective, the size of the task of evaluating these study effects may be consistent with our conclusion that the paradigm is inherently weak.

The methodologically flawed study by Rodin and Rodin aroused considerable interest in multisection validity studies, and focused attention on the methodological weaknesses of the design. Perhaps more than any other type of study, the credibility of SETs has rested on this paradigm. Researchers' preoccupation with the multisection validity study has had both positive and negative aspects. The notoriety of the Rodin and Rodin study required that further research be conducted. Despite methodological problems and difficulties in the interpretation of results, meta-analyses demonstrate that sections for which instructors are evaluated more highly by students tend to do better on standardized examinations; a finding which has been taken as strong support for the use of the ratings. Furthermore, because the lack of reliability of section-average achievement scores have not been taken into account, SET/achievement correlations in existing research are likely to underestimate—substantially we believe—true SET/ achievement correlations. Nevertheless, the limited generality of the setting, the inherent weakness of the design, and the possibility of alternative explanations all dictate that it is important to consider other criterion measures and other paradigms in student-evaluation research.

Evaluations of Teaching Effectiveness by Different Evaluators

Most researchers emphasize that teaching effectiveness should be measured from multiple perspectives and with multiple criteria. Braskamp, Brandenburg, and Ory (1985) identify four sources of information for evaluating teaching effectiveness: students, colleagues, alumni, and instructor self-ratings. Ratings by students and alumni are substantially correlated, and ratings by each of these sources appear to be moderately correlated with self-evaluations. However, ratings by colleagues based on classroom observations do not seem to be systematically related to ratings by the other three sources. Braskamp, Brandenburg, and Ory recommend that colleagues should be used to review classroom materials such as course syllabi, assignments, tests, texts, and Scriven (1981) suggests that such evaluations should be done by staff from the same academic discipline from another institution in a trading of services arrangement that eliminates costs. While this use of colleagues is potentially valuable, we know of no systematic research that demonstrates the reliability or validity of such ratings.

Instructor Self-Evaluations
Validity paradigms in student evaluation research are often limited to a specialized setting (e.g., large multisection courses) or use criteria such as the retrospective ratings of former students that are unlikely to convince skeptics. Hence, the validity of SETs will continue to be questioned until criteria are utilized that are both applicable across a wide range of courses and widely accepted as a indicator of teaching effectiveness (see Braskamp, Brandenburg, and Ory, 1985 for further discussion). Instructors' self-evaluations of their own teaching effectiveness is a criterion which satisfies both of these requirements. Furthermore, instructors can be asked to evaluate themselves with the same instrument used by their students, thereby testing the convergent and divergent validity of the different rating factors. Also, there is evidence to suggest that providing instructors with the discrepancies between their own self-evaluations and SETs by their students provides more incentive to improve teaching effectiveness than the SETs alone (see Marsh, 1987).

Despite the apparent appeal of instructor self-evaluations as a criterion of effective teaching, it has had limited application and many studies are not readily available in published form. In his meta-analysis based on 19 studies, Feldman (1989a) reported a mean r of .29 for overall ratings and mean rs of .15 to .42 in specific components of teaching effectiveness. Marsh (1982c; Marsh, Overall and Kesler, 1979b) apparently conducted the only studies where faculty in a large number of courses (81 and 329) were asked to evaluate their own teaching on the same multifaceted evaluation instrument that was completed by students. In both studies: a) separate factor analyses of teacher and student responses identified the same evaluation factors (see Table 1); b) student-teacher agreement on every dimension was significant (median rs of .49 and .45; Table 5) and typically larger than agreement on overall teaching effectiveness (rs of .32 in both studies); 3) mean differences between student and faculty responses were small and not statistically significant for most items, and were unsystematic when differences were significant (i.e., SETs were higher than faculty self-evaluations for some items but lower for others).

In MTMM studies, multiple traits (the student rating factors) are assessed by multiple methods (SETs and instructor self-evaluations). Consistent with the construct validation approach discussed earlier, correlations (see Table 5 for MTMM matrix from Marsh's 1982c study) between SETs and instructor self-evaluations on the same dimension (i.e., convergent validities—median rs of .49 and .45) were higher than correlations between ratings on nonmatching dimensions (median rs of −.04 and .02), and this is taken as support for the divergent validity of the ratings. In the second study, separate analyses were also performed for courses taught by teaching assistants, undergraduate level courses taught by faculty, and graduate level courses. Support for both the convergent

TABLE 5. Multitrait-multimethod matrix: Correlations between student ratings and faculty self-evaluations in 329 courses. (Reprinted from Marsh [1984b] by permission of the American Psychological Association.)

Factor	Instructor self-evaluation factor									Student evaluation factor								
	1	2	3	4	5	6	7	8	9	10	11	12	13	14	15	16	17	18
Instructor self-evaluations																		
1. Learning/Value	(83)																	
2. Enthusiasm	29	(82)																
3. Organization	12	01	(74)															
4. Group interaction	01	03	-15	(90)														
5. Individual rapport	-07	-01	07	02	(82)													
6. Breadth	13	12	13	11	-01	(84)												
7. Examinations	-01	08	26	09	15	20	(26)											
8. Assignments	24	-01	17	05	22	09	22	(70)										
9. Workload/Difficulty	03	-01	12	09	06	-04	09	21	(70)									
Student evaluations																		
10. Learning/Value	46	10	-01	08	-12	09	-04	08	02	(95)								
11. Enthusiasm	21	54	-04	-01	-02	-01	-03	-09	-09	45	(95)							
12. Organization	17	13	30	-03	04	07	09	00	-05	52	49	(93)						
13. Group interaction	19	05	-20	52	00	-02	-14	-04	-08	37	30	21	(98)					
14. Individual rapport	03	03	-05	13	28	-19	-03	-02	00	22	35	33	42	(96)				
15. Breadth	26	15	09	00	-14	42	00	09	02	49	34	56	17	15	(94)			
16. Examinations	18	09	01	-01	06	-09	17	-02	-06	48	42	57	34	50	33	(93)		
17. Assignments	20	03	02	09	-01	04	-01	45	12	52	21	34	30	29	40	42	(92)	
18. Workload/Difficulty	-06	-03	04	00	03	-03	12	22	69	06	02	-05	-05	08	18	-02	20	(87)

Note: Values in parentheses in the diagonals of the upper left and lower right matrices, the two triangular matrices, are reliability (coefficient alpha) coefficients (see Hull & Nie, 1981). The underlined values in the diagonal of the lower left matrix, the square matrix, are convergent validity coefficients that have been corrected for unreliability according to the Spearman Brown equation. The nine uncorrected validity coefficients, starting with Learning, would be .41, .48, .25, .46, .25, .37, .13, .36, and .54. All correlation coefficients are presented without decimal points. Correlations greater than .10 are statistically significant.

and divergent validity of the ratings was found in each set of courses (also see Howard, Conway, and Maxwell, 1985).

Feldman (1988) reviewed studies that evaluated a different aspect of agreement between student and faculty perspectives. He examined 31 studies in which both students and instructors indicated the specific components of teaching effectiveness that are most important to effective instruction. The average correlation of .71 between the patterns of importance ratings indicated substantial agreement between the two groups. There were, however, some systematic differences: students placed somewhat more importance on teachers stimulating interest, having good elocutionary skills, and being available and helpful, whereas faculty placed somewhat more emphasis on challenging students, motivating students, encouraging self-initiated learning, and setting high standards. These findings are important in countering the frequently voiced concern that students and instructors differ substantially on what constitutes effective teaching. Because students and faculty do agree on the relative importance of different components of effective teaching, this research offers additional support for the construct validity of SETs and for the importance of considering their multidimensionality. It is also interesting to note that the pattern of correlations between specific dimensions and achievement in multisection validity studies (Feldman, 1989a) is not very highly correlated with the pattern of importance ratings by either students (.42) or faculty (.31).

This research on instructors' self-evaluations has important implications. First, the fact that SETs show significant agreement with instructor self-evaluations provides clear evidence for their validity, and this agreement can be examined in nearly all instructional settings. Second, there is good evidence for the validity of SETs for both undergraduate and graduate level courses (Marsh, 1982c). Third, support for the divergent validity demonstrates the validity of each specific rating factor as well as of the ratings in general, and argues for the importance of using systematically developed, multifactor evaluation instruments.

In discussing instructor self-evaluations, Centra speculated that prior experience with SETs may influence self-evaluations (Centra, 1975, 1979, 1989). In particular, he suggested that instructors may initially overestimate their teaching effectiveness and that they may lower their self-evaluations as a consequence of having been previously evaluated by students so that their ratings would be expected to be more consistent with SETs (Centra, 1979). If instructors were asked to predict how students would evaluate them, then Centra's suggestion might constitute an important methodological problem for self-evaluation studies. However, both SEEQ studies specifically instructed the faculty to rate their own teaching effectiveness as they perceived it even it they felt that their students would disagree, and not to report how their students would rate them. Hence, the fact that most of the instructors in these studies had been previously evaluated does not seem to be a source of invalidity in the interpretation of the results (also see Doyle, 1983). Furthermore, given that the average of SETs is a little over 4 on a 5-point response scale, if instructor self-evaluations are substantially higher than SETs before they receive any feedback from SETs as suggested by Centra, then faculty on average may have unrealistically high self-perceptions of their own teaching effectiveness. A critical issue is whether exposure to prior SETs enhances or diminishes the validity of instructor self-evaluations. A systematic examination of how instructor self-perceptions change, or do not change, as a consequence of student feedback is a fruitful area for further research.

Ratings by Peers

Peer ratings, based on actual classroom visitation, are often proposed as indicators of effective teaching (Braskamp, Brandenburg, and Ory, 1985; Centra, 1979; Cohen and McKeachie, 1980; French-Lazovich, 1981; also see Aleamoni, 1985), and hence a criterion for validating SETs. In studies where peer ratings are *not* based upon classroom visitation (e.g., Blackburn and Clark, 1975; Guthrie, 1954; Maslow and Zimmerman, 1956), SETs and peer ratings are substantially correlated, but it is likely that peer ratings are based on information from students. Centra (1975) compared peer ratings based on classroom visitation and SETs at a newly established university, thus reducing the probable confounding of the two sources of information. Three different peers evaluated each teacher on two occasions, but there was a relative lack of agreement among peers (mean $r = .26$) which calls into question their value as a criterion of effective teaching and precluded any good correspondence with SETs ($r = .20$).

Morsh, Burgess, and Smith (1956)[3] correlated SETs, student achievement, peer ratings, and supervisor ratings in a large multisection course. SETs correlated with achievement, supporting their validity. Peer and supervisor ratings, though significantly correlated with each other, were not related to either SETs or to achievement, suggesting that peer ratings may not have value as an indicator of effective teaching. Webb and Nolan (1955)[3] reported good correspondence between SETs and instructor self-evaluations, but neither of these indicators was positively correlated with supervisor ratings (which the authors indicated to be like peer ratings). Howard, Conway, and Maxwell (1985) found moderate correlations between SETs and instructor self-evaluations, but ratings by colleagues were not significantly correlated with SETs, self-evaluations, or the ratings of trained observers.

Other reviews of the peer evaluation process in higher education settings (e.g., Centra, 1979; Cohen and McKeachie, 1980; Braskamp, Brandenburg, and Ory,

---

[3]These two studies were conducted in a military settings which may limit their generality. Feldman (1989b), for example, specifically excluded them in his review of research within a university setting.

1985; French-Lazovich, 1981) have also failed to cite studies that provide empirical support for the validity of peer ratings based on classroom visitation as an
indicator of effective college teaching or as a criterion for SETs. Cohen and
McKeachie (1980) and Braskamp, Brandenburg, and Ory (1985) suggested that
peer ratings may be suitable for formative evaluation, but suggested that they
may not be sufficiently reliable and valid to serve as a summative measure.
Murray (1980), in comparing SETs and peer ratings, found peer ratings to be
"(1) less sensitive, reliable, and valid; (2) more threatening and disruptive of
faculty morale: and (3) more affected by non-instructional factors such as research productivity" (p.45) than SETs. Ward, Clark and Harrison (1981; also
see Braskamp, Brandenburg, and Ory, 1985) suggested a methodological problem with the collection of peer ratings in that the presence of a colleague in the
classroom apparently affects the classroom performance of the instructor and
provides a threat to the external validity of the procedure. In summary, peer
ratings based on classroom visitation do not appear to be very reliable or to
correlate substantially with SETs or with any other indicator of effective teaching. While these findings neither support nor refute the validity of SETs, they
clearly indicate that the use of peer evaluations of university teaching for personnel decisions is unwarranted (see Scriven, 1981 for further discussion).

Behavioral Observations By External Observers
At the precollege level, observational records compiled by specially trained
observers are frequently found to be positively correlated with both SETs of
teaching effectiveness and student achievement (see Rosenshine, 1971; Rosenshine and Furst, 1973 for reviews), and similar studies at the tertiary level are
also encouraging (see Dunkin, 1986; Murray, 1980). Murray (1976) found high
positive correlations between observers' frequency-of-occurrence estimates of
specific teaching behaviors and an overall student rating. Cranton and Hillgartner
(1981) examined relationships between SETs and specific teaching behaviors
observed on videotaped lectures in a naturalistic setting; SETs of effectiveness of
discussion were higher "when professors praised student behavior, asked questions and clarified or elaborated student responses" (p.73); SETs of organization
were higher "when instructors spent time structuring classes and explaining
relationships"(p.73). Murray (1980) concluded that SETs "can be accurately
predicted from outside observer reports of specific classroom teaching behaviors" (p.31).
    In one of the most ambitious observation studies, Murray (1983) trained
observers to estimate the frequency of occurrence of specific teaching behaviors
of 54 university instructors who had previously obtained high, medium or low
SETs in other classes. A total of 18-to-24 sets of observer reports were collected
for each instructor. The median of single-rater reliabilities (i.e., the correlation

between two sets of observational reports) was .32, but the median reliability for the average response across the 18-24 reports for each instructor was .77. Factor analysis of the observations revealed nine factors, and their content resembled factors in SETs described earlier (e.g., Clarity, Enthusiasm, Interaction, Rapport, Organization). The observations significantly differentiated among the three criterion groups of instructors, but were also modestly correlated with a set of background variables (e.g., sex, age, rank, class size). Unfortunately, Murray only considered SETs on an overall instructor rating item, and these were based upon ratings from a previous course rather than the one that was observed. Hence, MTMM-type analyses could not be used to determine if specific observational factors were most highly correlated with matching student rating factors. The findings do show, however, that instructors who are rated differently by students do exhibit systematically different observable teaching behaviors.

Systematic observations by trained observers are positively correlated with both SETs and student achievement, even though peer ratings apparently are not systematically correlated with either SETs or student achievement. A plausible reason for this difference lies in the reliability of the different indicators. Class-average SETs are quite reliable, but the average agreement between ratings by any two students (i.e., the single rater reliability) is generally in the .20's. Hence, it is not surprising that agreement between two peer visitors who attend only a single lecture and respond to very general items is low. When observers are systematically trained and asked to rate the frequency of very specific behaviors, and there is a sufficient number of ratings of each teacher by different observers, then it is reasonable that their observations will be more reliable than peer ratings and more substantially correlated with SETs. However, further research is needed to clarify this suggestion. For example, Howard, Conway, and Maxwell (1985) examined both external observer ratings by trained graduate students and colleague ratings by untrained peers, but found that neither was significantly correlated with the other, with instructor self-evaluations, or with SETs. While peer ratings and behavioral observations have been considered as separate in the present article, the distinction may not be so clear in actual practice; peers can be trained to estimate the frequency of specific behaviors and some behavior observation schedules look like rating instruments.

The agreement between multifaceted observation schedules and multiple dimensions of SETs appears to be an important area for future research. However, a word of caution must be noted. The finding that specific teaching behaviors can be reliably observed and do vary from teacher to teacher, does not mean that they are important. Here, as with SETs, specific behaviors and observational factors must also be related to external indicators of effective teaching. In this respect the simultaneous collection of several indicators of effective teaching is important.

TABLE 6. Correlations between overall evaluations of teaching effectiveness by different groups based on Feldman's (1989a) review (below main diagonal) and on the Howard, Conway, and Maxwell (1985) study.

		1	2	3	4	5	6
1 Current students	Mean r	1	.74**	.19	.24	—	.34*
	No.						
2 Former students	Mean r	.69**	1	.33*	.08	—	.31*
	No.	6					
3 Colleagues	Mean r	.55**	.33^a	1	−.12	—	−.13
	No.	14	1				
4 External observers	Mean r	.50**	.08^b	−.12^b	1	—	.18
	No.	5	1	1			
5 Administrators	Mean r	.39**	c	.48**	c	1	—
	No.	11	c	5	c		
6 Self-evaluations	Mean r	.29**	.31^a	.15*	.22^b	.08	1
	No.	19	1	6	2	5	

[a]There were insufficient studies to compute significance across studies, but the correlation within each study was statistically significant.

[b]There were insufficient studies to compute significance, but the correlation within each study was not statistically significant.

[c]There were no studies of this relation.

Note. Coefficients below the main diagonal are a summary of information Feldman's (1989a, Table 1 and Figure 1) review and readers should refer to that study for further information. Feldman reported relations as rs based on overall ratings or an average r for specific components. A single r from each study is used in the averages and for computing statistical significance (two-tailed p-levels) across the studies. Coefficients from the Howard, Conway, Maxwell study are based on evaluations of the same set of 43 instructors by different raters (administrator ratings were not included in this study).

The Comparison of Ratings by Different Groups

Feldman (1989b) conducted an important review and meta-analysis of studies correlating overall evaluations of teaching effectiveness by current students, former students, colleagues, administrators, external observers, and instructor self-evaluations. Inspection of Table 6 (below the main diagonal) indicates that there are many combinations in which there are very few or no relevant studies. Of greater relevance to this chapter, the results are consistent with some conclusions offered here but appear to conflict with others. Consistent with research summarized here, the 3 highest correlations involve SETs by current students (the highest being the correlation between current and former students) whereas those involving self-evaluations are more modest. In contradiction to conclusions offered here, however, SETs were more highly correlated with ratings by colleagues, external observers, and administrators than with self-evaluations.

Important limitations noted by Feldman (1989b) in interpreting his results in terms of validity issues need to be considered. The most appropriate tests of validity are based on studies in which ratings by different groups are independent of knowledge of ratings by other groups. This is clearly not the case in most studies of colleague and administrator ratings. Feldman noted that SET/colleague and SET/administrator relations in his review were infrequently based on actual classroom observation, and the relations were probably inflated by colleagues and administrators basing their ratings in part on information from students (e.g., prior SETs, discussion with students, or discussions with the instructor about prior SETs). Feldman did not specifically take this issue into account in his review (i.e., did not relate results to a between-study variable reflecting this issue) in part because of the paucity of relevant studies, whereas conclusions in this chapter focus more specifically on studies actually based on classroom observation. In this sense, the two sets of conclusions are not comparable. Also, in some self-evaluation studies considered by Feldman, instructors made ratings of their teaching effectiveness in general rather than ratings in relation to the specific class that was evaluated by students (e.g., Blackburn and Clark, 1975) whereas the focus in this chapter has been on SETs and self-evaluations of the same course at the end of the term (also see earlier discussion).

The Howard, Conway, and Maxwell (1985) study is particularly relevant to understanding the apparent discrepancies between conclusions offered here and by Feldman because it simultaneously considered 5 of 6 sources included in Feldman's review (all but administrator ratings). Howard, Conway, and Maxwell contrasted SEEQ construct validity research like that summarized in this chapter that usually considers only two or three indicators of teaching effectiveness for large samples with their study that examined five different indicators in a single study for a small sample. Forty-three instructors from a variety of disciplines were each evaluated in one course by: current students in the course (mean N = 34 per class); former students who had previously taken the same course or one selected by the instructor as being similar (minimum N = 5); one colleague who was knowledgeable of the course content and who attended two class sessions; and 8 advanced graduate students specifically trained in judging teaching effectiveness who attended two class sessions. Howard, Conway, and Maxwell concluded (see Table 6, above the main diagonal) that "former-students and student ratings evidence substantially greater validity coefficients of teaching effectiveness than do self-report, colleague and trained observer ratings" (p.195). Whereas self-evaluations were modestly correlated with current SETs (.34) and former SETs (.31), colleague and observer ratings were not significantly correlated with each other, current SETs, or self-evaluations (colleague ratings were significantly correlated with ratings by former students but not current students). Howard, Conway, and Maxwell's conclusions are generally consistent with the present conclusions but less consistent with those based on the Feldman (1989b) review. The critical difference, apparently, is that the present conclusions and those by Howard, Conway and Maxwell are based on evaluations of teaching effectiveness in a particular classroom whereas those by Feldman—at least for ratings by nonstudents—are infrequently based on actual classroom observation. The apparent inconsistencies in methodology, results, and interpretations require more empirical studies like that of Howard, Conway, and Maxwell and more detailed meta-analyses that take into account between-study differences.

Experimental Manipulations

Researchers have considered the effects of experimentally manipulated components of teaching effectiveness on SETs and other indicators of effective teaching. Whereas some of this research has focused on the effects of potential biases to SETs (see subsequent discussion), studies of teacher clarity (Land, 1985; Land and Coombs, 1981; Marsh, 1987) and teacher expressiveness (Abrami, Leventhal, and Perry, 1982; Marsh and Ware, 1982; Marsh, 1987) demonstrate the important potential of this approach. Both these teaching behaviors are amenable to experimental and correlational designs, can be reliably judged by students and by external observers, are judged to be important components of teaching effectiveness by students and by teachers, and are related to student achievement in naturalistic and experimental studies. In experimental settings, scripted lessons which differ in these teaching behaviors are videotaped, and randomly assigned groups of subjects view different lectures, evaluate teaching effectiveness, and complete achievement tests. In studies of teacher clarity and teacher expressiveness, the manipulated teaching behaviors have been found to be systematically related to SETs and student achievement. Dunkin (1986), and Rosenshine and Furst (1973) were particularly impressed with the robustness of teacher clarity effects and their generality across different instruments, different raters, and different levels of education. The effects of teacher expressiveness are positively related to student achievement in both multisection validity studies already considered and the Dr. Fox studies considered below. Furthermore, when multiple dimensions of teaching effectiveness are evaluated, manipulations of these specific behaviors are substantially more strongly related to matching SET dimensions than to nonmatching SET dimensions. These patterns of findings support the inclusion of clarity and expressiveness on SET instruments, demonstrates that SETs are sensitive to natural and experimentally manipulated differences in these teaching behaviors, and support the construct validity of the SETs with respect to these teaching behaviors.

Research Productivity

Teaching and research are typically seen as the most important products of university faculty. Research helps instructors to keep abreast of new developments in their field and to stimulate their thinking, and this in turn provides one basis for predicting a positive correlation between research activity and SETs of teaching effectiveness. However, Blackburn (1974) caricatured two diametrically opposed opinions about the direction of the teaching/research relationship: (a) a professor cannot be a first rate teacher if he/she is not actively engaged in scholarship; and (b) unsatisfactory classroom performance results from the professor neglecting teaching responsibilities for the sake of publications. Marsh (1979, 1987; also see Centra, 1983; Feldman, 1987), in a review of studies that mostly used SETs as an indicator of teaching effectiveness, reported that there was virtually no evidence for a negative relationship between effectiveness in teaching and research; most studies found no significant relationship, and a few studies reported weak positive correlations. Marsh (1987; also see Frey, 1978) reported that the specific SET components most logically related to research were more highly correlated to research, but even these correlations were not substantial.

In trying to explain this lack of relation between teaching and research, Marsh (1987) argued that ability, effort, and reward structure were all critical variables. In a theoretical model of these relations, Marsh (1979, 1987) proposed that: a) the ability to be effective at teaching and research are *positively* correlated (a view consistent with the first opinion presented by Blackburn); b) time spent on research and teaching are *negatively correlated* (a view consistent with the second opinion presented by Blackburn) and may be influenced by a reward structure which systematically favors one over the other; c) effectiveness, in both teaching and research, is a function of both ability and time allocation; d) the positive relationship between abilities in the two areas and the negative correlation in time spent in the two areas will result in little or no correlation in measures of effectiveness in the two areas. Marsh reported some support for hypotheses (b), (c), and (d). In his review, Feldman (1987) found some indication that research productivity was positively correlated with time or effort devoted to research and, perhaps, negatively correlated with time or effort devoted to teaching. However, he found almost no support for the contention teaching effectiveness was related to time or effort devoted to either research or teaching. Thus, whereas there is some support for Marsh's model, important linkages were not supported and require further research.

In summary there appears to be a zero to low-positive correlation between measures of research productivity and SETs or other indicators of effective teaching, although correlations may be somewhat higher for student rating dimensions which are most logically related to research effectiveness. While these findings seem neither to support nor refute the validity of SETs, they do demonstrate that measures of research productivity cannot be used to infer teaching effectiveness or vice versa.

Summary and Implications of Validity Research
Effective teaching is a hypothetical construct for which there is no adequate single indicator. Hence, the validity of SETs or of any other indicator of effective

teaching must be demonstrated through a construct validation approach. SETs are significantly and consistently related to a number of varied criteria including the ratings of former students, student achievement in multisection validity studies, faculty self-evaluations of their own teaching effectiveness, and, perhaps, the observations of trained observers on specific processes such as teacher clarity. This provides support for the construct validity of the ratings. Colleague and administrator ratings not based on classroom observation show substantial agreement with SETs, but these results must be interpreted cautiously. In contrast, colleague and administrator ratings that were based on classroom visitation, and research productivity, were shown to have little correlation with SETs, and since they are also relatively uncorrelated with other indicators of effective teaching, their validity as measures of effective teaching is problematic.

Nearly all researchers argue strongly that it is absolutely necessary to have multiple indicators of effective teaching whenever the evaluation of teaching effectiveness is to be used for personnel/tenure decisions. This emphasis on multiple indicators is clearly reflected in research described in this chapter. However, it is critical that the validity of all indicators of teaching effectiveness, not just SETs, be systematically examined before they are actually used. It seems ironic that researchers who argue that the validity of SETs has not been sufficiently demonstrated, despite the preponderance of research supporting their validity, are so willing to accept other indicators which have not been tested or have been shown to have little validity.

Researchers seem less concerned about the validity of information that is given to instructors for formative purposes such as feedback for the improvement of teaching effectiveness. This perspective may be justified, pending the outcome of further research, since there are fewer immediate consequences and legal implications. Nevertheless, even for formative purposes, the continued use of any sort of information about teaching effectiveness is not justified unless there is systematic research that supports its validity and aids in its interpretation. The implicit assumption that instructors will be able to separate valid and useful information from that which is not when evaluating formative feedback, while administrators will be unable to make this distinction when evaluating summative material, seems dubious.

Marsh and Overall (1980) distinguished between cognitive and affective criteria of effective teaching, arguing for the importance of affective outcomes as well as cognitive outcomes. Those findings indicate that cognitive and affective criteria need not be substantially correlated, and appear to be differentially related to different SET components. Cognitive criteria have typically been limited to student learning as measured in the multisection validity paradigm, and there are problems with such a narrow definition. In contrast, affective criteria have been defined as anything that seems to be noncognitive, and there are even more problems with such an open-ended definition. Further research is needed to define more systematically what is meant by affective criteria, perhaps in terms of the affective domains described elsewhere (e.g., Krathwohl, Bloom and Masia, 1964), to operationally define indicators of these criteria, and to relate these to multiple student rating dimensions (Abrami, 1985). The affective side of effective teaching has not been given sufficient attention in SET research or, perhaps, in the study of teaching in general.

The disproportionate amount of attention given to the narrow definition of teaching effectiveness as student learning has apparently stifled research on a wide variety of criteria that are acceptable in the construct validation approach. While this broader approach to validation will undoubtedly provide an umbrella for dubious research as suggested by Doyle (1983), it also promises to bring new vigor and better understanding to SET research. In particular, there is a need for studies that consider many different indicators of teaching effectiveness in a single study. In his recent review of teaching and learning in the college classroom, McKeachie, et al. (1990) emphasized the need to expand traditional models to include recent emphases on student cognition and other educational outcomes such as motivation, self-concept, and self-regulated learning. Elaborating on this point, McKeachie (personal communication, 19 March, 1991) noted that "as I see it one of our major problems is that we've typically used final examinations constructed by instructors as the measure of learning or educational achievement." He indicated that there was insufficient research considering relations between a diverse array of educational outcomes (e.g., taking advanced coursework, independent reading, problem solving skills, attitude changes) and specific SET components. In future research, it is imperative that SET researchers substantially expand the range of validity criteria that are related to SETs.

POTENTIAL BIASES IN STUDENTS' EVALUATIONS

The study of potential biases to SETs is voluminous, typically atheoretical, frequently methodologically flawed, and often not based on an articulated definition of what constitutes a bias. This is, however, an important area of SET research. To the extent that SETs are biased it is important to understand the nature of the biases and how they can be controlled. Even though research suggests that SETs are not substantially biased, there is a belief among faculty that they are. For example, Marsh and Overall (1979b), consistent with other surveys of faculty (e.g., Jacobs, 1987), reported that faculty wanted teaching to be evaluated, but believed that SETs—as well as other indicators of effective teaching—were biased. Hence, it is important to counter such misconceptions. A comprehensive review of this research is beyond the scope of this chapter and interested readers are directed to the excellent series of articles by Feldman (1976a, 1976b, 1977, 1978, 1979, 1983, 1984, 1987, 1989a, 1989b), other review papers by Aubrect (1981), Cashin (1988), Marsh (1983, 1984b, 1985,

1987), and McKeachie (1973, 1979), monographs by Braskamp, Brandenburg, and Ory (1985), Centra (1979, 1989; Centra and Creech, 1976) and Murray (1980), and a chapter by Aleamoni (1981). Older reviews by Costin, Greenough and Menges (1971), Kulik and McKeachie (1975), and the annotated bibliography by de Wolf (1974) are also valuable.

Large-scale Empirical Studies
Marsh (1987) reviewed several large studies that have looked at the multivariate relationship between a comprehensive set of background characteristics and SETs. Between 5 percent and 25 percent of the variance in SETs could be explained, depending upon the nature of the SET items, the background characteristics, perhaps the academic discipline, and perhaps the institution(s) where the study was conducted. In comprehensive multivariate studies, Marsh (1980, 1983) found that a set of 16 background characteristics explained about 13 percent of the variance in the set of SEEQ dimensions. However, the amount of variance explained varied from more than 20 percent in the Overall Course rating and the Learning/Value dimension, to about 2 percent of the Organization and Individual Rapport dimensions. Four background variables were most important and could account for most of the explained variance; more favorable ratings were correlated with higher prior subject interest, higher expected grades, higher levels of Workload/Difficulty, and a higher percentage of students taking the course for General Interest Only. A path analysis demonstrated that prior subject interest had the strongest impact on SETs, and that this variable also accounted for about one-third of the relationship between expected grades and SETs. Marsh (1983) demonstrated a similar pattern of results in five different sets of courses (one of which was the set of courses used in the 1980 study) representing diverse academic disciplines at the graduate and undergraduate level, although the importance of a particular characteristic varied somewhat with the academic setting.

A Construct Approach to the Study of Bias
The finding that a background characteristic is correlated with SETs does not mean that the ratings are biased. Support for a bias hypothesis, as with the study of validity, must be based on a construct approach. This approach requires that the background characteristics that are hypothesized to bias SETs are examined in studies which are relatively free from methodological flaws using different approaches, and interpreted in relation to a specific definition of bias. Important and common methodological problems in the search for potential biases to SETs include the following:

1. Using correlation to argue for causation—the implication that some variable biases SETs argues that causation has been demonstrated, whereas correlation only implies that a concomitant relation exists.

2. Neglect of the distinction between practical and statistical significance—all conclusions should be based upon some index of effect size as well as on tests of statistical significance.
3. Failure to consider the multivariate nature of both SETs and a set of potential biases.
4. Selection of an inappropriate unit of analysis. Since nearly all applications of SETs are based upon class-average responses, this is nearly always the appropriate unit of analysis. The size and even the direction of correlations based on class-average responses may be different from correlations obtained when the analysis is performed on responses by individual students. Hence, effects based on individual students as the unit of analysis must also be demonstrated to operate at the class-average level.
5. Failure to examine the replicability of findings in a similar setting and their generalizability to different settings—particularly in studies based on small sample sizes or a single academic department at a single institution.
6. The lack of an explicit definition of bias against which to evaluate effects—if a variable actually affects teaching effectiveness and this effect is accurately reflected in SETs, then the influence is not a bias.
7. Questions of the appropriateness of experimental manipulations—studies that attempt to simulate hypothesized biases with operationally defined experimental manipulations must demonstrate that the size and nature of the manipulation and the observed effects are representative of those that occur in natural settings (i.e., they must examine threats to the external validity of the findings).

Theoretical Definitions of Bias

Inadequate definition of what constitutes a bias has hindered research. Demonstrating a relation—even a causal relation—is insufficient. For example, research reviewed earlier suggests that teacher clarity is causally related to SETs (as well as student achievement), but it makes no sense to argue that teacher clarity biases SETs. Support for a bias hypothesis must be based on a theoretically defensible definition of what constitutes a bias. Marsh (1987) reviewed alternative definitions of bias and their weaknesses. One common definition, for example, suggests that SETs are biased to the extent that they are affected by variables not under the control of the teacher. According to this definition, however, grading leniency (students giving better-than-deserved ratings to instructors as a consequence of instructors giving better-than-deserved grades to students) is not a bias, since grading leniency is clearly under the control of the instructor. This definition also confuses bias with what Marsh referred to as "fairness." If a variable X legitimately influences the effectiveness of instruction and this influence is validly represented in SETs, then the influence of X should not be interpreted as a bias. For example, prior subject interest apparently affects teaching effectiveness in a way that is accurately reflected by SETs (see discussion below). In this respect, prior subject interest is not a bias to SETs. It may not, however, be "fair" to compare ratings in courses that differ substantially in prior subject interest for personnel decisions unless the influence is removed using statistical control or appropriately constructed norm groups. While there is need for further clarification of the issues of bias and fairness, it is also important to distinguish between these two concepts so that they are not confused. The "fairness" of SETs needs to be examined separately from, or in addition to, their validity and susceptibility to bias. Some researchers (e.g., Hoyt, Owens, and Grouling, 1973; Brandenburg, Slindle, and Batista, 1977; also see Howard and Bray, 1979) seem to circumvent the problem of defining bias by statistically controlling for potential biases with multiple regression techniques or by forming normative (cohort) groups that are homogeneous with respect to potential biases (e.g., class size). Whereas this procedure may be appropriate in some instances, its use requires that a causal relation has been demonstrated and must still be defended in relation to a theoretically defensible definition of bias or fairness. Consistent with this approach, for purposes of feedback from SEEQ, separate normative comparisons are made within each academic unit for teaching assistants, for undergraduate courses, and for graduate level courses so long as each resulting norm group has a sufficient number of classes.

Approaches to Exploring for Potential Biases

McKeachie (1973) argued that SETs could be better understood if researchers did not concentrate exclusively on trying to interpret background relations as biases, but instead examined the meaning of specific relations. Following this orientation, several approaches to the study of background influences have been utilized. The most frequently employed approach is simply to correlate class-average SETs with a class-average measure of a background variable hypothesized to bias SETs. Such an approach can be heuristic, but in isolation it can never be used to demonstrate a bias. Instead, hypotheses generated from these correlational studies should be explored in further research that more fully tests the construct validity of bias interpretations.

One approach is to isolate a specific variable, simulate the variable with an experimental manipulation, and examine its effect in experimental studies where students are randomly assigned to treatment conditions. The internal validity (see Campbell and Stanley, 1973, for a discussion of internal and external threats to validity) of interpretations is greatly enhanced since many counter explanations that typically exist in correlational studies can be eliminated. However, this can only be accomplished at the expense of many threats to the external validity of interpretations: the experimental setting or the manipulation may be so contrived that the finding has little generalizability to the actual application of SETs; the size of the experimental manipulation may be unrealistic; the nature of the variable in question may be seriously distorted in its "operationalization"; and effects shown to exist when the individual student is the unit-of-analysis may not generalize when the class-average is used as the unit-of-analysis. Consequently, while the results of such studies can be very valuable, it is still incumbent upon the researcher to explore the external validity of the interpretations and to demonstrate that similar effects exist in real settings where SETs are actually employed. The most fully documented use of this technique is the series of "Dr. Fox" studies that are discussed below.

An alternative approach—a construct approach—recommended by Marsh (1987) has been the basis of much SEEQ research. Two aspects of this approach were emphasized. First, consistent with the multidimensionality of the SETs, specific variables should be differentially related to SEEQ factors. For example, class size is most logically related (inversely) to the Group Interaction and Individual Rapport factors, and this logical relation is empirically testable. Support for the predicted pattern of findings argues for the construct validity of the ratings. The second aspect is based upon the assumption that a "bias" that is specific to SETs should have little impact on other indicators of effective teaching. If a variable is related both to SETs and to other indicators of effective teaching, then the validity of the ratings is supported. Employing this approach, Marsh asked instructors in a large number of classes to evaluate their own teaching effectiveness with the same SEEQ form used by their students, and the SEEQ factors derived from both groups were correlated with background characteristics. Support for the interpretation of a bias in this situation requires that some variable be substantially correlated with SETs, but not with instructor self-evaluations of their own teaching (also see Feldman, 1984). Of course, even when a variable is substantially correlated with both student and instructor self-evaluations, it is still possible that the variable biases both SETs and instructor self-evaluations (Abrami, d'Apollonia, and Cohen, 1990), but such an interpretation requires that the variable is not substantially correlated with yet other valid indicators of effective teaching. Also, when the pattern of correlations between a specific variable and the SEEQ factors for students response is similar to the pattern based on faculty self-evaluations using SEEQ, there is further support for the validity of the SETs.

Effects of Specific Background Characteristics
Emphasized in SEEQ Research

Results summarized below emphasize the description and explanation of the multivariate relations that exist between specific background characteristics and multiple dimensions of SETs. This is a summary of findings based upon some of the most frequently studied and/or the most important background characteristics, and of different approaches to understanding the relationships. In this section the effects of the five background characteristics that have been most extensively examined and shown to be related to some SET components in SEEQ research are examined: class size; workload/difficulty; prior subject interest; expected grades; reason for taking a course.

Class Size.
Class size is moderately correlated with Group Interaction and Individual Rapport (negatively, rs as large as −.30), but not with other SEEQ dimensions or with the overall ratings of course or instructor (Centra and Creech, 1976; Feldman, 1978, 1984; Marsh, Overall, and Kesler, 1979a; Marsh, 1980, 1983). There is also a significant nonlinear component to this relation in which small and very large classes were evaluated more favorably. However, since the majority of class sizes occur in the range where the relation is negative, the overall correlation is negative. A similar pattern of results was found between class size and instructor self-evaluations of their own teaching (Marsh, Overall, and Kesler, 1979a; also see Table 7). The specificity of the class size effect to dimensions most logically related to this variable, and the similarity of findings based on SETs and faculty self-evaluations argue that this effect is not a "bias" to SETs; rather, class size does have moderate effects on the aspects of effective teaching (primarily Group Interaction and Individual Rapport) to which it is most logically related and these effects are accurately reflected in the SETs. This discussion of the class size effect clearly illustrates why SETs cannot be adequately understood if their multidimensionality is ignored (also see Feldman, 1984; Frey, 1978) and why it is important to evaluate potential biases within a construct approach.

Prior Subject Interest
Marsh (1987; Marsh and Cooper, 1981; also see Feldman, 1977; Howard and Maxwell, 1980; Howard and Schmeck, 1979) reviewed previous studies of the relation of prior subject interest to SETs and faculty self-evaluations. The effect of prior subject interest on SEEQ scores was greater than that of any of the 15 other background variables considered by Marsh (1980, 1983). In different studies prior subject interest was consistently more highly correlated with Learning/Value (rs about .4) than with any other SEEQ dimensions (rs between .3 and −.12). Instructor self-evaluations of their own teaching were also positively correlated with both their own and their students' perceptions of students' prior subject interest (see Table 7). The self-evaluation dimensions that were most highly correlated with prior subject interest, particularly Learning/Value, were the same as with SETs. The specificity of the prior subject interest effect to dimensions most logically related to this variable, and the similarity of findings based on SETs and faculty self-evaluations argue that this effect is not a "bias" to SETs. Rather, prior subject interest is a variable that influences some aspects

TABLE 7. Background characteristics: Correlations with student ratings (S) and faculty self-evaluations (F) of their own teaching effectiveness (N = 183 undergraduate courses). (Reprinted from Marsh [1984b] by permission of the American Psychological Association.)

Background Characteristic	SEEQ Factor										
	Learn	Enthu	Organ	Group	Indiv	Brdth	Exams	Assign	Wrkld	Over Crse	Over Instr
Faculty rating "Scholarly production in their discipline" (1 = well below average to 5 = well above average)											
S	17	07	18	04	06	21	04	17	11	14	16
F	-03	-04	03	03	00	00	21	15	—	17	09
Students rating course workload/difficulty (1 = low to 5 = high)											
S	20	08	01	04	06	18	04	23	53	26	16
F	-03	-04	03	03	00	00	21	15	—	17	09
Faculty rating course workload/difficulty (1 = low to 5 = high)											
S	08	02	01	-03	04	02	05	12	—	15	08
F	07	03	15	-09	10	-06	21	21	53	29	16
Students rating expected course grade (1 = F to 5 = A)											
S	28	20	05	38	16	01	28	24	-25	26	27
F	11	-03	-07	17	-10	-11	-11	02	-19	-01	00

Faculty rating of "Grading leniency" (1 = *easy/lenient* to 5 = *hard/strict*)											
S	−04	−16	−06	06	−08	−05	−05	−02	26	−06	−10
F	00	04	06	16	14	08	32	19	28	14	03
Class size/enrollment (actual number of students enrolled)											
S	−24	−04	−13	−36	−21	−09	−22	−09	−07	−18	−20
F	−02	03	10	−43	−17	−03	−03	−11	−04	−04	−09
Faculty rating "Enjoy teaching relative to other duties" (1 = *extremely unenjoyable* to 5 = *extremely enjoyable*)											
S	25	34	18	22	33	00	20	09	03	29	32
F	24	39	01	10	12	−21	−20	03	−03	15	22
Faculty rating "Ease of teaching particular course" (1 = *very easy* to 5 = *very difficult*)											
S	07	−01	10	11	06	09	09	01	05	03	08
F	−12	−16	−07	17	12	06	05	04	17	−14	−10

Note: SSEQ = Students' Evaluations of Educational Quality. Correlations are presented without decimal points; all those greter than .15 are statistically significant. For more detail, see Marsh and Overall (1979b).

of effective teaching, particularly Learning/Value, and these effects are accurately reflected in both the SETs and instructor self-evaluations. Higher student interest in the subject apparently creates a more favorable learning environment and facilitates effective teaching, and this effect is validly reflected in SETs as well as faculty self-evaluations.

Prior subject interest apparently influences teaching effectiveness in a way that is validly reflected in SETs, and so the influence should not be interpreted as a bias to SETs. However, to the extent that the influence is inherent in a particular course content, it may represent a source of "unfairness" when ratings are used for personnel decisions. If further research confirms these interpretations, then it may be appropriate to use normative comparisons or cohort groups to correct for this influence.

Workload/Difficulty

Workload/Difficulty is frequently cited by faculty as a potential bias to SETs in the belief that offering less demanding courses will lead to better SETs. For this reason, Workload/Difficulty has been considered as a potential bias in SEEQ studies even though it is also one of the SEEQ factors. Whereas the Workload/ Difficulty effect was one of the largest in SEEQ research, the direction of the effect was opposite to that expected if this variable was a bias; Workload/ Difficulty was positively correlated with SETS. Other research reviewed by Marsh (1987) was generally consistent with SEEQ results. Marsh and Overall (1979b) also reported that instructor self-evaluations of their own teaching effectiveness tended to be positively related to Workload/Difficulty (see Table 7). Results based on the large, multi-institution data base for the IDEA instrument suggest that SETs are even more positively related to Workload/Difficulty than are SEEQ results (see Cashin, 1988). Since the direction of the Workload/ Difficulty effect is opposite to that predicted as a potential bias, and since this finding is consistent for both SETs and instructor self-evaluations, Workload/ Difficulty does not appear to constitute a bias to SETs.

Expected Grades

SEEQ research and literature reviews (e.g., Centra, 1979; Feldman, 1976a; Marsh, Overall, and Thomas, 1976) have typically found class-average expected grades to be positively correlated with SETs. The critical issue is how this relation should be interpreted, and there are three quite different explanations for this finding. (1) The grading leniency hypothesis proposes that instructors who give higher-than-deserved grades will be rewarded with higher-than-deserved SETs, and this constitutes a serious bias to SETs. (2) The validity hypothesis proposes that better expected grades reflect better student learning, and that a positive correlation between student learning and SETs supports the validity of SETs. In multisection validity studies, for example, relations between grades and

SETs were interpreted as support for the validity of SETs although the grading leniency hypothesis may be a viable counter-explanation. (3) The student characteristics hypothesis proposes that preexisting student presage variables such as prior subject interest may affect student learning, student grades, and teaching effectiveness, so that the expected grade effect is spurious. While these explanations of the expected grade effect have quite different implications, it should be noted that grades, actual or expected, must surely reflect some combination of student learning, the grading standards employed by an instructor, and preexisting presage variables.

Path analyses. Marsh (1980, 1983) examined the relations among expected grades, prior subject interest, and SETs in a path analysis (also see Aubrect, 1981; Feldman, 1976a). Across all rating dimensions, nearly one-third of the expected grade effect could be explained in terms of prior subject interest. Since prior subject interest precedes expected grades, a large part of the expected grade effect is apparently spurious, and this finding supports the student characteristic hypothesis. Marsh, however, interpreted the results as support for the validity hypothesis in that prior subject interest is likely to impact student performance in a class, but is unlikely to affect grading leniency. Hence, support for the student characteristics hypothesis may also constitute support for the validity hypothesis; prior subject interest produces more effective teaching which leads to better student learning, better grades, and higher evaluations. This interpretation, however, depends on a definition of bias in which SETs are not "biased" to the extent that they reflect variables which actually influence effectiveness of teaching.

In a similar analysis, Howard and Maxwell (1980; also see Howard and Maxwell, 1982), found that most of the covariation between expected grades and class-average overall ratings was eliminated by controlling for prior student motivation and student progress ratings. In their path analysis, prior student motivation had a causal impact on expected grades that was nearly the same as reported in SEEQ research and a causal effect on overall ratings which was even larger, while the causal effect of expected grades on SETs was smaller than that found in SEEQ research. They concluded that "the influence of student motivation upon student performance, grades, and satisfaction appears to be a more potent contributor to the covariation between grades and satisfaction than does the direct contaminating effect of grades upon student satisfaction" (p. 818).

Faculty self-evaluations. Marsh and Overall (1979b) examined correlations among SETs and instructor self-evaluations of teaching effectiveness, SETs of expected grades, and teacher self-evaluations of their own "grading leniency" (see Table 7). Correlations between expected grades and SETs were positive and modest (rs between .01 and .28) for all SEEQ factors except Group Interaction (r = .38) and Workload/Difficulty (r = −.25). Correlations between expected grades and faculty self-evaluations were close to zero (rs between −.11

and .11) except for Group Interaction (r = .17) and Workload/Difficulty (r = -.19). Correlations between faculty self-perceptions of their own "grading leniency" (on an "easy/lenient grader" to "hard/strict grader" scale) with both student and teacher evaluations of effective teaching were small (rs between -.16 and .19) except for ratings of Workload/Difficulty (rs of .26 and .28) and faculty self-evaluations of Examinations/Grading (r = .32). In a separate study Marsh (1976) also reported small, generally nonsignificant correlations between faculty self-evaluations of their grading leniency and SETs, but found that "easy" graders received somewhat (significantly) lower overall course and Learning/value ratings. The correlations between grading leniency and SETs, and the similarity in the pattern of correlations between expected grades and ratings by students and by faculty, seem to argue against the interpretation of the expected grade effect as a bias. Nevertheless, the fact that expected grades were more positively correlated with SETs than with faculty self-evaluations may provide some support for a grading leniency bias.

Experimental manipulation of expected grades. Some researchers have argued that the expected grade effect can be better examined by randomly assigning students to different groups which are given systematically different grade expectations. Marsh (1987; also see Abrami, Dickens, Perry, and Leventhal, 1980) reviewed studies of this sort in which grades were experimentally manipulated by assigning grades that were different from the ones that students had earned or expected, or using different grading standards in different sections of the same course. Particularly when students received grades that were different from what they had earned, the nature of the experimental manipulations did not seem to match naturally occurring differences in grading standards. Even when grading standards were manipulated for different sections of the same course, it is likely that students from different sections realized they were being graded according to different standards.

Abrami et al. (1980) conducted what appears to be the most methodologically sound study of the effects of experimentally manipulated grading standards on SETs. After reviewing previous research they described two "Dr. Fox" type experiments in which grading standards were experimentally manipulated. Groups of students viewed a videotaped lecture, rated teacher effectiveness, and completed an objective exam. Students returned two weeks later when they were given their examination results and a grade based on their actual performance but scaled according to different grading standards (i.e., an "average" grade earning a B, C+, or C). The subjects then viewed a similar videotaped lecture by the same instructor, again evaluated teacher effectiveness, and took a test on the content of the second lecture. The manipulation of grading standards had no effect on performance on the second achievement test and weak inconsistent effects on SETs. There were also other manipulations (e.g., instructor expressiveness, content, and incentive), but the effect of grading standards accounted for no more than 2 percent of the variance in SETs for any of the conditions, and failed to reach statistical significance in some. Not even the direction of the effect was consistent across conditions, and stricter grading standards occasionally resulted in higher ratings. These findings fail to support the contention that grading leniency produces an effect that is of practical significance, although the external validity of this interpretation may also be questioned.

Other approaches. Marsh (1982a) compared differences in expected grades with differences in SETs for pairs of offerings of the same course taught by the same instructor on two different occasions. He reasoned that differences in expected grades in this situation probably represent differences in student performance, since grading standards are likely to remain constant, and differences in prior subject interest were small and relatively uncorrelated with differences in SETs. He found even in this context that students in the more favorably evaluated course tended to have higher expected grades, which argued against the grading leniency hypothesis. It should be noted, however, that while this study is in a setting where differences due to grading leniency are minimized, there is no basis for contending that the grading leniency effect does not operate in other situations. Also, the interpretation is based on the untested assumption that differences in expected grades reflected primarily differences in student performance rather than differences in the grading standards by the instructor.

Peterson and Cooper (1980) compared SETs of the same instructors by students who received grades and those who did not. The study was conducted at two colleges where students were free to cross-enroll, but where students from one college were assigned grades but those from the other were not. Class-average ratings were determined separately for students in each class who received grades and those who did not, and there was substantial agreement with evaluations by the two groups of students. Hence, even though class-average grades of those students who received grades were correlated with their class-average evaluations and showed the expected grade effect, their class-average evaluations were in substantial agreement with those of students who did not receive grades. This suggests that the expected grade effect was not due to grading leniency, since grading leniency was unlikely to affect ratings by students who did not receive grades.

Gigliotti and Buchtel (1990) tested SETs for a self-serving bias, an attributional effect in which individuals take credit for their successes (good grades) but attribute their failures (poor grades) to external causes. Thus, for example, students who do poorly or more poorly than they expect, may rate instructors more poorly than they deserve. Interestingly, this approach does not predict a grading-leniency bias in that students who do well or better than expected will take credit for their successes and not attribute them to the instructor. However, analyses based on the course grade and on differences between expected and actual course grades provided little consistent evidence for a self-serving bias.

Expected grades, actual grades, and grade violations were all unrelated to class-average ratings of instructor skills, instructor support, fairness of the course, and overall instructor ratings. Class-average grades were, however, related to ratings of "personal fit" (e.g., usefulness of course) and impact on self-feelings (e.g., how course affected feelings of self), but not in a way that was predicted by a self-serving bias. The authors interpreted their results as supporting Marsh's (1984) conclusion about the relative lack of bias in SETs due to actual or expected grades.

Summary. Evidence from a variety of different types of research clearly supports the validity hypothesis and the student characteristics hypothesis, but does not rule out the possibility that a grading leniency effect operates simultaneously. Support for the grading leniency effect was found with some experimental studies, but these effects were typically weak and inconsistent, may not generalize to nonexperimental settings where SETs are actually used, and in some instances may be due to the violation of grade expectations that students had falsely been led to expect or that were applied to other students in the same course. Consequently, while it is possible that a grading leniency effect may produce some bias in SETs, support for this suggestion is weak and the size of such an effect is likely to be insubstantial in the actual use of SETs.

Reason for Taking a Course

Courses are often classified as being elective or required courses, but preliminary SEEQ research indicated that this dichotomy may be too simplistic. On SEEQ students indicate one of the following as the reason why they took the course: a) major requirement; b) major elective; c) general interest; d) general education requirement; e) minor/related field; or f) other. All SEEQ factors tended to be positively correlated with the percentage of students taking a course for general interest and as a major elective, but tended to be negatively correlated with the percentage of students taking a course as a major requirement or as a general education requirement. After controlling for the effects of the set of 16 background characteristics, however, general interest was the only reason to have a substantial effect on ratings and it accounted for most of the variance that could be explained by the subset of five reasons. The percentage of students taking a course for general interest was also one of the four background variables selected from the set of 16 as having the largest impact on SETs and included in Marsh's (1980, 1983) path analyses. Marsh (1980, 1983) consistently found the percentage taking a course for general interest to be positively correlated with each of the SEEQ factors in different academic disciplines. However, the sizes of the correlations were modest, usually less than .20, and the effect of this variable was smaller than that of the other three variables (prior subject interest, expected grades, and workload/difficulty) considered in his path analyses. The correlations were somewhat larger for Learning/value, Breadth of Coverage, Assignments, Organization and overall course ratings than for the other SEEQ dimensions, but only the correlations with Breadth of Coverage were as large as or larger than those of the other variables considered in the path analysis.

Other researchers have typically compared elective courses with required courses, or have related the percentage of students taking a course as an elective (or a requirement) to SETs, but these approaches may not be directly comparable to SEEQ research. Large empirical studies have typically found that a course's electivity is positively correlated to student rating (e.g., Brandenburg, Slindle, and Batista, 1977; Pohlman, 1975; but also see Centra and Creech, 1976). These findings are also consistent with Feldman's 1978 review. Thus, these generalizations appear to be consistent with the SEEQ research.

Effects of Specific Background Characteristics Not Emphasized in SEEQ Research

Marsh (1980, 1983) examined the relations between a wide variety of background characteristics, but concluded that most of the variance in SETs that could be accounted for by the entire set could be explained by those characteristics discussed above. The effects of other characteristics, though much smaller, are considered briefly below. A few additional characteristics were examined in particular SEEQ studies (e.g., the faculty self-evaluation studies) that were not available for the large scale studies, and these are also discussed below. Finally, the results are compared with the findings of other investigators, particularly those summarized in Feldman's set of review articles.

Instructor Rank and Years Teaching Experience

SEEQ research has found that teaching assistants receive lower ratings than regular faculty for most rating dimensions and overall rating items, but that they may receive slightly higher ratings for Individual Rapport and perhaps Group Interaction (e.g., Marsh, 1976, 1980; Marsh and Overall, 1979b). Marsh and Overall (1979b) found this same pattern in a comparison of self-evaluations by teaching assistants and self-evaluations by regular faculty. Large empirical studies by Centra and Creech (1976) and by Brandenburg, Slindle, and Batista (1977) and Feldman's 1983 review also indicate that teaching assistants tend to receive lower evaluations than do other faculty (although Feldman also reported some exceptions).

Once teaching assistants are excluded from the analysis, relations between rank and SETs are much smaller in SEEQ research. There is almost no relation between rank and global ratings, while faculty rank is somewhat positively correlated with Breadth of Coverage and somewhat negatively correlated with Group Interaction. These results for the global ratings are consistent with large empirical studies (e.g., Aleamoni and Yimer, 1973; Brandenburg, Slindle, and Batista, 1977; Centra and Creech, 1976). Feldman (1983) reported that a majority of the studies in his review found no significant effect of instructor rank on global ratings, but that the significant relations that were found were generally positive. Feldman also reported that rank was not significantly related to more specific rating dimensions in a majority of studies, but that positive relations tended to be more likely for dimensions related to instructor knowledge and intellectual expansiveness whereas negative relations were more likely for ratings of encouragement of discussion, openness, and concern for students. Marsh and Hocevar (1991b; see earlier discussion) found that the ratings received by the same cohort of teachers who were evaluated continuously over a 13-year period showed little or no changes over this period.

Course Level

In SEEQ research, higher level courses—particularly graduate level courses—tend to receive slightly higher ratings (e.g., Marsh, 1976, 1980, 1983; Marsh and Overall, 1979b). Marsh and Overall (1979b) found that both SETs and faculty self-evaluations tended to be higher in graduate level courses than undergraduate courses. Marsh and Hocevar (1991b) also found this relation even when comparing SETs of the same teachers in graduate and undergraduate classes. In his review of this relation, Feldman (1978) also found that SETs tended to be positively related to course level. The effect of course level is typically diminished and may even disappear when other background variables are controlled (see Braskamp, Brandenburg, and Ory, 1985; Feldman, 1978; Marsh, 1980) but this finding is difficult to interpret without a specific model of the causal ordering of such variables.

Sex of Students and/or Instructor

Empirical studies (e.g., Centra and Creech, 1976; Pohlman, 1975) and Feldman's 1977 review indicate that student sex has little effect on SETs, although Feldman notes that when significant effects are reported women may give slightly higher ratings than men. Similarly, large empirical studies (e.g., Brandenburg, Slindle, and Batista, 1977; Brown, 1976) and McKeachie's 1979 review suggest that the sex of the instructor has little relation to SETs, although Dukes and Victoria (1989) and Feldman suggest a weak tendency for women teachers to receive higher ratings.

Feldman (1977) also considered student-gender by teacher-gender interactions, but few of the studies in his review provided relevant information. Since his review, however, additional research has examined this interaction. Because it is difficult to disentangle true sex differences from sex biases in correlational studies, it is particularly interesting to consider experimental studies. In three studies (Basow 1987; Basow and Distenfeld, 1985; Winocur, Schoen, and Sirowatka, 1989), Dr. Fox type designs were employed (see later discussion of Dr. Fox studies) in which male and female actors were videotaped presenting experimentally manipulated lessons and students were randomly assigned to different conditions. The design variables were student gender, teacher gender, and instructional style. Higher instructor ratings were associated with higher levels of instructor expressiveness in the two Basow studies and an affiliative (as opposed to an instrumental) presentation style in the Winocur study. The effects of teacher gender, student gender, and their interaction, however, were either nonsignificant or very small in all three studies. Dukes and Victoria (1989) presented written scenarios depicting a teacher who was either male or female. In different conditions, teachers were described as high or low in different components of teaching effectiveness (knowledge, enthusiasm, rapport, and organization) and differed in status (department chairperson or not). In none of the conditions were the effects of teacher gender, student gender or their interaction statistically significant. Dukes and Victoria concluded that ratings in their study were primarily a function of the components of teaching effectiveness rather than gender or status. These experimental studies are apparently consistent with survey studies in showing that student gender and teacher gender have little effect on SETs.

Administration and Stated Purpose of the Ratings
Feldman's 1979 review suggests that some aspects of the manner in which SETs are administered may influence the ratings. Feldman (also see Braskamp, Brandenburg, and Ory, 1985) reported that anonymous ratings tended to be somewhat lower than non-anonymous ratings, and this effect may be stronger when teachers are given the ratings before assigning grades, when students feel they may be called upon to justify or elaborate their responses, or, perhaps, when students view the instructor as vindictive. Feldman (1979) reported that ratings tend to be higher when they are to be used for administrative purposes than when used for feedback to faculty or for research purposes, but that the size of this effect may be very small (also see Centra, 1979; Frankhouser, 1984). Feldman (1979) reported that ratings tended to be similar whether collected in the middle of the term, near the end of the term, during the final exam or even after completion of the course. Marsh and Overall (1980), however, suggested that end-of-term ratings may be less valid than mid-term ratings. Whereas these influences may not be large, all aspects of the administration process should be standardized.

Academic Discipline
Feldman (1978) reviewed studies that compared ratings across disciplines and found that ratings are: somewhat higher than average in English, humanities, arts, languages, and, perhaps, education; somewhat lower than average in social sciences, physical sciences, mathematics and engineering, and business administration; and about average in biological sciences. The Centra and Creech 1976 study and the Cashin and Clegg (1987) studies are particularly important because they were based on a very large number of courses from many different insti-

tutions. Centra and Creech classified courses as natural sciences, social sciences and humanities and found that ratings were highest in humanities and lowest in natural sciences. However, even though these results were highly significant, the differences accounted for less than 1 percent of the variance in the SETs.

For global items, Cashin and Clegg (1987) reported a similar pattern of discipline differences to those reported by Feldman (1978): the highest ratings were for humanities and arts courses, followed by social science courses, with the lowest ratings for mathematics, science, and economics courses. Whereas discipline differences were not large for global summary items, there were large differences for SETs of their progress on particular objectives. For example, ratings of "developing skill in expressing myself orally and in writing" were substantially higher in English, Language, and Letters than other disciplines, ratings of "discovering the implications of the course materials for understanding myself" were higher in Arts, Letters, Psychology, and Sociology, whereas ratings of "gaining factual knowledge (terminology, classifications, methods, trends)" were higher in mathematics and Biology. Particularly for these progress items, there appears to be a logical correspondence between the item content and the observed differences. It should also be noted, however, that these items are not like those that typically appear on SET instruments.

Neumann and Neumann (1983), based on Biglan's 1973 theory, classified academic areas according to whether they had: a) a well-defined paradigm structure (hard/soft); b) an orientation towards application (applied/pure); and c) an orientation to living organisms (life/nonlife). Consistent with a priori predictions based on the nature of instruction in different combinations, the authors found that SETs were higher in soft, in pure, and in nonlife disciplines. While the effects of all three facets on SETs were significant, the effect of the hard/soft facet was largest. The authors indicated that teachers in paradigmatic areas where research procedures are not well-developed play a more major role than in paradigmatic areas where the content and method of research is well-developed. On the basis of this research, the authors argued that SETs should only be compared within similar disciplines and that campus-wide comparisons may be unwarranted since the role of teaching varies in different academic areas. The generality of these findings may be limited since the results were based on a single institution. Further tests of the generality of these findings are important. The findings also suggest that discipline differences observed in SETs may reflect the different roles of teaching in these disciplines that are accurately reflected in the SETs.

There may be consistent differences in SETs due to academic discipline, but the relations are generally small for typical SET items. Also, it is possible that such differences are inherent in the discipline rather than a function of differences in teaching effectiveness. Nevertheless, since there are few large, multi-institutional studies of this relation, conclusions must be tentative. The implications of such a relation, if it exists, depend on the use of the SETs. At institutions where SEEQ has been used, administrative use of the SETs is at the school or division level, and SETs are not compared across diverse academic disciplines. In such a situation, the relation between ratings and discipline may be less critical than in a setting where ratings are compared across all disciplines.

Personality of the Instructor
The relation between the personality of an instructor and SETs is important for at least two different reasons. First, there is sometimes the suspicion that the relation is substantial and that instructor personality has nothing to do with being an effective teacher, so that the relation should be interpreted as a bias to SETs. Second, if the relation is significant, then the results may have practical and theoretical importance for distinguishing between effective and ineffective teachers, and for a better understanding of teaching effectiveness and personality.

Feldman's review (1986), because of the limited number of studies, emphasized relations between overall SETs (rather than separate instructional dimensions) and 14 categories of personality as inferred from self-reports by the instructor or as inferred from ratings by others (students or colleagues). For studies of personality based on self-report measures, the only practically significant correlations were for "positive self-regard, self-esteem" (mean r = .30) and "energy and enthusiasm" (mean r = .27); the mean correlation was .15 or less between SETs of teaching effectiveness and each of the other 12 areas of personality. In contrast, when personality was inferred from ratings by students or colleagues, the correlations were much higher; the average correlations between SETs and most of the 14 categories of personality were between .3 and .6.

Murray, Rushton, and Paunonen (1990) conducted an important study of relations between teacher personality and SETs. Using archive data, overall ratings of 46 instructors in up to 6 different types of courses ranging from freshman lecture courses to graduate seminars were considered. For each instructor between 9 and 15 sets of colleague ratings were obtained on a set of 29 personality traits. Patterns of zero-order correlations varied substantially depending on course type; in a few instances the same personality trait (e.g., seeks help and advice) correlated significantly and in the opposite direction with teaching effectiveness for different course types. Stepwise multiple regressions conducted separately within each course type indicated that substantial proportions of the variance in overall ratings could be explained by the first five personality traits to enter the equation. Because the number of instructors representing each course type was small (ns of 29 to 40) relative to the number of personality traits, there is likely to be substantial capitalization on chance that was only partly controlled.[4] Factor analyses of the 29 personality traits identified five well-

[4]Using stepwise multiple regression, Murray, Rushton, and Paunonen (1990) used the best five of 29 personality traits to predict overall ratings of between 29 and 40 instructors for each course type. Recognizing the potential for capitalizing on chance, they presented adjusted R^2 values based

defined factors. Profiles of the instructors most effective in the various categories indicated substantial differences in the different course types—particularly undergraduate and graduate level courses. Instructors most effective in all undergraduate courses, for example, were high in Extroversion whereas instructors most effective in graduate level courses were only average in Extroversion.

Feldman's review and the Murray, Rushton, and Paunonen (1990) study suggest that there is a relation between SETs and at least some aspects of the instructor's personality, but does not indicate whether this is a valid source of influence or a source of bias. As noted with other sources of influence, if teacher personality characteristics influence other indicators of teaching effectiveness in a manner similar to their influence on SETs, then the relation should be viewed as supporting the validity of SETs. Murray, Rushton, and Paunonen interpreted their findings to mean that an instructor's personality is translated into specific teaching behaviors that are accurately reflected in SETs. In support of this claim, earlier research by Erdle, Murray and Rushton (1985) found that more than 50 percent of the relation between personality and SETs was mediated by specific classroom behaviors. Using a perspective similar to that used here, they argued that such relations support the validity of SETs and should not be viewed as a source of invalidity. Neither Feldman's review nor the Murray, Rushton, and Paunonen study examined the pattern of relations between specific components of personality and specific student evaluation factors, and this is unfortunate. Logically, some specific aspects of an instructor's personality should be systematically related to some specific student evaluation factors. For example, enthusiasm is frequently measured by personality inventories and SET instruments and so the two measures of enthusiasm should be substantially correlated. Feldman's review indicated that personality inferred by others—like those in the Murray, Rushton, and Paunonen study—is substantially more correlated with SETs than personality inferred from self-responses. This distinction would seem to be important in establishing the practical significance of these findings for SET research and the theoretical implications for personality research.

The Dr. Fox Paradigm
The Dr. Fox effect is defined as the overriding influence of instructor expressiveness on SETs. The results of Dr. Fox studies have been interpreted to mean that an enthusiastic lecturer can entice or seduce favorable evaluations, even though the lecture may be devoid of meaningful content. In the original Dr. Fox

on 5 predictor variables. In fact, however, there were 29 possible predictor variables—not 5—and so their correction substantially underestimated the likely capitalization on chance. Correcting for 29 predictor variables would result in trivial R^2, but this approach probably overcorrects for capitalization on chance. One better compromise would be to use the five personality factor scores (derived from the 29 traits) to predict overall ratings, but these results were not presented. Based on the information presented it is difficult to determine the strength of relations between personality ratings and SETs.

study by Naftulin, Ware, and Donnelly (1973), a professional actor called "Dr. Fox" lectured to educators and graduate students in an enthusiastic and expressive manner, and teaching effectiveness was evaluated. Despite the fact that the lecture content was specifically designed to have little educational value, the ratings were favorable. The authors and critics agree that the study was fraught with methodological weaknesses, including the lack of any control group, a poor rating instrument, the brevity of the lecture compared to an actual course, the unfamiliar topic coupled with the lack of a textbook with which to compare the lecture, and so on (see Abrami, Leventhal, and Perry, 1982; Frey, 1979; Marsh, 1987; Marsh and Ware, 1982; Ware and Williams, 1975). Frey (1979) notes that "this study represents the kind of research that teachers make fun of during the first week of an introductory course in behavioral research methods. Almost every feature of the study is problematic" (p.1). Nevertheless, reminiscent of the Rodin and Rodin (1972) study described earlier, the results of this study were seized upon by critics as support for the invalidity of SETs.

To overcome some of the problems, Ware and Williams (Ware and Williams, 1975, 1977; Williams and Ware, 1976, 1977) developed the standard Dr. Fox paradigm where a series of six lectures, all presented by the same professional actor was videotaped. Each lecture represented one of three levels of course content (the number of substantive teaching points covered) and one of two levels of lecture expressiveness (the expressiveness with which the actor delivered the lecture). Students viewed one of the six lectures, evaluated teaching effectiveness on a typical multi-item rating form, and completed an achievement test based upon all the teaching points in the high content lecture. Ware and Williams (1979, 1980) reviewed their studies, and similar studies by other researchers, and concluded that differences in expressiveness consistently explained much more variance in SETs than did differences in content.

Reanalyses and Meta-analyses
A reanalysis. Marsh and Ware (1982) reanalyzed data from the Ware and Williams studies. A factor analysis of the rating instrument identified five evaluation factors which varied in the way they were affected by the experimental manipulations. In the condition most like the university classroom, where students were told before viewing the lecture that they would be tested on the materials and that they would be rewarded in accordance with the number of exam questions which they answered correctly (incentive before lecture), the Dr. Fox effect was *not* supported. The instructor expressiveness manipulation only affected ratings of Instructor Enthusiasm, the factor most logically related to that manipulation, and content coverage significantly affected ratings of Instructor Knowledge and Organization/Clarity, the factors most logically related to that manipulation. Research by Perry (see Perry, 1991; Perry and Magnusson, 1987; Perry and Penner, 1990) provides empirical support for the broader implications

of this variable for student motivation and performance. When students were given no incentives to perform well, instructor expressiveness had more impact on all five student rating factors than when external incentives were present, though the effect on Instructor Enthusiasm was still largest. However, without external incentives, expressiveness also had a larger impact on student achievement scores than did the content manipulation (i.e., presentation style had more to do with how well students performed on the examination than did the number of questions that had been covered in the lecture). This finding demonstrated that, particularly when external incentives are weak, expressiveness can have an important impact on both SETs and achievement scores. In further analyses of the achievement scores Marsh (1984a, p.212) concluded that the study was one of the few to "show that more expressively presented lectures *cause* better examination performance in a study where there was random assignment to treatment conditions and lecturer expressiveness was experimentally manipulated." Across all the conditions, the effect of instructor expressiveness on ratings of Instructor Enthusiasm was larger than its effect on other student rating factors. Hence, as observed in the examination of potential biases to SETs, this reanalysis indicates the importance of considering the multidimensionality of SETs. An effect which has been interpreted as a "bias" to SETs seems more appropriately interpreted as support for their validity with respect to one component of effective teaching. Consistent with this interpretation, Feldman's (1988) review indicated that "teacher enthusiasm" was judged to be an important characteristic by both students (rated 5th of 18 components) and faculty (2nd) although it was only 11th highest in its relation with student achievement.

A meta-analysis. Abrami, Leventhal, and Perry (1982) conducted a review and a meta-analysis of all known Dr. Fox studies. On the basis of their meta-analysis, they concluded that expressiveness manipulations had a substantial impact on overall SETs and a small effect on achievement, while content manipulations had a substantial effect on achievement and a small effect on ratings. Consistent with the Marsh and Ware reanalysis, they also found that in the few studies that analyzed separate rating factors, the rating factors that were most logically related to the expressiveness manipulation were most affected by it. Finally, they concluded that while the expressiveness manipulation did interact with the content manipulation and a host of other variables examined in the Dr. Fox studies, none of these interactions accounted for more than 5 percent of the variance in SETs.

Extensions. The Dr. Fox paradigm is an apparently valuable procedure for studying a wide variety of teaching variables within the context of a controlled experimental design as demonstrated by the research program on college students perceptions of control conducted by Perry and his associates (see Perry, 1991, for an overview). The focus of this research was not the Dr. Fox effect nor even SETS, but how instructor expressiveness interacted with perceived control to influence achievement test scores. Within an educational context, perceived control is a student's perceived capacity to influence and predict events, particularly those contributing to academic achievement. An internal locus in which students take more responsibility for their outcomes is associated with more favorable academic behaviors and outcomes. Whereas perceived control is often conceptualized as a relatively stable individual difference variable, Perry (1991) demonstrated that perceived control is significantly lowered by giving students negative, noncontingent feedback on responses to multiple choice test items.

In Perry's (1991) basic paradigm, students completed individual difference instruments, were administered feedback manipulations designed to alter perceptions of control, were presented with Dr. Fox-type videotapes that varied in terms of instructor expressiveness, and then completed post-test materials consisting of a multiple choice achievement test and an attribution questionnaire. The results of different studies have consistently shown a aptitude-treatment interaction in which instructor expressiveness has no effect on achievement test scores for students who are low in perceived control whereas instructor expressiveness increases achievement test scores for other students.

Other research suggested that low perceived control that occurred naturally (i.e., an individual difference variable instead of the result of an experimental manipulation) produced a similar pattern of results. Interestingly, low perceived control that occurred naturally could be offset to some extent by the feedback manipulation and also by an attributional retraining program described by Perry and Penner (1990). Perry and Dickens (1984) also studied how this effect varied with the incentive level of students. In the no-incentive conditions, instructor expressiveness facilitated achievement for contingent-feedback (high perceived control) students but not for noncontingent-feedback (low perceived control) students. In the high incentive condition performance was consistently higher, but instructor expressiveness did not effect achievement performance for either contingent or noncontingent feedback conditions. Perry (1991), like Marsh and Ware (1982), concluded that under conditions of high external incentive, instructor expressiveness has little effect on achievement performance. Research by Perry and his associates is important in demonstrating that the effectiveness of the instructor expressiveness can vary systematically depending on individual differences of students within a class or environmental factors. More generally, the research demonstrates the broad applicability of the Dr. Fox paradigm to the study of teaching effectiveness.

Interpretations, Implications and Problems
How should the results of the Dr. Fox type studies be evaluated? Consistent with the present emphasis on the construct validity of multifaceted SETs, a particularly powerful test of the validity of SETs would be to show that each rating factor is strongly influenced by manipulations most logically associated with it

and less influenced by other manipulations. This is the approach used in the Marsh and Ware reanalysis of the Dr. Fox data described above, and it offers strong support for the validity of ratings with respect to expressiveness and, perhaps, limited support for their validity with respect to content.

Multiple ratings factors have typically not been considered in Dr. Fox studies even though researchers typically collect ratings that do represent multiple rating dimensions (i.e., the same form as was shown to have five factors in the Marsh and Ware reanalysis, and/or items from the 1971 Hildebrand, Wilson and Dienst study). However, this makes no sense when researchers also emphasize the differential effects of the experimental manipulations on the total rating score and the achievement outcome. According to this approach, SETs may be invalid because they are "oversensitive" to expressiveness and "undersensitive" to content when compared with achievement scores (but see Abrami, Leventhal, and Perry, 1982).

It is hardly surprising that the number of examination questions answered in a lecture (only 4 of 26 exam questions are covered in the low content lecture, while all 26 are covered in the high content lecture) has a substantial impact on examination performance immediately after the lecture, and less impact on SETs; more relevant is the finding that content also impacts SETs. Nor is it surprising that manipulations of instructor expressiveness have a large impact on the total rating score when some of the items specifically ask students to judge the characteristic that is being manipulated; more relevant is the finding that some rating factors are relatively unaffected by expressiveness and that achievement scores are affected by expressiveness. SETs are multifaceted, the different rating factors do vary in the way they are affected by different manipulations, and any specific criterion can be more accurately predicted by differentially weighting the student rating dimensions. Since most of the Dr. Fox studies are based upon total scores instead of separate components, reanalyses of these studies, as was done in the Marsh and Ware study, should prove valuable.

Summary of the Search for Potential Biases
The search for potential biases to SETs is plagued by methodological problems and the lack of definition of what constitutes a bias. For most of the relations, the effects tend to be small, the directions of the effects are sometimes inconsistent, and the attribution of a bias is typically unwarranted. There is clearly a need for meta-analyses, and systematic reviews such as those by Feldman, to provide more accurate estimates of the size of effects which have been reported, and the conditions under which they were found. Perhaps the best summary of this area is McKeachie's (1979) conclusion that a wide variety of variables that could potentially influence SETs apparently have little effect. Similar conclusions have been drawn by Centra (1979, 1989), Cashin (1988), Menges (1973), Marsh (1980, 1983, 1987), Murray (1980), Aleamoni (1981), and others.

There are, of course, nearly an infinite number of variables that could be related to SETs and could be posited as potential biases. However, any such claim must be seriously scrutinized in a series of studies that are relatively free from the common methodological shortcomings, are based upon an explicit and defensible definition of bias, and employ the type of logic used to examine the variables described here. Single studies of the predictive validity of psychological measures have largely been replaced by a series of construct validity studies, and a similar approach should also be taken in the study of potential biases. Simplistic arguments that a significant correlation between SETs and some variable "X" demonstrates a bias can no longer be tolerated, and are an injustice to the field. It is unfortunate that the cautious attitude to interpreting correlations between SETs and potential indicators of effective teaching as evidence of validity has not been adopted in the interpretation of correlations between SETs and potential biases as a source of invalidity.

UTILITY OF STUDENT RATINGS

Braskamp, Brandenburg, and Ory (1985) argued that it is important for universities and individual instructors to take evaluations seriously. They support this contention with a broad rationale based on organizational research. Key points are that institutional goals/values are reinforced through an evaluation process and that successful organizations are data-based and assessment-driven. In summarizing this perspective Braskamp et al. (p.14) stated that: "the clarity and pursuit of purpose is best done if the achievements are known. A course is charted and corrections are inevitable. Evaluation plays a role in the clarity of purpose and determining if the pursuit is on course." In a related perspective, Marsh (1984b, 1987) argued that the introduction of a broad institution-based, carefully planned program of SETs is likely to lead to the improvement of teaching. Faculty will give serious consideration to their own teaching in order to evaluate the merits of the program. Clear support of a program by the central administration will serve notice that teaching effectiveness is being taken seriously. The results of SETs, as one indicator of effective teaching, will provide a basis for informed administrative decisions and thereby increase the likelihood that quality teaching will be recognized and rewarded, and that good teachers will be given tenure. The social reinforcement of getting favorable ratings will provide added incentive for the improvement of teaching, even at the tenured faculty level. Finally, faculty report that the feedback from student evaluations is useful to their own efforts for the improvement of their teaching.

Murray (1987) presented a similar logic in making the case for why SETs improve teaching effectiveness, offering four reasons: (a) SETs provide useful feedback for diagnosing strengths and weaknesses, (b) feedback can provide the impetus for professional development aimed at improving teaching, (c) the use of SETs in personnel decisions provides a tangible incentive to improve teaching, and (d) the use of SETs in tenure decisions means that good teachers are more likely to be retained. In support of his argument, Murray (1987) summarized results of published surveys from seven universities that asked faculty whether SETs are useful for improving teaching and whether SETs have led to improved teaching. Across the seven studies, about 2/3 of the faculty said that SETs were useful and about 80 percent indicated that SETs led to improved teaching.

Dunkin (1990) looked at relations among sex, academic qualifications, teaching experience, the use of SETs, and self-perceived teaching effectiveness for newly appointed staff at an Australian University where the use of SETs was not required. Males, lecturers with doctorates, and lecturers with more teaching experience rated themselves as more competent teachers. Self-perceived teaching effectiveness, however, was negatively related to the use of SETs. This suggests that lecturers who perceived themselves to be poorer teachers chose to use SETs in the belief that they would provide a basis for improved teaching.

None of these observations, however, provides an empirical demonstration of improvement of teaching effectiveness resulting from SETs.

Changes in Teaching Effectiveness Due to Feedback from Student Ratings
In most studies of the effects of feedback from SETs, teachers are randomly assigned to experimental (feedback) and one or more control groups; SETs are collected during the term; ratings of the feedback teachers are returned to instructors as quickly as possible; and the various groups are compared at the end of the term on a second administration on SETs and sometimes on other variables as well. (There is considerable research on a wide variety of other techniques designed to improve teaching effectiveness which use SETs as an outcome measure; see Levinson-Rose and Menges, 1981).

SEEQ has been employed in two such feedback studies using multiple sections of the same course. In the first study results from an abbreviated form of the survey were simply returned to faculty, and the impact of the feedback was positive, but very modest (Marsh, Fleiner, and Thomas, 1975). In the second study (Overall and Marsh, 1979) researchers actually met with instructors in the feedback group to discuss the evaluations and possible strategies for improvement. In this study students in the feedback group subsequently performed better on a standardized final examination, rated teaching effectiveness more favorably at the end of the course, and experienced more favorable affective outcomes (i.e., feelings of course mastery, and plans to pursue and apply the subject). These two studies suggest that feedback, coupled with a candid discussion with an external consultant, can be an effective intervention for the improvement of teaching effectiveness. These SEEQ studies are atypical of most feedback research in which different courses from a variety of disciplines are considered so that student achievement normally cannot be considered as an outcome variable.

In his classic meta-analysis, Cohen (1980) found that instructors who received midterm feedback were subsequently rated about one-third of a standard deviation higher than controls on the Total Rating (an overall rating item or the average of multiple items), and even larger differences were observed for ratings of Instructor Skill, Attitude Toward Subject, and Feedback to Students. Studies that augmented feedback with consultation produced substantially larger differences, but other methodological variations had little effect. The results of this meta-analysis support the SEEQ findings described above and demonstrate that SET feedback, particularly when augmented by consultation, can lead to improvement in teaching effectiveness.

L'Hommediu, Menges, and Brinko (1990; also see L'Hommediu, Menges, and Brinko, 1988) noted Dunkin's (1986) call for more research on the effects of SETs on changes in teacher processes and for meta-analyses of the influence of design and contextual effects. In response to Dunkin, the authors updated Cohen's (1980) meta-analysis and critically evaluated the methodology used in the 28 studies. They concluded that the overall effect size (.342) attributable to feedback was probably attenuated by threats to validity in existing research and developed methodological recommendations for future research. Among their many recommendations, they emphasized the need to: use a larger number of instructors, more critically evaluate findings within a construct validity framework as emphasized by Marsh (1987), more critically evaluate the assumed generalizability of midterm feedback to end-of-term feedback, and to base results on well-standardized instruments such as SEEQ. They also noted that teachers in many studies had previously received SET feedback so that feedback/no-feedback comparisons actually tested the additive effects of the additional feedback from that study. In this respect, the results are likely to underestimate the gain due to feedback compared to a control group that had never received SET feedback. This serious threat to the internal validity of results was not systematically evaluated in any of the studies, but the authors noted the need to consider previous experience with SETs in future research.

In their meta-analysis, L'Hommediu, Menges, and Brinko (1988) considered three forms of feedback that differed systematically in their effect sizes: written feedback consisting of printed summaries of SETs (Mean effect = .18, SD = .24, N = 16); personal feedback consisting of summary material delivered in person, sometimes accompanied by interpretations, discussion, and advice (mean effect = .25, SD = .21, N = 6); and consultative feedback that combines SET feedback and professional development (mean effect = .86, SD = .554, N = 6). Consistent with Cohen (1980) they concluded that "the literature reveals a persistently positive, albeit small, effect from written feedback alone and a considerably increased effect when written feedback is augmented with personal consultation'' (1990, p.240), but that improved research that incorporated their suggestions would probably lead to larger, more robust effects.

Wilson (1986, 1987) described an alternative paradigm that appears to have considerable potential. A key element in his research was a set of 24 teaching packets that were keyed to the 24 items on the SET instrument used in his research. Each packet contained suggestions from teachers who had received Distinguished Teaching Awards or received multiple nominations as the ''best teacher'' by graduating seniors. Participants in the study were volunteers who had been evaluated previously in the same course they would again be teaching. Based on SETs and self-evaluations of their own teaching, participants nominated specific evaluation items on which they would like assistance at a preliminary consultation session. The main consultation was held shortly before the second time the instructors were to teach the same course. The consultant began the session by noting items on which the instructor received the highest ratings. The consultant then considered 3 to 5 items which the instructor had selected or had received the lowest ratings. For each item the three to six strategies from the corresponding teaching packet were described and the instructor was given copies of the two or three that were of most interest to the instructor. During the next week the consultant summarized the main consultation and strategies to be pursued in a letter that was sent to the instructor and subsequently telephoned the instructor during the term to ask how things were going. The results indicated that ratings were systematically better at time 2 for the targeted items—particularly those items that referred to concrete behaviors (e.g., states objectives for each class session)—and an overall rating item. Recognizing the need for a nonintervention comparison group, Wilson evaluated SETs for 101 courses that were taught by the same instructors (who had not volunteered to be in the study) on two occasions during the same period. For this large comparison group, there were no systematic changes in either specific or global SETs. Results for the comparison group supported Wilson's contention that SETS without a consultation intervention are not likely to lead to improved teaching. Wilson suggested that the key elements in the consultation intervention were providing instructors with information on how to improve teaching in areas in which they are weak and the interpersonal expectations that created for some instructors a desire to fulfill an implied contract with their consultant. Whereas there may be counter-interpretations[5] of the findings in this quasi-experimental study, the results sug-

---

[5]Wilson (1986, 1987) evaluated changes for only the specific rating items that had been targeted for change. Because these items were typically the ones on which instructors had the lowest ratings at time 1, regression effects alone would predict that changes in these items would more likely be positive than negative. This problem, however, apparently does not affect results for the overall rating items.

gest that this consultation intervention may be an effective method for improving teaching effectiveness.

The most robust finding from the feedback research reviewed here is that consultation augments the effects of written summaries of SETs. Other sources also support this conclusion. For example, in the Jacobs (1987) survey of Indiana University faculty, 70 percent of the respondents indicated that SETs had helped them improve their teaching but 63 percent indicated that even when teachers can interpret their ratings, they often do not know what to do in order to improve their teaching. Also, Franklin and Theall (1989), based on an 153 multiple-choice test of knowledge about SETs that was validated by experts in the field, concluded that many users lacked the knowledge to adequately use the SETs for summative or formative purposes. Nevertheless, insufficient attention in SET research has been given to nature of consultative feedback that is most effective (e.g., Wilson, 1986, 1987). This important deficit in existing research has tremendous practical implications and should prove a fruitful area for further research.

Several issues still remain unresolved in SET feedback research. First, whereas the combination of feedback and consultation is more effective than feedback alone, no studies have provided an adequate control for the effect of consultation without SETs (i.e., a placebo effect due to consultation, or a real effect due to consultation that does not depend upon feedback from SETs).[6] Second, the criterion of effective teaching in feedback studies is limited primarily to subsequent SETs; only the Overall and Marsh (1979) study demonstrated a significant effect of feedback on achievement (but also see McKeachie, et al., 1980). Most other studies were not based upon multiple sections of the same course, and so it was not possible to test the effect of feedback on achievement scores. Third, nearly all of the studies were based on midterm feedback from midterm ratings. This limitation probably weakens effects in that many instructional characteristics cannot be easily altered within the same semester. Furthermore, Marsh and Overall (1980) demonstrated in their multisection validity study midterm ratings were less valid than end-of-term ratings. Fourth, most of the research is based upon instructors who volunteer to participate; this further limits the generality of the effect, since volunteers are likely to be more motivated to use the feedback. In addition, reward structure is an important variable which has not been examined. Even if faculty are intrinsically motivated to improve their teaching effectiveness, potentially valuable feedback will be much less useful if there is no extrinsic motivation for faculty to improve. To the extent that salary, promotion, and prestige are based primarily on research productivity, the usefulness of SETs as feedback for the improvement of teaching may be

[6] McKeachie (personal communication, 9 April, 1991) noted that he had conducted a follow-up study that used consultation alone and that consultation without student ratings was nearly as effective as consultation with student ratings.

limited. Hildebrand (1972, p.53) noted that: "The more I study teaching, however, the more convinced I become that the most important requirement for improvement is incorporation of effective evaluation of teaching into advancement procedures." Realistically, particularly for faculty trying to get tenure in research-oriented universities, it may be counter-productive to place too much emphasis on improving teaching if this is accomplished by a diminished publication record. Finally, future research needs to evaluate the validity threats outlined by L'Hommedieu, Menges, and Brinko (1990) and to incorporate their suggestions about how to counter these problems.

Nearly all feedback studies have considered the effects of feedback from SETs within a single term, and this is unfortunate. SETs are typically collected near the end of the term so that the more relevant question is the impact of end-of-term ratings. A few studies have considered long-term follow-ups of short-term interventions, but these were apparently not designed for this purpose and were sufficiently flawed that no generalizations are warranted (see Marsh, 1987). No research has examined the effects of continued SET feedback over a long period of time with a true experimental design, and such research may be ethically dubious and very difficult to conduct. The long-term effects of SET feedback may be amenable to quasi-experimental designs (e.g., Voght and Lasher, 1973), but the difficulties inherent in the interpretation of such studies may preclude any firm generalizations. For short periods, however, it may be justifiable to withhold the SETs from randomly selected instructors or to require that some instructors not collect SETs at all. In particular, it is reasonable to evaluate the effects of feedback from end-of-term ratings—augmented, perhaps, with consultation—on SETs collected the next semester in relation to SETs for no-feedback controls. Particularly for ongoing programs that regularly collect SETs at the end of each semester, this type of study should be easier to conduct than the traditional midterm studies, and so it is surprising that this research design has not been implemented.

Usefulness in Tenure/Promotion Decisions

Since 1929, and particularly during the last 25 years a variety of surveys have been conducted to determine the importance of SETs and other indicators of teaching effectiveness in evaluating total faculty performance in North American universities. Reviews (Centra, 1979; Marsh, 1987; Leventhal, Perry, Abrami, Turcotte, and Kane, 1981; Seldin, 1975) suggest that the importance and usefulness of SETs as a measure of teaching effectiveness have increased dramatically during the last 60 years and particularly in the last two decades. Despite the strong reservations by some, faculty are apparently in favor of the use of SETs in personnel decisions—at least in comparison with other indicators of teaching effectiveness. For example, in a broad cross-section of colleges and universities,

Rich (1976) reported that 75 percent of the respondents believed that SETs should be used in tenure decisions. Rich also noted that faculty at major research-oriented universities favored the use of SETs more strongly than faculty from small colleges, suggesting that SETs were more threatening at small colleges because teaching effectiveness is a more important determinant of personnel decisions. However, Braskamp, Brandenburg, and Ory (1985) noted that university faculty place more emphasis on striving for excellence and are more competitive than faculty at small colleges, and these differences might explain their stronger acceptance of SETs.

In order to experimentally evaluate the importance of teaching effectiveness in personnel decisions, Leventhal, et al. (1981), and Salthouse, McKeachie, and Lin (1978) composed fictitious summaries of faculty performance that systematically varied reports of teaching and research effectiveness, and also varied the type of information given about teaching (chairperson's report or chairperson's report supplemented by summaries of SETs). Both studies found reports of research effectiveness to be more important in evaluating total faculty performance at research universities, although Leventhal, et al. found teaching and research to be of similar importance across a broader range of institutions. While teaching effectiveness as assessed by the chairperson's reports did make a significant difference in ratings of overall faculty performance, neither study found that supplementing the chairperson's report with SETs made any significant difference. However, neither study considered SETs alone or even suggested that the two sources of evidence about teaching effectiveness were independent. Information from the ratings and chairperson's report were always consistent so that one was redundant, and it would be reasonable for subjects in these studies to assume that the chairperson's report was at least partially based upon SETs. These studies demonstrate the importance of reports of teaching effectiveness, but apparently do not test the impact of SETs. As noted earlier, Lin, McKeachie, and Tucker (1984) used a similar design to compare the effects of statistical summaries of SETs and written comments. Those results suggested that written comments augmented the impact of statistical summaries—favorably for highly rated teachers and negatively for less highly rated teachers. Again, however, the researchers did not consider comments alone or comments that were inconsistent with the statistical summaries, so there was no basis for comparing the relative impact of the two sources of information. This paradigm, however, could be used to determine the most effective way to present information from SETs. These studies, for example, imply that augmenting the feedback provided by summaries of global SETs may increase their impact. An important, unresolved question that appears well suited to this paradigm is the comparison of global SET summaries recommended for personnel decisions by Abrami (1989a, 1989b, 1991; also see Marsh, 1991a) and profiles of SET scores like those resulting from SEEQ responses that are emphasized here.

Usefulness in Student Course Selection

Little empirical research has been conducted on the use of ratings by prospective students in the selection of courses. UCLA students reported that the Professor/ Course Evaluation Survey was the second most frequently read of the many student publications, following the daily, campus newspaper (Marsh, 1987). Similarly, about half the Indiana University students in Jacob's (1987) study generally consulted published ratings prior to taking a course. Leventhal, Abrami, Perry, and Breen (1975) found that students say that information about teaching effectiveness influences their course selection. Students who select a class on the basis of information about teaching effectiveness are more satisfied with the quality of teaching than are students who indicate other reasons (Centra and Creech, 1976; Leventhal, Abrami, and Perry, 1976). In an experimental field study, Coleman and McKeachie (1981) presented summaries of ratings of four comparable political science courses to randomly selected groups of students during preregistration meetings. One of the courses had received substantially higher ratings, and it was chosen more frequently by students in the experimental group than by those in the control group. Apparently, SETs are useful for students in the selection of instructors and courses.

Summary of Studies of the Utility of Student Ratings

With the possible exception of short-term studies of the effects of midterm ratings, studies of the usefulness of SETs are infrequent and often anecdotal. This is unfortunate, because this is an area of research that can have an important and constructive impact on policy and practice. Important, unresolved issues were identified that are in need of further research. For example, for administrative decisions SETs can be summarized by responses to a single global rating item, by a single score representing an optimally-weighted average of specific components, or a profile of multiple components, but there is no research to indicate which is most effective. If different components of SETs are to be combined to form a total score, how should the different components be weighted? Again there is no systematic research to inform policy makers. Debates about whether SETs have too much or too little impact on administrative decisions are seldom based upon any systematic evidence about the amount of impact they actually do have. Researchers often indicate that SETs are used as one basis for personnel decisions, but there is a dearth of research on the policy practices that are actually employed in the use of SETs. A plethora of policy questions exist (e.g., how to select courses to be evaluated, the manner in which rating instruments are administered, who is to be given access to the results, how ratings from different courses are considered, whether special circumstances exist where ratings for a particular course can be excluded either a priori or post-hoc, whether faculty have the right to offer their own interpretation of ratings, etc.) which are largely unexplored despite the apparently wide use of SETs.

Anecdotal reports often suggest that faculty find SETs useful, but there has been little systematic attempt to determine what form of feedback to faculty is most useful (although feedback studies do support the use of services by an external consultant) and how faculty actually use the results which they do receive. Some researchers have cited anecdotal evidence for negative effects of SETs (e.g., lowering grading standards or making courses easier) but these are also rarely documented with systematic research. Critics suggest that SETs lead to more conservative teaching styles, but Murray (1987) countered that highly rated teachers often use nontraditional approaches and that teaching is less traditional today than it was before SETs were used widely. McKeachie (personal communication, 19 March, 1991) noted that SETs are typically used constructively, encouraging instructors to think of alternative approaches and to try them out. He also suggested, however, that if SETs are used destructively so that teachers feel that they are in competition with each other—"that they must always be wary of the sword of student ratings hanging over their head"—poor ratings may increase anxiety and negative feelings about students so that teaching and learning may suffer. Again, research is needed to examine whether teachers react constructively or destructively to SETs and whether there are individual differences that influence these reactions. While SETs are sometimes used by students in their selection of courses, there is little guidance about the type of information which students want and whether this is the same as is needed for other uses of SETs. These, and a wide range of related questions about how SETs are actually used and how their usefulness can be enhanced, provide a rich field for further research.

OVERVIEW, SUMMARY, AND IMPLICATIONS

Research described in this chapter demonstrates that SETs are clearly multidimensional, quite reliable, reasonably valid, relatively unbiased, and seen to be useful by students, faculty, and administrators. The same findings also demonstrate, however, that SETs may have some halo effect, have at least some unreliability, have only modest agreement with some criteria of effective teaching, are probably affected by some potential sources of bias, and are viewed with some skepticism by faculty as a basis for personnel decisions. It should be noted that this level of uncertainty probably also exists in every area of applied psychology and for all personnel evaluation systems. Nevertheless, the reported results clearly demonstrate that a considerable amount of useful information can be obtained from SETs; useful for feedback to faculty, useful for personnel decisions, useful to students in the selection of courses, and useful for the study of teaching. As noted by Cashin (1988), "in general, student ratings tend to be statistically reliable, valid, and relatively free from bias, probably more so than any other data used for faculty evaluation'' (p.5).

Despite the generally supportive research findings, SETs should be used cautiously, and there should be other forms of systematic input about teaching effectiveness, particularly when they are used for tenure/promotion decisions. Whereas there is good evidence to support the use of SETs as one indicator of effective teaching, there are few other indicators of teaching effectiveness whose use is systematically supported by research findings. Based upon the research reviewed here, other alternatives which may be valid include the ratings of previous students, instructor self-evaluations, and colleague ratings that are *not* based on actual classroom observation, but each of these has problems of its own. Alumni surveys typically have very low response rates and are still basically SETs. Faculty self-evaluations may be valid for some purposes, but probably not for personnel decisions. (Faculty should, however, be encouraged to have a systematic voice in the interpretation of their SETs.) Colleague ratings that are not based on classroom observation apparently reflect second-hand student perceptions or, in some cases, impressions based on summaries of SETs. Consequently, while extensive lists of alternative indicators of effective teaching are proposed (e.g., Centra, 1979), few are supported by systematic research, and none is as clearly supported as SETs.

Why then, if SETs are reasonably well supported by research findings, are they so controversial and so widely criticized? Several suggestions are obvious. University faculty have little or no formal training in teaching, yet find themselves in a position where their salary or even their job may depend upon their classroom teaching skills. Any procedure used to evaluate teaching effectiveness would prove to be threatening and therefore criticized. The threat is exacerbated by the realization that there are no clearly defined criteria of effective teaching, particularly when there continues to be considerable debate about the validity of SETs. Interestingly, measures of research productivity, the other major determinant of instructor effectiveness, are not nearly so highly criticized, despite the fact that the actual information used to represent them in tenure decisions is often quite subjective and there are serious problems with the interpretation of the objective measures of research productivity that are used. As demonstrated in this overview, much of the debate is based upon ill-founded fears about SETs, but the fears still persist. Indeed, the popularity of two of the more widely employed paradigms in student evaluation research, the multisection validity study and the Dr. Fox study, apparently stems from an initial notoriety produced by claims to have demonstrated that SETs are invalid. This occurred even though the two original studies(Rodin and Rodin, 1972 and Naftulin, Ware and Donnelly, 1973) were so fraught with methodological weaknesses as to be uninterpretable. Perhaps this should not be so surprising in the academic profession where faculty are better trained to find counter explanations for a wide variety of

STUDENTS' EVALUATIONS OF UNIVERSITY TEACHING

phenomena than to teach. Indeed, the state of affairs has resulted in a worthwhile and healthy scrutiny of SETs and was heuristic in generating important research. The bulk of research, however, has supported their continued use as well as advocating further scrutiny.

REFERENCES

Abrami, P. C. (1985). Dimensions of effective college instruction. *Review of Higher Education* 8: 211–228.
Abrami, P. C. (1988). SEEQ and ye shall find: A review of Marsh's "Students' evaluations of university teaching." *Instructional Evaluation* 9(2): 19–27.
Abrami, P. C. (1989a). How should we use student ratings to evaluate teaching. *Research in Higher Education* 30: 221–227.
Abrami, P. C. (1989b). SEEQing the truth about student ratings of instruction. *Educational Researcher* 43: 43–45.
Abrami, P. C., Cohen, P. A., d'Apollonia, S. (1988). Implementation problems in meta-analysis. *Review of Educational Research* 58: 151–179.
Abrami, P. C., and d'Apollonia, S. (1991). Multidimensional students' evaluations of teaching effectiveness: Generalizability of N = 1 research: Comment on Marsh (1991). *Journal of Educational Psychology*.
Abrami, P. C., d'Apollonia, S., and Cohen, P. A., (1990). Validity of student ratings of instruction: What we know and what we do not. *Journal of Educational Psychology* 82: 219–231.
Abrami, P. C., Dickens, W. J., Perry, R. P., and Leventhal, L. (1980). Do teacher standards for assigning grades affect student evaluations of instruction? *Journal of Educational Psychology* 72: 107–118.
Abrami, P. C., Leventhal, L., and Perry, R. P. (1982). Educational seduction. *Review of Educational Research* 52: 446–464.
Aleamoni, L. M. (1981). Student ratings of instruction. In J. Millman (ed.), *Handbook of Teacher Evaluation*. Beverly Hills, CA: Sage. Aleamoni, L. M. (1985). Peer evaluation of instructors and instruction. *Instructional Evaluation* 8 (entire issue).
Aleamoni, L. M., and Yimer, M. (1973). An investigation of the relationship between colleague rating, student rating, research productivity, and academic rank in rating instructional effectiveness. *Journal of Educational Psychology* 64: 274–277.
Aubrect, J. D. (1981). Reliability, validity and generalizability of student ratings of instruction (IDEA Paper No.6). Kansas State University: Center for Faculty Evaluations and Development. (ERIC Document Reproduction Service No. ED 213 296).
Barnes, J. (1985). Experience and student achievement/teacher effectiveness. In T. Husen and T. N. Postlethwaite (eds.), *International Encyclopedia of Education: Research and Studies*. Oxford: Pergamon Press.
Basow, S. A. (August, 1987). Teacher expressiveness: Effects of teacher sex and student sex. Paper presented at the 1987 Annual Meeting of the American Psychological Association, New York, NY (ERIC Document No. ED 290 067).
Basow, S. A., and Distenfeld, M. S. (1985). Teacher expressiveness: More important for male teachers than female teachers? *Journal of Educational Psychology* 77: 45–52.
Benton, S. E. (1982). Rating college teaching: Criterion validity studies of student evaluation of instruction instruments. (ERIC ED 221 147)
Biglan, A. (1973). The characteristics of subject matter in different academic areas. *Journal of Applied Psychology* 57: 195–203.

Blackburn, R. T. (1974). The meaning of work in academia. In J. I. Doi (ed.), *Assessing Faculty Effort* (a special issue of New Directions for Institutional Research.) San Francisco: Jossey-Bass.

Blackburn, R. T., and Clark, M. J. (1975). An assessment of faculty performance: Some correlations between administrators, colleagues, student, and self–ratings. *Sociology of Education* 48: 242–256.

Brandenburg, D. C., Slindle, J. A., and Batista, E. E. (1977). Student ratings of instruction: Validity and normative interpretations. *Research in Higher Education* 7: 67–78.

Braskamp, L. A., Brandenburg, D. C. and Ory, J. C. (1985). *Evaluating teaching effectiveness: A practical guide*. Beverly Hills, CA: Sage.

Braskamp, L. A., Ory, J. C. and Pieper, D. M. (1981). Student written comments: Dimensions of instructional quality. *Journal of Educational Psychology* 73: 65–70.

Brookfield, S. (1989). Teacher Roles and Teaching Styles: Adult Education. In Husen, T. and Postlethwaite, T. N. (eds.) *The International Encyclopedia of Education*, Supplementary Volume 1. Oxford: Pergamon Press.

Brown, D. L. (1976). Faculty ratings and student grades: A university-wide multiple regression analysis. *Journal of Educational Psychology* 68: 573–578.

Campbell, D. T., and Stanley, J. C. (1963). Experimental and quasi-experimental designs for research on teaching. In N. L. Gage (ed.), *Handbook of Research on Teaching*. Chicago: Rand McNally.

Cashin, W. E. (1988). Student ratings of teaching. A summary of research. (IDEA paper No.20). Kansas State University, Division of Continuing Education. (ERIC Document Reproduction Service No. ED 302 567).

Cashin, W. E., and Clegg, V. L. (April, 1987). Are student ratings of different academic disciplines different? Paper presented at the 1987 Annual Meeting of the American Educational Research Association, Washington, DC. (ERIC Document Reproduction Service No. ED 289 935).

Centra, J. A. (1975). Colleagues as raters of classroom instruction. *Journal of Higher Education* 46: 327–337.

Centra, J. A. (1979). Determining faculty effectiveness. San Francisco: Jossey-Bass.

Centra, J. A. (1983). Research productivity and teaching effectiveness. *Research in Higher Education* 18: 379–389.

Centra, J. A. (1989) Faculty evaluation and faculty development in higher education. In J. C. Smart (ed.), *Higher Education: Handbook of Theory and Research*, Vol. V. New York: Agathon Press.

Centra, J. A., and Creech, F. R. (1976). The relationship between student, teacher, and course characteristics and student ratings of teacher effectiveness (Project Report 76–1). Princeton, NJ: Educational Testing Service.

Clarkson, P. C. (1984). Papua, New Guinea students' perceptions of mathematics lecturers. *Journal of Educational Psychology* 76: 1386–1395.

Cohen, P. A. (1980). Effectiveness of student–rating feedback for improving college instruction: a meta-analysis. *Research in Higher Education* 13: 321–341.

Cohen, P. A. (1981). Student ratings of instruction and student achievement: A meta-analysis of multisection validity studies. *Review of Educational Research* 51: 281–309.

Cohen, P. A. (April, 1987). A critical analysis and reanalysis of the multisection validity meta-analysis. Paper presented at the 1987 Annual Meeting of the American Educational Research Association, Washington, D. C. (ERIC Document Reproduction Service No. ED 283 876).

Cohen, P. A., and McKeachie, W. J. (1980). The role of colleagues in the evaluation of college teaching. *Improving College and University Teaching* 28: 147–154.

Coleman, J., and McKeachie, W. J. (1981). Effects of instructor/course evaluations on student course selection. *Journal of Educational Psychology* 73: 224–226.

Cooley, W. W., and Lohnes, P. R. (1976). *Evaluation Research in Education*. New York: Irvington.

Costin, F., Greenough, W. T., and Menges, R. J. (1971). Student ratings of college teaching: Reliability, validity and usefulness. *Review of Educational Research* 41: 511–536.

Cranton, P. A., and Hillgarten, W. (1981). The relationships between student ratings and instructor behavior: Implications for improving teaching. *Canadian Journal of Higher Education* 11: 73–81.

Cronbach, L. J. (1971). Test validation. In R. L. Thorndike (ed.), *Educational Measurement*. Washington, D. C.: American Council of Education.

d'Apollonia, S., and Abrami, P. C. (1987). An empirical critique of meta-analysis: The literature on sutdent ratings of instruction. Paper presented at the annual meeting of the American Educational Research Association.

de Wolf, W. A. (1974). Student ratings of instruction in post secondary institutions: A comprehensive annotated bibliography of research reported since 1968 (Vol.1). University of Washington Educational Assessment Center.

Dowell, D. A., and Neal, J. A. (1982). A selective view of the validity of student ratings of teaching. *Journal of Higher Education* 53: 51–62.

Doyle, K. O. (1975). *Student Evaluation of Instruction*. Lexington, MA: D. C. Heath.

Doyle, K. O. (1983). Evaluating teaching. Lexington, MA: Lexington Books.

Drucker, A. J., and Remmers, H. H. (1950). Do alumni and students differ in their attitudes toward instructors? *Purdue University Studies in Higher Education* 70: 62–74.

Dubin, S. S., and Okun, M. (1973). Implications of learning theories for adult instruction. *Adult Education* 21(1): 3–19.

Dukes, R. L., and Victoria, G. (1989). The effects of gender, status, and effective teaching on the evaluations of college instruction. *Teaching Sociology* 17: 447–457.

Dunkin, M. J. (1986). Research on teaching in higher education. In M. C. Wittrock (ed.), *Handbook of Research on Teaching* (3rd Edition). New York: Macmillan.

Dunkin, M. J. (1990). Willingness to obtain student evaluations as a criterion of academic staff performance. *Higher Education Research and Development* 9: 51–60.

Erdle, S., Murray, H. G., and Rushton, J. P. (1985). Personality, classroom behavior, and college teaching effectiveness: A path analysis. *Journal of Educational Psychology* 77: 394–407.

Feldman, K. A. (1976a). Grades and college students' evaluations of their courses and teachers. *Research in Higher Education* 4: 69–111.

Feldman, K. A. (1976b). The superior college teacher from the student's view. *Research in Higher Education* 5: 243–288.

Feldman, K. A. (1977). Consistency and variability among college students in rating their teachers and courses. *Research in Higher Education* 6: 223–274.

Feldman, K. A. (1978). Course characteristics and college students' ratings of their teachers and courses: What we know and what we don't. *Research in Higher Education* 9: 199–242.

Feldman, K. A. (1979). The significance of circumstances for college students' ratings of their teachers and courses. *Research in Higher Education* 10: 149–172.

Feldman, K. A. (1983). The seniority and instructional experience of college teachers as related to the evaluations they receive from their students. *Research in Higher Education* 18: 3–124.

Feldman, K. A. (1984). Class size and students' evaluations of college teacher and courses: A closer look. *Research in Higher Education* 21: 45–116.

Feldman, K. A. (1986). The perceived instructional effectiveness of college teachers as related to their personality and attitudinal characteristics: A review and synthesis. *Research in Higher Education* 24: 139–213.

Feldman, K. A. (1987). Research productivity and scholarly accomplishment: A review and exploration. *Research in Higher Education* 26: 227–298.

Feldman, K. A. (1988). Effective college teaching from the students' and faculty's view: Matched or mismatched priorities. *Research in Higher Education* 28: 291–344.

Feldman, K. A. (1989a). Instructional effectiveness of college teachers as judged by teachers themselves, current and former students, colleagues, administrators, and external (neutral) observers. *Research in Higher Education* 30: 137–194.

Feldman, K. A. (1989b). Association between student ratings of specific instructional dimensions and student achievement: Refining and extending the synthesis of data from multisection validity studies. Research in Higher Education 30: 583–645.

Feldman, K. A. (1990a). An afterword for "the association between student ratings of specific instructional dimensions and student achievement: Refining and extending the synthesis of data from multisection validity studies". Research in Higher Education 31: 315–318.

Feldman, K. A. (1990b). Instructional evaluation. The Teaching Professor. (December): 5–7.

Fincher, C. (1985) Learning theory and research. In J. C. Smart (ed.), Higher Education:Handbook of Theory and Research, Vol.1. (pp.63–96). New York: Agathon Press.

Firth, M. (1979). Impact of work experience on the validity of student evaluations of teaching effectiveness. Journal of Educational Psychology 71: 726–730.

Franklin, J., and Theall, M. (March, 1989). Who reads ratings: Knowledge, attitude and practice of users of student ratings of instruction. Paper presented at the 1988 Annual Meeting of the American Educational Research Association, San Francisco, CA. (ERIC Document Reproduction Service No. ED 306 241).

Frankhouser, W. M. (1984). The effects of different oral directions as to disposition of results on student ratings of college instruction. *Research in Higher Education* 20: 367–374.

French–Lazovich, G. (1981). Peer review: Documentary evidence in the evaluation of teaching. In J. Millman (ed.), *Handbook of Teacher Evaluation*. Beverly Hills, CA: Sage.

Frey, P. W. (1978). A two dimensional analysis of student ratings of instruction. *Research in Higher Education* 9: 69–91.

Frey, P. W. (1979). The Dr. Fox effect and its implications. *Instructional Evaluation* 3: 1–5.

Frey, P. W., Leonard, D. W., and Beatty, W. W. (1975). Student ratings of instruction: Validation research. *American Educational Research Journal* 12: 327–336.

Gage, N. L. (1963). Handbook on Research on Teaching. Chicago: Rand McNally.

Gigliotti, R. J., and Buchtel, F. S. (1990). Attributional bias and course evaluations. *Journal of Educational Psychology* 82: 341–351.

Gilmore, G. M., Kane, M. T., and Naccarato, R. W. (1978). The generalizability of student ratings of instruction: Estimates of teacher and course components. *Journal of Educational Measurement* 15: 1–13.

Guthrie, E. R. (1954). The Evaluation of Teaching: A Progress Report. Seattle: University of Washington Press.

Hayton, G. E. (1983). An investigation of the applicability in technical and further education of a student evaluation of teaching instrument. An unpublished thesis. Department of Education, University of Sydney.

Hildebrand, M. (1972). How to recommend promotion of a mediocre teacher without actually lying. *Journal of Higher Education* 43: 44–62.

Hildebrand, M., Wilson, R. C., and Dienst, E. R. (1971). Evaluating University Teaching. Berkeley: Center for Research and Development in Higher Education, University of California, Berkeley.

Howard, G. S., and Bray, J. H. (1979). Use of norm groups to adjust student ratings of instruction: A warning. *Journal of Educational Psychology* 71: 58–63.

Howard, G. S., Conway, C. G.,and Maxwell, S. E. (1985). Construct validity of measures of college teaching effectiveness. *Journal of Educational Psychology* 77: 187–196.

Howard, G. S., and Maxwell, S. E. (1980). The correlation between student satisfaction and grades: A case of mistaken causation? *Journal of Educational Psychology* 72: 810–820.

Howard, G. S., and Maxwell, S. E. (1982). Do grades contaminate student evaluations of instruction. *Research in Higher Education* 16: 175–188.

Howard, G. S., and Schmeck, R. R. (1979). Relationship of changes in student motivation to student evaluations of instruction. *Research in Higher Education* 10: 305–315.

Hoyt, D. P., Owens, R. E., and Grouling, T. (1973). Interpreting student feedback on instruction and courses. Manhattan, KN: Kansas State University.

Jacobs, L. C. (1987). University faculty and students' opinions of student ratings. Bloomington IN: Bureau of Evaluative Studies and Testing. (ERIC Document Reproduction Service No. ED 291 291).

Krathwohl, D. R., Bloom, B. S., and Masia, B. B. (1964). *Taxonomy of Educational Objectives: The Classification of Educational Goals. Handbook 2. Affective Domain.* New York, McKay, 1964.

Kulik, J. A., and McKeachie, W. J. (1975). The evaluation of teachers in higher education. In Kerlinger (ed.), *Review of Research in Education*, (Vol.3). Itasca, IL: Peacock.

L'Hommedieu, R., Menges, R. J., and Brinko, K. T. (1988). The effects of student ratings feedback to college teachers: A meta-analysis and review of research. Unpublished manuscript, Northwestern University, Center for the Teaching Professions, Evanston, IL.

L'Hommedieu, R., Menges, R. J., and Brinko, K. T. (1990). Methodological explanations for the modest effects of feedback. *Journal of Educational Psychology* 82: 232–241.

Land, M. L. (1985). Vagueness and clarity in the classroom. In T. Husen and T. N. Postlethwaite (eds.), *International Encyclopedia of Education: Research and Studies.* Oxford: Pergamon Press.

Land, M. L., and Combs, A. (1981). Teacher clarity, student instructional ratings, and student performance. Paper presented at the annual meeting of the American Educational Research Association, Los Angeles.

Leventhal, L., Abrami, P. C., Perry, R. P., and Breen L. J. (1975). Section selection in multi-section courses: Implications for the validation and use of student rating forms. *Educational and Psychological Measurement* 35: 885–895.

Leventhal, L., Abrami, P. C., and Perry, R. P. (1976). Teacher rating forms: Do students interested in quality instruction rate teachers differently. *Journal of Educational Psychology* 68: 441–445.

Leventhal, L., Perry, R. P., Abrami, P. C., Turcotte, S. J. C., and Kane, B. (1981, April). Experimental investigation of tenure/promotion in American and Canadian universities. Paper presented at the Annual Meeting of the American Educational Research Association, Los Angeles.

Levinson–Rose, J., and Menges, R. J. (1981). Improving college teaching: A critical review of research. *Review of Educational Research* 51: 403–434.

Lin, Y–G., McKeachie, W. J., and Tucker, D. G. (1984). The use of student ratings in promotion decisions. *Journal of Higher Education* 55: 583–589.

Mackie, K. (1981). The application of learning theory to adult teaching. *Adults: Psychological and Educational Perspectives Series*. Monograph No.2. University of Nottingham, Nottingham.

Marsh, H. W. (1976). The relationship between background variables and students' evaluations of instructional quality. OIS 76–9. Los Angeles, CA: Office of Institutional Studies, University of Southern California.

Marsh, H. W. (1977). The validity of students' evaluations: classroom evaluations of instructors independently nominated as best and worst teachers by graduating seniors. *American Educational Research Journal* 14: 441–447.

Marsh, H. W. (1979). Annotated bibliography of research on the relationship between quality of teaching and quality of research in higher education. Los Angeles: Office of Institutional Studies, University of Southern California.

Marsh, H. W. (1980) The influence of student, course and instructor characteristics on evaluations of university teaching. *American Educational Research Journal* 17: 219–237.

Marsh, H. W. (1981a). Students' evaluations of tertiary instruction: Testing the applicability of American surveys in an Australian setting. *Australian Journal of Education* 25: 177–192.

Marsh, H. W. (1981b). The use of path analysis to estimate teacher and course effects in student ratings of instructional effectiveness. *Applied Psychological Measurement* 6: 47–60.

Marsh, H. W. (1982a). Factors affecting students' evaluations of the same course taught by the same instructor on different occasions. *American Educational Research Journal* 19: 485–497.

Marsh, H. W. (1982b). SEEQ: A reliable, valid, and useful instrument for collecting students' evaluations of university teaching. *British Journal of Educational Psychology* 52: 77–95.

Marsh, H. W. (1982c). Validity of students' evaluations of college teaching: A multitrait-multimethod analysis. *Journal of Educational Psychology* 74: 264–279.

Marsh, H. W. (1983). Multidimensional ratings of teaching effectiveness by students from different academic settings and their relation to student/course/instructor characteristics. *Journal of Educational Psychology* 75: 150–166.

Marsh, H. W. (1984a). Experimental manipulations of university motivation and their effect on examination performance. *British Journal of Educational Psychology* 54: 206–213.

Marsh, H. W. (1984b). Students' evaluations of university teaching: dimensionality, reliability, validity, potential biases, and utility. *Journal of Educational Psychology* 76: 707–754.

Marsh, H. W. (1985). Students as evaluators of teaching. In T. Husen and T. N. Postlethwaite (eds.), *International Encyclopedia of Education: Research and Studies*. Oxford: Pergamon Press.

Marsh, H. W. (1986). Applicability paradigm: Students' evaluations of teaching effectiveness in different countries. *Journal of Educational Psychology* 78: 465–473.

Marsh, H. W. (1987). Students' evaluations of university teaching: Research findings, methodological issues, and directions for future research. *International Journal of Educational Research* 11: 253–388. (Whole Issue No.3)

Marsh, H. W. (1991a). Multidimensional students' evaluations of teaching effectiveness: A test of alternative higher-order structures. *Journal of Educational Psychology* 83: 285–296.

Marsh, H. W. (1991b). A multidimensional perspective on students' evaluations of teaching effectiveness: A reply to Abrami and d'Apollonia (1991). *Journal of Educational Psychology* 83: 416–421.

Marsh, H. W. and Bailey, M. (in press). Multidimensionality of students' evaluations of teaching effectiveness: A profile analysis. *Journal of Higher Education*.

Marsh, H. W., and Cooper, T. L. (1981). Prior subject interest, students' evaluations, and instructional effectiveness. *Multivariate Behavioral Research* 16: 82–104.

Marsh, H. W., Fleiner, H., and Thomas, C. S. Validity and usefulness of student evaluations of instructional quality. *Journal of Educational Psychology* 67: 833–839.

Marsh, H. W., and Hocevar, D. (1984). The factorial invariance of students' evaluations of college teaching. *American Educational Research Journal* 21: 341–366.

Marsh, H. W. and Hocevar, D. (1983). Confirmatory factor analysis of multitrait–multimethod matrices. *Journal of Educational Measurement* 20: 231–248.

Marsh, H. W. and Hocevar, D. (1985). The application of confirmatory factor analysis to the study of self–concept: First and higher order factor structures and their invariance across age groups. *Psychological Bulletin* 97: 562–582.

Marsh, H. W., and Hocevar, D. (1991a). The multidimensionality of students' evaluations of teaching effectiveness: The generality of factor structures across academic discipline, instructor level, and course level. *Teaching and Teacher Education* 7: 9–18.

Marsh, H. W., and Hocevar, D. (1991b). Students' evaluations of teaching effectiveness: The stability of mean ratings of the same teachers over a 13–year period. *Teaching and Teacher Education* 7: 303–314.

Marsh, H. W. and Overall, J. U. (1979a). Long–term stability of students' evaluations: A note on Feldman's "Consistency and variability among college students in rating their teachers and courses. " *Research in Higher Education* 10: 139–147.

Marsh, H. W. and Overall, J. U. (1979b). Validity of students' evaluations of teaching: A comparison with instructor self evaluations by teaching assistants, undergraduate faculty, and graduate faculty. Paper presented at Annual Meeting of the American Educational Research Association, San Francisco (ERIC Document No. ED177 205).

Marsh, H. W. and Overall, J. U. (1980). Validity of students' evaluations of teaching effectiveness: Cognitive and affective criteria. *Journal of Educational Psychology* 72: 468–475.

Marsh, H. W. and Overall, J. U. (1981). The relative influence of course level, course type, and instructor on students' evaluations of college teaching. *American Educational Research Journal* 18: 103–112.

Marsh, H. W., Overall, J. U., and Kesler, S. P. (1979a). Class size, students' evaluations, instructional effectiveness.*American Educational Research Journal* 16: 57–60.

Marsh, H. W., Overall, J. U., and Kesler, S. P. (1979b). Validity of students' evaluations of instructional effectiveness: A comparison of faculty self–evaluations and evaluations by their students. *Journal of Educational Psychology* 71: 149–160.

Marsh, H. W., Overall, J. U., and Thomas, C. S. (1976). The relationship between students' evaluations of instruction and expected grades. Paper presented at the Annual Meeting of the American Educational Research Association, San Francisco. (ERIC Document No. ED 126 140).

Marsh, H. W. and Roche, L. (1991). The use of students' evaluations of university instructors in different settings: The applicability paradigm. (In review.)

Marsh, H. W., Touron, J., and Wheeler, B. (1985). Students' evaluations of university instructors: The applicability of American instruments in a Spanish setting. *Teaching and Teacher Education: An International Journal of Research and Studies* 1: 123–138.

Marsh, H. W., and Ware, J. E. (1982). Effects of expressiveness, content coverage, and incentive on multidimensional student rating scales: New interpretations of the Dr. Fox effect. *Journal of Educational Psychology* 74: 126–134.

Maslow, A. H., and Zimmerman, W. (1956). College teaching ability, scholarly activity, and personality. *Journal of Educational Psychology* 47: 185–189.

McKeachie, W. J. (1963). Research on teaching at the college and university level. In N. L. Gage (ed.), *Handbook of Research on Teaching*. Chicago: Rand McNally.

McKeachie, W. J. (1973). Correlates of student ratings. In A. L. Sockloff (ed.), *Proceedings: The First Invitational Conference on Faculty Effectiveness as Evaluated by Students*. Measurement and Research Center, Temple University.

McKeachie, W. J. (1979). Student ratings of faculty: A reprise. *Academe*: 384–397.

McKeachie, W. J., Lin, Y–G, Daugherty, M., Moffett, M. M., Neigler, C., Nork, J., Walz, M., and Baldwin, R. (1980). Using student ratings and consultation to improve instruction. *British Journal of Educational Psychology* 50: 168–174.

McKeachie, W. J., Pintrich, P. R., Lin, Y–G., Smith, D. A. F., and Sharma, R. (1990). *Teaching and Learning in the College Classroom: A Review of the Research Literature* (2nd ed.). School of Education, University of Michigan.

Menges, R. J. (1973). The new reporters: Students rate instruction. In C. R. Pace (ed.), *Evaluating Learning and Teaching*. San Francisco: Jossey-Bass.

Morsh, J. E., Burgess, G. G., and Smith, P. N. (1956). Student achievement as a measure of instructional effectiveness. *Journal of Educational Psychology* 47: 79–88.

Murray, H. G. (1976). How do good teachers teach? An observational study of the classroom teaching behaviors of Social Science professors receiving low, medium and high teacher ratings. Paper presented at the Canadian Psychological Association meeting.

Murray, H. G. (1980). Evaluating university teaching: A review of research. Toronto, Canada: Ontario Confederation of University Faculty Associations.

Murray, H. G. (1983). Low inference classroom teaching behaviors and student ratings of college teaching effectiveness. *Journal of Educational Psychology* 71: 856–865.

Murray, H. G. (April, 1987). Impact of student instructions ratings on quality of teaching in higher education. Paper presented at the 1987 Annual Meeting of the American Educational Research Association, Washington, DC. (ERIC Document Reproduction Service No. ED 284 495).

Murray, H. G., Rushton, J. P., and Paunonen, S. V. (1990). Teacher personality traits and student instructional ratings in six types of university courses. *Journal of Educational Psychology* 82: 250–261.

Naftulin, D. H., Ware, J. E., and Donnelly, F. A. (1973). The Doctor Fox lecture: A paradigm of educational seduction. *Journal of Medical Education* 48: 630–635.

Neumann, L., and Neumann, Y. (1985). Determinants of students' instructional evaluation: A comparison of four levels of academic areas. *Journal of Educational Research* 78: 152–158.

Ory, J. C. and Braskamp, L. A. (1981). Faculty perceptions of the quality and usefulness of three types of evaluativeinformation. *Research in Higher Education* 15: 271–282.

Ory, J. C., Braskamp, L. A., and Pieper, D. M. (1980). Congruency of student evaluative information collected by three methods. *Journal of Educational Psychology* 72: 181–185.

Overall, J. U., and Marsh, H. W. (1979). Midterm feedback from students: Its relationship to instructional improvement and students' cognitive and affective outcomes. *Journal of Educational Psychology* 71: 856–865.

Overall, J. U., and Marsh, H. W. (1980). Students' evaluations of instruction: A longitudinal study of their stability. *Journal of Educational Psychology* 72: 321–325.

Overall, J. U., and Marsh, H. W. (1982). Students' evaluations of teaching: An update. *American Association for Higher Education Bulletin*: 35(4) 9–13.

Palmer, J., Carliner, G., and Romer, T. (1978). Learning, leniency, and evaluations. *Journal of Educational Psychology* 70: 855–863.

Perry, R. P. (1991). In J. C. Smart (ed.), *Higher Education: Handbook of Theory and Research*, Vol. 7. New York: Agathon Press.

Perry, R. P., and Dickens, W. J. (1984). Perceived control in the college classroom: Response–outcome contingency training and instructor expressiveness effects on student achievement and causal attributions. *Journal of Educational Psychology* 76: 966–981.

Perry, R. P., and Magnusson, J.-L. (1987). Effective instruction and students' perceptions of control in the college classroom: Multiple lecture effects. *Journal of Educational Psychology* 79: 453–460.

Perry, R. P., and Penner, K. S. (1990). Enhancing academic achievement in college students through attributional retraining and instruction. *Journal of Educational Psychology* 82: 262–271.

Peterson, C., and Cooper, S. (1980). Teacher evaluation by graded and ungraded students. *Journal of Educational Psychology* 72: 682–685.

Pohlman, J. T. (1975). A multivariate analysis of selected class characteristics and student ratings of instruction. *Multivariate Behavioral Research* 10: 81–91.

Prosser, M., and Trigwell, K. (1990). Student evaluations of teaching and courses: Student study strategies as a criterion of validity. *Higher Education* 20: 135–142.

Prosser, M., and Trigwell, K. (1991). Student evaluations of teaching and courses: Student learning approaches and outcomes as criteria of validity. Paper in review, University of Technology, Centre For Learning and Teaching, Sydney NSW Australia.

Remmers, H. H. (1931). The equivalence of judgments and test items in the sense of the Spearman–Brown formula. *Journal of Educational Psychology* 22: 66–71.

Remmers, H. H. (1958). On students' perceptions of teachers' effectiveness. In McKeachie (ed.), *The Appraisal of Teaching in Large Universities*. Ann Arbor: The University of Michigan.

Remmers, H. H. (1963). Teaching methods in research on teaching. In N. L. Gage (ed.), *Handbook on Teaching*. Chicago: Rand McNally. Rich, H. E. (1976). Attitudes of college and university faculty toward the use of student evaluation. *Educational Research Quarterly* 3: 17–28.

Rodin, M., and Rodin, B. (1972). Student evaluations of teachers. *Science* 177: 1164–1166.

Rosenshine, B. (1971). Teaching behaviors and student achievement. London: National Foundation for Educational Research.

Rosenshine, B., and Furst, N. (1973). The use of direct observation to study teaching. In

R. M. W. Travers (ed.), *Second Handbook of Research on Teaching*. Chicago: Rand McNally.

Rushton, J. P., Brainerd, C. J. and Pressley, M. (1983). Behavioral development and construct validity: The principle of aggregation. *Psychological Bulletin* 94: 18–38.

Ryans, D. G. (1960). Prediction of teacher effectiveness. In C. W. Harris (eds.), *Encyclopedia of Educational Research*. New York: Macmillan.

Salthouse, T. A., McKeachie, W. J., and Lin Y. G. (1978). An experimental investigation of factors affecting university promotion decisions. *Journal of Higher Education* 49: 177–183.

Scriven, M. (1981). Summative teacher evaluation. In J. Millman (ed.), *Handbook of Teacher Evaluation*. Beverly Hills, CA: Sage.

Seldin, P. (1975). *How Colleges Evaluate Professors: Current Policies and Practices in Evaluating Classroom Teaching Performance in Liberal Arts Colleges*. Croton–on–Hudson, New York: Blythe–Pennington, 1975.

Stephens, M. D. (1985). Teaching methods for adults. In T. Husen and T. N. Postlethwaite (eds.), *The International Encyclopedia of Education*, Vol 9. Oxford:Pergamon Press.

Voght, K. E. and Lasher, H. (1973). Does student evaluation stimulate improved teaching? Bowling Green, OH: Bowling Green University (ERIC ED 013 371)

Ward, M D., Clark, D. C., and Harrison, G. V. (1981, April). The observer effect in classroom visitation. Paper presented at the annual meeting of the American Educational Research Association, Los Angeles.

Ware, J. E., and Williams, R. G. (1975). The Dr. Fox effect: A study of lecturer expressiveness and ratings of instruction. *Journal of Medical Education* 5: 149–156.

Ware, J. E., and Williams, R. G. (1977). Discriminant analysis of student ratings as a means of identifying lecturers who differ in enthusiasm or information giving. *Educational and Psychological Measurement* 37: 627–639.

Ware, J. E., and Williams, R. G. (1979). Seeing through the Dr. Fox effect: A response to Frey. *Instructional Evaluation* 3: 6–10.

Ware, J. E., and Williams, R. G. (1980). A reanalysis of the Doctor Fox experiments. *Instructional Evaluation* 4: 15–18.

Warrington, W. G. (1973). Student evaluation of instruction at Michigan State University. In A. L. Sockloff (ed.), Proceedings: The first invitational conference on faculty effectiveness as evaluated by students. Philadelphia: Measurement and Research Center, Temple University.

Watkins, D., Marsh, H. W., and Young, D. (1987). Evaluating tertiary teaching: A New Zealand perspective. *Teaching and Teacher Education: An International Journal of Research and Studies* 3: 41–53.

Webb, W. B., and Nolan, C. Y. (1955). Student, supervisor, and self–ratings of instructional proficiency. *Journal of Educational Psychology* 46: 42–46.

Williams, R. G., and Ware, J. E. (1976). Validity of student ratings of instruction under different incentive conditions: A further study of the Dr. Fox effect. *Journal of Educational Psychology* 68: 48–56.

Williams, R. G., and Ware, J. E. (1977). An extended visit with Dr. Fox: Validity of student ratings of instruction after repeated exposures to a lecturer. *American Educational Research Journal* 14: 449–457.

Wilson, R. C. (1986). Improving faculty teaching: Effective use of student evaluations and consultants. *Journal of Higher Education* 57: 196–211.

Wilson, R. C. (1987). Toward excellence in teaching. In L. M. Aleamoni (ed.), *Tech-*

nique for Evaluating and Improving Instruction. New Direction for Teaching and Learning, no.31. San Francisco: Jossey-Bass.

Winocur, S., Schoen, L. G., and Sirowatka, A. H. (1989). Perceptions of male and female academics within a teaching context. *Research in Higher Education* 30: 317–329.

Yunker, J. A. (1983). Validity research on student evaluations of teaching effectiveness: Individual versus class mean observations. *Research in Higher Education* 19: 363–379.

Reputational Rankings of Colleges, Universities, and Individual Disciplines and Fields of Study, From Their Beginnings to the Present

David S. Webster
Oklahoma State University

"In the absence of a system of hereditary ranks and titles, without a tradition of honors conferred by a monarch, and with no well-known status ladder even of high-class regiments to confer various degrees of cachet, Americans have had to depend for their mechanism of snobbery far more than other peoples on their college and university hierarchy."
Paul Fussell, "Schools for Snobbery," *New Republic*, October 4, 1982, p. 25.

INTRODUCTION

America has more than 2,000 four-year colleges and universities, far more than any other nation in the world. These institutions are distributed across a large geographical area, and they vary enormously in quality. The nation's best universities are probably better than those anywhere in the world, and its very worst colleges and universities are probably about as bad as, or even worse than, those in any other developed nation in the world. Despite the large number of American colleges and universities, the immense range in quality among them, and the enormous number of students they serve, there are few sources available to provide students, prospective students, their parents, campus administrators, philanthropic organizations, policy makers, and other interested parties with accurate information about the relative quality of American colleges and universities. The federal government, with a few exceptions early in the 20th century,

For a great deal of help in finding material on academic quality rankings years ago, when I was first beginning to learn about them, I thank Mary Langenfeld of the University of Wisconsin at Madison; Judy Lawrence, then of the Higher Education Research Institute at UCLA; and Lorraine Mathies, then librarian of the Education/Psychology Library at UCLA. For a great deal of help in finding material about them more recently I thank Haifa El-Agha, then a graduate student in higher education at Oklahoma State University, and Jill Holmes, social science librarian at Oklahoma State University. I thank Carol Smith, then of Oklahoma State University, and Rilla Collins of Oklahoma State University for typing the manuscript and for much other help with it.

has never ranked colleges and universities; neither have the various states ranked the institutions, even the public institutions, located within their borders by their academic quality. Modern accrediting agencies stratify institutions into two main groups—those that are accredited and those that are not—without making much effort to distinguish any further among those in each group. Most major associations of colleges and universities, such as the Association of American Universities (AAU), the Council of Graduate Schools (CGS), and the Association of American Colleges (AAC), have never published rankings of their members. College catalogs, brochures, and view books seldom compare the institution they promote with any others. The numerous college guidebooks, although some of them stratify colleges and universities into several groups according to their selectivity in admitting new freshmen, seldom if ever rank them according to academic quality.

With so many colleges and universities of such varying degrees of academic quality, and with so little comparative information available about which are the best institutions or the best professional schools, departments, and programs at them, academic quality rankings are the best means available to provide such information. Although many criteria have been used to rank colleges and universities over the years (for a summary and critique of them, see Webster, 1981), one criterion has been used in all nine published multidisciplinary rankings—that of reputation for academic excellence. This chapter reviews reputational rankings, from the first one, published by Raymond Hughes (1925) to rankings published as recently as June, 1991.

Definitions Concerning Reputational Rankings

Reputational rankings are rankings of colleges, universities, or—far more often—individual departments or professional schools at them, according to how highly others regard them. Theoretically, one could rank undergraduate and master's level programs by such rankings. In practice, however, most reputational rankings—and certainly most of the best-known, most influential ones—have rated doctoral level education in the arts, sciences, and engineering. A smaller number of the best-known ratings have ranked various kinds of professional schools. (The rankings that *U.S. News and World Report* has published, since 1983, of colleges and universities based on the strength of their undergraduate education are an exception to this generalization.) Theoretically, one could use one or more of many different groups—students, prospective students, alumni, and the educated general public, for example—as raters. In practice, however, most reputational rankings have employed as raters either academic administrators—especially academic deans and department chairs—or professors, or some combination. Theoretically, the raters could be asked to rank institutions according to one or more of a large number of criteria—for example, day-to-day student advising, dissertation advising, extracurricular activities, service to the community, and so on. In practice, however, most reputational rankings have asked about either or both of two characteristics—the research prowess of a department's faculty and departments' overall educational effectiveness.

Several reputational rankings, over the years, have determined the top 10, 20, or whatever departments in a field and then have listed them not in descending order, from highest-ranked to lowest-ranked, but rather in alphabetical order. Such rankings have been excluded from this review, except for Hughes' second ranking (1934b). Although it did not rank in order the most highly regarded departments in each discipline, it is nonetheless included because of its historical importance. It was compiled by the inventor of reputational rankings, it was the second such ranking ever published, and it is possibly the only reputational ranking that was published for more than 30 years, from 1925 to 1957. However, the many rankings that have listed the top-rated departments in a field in descending order, then stratified the lower-rated ones into groups and arranged schools within each group in alphabetical order have been included.

Most of the rankings discussed here were entirely reputational—that is, they were based entirely on the departments', professional schools', or institutions' reputations in the eyes of others. Some, however, were not entirely reputational. Manly's (no date) rankings were based mostly on reputational measures, although he also used objective data. The National Academy of Sciences' (NAS) ranking (Jones, Lindzey, and Coggeshall [eds.], 1982) used, depending on the discipline being covered, anywhere from 12 to 16 measures, only four of which were based on reputation. Its reputational measures, however, have been by far the most frequently cited in analyses of these rankings in both scholarly journals and the popular press. Rankings which were based partly but not entirely on reputational measures have been included in this chapter if the reputational component was an important part of them. Most reputational rankings have ranked departments in only one discipline or professional field. A handful, however, have ranked them in many fields of study. We refer frequently to multidisciplinary reputational rankings. These are the nine rankings of American institutions published by Hughes (1925); Hughes (1934b); Keniston (1959); Cartter (1966a); Roose and Andersen (1970); Margulies and Blau (1973); Blau and Margulies (1974/75); Ladd and Lipset (in Scully, 1979); and the NAS (in Jones, Lindzey, and Coggeshall [eds.], 1982). These rankings all covered many disciplines and/or professional school fields, from 17 (Margulies and Blau, 1973) to 36 (Roose and Andersen, 1970). All of them thus covered far more disciplines than did any other reputational ranking of American colleges and universities. The large majority of American reputational rankings have ranked only a single discipline or professional school field, although a handful have ranked a few. For example, Solmon and Astin (1981) ranked six liberal arts fields; *U.S. News and World Report* has ranked, since 1987, the best professional schools in four areas; and "The Cartter Report . . ." (1977) ranked the best professional schools in three fields. Though the nine multidisciplinary rankings are by no means without faults, taken as a group they are considerably better methodologically than were most other reputational rankings published contemporaneously with them.

LITERATURE REVIEWS OF REPUTATIONAL RANKINGS

Three extensive reviews of reputational rankings have been published, those by Lawrence and Green (1980), Conrad and Blackburn (1985), and Tan (1986). Lawrence and Green (1980, pp. 4–22) discussed the reputational rankings of Ph.D.-granting departments in both the arts and sciences and professional schools. Of the three reviews, theirs devoted the most attention to the only book-length work about reputational rankings ever published, W. Patrick Dolan's harshly critical *The Ranking Game* (1976). Conrad and Blackburn's review (1985, pp. 288–294) is the most useful of the three in considering the major criticisms of reputational rankings, discussing (pp. 292–294) seven frequently made complaints about them. Tan (1986, pp. 226–244) drew heavily on both Lawrence and Green's (1980) and Conrad and Blackburn's (1985) reviews; his is the longest, the most recent, and probably the most useful of the three. Next we discuss reputational rankings over the years, beginning with Hughes' 1925 ranking, the first reputational ranking ever published and one of the earliest rankings of colleges and universities of any type. We proceed chronologically, for the most part, from 1925 to the present.

THE ACHIEVEMENT OF RAYMOND HUGHES[1]

The inventor of the reputational ranking was Raymond M. Hughes, longtime professor of chemistry at Miami University of Ohio. He is the only natural scientist ever to compile a multidisciplinary reputational ranking. He served as president of Miami University from 1913 to 1927 and as president of Iowa State College from 1927 to 1936. He is said to have been the first to propose that American colleges and universities establish artists-in-residence programs (Havighurst, 1958, pp. 190–191). Throughout his life Hughes was an inveterate compiler of rankings of colleges and universities according to a variety of criteria. Among numerous other rankings he produced, both published and unpublished, he listed 554 American colleges and universities in order of how much money they had spent in 1934–35 (Hughes, no date); 30 institutions in order of

---

[1] I have been greatly helped, in writing the section on Raymond Hughes, by Arthur Steven Higgins' excellent, unfortunately little known Columbia University Teachers College Ed.D. dissertation (1968).

the number of current presidents of 300 colleges and universities to whom they had granted doctoral degrees (Hughes, 1940); 96 institutions in order of how many doctoral degrees they had granted, 1937/38–1941/42 (Hughes, 1946); and all the states by the proportion of their residents who were graduate students in 1949/50 (Hughes, 1952).

Hughes' 1925 Ranking

In response to a request from the North Central Association of Schools and Colleges for a study of graduate schools, Hughes did such a study in 1924. He presented it to the AAC in January, 1925 (Robertson [ed.], 1928, p. 161), and published it, with inmates at the Ohio State Reformatory doing the printing, as *A Study of the Graduate Schools of America* in 1925. In this slim book, Hughes ranked departments in the 20 fields of study in which Miami University then had departments. Nineteen were liberal arts disciplines, the only professional field being education. By choosing to rank predominantly liberal arts disciplines Hughes began a custom that has lasted until the present—that multidisciplinary reputational rankings would usually rank mostly or entirely liberal arts disciplines, not professional fields. (A frequent exception to this generalization, however, is engineering.) He asked his raters to consider these departments' desirability for "graduate work" in each discipline, thereby establishing another custom, in which multidisciplinary rankings have ranked departments for the quality of their graduate, usually Ph.D.-level work, not their undergraduate education.

Hughes asked his raters to rank the departments in one of these fields of study at each of 36 institutions. They included 24 of the 26 institutions that were then members of the AAU, two Canadian universities (McGill and Toronto), and 10 additional American institutions: Bryn Mawr, California Institute of Technology, University of Cincinnati, University of Colorado, Massachusetts Institute of Technology, New York University, University of Pittsburgh, Rice Institute, the University of Texas, and the University of Washington. This group did not include Hughes' own institution, Miami of Ohio. By asking his raters to rate only these 36 institutions, Hughes prevented strong departments at institutions other than these from being ranked.

For each of the 20 disciplines he ranked, Hughes enlisted a faculty member from that discipline at Miami University to submit a list of 40 to 60 people who taught the subject in American colleges and universities. Half or more of the raters were supposed to be professors in colleges, not universities. Each respondent was asked to rank all the departments in these 36 institutions offering work in his or her discipline from 1 to 5, according to their quality. Then Hughes multiplied the number of 1 ratings "by 4, the number of 2 ratings by 3, the number of 3 ratings by 2" (p. 6), and the number of 4 and 5 ratings by 1. About half the professors who had received rating forms returned them. Hughes then calculated the top-ranked departments for graduate work in each discipline. He provided tables for every discipline listing each institution in order of the number of first, second, third, and so on ratings it received, but he did not aggregate these ratings and list an overall score for each department. Neither did Hughes aggregate his departmental data to make institution-wide rankings. However, Walter Crosby Eells, who over many years produced several of his own rankings of graduate departments and entire institutions based on how many doctoral degrees they had conferred, produced his own ranking, using Hughes' data, "for the sixteen universities which were given a rank in at least 10 of the 20 departments" (Eells, 1926, p. 535).

In not compiling institution-wide rankings, Hughes again established a precedent that has lasted until today. Of the eight multidisciplinary rankings published after Hughes' ranking of 1925, only one (Keniston, 1959) aggregated departmental rankings into institution-wide ones.

Hughes' 1934 Study

Several years after his 1925 ranking was published, Hughes produced another reputational study, the second one ever published. It came about as follows. In 1932 Hughes, as the American Council on Education's (ACE) representative from the Association of Land-Grant Colleges, was elected chairman of the ACE (Higgins, 1968, p. 20). Five months after he took office, the ACE appointed a Committee on Graduate Instruction, with Hughes chairman of it. In 1933, in an interim report to the ACE, Hughes wrote that "the committee had voted 'to prepare a list of graduate schools offering adequate facilities for work in the various fields' " (p. 20).

The 1934 report was considerably different from the 1925 ranking. Some of the differences were as follows:

1. The 1925 ranking had included 20 disciplines. The 1934 report covered 35 fields.
2. In 1925, Hughes had selected his raters rather informally, asking a Miami University professor in each field of study to recommend raters Hughes might poll. In 1934, he asked the secretary of each field's national learned society to provide him with a list of scholars in its discipline, "distributed, as far as possible, among the various special branches of the field" (Hughes, 1934b, p. 193).
3. Hughes employed considerably more raters in 1934. In 1925 he had received returns from about 27 raters per discipline. In 1934, he got responses from about 58 raters per field.
4. In 1925, Hughes asked respondents to rate the institutions in their field from one to five; in 1934, he asked them to indicate the departments in their field they thought were adequately equipped for graduate work and to "star"

approximately the best 20 percent of them. Whereas Hughes had published his 1925 rankings discipline by discipline in approximate order of the points each department received, he arranged his 1934 findings very differently. All institutions that at least half the respondents in that discipline had indicated were adequately equipped for graduate work were listed not in descending rank order but in alphabetical order; the ones that at least half the raters "starred" had a star placed next to their name. He made no attempt to rank the highest-scoring departments in a discipline.

All in all, Hughes' methodology was very different in his 1934 report than it had been in his earlier one, although he did not explain why in the brief remarks that prefaced his 1934 study. There are at least three reasons why he may have changed his methodology. First, the ACE, which sponsored the second ranking but not the first, may have requested the change (Somit and Tanenhaus, 1982, p. 106). Second, the ACE's Committee on Graduate Instruction may have asked for the change. Third, Hughes himself may have decided to make the changes (Somit and Tanenhaus, 1982, p. 106).

Hughes selected the fields he included in his 1934 report very strangely. By 1934, he had left Miami University to become president of Iowa State College, a land-grant school with its greatest strength in agriculture and engineering. Of the 15 fields that Hughes added in 1934, six were in engineering and five in agriculture. Some of the new "fields" were not really fields at all but rather sub-fields, such as animal nutrition, bacteriology, entomology, genetics, human nutrition, plant pathology, plant physiology, and soil science. Iowa State performed far better in the 15 newly added fields, as a group, than it did in the 20 fields that Hughes had ranked earlier. Of the 20 fields that had been included in 1925, it was starred in one (5%) and was listed, without being starred, in three (15%). Of the 15 fields added in 1934, Iowa State was starred in three (20%) and listed, without being starred, in seven (47%). Of the eight "fields" that were really sub-fields, Iowa State was starred in bacteriology, entomology, and soil science, and listed in all the others—animal nutrition, genetics, human nutrition, plant pathology, and plant physiology. The reason why Hughes added these sub-fields is almost certainly to make Iowa State look better than it otherwise would have. Webster aggregated the departmental rankings—or, in the case of Hughes' 1934 study, what could have been his departmental rankings, had Hughes calculated them—of seven multidisciplinary reputational rankings to get institution wide ones. Iowa State ranked higher in 1934—tied for 19th place—than it did in any of the other rankings (Webster, 1983, Table 11, p. 23).

In an article published shortly after his 1934 report appeared, Hughes listed what he considered the survey's faults. One was that the 35 fields represented were a very disparate group, consisting of what might be considered major fields, such as mathematics, physics, and history, which are carried on in a large way in many institutions; minor fields, such as anthropology, astronomy, fine arts, in which graduate work at the doctorate level is carried on in only a few institutions; and subfields, such as plant pathology, plant physiology, and entomology, which could certainly be looked upon as subordinate to the general fields of botany and zoology. . . . Owing to a lack of uniformity of policy in listing these subjects, it was very difficult to arrive at any list of fields which suitably represented the graduate work in all of the institutions really offering work in the subjects. (Hughes, 1934a, pp. 118–119)

While Hughes did not admit that his use of these sub-fields considerably improved his own institution's rating, his discussion of the fields he selected may have been a tacit admission that he realized that by choosing the fields he did he had certainly done so.

Hughes did not mention what may have been another fault of his survey. Reputational rankings are often criticized for using as raters too many leading, rather than ordinary, scholars in a field. Hughes himself, in his 1925 ranking, stipulated that at least half the raters in each discipline should be from colleges, not universities, in an apparent effort to make sure that he included a substantial number of rank and file scholars. But in 1934, when he asked national learned societies to provide lists "of 100 well-known scholars" (Hughes, 1934b, p. 193), he ended up polling a disproportionate number of the leading scholars in each field. His raters in psychology, for example, included Gordon Allport, Edwin Boring, Clark Hull, Lewis Terman, Edward Thorndike, Louis Thurstone, and Edward Tolman (pp. 221–222).

Hughes did not provide field-by-field rankings in 1934, much less institutional ones. But nature abhors a vacuum, and, as has been the case with all the multidisciplinary reputational rankings whose compiler(s) did not aggregate departmental rankings into institution-wide ones, others were ready to do what Hughes and his committee had not. One of them was Eells, who had already combined Hughes' 1925 departmental data into institution-wide totals. He took Hughes' 1934 data and ranked institutions by how many of their departments were at least adequately staffed. The University of California and the University of Wisconsin tied for first, each with 31 such departments (Eells, 1934, Table 1, p. 709).

A year later, Embree (1935, p. 655) published his own rating, loosely based on Hughes' 1934 results. In several cases, he combined some of Hughes' subfields into one department. Plant physiology, plant pathology, and soil science, for example, were all subsumed under botany. He also added, as one department, pathology and the clinical sciences of medicine, neither of which Hughes had included. Embree wound up with 24 departments, compared with Hughes' 35, and then ranked institutions according to the number of departments in which they were starred. His results were very different from those of Eells. Harvard, with 22 starred departments, Chicago, with 21, and Columbia, with 19, were the three leading universities. California tied for fourth, and Wisconsin tied for ninth.

Still a third scholar aggregated Hughes' departmental data into institution-wide totals. Foster determined those institutions that had the greatest proportion of their departments included among those Hughes had starred (1936, Table 18, p. 36). MIT, with 91 percent of its departments starred, Princeton, with 82 percent, and Chicago, with 81 percent, led the list. He also ranked institutions after crediting them with 10 points for each starred department and seven points for each adequate one (Table 19, p. 37). California, Harvard, and Columbia, in that order, led that list.

Hughes, along with Allan Cartter, is one of the two most important figures in the history of reputational rankings. He invented the reputational ranking and compiled what are possibly the only two reputational rankings ever published before 1957. He established many of the practices that most or all later multidisciplinary reputational rankings would follow, such as concentrating on graduate education; surveying predominantly liberal arts disciplines, not professional school fields; and not aggregating departmental data into institution-wide rankings. Keniston (1959) and Cartter (1966a) both published Hughes' 1925 rankings next to their own to show how the reputations of the departments they ranked compared to their reputations in his germinal ranking.

REPUTATIONAL RANKINGS, 1934–1959

Almost no reputational rankings were published in the quarter century from 1934–1959. What may possibly have been the third reputational ranking ever compiled was never published. More than a decade after it was completed the journalist Chesly Manly published this description of it in the *Chicago Tribune*:

> In 1946, members of the Association of American universities (*sic*) rated themselves according to the eminence of their faculties. Members of each department of instruction at each university were asked to evaluate the corresponding departments of other universities. Each department was given a numerical value and each university received an average score for all of its departments conferring the Pr.D. (*sic*) degree.
>
> Although this confidential rating was never published, a copy was shown to this reporter. Yale had the best score, an average of 1.39 for 24 departments. In the scoring method used, the lowest average was the best. Harvard, with 23 departments awarding the doctorate, was second, with a score of 1.43. Chicago, with 26 such departments, was tied with California for third place with a score of 1.49. Next was Cal Tech, with only seven departments, and following in order were Columbia, Princeton, Wisconsin, Pennsylvania, Illinois, Cornell, and Johns Hopkins. (Manly, no date, p. 3)

Possibly the next reputational ranking ever published was compiled by Manly himself. He was not an academician but rather a reporter for the *Chicago Tribune*. He wrote, among other books, *The Twenty-year Revolution: From Roosevelt to Eisenhower*, a product of the Cold War which argued that

> the primary menace to [America] is not the Soviet military threat, but internal subversion through control of foreign policy and related armaments programs. (Manly, 1954, p. 1)

In a series of articles published in the *Chicago Sunday Tribune* in spring, 1957, he ranked the United States' purportedly 10 best universities, coeducational colleges, men's colleges, women's colleges, law schools, and engineering schools (Manly, no date, pp. 1–2).

Manly did not report exactly how he arrived at his rankings. He seems to have compiled them mostly according to the opinions of a few dozen "consultants." They were not purely reputational rankings, however, for he wrote that he also collected "a great mass of objective data" (p. 1), which "was used to determine the order of rating when there was no clearly defined consensus" (p. 1). Writing for a Chicago newspaper, he seems to have selected a disproportionately large number of his "consultants" from the upper midwest. He listed 33 such consultants (an unknown number were not named), of whom 15 were currently employed in the upper midwest; fully seven of these were at the University of Chicago (p. 3).

Perhaps that is why colleges and universities from the upper midwest sometimes seem to be ranked higher than they "should" be. Of the 10 leading law schools in the United States, no fewer than five were from the upper midwest— Chicago (second), Michigan (fifth), Wisconsin (seventh), Illinois (ninth), and Northwestern (tenth). Of the 10 leading co-educational colleges, Oberlin was ranked first, ahead of Swarthmore, Reed, and Pomona, and Carleton was ranked third. Among men's liberal arts colleges, Kenyon was ranked third, ahead of Wesleyan (Connecticut), Hamilton, and Williams.

Manly's early reputational rankings were quite distinctive in three ways. First, four of his six rankings, all except those of law and engineering schools, were of "whole" colleges and universities, not, as most reputational rankings have been, of academic disciplines or professional fields. Second, while most reputational rankings have been of graduate level education, three of Manly's rankings— those of men's, women's, and co-educational colleges—ranked undergraduate, not graduate education. Third, while almost all reputational rankings have specified that they are either of graduate or undergraduate education, in Manly's rankings of universities and of engineering schools, he did not ask raters to distinguish between the two but rather to rate the whole institution, including both graduate and undergraduate education.

These six rankings may be the earliest reputational rankings ever published by anyone other than Hughes. However, perhaps because they were not compiled by an academician and appeared not in an academic publication but rather a newspaper, they are little known. They are seldom mentioned in the literature on academic quality rankings, not nearly as often as the two rankings by Hughes which preceded them and the one by Keniston which followed them.

KENISTON'S RANKING OF 1959

Hayward Keniston was the only humanities scholar ever to compile a multidisciplinary reputational ranking. He graduated *summa cum laude* from Harvard in 1904 and received his Ph.D. there in 1911. He taught Spanish for more than a decade (1914–25) at Cornell. He then moved to the University of Chicago, where he taught Spanish (1925–40), and afterwards to the University of Michigan, where he served as professor of Romance languages (1940–52) and Dean of the College of Literature, Science, and the Arts (1945–51). He was an outstanding scholar, and "for roughly 15 years (1925–1940), [he] ranked as this country's perhaps foremost, best-known spokesman for Spanish philology" (Malkiel, 1971, p. 677). Like Hughes, Keniston enjoyed making lists. Malkiel commented on Keniston's penchant for frequency lists and bibliographies, writing that "there is the same positivistic tidiness and meticulosity (also, on the reverse side, the same dryness) informing [Keniston's] frequency lists, bibliographies, guides . . ." (p. 679). Keniston, incidentally, was the father of Kenneth Keniston, Andrew Mellon Professor of Human Development at MIT, who wrote frequently from the late 1960s to the early 1970s about student activists.

Starting in 1956, Keniston served on the staff of the University of Pennsylvania's Educational Survey, an effort by that institution to take stock of its position among American research universities. In connection with his work there, he compiled, when he was well into his 70s, a multidisciplinary reputational ranking which was published as an appendix to his *Graduate Study and Research in the Arts and Sciences at the University of Pennsylvania* (1959). Except for Hughes' 1925 ranking, it was the only multidisciplinary reputational ranking ever compiled under the auspices of a college or university.

In contrast to all the other multidisciplinary reputational rankings, Keniston's was based on the opinions of department chairpersons only. He surveyed the chairpersons at 25 leading universities, which he used these criteria to choose: "(1) membership in the Association of American Universities, (2) number of Ph.D.'s awarded in recent years, (3) geographical distribution" (Keniston, 1959, p. 115).

In selecting the universities to include in his study, Keniston looked for comprehensive research universities like the University of Pennsylvania. He did not include Massachusetts Institute of Technology and California Institute of Technology since they were technical institutes, not universities. Some of the choices he made about institutions to include and exclude are open to question. He included Catholic University, for example, a charter member of the AAU, but not Michigan State (Harrington, 1957) or Brown.

Keniston provided the chairpersons of 24 departments at each of the 25 universities he included a list of these 25 universities, and he asked them to rank the 15 strongest departments in their discipline. He received replies from about 80 percent of the chairs, or about 20 per discipline, so his ranking was based on fewer respondents per discipline than any other multidisciplinary ranking. If an institution was not included among the 25, it was quite unlikely that any of its departments would be ranked, no matter how well-regarded they were, although a few strong departments at institutions Keniston excluded did get some write-in votes.

Keniston's ranking had several unusual features. First, he combined his departmental rankings into four area-wide rankings for the humanities, social sciences, biological sciences, and physical sciences. His ranking and the *Cartter Report* are the only ones that ever aggregated their disciplinary rankings into areawide ones.

Second, he was the only compiler of a multidisciplinary reputational ranking ever to aggregate his disciplinary rankings into institution-wide ones. He also aggregated Hughes'(1925) departmental rankings into institution-wide ones and displayed what would have been Hughes' institution-wide rankings, had Hughes aggregated his departmental rankings into institution-wide ones, next to Keniston's own rankings.

Third, as Harrington (1957), later the president of the University of Wisconsin, has pointed out, Keniston chose an exceptionally large proportion of the disciplines he ranked from the humanities. Eleven of his 24 (46%) were from this area, in comparison to Cartter's *Assessment of Quality in Graduate Education*, hereafter called the *Cartter Report*, published seven years later, in which only six of the 29 disciplines selected (21%) were from the humanities. Two of the humanities fields Keniston included, Oriental studies and Slavic studies, have never been included in any other multidisciplinary reputational ranking. He may have selected so many disciplines from the humanities because of his own background in Spanish language and literature. Or he may have chosen them because the University of Pennsylvania was stronger in the humanities than in any other area, ranking eighth in the humanities, 10th in biological sciences, 14th in the social sciences, and in some unspecified position lower than 17th in the physical sciences. Like Hughes in his 1934 ranking, Keniston may have wanted to include those fields in which his university was strongest in order to enable it to look better than it otherwise would have. Pennsylvania ranked 6th in Slavic studies and 8th in Oriental studies, for example, and in only five of the other 22 fields of study that Keniston included did it rank as high as 8th. Just as

Keniston selected an unusually large number of fields from the humanities, he selected an unusually small number from the biological sciences—only two (8%), botany and zoology. (By contrast, the *Cartter Report* [1966] included eight disciplines [28%] from the biological sciences.)

Fourth, along with Hughes (1925), Keniston is the only compiler of a multidisciplinary reputational ranking not to include engineering among the fields he ranked. The reason he failed to include it was probably because doing so would have lowered the University of Pennsylvania's standing. Although Pennsylvania ranked 11th among institutions, overall, on its strength in the 24 fields Keniston included, it almost certainly would have ranked far lower in engineering, because in the *Cartter Report*, published only seven years after Keniston's rating, it ranked 13th in electrical engineering, only "good" in mechanical engineering, and only "adequate plus" in both chemical and civil engineering.

Fifth, he assigned some of the disciplines he ranked to a broad area idiosyncratically—for example, he listed geography with the physical sciences, not the social sciences (Harrington, 1957) and history with the humanities, not the social sciences.

OTHER REPUTATIONAL RANKINGS, 1959–1966

Other than the rankings discussed so far, very few reputational rankings were compiled before the *Cartter Report*. This section describes five—four published and one unpublished—of the few that were.

The first of them was done by an Australian geographer and published in an Australian geography journal (Thomson, 1961). It was possibly the only ranking entirely of American departments in any discipline to be published in a foreign journal. Thomson interviewed 36 geographers, 16 of them the "administrative heads" of their departments, from 20 institutions. He asked them "to list the graduate departments where the student would receive the best general training" (p. 138). He then ranked the 20 departments that were mentioned at least once.

Somit and Tanenhaus, in a book-length study of the discipline of political science (1964), ranked the top 33 graduate political science departments based on responses from a sample of 430 members of the American Political Science Association. They found (Table 3, p. 34) that there was a close correlation between the rankings of these departments and Keniston's ranking of the institution as a whole. They also found that their respondents who were strongly pro-behavioral ranked behaviorally oriented political science departments very differently from the way strongly anti-behavioral political scientists did. Pro-behavioralists ranked Yale's and Northwestern's behaviorally oriented political science departments first and fifth, respectively, while anti-behavioralists ranked these departments respectively sixth and twentieth (pp. 38–39).

Sieber (with Lazarsfeld, 1966) asked education school deans and coordinators to name "schools or departments of education in the nation which they considered to be doing 'the most worthwhile and competent research'" (p. 30). Of the schools that were mentioned, they then ranked those that had at least 40 faculty members (Table 2, Appendix C-2).

Although the field of broadcasting has never been included in a multidisciplinary reputational ranking, it was the subject of one of the earliest reputational rankings. Kittross (1966) surveyed those subscribers and ex-subscribers to *Journal of Broadcasting* who he thought were most likely to be broadcasting professors, asking them which universities and colleges in this field they would recommend to a son or daughter. He ranked the top 20 institutions for graduate study (Table 1, p. 4) and the top several schools in four different geographical regions for undergraduate study (Table 2, pp. 5–6).

Clark Kerr compiled an unpublished ranking of medical schools ("Confidential Summary of Survey . . .") in 1966 when he was president of the University of California. He asked the deans of the 31 medical schools that were affiliated with universities which were AAU members to indicate whether each of these schools "should rank in the top ten, the second ten, the third ten, or lower" (p. 1). Some well-regarded medical schools, such as those at Western Reserve University and Yeshiva University, that were not affiliated with institutions belonging to the AAU, could not be ranked. The nine top-ranked medical schools and 11 of the top 12 were at private institutions. Considering the numerous rankings of all types that have been published in recent years for three social science disciplines—economics, psychology, and sociology—and for the professional field of business, especially Master's of Business Administration (MBA) programs, it is surprising that of the early reputational rankings of individual fields of study, none ranked any of these fields. Instead, they ranked fields like geography, broadcasting, political science, and medicine that have not been ranked nearly as often, in recent decades, as have other fields that were not covered by these early rankings.

Since, in recent decades, the best-known and most influential rankings have all been multidisciplinary reputational rankings, it is remarkable how few reputational rankings were published in the four decades after their invention. From 1925 to 1966, we have been able to find only eight published reputational rankings, the multidisciplinary ones by Hughes (1925; 1934b) and Keniston (1959), and the others by Manly (1957), Thomson (1961), Somit and Tanenhaus (1964), Sieber with Lazarsfeld (1966), and Kittross (1966). By 1966 dozens of rankings had already been published showing which colleges and universities had "produced," either in absolute numbers or in proportion to their graduates, the largest number of eminent alumni, as defined by those who were listed in *American Men of Science* or *Who's Who in America*, or in many other ways. Some of these rankings were very well-known indeed, such as the book by the eminent geographer Stephen Sargent Visher (1947) or those by the well-known psychologist Robert Knapp and his coauthors (1952; 1953; 1964). One reason why reputational rankings are so much more influential today than rankings using any other criterion or set of criteria is the extraordinary methodological advances made in them by Allan Cartter.

ALLAN CARTTER AND THE *CARTTER REPORT* (1966)

Allan Murray Cartter received his B.A. from Colgate University in 1946, his M.A. (1949) and Ph.D. (1952) from Yale University, and studied at Cambridge University from 1950 to 1952. He served as assistant and then associate professor of economics at Duke University from 1952 to 1958; as program associate for the Ford Foundation's program in economic development and administration from 1958 to 1959; as professor and Dean of the Graduate School at Duke from 1959 to 1962; and as vice president of the ACE from 1963 to 1966. From 1966 to 1972, he was chancellor of New York University; in 1973, he became professor of higher education at UCLA, where he worked until his death, at age 54, in 1976.

Although for much of his life he worked at demanding administrative jobs, he still wrote several important books, including *Redistribution of Income in Postwar Britain* (1956); *Higher Education: Who Pays? Who Benefits? Who Should Pay?* (1973); and *Ph.D.'s and the Academic Labor Market* (1976). In the field of higher education, however, he is best remembered for his ground-breaking reputational ranking, *An Assessment of Quality in Graduate Education* (1966a). He published it in 1966, announcing three reasons for doing so:

> . . . to bring earlier qualitative studies of graduate education up to date . . . to widen the assessment to include all major universities in the United States . . . to learn as much as possible about the vagaries and pitfalls of subjective assessments in the interest of improving such measurements for the future. (p. 3)

In many ways it was a great advance methodologically over the earlier multidisciplinary reputational rankings by Hughes and Keniston, perhaps because Cartter was the first social scientist to publish such a ranking. In any case, he established a precedent; since the *Cartter Report*, all the multidisciplinary reputational rankings have been compiled largely or entirely by social scientists. Roose, the senior compiler of the Roose/Andersen ranking, was an economist; Blau, co-compiler of the two Blau/Margulies rankings, is a sociologist; Ladd a political scientist and Lipset both a sociologist and political scientist; and the NAS ranking was done under the direction of Lyle Jones, a psychologist, and Gardner Lindzey, a psychologist and director and president of the Center for Advanced Study in the Behavioral Sciences.

Some of the ways in which the *Cartter Report* represented a methodological advance over the previous multidisciplinary rankings are as follows:

1. While the 1934 Hughes ranking had been based on a poll of only established scholars and Keniston had polled only department chairpersons, Cartter polled chairpersons, senior scholars, and also junior scholars.
2. While the first Hughes ranking had been based on returns from about 27 raters per discipline, the second Hughes rating from about 58, and the Keniston ranking from about 20, Cartter's ranking was based on returns from almost 140 per discipline.
3. While the first Hughes ranking had been limited to 36 institutions and the Keniston ranking to 25, the *Cartter Report* covered 106 institutions.
4. Cartter covered 29 academic disciplines, more than Hughes' 1925 ranking, which covered 20, and than Keniston's ranking, which covered 24 (though fewer than Hughes' 1934 ranking, which covered 35 fields).
5. Whereas the two Hughes rankings and the Keniston ranking had employed only a single criterion by which departments were rated, the *Cartter Report* used two—"quality of the graduate faculty" and "rating of the doctoral training program"—and ranked departments separately on each criterion.

While it is doubtful that it can be called a methodological advance, Cartter made at least one more major change from the earlier rankings. He labeled the departments he ranked according to how high they had scored. On a 5-point scale, with 5 being the highest score, he labeled all those departments ranked 4.01 or higher as "distinguished" and all those ranked from 3.01 to 4.00 as "strong." He grouped together all departments scoring from 2.51 to 3.00 in alphabetical order and labeled them "good," and he grouped together departments scoring from 2.01 to 2.50 in alphabetical order and called them "adequate plus." No other multidisciplinary reputational ranking has ever tagged departments scoring above certain cut-off points with descriptive labels.

In addition to the methodological advances he made, Cartter provided far more analysis of his own data than did the compilers of any other reputational ranking. (The NAS' ranking of 1982, while it provided an immense amount of data, in tables and figures, about its rankings for each discipline, provided little analysis of these data.)

He discussed in detail, for example, the relative strength of the institutions he ranked by broad areas—humanities, social sciences, biological sciences, physical sciences, and engineering (pp. 106–107); the relationship between departments' rated effectiveness of doctoral program and the number of "free choice" fellowship holders they attracted (pp. 107–109); the geographical distribution of the highest-ranked departments (pp. 109–111); the relationship between departments' ranking and their average faculty compensation (pp. 111–112); and the relationship between the rating of quality of graduate faculty in the *Cartter Report* and an institution's library resources (pp. 114–115).

Cartter selected four of the 29 disciplines whose departments he ranked for particularly close analysis—economics, English, physics, and political science. For these he discussed in detail the following:

1. how an additional small panel of experts ranked them as compared to his other respondents;
2. how those with a close institutional affiliation with the departments, either having earned a doctorate or currently employed at one of them rated them, compared to those not closely affiliated with them;
3. how raters from four geographical regions rated them;
4. how raters from departments that scored high in reputation ranked departments, compared with how raters from departments that scored low in reputation ranked them.

For all these disciplines except physics, he analyzed the relationship between departments' faculty publications and their ranking for rated quality of graduate faculty; for economics, he analyzed the relationship between departments' faculty salaries and their rated quality of graduate faculty; for English, he analyzed the differences between the ratings of those whose specialty was American literature and those whose specialty was British literature.

The *Cartter Report* sold some 26,000 copies and was reviewed far more widely than any previous reputational ranking. Most of the reviews were laudatory. Bowling, an historian at Washington University, called it "the most impressive compendium of informed opinion that we have to date on the increasingly important subject of quality in graduate education" (1966, p. 113). Ranz, Dean of Academic Affairs at the University of Wyoming, said it was "a highly significant work, recommended for every scholarly library and for every scholar's library" (1966, p. 3712). *Time* described it as "the most exhaustive assessment yet made of graduate education in the U.S." ("Who's Best At What?" 1966, p. 55). Walters, Vice-President of Academic Affairs at Boston University, called it an "authoritative document," one which "incorporates the most recent sophisticated techniques in sampling and takes into account almost every possibility of bias and prejudice" (1966, p. 75). *Science* stated that "for faculty and graduate students it will serve as a new Consumer's Guide to the academic marketplace" (Walsh, p. 1228).

Cartter not only analyzed his rankings in great detail in the report itself, but also in several speeches and articles he published shortly before and after the *Cartter Report*. He discussed the rankings of the leading economics departments in the *American Economic Review* (1965a); the rankings of the leading departments in the South in various fields, especially economics, in *Southern Eco-*

nomic Journal (1965b); of chemistry departments in *Science Education* (1966b); of psychology departments in a speech given to the American Psychological Association (1966c); and of rankings of Yale departments in *Ventures* (1966d).

Although Cartter declined to aggregate his departmental rankings into institution-wide ones, others performed that task. Magoun, dean of the Graduate Division at UCLA, published an article in the *Journal of Higher Education* (1966) in which, while he did not aggregate the departmental rankings into institution-wide ones, he came close to doing so. He aggregated Cartter's departmental rankings for the 25 arts and sciences disciplines, excluding the four engineering fields, which he ranked separately. The reason he did not include the engineering disciplines with the others is almost certainly because in doing so he would have lowered UCLA's ranking. According to Magoun's aggregation, for all the departments Cartter ranked except those in engineering, UCLA ranked 10th for quality of graduate faculty and 12th for educational effectiveness (Magoun, 1966, Table 1, p. 484). In engineering, however, it tied for 17th in quality of graduate faculty and was 20th for educational effectiveness (Table 6, p. 489). For the 25 disciplines excluding engineering, Magoun's top five institutions for quality of graduate faculty were as follows: 1. Harvard; 2. University of California (Berkeley); 3. Yale; 4. Princeton; 5. Chicago.

Ewell, Vice-President for Research at the State University of New York at Buffalo, aggregated the rankings differently (Ewell, no date) and determined that the top five universities in quality of graduate faculty were these: 1. University of California (Berkeley); 2. Harvard; 3. Wisconsin; 4. Michigan; 5. Stanford.

McCurdy, an AAU official, aggregated Cartter's departmental rankings still another way, considering both quality of faculty and educational effectiveness (DeBardeleben, 1966). He determined that the top four institutions were the same as those in Ewell's ranking, with Yale replacing Stanford for fifth place.

Cartter, in his preface to the *Cartter Report*, stated that the ACE's Advisory Committee on the Study of Graduate Education, which had overseen his ranking, intended to repeat the study within five years "to avoid 'fixing' reputations when in fact the academic scene is changing constantly" (p. x). Four years later that plan was realized. Under the auspices of the ACE, Kenneth Roose and Charles Andersen published a near replication of the *Cartter Report*, titled *A Rating of Graduate Programs* (1970), hereafter often called the Roose/Andersen study.

THE ROOSE/ANDERSEN STUDY (1970)

Kenneth D. Roose, the senior compiler of the Roose/Andersen study, graduated *summa cum laude* from the University of Southern California in 1940; received his Ph.D. from Yale in 1948; taught economics at Oberlin College from 1950 to 1961; served as dean of the College of Liberal Arts at Pennsylvania State University in State College from 1964 to 1968; and was vice-president of the ACE from 1968 to 1970. He left the ACE shortly before *A Rating of Graduate Programs* was published.

Charles J. Andersen has worked at the ACE since 1963. He assisted Cartter on the *Cartter Report*; Cartter called him "a worthy and tireless lieutenant . . . to whom I could delegate much of the data analysis" (*Cartter Report*, p. x). Since 1979, he has been director of the ACE's membership department and assistant to the director of the Division of External Relations.

Just as Hughes' 1934 ranking was deliberately less bold than his earlier one, listing the most highly regarded departments in each field in alphabetical, rather than descending rank order, so the Roose/Andersen study was deliberately less bold than its predecessor, the *Cartter Report*. Its authors announced that "in this new survey, we have tried to de-emphasize the pecking-order relationships. . . ." (p. 2). They certainly succeeded in doing so. By far the largest difference between the *Cartter Report* and the Roose/Andersen study is the numerous ways, including the following, in which the latter downplayed the pecking order of institutions:

1. Cartter's ranking was titled *An Assessment of Quality in Graduate Education*; Roose and Andersen called theirs *A Rating of Graduate Programs*, omitting the word "quality."
2. Cartter, in determining departments' rank order, rounded scores to two decimal places; Roose and Andersen rounded them only to one, resulting in their having far more departments tied than did the *Cartter Report*.
3. Cartter published departmental scores, on his 5-point scale of faculty scholarly quality and 3-point scale of program effectiveness, to two decimal places; Roose and Andersen published only departments' rank orders and did not publish departments' scores at all.
4. Cartter labeled departments that scored above certain cut-off points with descriptive adjectives. Roose and Andersen did not label any of their departments.
5. Cartter ranked departments by how well they scored on each of the two criteria he used—faculty quality and program effectiveness. Roose and Andersen ranked departments only by how well they scored on faculty quality, not by program effectiveness. For the criterion "effectiveness of doctoral program," they simply listed departments in order of how high they scored, without listing their ordinal position.

There were several other differences between the *Cartter Report* and the Roose/Andersen study. Most of them involved size. The latter ranking included substantially more disciplines, institutions, programs, and raters. Cartter included 29 disciplines, Roose and Andersen 36; Cartter included 106 institutions,

TABLE 1. How the top 50 institutions in the Roose/Andersen study, taken as a group, compare with the remaining 80 institutions, taken as a group, in quality of graduate faculty.

Faculties	All Institutions	Top 50	Remaining 80
Distinguished	204	198	6
Strong	598	546	52
Good	467	330	137
Adequate Plus	570	255	315
Unsatisfactory	787	106	681

ACE Graduate Program Rankings . . . , 1971, p. 20

Roose and Andersen 130; Cartter ranked 1,663 programs, Roose and Andersen 2,626; Cartter received about 4,000 usable responses, Roose and Andersen about 6,100.

In addition to these differences in size, Cartter listed separately the scores and rankings assigned by his department chairs, senior scholars, and junior scholars. Roose and Andersen listed only ordinal position, not scores, and they listed only the average score of their three groups of respondents, without listing the scores of each group separately. One finding of the Roose/Andersen ranking was that the distribution of strength at the 130 institutions they surveyed was very skewed. The top 50, taken as a group, were vastly superior in reputation for quality of graduate faculty to the other 80. This disparity can be seen Table 1.

While the Roose/Andersen study itself did not label groups of departments, Roose on one occasion did label them, using the same cut-off scores that the *Cartter Report* had used:

> These 50 institutions . . . have 97 per cent of the "distinguished" faculties, 91 per cent of the "strong" faculties, 71 per cent of the "good" faculties, 45 per cent of the "adequate plus" faculties and only 13 per cent of the "unsatisfactory" faculties. Overall, they have 72 per cent of the faculties "rated of sufficient quality to carry out a Ph.D. program. . . ."; they conduct 85 per cent of the graduate programs rated "adequate plus" or better in the humanities; 81 per cent in the social sciences; 70 per cent in the physical sciences; 66 per cent in engineering; and 64 per cent in the biological sciences. (Roose, quoted in "ACE Graduate Program Rankings . . . ," 1971, pp. 19–20)

Eleven of the 130 institutions surveyed by Roose and Andersen did not have even one department rated "adequate" (p. 20).

Although Roose and Andersen, as might be expected from their de-emphasis of disciplinary pecking orders, did not aggregate their departmental rankings into institution-wide ones, others did so. *Newsweek*, for example, listed the 10 institutions, in order, that "appeared most often in the top ranks and the number of disciplines in which they excelled" ("Still No. 1," 1971, p. 58). Fawcett, chairman of the AAU membership committee, sent a memo to the presidents of all AAU institutions showing the ranking of all 130 institutions in the Roose/ Andersen study. This ranking was based on departmental ratings in 20 of the 36 disciplines that Roose and Andersen had covered, the so-called "traditional liberal arts disciplines" (Fawcett, 1971, p. 1). The 16 disciplines that were omitted included all four engineering disciplines, eight of the 10 in the biological sciences, four of the 10 in the humanities, but none in the social sciences and physical sciences. The top five institutions were as follows: 1. University of California (Berkeley); 2. Harvard; 3. Michigan; 4. Wisconsin; 5. Chicago.

The *Journal of Higher Education* published a table showing, for all institutions that had been rated in both the *Cartter Report* and the Roose/Andersen study, what scores each achieved according to three different methods of totaling the departmental scores (Petrowski, Brown, and Duffy, 1974, Table 1, pp. 499–502). In addition, *Social Science Quarterly* published a table showing the 72 highest-ranking institutions for quality of graduate faculty in the Roose/ Andersen ranking (Morgan, Kearney, and Regens, 1976, Table 1, pp. 673– 674). The five highest-ranking institutions were these: 1. University of California (Berkeley); 2. Harvard; 3. Stanford 4. Yale; 5. Wisconsin.

For whatever reasons—possibly because it downplayed the "pecking order" of America's leading departments in the various disciplines, perhaps because it was methodologically very similar to the *Cartter Report*, perhaps because it was published only four years after the *Cartter Report*—the Roose/Andersen study, although it was widely covered in the press, did not receive nearly as much praise as had the *Cartter Report*. Indeed, it received a substantial amount of criticism from academics. A clinical psychologist (Derner, 1971, p. 857) bitterly criticized it for being unfair to the clinical psychology wing of psychology for two reasons. First, two of its four top-rated psychology departments and seven of its 30 top-rated ones did not have their clinical psychology programs accredited by the American Psychology Association. Second, in suggesting that "the various public institutions of a state should consider concentrating in single areas and not duplicate training in an area" (p. 857), the report was unfair to clinical psychology, because, far from having too many holders of doctoral degrees, as did some disciplines, clinical psychology did not even have enough.

At the University of Massachusetts, where the number of Ph.D.'s granted had increased from just three in 1960 to 204 in 1970, the graduate school dean argued that "the ratings are not sufficiently current to reflect the University's rapid, recent improvements" ("ACE Graduate Program Rankings . . . ," 1971, p. 23). In the 18 months it had taken to prepare the study, he said, his university's programs had "continued improving to a point where many departments might well have received higher ratings" (p. 23).

The Roose/Andersen study, like all the multidisciplinary reputational rankings published before it, ranked mostly disciplines in the arts and sciences. As of 1970, very few professional school fields, other than engineering, had ever been ranked, either as part of multidisciplinary rankings or in individual ones. Soon after the Roose/Andersen ranking was published, however, Peter Blau and Rebecca Zames Margulies published, in short order, two multidisciplinary reputational rankings of professional school fields.

BLAU AND MARGULIES' RANKINGS OF PROFESSIONAL SCHOOL FIELDS (1973 AND 1974/75)[2]

Peter Blau, co-author of the articles reporting these rankings, is an eminent sociologist, the author of *Exchange and Power in Social Life* (1964), *The Organization of Academic Work* (1973), and *On the Nature of Organizations* (1974), among many other books. Since 1988 he has been the Robert Broughton Distinguished Research Professor at the University of North Carolina at Chapel Hill. Rebecca Zames Margulies was a Ph.D. candidate in sociology at Columbia when the rankings were published.

The first ranking Blau and Margulies published (Margulies and Blau, 1973) included professional schools in 17 fields: architecture, business, dentistry, education, engineering, forestry, journalism, law, library science, medicine, nursing, optometry, pharmacy, public health, social work, theology, and veterinary medicine. For these fields, the study encompassed ''all American professional schools that are both accredited and university-affiliated'' (p. 22). Thus some professional schools were excluded because they were not accredited and others, like the Graduate Theological Union, because they were not affiliated with a university. Many of the fields Margulies and Blau covered, such as architecture, dentistry, optometry, public health, and veterinary medicine, have seldom if ever been covered in any ranking except this one and the one that the authors published about a year later (Blau and Margulies, 1974/75).

Margulies and Blau nowhere stated how many deans of each of the 17 types of professional school were polled and what proportion of them replied. They did provide, for each of the 17 types of schools, a tiny circle, 1/8″ in diameter, with a shaded area showing the proportion of its deans that responded. They also listed, for each field, the five most frequently mentioned departments, plus ties, in order of how often they were mentioned. For each of the top-ranked schools they listed the number of deans who responded in that field as well as the number naming it as one of the five best.

[2]In discussing the two rankings by Blau and Margulies and the one by Cartter and Solmon, I have relied heavily on an outstanding, unpublished UCLA Graduate School of Education course paper by Scheinberg (1977).

TABLE 2. Webster's calculations of the highest-ranking institutions in Margulies and Blau's 1973 ranking of professional schools.

Rank	Institution	Points
1.	Harvard	29
2.	Columbia	20.5
3.	University of California/Berkeley	19.5
4.	Chicago	17.5
5.	Stanford	15
6.	Michigan	14
7.	Yale	10
8.	Ohio State	9.5
9.	University of California/San Francisco	9
9.	Illinois (Urbana/Champaign)	9
9.	Massachusetts Institute of Technology	9

For some fields, the number of replies Margulies and Blau got was minuscule. They obtained only four ratings of optometry schools and five of public health schools. In other fields, the proportion of replies they received was very low. Although it is impossible to determine from the shaded portions of their circles the exact proportion of responses they obtained, their response rate in medicine must have been about 10 percent and in dentistry about 15 percent. They concluded that generally deans in high prestige fields, such as medicine, responded in smaller proportions than did deans in low-prestige fields.

Margulies and Blau did not combine their professional school rankings into institution-wide ones. Webster, however, aggregated their scores, giving institutions five points for a ranking of first, four points for a ranking of second, down to one point for a ranking of fifth. The top 11 institutions, including three tied for ninth place, according to his unpublished calculations, are shown in Table 2. Margulies and Blau's 1973 ranking of professional schools had numerous flaws, including these:

1. They did not publish the response rate to their question to deans asking them to rank schools. Not until their 1974/75 ranking did they reveal that their response rate to this question for the 1973 ranking was only 36 percent, and that "only 2 of the 17 fields in the original study had a response rate of more than 50 percent" (Scheinberg, 1977, p. 4).
2. They asked the deans only "to name the five most outstanding schools in their own profession" (Margulies and Blau, 1973, p. 21). They did not provide the deans with any information about what criteria they were supposed to use—for example, research, teaching, service, or some combination—to select the best schools (Scheinberg, 1977, p. 3).

3. They asked the deans only to list the five best schools, not to rank them, and then they ranked schools by the number of times each was mentioned. Thus a school that 70 percent of the deans thought was the nation's best and the other 30 percent did not list would have got a lower ranking than a school that 80 percent of the deans thought was the nation's fifth best school and the other 20 percent did not list.
4. They asked the deans to name the five best schools from memory; they did not provide them with a list of all the university-affiliated, accredited schools in their field (Scheinberg, 1977, pp. 3–4).
5. They surveyed only deans and no other group of respondents.

Margulies and Blau's 1973 ranking was severely criticized for the reasons listed above, especially the very small number and proportion of respondents they had in some of their fields. Responding to these criticisms, they published another ranking about a year later, this time with Blau as first author (Blau and Margulies, 1974/75). Whereas in 1973 the question upon which they based their ranking was one from a large instrument, this time their poll consisted of only one question: "What in your opinion are the five top schools in your profession?" (p. 43).

They ranked the 17 professional fields they had covered in 1973 and also music, receiving a response rate of 79 percent, as opposed to only 36 percent in their earlier ranking. Whereas in 1973 they had received only about 25 replies per field, in the later study they received about 55 replies per field. Whereas in 1973 they had listed only the five most frequently named schools in each field, plus ties, in 1974/75 they listed "the rankings of the professional schools named as the top five by at least 10 percent of the responding deans in their profession" (p. 43). This method resulted in their ranking about 10 or 12 institutions per field.

They found that the correlation between their first and second ranking was .94. They also found that the reputation of a professional school correlated only slightly with the reputation of the university of which it was part. For example, the correlation between the ranking of the professional field and the overall university for business was .21; education, .35; engineering, .20; law, .18; nursing, .27; pharmacy, .21; and social work, .23 (Table 2, p. 46). They stated (p. 47) that they got their ranking of universities from the Roose/Andersen study which, of course, did not publish university-wide rankings, never explaining how they aggregated Roose and Andersen's departmental totals into university-wide ones, or whose aggregation they used.

Webster, in unpublished calculations, determined the top 10 institutions based on the Blau/Margulies 1974/75 ranking, giving an institution 10 points for each first place rating, 9 points for each second place rating, and so on down to one point for each tenth place rating. Table 3 shows his rank order of the top 10 institutions.

TABLE 3. Webster's calculations of the 10 highest-ranking institutions in Blau
and Margulies' (1974/75) ranking of professional schools.

Rank	Institution	Points
1.	Michigan	75.5
2.	Harvard	61
3.	University of California/Berkeley	59.5
4.	Chicago	50.5
5.	Columbia	45.5
6.	Stanford	42
7.	Illinois	34
{ 8.	Minnesota	33.5 }
{ 8.	Ohio State	33.5 }
10.	Yale	31.5

Both Blau/Margulies rankings were criticized in letters to the editor of
Change, which had published the rankings. One letter argued (Austin et al.,
1975, p. 4) that it would have been fairer to ask not just deans but also faculty
and students to list schools. It also maintained that the reason the results of the
second ranking largely substantiated those of the first could have been because
the deans' opinions of the schools, in the second poll, were influenced by the
published rankings based on the first poll. Another letter observed (Peirce, 1975)
that in the field of social work, while all such schools were supposedly being
ranked, actually all 10 top-ranked schools had postmaster's level programs, and
not one was exclusively devoted to master's level education. "The top ten in
social work are thus the top ten of the 29 which offer post-master's programs"
(p. 4). The editors of *Change* took a hard line position in response to critical
letters. Replying to a letter criticizing the use of statistics in the 1973 ranking, by
far the weaker of the two, they replied that it was "from a statistical
viewpoint . . . easily defensible" (Editors of *Change*, 1974, p. 4). Answering
another letter criticizing the 1973 ranking's methodology, they replied that it was
"methodologically impeccable" (Editors of *Change*, 1974, p. 4).

THE CARTTER/SOLMON RANKING OF
PROFESSIONAL SCHOOLS (1977)

Allan Cartter, compiler of the *Cartter Report*, and Lewis C. Solmon did another
ranking of professional schools, publishing it in *Change* ("The *Cartter
Report* . . . ," 1977). For a good analysis of its methods and findings, including
some findings that were not published, see Munson and Nelson (1977). How-

ever, their opinion of "The *Cartter Report* . . ." of 1977 was much too rosy, probably because both of them had helped collect data for it and prepare it for publication (Munson and Nelson, 1977, p. 41).

The Cartter/Solmon ranking differed from the two Blau/Margulies rankings in several ways, including the following:

1. Instead of covering 17 or 18 professional school fields it covered only three— business, education, and law.
2. It polled not only deans but also senior and junior scholars.
3. It divided each field into six or more common subspecialties, and it asked deans to provide the name of a person from each subspecialty so that he or she could be sampled.
4. Instead of relying on respondents' "recall," it provided them with a roster of names of most or all of the major institutions in the field—in the case of business, for example, of the 51 business schools that granted Ph.D.'s.
5. It got a much larger number of responses than did either of the Blau/Margulies surveys—an average of 363 per field.

The compilers of this ranking tried hard, in a number of ways, to obtain more accurate results than had Blau and Margulies. But their study was by no means without flaws. The most serious one concerns the reason why the ranking was done. The Regents of the University of California were unhappy with how their flagship campuses, Berkeley and UCLA, had fared in the two Blau/Margulies rankings, so they asked the University of California at Berkeley's academic senate to conduct another ranking. The chair of the academic senate committee that wrote the first draft of the report was Cartter ("The *Cartter Report* . . . ," 1977, p. 44), then a UCLA professor. The cover letter sent out to people inviting them to participate was written on UCLA letterhead and signed by Cartter. It informed potential respondents that the rankings were being done "at the request of the University of California Board of Regents and the Faculty Assembly" (Cartter, 1975, p. 1).

Not surprisingly, with this kind of endorsement, of the six ratings of University of California schools—the business, education, and law schools at the University of California at Berkeley and UCLA—in four of them the University of California schools ranked higher in the Cartter/Solmon study in a combined score based on both faculty quality and educational attractiveness than they had in the second Blau/Margulies study. (In one rating they tied; in the sixth there is not sufficient information available to make a comparison.) In education, both University of California campuses improved their standing greatly from the second Blau/Margulies ranking to the Cartter/Solmon one. Berkeley was not even listed among the top 12 in the former, but was 5th in the latter; UCLA rose from tied for 12th in the former to 4th in the latter. In law, Berkeley rose from

7th in Blau/Margulies to 6th in Cartter/Solmon, and UCLA, which was listed at some unspecified position below 9th in the former, ranked 10th in the latter. In business, Berkeley was ranked 7th by Blau/Margulies and 6th by Cartter/Solmon, while UCLA ranked tied for 8th in Blau/Margulies and 8th in Cartter/Solmon.

Another flaw involved the way in which schools were chosen for the survey. Dartmouth's business school, Amos Tuck, was excluded from the ranking of business schools because it did not grant a doctorate, but if it had been included, based on where it ranked in other, nearly contemporaneous reputational rankings, it would almost certainly have ranked higher than most of the other business schools that were included (Scheinberg, 1977, p. 11).

Despite the many methodological differences between the second Blau/Margulies ranking and the Cartter/Solmon ranking, the two studies' results, for the three fields they both ranked, were reasonably similar. There was at least one spectacular exception, however, to this overall pattern. George Peabody College tied for 12th among colleges of education in Blau/Margulies, but ranked only 41st in the Cartter/Solmon study (Munson and Nelson, 1977, p. 46).

There are striking differences among the three fields Cartter and Solmon ranked concerning whether private or public universities dominated the rankings. In business and law, private institutions excelled. Nine of the top-ranked 11 business schools and 10 of the 15 top-ranked law schools were private. In education, the reverse was true; merely four of the top-ranked 14 institutions were private.

Only a few years after the second Blau/Margulies ranking was published, the *Chronicle of Higher Education* (Scully, 1979) published a highly idiosyncratic reputational ranking based on data collected by two of America's leading social scientists.

THE LADD/LIPSET RANKING (1979)

Everett Carll Ladd, Jr. is professor of political science at the University of Connecticut at Storrs and executive director and president of the Roper Center for Public Opinion Research. He is the author of, among other books, *Ideology in America: Change and Response in a City, a Suburb, and a Small Town* (1969); and co-author, with Seymour Martin Lipset, of *Professors, Unions, and American Higher Education* (1973) and *The Divided Academy* (1975).

Lipset is one of America's most distinguished social scientists, a world-class scholar in sociology and political science. He holds endowed chairs at both Stanford in political science and sociology and George Mason University in Virginia in public policy and sociology. He is the author or co-author of (with Martin Trow and James Coleman), *Union Democracy* (1956); *Political Man*

(1960); *Rebellion in the University* (1972); and many other books. For the years 1981–85, he received 25 percent more lines of citations in the *Social Science Citation Index* than did the next most cited American or Canadian political scientist (Klingemann, 1986, Table 3, p. 657). He has served as president of the American Political Science Association and as of this writing (1991) is president-elect of the American Sociological Association. He will have been the first person to head both organizations.

The Ladd/Lipset ranking was unusual in many respects. First, its 19 areas of study were selected differently from the way they were in all the other multidisciplinary reputational rankings. Instead of ranking departments only in separate disciplines, in several cases it combined two or more disciplines into one group. Thus agriculture and forestry were grouped together, as were mathematics and statistics. In addition, all the biological sciences were combined as "biological sciences," as were all the fields in engineering as "engineering" and all foreign languages as "foreign languages." Since an institution's department of, say, botany can be much stronger or weaker than its department of zoology, or its department of German much stronger or weaker than its department of Spanish, combining disciplines in this manner does not provide as much useful information as if disciplines were each ranked individually.

Second, while all the other multidisciplinary reputational rankings from the *Cartter Report* on have included either only departments from the liberal arts and engineering or only professional school fields, the Ladd/Lipset ranking included a substantial number of liberal arts disciplines and also a substantial number of professional school fields.

Third, while most other multidisciplinary reputational rankings have been done as separate projects, this one was compiled from some 4400 responses to exactly one question of a 128 item instrument, "The 1977 Survey of the American Professoriate" (Ladd and Lipset, 1977). In this respect it was like Margulies and Blau's 1973 ranking, which was also based on the responses to one question from a large instrument. (Unlike Margulies and Blau, though, who asked respondents to name the five best departments in their field, without necessarily listing them in order, Ladd and Lipset asked their respondents to list the five best departments in their field, in order.)

Fourth, this ranking was never published under either Ladd or Lipset's name. It appeared in an article in the *Chronicle of Higher Education* under the byline of a *Chronicle* staff member.

Fifth, the question upon which the ranking was based was not phrased nearly as well as it could have been. It was worded as follows: "Name the five departments nationally in your discipline that have the most distinguished faculties. (Please list the institutions in the order of their importance.)" (Ladd and Lipset, 1977, question 61, p. 10). The question thus did not specify what activities these faculties should be distinguished in—research, graduate-level teaching, under-

TABLE 4. The top 10 institutions in Ladd and Lipset's 1979 ranking, according to Callcott's aggregation.

Rank	Institution	Points
1.	Harvard	142
2.	University of California/Berkeley	118
3.	Stanford	106
4.	Yale	84
5.	Michigan	68
6.	Chicago	63
7.	Wisconsin	61
8.	Princeton	50
9.	Massachusetts Institute of Technology	46
10.	Illinois (Urbana/Champaign)	42

graduate teaching, or some combination. Also, the word "importance" was not well chosen. "Excellence" or "quality" would have been better.

Sixth, the criterion used for a department to be included in the *Chronicle* ranking was that at least 10 percent of the faculty in that field who responded to the question listed it as one of the five best in his or her discipline. As a result, instead of 15 or more departments in each discipline being ranked, as was generally the case with Cartter and Roose/Andersen rankings, the "field" with the most departments listed was agriculture and forestry, with 15; in two fields, law and sociology, only eight were listed. Thus the Ladd/Lipset ranking did not provide as much information about the most highly regarded departments in a field as do most of the other multidisciplinary rankings.

Seventh, although the *Chronicle of Higher Education* did not aggregate Ladd and Lipset's field-wide rankings into institutional totals, when a later scholar (Callcott, 1980) made such an aggregation (see Table 4), it had some strange results because Ladd and Lipset had ranked so few schools per field. According to Callcott, Juilliard School in New York City tied for the 19th best institution in the United States (p. 7) entirely because its music department had been ranked third among such departments.

Eighth, while one complaint about many or most reputational rankings is that those who compile them usually ask mostly or entirely scholars at well-known universities to rank departments, and these scholars may be predisposed to rank highly those departments that come closest to matching what is admired at the leading departments, the Ladd/Lipset ranking cannot be criticized on these grounds. Some 41 percent of the professors they sampled taught at liberal arts colleges, and about 5 percent—most unusual for a reputational ranking—taught at two-year colleges.

Appearing, as it did, in a two-page newspaper article, and having many idiosyncracies and methodological flaws, the Ladd/Lipset ranking did not receive nearly as much attention in either the scholarly or the popular press as did most other multidisciplinary rankings. It did, however, arouse strong criticism from the distinguished Yale University mathematician Serge Lang, who launched a years-long attack on the entire Ladd/Lipset survey of the American professoriate, culminating in a book-length anthology of invective against it (Lang, 1982). Elsewhere, Lang (1979) criticized the ranking's treatment of mathematics departments on a number of grounds, including the following: it made no distinction between pure and applied mathematics; it combined statistics with mathematics; and it made no sense to ask respondents to compare a small mathematics department like Harvard's with a large one like Berkeley's. In addition, he criticized the ranking as a whole because, in an evaluation of distinguished faculties, "no campus of the University of California was in the sample, but several state colleges were" (p. 4), and only "between 100 and 200 respondents 'rated' each field" (p. 4).

All in all, this ranking had many faults. Like the two rankings in *Change* in the mid-1970s in articles co-authored by Peter Blau, it did not come close to representing the best work of its compilers.

THE NATIONAL ACADEMY OF SCIENCES RANKING (1982)

After Hughes' 1925 ranking he declined, in his 1934 report, to rank the leading departments in any field of study. Similarly, after the *Cartter Report*, Roose and Andersen, in their 1970 ranking, went to considerable lengths to downplay departmental pecking orders. No multidisciplinary reputational ranking, however, ever went nearly as far to avoid pecking orders as the National Academy of Sciences' *Assessment of Research-Doctorate Programs in the United States* (Jones, Lindzey, and Coggeshall [eds.], 1982). This deliberately obfuscatory ranking was exceptionally difficult to decipher. Webster (1983) provided a kind of Rosetta Stone for it. He also provided a comparison of how its leading institutions—if its compilers had aggregated their program-wide scores into institutionwide ones—would compare to the leading institutions in most of the other multidisciplinary reputational rankings.

The NAS *Assessment* was sponsored by the Conference Board of Associated Research Councils, an umbrella organization including the American Council of Learned Societies; the ACE; the National Research Council (NRC); and the Social Science Research Council.

It was financed by the Andrew W. Mellon Foundation, the Ford Foundation, the Alfred P. Sloan Foundation, the National Institutes of Health, the National Science Foundation, and the NAS. At one time the compilers of the *Assessment* had planned for it to include considerably more than the 32 disciplines it ultimately covered. Like Hughes, however, who in 1934 cut back from the 50 fields he would have liked to include to 35 because of insufficient funds, they had to cut down on the number of disciplines they studied because of lack of money.

The NAS ranked programs, not departments, because occasionally, especially in the biological sciences, its compilers found that two, three, or even four programs in the same field of study were located in different departments. Biochemistry, for example, is sometimes studied in both a university's biology department and its chemistry department. Unlike the other multidisciplinary reputational rankings discussed in this chapter, the NAS *Assessment* was not purely a reputational ranking. For each discipline it covered, it employed from 12 to 16 measures, of which only four were reputational ones. These four concerned faculty scholarly quality; program effectiveness in educating research scholars or scientists; change in program quality during the previous five years; and raters' familiarity with the work of the program's faculty.

Nevertheless, although reputational measures were only a few of the criteria used, both scholars and journalists paid far more attention to them, especially the measures for quality of faculty and for program effectiveness, than to any others. For example, when the *Chronicle of Higher Education* reported the NAS' results, it published the scores that the programs in all 32 disciplines got on each of the four reputational measures, but it did not publish the results for any of the non-reputational criteria (Scully, 1982a, September 29; Scully, 1982b, November 10; "Evaluations of 326 Programs . . . ," 1982, December 1; "616 Doctoral Programs . . . ," 1983, January 12; "Final Report in Assessment . . . ," 1983, January 19). Similarly, Webster ("Lessons from the Presentation and Use of Data . . . ," 1991), reported that of the 12 scholarly books and articles he found that discussed the NAS' rankings, all of them used one or more of its reputational measures, and only three used any other measure (p. 4). In coverage of the NAS' rankings in 29 daily newspapers and popular magazines, Webster found that all of them, including *Time*, the *New York Times*, the *Boston Globe*, the *Chicago Tribune*, and the *Washington Post*, reported the rankings according to one or more of the reputational measures. Of the other eight to 12 measures the NAS employed, only seven of these 29 outlets published rankings based on even one of them (p. 4).

The NAS ranking of 1982 was, in many ways, the Rolls-Royce of academic quality rankings. It cost more than half a million dollars to compile, making it by far the most costly ranking ever done. Whereas the Roose/Andersen study had included 130 institutions, the NAS included 228; while Roose and Andersen had covered 2,626 departments, the NAS covered 2,699 programs. Whereas Roose and Andersen had, in most cases, ranked only the top 15 to 30 departments in a discipline, the NAS included detailed data, for the measures it used, about all the programs in each discipline which, in aggregate, had conferred about 95 percent

TABLE 5. The 10 leading institutions according to reputation for faculty quality in the NAS ranking, according to Webster.

Rank	Institution	Score
1.	University of California/Berkeley	45
2.	Stanford	34
{ 3.	Harvard	32 ⎫
{ 3.	Yale	32 ⎭
5.	Massachusetts Institute of Technology	29
6.	Princeton	28
7.	Chicago	27
{ 8.	UCLA	24 ⎫
{ 8.	Michigan	24 ⎬
{ 8.	University of Wisconsin (Madison)	24 ⎭

of the discipline's doctorates in a recent five-year span. Such programs numbered well over 100 in some disciplines.

By far the worst feature of the NAS ranking was that it failed to provide any easily understandable information about each program's standing in its discipline. Instead of ranking the programs in descending order of quality for each criterion, it listed them in alphabetical order, from Adelphi to Yeshiva, or whatever. It listed program ratings in standard scores, with 50 being the mean and with a standard deviation of 10. Thus almost all programs received a standard score between 30 and 70. However, since for most disciplines several dozen programs were listed, it was very difficult to determine where they ranked.

Other publications were quick to publish some of the NAS' data in more comprehensible form. *Changing Times* ("Best Places to Be for a Ph.D.," 1983), the *Washington Post* (Feinberg, 1983b), the *New York Times* (Fiske, 1983), the *Boston Globe* (Kindleberger, 1983), and *Time* ("The Brightest and the Best," 1983) all listed, in descending order, the top few programs in some or all 32 disciplines according to one or two of the reputational measures and occasionally one of the other measures.

Others summed the NAS' program-by-program scores and obtained institution-wide totals for the top-ranked institutions. For example, Webster (1983, Table 3, p. 18) listed the top 30 institutions, plus ties, according to reputation for faculty quality. He gave an institution two points for each program with a standard score of 70 or higher and one point for each program with a standard score of 60 or higher. The top 10 institutions, according to his method of aggregating program scores, are shown in Table 5.

Astin aggregated the NAS' scores differently (1985, Table 3, p. 30), by averaging, if they had at least 10 programs included, their mean scores on the NAS' 6-point scale. His top 10 institutions, plus ties, are shown in Table 6.

TABLE 6. The 10 highest-ranking institutions, plus ties, in the NAS (1983) ranking, according to Astin.

Rank	Institution	Score
1.	Massachusetts Institute of Technology	5.67
2.	Harvard	5.40
3.	University of California/Berkeley	5.39
4.	Stanford	5.18
5.	California Institute of Technology	5.17
6.	Yale	5.06
7.	Chicago	5.04
8.	Princeton	5.02
9.	UCLA	4.83
{ 10.	Columbia	4.79 }
{ 10.	Michigan	4.79 }

The NAS' ranking was covered very widely in daily newspapers and popular magazines, but—for reasons worthy of study in themselves—it was not analyzed nearly as often in scholarly publications as the *Cartter Report* and the Roose/Andersen study had been. (Perhaps one reason is that the *American Sociologist*, which during the years 1965–82 had published more articles on academic quality rankings than any other scholarly journal, suspended publication from 1982 to 1987. Thus it was not available as an outlet in which sociologists could publish articles about it.) The NAS' rankings of political science programs, however, have been analyzed more extensively than its rankings in any other discipline in a series of articles in *PS*, the navel-gazing journal for political science, as the *American Sociologist* is for sociology. Rudder (1983), Welch and Hibbing (1983), and Klingemann (1986) all analyzed its findings concerning political science programs. One of the longest analyses of the NAS ranking was the savage review of it by the sociologist Lionel Lewis in *Sociological Quarterly* (Lewis, 1984). He argued that it was conceived and designed largely by academic administrators, not, as it should have been, by scholars. Since it was designed according to the wishes of administrators, it neglected measures important to understanding faculty publication productivity, such as per capita publications, and also measures crucial to educational effectiveness, such as the nature of the curriculum. Some evidence he cited in support of his position was as follows:

1. Of 44 participants at a 1976 conference to determine if there was a need for such a study, only seven had professional [*sic*—but Lewis, from the context, clearly means "professorial"] titles. Thirty-two were identified as academic administrators . . . (p. 128).

2. The first of "four considerations" at the initial conference, which recommended that the research be undertaken, was "the importance of the study results to national and state bodies" (p. 128).
3. At every stage, the project was shaped by administrators. "Early in the study an effort was made to solicit the views of presidents and graduate deans at more than 250 universities. Their suggestions were most helpful to the committee in drawing up final plans for the assessment . . ." (p. 128).
4. Even in selecting judges for the reputational survey "preference was given to those faculty members whom the study coordinators [administrators] had nominated to serve as evaluators" (p. 128).

Since, according to Lewis, the study was conceived of and planned by administrators, not faculty members, "the question of the content of graduate programs is never considered, even in the most oblique way" (p. 128). That is also why expenditures for research and development activities and the number of published articles are reported without controlling for the size of a department. Certainly, a study carried out for the purpose of gauging the quality of academic programs would be interested in per capita, rather than aggregate, figures. This matter would not be important to some administrative office which was simply interested in input (how many dollars the department brought in) and output (how many times the department got its name in print). . . . (p. 129).

The NRC has recently begun work on another assessment of doctoral programs in the arts, sciences, and engineering. It should be published around 1994. At a planning meeting in Irvine, California in April, 1991, about 40 university administrators and faculty members discussed what measures of academic quality it should use. There was near unanimity that, whatever other criteria might be selected, reputational measures should be used, both because of their intrinsic usefulness and because they had been used in previous multidisciplinary rankings of doctoral education and could therefore serve as the basis of comparisons about how the reputations of programs had changed over the years.

INTERNATIONAL REPUTATIONAL RANKINGS

Academic quality rankings—both reputational ones and other types, as well— were invented in the United States. They were used extensively here and, to a much lesser extent, in Canada for decades before they became popular anywhere else in the world. (For a discussion of why academic quality rankings developed in the United States, rather than elsewhere, see Webster, 1982.) In recent years, however, journals, magazines, and newspapers published elsewhere than North America have started to publish academic quality rankings. In contrast to the United States, where reputational rankings are by far the best known and often the most carefully done of the various types of rankings, in Europe reputational rankings are seldom compiled. Rankings there usually are based on one of a large number of objective measures covering, for example, faculty publication productivity, cost per student, faculty/student ratio, graduates' starting salaries, and so on. For a good discussion of recent academic quality rankings, both reputational and other kinds, in the United States and four western European nations, see Frackmann and Muffo (1988, pp. 10–28). This section discusses rankings originally published elsewhere than the United States and Canada.

British Reputational Rankings

Although in Britain "the method of assessing contributions to scientific knowledge apparently most favored by scientists is that of peer evaluation" (Martin and Irvine, 1983, p. 72), few peer rankings of departments and institutions have been compiled. Still, England may have published more than any other European nation.

In 1976, the eminent sociologist Albert Halsey compiled a reputational ranking of British academic departments. In 1989, he compiled another (Halsey, 1990). In the second he ranked, according to the opinions of university faculty, the top few departments in each of 15 disciplines and fields of study (Table 3, pp. 392–395); the top few institutions in each of nine broad subject areas (Table 2, pp. 389–390); and the top 21 British universities, overall, counting the major University of London colleges as separate entities (Table 1, p. 388). The top five universities, overall, were as follows: 1. Oxford; 2. Cambridge; 3. Manchester; 4. Edinburgh; 5. Imperial College, London.

By far the best-known English reputational ranking was the series of eight articles the (London) *Times Higher Education Supplement* (*THES*) published over a period of more than six years (Scott, 1982; "Oxbridge Still Dominates . . . ," 1983; "Searching for an Elusive Quality," 1984; "Difficulties of Demarcation," 1985; "Top Ranking Universities and Polys," 1985; "Sixth of the Best . . . ," 1987; O'Leary and Scott, 1987; "Apples and Pears," 1988). The *THES* ranked departments in 30 fields of study, chosen about equally from four areas—the humanities, the social sciences, the natural sciences, and the applied sciences or professions ("Oxford Still Dominates . . . ," 1983) at universities, polytechnics, colleges, and other types of institutions of higher education in England, Ireland, Scotland, and Wales. Like Keniston (1959), the *THES* polled only department chairpersons. It asked them to rank the leading departments in their field separately for "mainly the output and quality of their research" and "mainly the quality of their teaching of undergraduate students."

The noteworthy features of this ranking included the following:

1. As opposed to those American reputational rankings like the *Cartter Report*, the Roose/Andersen study, and the NAS ranking, in which, when respondents were asked about quality of faculty research and program educational

effectiveness, the two almost always correlated at .98 or higher, the correlations between answers to the two questions the *THES* asked, if they were calculated, would be far lower. The main reason why is that the *Cartter Report*, the Roose/Andersen study, and the NAS ranking asked about the quality of faculty research and about program effectiveness of *doctoral-level* education, while the *THES* asked respondents to rank faculty research "output and quality," on the one hand, and "mainly the quality of their teaching of *undergraduate students*," on the other.

2. The *THES* rankings were based on the opinions of far fewer respondents than have been most recent American multidisciplinary reputational rankings. For example, its ranking of English departments was based on only 20 complete returns, of classics on only 21 complete returns, and of biological sciences on only 30 complete returns.

3. The rankings were complicated, and to an extent invalidated, because the institutions rated were located not only in England, but also in Ireland, Scotland, and Wales. The fact that Scotland has a different legal system than does England, for example, made it difficult for respondents to compare Scottish and English law schools.

4. The rankings aroused enormous controversy, perhaps even more than such rankings have aroused in the United States. One reason why, perhaps, is that English academics are less accustomed than those in the United States to having their departments ranked. Another is that some of the rankings were published when the University Grants Committee was reviewing the fields that had just been ranked, and many academics thought that publishing the ratings would unduly influence the Committee's decisions. The *THES* was unable to rank medical schools because of the very low response rate it received ("Searching for an Elusive Quality," 1984); it could not rank music departments because the National Association of University Music Staff boycotted the survey ("Apples and Pears," 1988); and its rankings in education were subjected to "a limited boycott by members of the Polytechnic Council on the Education of Teachers" ("Sixth of the Best . . . ," 1987, p. 10).

5. In several fields, some unheralded polytechnics ranked very high, better than most universities did in these fields, especially for the quality of their teaching of undergraduate students. In French, for example, Portsmouth Polytechnic tied for 12th in research and tied for 11th in teaching undergraduate students; in business and management, Kingston Polytechnic was 14th in teaching undergraduate students; in mathematics, Leicester Polytechnic and Sheffield City Polytechnic tied for 8th in teaching undergraduate students; and in computer science, Hatfield Polytechnic was 4th, North Staffs Polytechnic 6th, and Teesside Polytechnic 11th in quality of teaching of undergraduates. In addition, in German, Ealing College of Higher Edu-

cation tied for 16th in quality of undergraduate teaching, a very high ranking for a college.

In addition to being boycotted in some fields, the *THES* rankings were also criticized by many of the department heads to whom it was sent (Scott, 1982, p. 8).

Two of the few other reputational rankings of institutions published outside America are as follows:

Europe-wide

In 1989, the Paris magazine *Libération* issued a guidebook featuring a reputational ranking of the best European universities ("Les 100 Meilleures Universités en Europe," 1989). Based on responses from more than 600 European academicians, it listed the five to the 20 best institutions in each of 21 fields of study.

Worldwide

In 1986, Asian scholars ranked the 12 best universities in the world as follows (Rosovsky, 1990, p. 30): 1. Harvard; 2. Cambridge and Oxford; 3. Stanford; 4. University of California (Berkeley); 5. Massachusetts Institute of Technology; 6. Yale; 7. Tokyo; 8. Paris-Sorbonne; 9. Cornell; 10. Michigan and Princeton.

RANKINGS IN MASS CIRCULATION MAGAZINES

Until recently, academic quality rankings, including reputational rankings, were usually published in academic journals and occasionally in books and monographs with small circulations. In the last decade, though, rankings have begun to appear in mass circulation magazines and in books published by the companies that own these magazines. The circulation of these rankings dwarfs the circulation of any previous ones. *Business Week*, with a North American circulation of about 900,000, recently published two articles ranking the best MBA programs (Byrne, 1988; Byrne, 1990) based on two criteria, one of which was reputation in the eyes of officials at companies that "actively recruit at the top schools" (Byrne, 1990, p. 54). These rankings have stirred up considerable controversy. Both in 1988 and 1990 *Business Week* ranked Northwestern University's MBA program, seldom ranked first by anyone else, as America's best. Beyond doubt the best known and most influential of the rankings in mass circulation magazines are those in *U.S. News and World Report*, with a circulation of about 2.2 million. Since 1983, *U.S. News and World Report* has ranked undergraduate education at colleges and universities (Solorzano with Quick, 1983; "America's Best Colleges," 1985; Solorzano et al., 1987a; Bauer, Solorzano, and Soltz, 1988; Sheler, Toch, Morse, Heupler, and Linnon, 1989; Elfin et al., 1990).

Recently, *U.S. News and World Report* has published two books containing rankings of undergraduate education. They included the same rankings that appeared in the magazine but also provided a great deal of additional information (*America's Best Colleges*, 1990; *America's Best Colleges*, 1991).

Since 1987, *U.S. News and World Report* has also ranked the leading professional schools in four fields—business, engineering, law, and medicine (Solorzano et al., 1987b; ''America's Best Graduate and Professional Schools,'' 1990; Morse with Wagner and others, 1991).

From 1983 through 1987, the *U.S. News and World Report* rankings, both of undergraduate education and of professional schools, were based entirely on reputation. Its rankings of colleges and the undergraduate programs of universities were based on a poll of college presidents, and its 1987 ranking of professional schools was based on the opinions of professional school deans. Many college and university officials complained that these rankings were not accurate. They argued that objective measures should be used instead of or in addition to reputational ones; that presidents could not possibly know the academic quality of all the schools they were asked to rank; and that presidents were not the best people to evaluate institutions' academic reputations. Responding to these criticisms, in 1988 *U.S. News and World Report*, in its rankings of undergraduate education, used objective measures in addition to reputational ones. It also polled, for the reputational component of its rankings, deans and admissions officers in addition to presidents.

By any measure, *U.S. News and World Report*'s rankings of both undergraduate education and professional schools have improved enormously since they began. Its rankings of undergraduate education are now by far the best such rankings that have ever been published, and its rankings of the four professional school fields either the best or among the best that have ever been published for these fields. Mel Elfin, the *U.S. News and World Report* special projects editor who oversees both rankings, and Robert Morse, the magazine's senior editor who does most of the work on them, have been quite receptive to criticisms of their rankings that college officials have made over the years. They have changed the measures they use and the weights they have assigned to them frequently, partly in response to such criticisms.

Nonetheless, the rankings still have at least one troubling feature. In its most recent (1990) ranking of undergraduate schools, the magazine listed in order, as it had done before, the 25 top national universities (pp. 118–119) and the 25 leading top liberal arts colleges (pp. 122–123). These categories, like the other categories that *U.S. News and World Report* uses, are based on the Carnegie Foundation for the Advancement of Teaching's *Classification of Institutions of Higher Education* (1987). Most of the nation's best regarded colleges and universities fall into one of these two categories. *U.S. News and World Report* also ranked the top 15 regional colleges and universities, plus ties, in each of four regions, the north, south, midwest, and west (pp. 128–129); the top 10 regional liberal arts colleges in each of these regions (pp. 132–133); and the three top schools in America specializing in each of these areas: the arts, business, and engineering.

As a result, national universities and national liberal arts colleges that fail to rank among the top 25 institutions are left in limbo. They do not get ranked at all, anywhere in *U.S. News and World Report* (although the magazine does report the quartile in which they place), while institutions that are often, by most measures, not nearly as good can be listed at or near the top of the rankings of regional colleges and universities or regional liberal arts colleges. In the 1990 ranking of national universities, for example, such well-regarded universities as the University of California/San Diego, the University of Illinois at Urbana/Champaign, and the University of Wisconsin/Madison were not ranked at all, simply because they did not "make" the top 25 among national universities. Similarly, such well-regarded liberal arts colleges as Dickinson, Kenyon, and Scripps were not listed among the top 25 national liberal arts colleges. *U.S. News and World Report* has arranged its rankings this way partly to "share the wealth," to ensure that institutions which are not at or near the top of the national pecking order still can gain recognition by being listed among their region's top colleges or universities.

College and university administrators and professors have attacked the *U.S. News and World Report* rankings since the first one appeared in 1983, although they have not attacked it as ferociously in recent years as they did when the rankings were based solely on reputation. Indeed, one reason why *U.S. News and World Report* added objective measures was to mollify critics who complained that its rankings should not be based entirely on opinion. Recently, however, reports have circulated that many institutions have deliberately supplied *U.S. News and World Report* with false "objective" information in order to improve their chances for a high ranking. The president of Marshall University, J. Wade Gilley, complained that

> manipulative reporting now has expanded beyond SAT scores to graduation rates of athletes, the number of National Merit Scholars enrolled, and almost anything else that enhances an institution's public image. (Gilley, 1990a, p. 22)

A few months later, he wrote as follows:

> . . . all "objective data" used in the survey are self-reported by the colleges and therefore questionable. . . . there is growing evidence that officials at many institutions fudge or shade their data to build up their college's or university's image. (Gilley, 1990b, p. 35)

To stop what he believed to be the widespread practice of institutions reporting false "objective" data, Gilley went so far as to recommend that *U.S. News and*

World Report use only reputational measures in compiling its rankings (1990a, p. 22). Schmotter (1989) pointed out that one reason for the success of rankings like those in *U.S. News and World Report* has been the failure of colleges and universities themselves to provide useful information about their comparative quality:

> The fact is that higher education itself has not been able to develop a means of evaluating and certifying quality that is either relevant or intelligible to those who invest in it through their tuition payments or gifts. Accreditation, an arcane and mysterious system to nearly all students and alumni, screens out only the most obviously deficient institutions. Faculty reputations are made within individual academic disciplines, and people outside these communities are ill suited to make judgments about quality and reputation. (p. A40)

At any rate, rankings of colleges and universities, based on reputation and/or other measures, by magazines and other popular media, are clearly not going to disappear. In addition to the *Business Week* and *U.S. News and World Report* rankings, *Money* magazine, with a circulation of more than 1.8 million, has recently published a special issue listing America's 100 public and 100 private colleges and universities that are the best value for the money it costs to attend them (*Money Guide: America's Best College Buys*, 1990, pp. 72–73). *Business Week*, building on its magazine rankings of MBA programs, has published a book listing more programs and including far more information than its magazine articles do (Byrne, 1991). The newspaper *USA Today* ranks colleges and universities annually by how selective they are in admitting new freshmen.

OTHER REPUTATIONAL RANKINGS, 1967–1991

Up to now, we have discussed many of the rankings at some length, for a variety of reasons. They include the following: the rankings were compiled early in the history of reputational rankings; they ranked numerous fields of study; they were widely discussed by scholars, extensively covered in the popular press, or both; they appeared in mass-circulation media; or some combination. In this section, we briefly describe many of the other reputational rankings that appeared from 1967 to 1991. These rankings are organized alphabetically by discipline or professional field, and within each discipline in chronological order. If there are rankings for a discipline or field's sub-fields, as, for example, health education, higher education, and special education within the field of education, these rankings are arranged alphabetically by sub-field and in chronological order within each sub-field.

Most of the rankings listed in this section considered graduate-level education only. In a few cases, they covered both graduate-level and undergraduate-level education separately or they considered institutions' graduate and undergraduate education, taken as a whole. For the few rankings that are based on anything other than graduate-level education, we call attention to this fact in our discussion of them.

RANKINGS OF GRADUATE EDUCATION

Agricultural Economics
In 1976, Boddy ranked the top agricultural economics departments by both the quality of their graduate faculty and the attractiveness of their Ph.D. programs. Though he never published this ranking, his list of the 19 best departments according to graduate faculty quality is displayed in Owen and Cross (eds.), (1984, Table 8, p. 108).

Broadcasting
Kittross, who in 1966 had ranked schools of broadcasting, later (Kittross, 1973) ranked the leading schools for graduate study in radio and television (Table 2, p. 9). He also ranked the leading schools for undergraduate study in these fields (Table 3, p. 11) in each of four geographical areas.

Business
More reputational rankings of business schools, especially their MBA programs, have been published in recent years than of any other field, with the possible exception of education. Four of them appeared in the magazine *MBA* from 1974 to 1977 ("The Fifteen Top-Ranked Graduate Business Schools . . . ," 1974; "The Top 15," 1975; "Graduate Business Schools . . . ," 1976; Ross, 1977). In all four, deans, MBA holders, and readers of the magazine each ranked approximately the top 10 or 15 MBA programs. *MBA*'s 1974 issue included another ranking of MBA programs, this one by corporate recruiters (Harris and Jefferson, 1974, p. 24). The rankings in *MBA* were not very sophisticated methodologically. Its 1976 ranking was biased because the magazine's editors bound the questionnaires used for its readers' rankings of MBA programs into an issue that contained a laudatory story on Stanford Business School ("Graduate Business Schools," 1976, p. 42).

Business Sub-fields
Brooker and Shinoda (1976) ranked colleges and universities that belonged to the American Association of Collegiate Schools of Business (AACSB) which had the best master's programs and best doctoral programs in five areas: accounting; finance; management science/operations research; marketing; organization theory and behavior.

Accounting
Estes (1970) ranked the 10 best business schools in accounting from among those schools that offered a doctorate with a major or minor in accounting. He obtained evaluations from several groups of respondents: deans, chairs of accounting departments, full professors of accounting, other teachers of accounting, practitioners, and a panel of leaders of the accounting profession. He then aggregated their responses to rank the top 10 programs (Table 2, p. 88). Carpenter, Crumbley, and Strawser (1974) also ranked the leading accounting programs, both by the quality of their faculty (Table 1, p. 92) and the effectiveness of their doctoral programs (Table 2, p. 93). The newsletter, *Public Accounting Report,* has ranked accounting programs annually for 10 years. In its most recent survey, the University of Illinois (Urbana/Champaign) was regarded as having both the best undergraduate and the best graduate accounting program in the country ("U.S. Professors Rank Arthur Andersen . . . ," 1991, p. 3).

Executive Education
Maidment ranked the top 20 university-based programs of executive education by their reputations in the eyes of deans of schools and colleges of business administration accredited by the AACSB (Maidment, 1986, p. 118).

International Business
Ball and McCulloch ranked (1984, p. 178, Table 3) the top 21 programs in international business. Nehrt (1987, Table 4, p. 98) ranked the top 30 master's programs in this field. Ball and McCulloch, in a follow-up to their 1984 ranking, listed (1988, Table 2, p. 297) the top 25 American schools in international business. Finally, Nehrt, reanalyzing the data from which he had compiled his 1987 ranking, produced a new one of the top 27 American schools in international business (1989, Table 2, p. 167).

Communication
Probably the most prolific publishers of reputational rankings in any field is the team of Renee Edwards and Larry Barker, occasionally joined by Kittie Watson. All three are faculty members in communication or speech communication at universities in the American South. Since 1979, they have combined to publish at least five articles ranking doctoral programs in communication (Edwards and Barker, 1977; 1979; 1983; Edwards, Watson, and Barker, 1988; Watson, Edwards, and Barker, 1989). They have also published at least four more articles that contain reputational rankings of leading communication programs, but since their tables displayed these programs in alphabetical, not rank order, these articles are not considered here. In their rankings, they typically have listed outstanding communication programs in each of several sub-fields: they then have aggregated these rankings of subfields to obtain an overall ranking.

Computer Science

Conway (1978, Table 1, p. 4) ranked the top 10 American and Canadian computer science programs by the perceived quality of their graduate faculty and listed, in alphabetical order, three groups of lower-ranked schools.

Education

Walberg asked a random sample of 250 members of the American Educational Research Association to rank the institutions that "have been contributing the best educational research in their schools, colleges or departments of education during the past few years" (1972, p. 15). He then listed the top 12 such institutions (Table 1, p. 15).

A Ranking of Several Sub-fields of Education

Higgins (1968), in his Columbia University Teachers College dissertation, asked senior faculty members teaching in one or more of the areas he ranked, "how would you rate [doctoral programs at a selected list of institutions] if you were selecting a graduate school for doctoral work in your field today?" (Abstract, p. ii). Based on 413 responses, he then ranked the top 10 or so institutions in each of five areas: 1. Educational administration: Elementary, secondary, or general; 2. Counseling, guidance, and student personnel administration; 3. Social and philosophical foundations; 4. Curriculum and teaching: General supervision; 5. Administration of higher education, including community colleges or adult education. West (unpublished manuscript) ranked the 25 leading schools and colleges of education, plus ties, in each of eight sub-fields: administration; educational policy studies; educational psychology; elementary and early childhood education; post secondary education; secondary education; special education; vocational and technical education. He combined the ratings for these fields to obtain a ranking of the top 25 schools and colleges of education, overall (p. 23).

Rankings of Individual Sub-fields of Education

Art Education. Hardiman, Shipley, and Zernich (1975, Table 1, p. 27) ranked the United States' 10 top programs in art education.

Educational Administration. Gregg and Sims (1972), using a format closely resembling those used by Cartter and Roose and Andersen, ranked the top 30 departments of educational administration, plus ties, by faculty quality (Table 4, pp. 76–77) and also by program quality (Table 9, pp. 86–87).

Health Education. Fourouzesh, Creswell, and Price (1982), in a study that was apparently never published, included several tables ranking the top 10 doctoral programs and the top 20 master's programs in health education according to each of several criteria.

Higher Education. Johnson (1982, Table 7, unnumbered page) ranked the 10 leading programs of higher education. More recently, Newell and Kuh (1989, p. 84) also ranked the top 10 higher education administration programs.

Physical Education. Baker (1980, p. 32) ranked the top 20 doctoral programs in physical education in the eyes of professional physical educators. Massengale and Sage (1982, Table 1, p. 308) ranked the top 20 programs by graduate faculty quality.

Special Education. Sindelaar and Schloss ranked the 10 best doctoral programs in special education according to faculty distinction (1986, Table 3, p. 55) and also by those that graduated the best-prepared students (Table 4, p. 55).

Engineering
The magazine *New Engineer* ranked the top few graduate and undergraduate engineering schools in each of these areas: chemical/petroleum; civil; electrical; engineering science; industrial; mechanical; and "others"; ("Ranking the Engineering Schools," 1976, Table 1, p. 21). It then ranked separately the top 20 undergraduate engineering schools, plus ties, according to surveys of engineering school department heads and *New Engineer*'s readers (Table 5, p. 26).

Journalism
Clark, Alperstein, Haskins, and Lindeborg (1972, Tables 3–5, pp. 11–13) listed, in order, the top journalism schools according to their quality of faculty, effectiveness of graduate program in professional areas, and effectiveness of doctoral program.

Law
Juris Doctor ("The Popular Vote . . . ," 1976, Tables 1–4, p. 18) published four tables, each listing the dozen or so leading law schools by their academic quality and their "value in landing good jobs" (p. 17) in the eyes of law school deans and the magazine's readers.

Library Science
Carpenter and Carpenter (1970, Table 31, p. 42) ranked the 25 leading master's degree programs in library science. Years later, White (1987) ranked the 15 leading library science programs, plus ties, at the master's level (Tables 1 and 2, p. 260) and the 13 leading programs, plus ties, at the doctoral level (Tables 3 and 4, p. 261).

Medicine
The magazine *Medical Dimensions* ("The Popular Vote . . . ," 1976) ranked the medical schools with the best academic programs; the best clinical programs; and those that were most useful "in helping graduates land top residencies" (p. 32). It published separate rankings showing how the various schools fared in the eyes

of medical school deans; students; housestaff; and those in private practice and others, showing the top handful—in no case, more than five—schools in each category (p. 36).

In an unusually well-done ranking, Cole and Lipton (1977) ranked all 94 medical schools approved by the American Medical Association in 1971–72 (Table 2, pp. 669–671).

Nursing
Chamings (1984, Tables 1 and 2, p. 238) ranked the top 35 American nursing schools according to nursing school deans and nurse researchers.

Public Administration and Public Policy
Morgan et al. (1981, Table 1, p. 669) ranked the top 39 master's degree granting programs in public administration and public policy. Two authors of this study, Morgan and Meier, then polled two additional groups of respondents to learn how closely their rankings would correspond to those of the original group. Based on the second two polls, they listed the 50 best-regarded schools granting a master's degree in public administration in the eyes of practitioners and the 50 best-regarded schools in the eyes of academics (Morgan and Meier, 1982, Tables 1 and 2, p. 172.)

Theatre
Edwards, Watson and Barker, who combined to compile one of the rankings of communication discussed above, also ranked doctoral programs in theatre (1989). They asked respondents from the Association for Communication Administration and the Association for Theatre in Higher Education to rank the leading schools in various theatre sub-fields. They then listed the overall ranking obtained from each group (Table 8, p. 69 and Table 16, p. 72).

RANKINGS OF UNDERGRADUATE PROGRAMS AT FOUR-YEAR COLLEGES AND UNIVERSITIES

A Ranking of "Whole" Institutions
Krukowski Associates and Kane, Parsons Associates (1986) asked high school juniors in the eastern and midwestern United States to rank those colleges and universities they considered the academically strongest; the most prestigious; the best public institutions; and the most fun to attend. They listed the top 10 institutions in each category. This ranking may have been the only one ever published in which high school juniors were the raters. Not one institution that calls itself a college was named to any of the lists, with the exception of Dartmouth, which tied for seventh for "most prestigious." Every other institution

named was a university, except for MIT and Caltech. The University of Virginia was rated the best public college or university in the United States. The University of Southern California and Boston University, even though they are private, both made the list of the top 10 public institutions.

A Ranking of Six Departments

Solmon and Astin (1981) asked respondents to select, from a list of 80 to 150 departments provided them, the best in one of seven fields—biology, business, chemistry, economics, English, history, and sociology—according to each of six criteria concerning quality of undergraduate education. From the lists their respondents generated of the leading institutions in each of these seven fields, they eliminated all those institutions that had scored 3.0 or higher for "quality of graduate faculty" in the Roose/Andersen study. Excluding the field of business from those they analyzed, they then listed (*Change*, Table 2, p. 26) 42 institutions that their respondents had ranked among the top 10 in at least one of the six criteria in at least one of the six fields. They ranked these institutions by how many of the six fields in which they had been ranked among the top 10 on at least one criterion. Seven colleges tied for first, all of them ranking highly in five of the six fields. They were Amherst, Bryn Mawr, Carleton, Dartmouth, Haverford, Pomona, and Williams. Some colleges, often considered among the very best in the United States, ranked among the top schools in fewer than five fields, including Reed (4); Swarthmore (4); Oberlin (2); and Wellesley (2).

Rankings of Individual Fields

Business
Hunger and Wheelen (1980, Table 1, p. 26) compiled two rankings of the top undergraduate programs in business. One showed how they ranked in the eyes of business school deans at schools whose undergraduate business programs were accredited by the AACSB. The other showed how they ranked in the eyes of senior personnel executives.

Public Relations
Public relations educators ranked the 11 top undergraduate programs for public relations ("Educators Rank Public Relations Programs," 1989, p. 11).

A RANKING OF COMMUNITY COLLEGES

In one of the very few rankings, reputational or otherwise, ever published of community colleges, Rouche and Baker listed, in order, (1987, p. 10) the top five community colleges in terms of being "known nationally for success in classroom instruction" (p. 9).

CHARACTERISTICS OF THE "OTHER" RANKINGS, 1967–1991

Almost all the fields and sub-fields covered by the rankings in this section are in professional and vocational areas—broadcasting, business, education, law, library science, medicine, and so on. Few of the multidisciplinary reputational rankings have included many professional fields outside of engineering—the two by Blau and Margulies are exceptions—so rankings of professional school fields are certainly useful. Many liberal arts disciplines and sub-disciplines are not covered in most or all of the multidisciplinary rankings either, but the rankings discussed in the section, "Other Reputational Rankings, 1967–1991," include very few liberal arts disciplines or sub-disciplines. In addition to the six liberal arts disciplines covered by Solmon and Astin (1981), of the more than 40 rankings included in this section, the only ones that cover such disciplines are the three by Edwards and Barker and, in one case, Edwards, Watson, and Barker on communication; the one by Conway on computer science; and the one by Edwards, Watson, and Barker on theatre. Many rankings of liberal arts disciplines, especially in some of the social science fields such as economics, psychology, and sociology, have been published in recent years. However, for reasons that are worthy of study in themselves, they usually employed other measures, such as faculty publication productivity, than reputation.

A large proportion of the rankings discussed in this section were not of fields of study but of sub-fields, such as art education, educational administration, health education, higher education, and physical education. Such rankings are useful, because recent multidisciplinary reputational rankings have ranked *fields* of study, not sub-fields.

Methodologically, what is most striking about these rankings is that they made almost no advances on the *Cartter Report*, even though that ranking was published a quarter century ago. Some of them followed the *Cartter Report* closely in using two criteria for ranking fields—faculty quality and program effectiveness—and in using rating scales very similar to Cartter's 5-point scale for rating faculty quality and 3-point scale for rating program effectiveness. However, those modelled after the *Cartter Report* seldom improved upon it in any way, and those not modelled after it were, for the most part, far worse than it methodologically.

A few of these rankings were very good methodologically, such as those by Solmon and Astin (1981) and Cole and Lipton (1977). Many of them, however, especially those published not in academic journals but in magazines read by attorneys, business people, and physicians, were quite primitive.

Only a handful of the rankings considered in this section covered undergraduate education. Undergraduate education is an area in which rankings would be especially useful, since none of the multidisciplinary reputational rankings covered it. Just as rankings of individual liberal arts disciplines have been based, in recent years, more often on faculty publication productivity than on reputation, so rankings of undergraduate education have usually been based on other measures than reputation. Most often they have been based on the undergraduate origins of those who go on to earn Ph.D.s or become successful in later life.

CRITICISMS OF REPUTATIONAL RANKINGS

Most of the best known, most influential academic quality rankings have been based on reputation. As a result, reputational rankings have probably been the subject of more analysis and criticism by scholars than have all other types of rankings put together. Many of these criticisms have been made numerous times and have been capably reviewed by others. For discussion of some of the major criticisms of reputational rankings, see the following literature reviews: Lawrence and Green (1980), pp. 8–12; 15–16; Conrad and Blackburn, 1985, pp. 292–294; and Tan, 1986, pp. 243–244. Astin (1985, pp. 27–28) made eight generalizations about reputational rankings, a few of them critical. Some of the most frequently expressed criticisms of reputational rankings are these:

1. They are subject to various kinds of rater bias, so that raters will, for example, rank institutions where they serve on the faculty or from which they graduated higher than they "should" be.
2. Raters generally don't know enough about more than a handful of the institutions they are asked to consider to rate them accurately.
3. Rankings are subject to the "halo" effect, so that departments at well-regarded institutions may be ranked higher than they deserve to be, and departments at poorly-regarded institutions may be ranked lower than they deserve to be.
4. They are subject to time lag, so that raters may rank departments based on how good they were years earlier.
5. There is a very high correlation between a department's rating in reputational rankings and its size as measured, for example, by its number of faculty, full-time students, recent doctoral recipients, or some combination. Therefore, reputational rankings, for all practical purposes, rate departments based on their size more than on their quality.
6. "Quality" is a difficult word to define, and some of those who have compiled academic quality rankings made little effort to define it for the raters. What reputational rankings really rate, even when they purport to rank departments on some other criterion, is faculty research reputation, rather than faculty or departmental "quality."

These criticisms have all been made numerous times, and we will not dwell on them further here. Instead, we will discuss some criticisms that have not, as a group, been made nearly as often as those listed above. They are as follows:

The correlation between departments' and programs' rankings for faculty research prowess and for program effectiveness is exceptionally high. In the Roose/Andersen study, of the 36 disciplines covered, for 24 of them the correlation between these two measures was .99, and for the other 12 it was .98 (Roose and Andersen, 1970, Table 30, p. 34). For the 32 disciplines covered by the NAS rankings, taken as a group, the correlation between the two measures was .99 (Astin, 1985, p. 27). The extraordinarily high correlation between these two implies, as Dolan (1976, p. 41) has pointed out, that there is only one variable being measured, not two. It is reasonable to conclude that the "real" variable being measured is faculty research prowess, because it is much more visible than is program effectiveness.

It is remarkable that the correlation in reputational rankings between faculty research prowess and departmental educational effectiveness should be so high, because much research suggests that the actual correlation is much lower. Webster, for example, reviewed nine empirical studies published from 1970 to 1985 on the relationship between faculty members' undergraduate teaching effectiveness and their research productivity, finding that "all nine concluded that there is little or no positive correlation between research productivity and teaching effectiveness" (1985a, p. 61). Feldman, in an extraordinarily thorough review, examined more than 40 studies on the relationship between undergraduate teaching effectiveness and faculty research productivity and concluded that "there is a very small positive association" (1987, p. 227) between professors' research productivity and their teaching effectiveness.

All the studies that Webster reviewed, and all or almost all the studies that Feldman reviewed, examined the relationship between research productivity and *undergraduate* teaching effectiveness. The multidisciplinary reputational rankings, on the other hand, have been based on faculty research productivity and *graduate*-level or even *doctoral*-level teaching effectiveness. Nonetheless, the fact that there is almost no correlation between the two at the undergraduate level suggests that there may well be a considerably less than perfect relationship between them at the graduate level. Hartnett, Clark, and Baird found (1978) that peer ratings of departments' faculty, based largely on their publications, for the disciplines of chemistry, history, and psychology "appear to be unaffected by graduate student completion rates, student perceptions of the quality of teaching or degree of faculty concern for students" (p. 1313). They also concluded that reputational rankings "say little or nothing about the quality of instruction, the degree of civility or humaneness, the degree to which scholarly excitement is nurtured by student-faculty interactions, and so on'' (p. 1314).

Multidisciplinary reputational rankings, focussing, as they have, entirely on graduate level education, implicitly denigrate undergraduate education, because an institution's achievements in this area are not reflected in the rankings. Dolan (1976, pp. 36; 38) and Bowker (no date, p. 14) both argued this position. Dolan pointed out that Roose and Andersen themselves were much aware that their ranking might shift the public's attention away from undergraduate education, writing that:

> If, for example, the response to these rankings is to shift resources and attention in excessive amounts to the development of the quality of graduate programs, undergraduate teaching and education could be the ultimate losers. (Roose and Andersen, 1970, quoted in Dolan [1976], p. 36)

Reputational rankings, by motivating departments to imitate those ranked above them in an effort to improve their own position in subsequent rankings, reward conformity and orthodoxy, and they punish diversity, variety, and innovation (Dolan, 1976, pp. 35–36; Bowker, no date, p. 14). Webster (1984a, pp. 35–37), however, took the opposite position, pointing out that in several different fields unorthodox departments were ranked quite high.

Rankings provide a pecking order, but no information about how many departments in a field meet or exceed any absolute level of quality. They inform one what the top five, ten, twenty or whatever most highly regarded departments are, but they provide no information about how many departments are excellent, adequate to confer the doctorate, or whatever (Blackburn and Lingenfelter, 1973, p. 4). Though the *Cartter Report* did assign the adjectives ''distinguished,'' ''strong,'' ''good,'' and so on to departments scoring above certain cut-off points, these labels were assigned to departments whose scores exceeded a certain round number arbitrarily selected by Cartter; they did not correspond to any empirically-based definition of being a ''distinguished'' or ''strong'' department.

A related criticism is that since rankings provide only pecking orders, ''the rating information seldom makes for a better understanding of a specific program's strengths and weaknesses and therefore is not useful for program improvement'' (Hartnett, Clark, and Baird, 1978, p. 1310).

Most of whatever information reputational rankings provide concerns the most highly regarded departments in each discipline. These are the ones that are usually listed in rank order, rather than alphabetical order, and these are the departments on which those who analyze the rankings concentrate. So rankings tell much more about the best-regarded departments in any discipline than about the rank and file ones (Dolan, 1976, p. 17).

Very few reputational rankings have supplied raters with a list of the names of the faculty members in the departments they were supposed to rank. So it is not clear, as Cole and Zuckerman (1976, p. 16) pointed out, whether raters assign their rankings based on the research prowess of many or most of a department's faculty or just the few who are most visible. The compilers of the NAS ranking sought to find out which was the case, providing 90 percent of the raters with a list of all faculty members in the programs they were supposed to rate. They found that evaluators in most disciplines rated programs slightly higher when they were *not* supplied with the names of their faculty members, possibly because the faculty whose names evaluators could remember were better scholars than those whose names they could not. For a discussion of the results for disciplines in the social and behavioral sciences, see Jones, Lindzey, and Coggeshall [eds.], (1982), pp. 194–196.

Reputational rankings—based, as they are, largely upon the faculty's research prowess—"are unfair to doctoral programs which do not place primary emphasis on doing research and preparing their students to do research" (Hartnett, Clark, and Baird, 1978, p. 1310).

Reputational rankings favor large, comprehensive departments over those that are smaller and/or less comprehensive. As Logan Wilson argued, "high quality, but narrowly focused, programs or departments do not and cannot get as good a rating as they deserve" (no date, p. 2). They also reward "the single model full-university" (Dolan, 1976, p. 77) over smaller, more specialized institutions.

Reputational rankings have ranked only individual departments or programs. Dolan (1976, pp. 35–36) observed that interdisciplinary work has not been counted at all. He is generally correct, although there have been a handful of exceptions, such as Keniston's (1959) ranking Oriental studies and Slavic studies. Although "interdisciplinary" work is sometimes taught in a single department, as, for example, in departments of comparative literature or American studies, no multidisciplinary reputational ranking has ever included either of these fields.

While reputational rankings of professional school fields have often ranked sub-fields, rankings of liberal arts disciplines have almost always ranked entire departments. They have very seldom ranked parts of departments—for example, the American history wing of a history department or the American literature emphasis of an English department. But it can be argued that what is most important about graduate departments is what Welch (1971, pp. 95–96) called their sub-fields and what David Riesman called (1980, p. 243) their "microclimates." However, Hartnett, Clark, and Baird concluded the opposite. In their study of departments of chemistry, history, and psychology, they observed that "the correlations are generally so high [between the various subspecialties of a department and the whole department] that separate ratings would appear to be unnecessary" (1978, p. 1313).

Research activity in some fields, particularly in the sciences, does not always coincide with departmental or program units. As Cole and Zuckerman pointed out:

> Recent research in the soicology (*sic*) of science leads us to believe that disciplinary units such as physics, biology and chemistry are not the most meaningful divisions in science. Rather, the sciences appear to be divided into specialties and sub-specialties focussed on substantive problems. These form coherent units in cognitive and social terms. In this sense, the departmental structure of universities no longer corresponds to the structure of scientific investigation (1976, pp. 21–22).

The situation may be much the same in some other disciplines. In 1977, Cox and Catt ranked Ph.D.granting psychology departments based on their faculty members' research productivity, rating the University of Wisconsin at Madison department first. But later Levin et al. (1978) found that about 40 percent of the authors of articles for which the psychology department received credit had been situated elsewhere in the university. So the departmental and program units that are being ranked may not always correspond very well with faculty research and scholarship in the discipline.

Most of the criticisms discussed so far were made of reputational rankings in general, and most of them apply to many different disciplines. The criticism listed below, however, applies to a particular discipline.

Tyler (1972, p. 194) argued that in the Roose/Andersen study, experimental psychologists were overrepresented in the sample and clinical psychologists were underrepresented. Since experimental psychologists are more likely to hold university faculty positions than are clinical psychologists, the Roose/Andersen study therefore overrepresented the opinions of academic psychologists and underrepresented the opinions of non-academic psychologists.

WHO USES RANKINGS?

There is little empirical evidence available on who used reputational (or any other kind of) rankings in the past, how often, with what results, and who uses them now. However, much indirect evidence suggests that compilers of rankings seldom have had students, prospective students, and their parents—who are certainly by far the largest potential group of users for rankings—uppermost in their minds as the audience for their rankings. Some of this evidence is as follows:

1. The multidisciplinary rankings all ranked only graduate level programs, not undergraduate programs, although at any time far more students are planning to apply to undergraduate than to graduate school.
2. Some of them were published in outlets and formats less than readily acces-

sible to students. Hughes' 1934 ranking was published in the *Educational Record* and the Ladd/Lipset ranking in the *Chronicle of Higher Education*, both of which are read primarily by academicians. The NAS' (1982) ranking was published in a deliberately hard to understand format.

3. Partly as a result of the two reasons listed above, rankings have not, as a group, sold very well. The *Cartter Report* was considered a best-seller, as rankings go, because it sold about 26,000 copies.

4. Except for the Hughes (1934b) report, which did not rank *any* departments, and the NAS (1982) ranking, which provided data for almost all the doctorate programs in each discipline, each of the multidisciplinary reputational rankings has ranked only the better-regarded or best-regarded departments in each discipline. There rankings would have been more helpful to students, prospective students, and their parents had they ranked most or all of the departments in the various disciplines, not just some of them.

5. The sales success of the many spurious rankings that Jack Gourman has been publishing for almost a quarter of a century (for a debunking of Gourman's rankings, see Webster, 1984b) shows that there is a great demand for ratings of colleges, universities, and individual departments that is not being met by legitimate rankings.

6. The compilers of only one of all the multidisciplinary rankings placed much emphasis, in their discussion of their rankings, on its importance to potential students. That one was the Roose/Andersen study, whose authors wrote as follows:

> A fundamental purpose is to furnish prospective graduate students with information on faculties and programs. The study seems to us warranted if at the least it enables prospective consumers of graduate education to make more intelligent and informed choices of programs and institutions. (p. xi)

Cartter, although he mentioned his report's potential usefulness to prospective students, generally gave this group short shrift compared to other groups (pp. 3–4). The compilers of the NAS (1982) ranking, too, while they acknowledged that it could be useful to graduate students and prospective graduate students, also gave these groups relatively little emphasis:

> It is evident that the assessment of graduate programs is highly important for university administrators and faculty, for employers in industrial and government laboratories, for graduate students and prospective graduate students, for policymakers in state and national organizations, and for private and public funding agencies. (pp. 1–2)

Of the other multidisciplinary rankings, Hughes (1925) wrote that his report would be of interest to college presidents or deans who sought to fill vacancies (p. 3) or to "any one interested . . ." who could "turn to it readily for a rough estimate of the work in a given field," (p. 3), but did not mention students at all. Hughes (1934b), Keniston (1959), and Blau/Margulies (1973; 1974/75) did not discuss possible audiences. Ladd and Lipset (in Scully, 1979) wrote no report at all on the rankings that the *Chronicle of Higher Education* published, based on their data.

To the extent that these rankings came to the attention of graduate students, prospective graduate students, and their parents at all, it was probably more through college and university newspapers, metropolitan newspapers, and news-magazines, in which some of the recent multidisciplinary rankings have been very widely covered, than through the rankings themselves. Not until *U.S. News and World Report* began to rank undergraduate education in 1983 have actual rankings—rather than media coverage of them—reached a large audience of students, prospective students, and their parents. Since *U.S. News and World Report* wants its rankings to be useful to students and their parents, it has never, as of late 1991, ranked graduate programs in the arts and sciences. Rather, it has ranked undergraduate education and four professional school fields in which large numbers of students enroll.

THE USES OF REPUTATIONAL RANKINGS

Reputational rankings have many uses. One is to let department chairs and professors know where their department stands in its discipline in reputation for faculty research prowess. This is an important function of rankings. It rewards departments that are perceived as having increased their faculty research prowess since previous rankings, and it motivates them to try to increase their research prowess still more to improve their standing in future rankings. It is possible that many departments in disciplines regularly covered by reputational rankings have faculties that are more productive in research than they otherwise would be, because of the carrot-and-stick that rankings represent.

Rankings also influence university-wide resource allocation decisions. Theoretically, a department's low or declining ranking could motivate university administrators to put additional resources into it to improve it. Usually, however, what Robert Merton (1968) has described as the "Matthew effect" governs the situation; departments that are already "rich" in prestige get richer in resources; departments that are "poor" in prestige stay poor or get poorer in resources. University administrators generally try to maintain or improve their already best-regarded departments rather than bring their less well-regarded departments up to the level of the well-regarded ones. In doing so, they are acting in accordance with the suggestion made by the eminent economist George Stigler (1963), that universities should seek not to become outstanding in all fields, because that would be impossibly expensive, but rather to develop a few centers of excellence.

Generally, then, university administrators reward high-ranking departments with additional resources. When departments rank very low compared to others at the institution, or have slipped badly, university administrators may even abolish them. Washington University in St. Louis, for example, recently eliminated its sociology department, partly because it had fallen very badly in reputation between the *Cartter Report*, in which it ranked 16th in quality of graduate faculty, and the NAS ranking, in which it tied for 57th on this measure. Occasionally, however, university administrations put additional resources into poorly ranked programs to shore them up. Trow (1983) has described how, because the University of California at Berkeley's programs in the biological sciences slipped, some of them quite badly, between the Roose/Andersen study and the NAS ranking, the campus' administration provided them with extra resources in an attempt to improve them.

A third use of rankings is to let university-wide administrators and other concerned people know how a university's departments, taken as a group, are faring. They can show, for example, how well a university's doctorate-granting departments are regarded compared to those at nearby universities. After the NAS ranking appeared, for example, the *Washington Post* published an article (Feinberg, 1983a) showing how some nearby universities ranked, department by department, in each discipline covered by the NAS in which they offered doctoral work. Rankings also provide the raw material for others to show how institutions have changed in reputation over time, as Webster (1983, Table 11, p. 23) and Kerr (1991, Table 2, p. 13) have done.

Sometimes this use of rankings—providing campus-wide administrators with information about how their departments have fared since a previous ranking—can reveal dramatic changes. For example, the data for the *Cartter Report* were collected in 1964 and the data for the Roose/Andersen study in 1969. In those five years, the State University of New York at Buffalo, which in the mid-1960s had hired the University of California at Berkeley's former acting chancellor as president, set out to make itself "the Berkeley of the East." It received large increases in state funding for several years under Governor Nelson Rockefeller, and many of its departments quickly improved their reputations. In the Roose/Andersen study, published in 1970, 66 raters (out of 71 who expressed an opinion on the matter) considered its classics department "better than five years ago" for "quality of graduate faculty"; in English, the figures were 58 out of 61; in history, 41 of 49; in psychology, 46 of 53; in sociology, 39 of 52; in chemistry, 51 of 57.

Columbia University, on the other hand, fared disastrously in those five years. For faculty quality, of its 25 departments that were rated in both rankings, it received an improved ranking in one (astronomy), an identical rating in three, and a lower rating in fully 21, and many of its departments' declines were very steep. In classics, for example, it fell from tied for 6th to tied for 12th; in biochemistry, from 11th to tied for 26th; in physiology, from tied for 10th to tied for 27th; in zoology, from tied for 14th to tied for 28th; in geology, from 4th to 9th; in electrical engineering, from tied for 10th to tied for 21st. Although Columbia had suffered because of the student turbulence there in the late 1960s, that is probably not the whole, or even the major reason for its decline, because the University of California at Berkeley had suffered at least as much from student protest in the 1960s, and it underwent no decline at all between the *Cartter Report* and the Roose/Andersen study. Of the three people discussed in the section on the *Cartter Report* who aggregated most or all of Cartter's departmental scores into institution-wide ones, two—Ewell (no date) and McCurdy (in DeBardeleben, 1966)—ranked UC/Berkeley first, and the other (Magoun, 1966) ranked it second. Fawcett (1971), who aggregated Roose/Andersen's departmental scores in 20 liberal arts disciplines to get institution-wide scores, also ranked UC/Berkeley first.

In addition to its sharp drop in many departments in ratings for quality of graduate faculty, Columbia also fared very poorly in the Roose/Andersen ranking in how well its departments fared in their reputation for educational effectiveness compared to their reputation for faculty quality. It is axiomatic that in American reputational rankings which ask respondents to rate departments both for their faculty's research prowess and their programs' educational effectiveness, the rankings based on the two criteria are virtually identical.

At Columbia, however, fully 11 of its departments ranked four or more places lower in educational effectiveness than in faculty quality (Roose and Andersen, 1970, Table 26, pp. 22–23), far more than at any other institution in the country. (Runners-up—all, like Columbia, large universities located in or near large cities—were the University of California at Berkeley, five; the University of Chicago, four; and the University of Minnesota and the University of Pennsylvania, tied with three [Table 26, pp. 22–23]). In some cases at Columbia, the disparity between its departments' scores on these two measures was very great; English, for example, ranked tied for 6th in faculty quality but tied for 23rd in educational effectiveness, a drop of 17 places. No other department, of the 2,626 covered by Roose and Andersen, had a drop between its rating for faculty quality and its rating for educational effectiveness of more than 10 places. Columbia's physics department, too, ranked much lower in educational effectiveness than in faculty quality; it was tied for 7th in the latter and tied for 16th in the former.

So reputational rankings can be very helpful in alerting campus-wide officials not only to individual departments' gains or losses in reputation, but also to campus-wide patterns of rise and decline in reputations.

Another use of rankings is to supply statewide higher education officials with information with which they can make plans for discontinuing weak programs. For example, the Oklahoma State Regents for Higher Education announced in 1991 that all departments at the University of Oklahoma and Oklahoma State

University which did not rank within the top 50 in their disciplines were in jeopardy of being merged with other departments or eliminated. (The Regents did not announce what sources of information would be used to identify the top 50 such departments. Presumably reputational rankings would be among them, however, since they are by far the best-known and the most influential of modern rankings and since they have been used to rank many disciplines and fields of study, particularly in the humanities and some of the minor professions, that have seldom been included in any other kind of ranking.)

Increasingly, in recent years, colleges and universities have used good performances in rankings to market and advertise themselves. A recent *U.S. News and World Report* ranking of undergraduate colleges and universities, for example, based partly on reputation, called the University of Nevada at Las Vegas, along with two other institutions, one of the "rising stars of American higher education" in the western United States (Sheler, Toch, Morse, Heupler, and Linnon, 1989, p. 81). Based on this encomium, that institution has frequently placed large display ads in the *Chronicle of Higher Education*'s "Bulletin Board" section, which contains job announcements, headlined "UNLV—One of the 'rising stars of American higher education.' "

Philanthropic organizations, of course, both private and public, use the rankings to learn which departments in a discipline have the best-regarded research faculties, so they can make grants accordingly. Once again, as with campus-based resource allocation sessions, generally the rich get richer and the poor stay poor or get poorer, but not always. Allan Cartter, for example, reported the following:

> At least one major university has spent considerable time recently trying to convince a Federal agency that it is *not* (emphasis Cartter's) one of the top 20 universities in the country and thus is eligible for support as a "university of promise." (1966, p. 4)

Sometimes, selective organizations use rankings for information about which institutions are worthy of membership. For example, an administrator whose university was a member of the AAU distributed an unpublished memo (Baughman, 1968) comparing the 42 universities which were then members of the AAU with 11 well-regarded institutions which were not on several characteristics, including how high they had ranked in the Ewell (no date); McCurdy (in De-Bardeleben, 1966); and Magoun (1966) aggregations of the *Cartter Report*'s departmental scores. One objective of this memo seems to have been to help decide which, if any, of these 11 institutions should be invited join the AAU (p. 22).

Usually it is academic departments, broad fields of study at them, such as the social sciences and the humanities, or entire institutions that gain or lose prestige according to how high or low they are rated in reputational rankings. In at least one case, however, members of an academic discipline thought it was crucial to their discipline's prestige for its departments to be ranked. The NAS, as it prepared to compile its 1982 ranking, had decided not to include geography. Dwight A. Brown, chairperson of the geography department at the University of Minnesota, then wrote to the chairs of other geography departments, urging them to lobby the NAS to include geography. His grounds for doing so were that if geography were not covered, "cost-cutting administrators would be quick to cite [geography's] exclusion from the study to justify the elimination of geography programs, and the study would be cited as evidence that geography is not central to university education" (1980, p. 1). Ultimately, the NAS included geography, with the discipline of geography itself paying what it cost the NAS to rank its departments.

Another use of rankings can be to show how the nation's doctorate-granting departments, taken as a whole, are faring, and to compare their current standing with their standing in earlier rankings. An apparent improvement in departments between two rankings can be used as evidence that American doctoral-level education (and, by implication, all of American higher education) has improved and that the nation is getting its money's worth. For example, although the Roose/Andersen study itself did not emphasize the point, the ACE's press release on it stressed the fact that many departments had shown improvements in their "quality of graduate faculty" between the *Cartter Report* and the Roose/Andersen study.

> Three-fourths of the more than 1,600 programs surveyed in both studies show increases in their "quality of graduate faculty" scores in the new survey. In 1964, 1,161, or 69.8 percent, of the rated faculties achieved the score category "adequate plus" or better. In 1969, 1,306, or 80.0 percent, of the faculties included in both studies had equivalent scores.
>
> The report also notes that nearly one in six of the faculties that in 1964 were rated "good" or "adequate plus" showed 1969 scores equivalent to the "strong" category. More than a fourth of the faculties rated "good" in 1964 were rated "strong" in 1969, and 39 faculties rated "strong" in 1964 received scores in 1969 equivalent to the earlier report's "distinguished" category. (Skinner, 1970, p. 1)

Needed Rankings

For reasons worthy of study in themselves, multidisciplinary reputational rankings have usually ranked Ph.D. programs in arts and sciences disciplines plus engineering, and occasionally major professional schools other than engineering. What are needed now are well-done reputational (and other) rankings of a wider variety of disciplines and a greater range of levels. Additional rankings, for example, of colleges and the undergraduate offerings of universities would be very useful. Rankings of graduate programs that confer the master's as the highest degree would also be helpful. Many rankings have been compiled of

MBA programs and some of Master's of Library Science programs, but very few have been conducted of liberal arts departments that grant the master's as the highest degree.

In addition, rankings of what are sometimes called the "minor" professions would be very useful. Various engineering departments, of course, have been ranked in most of the multidisciplinary rankings, and business, education, and law have each been covered by several rankings, including one or more multidisciplinary reputational rankings. For most of the minor professions, however, very little is available except the two Blau/Margulies rankings, which were not very useful in the first place and are now almost two decades old.

POLICY IMPLICATIONS

Most of the policy implications discussed here are those that can be drawn from the multidisciplinary reputational rankings, rather than those done of a single discipline or field of study. Similarly, most of the policy implications to be discussed are those that can be drawn from many, most, or all of these rankings, rather than only one or a few of them. However, in a few cases we discuss, for one reason or another, policy implications that can be drawn from only one or two of these rankings.

The policy implications are divided into five groups, according to the policy makers that they primarily affect. These groups are as follows: university-wide administrators; statewide officials; officials at particular types of institutions; national officials; people who may compile future rankings.

University-wide administrators

1. Perhaps the most important policy implication of all is the following. Reputational rankings, as they have been done over the decades and as they are still done today, are almost always far more informative about a department's faculty research and publication prowess than they are about any other of its features. Even rankings based on "educational attractiveness" are probably based far more on faculty research prowess than on any other aspect of the department's education attractiveness. So campus administrators should regard them as such, and not believe that they reveal very much, if anything, about other aspects of their institution's departments' educational attractiveness.
2. University-wide administrators also use reputational rankings to increase their institutions' resources. They can use them when they approach state legislatures and/or private donors to argue that a particular department is outstanding and therefore deserves more support or that another one is slipping and needs

to be bolstered. As the chief academic officer of a major research university has said:

> With private donors or public bodies, it is easier to be able to point to external assessments that are independent of the self-interest of the university than it is to use private sources of information to support the arguments about the quality of work in the particular disciplines represented at that university. (Bradburn, 1988, p. 97)

Statewide Officials

1. Reputational rankings can inform state legislators which departments at which public universities in the state are the most productive in research, because such departments can often help the state's economic development (Bradburn, 1988, p. 94).
2. They can inform statewide higher education officials which programs at public universities are not well regarded, so that they can decide whether to eliminate them (Roose and Andersen, 1970, p. 25).

Officials at Particular Types of Institutions

1. After the publication of the Roose/Andersen study (1970), two well-known black educators, Andrew Billingsley and Elias Blake, Jr., objected to the fact that Roose and Andersen's sample of 130 institutions did not include even one predominantly black one. They argued that this omission gave the impression that such institutions did not even offer graduate education ("Report on Graduate Study Ignored Blacks," 1971). They also complained that the report, by suggesting that most support be given to the approximately 50 highest-rated institutions (Roose and Andersen, 1970, p. 25), hurt the aspirations of black universities, none of which was in or near that group.
2. While Billingsley and Blake contended that the Roose/Andersen study unfairly served to dampen the aspirations of predominantly black institutions, an editorial in the Jesuit monthly *America* took the opposite tack. It argued that the poor showing of Catholic universities in that ranking, and their "agonizingly slow" progress between the *Cartter Report* and the Roose/Andersen study, strongly suggested that Catholic universities should curb their ambitions. It suggested that Catholic universities should stop developing new Ph.D. programs and instead should concentrate their efforts on "developing two or three really outstanding divinity schools at Catholic universities" ("Catholic Universities Flunk the Ph.D. Exam," 1971, p. 84).

National Officials

1. Roose and Andersen expressed concern that their rating of Ph.D.-granting departments might focus too much attention on graduate education and lead to the comparative neglect of undergraduate education (1970, pp. 24–25).

2. They also argued that in the future a sufficient supply of Ph.D.'s "for most traditional uses" could be trained in the top-ranked 50 or so institutions (p. 25).

3. In addition, they suggested that America's doctoral-level education had improved greatly from 1966 to 1970, and that therefore, by implication, America was getting a good return for the money it spent on higher education (1970, pp. 16–24).

Those Who May Compile Future Rankings

Finally, there is a policy implication for those who may compile future rankings. In recent decades the purpose of most reputational rankings has changed markedly:

> . . . the original goal of national assessments was to determine which departments provided the best graduate education. Through a process of goal displacement, research in this area has become increasingly preoccupied only with scholarly productivity. (Rau and Leonard, 1990, p. 252)

While Rau and Leonard did not make the point themselves, certainly it can be argued that those who compile reputational rankings should pay more attention to assessing across-the-board quality in graduate (and other levels of) education and become less preoccupied than they are now with scholarly research productivity.

CONCLUSION

Reputational rankings, although not the oldest kind of academic quality rankings and far from the most numerous ones, since at least the mid-1960's have nevertheless been the most influential type of ranking. Still, they have many faults. The two most important ones are these. First, being based, as they are, upon faculty members' scholarly reputations,

> they can effectively rate only departments whose members have substantial research reputations. Such rankings are useful for differentiating, in a given discipline, between, say, Stanford and Berkeley, Duke and the University of North Carolina at Chapel Hill, and, arguably, Washington State University and Oregon State University. But once below the top few dozen or, at most, the top one hundred departments in a discipline, it is very hard to differentiate among departments on the basis of their faculty's research reputations, which are often slender or nonexistent. (Webster, 1981, p. 21)

Second, since they are based almost entirely upon faculty members' research reputations, they should not be interpreted, as they commonly are, as revealing very much, if anything, about all the other important aspects of departments other than their faculty members' research prowess. They should probably be employed, as the NAS' 1982 ranking did, as one or a few measures of academic quality, among several others.

REFERENCES

ACE graduate program rankings: Ammunition for increased or reduced support? (1971, February 10). National Association of State Universities and Land-Grant Colleges Circular Letter #4, pp. 17–28.

A Classification of Institutions of Higher Education. (1987). Princeton, N.J.: Carnegie Foundation for the Advancement of Teaching.

America's best colleges. (1985, November 25). *U.S. News and World Report*: 46–51; 54–60.

America's Best Colleges, 1990. (1990). Washington, DC: U.S. News and World Report.

America's Best Colleges, 1991. (1991). Washington, DC: U.S. News and World Report.

America's best graduate and professional schools. (1990, March 19). *U.S. News and World Report*: 46–50; 52–56; 59–62; 64–67; 70–72; 74–76; 78–79.

Apples and pears. (1988, June 24). *Times Higher Education Supplement*: 8–9.

Astin, A.W. (1985). *Achieving Educational Excellence*. San Francisco: Jossey-Bass.

Austin, L., et al. (1975, May). Letter to the editor, *Change* 7: 4.

Baker, J.A.W. (1980). Rating of doctoral programs in physical education in the United States. *International Journal of Physical Education* 17: 31–32.

Ball, D.A., and McCulloch, Jr., W.H. (1984). International business education programs in American schools: How they are ranked by members of the Academy of International Business. *Journal of International Business Studies* 15: 175–180.

Ball, D.A., and McCulloch, Jr., W.H. (1988). International business education programs in American and non-American schools: How they are ranked by the Academy of International Business. *Journal of International Business Studies* 19: 295–299.

Bauer, B., Solorzano, L., and Woltz, V. (1988, October 10). America's best colleges. *U.S. News and World Report*: C3–C9; C12–C13; C15; C18; C20–C25; C28–C32.

Baughman, G.W. (1968, October 16). Characteristics of size and quality of graduate education among members of the Association of American Universities. Unpublished manuscript, Ohio State University, Columbus.

Best places to be for a Ph.D. (1983, November). *Changing Times* 37: 64; 66–67.

Blackburn, R.T., and Lingenfelter, P.E. (1973). *Assessing Quality in Doctoral Programs: Criteria and Correlates of Excellence*. Ann Arbor, MI: Center for the Study of Higher Education.

Blau, P.M. (1964). *Exchange and Power in Social Life*. New York: John Wiley.

Blau, P.M. (1973). *The Organization of Academic Work*. New York: John Wiley and Sons.

Blau, P.M. (1974). *On the Nature of Organizations*. New York: John Wiley and Sons.

Blau, P.M., and Margulies, R.Z. (1974/75, December/January). The reputations of American professional schools. *Change* 6: 42–47.

Bowker, A.H. (no date). Measuring the quality of graduate programs. Unpublished manuscript.

Bowling, W.G. (1966). Review of *An Assessment of Quality in Graduate Education*. *College and University* 42: 110–113.

Bradburn, N.M. (1988). The ranking of universities in the United States and its effects on their achievement. *Minerva* 26: 91–100.

Brightest and the best, The. (1983, January 24). *Time*, p. 64.

Brooker, G., and Shinoda, P. (1976). Peer ratings of graduate programs for business. *Journal of Business* 49: 240–251.

Brown, D.A. (1980, November 19). [Unpublished letter to chairpersons of geography departments.] University of Minnesota, Minneapolis/St. Paul.

Byrne, J.A. (1988, November 28). The best B-schools. *Business Week* 76–80; 84–86; 92.

Byrne, J.A. (1990, October 29). The best B-schools. *Business Week* 52–58; 62–63; 66.

Byrne, J.A. (1991). *Business Week's Guide to the Best Business Schools*. (2nd ed.). New York: McGraw-Hill.

Callcott, G.H. (1980, April). The costs of excellence. University of Maryland Graduate School *Chronicle* 13: 29.

Carmody, D. (1987, November 25). Colleges' S.A.T. lists can be creative works. *New York Times*, section B, p. 10.

Carpenter, C.G., Crumbley, D.L., and Strawser, R.H. (1974). A new ranking of accounting faculties and doctoral programs. *Journal of Accountancy* 137: 90–94.

Carpenter, R.L., and Carpenter, P.A. (1970). The doctorate in librarianship and an assessment of graduate library education. *Journal of Education for Librarianship* 11: 3–45.

Cartter, A. (1956). *Redistribution of Income in Postwar Britain*. New Haven: Yale University Press.

Cartter, A.M. (1965a). Economics of the university. *American Economic Review* 55: 481–494.

Cartter, A.M. (1965b). Qualitative aspects of southern university education. *Southern Economic Journal*, Supplement on "Education and the Southern Economy," 32(1), part 2: 39–69.

Cartter, A.M. (1966a). *An Assessment of Quality in Graduate Education*. Washington, DC: American Council on Education.

Cartter, A.M. (1966b). Assessing quality in graduate education. *Science Education* 50: 251–258.

Cartter A.M. (1966c, September). The assessment of quality: A view in retrospect. Unpublished manuscript of an address presented to the American Psychological Association.

Cartter, A.M. (1966d). As others view Yale: An assessment of graduate education. *Ventures* 6: 15–20.

Cartter, A. (1973). *Higher education: Who pays? Who benefits? Who should pay?* New York: McGraw-Hill.

Cartter, A.M. (1975, December 1). Unpublished letter to faculty members accompanying the survey form for "The Cartter report on the leading schools of education, law, and business." University of California at Los Angeles, Los Angeles.

Cartter, A. (1976). *Ph.D.'s and the Academic Labor Market*. New York: McGraw-Hill.

Cartter report on the leading schools of education, law, and business, The. (1977, February). *Change* 9: 44–48.

Catholic universities flunk the Ph.D. exam. (1971, January 30). *America*: 84.

Chamings, P.A. (1984, September/October). Ranking the nursing schools. *Nursing Outlook* 32: 238–239.

Clark, W.C., Alperstein, G.S., Haskins, J.B., and Lindeborg, R.A. (1972). *Journalism Education Reputations*. Syracuse, N.Y.: Syracuse University S.I. Newhouse School of Public Communications.

Cole, J.R., and Lipton, J.A. (1977). The reputations of American medical schools. *Social Forces* 55: 662–684.

Cole, S., and Zuckerman, H. (1976, September). The use of ACE ratings in research on science and higher education. Unpublished manuscript prepared for the Planning Conference on Assessment of the Quality of Graduate Education Programs in the United States.

Conrad, C.F., and Blackburn, R.T. (1985). Program quality in higher education: A review and critique of literature and research. In J.C. Smart (ed.). *Higher Education: Handbook of Theory and Research*, vol. I. New York: Agathon Press.

Conway, R. (1978). *A Survey of Graduate Programs in Computer Science*. Ithaca, N.Y.: Cornell University Department of Computer Science.

Cox, W.M., and Catt, V. (1977). Productivity ratings of graduate programs in psychology based on publication in the journals of the American Psychological Association. *American Psychologist* 32: 793–813.

DeBardeleben, A. (1966, August 8). Unpublished letter sent to the Regents of the University of Wisconsin. Park Falls, WI.

Derner, G. (1971). Criticism of ACE report on university standings. *American Psychologist* 26: 856–857.

Difficulties of demarcation. (1985, February 8). *Times Higher Education Supplement*: 12–13.

Dolan, W.P. (1976). *The Ranking Game*. Lincoln: University of Nebraska Printing and Duplicating Service.

Editors of *Change*. (1974, April). Replies to letters to the editor. *Change* 6: 4.

Educators rank public relations programs. (1989). *Public Relations Journal* 45: 11–12.

Edwards, R., and Barker, L. (1977). A rating of doctoral programs in speech communication, 1976. *Bulletin of the Association for Communication Administration* 20: 59–69.

Edwards, R., and Barker, L. (1979, October). A rating of doctoral programs in speech communication, 1978: *Bulletin of the Association for Communication Administration*: 23–34.

Edwards, R., and Barker, L. (1983). Evaluative perceptions of doctoral programs in communication, 1982. *Bulletin of the Association for Communication Administration* 45: 76–91.

Edwards, R., Watson, K., and Barker, L.L. (1988). A rating of doctoral programs in selected areas of speech communication: 1987–88. *Bulletin of the Association for Communication Administration* 66: 23–36.

Edwards, R., Watson, K., and Barker, L.L. (1989). A rating of doctoral programs in selected areas of theatre: 1987–88. *Bulletin of the Association for Communication Administration* 67: 62–73.

Eells, W.C. (1926, April 24). A study of the graduate schools of America. *School and Society* 23: 535–536.

Eells, W.C. (1934, June 2). American graduate schools. *School and Society* 39: 708–712.

Elfin, M., et al. (1990, October 15). College guide, 1991. *U.S. News and World Report*: 103–109; 116; 118–134.

Elton, C.F., and Rodgers, S.A. (1971, November 5). Physics department ratings: Another evaluation. *Science* 17: 565–568.

Embree, E.R. (1935, June). In order of their eminence. *Atlantic Monthly* 15: 652–664.

Estes, R.W. (1970, July). A ranking of accounting programs. *Journal of Accountancy* 130: 86–90.

Evaluations of 326 programs in engineering. (1982, December 1). *Chronicle of Higher Education*: 8, 10.

Ewell, R.H. (no date). A quantified summary of the American Council on Education report, An assessment of quality in graduate education. Unpublished manuscript, State University of New York at Buffalo, Buffalo.

Fawcett, N.G. (1971, April 12). Quality of graduate programs. Unpublished memo sent to the presidents of member institutions of the Association of American Universities, Ohio State University, Columbus.

Feinberg, L. (1983a, March 20). Universities in D.C. rank poorly in survey. *Washington Post*: B1, B6.

Feinberg L. (1983b, April 1). Survey ranks Berkeley tops for graduate study. *Washington Post*: A-2.

Feldman, K.A. (1987). Research productivity and scholarly accomplishment of college teachers as related to their instructional effectiveness: A review and exploration. *Research in Higher Education* 26: 227–298.

Fifteen top-ranked graduate business schools in the United States, The. (1974, December). *MBA* 8: 21–25.

Final report in assessment of graduate education rates 639 programs in social, behavioral sciences. (1983, January 19). *Chronicle of Higher Education*: 12–14.

Fishman, K.D. (1983, September 13). Thirty deans choose the best state colleges and universities. *Family Circle*: 67–69.

Fiske, E.B. (1983, January 17). Berkeley tops scholars' rankings of graduate schools' reputations. *New York Times*: A1, B7.

Forouzesh, M., Creswell, Jr., W.H., and Price, J.H. (1982). Peer ratings of health education graduate programs excluding schools of public health. Unpublished paper.

Foster, L. (1936). *The Functions of a Graduate School in a Democratic Society*. New York: Huxley House.

Frackmann, E., and Muffo, J.A. (1988, August). Quality control, hierarchies and information: The context of rankings in an international perspective. Unpublished paper presented to the European Association for Institutional Research, Bergen, Norway.

Fussell, P. (1982, October 4). Schools for snobbery. *New Republic*: 25–31.

Gilley, J.W. (1990a, July/August). The numbers game and college rankings. *AGB Reports* 20: 20–22.

Gilley, J.W. (1990b, November/December). U.S. News moves up a rank—barely. *AGB Reports* 32: 34–35.

Graduate business schools: The top ten. (1976, December). *MBA* 10: 42, 44–45.

Graduate schools of arts, literature, and science. (1928). In D. A. Robertson (ed.). *American Universities and Colleges*. New York: Charles Scribner's Sons.

Gregg, R.T., and Sims, P.D. (1972). Quality of faculties and programs of graduate departments of educational administration. *Educational Administration Quarterly* 8: 67–92.

Halsey, Albert H. (1990). The ranking of university departments in Britain. *Beitrage zur Hochschulforschung* 4: 385–396.

Hardiman, G.W., Shipley, J.R., and Zernich, T. (1975). A ranking of graduate programs in art education: An exploratory survey. *Art Education* 28: 26–27.

Harrington, F. (1957, November 8). Unpublished memo to President Fred of the University of Wisconsin. University of Wisconsin, Madison.

Harris, L., and Jefferson, J.W. (1974, December). How recruiters rank them. *MBA* 8: 24.

Hartnett, R.T., Clark, M.J., and Baird, L.L. (1978, March 24). Reputational ratings of doctoral programs. *Science* 199: 1310–1314.

Havighurst, W. (1958). *The Miami Years, 1809–1959*. New York: G.P. Putnam's Sons.

Higgins, A.S. (1968). The rating of selected fields of doctoral study in the graduate schools of education: An opinion survey. Unpublished Columbia University Teachers College Ed.D. dissertation.

Hughes, R.M. (1925). *A Study of the Graduate Schools of America*. Oxford, Ohio: Miami University Press.

Hughes, R.M. (1934a). A survey of the existing equipment of the graduate schools. Association of American Universities, *Journal of Proceedings and Addresses of the Thirty-Sixth Annual Conference*. Chicago: University of Chicago Press, 116–129.

Hughes, R.M. (1934b). Report of the committee on graduate instruction. *Educational Record* 15: 192–234.

Hughes, R.M. (no date). *A List of Universities and Colleges Arranged in the Order of Their Expenditures for 1934–35*. Ames, Iowa: Collegiate Press.

Hughes, R.M. (1940, March 9). A study of university and college presidents. *School and Society* 51: 317–320.

Hughes, R.M. (1946). *A study of American graduate schools conferring the doctorate, 1937–38 to 1941–42*. Ames: Iowa State College Press.

Hughes, R.M. (1952). How many graduate students come from your state? *School and Society* 75: 278–279.

Hunger, J.D., and Wheelen, T.L. (1980). A performance appraisal of undergraduate business education. *Human Resource Management* 19: 24–31.

Johnson, J.A. (1982, March). A profile of faculty of doctoral programs in the study of higher education in the United States. Unpublished paper presented to the Association for the Study of Higher Education, Washington, DC.

Jones, L.V., Lindzey, G., and Coggeshall, P.E. (eds.). (1982). *An Assessment of Research-doctorate Programs in the United States*, 5 vols. Washington, DC: National Academy Press.

Keniston, H. (1959). *Gcraduate Study and Research in the Arts and Sciences at the University of Pennsylvania*. Philadelphia: University of Pennsylvania Press.

Kerr, C. (1966, June 22). Confidential summary of survey of relative excellence of medical schools in the United States. Unpublished memo, UCLA, Berkeley.

Kerr, C. (1991, May/June). The new race to be Harvard or Berkeley or Stanford. *Change* 23: 8–15.

Kindleberger, R.S. (1983, January 18). Scholars put MIT, Harvard in top 10. *Boston Globe*: 1, 12.

Kittross, J.M. (1966). What do we think of us? A rating of the schools of broadcasting by the teachers of broadcasting. Broadcast Education Association, *Feedback* 7: 1–8.

Kittross, J.M. (1973). What do we think of us . . . now? Broadcast Education Association, *Feedback* 15: 5–14.

Klingemann, H-D. (1986). Ranking the graduate departments in the 1980s: Toward objective qualitative indicators. *PS* 19: 651–661.

Knapp, R.H. (1964). *The Origins of American Humanistic Scholars*. Englewood Cliffs, N.J.: Prentice-Hall.

Knapp, R.H., and Goodrich, H.B. (1952). *Origins of American Scientists*. New York: Russell and Russell.

Knapp, R.H., and Greenbaum, J.H. (1953). *The Younger American Scholar: His Collegiate Origins*. Chicago: University of Chicago Press.

Knudsen, D.D., and Vaughan, T.R. (1969). Quality in graduate education: A re-evaluation of the rankings of sociology departments in the *Cartter Report*. *American Sociologist* 4: 12–19.

Krukowski, J., Associates and Kane, Parsons Associates. (1986, November). High school juniors in the eastern United States rate the nation's academically strongest and most prestigious colleges, 3: unpaginated flier.

Ladd, E.C., Jr. (1969). *Ideology in America: Change and Response in a City, a Suburb, and a Small Town.* Ithaca: Cornell University Press.

Ladd, E.C., Jr., and Lipset, S.M. (1973). *Professors, Unions, and American Higher Education.* Berkeley, CA: Carnegie Commission on Higher Education.

Ladd, E.C., Jr., and Lipset, S.M. (1975). *The Divided Academy.* New York: McGraw-Hill.

Ladd, E.C., Jr., and Lipset, S.M. (1977). The 1977 survey of the American professoriate. Unpublished questionnaire. Social Science Data Center, University of Connecticut, Storrs.

Lang, S. (1978, May 18). The professors: A survey of a survey. *New York Review of Books* 25: 38–42.

Lang S. (1979, December 3). Discredited ratings. *Princeton Alumni Weekly* 80: 4, 10.

Lang, S. (1982). *The File: Case Study in Correction.* New York: Springer-Verlag.

Lawrence, J.K., and Green, K.C. (1980). *A Question of Quality: The Higher Education Ratings Game.* AAHE-ERIC Higher Education Research Report No. 5. Washington, DC: American Association for Higher Education.

Levin, J.R., et al. (1978). University productivity ratings: A psychologist by any other name. *American Psychologist* 33: 694–695.

Lewis, L. (1984). Graduate education: Evaluating the evaluators—a review essay. *Sociological Quarterly* 25: 125–134.

Lipset, S.M. (1960). *Political Man: The Social Bases of Politics.* Garden City, NY: Doubleday.

Lipset, S.M. (1972). *Rebellion in the University.* Boston: Little, Brown.

Lipset, S.M., Trow, M.A., and Coleman, J.C. (1956). *Union Democracy.* Glencoe, IL: Free Press.

Mackay-Smith, A. (1985, October 11). Survey says top business schools may not be top business schools. *Wall Street Journal*: 31.

Magoun, H.W. (1966). The *Cartter Report* on quality in graduate education. *Journal of Higher Education* 37: 481–492.

Maidment, F. (1986). University-based executive education programs: A peer evaluation. *Personnel Administrator* 31: 117–118.

Malkiel, Y. (1971). Necrology: Hayward Keniston (1883–1970). *Romance Philology* 24: 677–680.

Manly, C. (1954). *The Twenty–Year Revolution: From Roosevelt to Eisenhower.* Chicago: Henry Regnery Company.

Manly, C. (no date). *Chicago Sunday Tribune* rates the nation's universities and colleges. Madison: University of Wisconsin News Service Reprint.

Margulies, R.Z., and Blau, P.M. (1973, November). America's leading professional schools. *Change* 5: 21–27.

Martin, B.R., and Irvine, J. (1983). Assessing basic research: Some partial indicators of scientific progress in radio astronomy. *Research Policy* 12: 61–90.

Massengale, J.D., and Sage, G.H. (1982). Departmental prestige and career mobility patterns of college physical educators. *Research Quarterly for Exercise and Sport* 53: 305–312.

Merton, R.K. (1968, January 5). The Matthew effect in science. *Science* 159: 56–63.

Money Guide: America's Best College Buys (1990, Fall)

Morgan, D.R., Kearney, R.C., and Regens, J.L. (1976). Assessing quality among graduate institutions of higher education in the United States. *Social Science Quarterly* 57: 670–679.

Morgan, D.R., and Meier, K.J. (1982). Reputation and productivity of public adminis-tration/affairs programs: Additional data. *Public Administration Review* 42: 171–173.

Morgan, D.R., Meier, K.J., Kearney, R.C., Hays, S.W., and Birch, H.B. (1981). Reputation and productivity among U.S. public adminstration and public affairs pro-grams. *Public Administration Review* 41: 666–673.

Morse, R.J. with Wagner, E.A., et al. (1991, April 29). The best graduate schools. *U.S. News and World Report*: 62–63; 65–66; 68–72; 74–75; 77–80; 82–84; 85; 88–91.

Munson, C.E., and Nelson, P. (1977). Measuring the quality of professional schools. *UCLA Educator* 19: 41–52.

Nehrt, L.C. (1987). The ranking of masters programs in international business. *Journal of International Business Studies* 18: 91–99.

Nehrt, L.C. (1989). The ranking of masters programs in international business—reply. *Journal of International Business Studies* 20: 163–168.

Newell, L.J. and Kuh, G.D. (1989). Taking stock: The higher education professoriate. *Review of Higher Education* 13: 63–90.

O'Leary, J., and Scott, P. (1987, July 24). Seventh wonders of academe. *Times Higher Education Supplement*: 6–7.

100 meilleures universités en Europe, Les. (1989, December). *Guide Libération* 1.

Owen, W.F., and Cross, L.R. (eds.). (1984). *Guide to Graduate Study in Economics, Agricultural Economics, and Doctoral Degrees in Business and Administration in the United States of America and Canada* (7th ed.). Boulder, CO: Economics Institute.

Oxbridge still dominates the quality league. (1983, August 5). *Times Higher Education Supplement*: 8–9.

Peirce, F.J. (1975, May). Letter to the editor. *Change* 7: 4.

Petrowski, W.R., Brown, E.L., and Duffy, J.A. (1974). "National universities" and the ACE ratings. *Journal of Higher Education* 44: 495–513.

Popular vote: Medical school survey, The. (1976, December). *Medical Dimensions* 5: 32, 34, 36.

Popular vote: Rankings of the top schools, The. (1976, December). *Juris Doctor* 6: 17–18; 21.

Ranking the engineering schools. (1976, December). *New Engineer* 5: 21, 25–27, 31.

Ranz, J. (1966). Review of *An assessment of quality in graduate education*. *Library Journal* 91: 3712.

Rau, W., and Leonard, II, W.M. (1990). Evaluating Ph.D. sociology programs: Theo-retical, methodological and policy implications. *American Sociologist* 21: 232–256.

Report on graduate study ignored blacks. (1971, January 30). *Philadelphia Tribune*, p. 3.

Review of an assessment of quality in graduate education. (1966, May 27). In National Association of State Universities and Land-Grant Colleges Circular Letter #15, pp. 16–17.

Riesman, David. (1980). *On Higher Education*. San Francisco: Jossey-Bass.

Roberts, L. (1983). Ranking doctorate programs in biological sciences. *BioScience* 33: 163–164.

Robertson, D.A. (ed.). (1928). *American Universities and Colleges*. New York: Charles Scribner's Sons.

Roose, K.D., and Andersen, C.J. (1970). *A Rating of Graduate Programs*. Washington, DC: American Council on Education.

Rosovsky, H. (1990). *The University: An Owner's Manual*. New York: W.W. Norton and Company.

Ross, S. S. (1977, December). Ranking the business schools. *MBA* 11: 19–22.

Roueche, J.E., and Baker, III, G.A. (1987). *Access and Excellence: The Open-Door College*. Washington, DC: Community College Press.

Rudder, C.E. (1983). The quality of graduate education in political science: A report on the new rankings. *PS* 16: 48–53.

Scheinberg, P.F. (1977, November 3). A critical evaluation of the ranking of American professional schools in studies by Peter Blau and Rebecca Margulies and Allan Cartter. Unpublished course paper for Administration 280H, Research and Evaluation in Higher Education Administration, University of California at Los Angeles Graduate School of Education.

Schmotter, J.W. (1989, August 16). Colleges have themselves to blame for the influence of journalistic rankings of their quality. *Chronicle of Higher Education*: A40.

Scott, P. (1982, December 3). A snapshot of current prejudices about ''quality.'' *Times Higher Education Supplement*: 8–9.

Scully, M.G. (1979, January 15). The well-known universities lead in faculties' reputations. *Chronicle of Higher Education*: 6–7.

Scully, M.G. (1982a, September 29). First major study since 1969 rates quality of graduate programs. *Chronicle of Higher Education*: 8–10.

Scully, M.G. (1982b, November 10). Quality of graduate programs rated in nine humanities disciplines. *Chronicle of Higher Education*: 4–6.

Searching for an elusive quality. (1984, January 20). *Times Higher Education Supplement*: 10–11.

Sheler, J.L., Toch, T., Morse, R.J., Heupler, K., and Linnon, N. (1989, October 16). America's best colleges. *U.S. News and World Report* 54–58; 65–84.

Sieber, S.D., with the collaboration of Lazarsfeld, P.F. (1966). *The Organization of Educational Research in the United States*. New York: Columbia University Bureau of Applied Social Research.

Sindelar, P.T., and Schloss, P.J. (1986). The reputations of doctoral training programs in special education. *Journal of Special Education* 20: 49–59.

616 doctoral programs in biological sciences rated in new assessment of quality of graduate education. (1983, January 12). *Chronicle of Higher Education*: 14–16.

Sixth of the best—as judged by your peers. (1987, January 23). *Times Higher Education Supplement*: 10–11.

Skinner, F. (1970, December 28). Press release for *A Rating of Graduate Programs*. Washington, DC: American Council on Education.

Solmon, L.C., and Astin, A.W. (1981, September). Departments without distinguished graduate programs. *Change* 13: 23–28.

Solorzano, L., et al. (1987a, October 26). America's best colleges. *U.S. News and World Report*, 49–56; 59–63; 66–70; 90.

Solorzano, L., et al. (1987b, November 2). America's best professional schools. *U.S. News and World Report*: 70–73; 75–76; 78–79; 81–83; 85.

Solorzano, L. with Quick, B.E. (1983, November 28). Rating the colleges. *U.S. News and World Report*: 41–46; 48.

Somit, A., and Tanenhaus, J. (1963). Trends in American political science: Some analytical notes. *American Political Science Review* 57: 933–947.

Somit, A., and Tanenhaus, J. (1964). *American Political Science: A Profile of a Discipline*. New York: Atherton Press.

Somit, A., and Tanenhaus, J. (1982). *The Development of American Political Science*. Boston: Allyn and Bacon.

Stigler, G.J. (1963). Meager means and noble ends. In *The Intellectual and the Market Place and Other Essays*. Glencoe, IL: Free Press, pp. 33–42.

Still no. 1. (1971, January 11). *Newsweek*, p. 58.

Summary of findings: Survey of journalism schools. (no date). Unpublished report. New York: Carl Byoir and Associates.

Tan, D.L. (1986). The assessment of quality in higher education: A critical review of the literature and research. *Research in Higher Education* 24: 223–265.

There's no accounting. (1985, December 16). *Philadelphia Inquirer*, p. 1-C.

Thomson, K.W. (1961). An assessment of graduate schools of geography in the United States of America. *Australian Geographer* 8: 138–139.

Top fifteen, The. (1975, December). *MBA* 9: 33–35.

Top ranking universities and polys. (1985, December 13). *Times Higher Education Supplement*: 10–11.

Trow, M.A. (1983, November/December). Reorganizing the biological sciences at Berkeley. *Change* 15: 28, 44–53.

Tyler, F.B. (1972). Knowledgeable respondents: Private club or public service? *American Psychologist*: 27 191–196.

UNLV—one of the "rising stars of American higher education." (1991, July 10). *Chronicle of Higher Education*: B13.

U.S. professors rank Arthur Andersen the top firm for new graduates. (1991, June 15). *Public Accounting Report* 15: 1–4.

Visher, S.S. (1947). *Scientists Starred, 1903–1943, in "American Men of Science."* Baltimore: Johns Hopkins University Press.

Walberg, H.J. (1972). University distinction in educational research: An exploratory survey. *Educational Researcher* 1: 15.

Walsh, J. (1966, May 27). Graduate education: ACE study rates departments qualitatively. [Review of *An Assessment of Quality in Graduate Education*] *Science* 152: 1226–1228.

Walters, E. (1966, June 18). Identifying the excellent. [Review of *An Assessment of Quality in Graduate Education*] *Saturday Review* 49: 75–76.

Watson, K.W., Edwards, R., and Barker, L.L. (1989). A rating of doctoral programs in selected areas of mass communication: 1987–1988. *Bulletin of the Association of Communication Administration* 67: 20–36.

Webster, D.S. (1981). Advantages and disadvantages of methods of assessing quality. *Change* 13: 20–24.

Webster, D.S. (1982). Academic quality rankings: Why they developed in the United States and not Europe. *History of Higher Education Annual* 2: 102–127.

Webster, D.S. (1983). America's highest ranked graduate schools, 1925–1982. *Change* 15: 14–24.

Webster, D.S. (1984a). Innovation in Ph.D. programs and scores in reputational rankings. In M.J. Pelczar and L.C. Solmon (eds.), *Keeping Graduate Programs Responsive to National Needs*. New Directions for Higher Education 46. San Francisco: Jossey-Bass.

Webster, D.S. (1984b, November/December). Who is Jack Gourman and why is he saying all those things about my college? *Change* 16: 14–19; 45–56.

Webster, D.S. (1985a). Does research productivity enhance teaching? *Educational Record* 66: 60–62.

Webster, D.S. (1985b). Institutional effectiveness using scholarly peer assessments as major criteria. *Review of Higher Education* 9: 67–82.

Webster, D.S. (1991, April). Lessons from the presentation and use of data from the 1982 National Research Council assessment of doctoral programs. Unpublished paper presented to the Workshop on the Assessment of Research-Doctorate Programs in the United States, Irvine, California.

Welch, C. (1971). *Graduate Education in Religion: A Critical Appraisal*. Missoula: University of Montana Press.

Welch, S., and Hibbing, J.R. (1983). What do the new ratings of political science departments measure? *PS* 16: 532–540.

West, C.K. (no date). Ranking departments within colleges of education: A final report to the University of Illinois/Urbana Champaign Research Board. Unpublished manuscript.

White: H.S. (1987). Perceptions by educators and administrators of the ranking of library school programs: An update and analysis. *Library Quarterly* 57: 252–268.

Who's best at what? (1966, May 27). *Time*, p. 55.

Wilson, L. (no date). Report of ad hoc committee to review the American Council on Education rating of graduate programs. Unpublished manuscript.

Using Alternative Paradigms: Four Case Studies

John H. Milam, Jr.

George Mason University

PART I

INTRODUCTION

Most of the scholarship on paradigms in higher education is devoted to defining a specific language of assumptions, including the constructivist, critical theory, ethnocentric, ethnographic, Eurocentric, feminist, functionalist, interpretive, liberationist, Neo-Marxist, phenomenological, post-modernist, post-positivist, post-structuralist, radical humanist, and radical sociology paradigms. Although some scholars such as Attinasi (1990), Barrow (1991), Glazer (1990), Lincoln (1989), Tierney (1991), and Townsend (1991) acknowledge specific paradigm assumptions as being central to their work, little research has been done which explores the fundamental tensions between paradigms and how these relate to the conduct of research in higher education. Part of the problem may be that few scholars adopt the same language of assumptions which would allow them to make sense of and explore different paradigm points of view at the same time. There are numerous examples of scholars engaged in dialogue about the differences between paradigms. However, most battle maps for the "paradigm wars" are one-sided.

The purpose of this chapter is to contribute to this paradigm dialogue, not by offering yet another set of definitions, but by presenting case studies which use the critical lenses of different research perspectives. This design for case studies is based, in part, on an idea which Morgan (1983) had for a conference on organizational inquiry. He hoped that participants would critically examine methodologies of organizational research using the Burrell and Morgan (1979) paradigm schema. The complexities of researchers' perspectives did not fit easily

The author wishes to thank David L. Clark, his dissertation advisor, and Clifton L. Conrad, a more recent advisor, for their assistance and encouragement in the preparation of this chapter.

into the paradigm definitions, however, and the participants abandoned Morgan's plan. Morgan asked:

> Was it possible to learn something from the assumptions underlying the different research perspectives? Although each perspective offered a logically coherent and internally consistent argument for conducting research in a particular way, this argument was ultimately derived from the ground assumptions on which it was based. Was it possible to raise and debate these assumptions? (Morgan, 1983, pp. 15–16).

The Burrell and Morgan (1979) paradigm schema has been shown to be useful in understanding the meta-theoretical assumptions of the core, higher education journal literature (Milam, 1991). With case studies of actual research within each paradigm, it may be possible to understand how scholars with an alternative paradigm might generate different research questions, assumptions, methods, and possibly findings. Perhaps interesting relationships, tensions, linkages, and dissonance between paradigms may be better understood by putting these questions in the context of actual research.

This chapter is divided into three sections. First, the theoretical framework of Burrell and Morgan (1979) for analyzing paradigms is presented. The literature about scholars' attitudes toward research perspectives is also discussed (Lincoln, 1989; Morgan, 1983; Schwandt, 1989; and Schwartz and Ogilvy, 1979). Next, four sets of case studies are presented which examine and critique examples of research from different paradigm perspectives. Finally, the results of the case studies are discussed. The dialogue about research which occurs in the case studies is analyzed according to the literature on attitudes about paradigms. The cognitive development theories of Perry (1970, 1981) and Belenkey, Clinchy, Goldberger, and Tarule (1986) are suggested as metaphors to portray possible positions, stages, or levels of paradigm development.

THEORETICAL BACKGROUND

Burrell and Morgan

In their work *Sociological Paradigms and Organisational Analysis*, Burrell and Morgan (1979) analyze organizational theory according to a two-dimensional paradigm schema. See Clark (1985), Conrad (1989), Griffiths (1983), and Milam (1989, 1991) for discussion of this schema for educational administration and higher education. Central to the Burrell and Morgan conception of paradigms is their belief that all social theories are based upon both a philosophy of science and a theory of the social world. These may be thought of in terms of different sets of implicit and explicit assumptions.

In the dimension of social science, the authors identify four types of assumptions:

(1) ontological assumptions about the nature and essence of what is being studied: *realism* versus *nominalism*;

(2) epistemological assumptions about the grounds for understanding knowledge: *positivism* versus *anti-positivism*;

(3) assumptions concerning human nature, about the relationship between human beings and their environment: *determinism* versus *voluntarism*;

(4) methodological assumptions about the ways to study and gather information about the social world: *nomothetic* versus *idiographic* methods.

These sets of opposite assumptions make up two sides of the social science dimension, which Burrell and Morgan label as the objective and the subjective. Methodological approaches which represent the objective approach include such techniques as causal modeling, survey questionnaires, and integrative literature reviews. Possible examples of subjective social science could include naturalistic inquiry, ethnography, and grounded theory building.

In the authors' work, sociological theory is considered under one of two mutually exclusive categories—the *sociology of regulation* versus the *sociology of radical change*. Regulation sociology is interested in understanding why society works the way it does and with integrating its mechanism and processes. Radical change sociology is based on the premise that conflict and contradiction are inherent in society and must form the basis for any social analysis. The seven sets of assumptions are identified as follows:

(1) Regulation sociology concerns the *status quo*, the way things currently are, and ways to maintain the patterns of the social system as a whole. Radical sociology is concerned with all elements of *radical change*, both at the structural level and at the level of subjective consciousness.

(2) Understanding and maintaining the functions and processes of the *social order* is the concern of regulation sociology, where radical sociology identifies *conflicts* such as class, gender, and race which are imbedded in the fabric of society.

(3) Regulation sociologists believe that values are developed autonomously. *Consensus* in terms of shared values is regarded as a positive indication of integration. Radical sociologists believe that shared values are the result of modes of *domination*.

(4) In regulation sociology, the *social integration and cohesion* of society are of primary concern. The radical sociology position recognizes that heterogeneity, imbalance, antagonistic and divergent forces are at work, and that these contribute to social, geopolitical, economic, and other kinds of structural *contradictions*.

(5) Maintaining the *solidarity* of how the patterns of society hold together is important to regulation sociology. *Emancipation* from the structures which limit potential is the concern of radical sociology.

(6) Where regulation sociology is interested in the *need satisfaction* of society

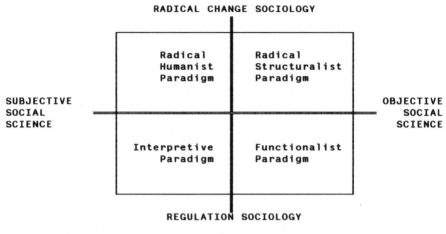

FIGURE 1.

as an organism, radical sociology focuses on psychic and material forms of *deprivation* and how the system erodes human fulfillment.

(7) Regulation sociology is rooted in understanding society as it already is, implicitly legitimizing the *actuality* of the status quo. Radical sociology offers visionary *potentiality* with alternatives to conflicts and contradictions.

Burrell and Morgan visualize their paradigm schema (Figure 1) as a grid with two dimensions and four cells. The four paradigms are defined by their position within the two dimensions of social science and sociology. The *functionalist* paradigm is based in objective social science and regulation sociology. The *radical structuralist* paradigm is also based in objective social science, but is rooted in radical change sociology. The *interpretive* and *radical humanist* paradigms both operate with subjective social science assumptions. While the interpretive paradigm is concerned with regulation sociology, the radical humanist holds a radical change sociological perspective.

SCHOLARS' ATTITUDES TOWARD PARADIGMS

The extensive scholarship by Lincoln (1985, 1986, 1989) and Lincoln and Guba (1985, 1989) on naturalistic inquiry, constructivism, and paradigms is a frequent starting point in scholars' discussions of the methodological choices and alternative paradigms which guide their work. Analyzing paradigm evolution in the various disciplines, Lincoln (1989) identifies four different types of attitudes toward multiple paradigm discussions. These include: denying that the debate is important; recognizing the debate, but affirming the primacy of the scientific method; denying that there is a debate, and continuing as always; and intense curiosity and interest in learning about the debate.

According to Lincoln, scholars who critique paradigms fall into four categories: those who feel that traditional methods are impoverished and need more richness; those who focus on the exclusion of gender in research, as this pertains to values and the portrayal of women; those who make an exception for one or two new axioms of inquiry within their existing paradigm; and those who are able to see a whole paradigm, discarding former methods of inquiry for a new world view.

In discussing approaches to understanding multiple paradigms, Morgan (1983) identifies attitudes among scholars which he labels as supremacy, synthesis, dialectic, contingency, and anything goes. In supremacy, there is a search for the merits of one method or perspective over another. Scholars challenge assumptions to refine a research strategy. This approach "encounters the same kind of relativism as that with which it is trying to deal" (p. 378). In synthesis, scholars work to find an optimum way to do research within an all-embracing paradigm, combining the strengths of some approaches and minimizing the weaknesses of others. The dialectical attitude recognizes that a diversity of approaches is inevitable. Scholars need to work with multisided approaches, counterpoising insights in order for new debates to emerge, and seeking a kind of theoretical pluralism. Another attitude, labeled contingency, involves the recognition that there is no one best set of assumptions. Research tools are used in a practical way according to their usefulness. Competing insights are used in complex analysis, and there is no search for foundational truth. A final attitude, labeled "Anything Goes" is one of complete relativism, believing that synthesis is unnecessary. Theoretical and methodological anarchy is welcomed. Only the researcher is in the position to choose an approach.

Schwandt (1989) modifies the work of Morgan (1983) in an article entitled "Solutions to the Paradigm Conflict: Coping with Uncertainty." He suggests slightly different attitudes about multiple paradigms: Denial, refusing to admit the problem; Co-optation, acknowledging paradigm differences but claiming that they are resolvable; Supremacy, claiming that one paradigm is ultimately better than another; Replacement, creating a new paradigm that blends the tensions between others; Primacy of method, extracting methods away from philosophy and science into a vision of problem solving, with the choice of methods as the primary concern; and Anarchism, admitting no authority to any paradigm and resisting the search for an ideal.

COGNITIVE DEVELOPMENT THEORY

Cognitive development theory also provides a lens for viewing the attitudes of scholars toward multiple paradigm discussions. The work of Perry (1970, 1981) on stages and levels of cognitive and ethical student development offers a language for discussing dualism and relativism. Belenky, Clinchy, Goldberger, and Tarule (1986) act on the criticisms of Gilligan (1982) and suggest that the metaphor of "finding a voice" is useful in mapping women's development. Working with Moore, Thompson (1991) combines Perry with Belenkey et al. in a revision of the Perry scheme used for student assessment at Evergreen State College. According to Thompson (1991, pp. 2–3), this does not fundamentally revise the cognitive epistemology used by Perry, but serves "to incorporate contemporary learning styles and styles of expression (along the lines of Belenkey et al.)."

Perry's stages are labeled as dualism modified, relativism discovered, and commitment in relativism. The key terms are dualism, multiplicity, relativism, and commitment. Explained simply, dualism divides meanings as right or wrong. Multiplicity recognizes that diverse opinions are legitimate when right answers are unknown. Relativism sees the full diversity of opinions, values, and judgments, viewing knowledge as "qualitative, dependent on context" (Perry, 1981, p. 80). Commitment involves decisions or choices made with awareness of relativism. These stages are broken out into nine positions, with the positions considered as less important to development than the transitions. The nine positions are labeled as: (1) basic duality; (2) multiplicity prelegitimate; (3) multiplicity legitimate but subordinate; (4) multiplicity correlate or relativism subordinate; (5) relativism correlate, competing or diffuse; (6) commitment foreseen; (7) initial commitment; (8) orientation in implications of commitment; and (9) developing commitments.

Belenky, Clinchy, Goldberger, and Tarule (1986) find metaphors for voice within women's development. These include: silence, received knowledge, subjective knowledge, procedural knowledge, and constructed knowledge. The reader should refer to the case study for definitions of these five metaphors of voice. Thompson (1991) presents modifications of positions two through five of the Perry scheme in his monograph *Learning at Evergreen*. Position two is relabeled as dualism or received knowledge. Knowledge is "information from Authorities" and is basically dualistic. Position three is relabeled as early multiplicity, or separate, procedural knowing. It is recognized that some answers are unknown. There is no sense of relationships between methods. Position four is relabeled as late multiplicity, or subjective and connected knowing. Concerned with "how to think," students recognize diversity of opinions. Authorities "are observed to differ because of their methods and assumptions, and particularly their gender, class, and culture, afford competing points of view" (Thompson, 1991, p. 3). Two sub-positions are suggested—an oppositional stance and an adherent stance. Position five is relabeled contextual relativism or constructivism, and involves metathinking, or "thinking about thinking." The belief in absolute knowledge is suspended, though it is possible to construct "tentative theories and models, some of which are demonstrably more appropriate than others to the context at hand'' (p. 4).

CASE STUDIES

Four case studies were developed as part of this author's dissertation research (Milam, 1989) and were revised for the purposes of this chapter. Each case study represents an example of research from one of the four Burrell and Morgan paradigms and consists of four parts.

These examples were located as part of a larger content analysis of the core, higher education journal literature (Milam, 1991). To determine the paradigmatic content of a piece of higher education research, 64 content analysis questions were used to look for implicit meta-theoretical assumptions. The language for each question comes directly from key phrases in the Burrell and Morgan definitions. Decision rules and dichotomous, a priori coding categories are used to catalog examples within the four paradigms, two dimensions, and eleven sets of assumptions. The content analysis techniques are chosen to ensure validity and replicability through extensive documentation and coding notes, peer debriefing, use of a methodological log, and memo-writing. The trustworthiness of the human author as a coding instrument is assessed and refined through pilot testing of the questions, memo-writing techniques, and decision rules.

Examples for case studies of the functionalist and radical structuralist paradigms were located in the content analysis of the journal literature. Other sources were required to locate a useful piece of research from the radical humanist and interpretive paradigm perspectives. All four research examples are coded as having a majority of the assumptions in their paradigm definitions for the social science and sociology dimensions.

Pascarella, Ethington, and Smart's (1988) article entitled "The Influence of College on Humanitarian/Civic Involvement Values" was chosen to represent the functionalist paradigm. For the radical structuralist paradigm, Loo and Rolison's (1986) article entitled "Alienation of Ethnic Minority Students at a Predominantly White University" was selected. Logan's (1988) article entitled "A Study of Four Undergraduate Computer-Writers" is an example of the interpretive paradigm. The monograph *Women's Ways of Knowing: The Development of Self, Voice, and Mind* by Belenky, Clinchy, Goldberger, and Tarule (1986) serves as an example of the radical humanist paradigm.

The first part of each case study consists of a synopsis of the research problem, methodology, and findings, using the language of assumptions of its particular paradigm. The research is then critiqued according to the critical lenses and language of the three alternative paradigms. The product of each case study consists of four different treatments of the same topic.

PART II

FUNCTIONALIST CASE STUDY: COLLEGE'S INFLUENCE ON VALUES

Pascarella, Ethington, and Smart's (1988) article entitled "The Influence of College on Humanitarian/Civic Involvement Values" represents an example of research in the functionalist paradigm. The authors present a longitudinal, causal model based on the work of Tinto, Astin and Kent, Lacy, and Chickering. This model posits that the type of institution attended by a student is a function of precollege characteristics, and that precollege characteristics and institution attended together influence many aspects of the college experience. Different college outcome characteristics are viewed as a function of these variables.

In order to observe the impact of institutional characteristics, the authors restricted the sample of students to those who had attended only one institution. The 4,843 students were enrolled in 379 four-year colleges and universities. Longitudinal data were collected from responses to the 1971 Cooperative Institutional Research Program (CIRP) Freshman Survey and to the 1980 CIRP Postcollege Survey. HEGIS files were used to gather matching institutional data.

The student precollege variables include: (1) scores on the 1971 humanitarian/civic involvement values measure, a factorially derived scale; (2) family socioeconomic status (SES); (3) age; (4) secondary school achievement; and (5) secondary school social accomplishment. The institutional characteristics include: (6) selectivity; (7) size; and (8) whether the college or university is predominantly black. The college experience variables include: (9) whether the student is a social science major; (10) college grade point average; (11) social leadership experiences; and (12) familiarity with faculty/staff. Student postcollege variables include: (13) highest degree attained; and (14) whether the student is employed in a social service occupation.

The dependent measure consists of scores on the 1980 humanitarian/civic involvement values measure, which uses the same 1971 scale. One post-college variable, employment in a social service occupation, is added to the 1980 survey. In the causal model, the measure of social leadership experiences is defined as the sum of four items assessing involvement. These include self-reports of being president of a student organization, serving on a university or department committee, editing a publication, or having a major part in a play. The 1971 and 1980 values involvement scales are based on the personal importance of six activities associated with civic and humanitarian involvement. These include activities such as cleaning up the environment, helping others who are in difficulty, participating in a community action program, becoming a community leader, influencing social values, and influencing the political structure.

The GEMINI statistical computer program is used by the authors to calculate indirect effects and estimate their significance. Structural equations are used to regress endogenous variables on exogenous variables and other antecedent endogenous variables in the causal model. These equations produce standardized and metric regression weights which are interpreted as direct effects. Preliminary analyses are performed to test whether or not direct effects vary by race and/or sex.

The results of the equations show that the causal model explains between 12.6 and 18.8 percent of the variance in scores on the 1980 humanitarian/civic involvement scale, depending on the subgroup population. Of the precollege variables, scores on the 1971 values measure are the only predictor which has a significant direct effect on all four sub-groups' 1980 scores. Most of the influence of these variables is indirect. None of the institutional characteristics has a significant direct effect on scores. Of the college experience variables, only social leadership experience shows a significant direct effect for all groups but black women. Some "pronounced racial differences" are found in the direct effects of the educational attainment and occupational outcome variables. For example, the effect on values development of being in a social service occupation is greater for whites than blacks. For whites, post-college employment has an impact on values development "above and beyond the influence of student precollege characteristics and the college experience;" whereas, for blacks, occupation has "little incremental impact on black student values" (p. 432). Highest academic degree awarded also has a significant indirect effect only for white males and females.

Based on the results, the authors conclude that "neither institutional selectivity nor predominant race had other than a trivial influence on the development of humanitarian/civic values" (p. 429). This means that:

> Irrespective of individual student race or gender, the humanizing of individual values is no more likely to occur at a selective college than at a nonselective college; nor does it appear to be much influenced by the institution's racial composition (p. 429).

Secondly, the findings suggest that:

> . . . the undergraduate college experience had a significant unique impact on the humanizing of values that is independent of the individual characteristics the student brings to college, the selectivity, size and predominant race of the institution attended, and subsequent educational attainment and postcollegiate occupation (p. 429).

Finally, Pascarella et al. conclude that: (1) social involvement has a positive impact on the development of humanitarian and civic values; (2) the type of involvement which most contributes to values development differs by race and sex; and (3) the indirect effects of outcome variables should be considered, since there are few direct effects.

Criticism of the Pascarella Study Employing the Interpretive Paradigm

From an interpretive standpoint, Pascarella et al.'s attempt to define variables and data elements of civic and humanitarian involvement values is futile and the use of sophisticated data analytic techniques inappropriate. To begin, the four sets of "variables" used in the causal model are simply labels for making sense of the world. Such data variables as "secondary school achievement" and "civic involvement values" are not "real." They are the result of the researchers' perceptions of the social world. In other words, Pascarella et al. fail to recognize that student experiences in college are the product of individual cognition and that reality is a social construction. Psychological processes of student and adult development are much more complicated than this research study allows for, or than most models and theories of student, adult, or human development allow for.

To an interpretive researcher, theory should be used differently than is done in this study. The interpretive researcher sees the need for grounded theory and theory as it relates to particularized situations, but the generalizability of theory is viewed as problematic. Functionalist researchers like Pascarella et al. believe that knowledge is expanded by the accumulation of new theories. This is why the research of Astin and Kent, Chickering, and Tinto is cited as a foundation of the study. However, the development of knowledge is not always a cumulative process.

Another criticism concerns the way in which civic and humanitarian values are separated out from other types of attitudes and values. How do the definitions used for humanitarian and civic values differ from other values? Why were these definitions chosen? The study places singular importance on one measure: graduates having been employed in a social service occupation. Is this to say that people employed in other occupations do not hold similar values? The scale used to measure values involvement consists of student responses to how important they rate "activities" associated with civic and humanitarian involvement. Hundreds of other college activities which are important to student development could have been included. The inherent value judgments of the CIRP survey must be questioned.

In their deterministic search for cause and effect relationships, the researchers are interested in environmental and situational behavioralism. The authors find a correlation between participation in an elite handful of social activities and scores on the values scale. An interpretive researcher would ask: Why are these "social leadership activities" particularly meaningful in terms of long-range values development. These activities seem to have been taken from an outdated image of college life. Also, there is no sense of the cultural diversity of human lives in a large university setting.

Where the results are interpreted in terms of direct and indirect effects, the researchers should have been looking from an interpretivist perspective into possible patterns and regularities. There is no need to "prove" anything about development, to establish one correct causal model. Pascarella et al. should have turned to qualitative techniques found in ethnography and naturalistic inquiry to examine research questions related to values and attitudes. Individual human nature and values development can only be understood from the point of view of students.

The findings of the study are suspect. For example, the interpretation is made that, for black alumni, post-college occupation has "little incremental impact on black student values" (p. 429). It is shown that the type of job obtained by blacks makes little difference to the values they hold about civic life and humanitarian concerns. This generalization is not credible. Of course employment has an effect on values, as does income level. What is important is not statistically measuring the degree of indirect effect for subgroups, but investigating and understanding the nature of racial differences in occupational outcome and educational attainment. The pre-existing constructs of the survey items may have prevented the researchers from exploring the pertinent, subjective data about students.

Another questionable finding is that there is no difference between traditionally black institutions and predominantly white institutions in how individual values are humanized. Certainly it is likely that the culture and experiences of the two institutional types differ greatly, just as the lives of black and white students differ. If the authors want to draw conclusions about black and white students in these institutions, then they should study real people, not just match HEGIS data to 15-year-old CIRP data. It seems as if the CIRP database guided the inquiry more than did any a priori research question and design.

In addition, from an interpretivist perspective, institutions are more relativistic than the authors are willing to admit. This apparent lack of appreciation for institutional complexity is evident in the interpretation that institutional selectivity has no influence on values. Selectivity does make a difference in how students develop values because this factor is related to many other things—institutional resources, diversity of the student body, quality of the faculty, and the role of teaching in the mission of the institution, to name a few. All of these aspects of the complex college world need to be taken into account. To isolate one aspect of college in a causal model is like looking at a painting without being able to see the picture as a whole, because the viewer is engrossed in trying to identify and label the brushes and pigments the artist used.

Criticism of the Pascarella Study Employing the
Radical Structuralist Paradigm

In the Pascarella study, values development is portrayed as an autonomous, voluntary, and spontaneous process; it is not. Radical structuralists assume that values are ordinarily imposed on some members of society by others. From this perspective, the question needs to be asked: Whose values are these that the authors are promoting? A radical structuralist analysis may show that the ideal humanitarian and civic involvement values promoted by Pascarella et al. are those of white, Anglo-Saxon, Protestant, middle class males between the ages of 18 and 22 attending quality, four-year institutions. It is important to note that, although the sample may have been random and diverse in sub-population representation, the causal model of values development is not that complex.

The article assumes that all students should hold the values of wanting to become involved in certain civic and humanitarian involvement activities. If students come to share these values, then the college environment is assumed to have been successful in its mission of student development. For the radical structuralist, these shared values are a sign of the success of the forces of domination. Individual values are subordinated for dominant values.

From a radical structuralist perspective, Pascarella et al. do not adequately recognize that many subtle forms of coercion are involved in the manipulation and control of students in order for them to develop the "correct" values. A number of economic, political, religious, and social forces work to socialize and indoctrinate students. What Pascarella and Astin label as "social leadership experiences," radical structuralists might term "conditioning." Student involvement in these traditional leadership activities reinforces norms and dominant codes of behavior by which students are taught to lead their lives.

The theoretical frameworks used for analyzing student involvement and student development are inadequate because these theories are fixed, stagnant, and overly rigid in their view of the human condition. This kind of research does not generate any new alternatives, nor is it truly concerned with student potential. Growth and development are considered by functionalists as everyday processes. Change is thought to be an ordinary, empirical reality. That Pascarella failed to introduce any form of radical change as a process in students' lives is understandable—due to the total lack of attention paid to the conflicts and contradictions embedded in college society. In fact, values of blacks, whites, men, and women are discussed without any reference to the contradictions among and between these different groups. The authors introduce variables of sex and race in the way all functionalists do. They do not understand or take into account the manner in which their limited view of gender and race issues affects the results. The college experiences of men and women will vary significantly because women are oppressed by a patriarchal society and because minorities are discriminated against. It is also necessary to account for the impact on students' lives of oppression from other sources, such as political systems, economic status, sexual orientation, family structures, and religious beliefs.

The authors find "pronounced racial differences" in educational attainment and occupational outcome. Of course whites go on to graduate and professional school at a greater rate. They do not face the same patterns of discrimination. Minorities do not have the same opportunities to hold elite, social service jobs. Instead, they are forced by the system to take lower-status, service employment. The study implies that all things are equal for those with a four-year college degree. What about "pronounced economic class differences" between low-income and high-income students and the effect of these on educational attainment and occupational outcomes?

Another example of differences in the viewpoints held by the radical structuralist and the functionalist is found in the way in which the authors interpret their finding that "predominant race" had only a trivial influence on values development. Is this to mean that there is no difference between predominantly white and traditionally black institutions when it comes to student development of values? Certainly, the environment faced by blacks in white universities is much less conducive to positive growth and development of self-esteem than that of black institutions, which support and nurture a community based in black culture. This finding is probably not accurate. Race does have a significant effect on values development.

The finding that none of the institutional characteristics has an effect on values development is only accurate from the point of view of the authors' narrow, functionalist definition of values. If the researchers had paid attention to institutional characteristics as these affect values through forces of domination, deprivation, and oppression, then significant direct and indirect effects would probably have been found. Once it is clear whose values are being reinforced, then findings may point out that predominantly white institutions cause greater problems for black students in terms of alienation of values than do traditionally black institutions. A different kind of institutional selectivity may, indeed, have a significant effect on values. Institutions may select those students who will fit into their value systems, and reject those who would challenge the value structure. Institutional selectivity probably does have a significant effect on values development.

A radical structuralist would not question the finding that participation in social leadership activities has a significant influence on values. The finding would be turned around, though, to question whether the influence is actually negative, not positive. Perhaps participation in such activities works in the other direction. Participation in these activities represents training in and acceptance of a particular political philosophy with inherent oppressive features which are ignored here.

The researchers could not change the data elements used in the original 1971

CIRP surveys. It may have been possible for them to have had input into the post-college 1980 survey. If they had the opportunity, they might have included items to determine whether black and women students had a "choice" in their having joined a service profession, or whether it is the only job they could get. Which of the "social service" jobs are high status and which are dead-end? Too many questions about social tensions are not addressed in the Pascarella study.

Criticism of the Pascarella Study Employing the Radical Humanist Paradigm

The Pascarella study fails to recognize the major theme of radical humanism: the alienation of human consciousness through domination by ideological super-structures. A radical humanist critique of the research addresses radical change issues of alienation, domination, deprivation, and oppression at the level of subjective consciousness. Each of these must be considered as part of any study of civic and humanitarian involvement values in college students.

In their functionalist perspective, the authors use data elements in the causal model to understand what happens to college students in their development of values. However, no such data elements as "socio-economic status" and "secondary school achievement" actually exist. These variables are a creation of the researcher, labels without meanings except for what the researchers assign to them. The only discernible data element to be studied is "human consciousness." The realist ontology needs to be exchanged in favor of a more nominalist perspective if the study is to deal with human beings.

From a radical change standpoint, consciousness is dominated by ideological superstructures which drive a wedge between the self and true consciousness. Radical humanists hope to change the social world by releasing consciousness from these forms of domination. Embedded in the functionalist sociology of regulation, this study offers little in understanding this dialectic of consciousness.

Idiographic methods would have been much more appropriate where nomothetic, quantitative methods are used. To the radical humanist, quantitative tests, measurements, and instruments do not fit the subjective nature of how civic and humanitarian values are developed in the consciousness of college students. Pascarella et al.'s positivist search for laws, causal relationships, and empirical hypotheses is without utility. The social world can only be understood by getting close to students' lives, by entering their frame of reference through such qualitative approaches as naturalistic inquiry and ethnography. The quantitative data gathering and analytic techniques chosen for this study are mismatched to the true purpose of such research, which is to understand the place of values in consciousness.

From a radical humanist point of view, the civic and humanitarian values discussed in the Pascarella article are part of the ideological constructions set up to control people by telling them how they should be and act in society. If students hold the "right" values about civic life, then they will want to influence other people's values and the political structure. The authors legitimize this form of domination. A radical humanist researcher would ask: Where do these ideals come from? Where does the language of values originate in the first place? What is the significance of this essentialist philosophy of cultural transmission within the mission of higher education? What purposes do values as an ideological construction serve in colleges and universities and in the larger society? To the radical humanist, all such ideological norms serve to alienate consciousness.

Radical humanist researchers would challenge the whole concept of what is being explored with the four sets of variables. From their perspective, the pre-college characteristics would fail to account for how human beings become alienated from their own selves. The variables on institutional characteristics would fail to recognize the ideological superstructures which stunt and limit potential. College experiences are discussed without any mention of contradictions and conflicts among different college constituencies. Finally, the post-college occupation variables consist of two elitist measures, degree attainment and employment in a social service occupation, neither of which acknowledges the inherent inequality and inequity of occupational class.

Pascarella et al. appear to have only a minimal understanding of how higher education has become a sort of "psychic prison" when they analyze the negative "psychosocial" effects of institutional size. Such psychosocial effects are part of the profound sense of alienation experienced by students.

None of the empirical findings of the study hold up to the scrutiny of the radical humanist's expectations for subjective social science and radical sociology. Too much is going on in the college world to expect that scores on the 1971 CIRP survey are any indication of values development. The college world is too complex for this kind of neat, sequential prediction. Similarly, the statement that institutional characteristics, especially selectivity and predominant race, have no significant effect on values development is not credible. Of course, all of these factors and many more will influence any individual's attitudes and values about civic life and humanitarian concerns. The oppressive nature of these factors, such as the world of discrimination at a southern, predominantly white university, will certainly affect values formation. Human actions are just too complex to be explained in a linear, causal model of values development.

The authors' findings about racial differences in educational attainment and occupational outcomes are probably useful on a surface level. Racial differences, as discussed in these findings, fail to include larger issues such as Afrocentricity. A radical humanist critique of this study might agree with the findings as somewhat true; but would have to ask: So what? The findings do not tell the reader anything about the sociological problems faced by minority students. That social leadership activities have an effect on values development seems correct on the surface. Generalization of these findings to other contexts is not appropriate.

RADICAL STRUCTURALIST CASE STUDY: ALIENATION OF ETHNIC MINORITIES

The article by Loo and Rolison (1986) entitled "Alienation of Ethnic Minority Students at a Predominantly White University" was chosen to represent the radical structuralist paradigm. This article begins with an analysis of the social processes and structures which influence the university environment for ethnic minority students. The authors recognize that goals for civil rights and equal access have not been realized for ethnic minorities. They suggest that some of the forces which preclude equal opportunity and academic success are ethnic isolation, sociocultural alienation, malintegration, racism, discrimination, cultural domination, and socioeconomic class disadvantages. Tinto's concept of academic and social integration is applied to the study of ethnic minorities in predominantly white institutions. What Tinto terms malintegration, Loo and Rolison define as alienation. The authors depart from Tinto in their focus on academic alienation, examining "perceptions of academic difficulty and satisfaction" instead of grade performance. Willie's theory of race relations also guides the research.

A small, public university in the University of California system was chosen as the site for the study. This institution has unique features which make it appropriate for the research problem, including "segregated" cluster colleges, a disproportionately small number of minorities, and non-traditional use of narrative evaluations in place of grades.

Semi-structured interviews are considered to be an appropriate data gathering method, because "for a sensitive topic like alienation, interviews that used ethnically relevant, open and closed questions were deemed preferable to alienation scales" (p. 62). Random sampling and stratification are used to choose students for interviews. Intentional oversampling of the minority population is done in order to detect differences between minority groups. The final sample consists of 163 undergraduate students, of whom 67 percent are members of minority groups and 33 percent are white. Examination of between group differences in the data is done with Chi-Square analyses.

For the most part, the interviewing is done by students of the same race. This is an important consideration, the authors argue, because with white interviewers there may be a "tendency" for "responses to be affected by a 'white socially desirable bias'" (p. 63). A structured schedule of both closed and open-ended questions is used. These questions are broken out into six theoretically derived categories, including sociocultural alienation, academic difficulties, thoughts of dropping out, academic satisfaction, university supportiveness and unsupportiveness, and ethnic representation.

Demographic characteristics are described first. The authors show that white and minority students differ significantly in terms of class backgrounds, parental occupation and education, ethnicity of home community, and whether the university's location is their hometown. They conclude that minority students feel significantly greater sociocultural alienation than do white students. Approximately 40 percent of the minorities interviewed state that their values are reflected just "a little" or "not at all" by the university. Greater social isolation is also experienced by these students.

A majority of the black and Chicano students interviewed believe that minorities experience greater academic difficulties than whites. White students' perceptions of these difficulties for minorities are evenly divided, with 53 percent believing that whites face the same difficulties as minorities. Academic difficulties are traced by some Chicano and black students to poor high school preparation. Others point to the socioeconomic and cultural differences between minorities and whites as variables affecting academic problems. Some ethnic minorities say that they have to deal with a kind of "culture shock" which requires them to expend energies that could go to other things.

There are no significant differences between the percentages of white and minority students who consider dropping out, but there are differences in the reasons for leaving. White students usually think about dropping out because of academic factors. For ethnic minorities, sociocultural alienation is as much a reason for dropping out as any academic factor.

The university environment is perceived from "vastly different perspectives" by whites and minorities. Sixty-three percent of white students feel that the university is supportive of minorities, as opposed to only 28 percent of Chicanos and blacks. The greatest sources of support, according to minorities, come through student services. Whites and minorities also have "vastly different views about how the university lacked support for minority students." One student feels that there is more "lip service" than "actual service." Another feels that "The university is doing the minimum." Two related problems are brought out by the interviews: the small number of minorities on campus; and the fact that there are "few social activities geared towards minority students" (p. 68).

The authors conclude that minority students experience significantly greater feelings of alienation than do white students, and that these feelings are the result of ethnic isolation and cultural domination. This form of sociocultural alienation is different than alienation which is caused by academic dissatisfaction. Even when minorities are doing well academically, they may experience feelings of alienation when the proportion of minorities on campus is small. When minority students feel alienated academically, this may be related to poor high school preparation, lower socioeconomic status, parental educational attainment, and the "culture shock" of "encountering a class and culture distinctly different from their background" (p. 72). In their analysis of white and minority students' perceptions about academic and sociocultural alienation, Loo and Rolison find that whites are basically unaware of the greater academic difficulties faced by minorities.

Criticism of the Loo and Rolison Study
Employing the Functionalist Paradigm

From a functionalist perspective, the topic explored in this study is important to fulfilling higher education's mission of equal opportunity and access. It is unfortunate that, in their efforts to understand the problems felt by ethnic minority students at predominantly white universities, Loo and Rolison employ a radical sociological perspective. This makes the study less useful to scholars who may wish to build on their research.

The authors cite Tinto's early work on attrition as relevant to their study. Because the adaptation of Tinto focuses on a different definition of academic satisfaction, one must question the theoretical framework. It is difficult to believe that Tinto's concept of malintegration is the same problem which the authors discuss. Sociocultural domination of values is not really part of Tinto's work. Willie's theory of how white values suppress minority values is what the authors are really interested in investigating. Use of this second theoretical framework, however interesting it may be to the authors, involves a major departure from Tinto's empirical model.

A functionalist believes that the conflict between white and minority students is only one of many processes and functions in college; that students' values are developed autonomously and spontaneously, not as a result of values domination; and that there are no contradictions between campus groups which cannot be worked out. The radical structuralist perspective on cultural domination is simply too radical. To a functionalist, it seems almost paranoid and conspiratorial in tone.

The choice of university for the case study is a problem. The university represents all of the anomalies of the minority experience in higher education, such as the formation of ethnic enclaves. The use of a narrative evaluation system by the university instead of grades makes the study of academic satisfaction questionable, since the Tinto model uses grades, not evaluations, as the measure of academic integration.

The results suggest that some minorities in this setting feel alienated and/or isolated by the university community. Issues of ethnic isolation are confused by the discussion of "segregated" enclaves within the university's eight colleges. These residential communities present fascinating portraits of integration and socialization at work in a complex, multiracial setting. What is the relationship between membership in an ethnic enclave and academic satisfaction? There are many different factors which could affect the academic satisfaction and integration of students, including experiences of discrimination and racism in the social world outside the university walls.

These peculiar features in the university setting make its use for data gathering inappropriate. From a functionalist standpoint, the case study has minimum generalizability. If external validity is important to the researchers, then the contextual features of the case work are far too idiosyncratic. Perhaps the oversampling of minorities should have been left for another study focusing on between-minority group differences.

The use of same-race interviewers was intended to alleviate what the authors call a "white socially desirable bias" in responses. There are many other types of problems which occur with this kind of interview. Deviation from a structured interview protocol may be a problem, due to the authors' (and perhaps the interviewers') ideological predisposition. This makes all of the data suspect.

The major finding of the research, that some minority students experience social and academic alienation that may be related to isolation and culture shock, is probably true, but certainly not new. This has been a concern of affirmative action, access, remediation, and retention programs for some time. The authors' radical position makes it sound as if nothing has ever been done to alleviate these problems.

All of the findings are supported with Chi-Square analyses, though more robust statistical tests would be welcome. The study's results are incomplete, though. For instance, the finding that white and minority students think about dropping out for different reasons is quite striking. There is a major difference, however, between thinking about dropping out and actually doing so. The authors do not interview students who dropped out, so it is impossible to tell if their reasons are not as much academic as cultural. Tinto's conception of attrition has much to say about drop-out behavior, but this use of Tinto's model is so convoluted by the radical sociology position that it is difficult to know where it should be applied.

Some of the other findings may be more easily assimilated within a functionalist view. It is highly probable that ethnic clustering is perceived differently by whites and minorities. This is because whites are not part of these enclave experiences, and therefore do not have adequate mechanisms for understanding what is happening in them. The finding that minorities experienced greater social isolation needs to be examined more fully. Perhaps there are other types of social interactions which take place which need to be included in the data gathering. Since the definition of isolation is not clear, the finding about social isolation is unclear. It seems obvious that whites would favor enrollment of more minorities on campus, especially since this sample is from California.

The finding that some minorities do not feel that the university is supportive of them is too general. The same is true of the finding that 40 percent of the minorities interviewed feel that their values are not reflected or are reflected just "a little" by the university. This interpretation is weak. It tells the reader nothing except that the university environment is culturally diverse and perceived in different ways.

Criticism of the Loo and Rolison Study
Employing the Interpretive Paradigm

Since the interpretive paradigm represents the exact opposite of the assumptions of the radical structuralist paradigm, both sociology and social science criticisms of the Loo and Rolison study would be raised by an interpretivist. To begin, the research is too bound by theory, too grounded in a particular social analysis. A priori definitions of social determinants limit the exploration of possible social forces and shape the researchers' perceptions of them. This discussion of minority alienation is therefore one-sided. The authors fail to look for larger patterns and processes which are part of the coordinating, integrating, and cohesive mechanisms of society.

To an interpretive researcher, the discussion of conflict, domination, and contradiction must be moved from the structural to the subjective. Research problems and questions should be concerned with understanding subjective experiences, examining the university in all of its multidimensional complexity. Psychological processes such as feelings of alienation and isolation may be part of the college experience. However, these processes are much more complicated than these theories suggest. The environmental, situational, and behavioral variables which are discussed offer, at best, an incomplete portrait of human activities. Such determinants may play a role in patterns of integration, but to attribute any person's actions or feelings to one or more of these variables is to deny the depth and complexity of human affairs.

Shared values are seen by the interpretive researcher as a sign of integration, whereas the radical structuralist views them as a sign of the success of the forces of domination. Although heterogeneity and imbalance may be pointed out as incongruities within the university, these problems are actually part of the integrating and cohesive processes being worked out in society as a whole. Radical structuralists believe that racial conflicts are evidence of deep, societal contradictions. They do not understand that, over time, different constituencies can co-exist peacefully and compatibly. What radical structuralists label as conflict and contradiction are simply pieces of the puzzle of integration which keep the social world moving forward, albeit somewhat slowly at times.

The emphasis on sociocultural domination is far too mechanistic, deterministic, and radical for an investigation of how values may or may not be influenced by culture. Cultural domination does not occur simply because social efforts exist to preserve and protect values and norms. It is clear that the researchers operate with value judgments about what constitutes minority alienation and that their efforts to be "objective" are unsuccessful since it is impossible for them to be detached.

The definitions and labels used by Loo and Rolison to describe alienation, academic difficulties, university supportiveness, and attitudes toward minority admissions are not "real," because empirical definitions are themselves the product of subjective value judgments. The interpretivist views these labels as the result of researchers' perceptions of the social world and of their theoretical frameworks. The search for significant differences between whites and minority groups through Chi-Square analyses is futile. Researchers must recognize that experiences in higher education are the creation of individual cognition and consciousness and part of the social construction of reality. It is only at the subjective level that the problem of alienation may be understood in a meaningful way.

Research on minority experiences should be based upon first-hand evidence from subjective accounts. Principles of ethnography and naturalistic inquiry should guide the inquiry. With the interviews, Loo and Rolison should have tried to get inside the university's frame of reference, to learn the language of today's minority and white college students, and to tell their stories.

It is unfortunate that the authors spend so much time trying to generalize from data that do not lend themselves to this kind of nomothetic analysis. Interpretation should have been left to the reader, based on her or his own feelings about the study's trustworthiness. No attempts to form conclusions should have been made, as these are inappropriate.

Criticism of the Loo and Rolison Study
Employing the Radical Humanist Paradigm

To a radical humanist, the determinist reliance on examining the social world from environmental, situational, and behavioral perspectives is a major weakness of the Loo and Rolison study. Human actions are much more complex than the Tinto and Willie theories imply. The social world of domination and deprivation in the university must be analyzed from a more contextual and relativistic perspective. It is of utmost importance that researchers be able to understand the sources of alienation which are inherent in the totality of universal consciousness and which converge in the context of the social construction called "higher education."

Radical humanists believe that only by entering the minority student frame of reference and getting to know students who are oppressed can researchers investigate issues of alienation. Quantitative measures, tests, and data analytic techniques do not fit this kind of subjective inquiry. Social science knowledge is not be expanded by the accretion and accumulation of hypotheses and the acknowledgement of Chi Square differences. The creation of a radical humanist perspective on alienation is an holistic process.

Alienation is not a variable to be measured. If scholars are to participate in alleviating oppression, then research must focus on subjective consciousness, in all its dark and human frailty. Essentially, the world of the university acts as a sort of cognitive wedge, driven between the consciousness of minorities and their true selves. In the psychic prison of higher education, all people are alienated from their true selves and from each other.

The findings of the Loo and Rolison study are not surprising to a radical humanist. Minorities do feel culturally alienated and socially isolated. Their values are certainly not reflected by the university. It is no wonder that they have more academic difficulties, or that they drop out for different reasons than white students do. The university does not support them, just as it denies their cultural values. Ethnic clustering seems to have been the only way in which they have been able to survive amidst domination and oppression.

The results of the study actually tell the radical humanist reader very little about the nature of the alienation and isolation which minorities experience. The radical structuralist approach is useful only up to a certain point because of its positivist orientation. To really understand oppression at the level of consciousness, it is necessary that subjective assumptions about social science replace the traditional, positivist assumptions.

INTERPRETIVE CASE STUDY:
FOUR UNDERGRADUATE COMPUTER-WRITERS

In the article entitled "A Study of Four Undergraduate Computer-Writers," Logan (1988) uses ethnographic techniques and case studies to present a portrait of four undergraduate students who learn to use computers in their writing. The author's approach to educational research is based on assumptions underpinning what she describes as "interpretive inquiry."

The study focuses on one semester's writing class in a computer lab. Document analysis, observation, and interviews are used as ethnographic techniques. First, a computerized form of questionnaire is designed to elicit comments and reflections from students about their computer-writing skills. This procedure is abandoned because it does not gather the kind of information in which the researcher is interested. As part of her participation as instructor, the author then uses observation techniques to look for clues to the computer-writing processes at work for different students. Field notes of these observations are recorded. However, the author believes that this technique also does not offer the kinds of information she hopes to gather. Therefore, a series of informal "casual conversations'' are initiated with students during the lab time. Out of these conversations comes the author's decision to do interviews.

Students' selection for interviews is based on three criteria, including: (1) their "ability to articulate" their experiences using computers in writing; (2) their not having a computer at home to use; and (3) their having time to work in the lab and be interviewed. Two students who met these criteria are interviewed twice; once three weeks into the semester, and again two weeks before the end of the semester. Two additional students are chosen for one-time interviews to serve as "sources of 'disconfirming or confirming evidence' " (p. 136). It is hoped that these different data gathering methods will serve as forms of "triangulation."

The design of the open-ended interviews is "guided by the same general topic, but the sequence and nature of questions are determined by the subject's responses." The first question Logan uses is: "I was wondering if you would tell me something about your experiences with writing at a computer." During the progress of the interview, efforts are made to incorporate Spradley's three types of ethnographic questions. The interviews are recorded and transcribed. In addition, the author has access to students' written work for document analysis.

The data analytic approach involves "descriptive analysis of the meanings which these four writers assign to the activity of writing at a computer" (p. 138). In the article, case studies are presented for the two main students, Karen and Ellen. The case description is broken up into the two topics of attitudes about computers and writing strategies.

An example of how attitudes about computers are described is found in the following passage: "She [Ellen] expresses some ambivalence about the impact of computers on society in general, implying that somehow they are less authentic, not the real thing." Ellen explains:

> I think it would be a good idea to go back and see how it is to do it on a typewriter. . . . To open their minds up and say "Wow, look what it is that this thing can do." They take it for granted. And I think it's really important as computers become the pencil of the future that they learn the process of what they're really doing (p. 138)

The data on writing strategies are illustrated in this interview with Karen:

> Slow, just when you think you're halfway across, it sucks you back in. And it's a never ending process. For me it is. I have to keep going back through the manual that you gave us and re-read everything. . . . I always have to go back through to move text or to make any of the changes. For me it's just, ugh! I still don't like them [computers] (p. 142).

In her analysis, Logan writes that Karen "seems to want to blame the computer for some of her writing problems" (p. 143). During the second interview,

Karen "seemed a lot more antagonistic toward computers" (p. 142). Logan explains that:

> For Karen, the computer seems to represent the enemy out there to be conquered because it's so "up and coming." Perhaps because she sees it this way, it presents more difficulty for her. She seems more willing to accept her inability to "learn the computer," just as she is willing to accept her writing deficiencies as a "fact of life." One of her final remarks to me as she turned in her typed final paper was, "Well, I guess the computer won!" This comment along with the one in her last interview ("I still don't like them") suggests that she took the endeavor to be a personal confrontation, likened to "trudging through a swamp" (p. 144).

Summarizing the results of different ethnographic techniques, Logan explains that:

> Some dominant patterns of meaning surface in the description of these four computer-writers. As we consider these patterns, it is important to remember that they are offered not as findings, results, or conclusions . . . (p. 144).

Three important patterns of meaning emerge from this study. The first is that Ellen sees the computer as a technical "tool, something which she can use to write more efficiently." Second, Karen is interested in learning about the computer because it is "up and coming." For her, the computer also "seems to represent the enemy out there to be conquered . . ." Learning the computer is "a personal confrontation." In the cases of Bob and Angie, "the computer is not at issue; it is a given" (p. 144). Both have prior computer experience and, unlike Ellen and Karen, are primarily interested in getting the system to work for them.

Logan concludes by analyzing the patterns of meanings in terms of their implications for practice. No attempt is made to generalize from these case studies. The author warns that:

> Knowing how four writers perceived a semester's experience of writing with a computer does not tell us how four other students during a different semester or even during the same semester perceived it. Nor does it tell us how these same four students might perceive it in another setting. . . . One value, it seems, of such an irreplicable [sic] study is that knowing how meaning was made in this classroom community might provide us with new lenses for looking at others (p. 145).

Criticism of the Logan Study Employing the Functionalist Paradigm

To a functionalist, the Logan study of computer-writers is poor research; the research problem is framed in such a subjective manner that the study does not accomplish anything. Methodologically, there are problems in the data gathering and data analytic techniques.

A functionalist would question whether case studies of this sort can generate information that is useful in any cumulative sense. There are a number of disciplines which can be brought to bear on the problem of understanding how learning labs may be used in teaching computers and writing. Sociology, psychology, education, along with the sub-fields of educational technology and cognitive development, have much to offer this topic of study, which better fits a behavioral treatment.

It is important to question whether the methodological design could have sustained the author's conclusions. First, the author tries a computerized questionnaire. The data on this procedure are not even reported. The reader is simply told that the data are not reported because the author didn't get the kind of data she was looking for. Then, the author tries to observe students in the lab. Again, the reader is told that this procedure does not obtain the type of information desired. Logan settles on interviews for data gathering. This might be an appropriate choice, using interviews to gather exploratory, qualitative data. The choice to interview only two students may limit the amount of insight to be gained into patterns in the data, since there is little room for redundancy.

Numerous problems may be expected in the data analysis when interviews are completely open-ended and non-sequential. It is impossible to know how problems in the content analysis are worked out by the author. The methods of document analysis of students' writings are not discussed. The cases are filled with the instructor's personal, subjective interpretation, despite statements to the contrary about not wanting to generalize. Logan's use of "descriptive analysis" is inadequate. All that the reader is left with is a sequence of simplistic anecdotal quotes about students' perceptions of their attitudes about computers and their writing strategies. Overall, the structure of the case studies is not useful.

One might predict that the results of such data gathering and analysis would be poor, and this is the case in the concluding sections of the article. There are no correlations, laws, or relationships to be found in the data, only what Logan calls "patterns of meanings." These three "meanings" are basically "meaningless." So what if Ellen sees computers as a tool and Karen used computers because they are trendy? The reader is told that Bob and Angie already know about computers. How does this affect their use of the lab? What about the four students' learning processes? Do they do anything in the lab? Does the curriculum meet their needs? Do they develop any skills? Do computers make a difference in their writing? These subjective accounts fail to illustrate any of these basic questions, or, for that matter, to be of interest to the reader.

Since the study's findings consist only of patterns of meanings, a functionalist researcher would question whether the data from two students represent a pattern. It is possible that these meanings are entirely idiosyncratic. For example, Karen's attitudes about computers being "trendy" may represent nothing at all but an off-hand remark. For this reason, all of the findings about patterns of meanings which Logan discusses are suspect. How does the reader know if students accept computers as writing tools? The fact that Angie has a computer at home may not be linked to her success in using computers or her acceptance that they are "a given." The relationship between Bob's having a background of computer science courses and his success in the lab is not substantiated by the "pattern" of his interview comments.

Even though Logan says she isn't going to generalize, the implications of the study sound like concluding recommendations. Any possible links between the implications, the "patterns of meaning," and the data are missing from the article. To make these kinds of recommendations, a researcher is expected to have analyzed data with some degree of precision.

Criticism of the Logan Study Employing the
Radical Structuralist Paradigm

For the radical structuralist, any form of critical analysis must recognize the inherent contradictions and conflicts which plague the college environment. Logan neglects to mention the role of technology in reinforcing class structures or the influence of computer technology in maintaining and preserving racial, gender, class, economic, and geopolitical superstructures in society. There is no understanding in this research of the ways in which technology is used to control and manipulate people's lives by dehumanizing work and reifying technical knowledge. Human worth is devalued in favor of technological competency. Also, there is no appreciation of the dominating power relationship which is the basis for pedagogy—that of professor over student.

To the radical structuralist, Logan's study simply reinforces the status quo, accepting that this is the way things are in society and that nothing can or should be done to change it. The learning laboratory, which is supposed to help teach students to use computers in their writing, does something entirely different, though. Students are conditioned into believing that technology will help them, that it will make them better students, that if they learn to use computers they will get better jobs because of their new skills. Through computer-writing, students come to accept a dominant belief system about the role of technology which subtly and unconsciously degrades the human condition. These mechanisms of oppression are legitimized by Logan, who accepts technology without questioning its impact. This is not to say that there is no place for computers or computer-writing software, but that their use should not facilitate oppressive class structures.

Both of the students in the case studies are women. It is obvious that neither of them is successful from the instructor's point of view in learning to use computers in their writing. One woman, Karen, even says that she does not like computers. Why should she? The expectation of the author, who seems unable to "objectively" separate herself from her role as instructor, is that Karen should like computers because they are good for her. The truth is that her experience with the computer has led to her self-image being belittled. Computers are described by Karen as the "enemy." For her, trying to learn word processing becomes a big "confrontation." These are not just words. They are cries for help, statements about the profound feelings of oppression and domination experienced by this student. The computer lab confronts her with sexist stereotypes and self-fulfilling prophecies of women's science abilities. The computer program tries to make her writing into what the programmer thinks it should be, grammatically and anatomically correct. No wonder she does not feel particularly creative. The learning laboratory is an artificial and dehumanizing setting. There are probably no windows in the lab. Certainly, there are no feelings of liberation or empowerment being developed as part of this new technology.

Two additional students are interviewed for confirmation of the data. It is interesting to note that both of these students seem to have met Logan's unspoken criteria of success in computer-writing. One of these students, Bob, faces none of the fears of success with technology that the two women feel, in part because he has already had computer courses. Angie does well, according to Logan, because she owns her own computer and regularly uses Wordperfect for word processing.

A radical structuralist reading of these limited, subjective data would suggest that Ellen and Karen are oppressed by computer technology. The computer-writing lab reinforces a particular form of domination. Bob is privileged because he fits into the norms of the technological elite. He also has an easier time of it because he is part of male-dominated society. Angie definitely fits into the researcher's bias for a middle class image of students, since she has the luxury to buy her own home computer and software. Through these four examples, one glimpses the processes by which training in technology legitimizes oppressive power. Ellen and Karen are deprived of their potential as producers and consumers of technology because they do not fit into the mold of computer "user." Since they are women, can not afford to buy their own computers, and are de-selected out of other computer science prerequisites, they lose this opportunity to become "computer literate." As an interpretive researcher, Logan fails to address these problems of class and gender.

There are certain expectations about the conduct of social science which Logan obviously does not meet. To the radical structuralist, Logan's subjective approach to social science does not constitute good research. The only data offered in the case studies are anecdotal. The scientific approach requires that data elements and variables be empirically grounded and defined with precise, technical language. Logan's observation procedures did not solicit the type of data she desired. This may be because the techniques are not very rigorous or objective. Open-ended interviews may be useful for data exploration, but these are inappropriate for prediction and explanation. Logan has no hypotheses, no empirical data, no conclusions, and no generalizations.

The "pattern of meaning" that Ellen sees computers as an effective writing tool also shows something the interpretive researcher is not looking for—students' resigned indifference to giving up their freedom in exchange for technological bondage. Bob and Angie, who both see computers as "a given," readily accept Logan's values about computers. It is possible that these are not patterns at all, but entirely idiosyncratic, since each pattern comes from only one subject.

Criticism of the Logan Study Employing the Radical Humanist Paradigm

Logan describes computers and technology as if they are value-free. From a radical humanist perspective, this is simply not the case. Where computer technology is discussed as a liberating element in society, it needs to be recognized as a negative and dominating force as well. In Logan's mind, only good could come from technology. The author seems to be blind to the reality that the two women interviewed for the case studies are alienated by their experiences with computers. She does not see that there are many forms of deprivation, oppression, and domination at work in the computer lab.

There is something to be learned from the data, though. Karen's comment that she did not like computers is a clue. The computer is the "enemy." She admits that "the computer won," and that learning to write on a computer is a "personal confrontation," like "trudging through a swamp" (p. 144).

Here, technology is reified and Karen's human worth devalued. She is alienated by her experience with computers. The dialogue between the student and professor, as depicted in the article, is an example of the communicative distortion which takes place in power relationships. The author's attitudes about computers do not allow her to observe what is taking place in the form of technological domination and oppression. Logan legitimizes the status quo of technological domination by criticizing Karen for her lack of acceptance of technology.

The author does not express much concern for creativity. In the context of a single classroom experience, Karen's potential as a computer user, her feelings of ability and talent as a writer, and her self-esteem as a person, are eroded. What if she has a learning disability? Like many others, she will be quickly passed over for selection into the technological elite because she does not meet the expectations of the professor, who acts as expert and judge. The lab staff serve as the gatekeepers of potential, passing out grades and possibilities for development and fulfillment.

Most researchers, like Logan, fail to understand what technology does to people. Karen sees computers as the enemy. The learning lab is not educating her to the possibilities of writing poetry, novels, or non-fiction. She is being trained to take her place as a second-class citizen. This higher education experience is inculcating her with values of passivity, submissiveness, low self-esteem, and low self-worth.

Moreover, from a radical humanist perspective, this kind of research perpetuates ideological hegemony by stultifying human creativity. To the radical humanist, the computer lab represents a kind of "psychic prison." The computer-writing curriculum drives a cognitive wedge between the self and true consciousness. There is no appreciation of cognitive development or of the psychology of critical thinking and writing skills. Through using these computer programs, students are taught to write correctly. Ideas are not important; grammar, spelling, and correct text analysis are. Engagement with any of the fundamental questions of human life is devalued. What is important to Logan is that Ellen and Karen learn to subordinate their originality and creativity by using a word processor, spelling checker, and text analyzer.

These case studies of how four undergraduates learned to do computer-writing represent larger societal tensions between science and the humanities, a false duality which is being played out in the totality of higher education. Science and computer technology triumph over the arts and humanities in general education and in the major. This new technology curriculum has become anti-human.

To an interpretive researcher like Logan, change is a superficial, ephemeral, everyday part of life. To a radical humanist, change means much more. True change takes place through the development of new modes of cognition and consciousness. Scholars have a responsibility to encourage alternatives to the status quo by envisioning radical changes in the ideological superstructures of technology. Subjective data gathering and analytic techniques such as used by Logan have a unique place in mapping the alienation of human consciousness. In this study, however, the technological bias of the researcher seems to reinforce and compound the profound sense of alienation felt by the two women.

RADICAL HUMANIST CASE STUDY:
WOMEN'S WAYS OF KNOWING

In their book *Women's Ways of Knowing: The Development of Self, Voice, and Mind*, Belenky, Clinchy, Goldberger, and Tarule (1986) present the results of a five-year research study on women's epistemology. From their perspective, most theories of development fail to identify "aspects of intelligence and modes of thought that might be more common and highly developed in women" (p. 7). This lack of significant research on women's development is a result of the male-dominated world of scholarship in developmental psychology and in all of the academic disciplines.

An emergent, naturalistic design using interviews and case studies was chosen in order to "explore with the women their experience and problems as learners and knowers as well as to review their past histories for changing concepts of the self and relationships with others" (p. 11). The authors describe their developmental assessment approach as being similar to that used by Perry (1970), which involves "an open and leisurely interview that establishes rapport and allows presuppositions and frames of reference of the interviewee to emerge. We share Perry's commitment to this phenomenological approach" (p. 10).

Gilligan's conception of women's development, portrayed as a process of "finding a voice," is crucial to the authors' understanding of gender differences and to their articulation of women's development, as distinct from men's. Rather than be guided in their data gathering and analysis by existing theoretical constructs and developmental research, the researchers "wanted to hear what the women had to say in their own terms rather than test our own preconceived hypotheses" (p. 11).

A total of 135 women were selected for interviews, including 90 women who attended or were recent alumni from one of six colleges, and 45 women who were being served by one of three family agency programs. The academic institutions encompass a wide variety of educational philosophies. The family agencies are considered as "invisible colleges." All of the agency programs are organized and run by women. This gives the authors a chance to find out "what kinds of institutions for promoting growth and development women would create for themselves if they were not so dominated by masculine images, theories, founders, or administrators" (p. 13). Also, by paying attention to mothering, which is the focus of various program services, it might be possible to "hear themes that were especially distinctive in the woman's voice" (p. 13). This diversity of respondents allows the researchers to "see the common ground that women share, regardless of background" (p. 13).

All 135 women are interviewed in-depth at least once, sometimes twice. The sets of interviews offered comparison data that could be used in case studies of development over time for approximately one-third of the women. A series of qualitative content analysis procedures are used to code and classify the interview data. First, the interview sections for assessing scores on the Perry, Kohlberg, and Gilligan development schemes are separated out and blind coding of these sections is done. Where Perry focuses on stages and positions of development which followed a clear sequence, Belenky et al. are interested in "epistemological *perspectives* from which women know and view the world" (p. 15). Applying the Perry scheme to Gilligan's concept of "finding a voice," the authors identify five distinct epistemological perspectives which they call "women's ways of knowing."

The interview transcripts are coded into a number of emergent and a priori categories. Contextual analysis follows the use of ethnographic techniques to preserve the data intact and place them into epistemological categories. Two other kinds of analyses are done. One of the a priori coding categories distinguishes women's epistemologies in terms of what the authors call "educational dialectics." These eleven educational dialectics consist of "bimodal dimensions." Each side of the dimensions represents a preferred mode of learning.

Statements from each woman are grouped under each dialectical mode. Throughout the interviews, the authors also pay attention to the influence of two social institutions on women's development—the family and formal education.

One result of the data analyses surprises the authors. They recognize the notion of "finding a different voice" which Gilligan heard "as women talked about personal moral crises and decisions." But, as they note, "What we had not anticipated was that 'voice' was more than an academic shorthand for a person's point of view . . ." but a "metaphor that can apply to many aspects of women's experience and development" (p. 18).

In their description of five "epistemological perspectives from which women know and view the world" (p. 15), the researchers caution that these are not to be interpreted as stages, positions, or sequences of development. The categories are not intended by the authors to be fixed or exhaustive. The authors state that their "intention is to share not prove our observations" (p. 16).

These five epistemological perspectives are: (1) silence; (2) received knowledge, or listening to the voices of others; (3) subjective knowledge, including the inner voice, and the quest for self; (4) procedural knowledge, including the voice of reason, separate knowing, and connected knowing; and (5) constructed knowledge, or integrating the voices.

Approximately one-third of the book *Women's Ways of Knowing* is devoted to understanding the effects of family life and formal education on women's development. Stories of family life are told as case studies of each epistemological perspective.

For the silent women, there is violence instead of dialogue at home. "Everyone in this small group experienced some form of gross neglect and/or sexual abuse, by one or both of their parents" (p. 159). These women need, somehow, to gain a voice if they are to break out of the cycle of being a victim or perpetrator of family violence. For received knowers who listen to the voices of others, there is one-way talk, inequality, and male domination, without any hope of rebellion against oppressive and sexually abusive authority. Those subjective knowers who listen to their inner voice are, on the contrary, able to "revolt and rebel against their parents" (p. 168), questioning authority. In this position, there comes the first "criticism of conventional female goodness," (p. 174) as the ideal of selflessness is questioned. In the family life of procedural knowers who are working to integrate the voices of reason and feeling, there is more of a dialogue and connectedness between mothers and daughters. Integrating the voices of reason and feeling, constructed knowers have themes of connectedness between mothers and daughters, using mothers in developing the voice of reason and fathers in developing the voice of emotion.

The authors observe that "women often feel alienated in academic settings and experience 'formal' education as either peripheral or irrelevant to their central interests and development" (p. 4). Most of the women who are interviewed feel that they have "often been treated as if they were stupid" (p. 194). In college, the focus on knowing does not involve development of the self and of voice, but acceptance of a new form of authority, that of faculty over student. Rarely are school experiences considered as "powerful learning experiences" (p. 200). A "tyranny of expectations" is at work, the authors find, in which connected knowing is devalued as a dialectic and separate knowing is praised. The masculine preference in each dimension is promoted as the mode for both sexes, and the modes preferred by women are down-played and/or criticized.

The differences between male and female students are contrasted in the chapter entitled "Toward an Education for Women." For women, confirmation of the self as a knower and acceptance into the college community of relationships are "prerequisites rather than consequences of development" (p. 194). In the concluding chapter entitled "Connected Teaching," the authors envision a philosophy of education for women's development that replaces "traditional separate education" with "connected teaching," and which pays attention to women's educational dialectics of connected knowing.

Criticism of the Belenky Study Employing the Interpretive Paradigm

To an interpretivist, this analysis is unmistakably based on a combination of feminist critique, radical sociology, Gilligan's and Perry's theories of development, and psychoanalytic theory. The researchers make a number of radical sociological assumptions about the existence of domination, contradiction, deprivation, emancipation, and potentiality—criticisms that do not have a place within the interpretive paradigm. They simply represent the views of one particular ideological perspective on the problems of the social world.

The primary goal of developmental research on women should be to understand the subjectively created social world, as it is, in terms of ongoing patterns and processes of human growth and development. The power relationships of male domination discussed by the radical humanist position are a theoretical interpretation. To an interpretivist, values about home, family, and education are acquired more autonomously than is suggested.

As for the overall findings of the study, these are frightening in their depiction of possible barriers to development which some women face. The metaphor of "voice" is useful in understanding part of what women feel is going on in their lives. It is interesting to look at the metaphor of voice from five different epistemological perspectives. Although this epistemology is grounded in a nominalist, constructivist approach to subjective knowing, it seems that the authors could not resist implying sequential stages and hierarchical levels of development.

The description of modes of how some women learn is interesting, but still somewhat Manichean. Although these polarities may be useful as a starting point, gender issues in learning are much more complex. It is probably true that some women learn in modes which are different from how some men learn, although it is questionable whether the two are at opposite poles. Here the radical sociological position intrudes in the interpretation of the data. Perhaps institutions of higher education do favor certain modes, as the authors suggest. It is implausible, though, to attribute complex processes to male domination and hierarchical power relationships. To the interpretivist, research with women about their development is only useful up to a point. The very nature of developmental psychology is hierarchical. The authors' methodological ideals for subjective inquiry are compromised because they are so engaged with their ideological approach.

Criticism of the Belenky Study Employing the Functionalist Paradigm
From a functionalist perspective, the sociological assumptions which undergird the Belenky study are simply unfounded. Instead of taking the traditional approach to the topic, they are interested in male domination and oppression. Values are acquired much more autonomously than the research suggests. The preferred learning modes which the authors describe are probably not the result of domination, deprivation, and oppression. It is absurd to assume that any of these learning dialectics exist as polar opposites between the sexes.

Significant gender-related behavioral problems do occur within the psychosocial process of integration, but these are not a sign of inherent contradictions or conflicts. These are natural imbalances and problems of heterogeneity which are caused by tensions between the sexes and by the panoply of human activities. Natural gender differences, which have both a physiological and psychological basis, should not be construed as representing any kind of authoritarian power relationship of men over women. Research needs to be done on differences between the sexes that can be attributed to the processes of growth and development, and to gender-specific developmental behavior. Research must pay attention to the environmental, situational, and behavioral determinants which are part of the integrating, coordinating, and cohesive mechanisms built into society.

Through the institutions of the family unit and higher education, the status quo of the social world is maintained. Men and women complement one another in their social lives, and their psychological development is basically compatible. This is not to make light of the tragic data about incest, sexual abuse, and family violence which the interviews bring out. One must recognize, though, that these deviations are not the norm. For many women, family life and education are developmentally stimulating and fulfilling parts of normal human existence. Belenky et al. criticize the institutions of family life and education for legitimizing and reinforcing oppression. A functionalist views the family unit and colleges and universities as important societal mechanisms which help balance divergent social processes.

To the functionalist, the entire approach to research used in the Belenky study is too subjective. Empirical data should be gathered which describe the relationship between the sexes in quantitative terms. Self-reports of how women learn and know about the world can be a useful source of data which might, conceivably, serve as a starting point in developmental research; but these are just subjective accounts. How can the reliability of these anecdotal reports be adequately measured? Other data sources with more integrity, such as instruments and tests, should be used to assess the validity of the interview data. If the interview protocol is valuable, then the data may be used to determine whether they support the epistemological schema.

The authors' "observations" are not objective. As researchers, their perceptions about women's development and their feminist belief structures influence their ability to gather and analyze the data dispassionately and rationally. Empirical precision should be of the utmost importance if any form of interpretation is to be done. All of the data coding is suspect. It is unclear which coding categories emerged and which were guided by theory.

The authors state that they do not want to make hypotheses, but that they want the data to speak for themselves. Still, subtle, hidden causal models are being defined in the description of the five epistemological positions. While attempting to be naturalistic and subjective on the surface, the feminist ideology implies that domination is a cause and that oppression is an effect. The authors are not successful in maintaining both a subjective and a radical change perspective. Perhaps they do not intend to. From a functionalist point of view, however, the mix of methods and ideology is problematic and makes the results much less useful.

Based on the data presented, it is difficult for the functionalist reader to accept the conclusion that women learn best through dialectical modes which support "connected knowing," or that "connected teaching" is useful in facilitating women's development. Overall, this study fails to substantiate any interpretations or conclusions that might be useful in future research. Researchers wishing to build on this developmental schema will have to remove the data from the many radical sociology interpretations which surround them. Any reporting of results should be done in a straight forward and scholarly manner that is not embedded in social commentary.

Criticism of the Belenky Study Employing the
Radical Structuralist Paradigm

From a radical structuralist point of view, this study of *Women's Ways of Knowing* is an excellent example of feminist discourse. It offers an original and compelling argument about family life and higher education as barriers to the development of women. Several general criticisms need to be raised, though, about the social science assumptions.

The devastating effects of male domination are discussed at a microcosmic level which is too subjective. Research on women's development should not fall victim to the "tyranny of data." In this study, the subjective data overshadow the a priori theoretical framework of radical sociology. The primacy of theory should be maintained. The authors incorporate a theoretical perspective, but fail to fully admit it that it guides their methodological choices. The subjectivity which is at the heart of this study must be avoided. If the male academic establishment is to be confronted, it should be done with empirically sound documentation of oppression.

Some of the findings of the study are more credible than others. It is important for scholars to document the fact that women learn differently than men, that men's ways of learning and knowing about the world have been valued, while women's ways have been criticized and scorned. The eleven educational dialectics and dimensions represent modes by which men oppress and devalue women's ways of knowing.

To a radical structuralist, the concept that human beings subjectively create their own reality is fundamentally unsound. The world is not a social construction. Here, the subjective nature of the data lead to misinterpretations about the nature of oppression in the social world. Barriers to development are real and tangible. They may be empirically tested and measured with nomothetic precision. Reality is the same, whether or not people develop different epistemological perspectives with which to see it.

The force and power of the critique is greatly diminished by the authors' nominalist assumptions about the social world. If this kind of research is to be taken seriously by the scholarly community, it is imperative that researchers remain objective social scientists who dispassionately employ methodological rigor to find new ways of tearing down barriers to women's development.

An alternative feminist model of women's development could be envisioned which suggests women's potential once they are emancipated from the structures of patriarchal society. Once an alternative feminist vision is put forward, it is possible to facilitate education for development by fostering activities which have a positive effect on women's development.

DISCUSSION

Using the Burrell and Morgan definitions to develop alternative research strategies, the case study approach produces interesting illustrations of relationships, tensions, linkages, and dissonance between paradigms. The two dimensional schema seems to be useful for critiquing and defending the problem, questions, methods, and findings of higher education research.

There are a number of limitations in the Burrell and Morgan schema and in the content analysis methodology. It is not possible to translate all of the different paradigm languages (constructivist, neo-Marxist, feminist, etc.) into the two dimensions and eleven sets of assumptions. Rather, the schema is offered as a starting point to help scholars share a common language to explore what it is to have a different paradigm perspective. The context of the case studies in actual research is designed to breathe life into the language of assumptions.

Sometimes, the cases read like caricatures of a perspective. While this is not intended, it is recognized that each paradigm critique could be made more complex. Except for Pascarella et al.'s example of functionalism, the content analysis results show that none of the authors are "pure" in their reflection of only one paradigm. In the case studies, each piece of research is treated as if it were. This undoubtedly holds authors to an idealistic standard with which they might not choose to be identified.

Another limitation of the case study process is its fundamentally dualistic nature. From one paradigm perspective, the other three are always inadequate in one or both dimensions of assumptions. All four cases are written as dualistic, black/ white, right/wrong treatments. Morgan (1983) and Schwandt (1989) label this attitude among scholars as one of supremacy. The cases are seen as "some sort of decisive test to determine which is superior" (Schwandt, 1989, p. 384). One purpose behind writing the four cases is to foster what Morgan (1983) defines as a dialectical attitude, trying to facilitate a multisided diversity of approaches in a sort of "theoretical pluralism." The case study method does not, though, allow the reader to weigh the merit of two opposing paradigm perspectives at the same time.

Morgan describes the problem of "reframing our view of knowledge." Scholars need to:

> find a way of dealing with the possibilities that relativism signifies. In order to find such an approach, it is necessary to reframe our view of knowledge in a way that gets beyond the idea that knowledge is in some sense foundational and can be evaluated in an absolute way, for it is this idea that ultimately leads us to try and banish the uncertainty associated with relativism, rather than simply to deal with it as an inevitable feature of the process through which knowledge is generated (Morgan, 1983, pp. 372–373).

Do arguments for reframing the discussion of multiple paradigms reflect only the interpretive point of view? Functionalists may not believe that the dominance of one paradigm in research is a limitation. Rather, this may be seen as a sign of the field of higher education's maturation and coherence. If scholars decide that something important is to be learned from challenging the dominant paradigm and exploring alternative paradigms, then the dynamic for change may mean moving from dualism to relativism.

There are interesting similarities between the cognitive development literature and the discussions of Morgan (1983), Schwandt (1989), and Lincoln (1989) about scholars' attitudes toward paradigms. Translating Belenkey et al. (1986), Perry (1970, 1981), and Thompson (1991) to attitudes about multiple paradigms, an interesting developmental map may be created which explains possible movement between dualism, multiplicity, relativism, and commitment in regard to a particular research paradigm.

While it is inappropriate here to suggest any empirical basis to this developmental approach to paradigms, it may be useful to explore the similar language of paradigmatic and developmental assumptions. If scholars are to be able to reframe their view of knowledge, then it is necessary to move away from dualism to multiplicity to simple relativism to more advanced stages of paradigm development.

Perry's idea of fostering development by presenting concepts which are one stage above students' current developmental level may be useful for thinking of the debate as an educational process. Rather than confronting other scholars over their lack of sensitivity to oppression or their not having recognized the utility of new axioms of inquiry, it may be more useful to take up the debate with language which is one stage above many listeners' or readers' current level of paradigm development. Dualists would be exposed to multiplistic perspectives, multiplistic scholars would encounter relativists, and relativists would be exposed to scholars who have made a commitment to conducting research in an alternative paradigm.

Such a strategy might use the case studies of this chapter in the following manner: To those dualists who believe that functionalism is the essence of good research, the case studies suggest that there are multiple perspectives on paradigms which are worth paying attention to. It is interesting to note that entirely different findings might result if an alternative problem statement and methodology were used. Multiplistic scholars who are already beginning to explore the language of different paradigms might be struck with the limitations of the case studies as being dependent on the context of theory and methodology. To relativistic scholars who recognize and appreciate the diversity of paradigms, the cases might allow them to explore approaches and make tentative commitments to a paradigm. Scholars who have made a commitment to a research paradigm may find it too limiting, and move back into relativism.

Perry's definitions of ways in which students deflect cognitive development might help scholars in understanding their own and others' problems in adjusting to different attitudes toward paradigms. A possible rephrasing of Perry might be: (1) Temporizing—in which scholars postpone movement away from their traditional paradigm. (2) Escape—where scholars abandon their responsibility to be aware of and debate paradigm issues. On a higher level, the multiplicity and relativism of the debate are exploited in order to avoid commitment. (3) Retreat—in which scholars avoid the complexity and ambiguity of the paradigm debate by retreating to dualism, showing little tolerance for other paradigms.

It is important to recognize and move beyond these possible barriers to paradigm development. The primary purpose of this chapter has been to use case studies to help the reader explore multiple paradigm perspectives. Reviewing this chapter, it is obvious that it meets the definitions of a functionalist approach to paradigms. The chapter is limited by its search for a rational, positivist explanation of what paradigms have to offer scholars in their research.

The use of a hierarchical developmental scheme is inherently functionalist. While Belenkey et al. state specifically that their model of women's development is not intended to be hierarchical, it is easy to fall into using the language of sequences, stages, levels, and positions. Most researchers who offer modifications of Perry retain the same sequence, though others may add or modify some positions. It may be most useful to think of this model of paradigm development as a metaphor. While it brings images and ideas to mind, human nature is much too complex to be discussed in this manner.

It is important that continued dialogue about paradigms be moved to a higher level. Too often, the mode of discussion has been one of confrontation. Feminists such as Glazer (1990) and Townsend (1991) confront scholars with the exclusion of gender in research and the patriarchal nature of the research enterprise. Lincoln (1985, 1989) confronts positivists with the axioms of naturalistic inquiry. This type of scholarship is critical to the evolution of paradigms. As the modified Perry/Belenkey developmental scheme suggests, though, a confrontational posture will not necessarily foster development. Instead, the debate must be taken to a variety of levels and involve learning different paradigm development languages.

Perry's positions seven through nine for commitment in relativism suggest a language for a higher level of discussion about multiple paradigms. How might this level of discussion take place among higher education scholars? In Pascarella and Terenzini's (1991) synthesis of research, *How College Affects Students*, they discuss research on Perry's theory of intellectual and ethical student development. Some striking parallels to attitudes about paradigms may be seen in the authors' description of position nine, commitment. Translating their language to the attitudes about paradigms, the following image of higher education researcher/scholars may be drawn:

Having affirmed their lives and responsibilities as researchers in a pluralistic society, scholars make commitments to specific ideas, ideologies, perspectives, methods, and assumptions. These commitments are seen as "dynamic and changeable." Scholars must believe in their own assumptions, yet be open and willing to learn about alternative approaches. Commitments to the social science or sociological perspective of a specific paradigm point of view are "modifiable, subject to new evidence and understanding about who one is and how the world is. Commitments may be made, but they are not immutable . . ." "This process of construction and reconstruction does not end with college. Indeed, it is a lifelong process'' (Pascarella and Terenzini, 1991, p. 30). Scholars should recognize that they will retrace the paradigm journey over and over, but hopefully ''more wisely.''

As Perry explains, the path of development is ''neither the straight line nor the circle, but a helix, perhaps with an ever expanding radius to show that when we face the 'same' old issues we do so from a different and broader perspective'' (Perry, 1981, p. 97).

REFERENCES

Attinasi, L.C., Jr. (1990). Phenomenological inquiry and higher education research. Paper presented at the Annual Meeting of the Association for the Study of Higher Education, Portland, Oregon, November 2, 1990.

Barrow, C.W. (1991). *Universities and the Capitalist State: Corporate Liberalism and the Reconstruction of American Higher Education, 1892–1928*. Madison: University of Wisconsin Press.

Bateson, G. (1972). *Steps Toward an Ecology of Mind*. New York: Ballantine.

Belenkey, M.F., Clinchy, B.M., Goldberger, N.R., and Tarule, J.M. (1986). *Women's Ways of Knowing: The Development of Self, Voice, and Mind*. New York: Basic Books.

Burrell, G., and Morgan, G. (1979). *Sociological Paradigms and Organisational Analysis*. London: Heinemann Educational Books.

Clark, D.L. (1985). Emerging paradigms in organizational theory and research. In Y.S. Lincoln (ed.), *Organizational Theory and Inquiry: The Paradigm Revolution*. Beverly Hills: Sage Publications.

Conrad, C.F. (1989) Meditations on the ideology of inquiry in higher education: exposition, critique, and conjecture. *Review of Higher Education* 12(3): 199–220.

Gilligan, C. (1982). *In A Different Voice: Psychological Theory and Women's Development*. Cambridge: Harvard University Press.

Glazer, J.S. (1990). Feminism and professionalism: the case of education and business. Paper presented at the Annual Meeting of the Association for the Study of Higher Education, Portland, Oregon, November 1, 1990.

Griffiths, D.E. (1983). Evolution in research and theory: a study of prominent researchers. *Educational Administration Quarterly* 19(3): 201–221.

Kuhn, T.S. (1970) *The Structure of Scientific Revolutions*. Second Edition. Chicago: University of Chicago Press.

Lincoln, Y.S. (1986). A future-oriented comment on the state of the profession. *Review of Higher Education* 10(2): 135–142.

Lincoln, Y.S. (ed.). (1985). *Organizational Theory and Inquiry: The Paradigm Revolution*. Beverly Hills: Sage Publications.

Lincoln, Y.S. (1989). Trouble in the land: the paradigm revolution in the academic disciplines. In J.C. Smart (ed.), *Higher Education: Handbook of Theory and Research in Higher Education*, Vol. V. New York: Agathon Press.

Lincoln, Y.S., and Guba, E.G. (1989). Ethics: the failure of positivist science. *Review of Higher Education* 12(3): 221–240.

Lincoln, Y.S., and Guba, E.G. (1985). *Naturalistic Inquiry*. Beverly Hills: Sage Publications.

Logan, S.W. (1988). A study of four undergraduate computer-writers. *Collegiate Microcomputer* 6(2): 135–146, 176.

Loo, C.M., and Rolison, G. (1986). Alienation of ethnic minority students at a predominantly white university. *Journal of Higher Education* 57(1): 58–77.

Milam, J.H., Jr. (1989). *Paradigms of Theory in Higher Education*. Doctoral Dissertation, University of Virginia. Ann Arbor: University Microfilms International. #9023474.

Milam, J.H., Jr. (1990). Paradigms of theory in higher education. Paper presented at the Annual Meeting of the Association for the Study of Higher Education, Portland, Oregon, November 2, 1990.

Milam, J.H., Jr. (1991). The presence of paradigms in the core higher education journal literature. *Research in Higher Education* 32(6): 651–668.

Morgan, G. (1983). *Beyond Method: Strategies for Social Research*. Beverly Hills: Sage Publications.

Overman, E.S. (1987) Policy physics: exploring the convergence of quantum physics and policy science. *Management Science and Policy Analysis Journal* 4(2): 30–39.

Pascarella, E.T., Ethington, C.A., and Smart, J.C. (1988). The influence of college on humanitarian/civic involvement values. *Journal of Higher Education* 59(4): 412437.

Pascarella, E.T., and Terenzini, P.T. (1991). *How College Affects Students*. San Francisco: Jossey-Bass Publishers.

Perry, W.G. (1970). *Forms of Intellectual and Ethical Development in the College Years: A Scheme*. New York: Holt, Rinehart, and Winston.

Perry, W.G. (1981). Cognitive and ethical growth. In A. Chickering (ed.), *The Modern American College: Responding to the New Realities of Diverse Students and a Changing Society*. San Francisco: Jossey-Bass Publishers.

Schwandt, T.A. (1989). Solutions to the paradigm conflict: coping with uncertainty. *Journal of Contemporary Ethnography* 17(4): 379–407.

Schwartz, P., and Ogilvy, J. (1979). *The Emergent Paradigm: Changing Patterns of Thought and Belief*. Menlo Park, CA: SRI International.

Terenzini, P.T., and Pascarella, E.T. (1991) Twenty years of research on college students: lessons for future research. *Research in Higher Education* 32(1): 83–92.

Thompson, K. (1991). *Learning at Evergreen: An Assessment of Cognitive Development*. Olympia, Washington: Washington Center for Improving the Quality of Undergraduate Education.

Tierney, W.G. (1991). *Official Encouragement, Institutional Discouragement: Minorities in Academe—The Native American Experience*, Norwood, NJ: Ablex. Working Draft.

Townsend, B.K. (1991). The impact of feminist scholarship upon the study of higher education: an analysis of two higher education journals. Paper presented at the Annual Meeting of the Association for the Study of Higher Education, Boston, MA, November 2, 1991.

Bibliometrics: A Method for the Study of the Literature of Higher Education

John M. Budd
Louisiana State University

INTRODUCTION

Research in higher education, as is true of the social sciences generally, has its quantitative side. As a discipline depending on formal communication processes, higher education literature itself can be the target of quantitative analysis. The products of research and scholarship, primarily books and periodicals, exhibit a number of physical characteristics that may illustrate some aspects of social networks of researchers, the trails of influence from researcher to researcher over time, or the interdisciplinary dependence of the field. Given that these aspects are important to the functioning of researchers and their products, study of the transfer of information as evidenced by the documents themselves is a potentially illuminating endeavor.

The formal study of the properties of literatures is usually given the generic name "bibliometrics." This term was first used by Pritchard (1969) to replace the previously used, but less descriptive, "statistical bibliography" (which was used in the title of an essay by Hulme (1923)). As is the case with many methodologies or approaches to research, the history of bibliometrics is not absolutely agreed upon. Broadus (1987) offers a history of the field which mentions some very early instances of the counting of bibliographic units. In general, though, bibliometrics is a twentieth-century phenomenon, so its history, while active, is quite brief. What may be the earliest formal statistical analysis of a literature may be that of Cole and Earles (1917), who examined writings on comparative anatomy from 1550 to 1860. This work was followed by that of Hulme (1923), who analyzed the contents of the *International Catalogue of Scientific Literature*. A subsequent study by Gross and Gross (1927) had the pragmatic aim of attempting to identify which journals a college library should subscribe to based on citations received by the journals.

Work related to the quantitative analysis proceeded almost simultaneously with these early efforts. Lotka (1926), for instance, was interested primarily in the productivity of authors writing in selected scientific fields. Part of his research focused on attempting to derive a predictive algorithm of productivity.

345

Zipf (1932, 1949) looked at word frequency in texts as a measure of statistical regularity within linguistics. One of the most influential of these early bibliometricians has been Bradford (1934, 1948). Bradford's attention centered on phenomena of scatter in literatures—specifically on the declining productivity of groups of journals in the sense of their relevance to or impact on a literature. The work of these three will be discussed in greater detail later.

Narin and Moll suggest that

> The field of bibliometrics has grown in close association with its applications. Many of the early bibliometric papers resulted from an innate curiosity about the functioning of the scientific enterprise. The most basic bibliometric data, a count and elementary categorization of publications by country and field, is still of interest today. (1977, p. 36)

Within the last three to four decades the majority of bibliometric research has dealt with citations within literature and what they can tell investigators about the products and producers of research. This has grown, however, to what is by no means a simplistic approach to literatures and authors. The applications of citation studies have been quite far ranging and have led researchers to sophisticated measures of information transfer and influences. The sophistication of the method had matured to the point that it can be used, as White and McCain (1989, pp. 119–20) point out, to result in

- An ability to map literature intelligibly at different levels of scale;
- Encouraging results of mapping at the "full-text" level where knowledge claims are made;
- An ability to create useful indicators of developments in science and, increasingly, in technology;
- An ability to model dynamic aspects of literatures mathematically, with good-to-excellent fits;
- Increasing relevance to practical information science;
- Growing skill in using computerized databases and statistical software for bibliometric ends; and
- A multinational base of contributors as the relevance of bibliometric indicators to national science and engineering policies is perceived.

Wallace (1987) focused on two particular concepts relevant to bibliometrics: scatter (the dispersion or measures of productivity inherent in literatures) and obsolescence (how materials in a literature age). Wallace emphasizes that "bibliometric studies will find their place as part of the science and sociology of scholarship" (1987, p. 47).

The remainder of this paper will discuss at some length the development of observed regularities (frequently called laws), the use of those regularities in studies of impact and influence, the many applications of citation analysis over the years, the more recent paths taken by bibliometric research, and the importance of bibliometrics as a method for studying higher education.

BIBLIOGRAPHIC UNITS

In order to examine any literature the researcher has to understand what entities comprise the pieces of the literatures. Since the majority of bibliometric studies have focused on the sciences, attention has been paid primarily to journals. There are some obvious properties of journals that can be fodder for bibliometric study: author(s); journal title (which may be viewed as source); date of publication (if time is of interest in a particular study); references; citations; descriptors or index terms; abstract; and text. Most of these properties exist, perhaps in a somewhat altered form, for books as well. For instance, instead of descriptors used for access in a printed index or machine-readable file, books are assigned subject headings for use in library catalogs. There is a distinction made here between references and citations; the distinction can be seen as one of time or direction. An author including works of the past in a paper makes reference to those earlier works. That author's paper may, in turn, receive citations from later works. In terms of any author's paper, reference is made to the past and citations are received from future works. As Price writes:

> It seems to me a great pity to waste a good technical term by using the words *citation* and *reference* interchangeably. I, therefore, propose and adopt the convention that if paper R contains a bibliographic footnote using and describing Paper C, then R contains a *reference* to C, and C has a citation from R. The number of references a paper has is measured by the number of items in its bibliography as endnotes, footnotes, etc., while the number of citations a paper has is found by looking it up in some sort of citation index and seeing how many other papers mention it. (1970, p. 7, emphasis in original)

These measures form a starting point for bibliometrics; early studies were primarily descriptive and involved counting aspects of one or more of the properties. They constituted early steps at analyzing the structures of subject literatures. As basic descriptions began to be accepted and truisms were established (for instance: the journal literature is important to scientists), researchers began asking more complex questions. one such question is: How do materials age in a given literature? One intent in answering this question is to discover the community's reliance on recent works. Many bibliometric studies still look at literatures in the aggregate; that is, they examine large sets of data so as to determine characteristics of information transfer in specific disciplines. Other, more recent, studies look at individual bibliographic units, such as one key or seminal paper, and track the influence of that paper and its content in a field. Variations on approaches, of course, exist, depending on the questions to be answered. Some researchers have attempted to identify the equivalent of social networks by examining the authors of published works.

A key consideration in bibliometric studies, though, is the bibliographic unit and its source. Is the researcher using physical issues of journals for the information regarding the properties of articles? Is the researcher relying on information from various indexing or abstracting tools for the information? Is accuracy assured? At the outset of any study these questions need to be addressed and potential problems of quality control need to be anticipated. in the social sciences (as well as the sciences) conclusions are dependent on the quality of the data. This is no less true for bibliometrics.

CITATIONS

Since this paper is essentially about means of studying communication patterns, a bit of background into such communication is necessary. Cronin, in writing on the topic of the citation process, uses as a "starting point the view that science needs to be looked at as a large social system. If we are to understand how science works, then we have something about the norms and values which guide and constrain the actions of individual scientists" (1984, p. 1). He further offers that "The term science will be used throughout as a convenient shorthand for the formalized and institutionalized process of systematic investigation, knowledge creation and research dissemination, both in relation to the natural ('hard') sciences and the social ('soft') sciences" (1984, p. 1). Cronin's caveat will serve well here in the discussion of the application of bibliometrics to higher education. His concept of "science" as a social system is also important to the study of communication which, after all, is a social act. Part of the recognition of the behavioral norms and values of a discipline includes Ziman's observation that "a scientific paper does not stand alone; it is imbedded in the 'literature' of the subject" (1968, p. 58).

One of the norms related to the literature and a paper's place in it is the process of acknowledging the work of those that have gone before. A reference in a paper is a formal notation of this debt, intellectual or other. Some writers have used analogies to describe citations (references). Smith, for instance, says that "Citations are signposts left behind after information has been utilized and as such provide data by which one may build pictures of user behavior without ever confronting the user himself" (1981, p. 85). Cronin states, "Metaphorically speaking, citations are frozen footprints on the landscape of scholarly achievement; footprints which bear witness to the passage of ideas" (1984, p. 25). Whatever figure of speech is used, the references in a paper indicate, in some way, which of the intellectual, political, or social debts the author is choosing to pay. Several writers have observed that the method of payment (that is, the specific citation practices) may vary from discipline to discipline because of the varying nature of research across fields. This process can be complex, as Ravetz finds,

> . . . since citations must convey some very subtle messages by a very crude device, the etiquette of each field will impose a code for their interpretation, whereby the entries and their possibly brief comments will convey the requisite meanings to those in the field. Each such node will depend on the character of the problem in the field, on the types of mutual dependence, and also on the ruling conception of the right division of intellectual property. In every case it will be a purely informal, perhaps tacit and unselfconscious, craft knowledge shared by members of the field. Thus, in the last resort, this aspect of the system of the protection of property depends like others on an informal etiquette as well as on a formal system of rules. (1971), p. 257)

Any author can attest that there are various reasons for making reference to certain works. The primary determining factor is probably the context of the author's work, as indeed it should be. This is, however, by no means the sole reason for citation behavior. One assumption that can be made is that referring to a particular work creates or designates some sort of relationship between the two documents and, possibly, between the authors of the two documents. The nature of such a relationship is illusive, since the process of citing other works is not an altogether objective one. The subjectivity that can enter into the process prevents the researcher from making categorical determination as to the purpose an author may have for referring to certain works. Sometimes the link between the two is relatively clear, but it is incumbent upon the investigator to resist the temptation to be a citation casuist; that is, it is not likely that a researcher can ascertain the inner workings of the author's mind and know why particular behavior results.

There are some common reasons why authors refer to the works they do, however. Certain functions of the reference process recur with sufficient frequency that they can be identified. Garfield enumerates fifteen common reasons for authors' behavior:

1. Paying homage to pioneers
2. Giving credit for related work
3. Identifying methodology, equipment, etc.
4. Providing background reading
5. Correcting one's own work
6. Correcting the work of others
7. Criticizing previous work
8. Substantiating claims
9. Alerting researchers to forthcoming work
10. Providing leads to poorly disseminated, poorly indexed, or uncited work

11. Authenticating data and classes of fact—physical constants, etc.
12. Identifying original publications in which an idea or concept was discussed
13. Identifying the original publication describing an eponymic concept or term as, e. g., Hodgkin's disease
14. Disclaiming the work or ideas of others (negative claims)
15. Disputing priority claims of others (negative homage). (1965, p. 185)

There is no suggestion or pretense that this constitutes an exhaustive list, but it does provide a starting point for the examination of the role played by the citation process in scholarly communication. Also, the differences that may exist among disciplines with regard to citation behavior generally may be reflected in the reasons exhibited by authors. For example, in a particular discipline it may be relatively common practice to criticize previous work or to dispute claims; in another, the operative behavior may be to ignore such works and, thus, to see to it that they do not continue to be a part of the literature. The nature of the discipline under scrutiny must be understood by the researcher so that the overt behavior is not assigned erroneous cause or purpose.

Just as no one list of reasons for citing can be complete, neither can one always assign a single reason to an author's citing of a particular work. There may well be more than one factor motivating the author to behave in a certain way, as Brooks (1986) has observed. He used a list of seven motives for citing—currency, negative credit, operational information, persuasiveness, positive credit, reader alert, and social consensus—and found that, in a majority of instances, the author's citing behavior is the result of multiple factors. He identified correlated groups of motivating factors; for example, persuasiveness, positive credit, currency, and social consensus tended to be grouped together. Also, reader alert and operational information correlated positively. Negative credit stood alone, perhaps because the kind of "deconstruction" an author may apply to a specific work does not fit well with the other categories. Moravcsik and Murugesan (1975) devised another set of citation types: perfunctory, organic, conceptual, operational, evolutionary, juxtapositional, confirmative, and negational. Cano (1989) employed this list in an investigation and found that perfunctory citations outnumbered others in her study and negational citations trailed the pack. Chubin and Moitra (1975) based their study on the classification by Moravcsik and Murugesan and reached somewhat different conclusions. Based on the typology and application they developed, a smaller percentage of references were determined to be perfunctory. Further, Chubin and Moitra noticed variances in referencing and citation practices based on the form, content, and outlet of the papers examined. Specifically, full-length articles exhibited different patterns from "letters," or brief communications.

When dealing with the examination of citation, researchers frequently default to a set of assumptions, since the true nature of reasons for citing, among other phenomena, is elusive. Smith enumerates some of the more common assumptions underlying the practice of citing:

1. *Citation of a document implies use of that document by the citing author.* This assumption actually has two parts: (1) the author refers to all, or at least to the most important, documents used in the preparation of [one's] work; and (2) all documents listed were indeed used, i. e., the author refers to a document only if that document has contributed to [one's] work.
2. *Citation of a document (author, journal, etc.) reflects the merit (quality, significance, impact) of that document (author, journal, etc.).*
3. *Citations are made to the best possible works.*
4. *A cited document is related in content to the citing document; if two documents are bibliographically coupled, they are related in content; and if two document are co-cited, they are related in content.*
5. *All citations are equal.* (1981, pp. 87–89, emphasis in original)

There may, naturally, be problems with these assumptions as they relate to specific cited works. An author may incorporate a document into published work because of the availability of the document and not incorporate others because of their unavailability. This phenomenon is relevant to the first and third assumptions. The second assumption is borne out by some studies, such as that of Bayer and Folger (1966). More will be said about bibliographic coupling and co-citation later. The fifth assumption is addressed in part by the aforementioned papers dealing with reasons and motives for citing. While the assumptions are problematical, especially when considering one particular cited work, aggregated citations may include many of the factors that are cause for concern and may help to diminish the impact of anomalous phenomena. Of interest, though, for future study of citations is the widespread accessibility of certain items or documents and the correlation of that accessibility and their citation in other documents.

Many of these assumption have been challenged by writers on the topic. Voos and Dagaev (1976), for example, question the equality of citations and the assumption that multiple citations to the same paper are of equal value to single citations. They maintain that multiple mentions of a particular paper may be indicative of a stronger relationship between citing and cited articles than is the case with a single mention. Herlach (1978) agrees, noting, "On the basis of a statistical test, multiple mention of a relevant reference within the same research paper can be taken as an indicator of a close relationship between a given cited paper and the citing papers in which the reference is mentioned more than once" (p. 310). A similar finding was arrived at by Bonzi (1982), whose work indicated a predictive connection between the number of times a paper is cited in a text and the relatedness between cited and citing items. This observation carries two implications for researchers of citing processes. If these authors are correct and one wishes to account for the phenomenon of subsequent citation, how is one to arrive at a weighting algorithm which accurately measures the relative strength of the connectedness of papers? In asking this question I do not mean to imply that it is impossible to arrive at such an algorithm, but its formulation would be problematic. The second implication is that the examination of subsequent citations is likely to have more importance for the study of influence or interrelatedness of small sets of papers; studies of literatures in the aggregate may not be affected by the larger scale. While both Herlach and Voos and Dagaev focused on scientific literature, Budd (1986) found, in a large-scale study of American literature, that the rank order of most frequently cited journal titles does not change when subsequent citations are accounted for. More study is needed in other literatures to determine if there are influences exerted by subsequent citation in particular disciplines.

Of greater interest to researchers may be errors in citations. Goodrich and Roland (1977) examined citations in ten U. S. medical journals in 1975 and found 634, 29 percent of the total, to be erroneous. Key and Roland (1977) looked at one major medical journal and found errors in 54 percent, 1,005, of the citations. Boyce and Banning (1979) examined all 1976 issues of the *Journal of the American Society for Information Science* and *Personnel and Guidance Journal* and found errors in 13.6 percent of the citations in the former title and 10.7 percent of the citations in the latter. They found that the most common error in both journals was wrong entry; that is, incorrect volume numbers, years, and pages. The problems errors signify for retrieval of cited papers are obvious; what they mean for citation studies is less clear. It cannot be determined if the errors might affect the results of research; no studies exist that both search for errors and examine the characteristics of cited works. Of concern also is a finding by Boyce and Banning that 23 percent of the citations in the *Journal of the American Society for Information Science* and 18.5 percent of those in *Personnel and Guidance Journal* could not be verified. It is not determined if the difficulty stems from the obscurity or lack of availability of the work cited, or errors which make retrieval impossible.

One question that arises is whether incorrect citation is a product of unintentional human error or some purposeful act. This is addressed by Broadus (1983), who traced one erroneous citation throughout the literature. In his book *Sociobiology*, Edward O. Wilson cites a paper by W. D. Hamilton, entitled "The Genetical Evolution of Social Behaviour." Wilson, however, refers to it as "The Genetical Theory of Social Behaviour." Of the 180 papers that cited both Wilson's book and Hamilton's paper (at the time of Broadus' study), 34 carry the erroneous word "theory." Broadus does not conclude that there is evidence of a breach of ethics, but does note that "Even if 4–8 percent of authors engage in this kind of [plagiarism of citations], that presents an important problem for scholars performing certain kinds of citation studies'' (p. 135). Sweetland (1989) maintained that at least some of the responsibility for error and their correction rests with the publishing process itself and that editors and referees need to be more attentive to citations as communication mechanisms.

Another assumption—that authors cite the most important documents and cite *only* important documents—has been frequently refuted with anecdotal evidence. It is a difficult assumption to test; a researcher would have to be able to identify the universe of relevant documents and then determine if these and only these are cited. It is an impossible task. Some may argue that at least a few of the papers cited are included for political reasons, such as citing the works of potential referees of the author's paper. Others may argue that some papers are intentionally or unintentionally omitted. One study, by Soper (1976), seeks to make some determinations regarding this aspect of citing practice. In her study of scholars she found that approximately three-quarters of the citations included in works by scientists and social scientists are to works they own and have access to in their offices. Another paper, by Prabha (1983), focuses on faculty in business administration at one institution and found that 57 percent of cited items were owned by the authors. Prabha's conclusions include:

> (1) the fact that less than one-third of the sources cited were considered essential raw material by those who cite them; (2) if an item is of critical importance, it is likely to be owned by the author; and (3) if a source is of critical importance it is likely to have been consulted specifically in the preparation of the citing article, but "criticality" is no guarantee that it has been used heavily by the author (p. 205).

If such findings were verified it would have important implications for the entirety of transfer of information. On the one hand, it may indicate that many scholars do a good job of collecting essential information themselves, through subscription, purchase, or a very effective invisible college. On the negative side, it could indicate a false reliance on ineffective means of information gathering. With Prabha's findings, for instance, the subjectivity of "critical importance," as determined by the authors, must be noted. Further study in this area could be illuminating.

Examples of Citation Studies

Citation analyses are quite common in virtually all disciplines. Many of these are designed to describe the characteristics of the literature of a certain field; the implication is that such a description will add to the knowledge of how scholars and researchers communicate. Some very early studies are noted above. Subsequent studies frequently focused on specific literatures. Fussler (1949 and 1949), for instance, looked at chemistry and physics in order to identify reliance on certain formats (journals form an overwhelming majority of cited items), age of cited documents (most citations are to the most recent ten years of material), and other characteristics. Broadus (1967), Lin and Nelson (1969), and Baughman (1974) conducted similar studies of the literature of sociology. Garfield (1984) examined anthropology journals to determine which are the most frequently cited, and which journals are citing them. This effort to identify the core journals in a field dates back to some of the earliest citation studies. The purpose of this kind of study is usually to derive a set of journals essential to scholars in the field, to suggest a set of journals to which libraries should subscribe, or to compare this objective means of ranking journals with other, subjective, ratings. Examples of these kinds of analyses include the study by White and White (1977) of psychology literature and the analysis of Walberg, Vukosavich, and Tsai (1981) of educational research journals. Other applications of citation analysis include studying the interrelationships among journals in a given discipline. Summers (1984) looked at the journal literature of reading research to determine not only core journals, but also how these highly cited journals are related to one another and to other journals in cognate areas with which they share citation patterns. The concept of interrelatedness is further developed by the work of Rice, Borgman, and Reeves (1988). They employed network analysis to examine clustering patterns and discover sub-field distinctions between interpersonal and mass media communication and a fairly high level of inbreeding (that is, within group citing) for each sub-field.

Other forms of social networking form the focus of citation studies of some literature. So (1988) builds on previous work in the field of communication and establishes linkages among several social science disciplines. A different means of analysis was employed by Neeley (1981), who studied cross-citation patterns (the citing of the literature of one field by the literature of another) of management and social science literatures. He found a statistically significant measure of interdisciplinarity by the management literature with regard to the social science literature; that is, management literature borrows from other disciplines in the social sciences as well as using its own literature. Thyer and Bentley (1986) looked at the institutional affiliations of cited authors in social work to determine which universities' faculties contribute most to the literature. Budd (1991) examined citations in the field of academic librarianship and was able to list the most frequently cited authors.

The citation structure itself has provided fodder for study by some researchers. Some, noted above, have examined authorial intent for citing. Peritz (1983), for example, devised a classification system for citations based on the following categories: setting the stage for the present study; background information; methodological; comparative; argumentative; speculative; hypothetical; documentary; historical; and casual. She applied this system to the literatures of sociology, education, demography, epidemiology, and librarianship. Others, such as Frost (1979), have incorporated what is essentially content analysis into the study of citations. Frost looked at citations in the context of the citing documents in the area of German literature to arrive at a classification scheme for citations. She writes:

> The scheme outlined organizes the citation usages into related groups. Three considerations govern the establishment of these groups: (1) whether a cited work is used as a primary or secondary source; (2) whether the work is used as a basis for a statement of fact or of opinion; and (3) where we are dealing with secondary works, whether the disposition of cited work was positive or negative (Does the citing author agree or disagree with his source?)'' (p. 405).

She found that the majority of the citations to both monographs and journals were for the purpose of establishing the current state of research and opinion, establishing supportive factual evidence, or providing further reading. Frost's classification was modified by Budd (1986) in his study of American literature. The finding of this study were consistent with those of Frost; only a total of 5.1 percent of the citations represent authorial approval or disapproval of cited works.

A variation of this classification scheme has been devised by Peritz (1983). Her research focused on the disciplines of sociology, education, demography, epidemiology, and librarianship. Her purpose, as was Frost's, was to objectify the process of identifying citation function. The eight categories used were: setting the stage for the present study; background information; methodological; comparative; argumental, speculative, hypothetical; documentary; historical; and casual. In all disciplines, ''setting the stage'' was the most frequently occurring category. The percentage of citations so classified ranged from 33.4 percent in epidemiology to 49.5 percent in demography. Other citations were dispersed among the other categories (and not consistently dispersed across the disciplines).

Citation Studies in Education and Higher Education
The above studies are noted to provide an indication of the range of purpose and application citation analysis may have. Researchers interested in describing characteristics of literatures or examining communication networks within or among disciplines may use these studies as examples of uses of the methodology to a variety of research questions. Scholars and researchers in the field of education in general and of higher education in particular have not been loath to incorporate citation analysis into their own study of the field's literature. Smart and Elton (1981) looked at citation patterns of education and found that the core of education literature is easily identified by the fact that nearly half of all citations to articles in education journals are received by articles in only ten journals. They also found that five structural factors—number of articles published, self-citation rate, reference ratio, immediacy factor, and Price index—account for nearly two-thirds of the variability of citation frequency. Smart (1983a, 1983b) built on

this research and determined that these characteristics tend to be highly stable over time. Smart also examined the relationship between perceived quality of journals and rankings by citation rate and found a weak positive correlation between the two, possibly because of the existence of important review or news-oriented titles in the field, which may be infrequently cited.

The definition of a core journal literature was attempted by Bayer (1983), who employed three strategies, including citation analysis. He found little agreement among the three, due in part to the variety of emphasis each of the strategies places on the construction of the journal literature. Silverman has also examined the literature of higher education. In one paper (Silverman, 1982) he attempted to establish a framework of manuscripts in the field, resulting in a matrix based on the focus of the manuscript (semantic, syntactical, cultural, or expressive) and method (analytical science, conceptual theory, conceptual humanism, or particular humanism). In a later paper (Silverman, 1985) he examined citation patterns relevant to this matrix of sixteen attributes. One conclusion is that the literature of higher education is too diverse and complex for a single model to fit the entirety of the literature. He mentions that the following factors need to be considered when assessing the specifics of the literature: ". . . the purposes of the journal; their interpretation of the relevance and construction of article types; the state of the field as relating to contemporary topics, methodologies, and substantive bases that themselves are in some stages of development; and the authors' intents" (pp. 174, 181). A recent article by Budd (1990) examined a variety of citation characteristics in the literature of higher education and compared them with those of other disciplines. The interdisciplinarity of the field is noted, as is the consistency with the social sciences generally.

Citation Analysis: Criticisms and Problems

Assuming that the authors of papers cite other papers correctly—that the kinds of errors noted above are minimal and minor (which, admittedly, is not necessarily a safe assumption)—there are still some difficulties associated with citation studies. Some of these have to do with the mechanics of doing the study itself. Cole and Cole (1971) and Smith (1981) discuss a number of characteristics of publishing and citing and what they portend for citation analysis. For instance, many papers have multiple authors; this phenomenon makes attributing authorship credit more difficult. Did all listed authors do equal work and, if not, is there any way to give weighted credit? Multiple authorship is also a problem when secondary sources list only first authors. Self-citations present a dilemma for researchers; the implications of an author citing himself or herself, a coauthor citing a coauthor's work, or even journal self-citation may be difficult to assess. When using secondary sources, such as indexes, homographs and synonyms obstruct the accurate identification of authors, especially when initials are used. Citation analysis is almost always focused on explicit citations—those appearing in reference lists or notes. In some disciplines, usually in the humanities, implicit citation—note taken of a work in the text—is not uncommon. The researcher should be aware that the text itself may be a source of citations. Patterns of citation, even within a fairly narrow discipline, may fluctuate over time; studies should take this into account when establishing a time-frame for the analysis. Of course, citation rates and patterns vary by field; it is important not to impose the structure of one discipline onto another as a means of evaluation.

MacRoberts and MacRoberts (1989) enumerate problems they see with citation analysis:

1. Formal influences not cited.
2. Biased citing.
3. Informal influences not cited.
4. Self-citing.
5. Different types of citations.
6. Variations in citation rate related to type of publication, nationality, time period, and size and type of specialty.
7. Technical limitations of citation indices and bibliographies.
   a. Multiple authorship.
   b. Synonyms.
   c. Homonyms.
   d. Clerical errors.
   e. Coverage of literature (p. 343).

There is considerable overlap in these lists; several of the problems are perceived by more than one writer. The difficulties are sufficiently serious that their potential effects should be noted.

Lawani (1983) elaborates on the forms which self-citation may take. First, he divides self-citation into two genera: synchronous (those self-citations contained in the citations, or references, that the author gives) and diachronous (those included in the citations the author receives). Each genus then includes four species:

Species I is a self-citation in which the first-named author of the citing paper is also the first-named author of the cited paper. This may be called the classic author self-citation and it is probably the only type which most investigators consider.
Species II self-citation is one in which any of the coauthors of the citing paper is the first-named author of the cited paper.
Species III is a self-citation in which the first-named author of the citing paper is a coauthor of the cited paper. It is possible, however, to have a self-citation in which a coauthor of the citing paper is the first-named author of the cited paper (Species II) and the first-named author of the same citing paper is a coauthor of the same cited paper. To ensure mutually exclusive classes, the author recommends and adopts the conven-

tion that only self-citations in which the first- named author of a citing paper is a coauthor of the cited paper, but where the first-named author of the cited paper is not a coauthor of the citing paper will be described as Species III self-citation.

Species IV self-citation is one in which a coauthor of the citing paper is also a coauthor of the cited paper. Note that the conditions for Species I and IV, and Species II, III, and IV may hold concurrently. Therefore, again adopt the convention that a self-citation will belong to Species IV if and only if it is not Species I, II, or III (p. 283).

Lawani's scheme also includes the problem of multiple authorship. The underlying dilemma of self-citation is the researcher's ignorance of citer motivation. It may be that an author, or team of authors, has done ground-breaking work and must cite themselves in order to develop the established research track. On the negative side, vanity may be the prime motivation. A researcher might ask authors about motivation, but should be aware of the possible dichotomy between rhetoric and action. Budd's (1990) citation study of higher education shows that lists of most frequently cited authors change when self-citation is controlled for.

The problem with homonyms and synonyms is, in part, due to some indexing sources. Moed and Vriens (1989) point out some of the inconsistencies in such products as the Science Citation Index and the Social Sciences Citation Index. In practical terms this means that the researcher must be aware that variant spellings of cited authors' names frequently occur and that transcription error may affect the indexed volume or page numbers. The difficulty, especially of homonyms, in the cited works themselves stems from the practice in many disciplines of using an author's initials rather than names. Biglan (1973a and 1973b) associates the use of initials with the "hardness" of disciplines and, in some circles, such "hardness" is deemed a desirable quality. The "hardness" or "softness" of disciplines is an example of imposing the behavior patterns of one group upon another. Differences, such as those illustrated by citation characteristics, may point to uniqueness by disciplines and, thus, may be directly comparable. This does mean that it is frequently difficult to distinguish among people with commonly occurring surnames, such as Smith or Johnson.

Another aspect of citation analysis to be aware of is the fluctuations of citation rates over time. Price (1976) examined scientific literature in the light of various bibliometric and citation models and found a cumulative advantage process at work; that is, a pattern of success breeding success. Scientific literature has tended to grow at a rate of about 7 percent per year, which results in a doubling in size every 14 years. Price maintained that citation practices, in the aggregate, tend to mirror this growth and this growth rate formed an essential component of his computational approach to citation growth. In effect, he argued, as Feidler and Hurt (1986) note, "that, beyond the 'first pulse' of citations, the citation rate will grow at the same rate as the literature" (p. 246). Price's formula is expressed as $n = n_0 e^{kt}$, where t is the time from the first pulse of n_0 citations and k is a constant which equals 0.07 (the rate of overall literature growth). Feidler and Hurt (1986) and Budd (1989) showed that this formulation is not applicable to specific instances in literatures, such as the impact of individual papers. Growth is a more complex function for influential papers. Moreover, with such specific instances, growth is by no means linear, but is in some way curvilinear. Kuhn (1970) offered a verbal construction of a complex fluctuating pattern in his classic work on scientific revolutions. Budd and Hurt (1991) looked at one specific sub-field of physics in this context, but found that actual citation data departed obviously from Price's model and did not fit Kuhn's, although the fit, as graphically represented, is closer to Kuhn's. The complexities of fluctuation have yet to be fully described, much less predicted.

Along with difficulties in determining citer motivation goes bias in citation. Bias can be bi-directional; authors may avoid citing some individuals for personal or political reasons or may choose to cite others for the same reasons. One instance of potential bias was described by Merton (1967) as the "Matthew Effect," the phenomenon of attributing credit, sometimes in the form of citations, to a person based on the totality of that person's contributions to the field and the recognition of that person as an influential author. The relevance of a particular cited work to the citing paper may be marginal. A specific example of potential bias, or at least the omission of crediting an author for cited work, occurs in the literature of citation analysis. Weinstock (1971), in writing about citation indexing, listed the fifteen reasons individuals may have for citing, as formulated by Garfield (1965) and noted above. Weinstock, however, did not cite Garfield. Some subsequent authors, such as Martyn (1975), have attributed the list to Weinstock. A researcher following the literature may or may not discover the anomaly; the discovery may well depend on serendipity.

Bibliographic Coupling and Co-Citation Analysis
These two concepts are related to an assumption by Smith, stated above, dealing with the interconnectedness of documents. Bibliographic coupling, as a notion, appeared in a paper by Fano (1956) about three-and-a-half decades ago. Though he did not use that term, he wrote of frequencies of association among documents. Kessler (1963) then articulated the idea of bibliographic coupling in a way that could have some operational use. He stated that papers

> . . . bear a meaningful relation to each other (they are coupled) when they have one or more references in common. We define a unit of coupling: Two papers that share one reference contain one unit of coupling. A coupling criterion is defined by the combination of coupling units between two or more papers (p. 49).

The assumption underlying bibliographic coupling is that the sharing of references implies a sharing of content as well, although this certainly need not be true. Martyn (1964) wrote that bibliographic coupling is "merely an indication of the existence of probability, value unknown, of relation between two documents" (p. 236). If two papers have one reference in common, they may well incorporate different bits of information from the common reference. If, on the other hand, two papers share ten references in common, and those ten common references constitute half of all references in each paper, the likelihood of a content relationship is greater. Probability would be very difficult to calculate with any precision, however. Few studies based on bibliographic coupling exist.

Co-citation is similar in principle to bibliographic coupling, but it approaches the matter from a slightly different angle. The determination of co-citation frequency also seeks to measure the relatedness of documents. Small (1973) writes:

> Unlike bibliographic coupling which links source documents, co-citation links cited documents and is, therefore analogous to a measure of descriptor or word association. . . . The number of identical citing items defines the strength of co-citation between the two cited papers. An identical citing item is simply a new document which has cited both earlier papers; therefore, co-citation is the frequency with which two items of earlier literature are cited together by the later literature (p. 265).

The germ of the idea for co-citation analysis lies in a paper by Price (1965), who proposed that each group of papers published in any given year is

> . . . "knitted" to a small, select part of the existing scientific literature but connected rather weakly and randomly to a much greater part. Since only a small part of the earlier literature is knitted together by the new year's crop of papers, we may look upon this small part as a sort of growing tip or epidermal layer, an active research front. (p. 59)

The purposes of co-citation vary with the researcher, but, as Bellardo (1980) observes, the primary thrust of most co-citation analyses is the study of the sociology or history of science, and especially the structure of scientific specializations. One assumption underlying this use of co-citation analysis is that the changes in citation patterns reflect alterations in the social structure of the area of specialization and, possibly, the cognitive structure as well. In this sense, the study of co-citation patterns may be used to determine the extent of use of an invisible college in a given sub-field (Noma, 1984). Existing citation indices are most frequently used to generate co-cited works. As search techniques and protocols for online or other means of retrieval, the construction of a data set becomes easier and (relatively) less expensive, plus there is the potential for the study of interdisciplinary influences.

Co-citation as an indication of the social structure of a discipline (as evidenced through formal communication patterns) is shown in the mapping of the invisible college. Mapping cognitive structures is problematic; White and McCain (1989) observed the examination of citation contexts—how the cited material is used in the citing document—to move towards analysis of the cognitive structures of formal communication. Small (1980) has inferred a logical system in the practice of co-citation, which has led him to describe specific types of content links:

> A is contained in B; A and B differ in their relation to C; A undergoes or is subject to B; and A is used to perform B. Other types of links we might expect to find are: A causes B; A follows from B; and A agrees with B. These links, particularly the deductive type (A follows from B), would be especially interesting in view of their implications for the philosophy of science. It would suggest that a co-citation network may consist of deductive chains, and the structure of network itself might indicate the completeness of that deductive system (pp. 191–92).

From this typology, Small maintained that co-citation analysis would help researchers identify paradigms in individual disciplines and sub-disciplines. He then made the lofty claim that "Bibliometrics could truly become a branch of epistemology" (p. 194). Others, such as De Mey (1982), are somewhat skeptical of the elaborate claims made by Small. De Mey stressed that such examination of the communication process must focus on past knowledge as embodied in the media of communication, such as books and journals. He cautioned that co-citation analysis is best fitted for the detection of specialties and is inadequate for the identification of paradigms. This skepticism may seem to deflate the utility of co-citation, but, as a means for exploring paths of knowledge, co-citation analysis is still in its early stages; considerable work remains to establish its ultimate utility. Some of the work has been extended by Small (1986) in an innovative study involving the synthesis of research reviews in one scientific sub-field.

One direction that co-citation analysis has taken in recent years has been to focus on authors as well as documents. Rather than an emphasis on specific documents, as described above, this research track seeks to establish links between and among authors. For instance, in the information science field if people cite any of the works of Derek Price and Henry Small, there is a link between these two individuals. (Actually, it should be noted that, with author co-citation, "author" is taken to signify the body of work produced by an individual.) As with other types of co-citation analysis, the strength of the link is determined by the frequency of author co-citation. White (1990) pointed out advantages of this kind of study, some of which are noted here:

- Authors (oeuvres) are a viable unit of analysis standing between the better-known units in citation and co-citation studies—articles on the one hand and journals on the other.
- Co-cited author searching—whether of single pairs of authors or of groups of pairs—is an effective technique for subject retrieval when carefully used. It usually retrieves "hits" not findable through conventional subject searches.
- Clustered authors on author maps have high potential for fruitful retrievals when systematically paired.

- Author maps reveal the "cognitive" or "intellectual" structure of a field by showing the consensus of citers as to important contributors and works.
- Author maps show who is central and who is peripheral to a field.
- The maps show who is central and who is peripheral within clusters representing specialties or schools of thought (p. 103).

Author co-citation analysis is sometimes accompanied by factor analysis, which permits examination of more than one area of specialization at a time and may indicate multidisciplinary clustering. These tools are used to produce intellectual maps of a research community, as McCain (1986 and 1990) did in her studies of the literature of genetics. Rogers and Cottrill (1990) employed the method to illustrate how two areas which share a common interest have divergent communication patterns.

As is true of many research methodologies, co-citation analysis has its detractors. The most vocal and articulate has been Edge (1977). He took issue with claims of objectivity and maintained that citation data are simply among the range of empirical data available to the researcher. He also disputed notions of inherent interrelatedness evidenced from co-citation and stated that co-citation studies, in focusing on aggregate data, lose sight of particularities in the quest for a model of the structure of science. Further, he rejected any idea that the method could establish boundaries of specializations since these are apt to be transient, and stressed the need to take into account informal, as well as formal, communication mechanisms. Mulkay 1991) also criticized the method generally because

> . . . the claimed correspondence between scientists' actions and the patterns of citations is not itself demonstrated, but is established solely by means of an analyst's fiat. . . . Citation analysis appears to deal with scientists's actions only because the analysts involved have consistently hidden away their speculative interpretations behind methodological fiats (pp. 16, 17).

Co-citation analysis, however, is not a simplistic endeavor and some of these criticisms ignore efforts to incorporate content and context into the analysis.

OTHER BIBLIOMETRIC PHENOMENA

While citation analysis, in one form or another, is the most common application of bibliometrics to the study of literatures, it is, by no means, the sole method of seeking bibliographic regularity. Before bibliometrics as a term existed, individuals were observing certain phenomena exhibited by literatures or their producers. Early efforts focused on specific aspects of the literature and sought to uncover an underlying mathematical regularity which, it has been hoped, would have not only descriptive, but predictive, significance. While these efforts have been labeled "laws," this is something of a misnomer, since the formulations have far from universal applicability. Even though the existing laws, which are empirically based, are imperfect formulations, they do describe some very basic and important characteristics of literatures. The articulation of regularities that will be discussed in turn are: Bradford's Law, Lotka's Law, and Zipf's Law.

Bradford (1934 and 1950) paid special attention to scatter when he turned his attention to scientific journal literature. His law is based on the premise that

> the use of any collection of items is generally not distributed evenly among those items; that is, some items may be used fairly heavily, others may receive moderate use, and some may hardly be used at all (p. 43).

In articulating his ideas and observations dealing with scatter he derived both verbal and graphical representations of his model. The verbal formulation, which was theoretical rather than empirical, stated:

> If scientific journals are arranged in order of decreasing productivity of articles on a given subject, they may be divided into a nucleus of periodicals more particularly devoted to the subject, and several groups or zones containing the same number of articles as the nucleus, where the number of periodicals in the nucleus and succeeding zones will be 1: a: a^2 (p. 116).

This is to say that the zones will increase in size according to an algorithm that is in part arithmetic and in part geometric. The verbal expression has been reinterpreted in mathematical terms by several writers, such as Vickery (1948), Leimkuhler (1967), and Brookes (1968 and 1969). These interpretations are not identical; in the process of translating Bradford's words into mathematical expressions different derivations of the relevant variables and their relationships have arisen.

To complicate matters further, Bradford's own graphical representation of scatter does not agree with his verbal formulation. There are mathematical irregularities between the two. Maia and Maia (1984) claimed that the discrepancy does not result in ambiguity, but their mathematical derivation is seriously flawed, largely because they redefine certain variables so as to produce a tautology that will, naturally but falsely, be equivalent. Wilkinson (1972) has simplified the equations for comparative purposes so that data for only two variables, the number of journals and the cumulative number of papers (or citations), need be known. In applying her equations Wilkinson notes that

> the graphical formulation more closely describes the practical situation, or at least describes it equally well. There would be advantages, also, in applying Bradford's law as manifested by the graphical formulation. There is a simple mathematical equation; a minimum of observed data is necessary to estimate the total numbers of journals and papers; the nucleus is definable (p. 128).

Cline (1981) modified Wilkinson's equations in her study of the literature of library science. She wrote that her formulation

> . . . utilized simple formulas for calculating N (the estimated total number of papers containing articles relevant to the subject of the search) and R(N) (the estimated total number of papers produced by N). Only p (number of journals) and S (the corresponding cumulative number of papers) had to be known in order to apply the formulas. Both p and S were obtained from a plot of the empirical data on semilog paper. Although the value of p could be chosen anywhere in the linear portion of the curve, the point at which the initial concave portion of the curve turned into the linear region ($n = n_m$) was arbitrarily chosen to equal to p and was used in determining the corresponding value of S. By identifying on the plot 2S papers, the corresponding number of journals required to supply 2S, called q, was ascertained. The values obtained for S, p, and q were then used to calculate N and R(N) for both the verbal and graphical expressions of Bradford's law (p. 56).

Cline's equations are as follows:

Verbal Formulation

$$N = \frac{S}{\log \alpha} - \frac{p}{\alpha - 1}$$

$$\text{where } \alpha = \frac{q - p}{p}$$

$$R(N) = \frac{S}{\log \alpha} \times \log \frac{S}{\log \alpha} \times \frac{(\alpha - 1)}{p}$$

Graphical Formulation

$$N = \frac{S}{\log \beta}$$

$$\text{where } \beta = \frac{q}{p}$$

$$R(N) = \frac{S}{\log \beta} \times \log \frac{S}{\log \beta} \times \frac{\beta}{p}$$

Budd (1988) employed Cline's equations and found that, for the literature of higher education, the graphical representation of Bradford's Law provides a closer approximation to observed data than does the verbal representation.

While Wilkinson's formulations illustrate the quantitative differences of the verbal and graphical representations of Bradford's Law, neither representation provides an actual model of empirical observation or of theoretical predictability.

Bradford's Law is quite limited due to its sensitivity to such factors as sample size, area of specialization, and time. Pratt (1977) derived a formulation purporting to measure the degree of concentration of the literature of a particular field, but the measure is largely dependent on sample size. Drott (1981) used the studies by Lawani (1972 and 1973) of the literature of tropical agriculture (using two different samples) and concluded that Pratt's measure would demonstrate,paradoxically, that tropical agriculture is more concentrated than tropical agriculture. Ignorance or avoidance of the sensitivity of Bradford's Law to these conditions have led to some false "application" of the Law. Drott maintained that

> Between theory and empiricism lies a gap. This gap is the fact that at present, the intellectual richness of real situations is not represented in the mathematical austerity of the theoretical equations. It remains to be seen if this gap can be bridged by further research. . . . On one hand, [Bradford's Law] is easy to observe in real situations and can be represented with a fairly simple mathematical formula. On the other hand, Bradford-type data resist statistical testing, and the model fails to reveal the underlying process which "causes" the distribution. In any case, the wise reader will examine any study of Bradford's law closely before rushing to believe more than is actually stated and supported (p. 51).

Lotka (1926) was more interested in the producers of literatures and so paid attention to author productivity. The statement that has come to be known as his Law asserted that "the number (of authors) making n contributions is about $1/n^2$ of those making one; and the proportion of all contributors, that make a single contribution, is about 60 per cent" (p. 323). This means that approximately one-fourth of the authors contributing one paper to a subject literature will make two contributions. (This same proportion can apply to cited works in a literature and the relative frequency of cited authors.) Lotka's Law included the computation of the percentage of the total number of contributors making n contributions. This computational formula is as follows: $f = 600/\pi^2 n^2$. Lotka examined a set of authors from the 1907–16 *Decennial Index to Chemical Abstracts* and a set from Auerbach's *Geschichtstafeln der Physik* and found, when the equation was applied, an empirical approximation of his stated law. Potter (1981) reviewed the literature on Lotka's Law and quoted writers who affirmed the empirical consistency with the theoretical law. Some stated the following:

> It (Lotka's law) has been shown to hold for the productivity patterns of chemists, physicists, mathematicians, and econometricians (Krisciunas, 1977, p. 65). Lotka's "inverse square law" of scientific productivity has since been shown to fit data drawn from several widely varying time periods and disciplines (Allison and Stewart, 1974, p. 596).

Lotka's Law, unlike Bradford's, can be subjected to some statistical analysis. Coile (1977) examined studies applying Lotka's Law to several disciplines and found some misinterpretations of the Law, for instance in Schorr's (1975) study of map librarianship. One common departure from Lotka in subsequent research is the inclusion of co-authors in the examination of productivity. This does not mean that co-authors should not be studied in terms of productivity, but Lotka's formulation was based on principal authors only. Lotka's law is somewhat sensitive to sample size and Coile demonstrated that the Kolmogorov-Smirnov (K-S) goodness-of-fit test is the most powerful and most appropriate to determine the conformity of observed data with Lotka's prediction. As Potter (1981) stated:

> The K-S test determined the maximum deviation, D:
> $$D = \text{Max} \ |F_o \ (X - S_n \ (X))|$$
> where $F_o(X)$ is the theoretical cumulative frequency function and $S_n(X)$ is the observed cumulative frequency function of a sample of n observation. At a 0.01 level of significance, the K-S statistic is equal to $1.63/n^2$. If D is greater than the K-S statistic, then the sample distribution does not fit the theoretical distribution. (pp. 22–23)

When Coile applied the K-S test to Lotka's own data he found that, while the predicted model fit the physics literature, it did not fit the chemistry literature.

Pao (1986) examined many studies applying Lotka's Law to discover which of them exhibited a statistically significant conformity with the Law. She restated the Law as an inverse exponential function, $x^n \cdot y = c$, where n—the regression line—and c—a constant— must be calculated from the observed data. The regression line can be derived using a standard linear regression equation and r^2, the coefficient of determination, can be computed to determine the proportion of variation in y that can be explained by the regression formula. Pao then offered a formula to compute c, which employs the calculated value of n, which she derived in an earlier paper (Pao, 1985). In her conclusion she wrote:

> Over 80 percent of the data sets conformed to Lotka's law. From the empirical evidence, it is recommended that data should be compiled from a comprehensive source to capture a true representation of the target population. Either quality or quantity may be used as selection criteria. If only a single major primary journal is used to collect data, a longer period of coverage is advised. (p. 32)

The third of the bibliometric laws discussed here is that attributed to Zipf. The principle of his law was articulated in a book entitled *The Psycho-Biology of Language* (Zipf, 1935) and applied in *Human Behavior and the Principle of Least Effort* (Zipf, 1949). As Ikpaahindi said, "His principle suggests that people find it easier to choose and use familiar words, rather than unfamiliar words and that the probabilities of occurrence of familiar words are therefore higher than those of unfamiliar ones" (p. 171). Zipf used the text of Joyce's *Ulysses* and calculated the frequency of occurrence of the 29,899 unique words used in the novel. He then formulated the relationship of rank and frequency as rf = c, where r is the rank of a word, f is the frequency of occurrence, and c is a constant. When graphically represented the Law usually takes the following form: $\log r + \log f = \log c$. Zipf assumed that the "true" slope of a curve on which the data would be plotted is -1. Wyllys (1981) maintained that Zipf's Law, as do those of Bradford and Lotka, could be expected to follow a Poisson-like distribution since it basically follows a stochastic process formulated on the occurrence of events whose individual probabilities are usually small. He further notes that such a basis was observed a number of years ago by Simon (1955).

The stochastic models that are evident in the bibliometric laws are not limited to communication and language. As Bookstein (1979) pointed out, similar regularities have been observed of other phenomena, such as income distribution in society (Pareto, 1897) and island size in an archipelago (Mandelbrot, 1963). In light of the recognition of the similarities of these processes, some writers have sought some sort of unity in bibliometric measures. One such effort was that of Brookes (1968), who looked at the relationship of Bradford and Zipf distributions. Egghe (1985) focused on the implications of Lotka's Law for Bradford's Law. Egghe (1987) also examined the concept of class concentration of literatures as set forth by Pratt (1977) and the implication of concentration for the laws of Zipf, Lotka, and Mandelbrot. In a broader study, Tague (1990) looked at size and rank as means of studying and modeling bibliometric phenomena and found that such approaches can be useful in designing information storage and retrieval systems. One of the most ambitious efforts was that of Price (1976) who tried to use existing laws as a groundwork for the formulation of a central, uniform theory on which to base the modeling of information processes. While the model has some application to literatures in the aggregate, it has little to say about the specifics of a literature, especially a literature that breaks the pattern of "normal science."

USES OF BIBLIOMETRIC STUDIES

The above discussion briefly summarizes the methodology (or methodologies) of bibliometrics as a means of investigating formal communication mechanisms and patterns. It is evident from the works cited that bibliometrics holds some intellectual appeal as a way to look at some tangible evidence of information transfer. A question that remains is: To what uses are these studies put? In other words, what are the applications of the methodology; what are some of the questions asked (beyond identification of the basic structure of literatures as evidenced by bibliometric properties)? Once some of the characteristics of a literature had been identified the curiosity of the research community began to move forward. Most investigations have used bibliometrics to examine communication between and among disciplines. Some of these have already been discussed; others, with particular purposes, will be noted.

More than two decades ago Price (1970) used citation data to create a matrix of literatures based on characteristics of formal communication patterns. He placed journals on a grid which included an archival-research front axis and a review-ex cathedra axis. The former axis was based on recency of citations and the latter on number of citations. Using this matrix he identified a value called Price's Index for a number of journals in many different fields. The "hard" disciplines were those with citation to more recent materials. The labels of "hard" and "soft" have proved both enduring and problematic. One of the problems can be seen in the application of the terms in papers subsequent to Price's. Noted above are Biglan's (1973a and 1973b) studies which attempted to place disciplines on a "hard-soft" continuum. This classification has had some degree of influence and has spawned further research using the terminology. Papers, such as those by Smart and Elton (1975 and 1982), have sought to use Biglan's schema and labeled the classification the "Biglan model." Bayer employed citation analysis to examine the pervasiveness, not only of Biglan's work, but of the mischaracterization of it as a model by Smart and associates. Bayer (1987) illustrated how the notion of hardness and softness was transformed into a perceived theoretical model in the literature.

Related to one of the concepts used by Price is the study of obsolescence of a literature; that is, the rate at which information ages in a discipline as characterized by cited works. One of the most important papers on the aging of literatures was that of Line and Sandison (1974). Among other things, they observed that there are two ways to examine literature aging: synchronously and diachronously. A synchronous study records uses or citations at a single point in time and examines the age distribution of materials at that point. A diachronous study follows the use or citation of items through time or at different points in time. In the former, the user or citer population is fixed; in the latter the materials used or cited are fixed. Line and Sandison proposed some hypotheses regarding aging that studies of obsolescence might focus on:

Literature may decline in use faster when
(a) it deals with data of ephemeral relevance (e. g. prices, stocks, experimental data filling in a theory)
(b) it is in the form of a "report," thesis, "advance communication" or preprint (which may be written up more fully or in more accessible form later)
(c) it is in a rapidly advancing technology.

Literature may decline in use more slowly when
(a) it is descriptive (e. g. taxonomic botany, properties of materials, basic methodology)
(b) it deals with concepts (e. g. philosophy, political theory, new or seminal ideas)
(c) it is critical (e.g., literary criticisms, historiography).

It is difficult on present evidence to hypothesize about
(a) 'syntheses' (textbooks, manuals, and treatises—revisions not counting as evidence of decline in use)
(b) pure as compared with applied fields. (pp. 317–18)

Some studies have focused on points brought up by Line and Sandison. Stinson and Lancaster (1987), for instance, examined potential differences between synchronous and diachronous studies. They found the synchronous method easier to employ and yielding of results equivalent to the diachronous method and concluded that a synchronous study could result in an accurate measure of decline in use with age as measured by citation data. Griffith and others (1979) tested an aging model originally set forth by Brookes (1970) and found that, with citation data, scientific literature does indeed age, and age fairly rapidly. They discovered that half of all citations occur within five years of publication and ninety percent of citations occur within twenty years of publication. While there are implications for formal communication patterns from this study, it is not as clear whether other communication mechanisms or forms of literature use exhibit similar patterns.

Another use of bibliometrics, touched on earlier, is the evaluation of literatures. Bradford's Law, which focuses on the determination of a core literature, is one means by which such evaluation may be undertaken. More specifically, citation data may be used to apply Bradford's Law to a literature. Singleton (1976) used citations to try to arrive at a ranking of journal in physics. While such a means can be employed to rank journals, there are some implications of this, as Singleton pointed out. Not the least of the potential objections to using citations is the likelihood of bias in favor of older, larger journals. Reliance on an "impact factor" (examining citations relative to the number of articles published in a journal) helps to control for the size variable, but not for maturity. Because of some of the objections that can arise from bibliometric data, some researchers have sought to determine if there can be a general agreement among means of evaluation. McAllister and others (1980) looked at subjective prestige rankings of a number of scientific journals in concert with citation data from the same set of journals. They found close agreement between the two. It may be that the same factors influence both citation (the incorporation of published works into citers' papers) and prestige (the publication of papers perceived as important). Weisheit and Regoli (1984) warn that "even the best measures of journal rankings are relatively crude. In most cases scholars would be well advised to rank journals in sets or clusters rather than by assigning artificially precise indicators or ranks" (p. 323).

Beyond the determination of the core of a literature, as defined by the productivity of a set of journals, there are questions researchers ask regarding the influence and quality of a literature. The basic strengths and weaknesses of using citation as an evaluation tool have been discussed by Garfield (1979). He maintained that citation analysis is a solid and economical evaluation tool, as long as some of the problems of citations can be overcome. Hurt (1984) reviewed the use of bibliometric measures as a means of identifying important literature. Objections to the method (many of which are included in this paper) are noted and Hurt concluded that, while such means as citation analysis can be valuable in producing a set of indicators, they are limited by the possibility of bias introduced into the measurement. Thus, multiple perspectives provide a richer indication of the sociological and intellectual landscape of a literature. Lawani and Bayer (1983) approach the identification of influential literature by comparing citations and peer assessment. They observed that, while the two measures correlate positively, the information provided has implications for literatures in the aggregate, not for individuals or individual contributions. Lawani (1986) affirmed the positive correlation of the two variables and further noted that self-citation among quality papers is proportionally lower than for other papers. In a somewhat different methodological approach, Porter, Chubin, and Jin examined the output of some prominent scientists and found relatively little overlap in the listing of ''best'' (as perceived by the scientists themselves) and most cited papers. These findings enhance Hurt's admonition that no single means of investigation can uncover the entirety of the culture of a discipline's literature.

Bibliometric data have also been used in some studies for comparative purposes. Basically, some writers have sought to employ bibliometrics as an evaluation mechanism. Moed and others (1985), for example, looked at the uses of bibliometric data to examine and, perhaps, alter organizational research policy for universities. There are some problems with the method, such as the variance in practice from field to field, the completeness of any one source, and the necessity of identifying all members of research groups, so that comparisons can be made. They found that, although limited, bibliometrics can be a reasonable monitoring device, especially of the products of active communication. Narin (1987) agreed that the method can be used as an evaluative mechanism. He compared perception and citation within scientific disciplines and found that, with regard to the funding patterns of the National Institutes of Health, bibliometrics provides a valid performance measure and can be used to evaluate funding policy. On a larger scale, bibliometrics has been used to assess the performance of universities. Anderson, Narin, and McAllister (1978) discovered that bibliometric measures of size (numbers of papers published) and quality (citation rates) are components of some peer rating scores. They also found that prestige in one department is dependent on the prestige of other departments, and that bibliometric size is a factor that influences this phenomenon. Muffo, Mead, and Bayer (1987) looked to compare five universities across disciplinary lines, using publication data. They were able to make distinctions, but warned that comparisons need to be viewed in the light of institutional mission, faculty size, the classification of disciplines, disciplinary overlap, and multiple authorship.

Some uses of bibliometrics can have more specific purposes. Whereas some of the aforementioned studies have focused on institutional assessment, some have as their central area of examination the evaluation of the research output of individuals. The application of bibliometrics was one emphasis of a paper by King (1987), who recognized that many institutions perceive the need for more objective measures in the peer review process. Such measures should, ideally, be field independent (applicable across disciplinary lines), which is a problem for bibliometrics as a whole. Also, the measures should be useful at a particular, rather than an aggregate, level. There are some other caveats to be aware of if bibliometrics is going to be applied to the evaluation of individuals. As Garfield (1983) pointed out, some sort of weighting mechanism should be employed so that young faulty are not evaluated on the basis of the productivity of mature faculty. Because of this, years of experience should be a factor in any analysis. On a more general note, evaluators need to be conscious of the time lag built into the submission-acceptance-publication-citation process and not expect an immediate database of citations before the communication machine is able to generate it. Garfield further noted that the differing behavior patterns of the various disciplines should be taken into account so that the standards of one field, which may include a phenomenon that has come to be known as "least publishable unit" (reducing a research project to the smallest bits of information that can be published separately), are not applied to another.

The above factors, save the last, address some of the mechanical aspects of using bibliometric measures in individual performance evaluation. Some other authors have been attentive to policy issues that arise with such an assessment method. Dill (1986), for example, observed that citation is not only a potential measure of performance, but a potential incentive to produce. If academic units foster early citation of the work of junior faculty, the stimulus is likely to have an effect on the overall evaluation mechanism. This is an especially important point when comparing members of one unit where supportive effort exists with those in whose units such support is absent. Webster and Conrad (1986) pointed out that, while citation study provides an objective measure that can be used for evaluative purposes, each study must be scrutinized to see what is *not* being measured. In those studies where a relatively small set of journals are analyzed it is difficult to extrapolate the findings to all journals and, further, to all means of publishing. Braxton and Bayer (1986) maintained that citation analysis can be used to "provide an objective measure of productivity, significance, quality, utility, influence, effectiveness, or impact of a scholar and his or her scholarly products" (p. 35). They did, on the other hand, recognize some difficulties of the method, such as limitations of secondary indexing sources, time delay, self-citation, and the lack of a normative standard that could be applied across disciplines. Moreover, they insisted that citation data be used as one component in a set of evaluative criteria. On its own, citation analysis may not be able to differentiate sufficiently among individuals and their accomplishments.

CONCLUSION

Bibliometrics, while a relatively recent methodological development, has received a great deal of attention by the scholarly and research community. As a means of examining information transfer bibliometrics, on the whole, has proved itself to be an intellectually interesting approach and a useful empirical means of studying tangible phenomena related to communication. Its application has grown from description of the characteristics of a field's literature use to the intellectual mapping of communication across disciplines. it is likely that, in the future, more attention will be paid to the influence of individual authors or individual documents, both as they depart form "normal science" and as they may typify it. Acquiring the data to employ bibliometric techniques has become faster, easier, and cheaper; this has undoubtedly influenced both the number and the complexity of bibliometric studies.

The more widespread use of bibliometrics and the broader applications of research findings prompt some important questions. For instance, will the ready availability of data lead to policy changes on college and university campuses? Will the objectivity of bibliometrics as a methodology obscure the subjectivity that not infrequently underlies the phenomenon providing data for studies? Regarding citations, Smith (1981) asked two questions for which complete answers still do not exist: "Is it possible that increased use of citation analysis will cause a change in citation behavior? How will citation behavior be affected by the increased use of electronic media for generation, storage and dissemination of information" (p. 99)? These questions can provide bibliometric studies with some direction in dealing with some basic design and implementation implications. Since these questions, along with less global questions regarding information transfer, have not been answered thoroughly and satisfactorily, researchers using bibliometrics as a methodology can look forward to creative and stimulating opportunities for investigation.

REFERENCES

Anderson, R. C., Narin, F., and McAllister, P. (1978). Publication ratings versus peer ratings of universities. *Journal of the American Society for Information Science* 29(2): 91–103.

Baughman, J. C. (1974). A structural analysis of the literature of sociology. *Library Quarterly* 44(4): 293–308.

Bayer, A. E. (1987). The 'Biglan model' and the smart messenger: A case study of eponym diffusion. *Research in Higher Education* 26(2): 212–23.

Bayer, A. E. (1983) Multi-method strategies for defining 'core' higher education journals. *Review of Higher Education* 6(2): 103–13.

Bayer, A. E., and Folger, J. (1966). Some correlates of a citation measure of productivity in science. *Sociology of Education* 36: 381–90.

Bellardo, T. (1980–81). The use of co-citations to study science. *Library Research* 2: 231–37.

Biglan, A. (1973a). The characteristics of subject matter in different academic areas. *Journal of Applied Psychology* 57: 195–203.

Biglan, A. (1973b). Relationships between subject matter characteristics and the structure and output of university departments. *Journal of Applied Psychology* 57: 204–13.

Bonzi, S. (1982). Characteristics of a literature as predictors of relatedness between cited and citing works. *Journal of the American Society for Information Science* 33(4): 208–16.

Bookstein, A. (1979). Explanation of the bibliometric laws. *Collection Management* 3(2/3): 151–62.

Boyce, B. R., and Banning, C. S. (1979). Data accuracy in citation studies. *RQ* 18: 349–50.

Bradford, S. C. (1950). *Documentation*. Washington, DC: Public Affairs Press.

Bradford, S. C. (1934). Sources of information on specific subjects. *Engineering* 137: 85–86.

Braxton, J. M., and Bayer, A. E. (1986). Assessing faculty scholarly performance. *New Directions for Institutional Research* No. 50: 25–42.

Broadus, R. N. (1967). A citation study for sociology. *American Sociologist* 2: 19–20.

Broadus, R. N. (1987). Early approaches to bibliometrics. *Journal of the American Society for Information Science* 38(2): 127–29.

Broadus, R. N. (1983). An investigation of the validity of bibliographic citations. *Journal of the American Society for Information Science* 34(2): 132–35.

Brookes, B. C. (1969). Bradford's law and the bibliography of science. *Nature* 224: 953–56.

Brookes, B. C. (1968). The derivation and application of the Bradford-Zipf distribution. *Journal of Documentation* 24(4): 247–65.

Brookes, B. C. (1970). Obsolescence of special library periodicals: sampling errors and utility contours. *Journal of the American Society for Information Science* 21:20–29.

Brooks, T. A. (1986). Evidence of complex citer motivations. *Journal of the American Society for Information Science* 37(1): 34–36.

Budd, J. (1986). A citation study of american literature: implications for collection management. *Collection Management* 8: 49–62.

Budd, J. M. (1988). A bibliometric analysis of higher education literature. *Research in Higher Education* 28(2): 180–90.

Budd, J. M. (1990). Higher education literature: characteristics of citation patterns. *Journal of Higher Education* 61(1): 84–97.

Budd, J. M. (1989). Information transfer and scholarship: the impact of the Peters and Ceci paper. *Library & Information Science Research* 11(4): 357–68.

Budd, J. M. (1991). The Literature of academic libraries: an analysis. *College & Research Libraries* 52(3): 290–95.

Budd, J., and Hurt, C. D. (1991). Superstring theory: information transfer in an emerging field. *Scientometrics* 21(1):87–98.

Cano, V. (1989). Citation behavior: classification, utility, and location. *Journal of the American Society for Information Science* 40(4): 284–90.

Chubin, D. E., and Moitra, S. D. (1975). Content Analysis of References: Adjunct or Alternative to Citation Counting? *Social Studies of Science* 5(4): 423–41.

Cline, G. S. (1981). Application of Bradford's law to citation data. *College & Research Libraries* 42(1): 53–61.

Coile, R. C. (1977). Lotka's frequency distribution of scientific productivity. *Journal of the American Society for Information Science* 28(6): 366–70.

Cole, F. J., and Earles, W. B. (1917). The history of comparative anatomy. Part I. A statistical analysis of the literature. *Science Progress* 11: 578–96.

Cole, J., and Cole, S. (1971). Measuring the quality of sociological research: problems in the use of the science citation index. *American Sociologist* 6: 23–29.

Cronin, B. (19984). *The Citation Process: The Role and Significance of Citations in Scientific Communication*. London: Taylor Graham.

de Mey, M. (1982). *The Cognitive Paradigm*. Dordrecht, Holland: D. Reidel Publishing Company.

Diamond, A. M., Jr. (1985). What is a citation worth? *Journal of Human Resources* 21: 200–15.

Dill, D. D. (1986). Research as a scholarly activity: context and culture. *New Directions for Institutional Research* No. 50: 7–23.

Drott, M. C. (1981). Bradford's law: theory, empiricism and the gap between. *Library Trends* 30(1): 41–52.

Edge, D. (1980). Why I am not a co-citationist. In Garfield, E., *Essays of an Information Scientist, Vol. Three—1977–1978*. Philadelphia: ISI Press, pp. 239–46.

Egghe, L. (1985). Consequences of Lotka's law for the law of Bradford. *Journal of Documentation* 41(3): 173–89.

Egghe, L. (1987). Pratt's measure for some bibliometric distributions and its relation with the 80/20 rule. *Journal of the American Society for Information Science* 38(4): 288–97.

Fano, R. M. (1956). Information theory and the retrieval of recorded information. In J. H. Shera, A. Kent, and J. Percy (eds.), *Documentation in Action*. New York: Reinhold, pp. 238–44.

Feidler, A., and Hurt, C. D. (1986). Stratospheric aerosols: the transfer of scientific information. *Library & Information Science Research* 8: 243–60.

Frost, C. O. (1979). The use of citations in literary research: a preliminary classification of citation functions. *Library Quarterly* 49(4): 399–414.

Fussler, H. H. (1949a). Characteristics of the research literature used by chemists and physicists in the United States. *Library Quarterly* 19(1): 19–35.

Fussler, H. H. (1949b). Characteristics of the research literature used by chemists and physicists in the United States. Part II. *Library Quarterly* 19(2): 119–43.

Garfield. E. (1983). How to use citation analysis for faculty evaluations, and when is it relevant? Part 1. *Current Comments* No. 44: 354–72.

Garfield, E. (1984). Anthropology journals: what they cite and what cites them. *Current Anthropology* 25: 514–28.

Garfield, E. (1965). Can citation indexing be automated? In M. E. Stevens, V. E. Giuliano, and L. B. Heilprin (eds.), *Statistical Association Methods for Mechanized Documentation*. Washington, DC: U. S. Department of Commerce, National Bureau of Standards; 1965: 189–92. (NBS Misc. Pub. 269).

Garfield, E. (1979). Is citation analysis a legitimate evaluation tool? *Scientometrics* 1(4): 359–75.

Goodrich, J. E., and Roland, C. G. (1977). Accuracy of published medical reference citations. *Journal of Technical Writing and Communication* 7(1): 15–19.

Griffith, B. C., Servi, P. N., Anker, A. L., and Drott, M. C. (1979). The aging of scientific literature: a citation analysis. *Journal of Documentation* 35(3): 179–96.

Gross, P. L. K., and Gross, E. M. (1927). College libraries and chemical education. *Science* 66: 385–89.

Herlach, G. (1978). Can retrieval of information from citation indexes be simplified? *Journal of the American Society for Information Science* 29: 308–10.

Hulme, E. W. (1923). Statistical bibliography, etc.'' *Library Association Record* 1(4): 262–63.

Hurt, C. D. (1984). Important literature identification in science: a critical review of the literature. *Advances in Librarianship* 13: 239–58.

Ikpaahindi, L. (1985). An overview of bibliometrics—its measurements, laws and their applications. *Libri* 35(2): 163–77.

Kessler, M. M. (1963). Bibliographic coupling between scientific papers. *American Documentation* 14: 10–25.

Key, J. D., and Roland, C. G. (1977). Reference accuracy in articles accepted for publication in the *Archives of Physical Medicine and Rehabilitation*. *Archives of Physical Medicine and Rehabilitation* 58(3): 136–37.

King, J. (1987). A review of bibliometric and other science indicators and their role in research evaluation. *Journal of Information Sciences* 13: 261–76.

Kuhn, T. S. (1970). *The Structure of Scientific Revolutions*, 2nd ed. Chicago: University of Chicago Press; 1970.

Lawani, S. M. (1973). Bradford's law and the literature of agriculture. *International Library Review* 1973; 5: 341–50.

Lawani, S. M. (1982). On the heterogeneity and classification of author self-citations. *Journal of the American Society for Information Science* 33(5): 281–84.

Lawani, S. M. (1972). Periodical literature and subtropical agriculture. *Unesco Bulletin for Libraries* 26: 88–93.

Lawani, S. M. (1986). Some bibliometric correlates of quality in scientific research. *Scientometrics* 9(1–2): 13–25.

Lawani, S. M., and Bayer, A. E. (1983). Validity of citation criteria for assessing the influence of scientific publications: new evidence with peer assessment. *Journal of the American Society for Information Science* 34(1): 59–66.

Leimkuhler, F. F. (1967). The Bradford distribution. *Journal of Documentation* 23: 197–207.

Lin, N., and Nelson, C. E. (1969). Bibliographic reference patterns in core sociological journals, 1965–1966. *American Sociologist* 4: 47–50.

Line, M. B., and Sandison, A. (1974). 'Obsolescence' and changes in the use of literature with time. *Journal of Documentation* 30(3): 283–350.

MacRoberts, M. H., and MacRoberts, B. R. (1989). Problems of citation analysis: a critical review. *Journal of the American Society for Information Science* 40(5): 342–49.

Maia, M. J. F., and Maia, M. D. (1984). On the unity of Bradford's law. *Journal of Documentation* 40(3): 206–16.

Mandelbrot, B. (1963). New methods in statistical economics. *Journal of Political Economy* 71: 421–40.

Martyn, J. (1964). Bibliographic coupling. *Journal of Documentation* 20(4): 236.

Martyn, J. (1975). Citation analysis. *Journal of Documentation* 31(4): 291–97.

McAllister, P. A., Anderson, R. C., and Narin, F. (1980). Comparison of peer and citation assessment of the influence of scientific journals. *Journal of American Society for Information Science* 31(3): 147–52.

McCain, K. W. (1990). Mapping author in intellectual space: population genetics in the

1980s. In C. L. Borgman (ed.), *Scholarly Communication and Bibliometrics*. Newbury Park, CA: Sage Publications, Inc., 1990, pp. 194–216.

McCain, K. W. (1986). The paper trails of scholarship: mapping the literature of genetics. *Library Quarterly* 56(3): 258–71.

Merton, R. K. (1968). The Matthew effect in science. *Science* 159: 56–63.

Moed, H. F., Burger, W. J. M., Frankfort, J. G., and Van Raan, A. F. J. (1985). The use of bibliometric data for the measurement of university research performance. *Research Policy* 14: 131–49.

Moed, H. F., and Vriens, M. (1989). Possible inaccuracies occuring in citation analysis. *Journal of Information Science* 15: 95–107.

Moravcsik, M. J., and Murugesan, P. (1975). Some results on the function and quality of citations. *Social Studies of Science* 5: 86–92.

Muffo, J. A., Mead, S. V., and Bayer, A. E. (1987). Using faculty publication rates for comparing 'peer' institutions. *Research in Higher Education* 27(2): 163–75.

Mulkay, M. (1991). *Sociology of Science: A Sociological Pilgrimage*. Buckingham: Open University Press.

Narin, F. (1987). Bibliometric techniques in the evaluation of research programs. *Science and Public Policy* 14(2): 99–106.

Narin, F., and Moll, J. K. (1977). Bibliometrics. *Annual Review of Information Science and Technology* 12: 35–58.

Neeley, J. D., Jr. (1981). The management and social science literatures: an interdisciplinary cross-citation analysis. *Journal of the American Society for Information Science* 32(3): 217–23.

Noma, E. (1984). Co-citation analysis and the invisible college. *Journal of the American Society for Information Science* 35(1): 29–33.

Pao, M. L. (1986). An empirical examination of Lotka's law. *Journal of the American Society for Information Science* 37(1): 26–33.

Pareto, V. (1897). *Cours D'économie Politique*, Vol. 2. Lausanne: 1 Universite de Lausanne.

Peritz, B. C. (1983). A classification of citation roles for the social sciences and related fields. *Scientometrics* 5: 303–12.

Porter, A. L., Chubin, D. E., and Jin, X-Y. (1988). Citations and scientific progress: comparing bibliometric measures with scientist judgments. *Scientometrics* 13(3–4): 103–24.

Potter, W. G. (1981). Lotka's law revisited. *Library Trends* 30(1): 21–39.

Prabha, C. G. (1983). Some aspects of citations behavior: a pilot in business administration. *Journal of the American Society for Information Science* 34: 202–06.

Pratt, A. D. (1977). A measure of class concentration in bibliometrics. *Journal of the American Society for Information Science* 28(5): 285–92.

Price, D. J. de S. (1970). Citation measures of hard science, soft science, technology, and nonscience. In C. N. Nelson, and D. K. Pollock (eds.), *Communication Among Scientists and Engineers*. Lexington, MA: Heath Lexington Books, pp. 3–22.

Price, D. de S. (1976). A general theory of bibliometric and other cumulative advantage processes. *Journal of the American Society for Information Science* 27(5): 292–306.

Price, D. de S. (1965). Networks of scientific papers. *Science* 149: 56–64.

Pritchard, A. (1969). Statistical bibliography or bibliometrics? *Journal of Documentation* 24(4): 348–49.

Ravetz, J. R. (1971). *Scientific Knowledge and Its Social Problems*. Harmondsworth: Penguin.

Rice, R. E., Borgman, C. L., and Reeves, B. Citation networks of communication journals, 1977–1985: cliques and positions, citations made and citations received. *Human Communication Research* 15(2): 256–83.

Rogers, E. M., and Cotrill, C. A. (1990). An author co-citation analysis of two research traditions: technology transfer and the diffusion of innovations. In C. L. Borgman (ed.), *Scholarly Communication and Bibliometrics*. Newbury Park, CA: Sage Publications, Inc., pp. 157–65.

Schorr, A. E. (1974). Lotka's law and library science. *RQ* 14: 32–33.

Silverman, R. J. (1985). Higher education as a maturing field? evidence from refereeing practices. *Research in Higher Education* 23(2): 150–83.

Silverman, R. J. (1982). Journal manuscripts in higher education: a framework. *Review of Higher Education* 5(4): 181–96.

Simon, H. A. (1957). On a class of skew distribution functions. In *Models of Man: Social and Rational*. New York: Wiley, pp. 145–64.

Singleton, A. (1976). Journal ranking and selection: a review in physics. *Journal of Documentation* 32(4): 258–89.

Small, H. (1973). Co-citation in the scientific literature: a new measure of the relationship between two documents. *Journal of the American Society for Information Science* 1973; 24(4): 265–69.

Small, H. (1980). Co-citation context analysis and the structure of paradigms. *Journal of Documentation* 36(3): 183–96.

Small, H. (1986). The synthesis of specialty narratives from co-citation clusters. *Journal of the American Society for Information Science* 37(3): 97–110.

Smart, J. C. (1983a). Perceived quality and citation rates of education journals. *Research in Higher Education* 19(2): 175–82.

Smart, J. C. (1983b). Stability of education journal characteristics: 1977–1980. *Research in Higher Education* 19(3): 285–93.

Smart, J. C., and Elton, C. F. (1975). Goal orientations of academic departments: a test of Biglan's model. *Journal of Applied Psychology* 60(5): 580–88.

Smart, J. C., and Elton, C. F. (1981). Structural characteristics and citation rates of education journals. *American Educational Research Journal* 18(4): 399–413.

Smart, J. C., and Elton, C. F. (1982). Validation of the Biglan model. *Research in Higher Education* 17(3): 213–29.

Smith, L. C. (1981). Citation analysis. *Library Trends* 30(1): 83–106.

So, C. Y. K. (1988). Citations patterns of core communication journals: an assessment of the developmental status of communication. *Human Communication Research* 15(2): 236–55.

Soper, M. E. (1976). Characteristics and use of personal collections. *Library Quarterly* 46(4): 411–13.

Stinson, E. R., and Lancaster, F. W. (1987). Synchronous versus diachronous methods in the measurement of obsolescence by citation studies. *Journal of Information Science* 13: 65–74.

Summers, E. G. (1984). A review and application of citation analysis methodology to reading research journal literature. *Journal of the American Society for Information Science* 35(6): 332–43.

Sweetland, J. H. (1989). Errors in bibliographic citations: a continuing problem. *Library Quarterly* 59(4): 291–304.

Tague, J. (1990). Ranks and sizes: some complementarities and contrasts. *Journal of Information Science* 16: 29–35.

Thyer, B. A., and Bentley, K. J. (1986). Academic affiliations of social work authors: a citations analysis of six major journals. *Journal of Social Work Education* 22(1): 67–73.

Vickery, B. C. (1948). Bradford's law of scattering. *Journal of Documentation* 4(4): 198–203.

Voos, H., and Dagaev, K. S. (1976). Are all citations equal? Or, did we op. cit. your idem? *Journal of Academic Librarianship* 1(6): 19–21.

Walberg, H. J., Vukosavich, P., and Tsai, Shiow-Ling. Scope and structure of the journal literature in educational research. *Educational Researcher* 10(8): 11–13.

Wallace, D. P. (1987). A solution in search of a problem: bibliometrics and libraries. *Library Journal* 112: 43–47.

Webster, D. S., and Conrad, C. F. (1986). Using faculty research performance for academic quality rankings. *New Directions for Institutional Research* No. 50: 43–57.

Weinstock, M. (1971). Citation indexes. In *Encyclopaedia of Library and Information Science*, vol. 5. New York: Marcel Dekker, pp. 16–40.

Weisheit, R. A., and Regoli, R. M. (1984). Ranking journals. *Scholarly Publishing* 15: 313–25.

White, H. D. (1990). Author co-citation analysis: overview and defense. In C. L. Borgman (ed.), *Scholarly Communication and Bibliometrics*. Newbury Park, CA: Sage Publications, Inc., pp. 84–106.

White, H. D., and McCain, K. W. (1989). Bibliometrics. *Annual Review of Information Science and Technology* 24: 119–86.

White, M. J., and White, K. G. (1977). Citation analysis of psychology journals. *American Psychologist* 32: 301–05.

Wilkinson, E. L. (1972). The ambiguity of Bradford's law. *Journal of Documentation* 28(2): 122–30.

Wyllys, R. E. (1981). Empirical and theoretical bases of Zipf's law. *Library Trends* 30(1): 53–64.

Ziman, J. M. (1968). *Public Knowledge: An Essay Concerning the Social Dimension of Science*. Cambridge: Cambridge University Press.

Zipf, G. K. (1949). *Human Behavior and the Principle of Least Effort*. Cambridge, MA: Addison-Wesley.

Zipf, G. K. (1932). *Selected Studies of the Principle of Relative Frequency in Language*. Cambridge, MA: Harvard University Press.

Logistic Regression for Research in Higher Education

James T. Austin
The Ohio State University

Robert A. Yaffee
Academic Computing Facility, New York University

and

Dennis E. Hinkle
Butler University

INTRODUCTION

The general linear model (GLM) is widely used by researchers in higher education (Ahlgren and Walberg, 1975; Cohen, 1968; Darlington, 1968; Kerlinger, 1985). Such statistical models relate a linear combination of explanatory or predictor variables with varying intercorrelations to an interval response variable. When the explanatory variables are continuous, the procedure is *regression*; when the explanatory variables are categorical, the procedure is *analysis of variance*; when the explanatory variables are a combination, the procedure is *analysis of covariance*. All these techniques are special cases of ordinary least squares (OLS) regression and their range of capabilities provides researchers with a powerful tool for analyzing experimental and nonexperimental data. But OLS regression assumes an interval-level response variable, which is not always the case for data collected in higher education research. In this chapter we will argue that, when the response variable is dichotomous, logistic regression is one appropriate technique.

This chapter was begun while the first author was a postdoctoral trainee in the Quantitative Methods Program of the Department of Psychology, University of Illinois, Lawrence E. Jones, Training Program Director. During this time, J.T. Austin was supported by a National Research Service Support award, MH14257. Additional work was supported while the first author was a Visiting Assistant Professor at New York University. The authors are grateful to Ulf Bockenholt for critically reading an earlier draft and substantially improving the final version. Elizabeth G. Lewis of the RAND Corporation provided assistance during the formative stages of the paper. Address all correspondence to the first author at the Department of Psychology, The Ohio State University, 142 Townshend Hall, 1885 Neil Avenue, Columbus, Ohio, 43210–1222.

This chapter presents an intermediate-level exposition that will enable researchers in higher education to use logistic regression as implemented via mainframe and personal computer software. This technique relates one or more predictors to a dichotomous criterion or response variable. There is wide usage of logistic regression in other scientific disciplines, including econometrics and epidemiology, but the two prominent regression texts for behavioral researchers do not provide any coverage of logistic regression (e.g., Cohen and Cohen, 1983; Pedhazur, 1982). The omission reinforces the need for this presentation.

In order to achieve our didactic goals, we deliberately maintain the complexity of the presentation at an intermediate level; additional sources are provided for interested readers. We try to follow the advice of Buchanan (1974), who proposed three criteria for determining appropriate analyses for a contingency table: (a) *statistical, practical,* and *communicable.* Many writers focus on the first to the exclusion of the others; we will balance the three in both the discussion and examples.

The chapter is organized as follows. The first section describes dichotomous response situations for which logistic regression is appropriate, discusses problems encountered when using OLS to estimate regression models for such responses, and briefly reviews additional sources on logistic regression. We then describe a hypothetical dataset consisting of a dichotomous response variable and several predictors. The core of the presentation develops and illustrates the logistic regression model, including assumptions, estimation, model evaluation, using a single and a multiple predictor example. Diagnostics for checking the tenability of the logistic model, including numerical and graphical techniques, are described briefly. In the following section we consider discriminant function analysis as an alternative to logistic regression. We then describe several computer software packages that estimate and test logistic regression models. The conclusion section summarizes our presentation.

BINARY RESPONSES

When analyzing data from experimental or nonexperimental research, researchers in higher education often face situations in which the response variable is restricted to two values, say 0 and 1. The choice of reference category, or the category labeled 0, is arbitrary and can be changed easily through recoding. Such variables are termed *binary* or *dichotomous.* The two levels may be ordered or unordered, and may result from naturally occurring dichotomies or from collapsing multicategory or continuous responses. In describing data of this form, the sufficient statistic is the proportion, which reflects the responses that fall in one level of the dichotomous variable (Fleiss, 1981; Gart, 1971). Given the statistical problems that occur when OLS regression is applied to such data (see below), researchers require alternative techniques to analyze their data. Logistic regression is the major alternative to OLS regression for analyzing binary criterion variables as a function of one or more predictors.

Binary Response Variables in Higher Education Research

Many response variables of interest in higher education are binary decisions or choices by individuals, including the decision to remain in or to withdraw from an academic program, to promote or not to promote an assistant professor, and responding or not responding correctly to a test item. Logistic regression models were first developed in epidemiology to estimate the probabilities of contracting a disease as a function of a risk factor, conditional on a set of covariates (Berkson, 1944; Cornfield, 1951; Kelsey, Thompson, and Evans, 1986; Kleinbaum, Kupper, and Morgenstern, 1982; Walker and Duncan, 1967). Binary behavioral responses in related settings include separation and reenlistment in the military (Nord et al., 1986), turnover and retention in work organizations (Olian, Taylor, and Trader, 1985), repeating/not repeating a crime for parolees, or voting/not voting in an election. In economics and psychology logistic regression models are used to estimate personal "thresholds" from choice data (e.g., to purchase or not purchase a consumer good) under the heading of qualitative response models (e.g., Bock and Jones, 1968; P. Kennedy, 1986; Luce and Suppes, 1965; Maddala, 1983; Maxwell, 1974; McFadden, 1974, 1984). Finally, logistic regression has been applied to the analysis of stratified survey data (e.g., Passmore and Mohamed, 1984; Roberts, Rao, and Kumar, 1987).

A more concrete example illustrating the application of a logistic regression model is a choice setup in which individuals must choose one of two alternatives. Choice is assumed to be a function of a comparison between some internal standard and a threshold. Below the threshold, one alternative is chosen; above the threshold the other alternative is chosen. If the subjective threshold value is assumed to be a function of multiple, independent factors, then the cumulative normal distribution is appropriate for modeling the relation of the underlying process and the observed values. The similarity of the logistic and cumulative normal distributions supports the use of the logistic distribution (Bock, 1975; Cox, 1970; Judge et al., 1985).

Even more concretely, in voluntary college attrition, an important higher education research topic, the rationale for such a choice model is as follows. A choice to remain or to leave during the first year of an academic program is made when a subjective distribution is compared to a threshold or cutpoint that divides the distribution into two parts. Below the threshold, persistence in school is chosen; above the threshold, the alternative decision to drop out is chosen. Work by Terenzini and Pascarella (1977, 1978, 1980; Pascarella, 1980) that validates and extends Tinto's (1975) model of college attrition represents a situation where logistic regression could be used to model the probability of a first-year undergraduate or graduate leaving college. For example, students from minority ethnic groups may experience multiple events that lead them to evaluate their continued persistence in college. At some point, the threshold is reached and a decision to withdraw is made. An alternative theoretical perspective on voluntary attrition is the work of Finn (1989). He reviewed two models, *frustration–self-esteem* and *participation-identification*, that reflect alternative developmental perspectives on dropping out of school. Both Tinto's and Finn's models attempt to explain the binary outcome of attrition from school and could be tested appropriately using logistic regression models.

Binary Responses and OLS Regression

The motivation for using logistic regression is easily seen by examining problems that are encountered when OLS regression is applied to a binary response variable. This application is called the Linear Probability Model (LPM). Goodman (1975) has advocated the LPM when predicted proportions range between .25 and .75 because of the similarity of logistic and OLS regression results within this interval. However, a major problem is that predicted proportions can be greater than 1.0 or less than 0.0; such values are illogical and uninterpretable. Second, it is impossible to obtain an approximately normal distribution for the residuals. A third problem is that the residual variance is nonhomogeneous along the regression function because the variance is systematically related to the mean criterion proportion at each level of the explanatory variable. This relationship results in inefficient estimates of the error variance. Significance tests for regression coefficients are thus invalid, even though the OLS estimates are unbiased, because the standard errors fluctuate. The R^2 index of variance explained is neither meaningful nor applicable (Aldrich and Nelson, 1984; Fienberg, 1980; Haberman, 1978; Judge et al., 1985; Maddala, 1983).

Several solutions for these problems have been proposed. One solution is to truncate predicted values outside the 0–1 range of probability (cf. Aldrich and Nelson, 1984; Anderson et al., 1980; J.J. Kennedy, 1985). On the other hand, Smith and Cichetti's (1975) unpublished results suggested that truncation and other methods for improving out-of-range predicted values do not always work well in practice. A two-step weighted least squares (WLS) approach, in which the variability of the predictors is incorporated into the regression, has also been suggested (Goldberger, 1964), but this procedure is somewhat unwieldy. Moreover, in the end there are still problems with assuming linear relationships for response probabilities (cf. Aldrich and Nelson, 1984; Hanushek and Jackson, 1977). Logistic regression models seem to be a more appropriate solution than patched-up LPMs.

Another general means of analyzing binary responses are the family of loglinear models for contingency table data (cf. Fienberg, 1980; Hinkle, Austin, and McLaughlin, 1989; J.J. Kennedy, 1985; Marascuilo and Busk, 1987). Haberman, Goodman, and other writers refer to logit models as loglinear models using binary dependent variables, but with the explanatory variables all categorical. It has been shown by Haberman (1978) and Anderson et al. (1980) that logistic regression models can be expressed in loglinear form. However, we do not advocate automatically collapsing continuous variables into ordinal or categorical form merely to employ loglinear analysis because of the potential loss of information and the arbitrary nature of the cutpoints.

Thus far we have considered only dichotomies for responses. If a categorical dependent variable spans three or more levels, it is termed polytomous or polychotomous. The levels of a polytomous response variable may be ordered or unordered. OLS regression is still inappropriate for the reasons stated above, specifically, lack of normality and nonhomogeneous error variance. Ordinal logit and multinomial logit models are appropriate for such responses. We do not present logistic models for polytomous response variables in this chapter, but the extension is straightforward and relies on logits that are based on cumulating levels of the categories (cf. Bock, 1975; Hosmer and Lemeshow, 1989). Alternatives for ordinal responses such as loglinear analysis, ordinal logistic regression, least squares regression, or latent variable modelling may be appropriate depending on: (a) the level of measurement of the explanatory variables, (b) the tenability of statistical assumptions, (c) the goals of the researcher, and (d) whether the variables are latent or manifest (e.g., Agresti, 1984, 1989; Aldrich and Nelson, 1984; Muthen, 1984).

Additional Sources

Numerous expository materials address logistic regression topics. The major books are by Agresti (1984, 1989), Aldrich and Nelson (1984), Cox and Snell (1989), Haberman (1978), and Hosmer and Lemeshow (1989). The reader is warned that these sources range across disciplines and that differences in terminology exist. Specifically, most work on the topic has been published in econometrics, biometrics, and statistics journals.

In econometrics, texts by Maddala (1983), Judge, Griffiths, Hill, Lutkepohl, and Lee (1985), Amemiya (1985), and Gujarati (1988) are useful but technical. An article by Amemiya (1981) and two chapters in the *Handbook of Econometrics* (Dhrymes, 1986; McFadden, 1984) review qualitative response models for both dichotomous and polytomous situations. One of the more accessible of the econometrics sources is P. Kennedy (1986). Sources for epidemiological discussions of logistic regression include Kelsey et al. (1986), Kleinbaum et al. (1982), Schlesselman (1982), Greenberg and Kleinbaum (1985), Kleinbaum, Kupper, and Chambless (1982), and Rothman (1986). Many articles on these topics also appear in the journals *Biometrika*, *Biometrics*, and the *American Journal of Epidemiology*. Finally, we recommend Bishop, Fienberg, and Holland (1975), Fienberg (1980), Haberman (1978, 1979), and Agresti (1984, 1989) for the statistically-minded, with the caveat that they require some mathematical sophis-

TABLE 1. Hypothetical Data for an Example

Case	Response Tenure	Explanatory Variables		Publications
		Gender	Race	
001	1	1	0	8
002	1	1	1	9
003	0	0	1	10
004	1	1	0	6
005	0	1	1	7
006	0	1	1	9
007	0	0	0	12
008	1	1	0	18
009	1	1	0	22
010	0	1	0	3
011	1	1	2	17
012	1	0	0	10
013	0	1	1	12
014	0	1	1	10
015	0	1	0	14
016	0	1	1	9
017	0	1	0	8
018	0	1	0	6
019	0	0	1	7
020	0	1	1	9
021	1	1	0	24
022	0	1	0	2
023	0	1	2	10
024	1	1	2	14
025	1	1	1	16
026	0	1	0	17
027	1	0	1	20
028	0	0	0	4
029	1	0	1	14
030	0	1	0	9
031	1	1	0	10
032	1	1	0	12
033	0	0	0	11
034	0	0	1	9
035	0	0	0	5
036	0	1	0	8
037	0	0	0	13
038	1	0	2	19
039	0	1	1	4
040	1	1	0	12
041	0	0	0	13
042	0	0	0	10
043	0	0	0	7
044	0	0	0	9

(continued)

TABLE 1. Hypothetical Data for an Example (*continued*)

Case	Response Tenure	Explanatory Variables		Publications
		Gender	Race	
045	0	0	0	2
046	0	1	1	10
047	1	1	0	18
048	0	1	0	9
049	1	1	2	20
050	0	0	0	11
051	0	1	0	9
052	1	1	0	14
053	1	1	0	11
054	0	0	1	5
055	0	1	2	7
056	1	1	0	6
057	0	0	1	4
058	1	0	2	10
059	0	1	1	7
060	0	1	2	9
061	0	1	1	6
062	0	0	0	13
063	0	1	0	11
064	1	1	0	14
065	0	0	0	7
066	1	1	1	14
067	1	0	2	32
068	1	1	0	12
069	0	1	2	8
070	0	0	1	8
071	0	1	0	5
072	1	1	1	9
073	0	1	2	12
074	0	0	1	14
075	1	1	0	15
076	0	0	0	6
077	0	0	0	11
078	0	0	0	3
079	0	1	2	7
080	1	1	1	17
081	0	1	0	12
082	0	1	0	8
083	0	1	0	11
084	1	0	1	21
085	1	0	0	11
086	0	1	2	7
087	0	1	0	15
088	0	1	1	4
089	0	1	0	5
090	0	1	0	6

tication. Cox and Snell's (1989) update of Cox (1970) is excellent in terms of scope and level of discussion, from a statistical orientation.

In the social sciences, books by Aldrich and Nelson (1984), Neter, Wasserman, and Kutner (1989), J.J. Kennedy (1985), Bock (1975), and Hanushek and Jackson (1977) are useful. Aldrich and Nelson (1984) and Hanushek and Jackson (1977) use econometrics perspectives; Neter et al. (1989) approach the topic from a statistical and business orientation. The treatment by Bock (1975) is comprehensive and represents a very flexible approach. It can accommodate "single" and "multiple" responses by subjects, as well as the small samples that occur in practical work.

An Example

For the pedagogical purposes of this chapter, an hypothetical data set will be used for both a one-predictor and a multi-predictor example. The binary response or criterion variable (Y) is the departmental recommendation for academic tenure ($Y = 0$ = no; $Y = 1$ = yes). Three relevant predictor or explanatory variables were included in the data set: gender (G), race (R), and number of refereed publications (P). Gender is a dichotomous variable ($G = 0$ = male; $G = 1$ = female). Race is categorical ($R = 0$ = white; $R = 1$ = black; $R = 2$ = other). Number of publications is a discrete variable which, for the purposes of this discussion, is assumed to have underlying continuity. The observations represent 90 assistant professors who are in the final year of their probationary period. These data are contrived, but analyses of such data can be used in higher education to study cases of academic discrimination or to monitor tenure policies within colleges and universities (cf. J.J. Kennedy, 1983; Kriska and Milligan, 1982). The data set is listed in Table 1 and summary statistics for the variables are provided in Table 2.

LOGISTIC REGRESSION CONCEPTS AND MODELS

As noted above, the goal of logistic regression is to relate one or more explanatory variables (X_i) to the binary response variable (Y). For a sample of size n, the responses are observed counts f_1 and f_2, where $f_1 + f_2 = n$. Corresponding sample proportions are p and q where $p = f_1/n$ and $q = 1-p = f_2/n$ and $p+q = 1.0$. Constraining the sum of p and q to be 1.0 makes a probability interpretation valid. The sample mean of a binary variable is n*p, which equals the number of observations coded as 1's (f_1); the sample variance is n*p*q. From this formula it is easy to see that the variance is systematically related to the value of p. Specifically, maximum variance occurs when $p = q = .50$, and as p shifts in either direction from .50 the variance decreases (Gart, 1971; Hinkle, Wiersma, and Jurs, 1988).

TABLE 2. Simple Statistics for Explanatory Variables

Variable	Mean	S.D.	Minimum	Maximum
GENDER	.655556	.477849	.00000	1.0000
BLACK	.288889	.455785	.00000	1.0000
OTHER*	.144444	.353509	.00000	1.0000
NUMPUBS	10.60000	5.194639	2.0000	32.000

*OTHER refers to the second category required to represent the three-level race variable.

Basic Concepts

Use of logistic regression requires the understanding of three concepts: (a) the odds ratio, (b) the logit transformation of the response variable, and (c) the logistic function that is used to model the observed responses. We discuss these concepts and then present the logistic regression model for one and several predictors.

Odds Ratio

In the logistic regression model the ratio p/q is called the "odds." The odds ratio, which is the ratio of two simple odds, was proposed by Yule in 1900 to summarize the association in a 2 × 2 contingency table in terms of conditional probability (Goodman and Kruskal, 1954). In logistic regression with one predictor variable the odds ratio is interpreted as the ratio of the probability of being at one level of the response, say $(Y_i = 1)$, to the probability of being at the other level, $(Y_i = 0)$, conditional on the levels of the explanatory variable. In the example we have just analyzed, the odds ratio would be interpreted as the change in the probability of being recommended for tenure that is associated with changes in the number of refereed publications. Furthermore, the sample odds ratio is a useful estimator for the product binomial and multinomial distributions (Bishop et al., 1975). For multiple predictors, conditional 2 × 2 tables can be used to represent marginal associations. These represent the association between the criterion and each predictor while controlling for the other predictors, similar to the interpretation of the partial regression coefficient in OLS multiple regression. The flexibility of the odds ratio can be seen in its extension to represent "higher-order" odds ratios or "ratios of odds ratios" (Page, 1977).

Logit Transformation

The criterion or response variable that is analyzed in logistic regression is a logarithmic transformation of the odds ratio, called the logit:

$$logit = \ln (p/q), \tag{1}$$

where ln is the natural logarithm or log to the base e. The term "logit" is a shortening of "logistic unit" (Berkson, 1944). The logit is verbally defined as the natural log of the "odds," and forces the response variable to lie in the 0–1 interval without constraining the values of explanatory variables or parameter estimates. It is these log-transformed data, not the original raw data, that are linearly related to the regression function. Following the estimation of the regression model, the specific log-transformed coefficients can be transformed back into the original units for interpretation.

Logistic Function and Distribution

The logistic function is an S-shaped or sigmoidal curve used as a model of the distribution of the response variable (P. Kennedy, 1986). If the relationship between the explanatory variable and the response probability is negative then the logistic curve is inverted just as in OLS regression, and the meaning is that high values of the predictor variable are associated with the lower category for the response variable. This is totally arbitrary because a recoding of the binary response reverses the logistic curve. The logistic function is essentially linear between p's of .20 to .80, but tapers off toward 0 and 1 outside of this range. Only at the tails are there likely to be large differences between the logistic and normal cumulative distribution functions. Because of its form, the logistic function is ideally suited for predicting probabilities—it asymptotically approaches but never exceeds 0 and 1 (Cox, 1970).

Logistic Regression with One Predictor

The logistic regression model with one predictor variable is given by:

$$\ln (p/q) = b_0 + (b_1 * X). \tag{2}$$

Following the logarithmic transformation, this model becomes:

$$p = \exp(b_0 + [b_1 * X]) / [1 + \exp(b_0 + [b_1 * X])] \tag{3}$$

where p = the expected probability of being in category $Y_i = 1$,
  b_0 = regression constant, b_1 = regression coefficient,
  X = observed values for the predictor variable, and
  $\exp$ = 2.7183 raised to the power of the term in parentheses.

As in OLS regression, b_0 is the estimated intercept and b_1 is the estimated slope of the regression function. The intercept b_0 is a scaling factor that locates the logistic function on the Y-axis (Dillon and Goldstein, 1984). Usually this parameter is of limited value in behavioral research because many of the predictor variables are measured on arbitrary scales. The interpretation of the regression coefficient, b_1, is not as simple as in OLS regression due to the nonlinearity of the logistic function. Specifically, the change in Y associated with a unit increase in X, the predictor variable, varies according to the position on the x scale where the increase occurs. We note that it takes a greater influence from a predictor variable to change the response probabilities at the extremes, near 0 or 1, than it does to change the response probabilities near the middle of the function near p = .5 (Dillon and Goldstein, 1984). Also, as can be seen from equation 3, interpretation of b_1 requires transformation back into percentage changes of original units by using the transformation $(e^{b_1} - 1) * 100$ (cf. Neter et al., 1989), as shown in the one-predictor example below.

A Simple Example with One Predictor
To illustrate logistic regression using a single predictor or explanatory variable, consider the hypothetical data set described above. For this simple example, the response variable (Y) is the departmental recommendation for academic tenure; the single explanatory variable will be number of refereed publications (P). This model could be called the "merit" or "competence" model because it relates the departmental recommendation to research productivity, although it does not make any provision for teaching or service performance by the probationer. Summary output for the logistic regression analysis is found in Table 3; it includes the X^2 values for the null and the one-predictor models, the logistic regression slope estimate and its standard error, the exponentiated value of the slope estimate, and a classification table of observed and predicted values of the response variable.

Logistic Regression with Multiple Predictors
Most research situations in higher education are likely to involve more than one explanatory variable. The model for multiple logistic regression is given as follows:

$$p = \exp(b_0 + \mathbf{x}'\mathbf{b}) / [1 + \exp(b_0 + \mathbf{x}'\mathbf{b})]. \qquad (4)$$

The major change from the one-predictor case is the use of matrix notation to represent the multiple slope coefficients. Thus $\mathbf{b}$ is a vector of estimated regression coefficients and $\mathbf{x}'$ is a matrix of values of explanatory variables. Interpretation of the intercept is unchanged from above. The slopes for the multiple-predictor case represent changes in the response probability attributable to specific explanatory variables, controlling for the other explanatory variables that are in the model.

An Extended Example
Here we present an extension of the previous example with all three predictors. This example will demonstrate the points just made concerning the multiple logistic regression model and illustrate interpretation of the partial regression coefficients. Again, the research questions concern the following,'' Is there a

TABLE 3. Exemplary Output for the One-Predictor Example

```
Model Fit Statistics:

-2 LL (Intercept Only)                    115.909
-2 LL (Intercept + Covariates)             80.827

X² for Covariates                          35.082  df=1


Estimates:

Term    Parameter    SE      Wald X²    Prob.    Exp(b1)

Pubs     .3582      .0820    19.08      .0001    1.43


Classification Table:
```

		PREDICTED	
		EVENT	NO EVENT
	EVENT	18	13
Observed			
	NO EVENT	7	52

---

predictive relationship between the dichotomous criterion and the set of predictors: number of publications, race, and gender?''

We estimated a main effects model for this data using SAS PROC LOGISTIC (SAS, 1990), BMDP LR (BMDP Inc., 1990), SPSS LOGISTIC REGRESSION (SPSS, 1990), and a supplementary module (Steinberg and Colla, 1991) for the PC program SYSTAT (Wilkinson, 1988). All four packages provide stepwise routines but will estimate user-specified models. However, several programming caveats should be noted before the output is presented. First, researchers are advised to dummy code categorical variables themselves to be sure that the exp(b) coefficient for each variable is in fact the odds ratio. Otherwise, the program may choose a reference category that the analyst does not intend. This caveat pertains in our example to the three-level race variable, which requires two dummy variables to represent its effects on the tenure decision. You will note our recoding statements in the input programs for each package. Second, SYSTAT requires that binary variables be coded 1 and 2 rather than the familiar 0 and 1 coding. This detail pertains only to the response variable, in this case tenure recommendation. Third, some programs model the upper probability (category coded 1) while others model the lower probability (category coded 0). This choice reverses the signs of the coefficients between packages, but has no substantive effect.

The edited input and output programs for the analyses using the four packages are given in several appendices. Table 4 contains a summary table that presents the information from the analyses. Note that the only statistically significant predictor is number of publications ($p < .0001$), but that the coefficient for gender produces a p-value around .14. For refereed publications, the estimated logistic regression coefficient (b_1) of .365 and the standard error of .0834 converge across all packages, with positive signs given those programs that model the lower probability (i.e., as number of publications increases, the probability of getting tenure increases and the complementary probability of not getting tenure decreases). The reverse holds for the negative coefficients.

The exponentiated value of the regression coefficient for refereed publications, $\exp(b_1)$, is 1.44. This value is interpreted as the change in the odds ratio associated with an increase of one unit in the predictor variable. The transformation of $(e^{b_1} - 1) * 100$ is interpreted as the percentage change in the dependent variable per unit change in the predictor variable. Specifically, as number of refereed publications increases one unit, the probability of a favorable tenure recommendation increases 44 percent. The 1 in 1.44 is disregarded because 1 is the baseline for ratios, meaning that it yields an equal probability of either decision. We did not estimate interactions effects, but given the paucity of significant main effects, there may not be any interactions. Interested readers could evaluate our conjecture for themselves using the actual data as listed in the appendices.

Other output in the appendices has been selectively provided to demonstrate the unique features of the various programs. As a general observation, SAS and BMDP provide more detail than SPSS and SYSTAT, but all of the programs have useful features. All of the programs present a classification table for comparing actual and predicted values for the response variable, but there are differences in how this is accomplished. For example, BMDP prints a ''cost'' analysis, consisting of a table and a figure, for which the user can control the costs of the misclassification cells; the default is -1.0 for each, which implies equal weighting of false positives and false negatives. We found that SAS provided the best classification table, which included measures of sensitivity, specificity, and association. Finally, note that graphic plots are relatively difficult to obtain with SPSS and SYSTAT, requiring an additional step to save output data to a plotting program. SAS and BMDP provide plots within the logistic routine.

TABLE 4. Exemplary Output for the Three-Predictor Example

```
Model Fit Statistics:

-2 LL (Intercept Only)                    115.909
-2 LL (Intercept & Covariates)             78.490

X² for Covariates                          37.419    df=4
```

Estimates:

Term	Parameter	SE	Wald X²	Prob.	Exp(b1)
Sex	.9315	.637	32.136	.14382	.53
R1	-.1492	.6481	.053	.8179	.86
R2	-.1271	.8395	.023	.8797	.88
Pubs	.3654	.0834	19.175	.0001	1.44

Classification Table:

		PREDICTED	
		EVENT	NO EVENT
	EVENT	17	14
Observed			
	NO EVENT	6	53

Assumptions

The four major assumptions required in order to use logistic regression are (1) linearity in the logits, (2) no multicollinearity, (3) statistical independence of the responses, and (4) large sample size (at least $n > 30$ per each independent variable). A computer program to evaluate the first assumption was written by Harrell and Lee (1985). The simplicity of assumptions is a persuasive rationale for the use of logistic regression (Haberman, 1978; Press and Wilson, 1978). The logistic function derives additional value because of its close match to the cumulative normal distribution and its computational simplicity relative to the normal distribution. We should note, however, that there is little research addressing the robustness of the technique against violations of these assumptions.

Estimation

In considering estimation for the logistic regression model, the two major techniques are both iterative: weighted least squares (WLS) and maximum likelihood (ML). Details of computations may be found in Thisted (1988) or Kennedy and Gentle (1980). Pregibon (1981) lists the typical output of maximum likelihood estimation, including the parameters and their standard errors, the covariance matrix of the parameters, an overall likelihood ratio goodness-of-fit statistic, and the "deviance" or difference between the maxima of the observed and fitted log-likelihoods (Pregibon multiplies this difference by -2, as do several of the computer packages that we will be discussing below). The log-likelihood, when multiplied by -2, is distributed as X^2 with degrees of freedom equal to N-p-1; it represents the difference between observed and fitted values. A useful property of the deviance and the likelihood ratio X^2 statistics is that they can be decomposed into components.

To summarize, there are advocates of both estimation methods. Harrell and Lee (1985), Haberman (1978), and Schlesselman (1982) recommend ML estimation while Berkson (1949, 1955) and Cox (1970) prefer WLS. Recently, Cox and Snell (1989) noted that with the increase in computational power available to the typical research, ML methods are to be preferred. Another reason to prefer ML is that it can estimate zero cells (although not zero marginals), while WLS cannot. However, both estimation methods rely on similar large sample, asymptotic arguments to justify standard errors and significance tests.

Model Evaluation

Assessing the results of a logistic regression analysis is not as straightforward as with OLS regression, for which tests and measures of goodness-of-fit are widely known. There are several different approaches to model evaluation for logistic regression. The better-known approaches include (1) using a likelihood-ratio chi-square (L^2) to test the significance of a set (or subset) of variables, (2) comparing observed and predicted probabilities using a classification table, and (3) constructing a correlation-like measure as a function of likelihood L^2 values (Amemiya, 1981; Harrell, 1986). For testing hierarchically-nested models (i.e., models that range from less to more restrictive) the "chi-square difference" approach is often used because the difference between two chi-squares is distributed as X^2 with the degrees of freedom equal to the difference in the number of variables estimated under the two models.

Hosmer and Lemeshow (1980) compared several tests of fit for multiple logistic regression, concluding that all test statistics followed an X^2 distribution.

However, the appropriate degrees of freedom depend on the particular test statistic and the distributional assumptions the researcher is willing to make. Brown (1982) proposed and evaluated an X^2 test based on Rao's (1973) score statistic. This test yields an assessment of the adequacy of the logistic distribution assumption and is provided as part of the BMDP LR output. In summary, the best advice is to use a combination of measures as a system of checks and balances and to know what information each measure provides.

Regression Diagnostics

Diagnostic measures for OLS regression (cf. Belsley, Kuh, and Welsch, 1980; Stevens, 1984) have been extended to the logistic regression case by Pregibon (1981). These measures are helpful in assessing the correctness of the logistic model specification. We do not discuss these techniques in depth, but in general they can be used to assess the appropriateness of the regression model. One prominent diagnostic is the residual, which can be used to detect outliers in the response variable distribution. Another diagnostic is the identification of influential data points in the distribution of the explanatory variables. Influential data points are those that exert a large effect on the estimated values of the regression coefficients. The two diagnostics termed "most helpful" by Pregibon (1981) were the components of X^2 and the components of deviance. These diagnostics are especially important with the application of maximum likelihood estimation to survey data with small sample sizes. This situation is likely to be the case for many readers, therefore this section has been included as part of the presentation.

Three graphical methods to suggest remedial steps were presented by Landwehr, Pregibon, and Shoemaker (1984, with peer commentary). These methods are straightforward generalizations of OLS diagnostics, and consist of local mean deviance plots, empirical probability plots, and partial residual plots. The local mean deviance plots are the analog of partitioning the global deviance, which gives the disagreement between the observed and fitted data, into pure error and lack-of-fit components for each case. The empirical probability plots are analogous to normal probability plots of residuals. Landwehr et al. (1984) recommended using the local deviance, or the amount that the individual observation contributes to the global deviance (because the global deviance can be decomposed), standardized by its appropriate standard error and plotted against the X^2 distribution with one degree of freedom. Finally, the partial residual plot depicts the relationship between the response variable and an explanatory variable while controlling for the other variables in the model.

Several other diagnostics have been suggested and are implemented in various computer packages. Harrell and Lee (1985) wrote a SAS macro program named EMPTREND that assesses nonlinearity in the relation between the logit-transformed criterion and the regression function. SAS PROC LOGISTIC provides both the DFBETA, which gives the change in the estimated regression coefficient associated with dropping an individual observation, and the diagonal elements of the hat matrix (discussed in the papers by Belsley et al., 1980, and Stevens, 1984). Both statistics are plotted against cases. Such statistical and graphical measures help to identify individual subjects for further inspection and possible removal. BMDP LR provides Hosmer's test as part of its standard output, allowing a test of the fit of the observed data to a logistic distribution. Smaller values of this test statistic indicate better fit of the logistic distribution. It is noteworthy that the use of OLS-type residuals alone may not be as infor mative in logistic regression as it is with OLS regression. This problem o.·c ·· because the response variable takes on only two values (Neter et al., 1989). A solution is to define residuals either as components of chi-square or as "components of deviance," both of which can be broken down into constituents (Pregibon, 1981, p. 711).

An Alternative to Logistic Regression

The most common alternative to logistic regression analysis is discriminant function analysis (DFA), which assumes a multivariate normal distribution of the explanatory variables. Discriminant function analysis can be applied to a binary response, in which case one goal is to develop a linear discriminant function that will classify observations into one or the other levels of the response variable (Tatsuoka, 1988). Thus, the purpose of DFA is to define a function or functions that maximally discriminates between groups of respondents defined by the response variable. Usually the discriminating variables are all continuous, because there may be violations of multivariate normality if mixed sets of variables are used (cf. Dillon and Goldstein, 1978; Goldstein and Dillon, 1978). Moreover, an assumption of equal covariance matrices is made for DFA, although there are alternative techniques for when this specific assumption is not met. A canonical formula is based on a multivariate approach to an F-ratio in which the ratio of variance between groups to variance within groups is maximized. The model for discriminant analysis is:

$$(W^{-1}B - \lambda I)\underline{v} = \underline{0}$$

where W = within groups error variance-covariance matrix
B = between groups variance-covariance matrix
λ = matrix of eigenvalues
$\underline{v}$ = matrix of eigenvectors

By factor analyzing this equation, r eigenvalues (in descending order of magnitude) and r associated eigenvectors $Y_i' = [v_1, v_2, \ldots, v_p]$ are extracted. Each eigenvector contains discriminant coefficients of the independent variables that together serve to discriminate maximally among the groups of the polytomous variables $Y_i = v_{11*}X_1 + v_{12*}X_2 + \ldots + v_{1p}*X_p$. The Y_i from Y_1 to Y_r are the uncorrelated linear discriminant functions that are used to differentiate among the levels of the grouping variable.

In commenting on Landwehr et al.'s (1984) proposals for the graphical assessment of logistic regression models, Rubin (1984) noted an essential difference between logistic regression and DFA. Specifically, logistic regression directly estimates a conditional distribution: $P(Y_i = 1 \mid \mathbf{x})$. On the other hand, discriminant analysis reverses this logic and first estimates $P(\mathbf{x} \mid Y_i = 1)$ and $P(\mathbf{x} \mid Y_i = 0)$, then combines these two estimates using Bayes' theorem to estimate indirectly the probability that logistic regression estimates directly. Rubin states that the preferred model depends on the question to be answered and gives two reasons to prefer logistic regression when the objective is to estimate $P(Y_i = 1 \mid \mathbf{x})$. First, simple models such as normality for the distribution of $\mathbf{x}$ given y are harder to justify when the number of parameters is large and the sample size is small. Second, the number of parameters to be estimated for a discriminant analysis is larger because a joint distribution rather than a conditional one is used.

Logistic regression results are often quite close numerically to alternative techniques (Chambers and Cox, 1967). This finding leads some writers to argue that logistic regression is preferred because it requires fewer assumptions and is therefore more robust (e.g., Haberman, 1978). Fienberg (1980) discusses the results of several studies that have reported logistic regression performance to be superior to that of discriminant analysis for classification and prediction problems, except where all DFA assumptions are met (e.g., Chambers and Cox, 1967; Halperin, Blackwelder, and Verter, 1971; Harrell and Lee, 1985; Press and Wilson, 1978). Therefore we recommend that the choice between these procedures should be made on the basis of the tenability of the multivariate normality and equality of the error covariance matrices assumed by DFA. One decision rule would be if the predictor variables include continuous and categorical levels of measurement, then logistic regression is preferred. On the other hand, if there are only continuous predictors, the choice is difficult and could be based on individual preference.

Computer Packages

In general, statistical software packages are improving rapidly, including those for logistic regression. Because the logistic regression equation is nonlinear in the parameters due to its exponential form, iterative methods are needed to estimate the regression model and corresponding parameters, thus progress in statistical software for logistic regression is constrained by computational capabilities.

The Statistical Analysis System (SAS) routine called PROC LOGISTIC appears to be the best package at the present time (SAS Institute, 1990). It replaces the Supplemental Library LOGIST procedure of Harrell (1986). The new SPSS subroutine LOGISTIC REGRESSION removes the need to use the PROBIT procedure as in past versions (SPSS Inc., 1990). BMDP LR estimates logistic regression and BMDP PR performs polytomous logistic regression (BMDP, 1990). The Generalized Linear Interactive Modeling (GLIM) program written by the British Numerical Algorithms Group (GLIM, Ver. 3.77, 1986; Aitkin, Anderson, Francis, and Hinde, 1989; McCullagh and Nelder, 1983; Nelder and Wedderburn, 1972) is available for logistic regression on both mainframes and PCs. Two drawbacks of GLIM include its unfamiliar operating terminology and the fact that it is not as well-known in the United States. Hosmer and Lemeshow (1989) reported small differences between program output overall, but did note that estimated standard errors deviated slightly between the packages they used. Before briefly describing the computer packages, we note that increased understanding on the part of readers will best be gained through studying the manuals and performing analyses on datasets of interest.

SAS. PROC LOGISTIC in SAS requires minimal assumptions and fits specified models to a binary response variable or an ordinal response variable. Multinomial logistic models cannot be estimated. Options control the use of a stepwise, backward elimination, or user-provided models. User-defined models are obtained by *not* specifying a variable selection method.

BMDP. BMDP LR fits logistic models to binary responses with either stepwise variable selection or user-selected models. BMDP PR fits polytomous logistic models. Both routines are provided as part of the standard BMDP mainframe package and are also available for PC. Input data may either be in tabular form or in a typical raw data matrix with subjects as rows and variables as columns. Both forward and backward selection algorithms are available, with two options for entering or removing variables. Two iterative algorithms, the method of Jennrich and Moore (1975) or an approximation to the asymptotic covariance matrix of the estimates (ACE), are available. A table summarizing the stepwise results is included in the output as well as several goodness-of-fit statistics and tests for variables in and out of the model. Graphical displays are provided that can be helpful in the interpretation of the models, including a plot of the percent correct as a function of the cutpoint. If certain cases are weighted so that they are not used in estimation, cross-validation of the model is possible.

SPSS. The SPSS subroutine LOGISTIC REGRESSION estimates only binary logistic models. It is described in the Advanced Statistics User's Guide (SPSS Inc., 1990). Either tabulated data or data with one subject per case is accepted.

PC Programs

Because of the growing use of PCs to perform statistical analyses that were once the exclusive province of mainframe packages, we briefly discuss several PC programs here. Currently there are many available programs, but little knowledge of comparative performance. The general-purpose SYSTAT program (Wilkinson, 1988) provides logistic regression. We demonstrate its use in analyzing the example data below. The BMDP/386 PC package now provides the

LR and PR routines of the mainframe program. The GLIM package mentioned above is available in a PC version. Econometric programs, including SHAZAM (White, 1987; White and Bui, 1988) and LIMDEP (Greene, 1990), perform logistic regression, but these are less familiar to researchers outside of economics. Kikuchi (1985) and Dallal (1988) have written programs for IBM PCs. Kikuchi (1985) synthesized WLS and ML estimation approaches. Not enough is known about PC programs to recommend any of these programs for users at the present.

Two other general points bear mentioning to conclude this section on computer packages. First, we must state some reservations concerning the stepwise nature of several of the programs discussed above. Primarily, stepwise procedures are statistically, and not theoretically, driven. Also, exact significance rates using a stepwise variable selection algorithm are not known, even for OLS procedures. Given that less is known about maximum likelihood estimation, one is probably better off to assume that the situation is at least as bad for logistic regression. Therefore, *unless* a frankly exploratory search for significant predictors with a large number of cases *and* a suitable cross-validation sample is available, in our opinion it is preferable to estimate a specific model. Second, BMDP LR does not provide WLS estimation, although SAS does in the PROC CATMOD routine.

SUMMARY

Our aim was to provide an intermediate-level exposition of the logistic regression model. Several situations in which higher education researchers might employ logistic regression were described. We discussed several problems encountered when ordinary least squares (OLS) regression is used to fit the linear probability model (LPM) to binary response variables. Such problems support the utility of logistic regression as an alternative to the LPM. In this section we also mentioned more advanced sources from a variety of disciplines outside of the education area.

Basic concepts underlying logistic regression, including the logit transformation of the dichotomous responses, the logistic function, simple and multiple logistic regression models, and the assumptions of logistic regression, were discussed and examples given. Two major approaches to estimation, maximum likelihood and weighted least squares, were discussed. Approaches to model evaluation were detailed. Several computer programs and their output were described. Regression diagnostics were briefly presented In a subsequent section we compared discriminant function analysis and logistic regression. Finally, an extended example was presented to allow readers to see how logistic regression is implemented.

There were several topics that we did not present in order to minimize the complexity of the presentation. First, we covered only the binary response situation, but extension of logistic models to ordinal (Agresti, 1984) and polytomous (Agresti, 1989) cases is straightforward. SAS PROC CATMOD and BMDP PR can estimate the polytomous models, while SAS PROCS CATMOD and LOGISTIC can estimate ordinal models. Second, experimenters often measure multiple response variables. For situations in which a number of correlated binary responses are measured on each sampling unit, a multivariate setup is the appropriate analysis. Treatments of multivariate logistic models are contained in Nerlove and Press (1973) and Bock (1975). Bonney (1987) presents a related approach that decomposes dependence among the response variables in terms of conditional probabilities, each of which is modeled with a univariate logistic regression model. Third, latent variable or structural equation models that regard dichotomous and polytomous variables as indicators of underlying continua are another recent development (Muthen, 1984). In some ways this development is reminiscent of the dispute between Yule and Pearson concerning the appropriateness of assuming an underlying continuum for an observed categorical variable (cf. Pearson and Heron, 1913; Yule, 1912; cited in Goodman and Kruskal, 1954).

We believe that the flexibility of regression models is extended to the binary, ordinal, or polytomous response cases quite easily through the use of logistic regression analysis. Although the technique differs from OLS regression in several important features, there is enough similarity so that readers should be able to estimate and use a logistic regression analysis after reading this chapter. As a practical suggestion, we recommend that interested readers input the data in Table 1 and estimate a model that includes the interaction terms. Obviously, study of the source references is recommended to understand the technique in greater detail.

APPENDIX 1. Edited SAS Input and Output

1. Input Program:

```
1     OPTIONS LS=80 PS=55;
2     TITLE 'SAS LOGISTIC REGRESSION EXEMPLAR';
3     PROC FORMAT;
4         VALUE TEN 1='Granted' 0='Not granted';
5         VALUE GEN 0='Male' 1='Female';
6         VALUE RA 0='White' 1='Black' 2='Other';
7     DATA ONE;
8       INPUT ID TENURE GENDER RACE NUMPUBS;
9         LABEL   TENURE='Tenure granted'
10                GENDER='Sex of candidate'
11                RACE='Race of candidate'
12                NUMPUBS='Number of publications';
13    Black = 0; If race = 1 then black = 1;
14    Other = 0; If race = 2 then other = 1;
15        FORMAT TENURE TEN.;
16        FORMAT GENDER GEN.;
17        FORMAT RACE RA.;
18    CARDS; (data lines after this statement)
108   PROC LOGISTIC CT;
109   MODEL TENURE=GENDER BLACK OTHER NUMPUBS /
                   CORRB IPLOTS;
110   RUN;
```

Data Set:	WORK.ONE
Response:	TENURE (Tenure granted)
Levels:	2
Link Function:	Logit

2. Response Profile:

Ordered Value	TENURE	Count
1	Granted	31
2	Not granted	59

3. Simple Statistics for Explanatory Variables:

Variable	Mean	S.D.	Minimum	Maximum
GENDER	0.655556	0.477849	0.00000	1.0000
BLACK	0.288889	0.455785	0.00000	1.0000
OTHER	0.144444	0.353509	0.00000	1.0000
NUMPUBS	10.60000	5.194639	2.00000	32.0000

APPENDIX 1 (continued)

4. Criteria for Assessing Model Fit:

Criterion	Intercept Only	Intercept and Covariates	X^2 for Covariates			
AIC	117.909	88.490	.			
SC	120.409	100.989	.			
-2 LOG L	115.909	78.490	37.419	4 DF	p=.0001	
Score	.	.	31.309	4 DF	p=.0001	

5. Analysis of M.L. Estimates:

Variable	Parameter Estimate	S.E.	Wald X^2	Pr > X^2	Standard. Estimate
INTERCPT	-5.2761	1.1419	21.3472	.0001	.
GENDER	.9315	.6373	2.1366	.1438	.245415
BLACK	-.1492	.6481	.0530	.8179	-.037502
OTHER	-.1271	.8395	.0229	.8797	-.024763
NUMPUBS	.3654	.0834	19.1754	.0001	1.046379

6. Predicted Probabilities & Observed Responses:

```
Concordant = 83.4%        Somers' D = 0.683
Discordant = 15.0%        Gamma     = 0.694
Tied       =  1.6%        Tau-a     = 0.312
(1829 pairs)              c         = 0.842
```

7. Classification Table:

		Predicted EVENT	NO EVENT	Total
Observed	EVENT	17	14	31
	NO EVENT	6	53	59
	Total	23	67	90

Sensitivity=54.8%, Specificity=89.8%, Correct=77.8%
False Positive Rate=26.1%, False Negative Rate=20.9%
EVENTS are outcomes with response values of 1

APPENDIX 2. Edited SPSSX Input and Output

1. Input Program:

```
 1   SET WIDTH 80/LENGTH 55
 2   TITLE 'SPSS LOGISTIC REGRESSION EXEMPLE'
 3   DATA LIST / ID 2-4 TENURE 17 GENDER 33
     RACE 49 NUMPUBS 63-65
 4   VAR LABELS TENURE 'Tenure Granted'/
 5    GENDER 'Sex of cand'/RACE 'Race of cand'
 6   VALUE LABELS
      TENURE 0 'Not granted' 1 'Granted'/
      GENDER  0 'Male' 1 'Female'/
      RACE 0 'White' 1 'Black' 2 'Other'
 7   COMPUTE BLACK = 0  IF (RACE = 1) BLACK = 1
 8   COMPUTE OTHER = 0  IF (RACE = 2) Other = 1
 9   BEGIN DATA (data lines after this statement)
99   END DATA
100  LOGISTIC REGRESSION
        TENURE WITH GENDER BLACK OTHER NUMPUBS/
101     CLASSPLOT/ PRINT=CORR/
102     CASEWISE = ZRESID OUTLIER DFBETA
```

```
Dependent Variable Encoding:
Original Value      Internal Value
        0                   0
        1                   1
```

2. Dependent Variable & M.L. Estimates:

```
TENURE      Tenure Granted
Beginning Blk No. 0. Initial loglikelihood Function
-2 Log Likelihood:  115.90912 [Constant included]
```

```
Beginning Block Number  1.  Method:   Enter
Variable(s) Entered on Step Number
1..       GENDER     Sex of candidate
          BLACK
          OTHER
          NUMPUBS
```

Estimation terminated: loglikelihood decreased < .01

	X^2	df	Significance
-2 Log Likelihood	78.490	85	.6777
Model Chi-Square	37.419	4	.0000
Improvement	37.419	4	.0000
Goodness of Fit	80.440	85	.6197

APPENDIX 2 (continued)

3. Variables in the Equation:

Variable	B	S.E.	Wald	df	Sig	R	Exp(B)
GENDER	.9315	.6373	2.1364	1	.1438	.0343	2.5382
BLACK	-.1492	.6481	.0530	1	.8179	.0000	.8614
OTHER	-.1271	.8394	.0229	1	.8796	.0000	.8806
NUMPUBS	.3653	.0834	19.1746	1	.0000	.3849	1.4410
Constant	-5.2755	1.1418	21.3464	1	.0000		

4. Correlation Matrix:

	Constant	GENDER	BLACK	OTHER	NUMPUBS
Constant	1.000				
GENDER	-.51025	1.000			
BLACK	-.16405	-.00442	1.000		
OTHER	-.04438	-.12230	.25410	1.000	
NUMPUBS	-.86436	.15103	-.02461	-.06377	1.000

5. Individual Case Analysis:

CASE	Obs TENURE	ZResid	Const DFB0	Gender DFB1	Black DFB2	Other DFB3	NumPubs DFB4
4	S G **	2.9331	.4051	.0767	-.1212	-.1245	-.0301
26	S N **	-2.5426	.4271	-.1566	.1333	.1681	-.0402
56	S G **	2.9331	.4051	.0767	-.1212	-.1245	-.0301
58	S G **	2.3982	.4198	-.3417	.0034	.5920	-.0165

S=Selected; U=Unselected cases; ** = Misclassified
Studentized residuals greater than 2.000 are listed.

6. Observed Groups and Predicted Probabilities:

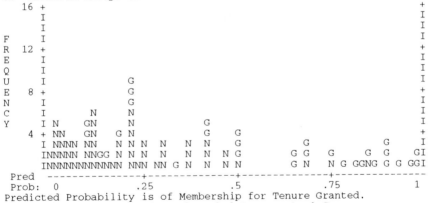

Predicted Probability is of Membership for Tenure Granted.
N=Not granted, G=Granted; Each Symbol Represents 1 Case.

APPENDIX 3. Edited BMDP Input and Output

1. Input Program:
```
/ INPUT      VARIABLES = 5.  FORMAT IS FREE.  UNIT=11.
  VARIABLE NAMES CASENUM,TENURE,GENDER,RACE,NUMPUBS.
/ GROUP
  CUTPOINTS(TENURE)=0.NAMES(TENURE)=REFUSED,GRANTED.
  CUTPOINTS(GENDER)=0.NAMES(GENDER)=MALE,FEMALE.
  CUTPOINTS(RACE)=0,1.NAMES(RACE)=WHITE,BLACK,OTHER.
/ REGRESS  DEPEND = TENURE.
           MODEL = GENDER,RACE,NUMPUBS.
           INTERVAL=NUMPUBS.
           METHOD = MLR.  ITER = 30.  LCONV = .001.
/ PRINT   LINESIZE = 72.  CELLS = MODEL.  PLOT.  COST.  HIST.
/ PLOT    SIZE = 40, 35.
/ END.
```

2. Case Analysis:
Number of cases to be printed   10

CASE NO.	1 CASENUM	TENURE	2 GENDER	3 RACE	4	5 NUMPUBS
1	1.00	GRANTED	FEMALE	WHITE		8.00
2	2.00	GRANTED	FEMALE	BLACK		9.00
3	3.00	REFUSED	MALE	BLACK		10.00
4	4.00	GRANTED	FEMALE	WHITE		6.00
5	5.00	REFUSED	FEMALE	BLACK		7.00
6	6.00	REFUSED	FEMALE	BLACK		9.00
7	7.00	REFUSED	MALE	WHITE		12.00
8	8.00	GRANTED	FEMALE	WHITE		18.00
9	9.00	GRANTED	FEMALE	WHITE		22.00
10	10.00	REFUSED	FEMALE	WHITE		3.00

Number of Cases Read. 90
Total Number of Responses Used in the Analysis 90.
Refused . . . . . .   59.
Granted . . . . . .   31.
Number of distinct covariate patterns . . . . . 55.

3. Analysis of M.L. Estimates:
```
Step 0        LOG LIKELIHOOD    = -39.24
GF CHI-SQ (2*O*LN(O/E))         = 36.76 df 50  P=.918
GF CHI-SQ (HOSMER-LEMESHOW)     = 6.535 df  8  P=.588
GF CHI-SQ ( C.C.BROWN )         = 0.311 df  2  P=.856
```

Term	Coeff	S.E.	Coef/SE	Exp (coef)	95% CI Exp(coef) Lower	Upper
GEND	-0.9315	.637	-1.46	0.394	0.111	1.40
RACE(1)	0.1492	.648	0.230	1.16	0.320	4.21
(2)	0.1271	.839	0.151	1.14	0.214	6.03
PUBS	-0.3654	.834E-01	-4.38	0.694	0.588	0.82
CONST	5.276	1.14	4.62	196.	20.2	.189E+04

APPENDIX 4. Edited SYSTAT Input and Output

1. Input Program:

```
OUTPUT NEWLOGIS
USE NEWLOGIS
NCAT = 2
MODEL
 TENURE = CONSTANT+GENDER+BLACK+OTHER+NUMPUBS
ESTIMATE
```

2. Multinomial Logit Analysis:

```
Dependent Variable:              TENURE
Number Of Records Processed:     90
Number of Choices in Each Category
==================================
        1           59
        2           31
```

Independent variable means:

	Variable	D = 1	D = 2
1	CONSTANT	1.000	1.000
2	GENDER	.6102	.7419
3	BLACK	.3051	.2581
4	OTHER	.1186	.1935
5	NUMPUBS	8.458	14.68

3. M.L. Estimates:

```
log likelihood at iteration 1 is  -62.383246
log likelihood at iteration 2 is  -41.604985
log likelihood at iteration 3 is  -39.410306
log likelihood at iteration 4 is  -39.246274
log likelihood at iteration 5 is  -39.244825
convergence achieved.  L.L.: -39.24482515616
```

	Parameter	Estimate	S. E.	t
1	CONSTANT	5.276057	1.141831	4.6207
2	GENDER	-.9315358	.6372641	-1.4618
3	BLACK	.1492401	.6480681	.23028
4	OTHER	.1270554	.8394237	.15136
5	NUMPUBS	-.3653616	.8342737E-01	-4.3794

-2 log likelihood ratio (X^2) :   37.419465 4 DF

4. Choice Probabilities for Each Category:

(Actual & Predicted Using Mean X's)

	Observed	Predicted
1	.6555556	.7014092
2	.3444444	.2985908

REFERENCES

Agresti, A. (1984). *Analysis of Ordinal Categorical Data*. New York: Wiley.

Agresti, A. (1989). *Categorical Data Analysis*. New York: Wiley.

Ahlgren, A., and Walberg, H.J. (1975). Generalized regression analysis. In D.J. Amick and H.J. Walberg (eds.), *Introductory Multivariate Analysis*. Berkeley: McCutchan.

Aitkin, M., Anderson, D., Francis, B., and Hinde, J. (1989). *Statistical Modelling in GLIM*. Oxford, England: Clarendon Press.

Aldrich, J.H., and Cnudde, C.F. (1975). Probing the bounds of conventional wisdom: A comparison of regression, probit, and discriminant analysis. *American Journal of Political Science* 19: 571–608.

Aldrich, J.H., and Nelson, F.D. (1984). *Linear Probability, Logit, and Probit Models*. Beverly Hills: Sage.

Amemiya, T. (1981). Qualitative response models: A survey. *Journal of Economic Literature 19*: 1483–1536.

Amemiya, T. (1985). *Advanced Econometrics*. Cambridge, MA: Harvard University Press.

Anderson, S., Auquier, A., Hauck, W.A., Oakes, D., Vandaele, W., and Weisberg, H.I. (1980). *Statistical Methods for Comparative Studies*. New York: Wiley.

Belsley, D.A., Kuh, E., and Welsch, R.E. (1980). *Regression Diagnostics: Identifying Influential Data and Sources of Collinearity*. New York: Wiley.

Berkson, J. (1944). Application of the logistic function to bioassay. *Journal of the American Statistical Association* 39: 357–365.

Berkson, J. (1949). Minimum X^2 and maximum likelihood solution in terms of a linear transform, with particular reference to bioassay. *Journal of the American Statistical Association* 44: 273– 278.

Berkson, J. (1951). Why I prefer logits to probits. *Biometrics* 7: 327–339.

Berkson, J. (1955). Maximum likelihood and minimum X^2 estimates of the logistic function. *Journal of the American Statistical Association* 50: 130–162.

Bishop, Y.M.M., Fienberg, S.E., and Holland, P.W. (1975). *Discrete Multivariate Analysis*. Cambridge, MA: MIT Press.

BMDP Statistical Software Manual (Vol. 2). (1990). Berkeley, CA: University of California Press.

Bock, R.D. (1975). *Multivariate Statistical Methods in Behavioral Research*. New York: McGraw-Hill.

Bock, R.D., and Jones, L.V. (1968). *The Measurement and Prediction of Judgment and Choice*. San Francisco: Holden-Day.

Bonney, G.E. (1987). Logistic regression for dependent binary observations. *Biometrics* 43: 951–973.

Brown, C.C. (1982). On a goodness of fit test for the logistic model based on score statistics. *Communications in Statistics, Theory and Method* 11: 1087–1105.

Buchanan, W. (1974). Nominal and ordinal bivariate statistics: The practitioner's view. *American Journal of Political Science*: 18, 625–646.

Chambers, E.A., and Cox, D.R. (1967). Discrimination between alternative binary response models. *Biometrika* 54: 573–578.

Cohen, J. (1968). Multiple regression as a general data-analytic system. *Psychological Bulletin* 70: 426–443.

Cohen, J., and Cohen, P. (1983). *Multiple Regression/Correlation Analysis for the Behavioral Sciences*. Hillsdale, NJ: Erlbaum.

Cornfield, J. (1951). A method of estimating comparative rates from clinical data: Applications to cancer of the lung, breast, and cervix. *Journal of the National Cancer Institute* 11: 1269–1275.

Cox, D.R. (1970). *Analysis of Binary Data*. London: Methuen.

Cox, D.R., and Snell, E.J. (1982). *Applied Statistics: Principles and Examples*. London: Chapman and Hall.

Cox, D.R., and Snell, E.J. (1989). *Analysis of Binary Data* (2nd ed.). London: Methuen.

Dallal, G.E. (1988). LOGISTIC: A logistic regression program for the IBM PC. *American Statistician* 42: 272.

Darlington, R.B. (1968). Multiple regression in psychological research and practice. *Psychological Bulletin* 69: 161–182.

Davis, J.A. (1974). Hierarchical models for significance tests in multivariate contingency tables: An exegesis of Goodman's recent papers. In *Sociological Methodology 1973– 1974*. San Francisco: Jossey-Bass.

Dhrymes, P.J. (1986). Limited dependent variables. In Z. Griliches and M.D. Intriligator (eds.), *Handbook of Econometrics*, Vol. III. New York: Elsevier.

Dillon, W.R., and Goldstein, M. (1978). On the performance of some multinomial classification rules. *Journal of the American Statistical Association* 73: 305–313.

Dillon, W.R., and Goldstein, M. (1985). *Multivariate Analysis*. New York: Wiley.

Efron, B. (1975). The efficiency of logistic regression compared to normal discriminant analysis. *Journal of the American Statistical Association* 70: 892–898 Efron, B. (1978). Regression and ANOVA with zero-one data: Measures of residual variation. *Journal of the American Statistical Association* 73: 113–121. Fienberg, S.E. (1980). *The Analysis of Cross-Classified Categorical Data* (2nd ed.). Cambridge, MA: MIT Press.

Finn, J.D. (1989). Withdrawing from school. *Review of Educational Research* 59: 117–142.

Finney, D.J. (1971). *Probit Analysis* (3rd ed.). Cambridge: Cambridge University Press.

Fleiss, J.L. (1981). *Statistical Methods for Rates and Proportions* (2nd ed.). New York: Wiley.

Fowlkes, E.B. (1987). Some diagnostics for binary logistic regression via smoothing. *Biometrika* 74: 503–515.

Gart, J.J. (1971). The comparison of proportions: A review of significance tests, confidence intervals, and adjustments for stratification. *Review of the International Statistical Institute* 9: 148–169.

Goldstein, M., and Dillon, W.R. (1978). *Discrete Discriminant Analysis*. New York: Wiley.

Goodman, L.A. (1963). On methods for comparing contingency tables. *Journal of the Royal Statistical Society*, A 126: 94–108.

Goodman, L.A. (1970). The multivariate analysis of qualitative data: Interactions among multiple classifications. *Journal of the American Statistical Association* 65: 225–256.

Goodman, L.A. (1975). A new model for scaling response patterns: Application of the quasi-independence concept. *Journal of the American Statistical Association* 70: 755–768.

Goodman, L.A. (1978). *Analyzing Qualitative/Categorical Data*. Cambridge, MA: Abt.

Goodman, L.A., and Kruskal, W.H. (1954). Measures of association for cross-classifications. *Journal of the American Statistical Association* 49: 732–764.

Greenberg, R.S., and Kleinbaum, D.G. (1985). Mathematical modeling strategies for the analysis of epidemiologic research. *Annual Review of Public Health* 6: 223–245.

Greene, W. (1990). *LIMDEP: A Program for the Analysis of Limited Dependent Variables*. New York: New York University.

Gujarati, D.N. (1988). *Basic Econometrics* (2nd ed.). New York: McGraw-Hill.

Haberman, S. (1978). *Analysis of Qualitative Data* (Vol. 1). New York: Academic Press.

Haberman, S. (1979). *Analysis of Qualitative Data* (Vol. 2). New York: Academic Press.

Halperin, M., Blackwelder, W.C., and Verter, J.I. (1971). Estimation of the multivariate logistic risk function: A comparison of the discriminant and maximum likelihood approaches. *Journal of Chronic Diseases* 24: 125–158.

Hanushek, E.A., and Jackson, J.E. (1977). *Statistical Methods for Social Scientists*. New York: Academic Press.

Harrell, F.E. (1986). The LOGIST procedure. In S. Joyner (ed.), *SUGI Supplemental Library User's Guide* (1986 Edition). Cary, NC: SAS Institute.

Harrell, F.E., and Lee, K.L. (1985). The practical value of logistic regression. *SUGI Proceedings* 031–1036.

Hinkle, D.E., Austin, J.T., and McLaughlin, G.R. (1989). Using loglinear models in research. In J.C. Smart (ed.), *Higher Education: Handbook of Theory and Research*, Vol. VI. New York: Agathon Press.

Hinkle, D.E., Wiersma, W., and Jurs, S.G. (1988). *Applied Statistics for the Behavioral Sciences* (2nd ed.). Boston: Houghton Mifflin.

Hoaglin, D.C., and Welsch, R.E. (1978). The hat matrix in regression and ANOVA. *American Statistician* 32: 17–22.

Hosmer, D.W., and Lemeshow, S. (1980). Goodness of fit tests for the multiple logistic regression model. *Communications in Statistics, Theory and Method* 9: 1043–1069.

Hosmer, D.W., and Lemeshow, S. (1989). *Applied Logistic Regression*. New York: Wiley.

Jennrich, R.I., and Moore, R.H. (1975). Maximum likelihood estimation by means of nonlinear least squares. *Proceedings of the American Statistical Association, Statistical Computing Section*: 7–65.

Judge, G.J., Griffiths, W.E., Hill, R.C., Lutkepohl, H., and Lee, T-C. (1985). *The Theory and Practice of Econometrics* (2nd ed.). New York: Wiley.

Kelsey, J.L., Thompson, W.D., and Evans, A.S. (1986). *Methods in Observational Epidemiology*. New York: Oxford University Press.

Kennedy, J.J. (1985). *Analysis of Qualitative Data*. New York: Praeger.

Kennedy, P. (1986). *A Guide to Econometrics* (2nd ed.). Cambridge, MA: MIT Press.

Kennedy, W.J., and Gentle, J.E. (1980). *Statistical Computing*. New York: Marcel Dekker.

Kerlinger, F. (1985). *Foundations of Behavioral Research* (3rd ed.). New York: Holt, Rinehart, and Winston.

Kikuchi, D.A. (1985). Alleycat: Logistic regression on the IBM PCJr. *Proceedings of the American Statistical Association, Statistical Computing Section*: 165–167.

Kleinbaum, D.G., Kupper, L.L., and Chambless, L.E. (1982). Logistic regression analysis of epidemiologic data: Theory and practice. *Communications in Statistics, Theory and Method* 1: 485–547.

Kleinbaum, D.G., Kupper, L.L., and Morgenstern, H. (1982). *Epidemiologic Research: Principles and Quantitative Methods*. Belmont, CA: Lifetime Learning Publications.

Knoke, D., and Burke, P.J. (1980). *Log-linear Models*. Beverly Hills: Sage.

Koch, G.G., and Edwards, S. (1985). Logistic regression. In C. Read (ed.), *Encyclopedia of Statistical Sciences*, Vol. 5. New York: Wiley.

Kriska, S.D., and Milligan, G.W. (1982). Multiple regression analysis for categorical data with an illustrative application in personnel selection. *Psychological Bulletin 92*: 193–202.

Landwehr, J.M., Pregibon, D., and Shoemaker, A.C. (1984). Graphical methods for assessing logistic regression models. *Journal of the American Statistical Association* 79: 61–83.

Luce, R.D., and Suppes, P. (1965). Preference, utility, and subjective probability. In R.D. Luce, R. Bush, and E. Galanter (eds.), *Handbook of Mathematical Psychology*, Vol. 3. New York: Wiley.

Maddala, G.S. (1983). *Limited-dependent and Qualitative Variables in Econometrics.* Cambridge, England: Cambridge University Press.

Malik, H.J. (1985). Logistic curves and logistic distributions. In S. Kotz and N.L. Johnson (eds.). *Encyclopedia of Statistical Sciences,* Vol. 4. New York: Wiley.

Mantel, N., and Hankey, B.F. (1975). The odds ratio of a 2 × 2 contingency table. *Journal of the American Statistical Association* 29: 143–145.

Marascuilo, L.A., and Busk, P.L. (1987). Loglinear models: A way to study main effects and interactions for multidimensional contingency tables with categorical data. *Journal of Counseling Psychology* 34: 443–455.

Maxwell, A.E. (1974). The logistic transformation in the analysis of paired-comparison data. *British Journal of Mathematical and Statistical Psychology* 7: 62–71.

McCullagh, P. (1980). Regression models for ordinal data (with discussion). *Journal of the Royal Statistical Society* B, 42: 109–142.

McCullagh, P., and Nelder, J.A. (1983). *Generalised Linear Models.* London: Chapman and Hall.

McFadden, D. (1974). Conditional logit analysis of qualitative choice behavior. In P. Zarembka (ed.), *Frontiers in Econometrics.* New York: Academic Press.

McFadden, D. (1984). Econometric analysis of qualitative response models. In Z. Griliches and M. Intriligator (eds.), *Handbook of Econometrics,* Vol. 2. Amsterdam: North-Holland.

Mosteller, F. (1968). Estimation and association in contingency tables. *Journal of the American Statistical Association* 63: 1–28.

Muthen, B. (1984). A general structural equation model with dichotomous, ordered categorical, and continuous latent variable indicators. *Psychometrika* 49: 115–132.

Nelder, J.A., and Wedderburn, R.W.M. (1972). Generalized linear models. *Journal of the Royal Statistical Society,* A 135: 370–384.

Nerlove, M., and Press, S.J. (1973). *Univariate and Multivariate Loglinear and Logistic Models.* Technical Report R-1306 EDA/NIH. Santa Monica, CA: Rand Corporation.

Neter, J., Wasserman, W., and Kutner, M.H. (1985). *Applied Linear Statistical Models* (2nd ed.). Homewood, IL: Irwin.

Neter, J., Wasserman, W., and Kutner, M.H. (1989). *Applied Linear Regression Models* (3rd ed.). Homewood, IL: Irwin.

Nord, R.D., et al. (1986). *Propensity and the Reenlistment Decision.* TR 723, Army Research Institute for the Behavioral and Social Sciences, Alexandria, Virginia.

Olian, J.D., Taylor, M.S., and Trader, R.L. (1985). Special problems in analyzing dichotomous dependent variables: A conceptual and empirical discussion. Unpublished manuscript, Department of Management, University of Maryland, College Park, MD.

Oliver, J.D., and Hinkle, D.E. (1986). Regression analysis with dummy variables: Use and interpretation. *Journal of Vocational Education Research* 11: 17–32.

Page, W.F. (1977). Interpretation of Goodman's log-linear model effects: An odds ratio approach. *Sociological Methods and Research* 5: 419–435.

Pascarella, E.T. (1980). Student-faculty informal contact and college outcomes. *Review of Educational Research* 50: 545–595.

Passmore, D.L., and Mohamed, D.A. (1984). Application of logistic regression techniques in survey research. *Journal of Vocational Education Research* 8: 1–9.

Pearson, K., and Heron, D. (1913). On theories of association. *Biometrika* 9: 159–315.

Pregibon, D. (1981). Logistic regression diagnostics. *Annals of Statistics* 9: 705–724.

Press, S.J., and Wilson, S. (1978). Choosing between logistic regression and discriminant analysis. *Journal of the American Statistical Association* 73: 699–705. Pindyck, R.S., and Rubinfeld, D.L. (1981). *Econometric Models and Economic Forecasts* (2nd ed.). New York: McGraw-Hill.

Rao, C.R. (1973). *Linear Statistical Inference and Its Applications* (2nd ed.). New York: Wiley.

Roberts, G., Rao, J.N.K., and Kumar, S. (1987). Logistic regression analysis of sample survey data. *Biometrika* 74: 1–12.

Rothman, K.J. (1986). *Modern Epidemiology*. Boston: Little, Brown.

SAS Institute. (1986). *SUGI Supplemental Library User's Guide* (1986 Edition). Cary, NC: SAS Institute.

SAS Institute. (1990). *User's Guide* (Ver. 6, Vol. 2, 4th ed). Cary, NC: SAS Institute.

Schlesselman, J.J. (1982). *Case Control Studies: Design, Conduct, Analysis*. New York: Oxford University Press.

Smith, V., and Cichetti, C. (1975). Regression analysis with dichotomous dependent variables. Paper presented at the Third World Congress of the Econometric Society, Toronto, Canada.

Snell, E.J. (1987). *Applied Statistics: A Handbook of BMDP Analyses*. London: Chapman and Hall.

Somes, G.W., and O'Brien, K.F. (1985). Odds ratio estimators. In S. Kotz and N.L. Johnson (eds.), *Encyclopedia of Statistical Sciences*, Vol. 5. New York: Wiley.

SPSS Inc. (1990). *Advanced Statistics User's Guide*. Chicago: McGraw-Hill.

Steinberg, D., and Colla, P. (1991). *Logistic Regression: A Supplementary Module for SYSTAT and SYGRAPH*. Evanston, IL: SYSTAT Inc.

Stevens, J.P. (1984). Outliers and influential data points in regression analysis. *Psychological Bulletin* 95: 334–344.

Tatsuoka, M.M. (1988). *Multivariate Analysis for Education and Psychology* (2nd ed.). New York: McGraw-Hill.

Terenzini, P.T., and Pascarella, E.T. (1977). Voluntary freshman attritition and patterns of social and academic integration in a university: A test of a conceptual model. *Research in Higher Education* 6: 25–43.

Terenzini, P.T., and Pascarella, E.T. (1978). The relation of students' precollege experiences and freshman year experience to voluntary attrition. *Research in Higher Education* 9: 347–366.

Terenzini, P.T., and Pascarella, E.T. (1980). Toward the validation of Tinto's model of college student attrition: A review of recent studies. *Research in Higher Education* 12: 271–282.

Theil, H. (1971). *Principles of Econometrics*. New York: Wiley.

Thisted, R.A. (1988). *Elements of Statistical Computing*. New York: Chapman and Hall.

Tinto, V. (1975). Dropout from higher education: A theoretical synthesis of recent research. *Review of Educational Research* 45: 89–125.

Walker, S.H., and Duncan, D.B. (1967). Estimation of the probability of an event as a function of several independent variables. *Biometrika* 54: 167–179.

White, K.J. (1987). SHAZAM: A general computer program for econometric methods. *American Statistician* 41: 80.

White, K.J. and Bui, L.T.M. (1988). *Basic Econometrics: A Computer Handbook Using SHAZAM*. New York: McGraw-Hill.

Wilkinson, L. (1988). *SYSTAT: The System for Statistics*. Evanston, IL: Systat Inc.

Yaffee, R.A. (1990). Profile of pathological gamblers undergoing treatment. In *Final Report: Task Force on Gambling Addiction in Maryland* Baltimore: Alcohol and Drug Abuse Administration, Maryland Department of Health and Mental Hygiene.

Young, F.W., deLeeuw, J., and Takane, Y. (1976). Regression with qualitative and quantitative variables: An alternating least squares algorithm with optimal scaling features. *Psychometrika 1*: 505–529.

Yule, G.U. (1912). On methods of measuring association between two attributes. *Journal of the Royal Statistical Society* 75: 579–642.

A Critique of Intensive Courses and an Agenda for Research

Patricia A. Scott

and

Clifton F. Conrad
University of Wisconsin-Madison

Traditional course formats have remained relatively unchanged in American higher education: most colleges and universities schedule their courses several times per week for 12 to 16 weeks. Although there has been little evidence to support their use over various alternatives, traditional course formats continue to dominate in higher education owing to long-standing collegiate and bureaucratic traditions (Hefferlin, 1972).

Recently, however, changing student demographics have prompted a rapidly growing interest in intensive courses—semester- or quarter-equivalent classes offered in compressed formats. Concerned with maintaining enrollments, colleges and universities are courting adult and part-time students by offering intensive courses which better accommodate students' schedules. As a result, thousands of students have been afforded the opportunity to pursue a baccalaureate or post-baccalaureate degree which otherwise might have been impossible.

Yet, the growing presence of intensive courses on many college and university campuses has generated disapproval among many faculty and administrators. Conventional wisdom has long criticized intensive courses as being too compressed "to produce anything of educational value" (Slichter in Schoenfeld, 1967, p. 160). They have been reproached for sacrificing breadth, short-shrifting academic standards to accommodate time constraints, and obliging students to "cram" information at the expense of genuine learning and development.

Nevertheless, given adult and part-time student demographic trends, intensive courses probably will proliferate in the future. According to the National Center for Education Statistics (1989a), adult student enrollments increased 114 percent between 1970 and 1985 and now constitute an estimated 42 percent of post-

This project was supported by the Division of Summer Sessions and Inter-College Programs at the University of Wisconsin-Madison. We wish to express our sincere appreciation to Dean Harland Samson for his valued contributions.

secondary enrollments. Meanwhile, part-time student enrollments rose nearly 87 percent during the same time period and now comprise approximately 43 percent of enrollments in postsecondary education. Thus, there is every reason to expect that colleges and universities will continue to experiment with time-intensive course formats.

As intensive course formats grow, so too does the body of research which compares intensive and traditional courses. These investigations cut across a range of disciplines, fields of study, course formats, and degrees of intensiveness. Yet there have been no major attempts to conceptualize and synthesize the scattered literature, much less serious efforts to critique the extant research and suggest new avenues for future investigations. This paper sets out to address this lacuna.

PROCEDURE

This review of the literature was drawn from numerous sources. As a point of departure, we used the Educational Research Information Clearinginghouse (ERIC) to identify studies on intensive courses. We then conducted computerized searches in the *Social Science Index*, *PsycLit*, and *Dissertation Abstracts* data bases to locate additional articles and dissertations. References cited throughout these sources pointed to additional articles, chapters, and unpublished studies. Altogether, we found roughly 100 publications that, in varying degrees, addressed intensive courses. After reviewing the collective literature, we identified four major lines of related inquiry: 1) time and learning studies; 2) studies of educational outcomes comparing intensive and traditional formats; 3) studies comparing course requirements and practices between intensive and traditional formats; and 4) studies of student and faculty attitudes toward intensive courses.

We begin our discussion by tracing the origins and development of intensive courses. We then briefly touch on related educational research on time and learning. Our review of intensive course research begins by focusing on studies of educational outcomes, which are reviewed based on the type of intensive format investigated (summer, interim, modular, regular term, and weekend), the discipline studied, and the long-term learning effects. We then briefly examine research comparing course requirements and practices between traditional and intensive formats, after which we examine the literature on student and faculty attitudes regarding different types of intensive formats. We conclude with a critique of the literature, some proposed research questions, and a discussion of intensive courses as they pertain to educational policy and practice.

HISTORY OF INTENSIVE COURSES

Present day intensive courses evolved from several antecedents including summer sessions, interim sessions, modular calendar systems, weekend colleges, and foreign language training programs developed during World War II. Each of these educational innovations introduced a distinct form of intensive collegiate learning.

Summer Sessions

Summer sessions, the earliest expression of concentrated study, were instrumental in legitimizing intensive courses in American higher education. Summer sessions emanated from several historical sources. Teacher institutes, which first appeared in 1839, were one of the earliest influences. These institutes, which were designed to upgrade elementary and secondary school teaching skills, later "evolved into summer normal schools" at many colleges and universities (Schoenfeld, 1967, p. 10). Other precipitating forces responsible for the emergence and expansion of summer schools included the Chautauqua movement of the 1870s; mechanical and agricultural institutes, popular during the 1880s and 1890s; the rapid rise and expansion of graduate education; and the growth of university extension programs beginning in 1907 (Davis, 1972).

Private universities were the early pioneers of summer sessions. Harvard University was the first postsecondary institution to offer summer courses beginning in 1869, courses which were initially short-term, non-credit, refresher classes for teachers (Schoenfeld, 1967). Johns Hopkins University (which utilized the summer months for the pursuit of scholarly research) and the University of Chicago (which introduced a four quarter system in 1892) also helped popularize summer sessions in the United States. Most public institutions did not incorporate summer terms until the late nineteenth century but gradually colleges and universities adopted a summer session as a means to bolster enrollments and spread fixed-costs over the entire year (Gleason, 1986). Currently, the vast majority of all higher education institutions offer a summer term—most of which utilize intensive course designs.

Interim Sessions

A more recent departure from traditional semester and quarter terms is the interim session, one of the first calendar innovations to have "lasting and broad impact" (Conrad, 1978, p. 183). Colleges and universities originally designed this three- to four-week term as an innovative alternative to concurrent scheduling, which allowed students to concentrate exclusively and intensively on a single subject. Interim sessions developed out of a "dissatisfaction with [the] arbitrary temporal patterns" imposed by most colleges and universities and "represent[ed] an effort to [temporally] match term structure" with varying educational objectives (Conrad, p. 182). Since their inception at Florida Presbyterian College (now Eckerd College) in 1961, interim sessions have proliferated and many postsecondary institutions now offer some type of interim term.

Modular Calendar Systems

The belief that intense, concentrated study enhances learning led some colleges and universities to adopt modular calendars, bringing interim-like sessions to the academic year. Scio College in Ohio was the first to adopt a modular calendar. Its "One-Study Plan," which it introduced following the Civil War, required students to explore one subject until they "mastered" the content (Powell, 1976, p. 7). In 1877, Williamston Female College in South Carolina also introduced an intensive calendar system. Williamston divided its school year into seven terms, and students studied one subject each session. For more than 30 years, this plan was followed, and Williamston claimed it significantly increased students' attention and retention (Powell, 1976).

The first college in the twentieth century to adopt a modular-type calendar was Hiram College in Ohio. The Hiram Study Plan divided the academic year into four quarters of nine weeks each; students studied one intensive course each term along with a "running course" that continued throughout the entire year (Eckleberry, 1958, p. 225). Despite strong student support for the plan, faculty and administrative discontent led Hiram College to revert to a more traditional calendar in 1958 (Powell, 1976). Meanwhile, a number of other colleges have introduced modular calendar systems in the last several decades. Three of the most notable examples are Colorado College in Colorado, Martin College in Tennessee, and Mount Vernon College in Washington, D.C.

Language Acquisition Programs

Also significant in the evolution of intensive courses were the World War II foreign language training programs developed by the United States and British armies. These programs were considered highly successful; indeed, the United States Army's Special Training Program (ASTP) reportedly could train interpreters to fluency within months (Powell, 1976). Success with concentrated language programs suggested that intensive study could be a powerful alternative to traditional learning formats. Consequently, following the war, many college faculty who had experienced these programs introduced intensive coursework in their colleges and universities (Powell, 1976).

Weekend Colleges

In the mid-1960s, still another intensive format emerged—the weekend college, which catered primarily to working adult students. Miami-Dade Junior College offered the first such program in 1965, but weekend colleges did not proliferate until the 1970s (East, 1988). Recent surveys indicate that weekend colleges are currently experiencing rapid growth. According to a 1986 survey of both two-year and four-year institutions, there are approximately 225 weekend colleges nationwide, 55 of which emerged in 1985 or 1986 (East in Watkins, 1989). As a result of their proliferation, thousands of adults, primarily between 25 and 50 years of age, are matriculating in weekend colleges (Watkins, 1989).

TIME AND LEARNING

Educational researchers have long been interested in the concept of time and learning. Four areas of time-related inquiry and research have engaged scholars: massed versus spaced learning, concentrated study, interference theory, and allocated time and learning. A brief synopsis of each provides a useful context that helps to frame our critique and inform future research.

Massed Versus Spaced Learning

In study after study, researchers have found that distributing information over several spaced presentations is far superior to learning material in a single "massed" session.

Massed versus spaced learning research dates back to Ebbinghaus's classical learning experiments in the late nineteenth century. Ebbinghaus (1964) found that spaced practice was clearly superior to massed practice with regard to learning nonsense syllables. Ebbinghaus's findings have been replicated in dozens of studies under myriad conditions. According to Dempster and Farris (1990), one of the "most dependable and robust phenomena in experimental psychology" is the spacing effect (p. 97).

In summarizing the literature, Dempster and Farris (1990) conclude: "two spaced presentations are about twice as effective as two massed presentations, and the difference between them tends to increase as the frequency of repetition increases" (p. 97). Many theories have been offered to explain this phenomenon. Anderson (1990), for example, contends that spaced learning promotes variable encoding in memory. In this instance, encoding refers to the conversion of information into a form of code which is then stored in memory. Variable encoding increases the avenues of access to stored information which in turn, increases the opportunity for retrieval from memory at a later date.

Glover's and Corkill's (1987) study is representative of massed versus spaced investigations. Glover and Corkill required "massed" groups to read a 99–word paragraph or listen to a brief tape-recorded lecture twice during one intensive session, while the "spaced" groups read or heard the same material in two sessions separated by a 30–minute interval. Glover and Corkill found that "spaced" subjects recalled significantly more of the written/lecture material than the "massed" groups, which the researchers attributed to variable encoding.

In the same vein, Bahrick's and Phelps's (1987) study found that the differential effects of massed and spaced practice are long-lasting. Bahrick and Phelps tested subjects' retention of English-Spanish word pairs they learned 8 years earlier under spaced (30–day intervals) and massed (24 hour and no interval) learning conditions. Their findings revealed that the subjects who learned under spaced conditions recalled nearly two to three times as much as the "massed" groups.

It is tempting to hypothesize from this research that traditional-length courses are likely to yield superior long-term learning outcomes over intensive courses. However, as Hefferlin (1972) noted, intensive courses do not reflect massed practice as defined in many of these experiments. In his words:

> Instead they actually illustrate distributed [i.e., spaced] practice, since they employ daily cycles of rest and effort comparable to the 24 hour cycle sometimes used in distributed practice experiments (Hefferlin, 1972, p. 94).

Thus, it remains unclear how massed and spaced research relates to intensive courses. However, the scant research indicates this is an important area for further study.

Concentrated Study

Walberg's (1988a, 1988b) and Csikszentmihalyi's (1982) research on creativity and subjective experiences suggests that intensive periods of concentrated study may benefit students in ways not yet understood. Walberg (1988b), whose research has explored the origins and nature of creativity, notes that:

> psychological studies of the lives of eminent painters, writers, musicians, philosophers, religious leaders, and scientists of previous centuries, as well as prizewinning adolescents in this country today, reveal early, intense concentration on previous work in their fields, often to the near exclusion of other activities (p. 76).

Similarly, Csikszentmihalyi's (1982) research suggests that "deep concentration," "immersion" in an activity, and "undivided intentionality" lead to intrinsically rewarding "optimal experiences" which nourish and strengthen the self (p. 22). Csikszentmihalyi comments:

> Optimal experience stands out against this background of humdrum everyday life by excluding the noise that interferes with it in normal existence. Thus the first characteristic mentioned by people who describe how they feel at the height of enjoyment is a *merging of action and awareness*; a concentration that temporarily excludes irrelevant thoughts, feelings from consciousness. This means that stimuli outside the activity at hand have no access to consciousness; past and future cease to exist subjectively. This continuous focus on the present produces a *distortion of time* perspective. Minutes seem to stretch for hours, or hours elapse in minutes: Clock time is replaced by experiential sequences structured according to the demands of the activity (p. 22).

According to Csikszentmihalyi, optimal experiences result in a *"loss of self consciousness"* which yields true enjoyment and satisfaction (p. 22). Moreover, once felt, optimal experiences are self-perpetuating since high levels of satisfaction motivate the individual to seek additional experiences of a similar nature.

To be sure, such research is still in its infancy, and the question remains whether all students can benefit from intense, concentrated study. These investigations suggest, nonetheless, that concentrated study may cultivate skills and understandings which might remain untapped and undeveloped under the traditional system.

Interference

Interference theory guided a number of studies in the 1950s and 1960s, and was investigated under a wide variety of conditions and situations. In brief, interference theory predicts that similar tasks preceding or following a learning activity will "interfere" with an individual's long-term retention of the learned material. For example, Underwood (1957) found that the more lists (such as nonsense syllables and geometric forms) subjects learned, the less they recalled. He attributed this to "proactive interference," defined as interference from previously learned material (p. 53). Researchers speculate that interference weakens encoding which, in turn diminishes an individual's ability to retrieve stored information from memory.

With regard to education, some have speculated (Boddy, 1985; Hefferlin, 1972) that interference may diminish learning under concurrent scheduling, where students divide their attention between four to five courses each semester. According to Hefferlin (1972), concurrent schedules distract students and promote fragmented learning while, in contrast, intensive schedules foster uninterrupted and concentrated learning.

In one of the few studies to apply interference theory to intensive scheduling, Boddy (1985) studied students' performance in four intensive summer courses and four matched semester-length classes. He predicted an inverse relationship between course load and achievement and hypothesized that larger course loads would encumber learning because of increased levels of "interference." However, Boddy found no relationship between course load and achievement. Thus, without additional research, the connection between interference theory and course scheduling remains unclear.

Allocated Time and Learning

Finally, many researchers have studied the quantity of time needed to learn. Most educators believe more time fosters more learning. This argument has been advanced in support of the semester versus the quarter calendar system. However, research indicates that the relationship between time and learning is less than clear-cut. For example, Karweit's (1984) review of the time and learning literature concluded that "time is a necessary, but not sufficient, condition for learning" (p. 33). Walberg's (1988b) review concurred, and further emphasized that time in and of itself is only a "modest" predictor of achievement. Other factors, including "student aptitude," "quality of instruction," the amount of "productive classroom time," and the classroom and home environments, are equally important to achievement (p. 84). In addition, Gettinger (1984) argued that educators must also consider the "time needed to learn" (p. 15). This, she contends, is important since student learning rates differ depending on the task and learner characteristics. In short, these studies suggest that while the quantity of time spent is a contributing factor, other factors may be equally or more important in predicting student achievement. They also suggest that simply allocating fixed amounts of time to learning—without considering the factors listed above—diminishes every student's learning potential.

RESEARCH ON INTENSIVE COURSES

Many writings and a substantial number of studies compare various intensive and traditional course formats in higher education. The literature includes case studies as well as research using experimental, quasi-experimental, and cross-sectional survey designs. The emphasis, however, has clearly been on non-experimental and quasi-experimental research.

Our review of these studies is divided into six sections. The first section deals with studies measuring short-term intensive learning outcomes associated with five intensive course formats. [The reader is directed to Appendix A, which summarizes this research in tabular form.] Next, these same studies are re-examined by discipline to compare outcomes across disciplines and fields of study. The third section briefly explores the few studies that have examined the long-term effects of intensive courses. The fourth section summarizes research comparing course requirements and practices between intensive and traditional formats, and the last two sections look at the literature on student and faculty attitudes concerning intensive courses.

Outcomes by Type of Intensive Course

This section reviews the research on the educational outcomes of intensive courses. The research falls into five formats: summer, interim, modular, regular term, and weekend formats. Three representative studies will be discussed under each format including a case study and two experimental investigations.

Summer

Summer courses typically last from three to eight weeks and find expression in a variety of intensive designs. Formats range from total immersion to semi-intensive programs enrolling students concurrently in two or three classes. In the last several decades, there have been a number of experimental studies investigating intensive summer courses. Most of these studies have found no statistical differences between intensive and traditional course formats (Austin, Fennell, and Yeager, 1988; Bester, 1965; Kanun, Ziebarth, and Abrahams, 1963; and

Murphy, 1979), but three have found modest differences in favor of intensive learning (Boddy, 1985; Gaston, 1974; and Gleason, 1986). In addition to the experimental research, a number of case studies have found in favor of intensive summer courses (Deveny and Bookout, 1976; Eller, 1983; Keilstrup, 1981; Parlett and King, 1971; Solecki, 1971; Stephens, 1978; Troiani, 1986). The following three studies are representative of the intensive summer course research.

Kanun et al. (1963) were among the first to investigate intensive course formats in higher education. Kanun et al. compared the test scores of three sections of a psychology class after controlling for instructor, lectures, textbooks, and examinations. The only difference between the classes was that two of the sections were taught during a ten-week quarter (28 hours of instructional time) and the third section was taught during a five-week summer session (24 hours of instructional time). They found no significant differences in achievement between the three groups—findings which replicated the results of a pilot study they conducted one year earlier. Kanun et al. concluded that the spacing effect had little impact on outcomes as it relates to summer and traditional-length classes. They called for continued research to identify the optimal factors in learning.

Gleason (1986) compared student achievement between three sections of a summer macroeconomics course taught in either a 3– or 5–week format and four sections of the same course taught during the regular semester. She administered the nationally normed Revised Test of Understanding in College Economics (TUCE) as a pre-test measure of aptitude and post-test measure of achievement. Gleason found that students in the 3– week macroeconomics course scored significantly higher on the post-test than the 15–week class, although she noted that the groups were not statistically equivalent. She found no outcome differences between the 5– and 15–week courses. Gleason concluded that the calendar period had no impact on achievement in economics and that "intensive [summer] courses are at least as effective as semester-length courses taken concurrently with other subjects" (p. 98).

Foreign languages have been studied vis-a-vis intensive instruction more than any other discipline, and most investigations have found intensive courses to be effective alternatives to traditional course formats. For example, Eller (1983) described a 16–credit summer Spanish course offered at the University of Nebraska-Omaha. The class met six hours a day, five days a week, for eight weeks, incorporating a total of 240 hours of instruction. That was the equivalent of two years of Spanish instruction taken under the traditional format. According to Eller, the summer students' test scores were equal to, if not better, than those earned in regular courses, attrition rates were lower, and summer students exhibited greater conversational skills at the end of the course "probably because the students had been given the opportunity to concentrate fully on the subject"

(p. 226). Due to constant planning requirements, intensive courses were more demanding of instructors, Eller noted, but he concluded that intensive Spanish summer courses were highly successful options to traditional formats.

Interim

Interim courses are unique because they often exhibit a quasi-immersion design which intensively involves students in one course for three to four weeks. Our literature review found three experimental studies which compared intensive interim courses with semester or quarter-length classes. Two of these studies found no differences in outcomes between these two formats (Masat, 1982; Studdard, 1975); one reported mixed results (Richey, Sinks, and Chase, 1965). There have also been several case studies describing intensive interim courses, and all positively recommended intensive formats (DuVerlie, 1973; Tyler, 1970; Wallace, 1972). The following studies are representative of the research in this area.

Richey et al. (1965) were among the first to investigate student achievement in the intersession. Richey and his colleagues compared the course grades of students in 11 "matched" courses, one-half of which were offered during a 17–week spring semester and one-half of which were offered during a 13– day intersession. Courses were matched based on the course number, instructor, and content. Although analysis revealed nonsignificant differences in seven of the 11 pairs of courses, significant outcomes were found in the remaining four: intersession courses were favored by a three-to-one margin.

Richey and his colleagues then compared intersession and semester student achievement after grouping students according to class standing, grade point average, gender, age, and college enrollment. Altogether, the researchers studied 18 separate groups of students registered for either intersession or semester classes. Ten intersession groups earned significantly higher grades than their semester counterparts. Exclusive subject groups included junior and senior students, male and female students, students aged 22 and younger, and students registered for arts and sciences and business courses. Conversely, two groups of semester students—those registered for education classes and graduate students with a grade point average of 3.0 or less—outperformed the same groups enrolled in intersession classes. Six of the 18 groups exhibited nonsignificant achievement differences.

Richey et al. concluded that student performance in the intersession equaled that of the semester term and suggested that "consideration . . . be given to the possibilities of expanding course offerings in the Intersession so that the needs of a greater number of students may be met" (p. 41). They also cautioned that intersession courses "should be taught by enthusiastic, experienced and competent instructors, who are able to adapt themselves to the concentrated nature of

Intersession, and who have positive feelings toward teaching in a short term'' (pp. 41–42).

Masat (1982) examined a computer science "immersion" course that was offered during a 12–day interim term at Glassboro State College. The class met four full days per week for three weeks. Masat compared the interim students' final grades with grades earned in matched semester-length and 6–week summer courses with the same content, homework, and examinations. He found that the intersession class "compare[d] favorably" to the other formats and that the "intensive" students' mean course grade was slightly higher than that earned in either the matched semester or summer courses (p. 328). Moreover, he observed closer relationships among class members and increased student productivity; which he attributed to fewer interruptions and greater "inherent cohesiveness" in the intensive class (p. 328). Masat concluded that "students [in the intersession course] learned as well or better than in either a semester or summer session course" and that "three weeks can be used to teach an introductory computer science course efficiently and effectively without any loss in academic integrity" (p. 328).

Finally, Wallace (1972) examined seven intensive courses in French, German, Russian, and Spanish offered at The School for International Training during a January interim session. These courses were offered to both beginning and intermediate-level students. The classes met six hours a day, six days a week, for three weeks; the nationally normed MLA Cooperative Foreign Language Test was given as a post-test measure of achievement. Wallace found that beginning foreign language students scored above the 50th percentile for one year college general norms in three of the four areas tested. Moreover, students with only one year of previous language instruction scored just below the 2½-year norms. He concluded that three weeks of intensive language instruction could yield equal if not superior learning outcomes to a 30–week class offered in a traditional semester-length format.

Modular

Modular systems represent a unique learning environment where intensive courses are the norm, not the exception. Typically, the academic year is divided into five to ten modules and students concentrate intensively on one or two courses each term. Of the studies reviewed comparing modular and traditional schedules, three found no significant differences in outcomes, (Blackburn, Armstrong, and Dykes, 1977; Haney, 1985; Waechter, 1966) and two reported superior results in favor of modular scheduling (Kuhns, 1974; Mazanec, 1972). The literature review also revealed one case study which endorsed intensive courses (Richardson, 1973). Three representative studies of modular formats are discussed below.

In 1975, along with its semester-length classes, the University of Wisconsin-

TABLE 1. Summary of Mazanec's Findings

	Pre- and Post-Test Scores	Final Grades
Algebra	no differences in outcomes	no differences in outcomes
Speech	no differences in outcomes	6-week class exceeded 15-week class
English	6- and 15-week classes exceeded 3-week class	3-week class exceeded 15-week class
Political Science	3-week class exceeded 6- and 15-week classes	3- and 6-week classes exceeded 15-week class

Oshkosh instituted a modular schedule which divided the fall and spring semesters into two 7–week and one 3– week term, and the summer session into two 4–week terms. As a result of the new system, courses during the regular academic year were scheduled for either 3, 7, or 14 weeks. To evaluate educational outcomes in intensive courses, an evaluation team compared course grades between 3– , 7–, and 14–week matched classes. According to their analysis, none of the course formats exerted a "differential impact on either student learning or student assessment of instruction" (Blackburn et al., 1977, p. 40). However, the evaluation team noted that 3– week courses produced slightly higher course grades than their 14–week or 7–week counterparts, and 7–week classes yielded higher course averages than 14–week courses. In addition, students earned higher grades in courses offered in the first 7 weeks than in the same course scheduled in the second 7 weeks of the semester (p. 26). Finally, 14–week classes had greater percentages of incompletes and withdrawals than either the matched 7– or 3– week courses.

Mazanec's (1972) study also investigated modular and concurrent scheduling formats. He randomly assigned 75 students to one of two formats—an intensive or a semi-intensive schedule. The "intensive" group took four consecutive courses (speech, algebra, English, and political science) during the semester and each class met three hours a day for three weeks. The "semi-intensive" group took the same four courses, but two at a time, and each class met seven hours per week for six plus weeks. A control group studied the same four subjects, but classes were scheduled concurrently over the entire semester. The same instructors taught corresponding classes in each of the three formats.

Mazanec compared pre-to post-test scores and final course grades in the intensive, semi-intensive, and semester-length classes. Only three analyses yielded nonsignificant outcomes, while the other five yielded significant findings in favor of intensive courses. Table 1 summarizes Mazanec's findings based on course and outcome measures.

Mazanec concluded that "it appears that certain courses are indeed taught in a more effective manner under the intensified and semi-intensified systems of instruction than under the conventional semester system'' (p. 144).

Richardson (1973) described an intensive German course offered at Colorado College, which had adopted a modular calendar system in 1970. Under its modular system, each academic year was divided into nine 3½-week blocks. Consequently, the previously required two-semester sequence of German was modified into an eight-week, two block sequence. The resultant German course incorporated 14–16 contact hours per week, which Richardson likened to the U.S. Army language training methods. According to Richardson, the modular system allowed instructors to re-create German culture within the classroom, promoted experimentation and diversification of teaching methods, and freed instructors from the "tyranny of the bell" (p. 192). In turn, these attributes prompted in-depth class discussions, and freed students from competing demands from other courses, allowing them to concentrate exclusively on German. However, Richardson inferred that students' retention of intensively learned material was inferior to that learned in longer, less concentrated courses. Indeed, he recommended "maintenance courses" to insure long-term retention (p. 193).

Regular Term
Intensive courses offered during the regular semester or quarter represent another interesting variation, since these courses are often taken concurrently with traditional-length classes. A number of researchers have studied intensive courses offered during the regular semester. With only one exception, the experimental research reviewed has found no significant differences in learning outcomes between compressed courses and quarter- or semester-length classes (Allen, 1974; Austin et al., 1988; Brackenbury, 1978; Doyle and Sanders as reported in Doyle, 1978; Kirby-Smith, 1987; Knowles, 1972). However, one study reported significant outcomes in favor of intensive courses (Ray and Kirkpatrick, 1983). The literature search also found one case study which also positively recommended intensive courses (Frank, 1973). The following three studies are representative of the research in this tradition.

Knowles (1972) used five different measures of achievement to compare 18 public administration students enrolled in a semester-long research methods course with 15 students enrolled in the same course meeting seven hours a day for seven days. Course content and class requirements were the same for each class. Knowles found no statistical differences between the two groups on any of his outcome measures (which included grades on quizzes, a term project, a critique of an article, a "mini-study," and the final course grade), and recommended that intensive formats "become a permanent part of a graduate school curriculum" provided that research continued to yield similar results (p. 114).

Ray's and Kirkpatrick's (1983) study assessed the impact of different time formats on both learning and attitudinal change. They measured students' anxiety, knowledge, and attitudes regarding human sexuality after taking either a 3–week or 15–week human sexuality course held during the regular semester. The 3– week class met for 3 hours a day, 5 days a week; the semester-length course met 3 hours each week for 15 weeks. Both courses had the same instructors. Ray and Kirkpatrick administered the Sex Knowledge and Attitude Test (SKAT) and the State-Trait Anxiety Inventory (STAI) as pre- and post-tests to measure students' sexually related anxiety, sexual knowledge, and sexual attitudes. They found that both groups exhibited significant decreases in anxiety, greater tolerance for a variety of sexual behaviors, and increases in sexual knowledge. But, the students in the intensive course exhibited significantly higher pre-to post-test gain scores in sexual knowledge than students in the semester-length class. Ray and Kirkpatrick concluded that "the duration of the course is less important than the method of teaching it" (p. 84).

Finally, Frank (1973) reported on an intensive course in German which concentrated four semester-long German courses into one 14–credit-hour intensive course. The course met 20 hours per week through the semester. According to Frank, students found the course to be highly rewarding but difficult compared with their other university courses. Despite its difficulty, students in the intensive course consistently scored higher on comprehensive examinations and found the intensive course more stimulating than traditional-length German courses. As a result of its success, a higher proportion of students enrolled in upper-division German courses, and other foreign language disciplines within the department inaugurated their own intensive foreign language courses.

Weekend

In many respects, weekend programs exhibit the most concentrated form of intensive learning. At the one extreme, courses can be compressed into two weekends and still amass up to 40 hours of classroom time. This has led to widespread concern that achievement levels between weekend and traditional formats are not comparable.

A number of investigators have researched intensive weekend courses. Without exception, experimental studies comparing weekend and traditional-length courses have found no significant differences in learning outcomes (Austin et al., 1988; Brackenbury, 1978; Doyle, 1978; Doyle, Moursi, and Wood, 1980; Doyle and Yantis, 1977; Shapiro, 1988). Of the three case studies reviewed, all reported positive outcomes and endorsed intensive formats (Berk, 1979 and Lasker, Donnelly, and Weathersby, 1975; Pflanzer and East, 1984). The following experimental and case studies exemplify the research in this tradition.

Brackenbury (1978) compared final examination grades in eight sections of a philosophy of education class. All sections had the same instructor, course requirements, textbook, and final examination. The duration of the classes was the only difference. There were three 15–week sections, two 8–week , and three weekend sections that met over four consecutive weekends. Brackenbury reasoned that philosophy required "lengthy exposure" to "internalize such perspectives" and predicted that students in the semester-length sections would outperform those in the intensive sections (p. 93). Instead, he found no significant association between final exam grades and course format and concluded that varying course formats did not significantly impact on learning.

Doyle, Moursi, and Wood (1980) randomly assigned 39 students enrolled in a graduate class in business administration to one of two groups. The control group met two hours a week for 16 weeks; the intensive group completed the class over the course of two weekends. Instructor, total classroom time, content, and instructional methods were identical. Doyle and his colleagues compared students' course grades and scores on a cognitive achievement test designed to measure knowledge and understanding of administrative concepts. While no significant differences between the two groups on outcome measures were found, the intensive group's mean course grade was slightly higher than the traditional group's, and the traditional group scored higher on the cognitive achievement test. Doyle et al. concluded that "students in this format apparently learn as much as well as students in traditional formats and do not seem to be unduly exerted in doing so" (p. 14). Furthermore, they recommended that intensive courses remain in the curriculum.

Berk (1979) described an intensive statistics class offered at the University of Southern California in which students met for eight hours each day for eight consecutive Saturdays. One month prior to the beginning of the class, students received the textbook and course outline along with reading assignments to be completed by the first class session. Once the class began, each eight hour session consisted of lectures of 45 minutes to 1½ hours, alternated with problem-solving sessions. According to Berk, the statistics course

> "received consistently high ratings by students and positive comments by faculty members who teach courses for which statistics is a prerequisite. Its structure and applied orientation, in fact, have been instrumental in attracting students from sociology, political science, and criminology programs at other area universities" (p. 88).

In summary, the short-term outcome studies comparing intensive and traditional course designs suggest that intensive courses are effective alternatives to traditional course formats. If one accepts course grades, final examination scores, and pre- and post-tests as valid measures of achievement, then there is modest—but consistent—evidence that intensive courses yield equivalent, and sometimes superior, outcomes in comparison with traditional formats. The case studies also point to the relative effectiveness of intensive course designs. Without exception, these studies report that students benefit from the concentrated, unfragmented, and uninterrupted learning associated with intensive classes.

When these findings are broken down further, the research suggests that intensive courses also yield equal if not superior outcomes regardless of their format. As shown in Appendix A, which categorizes all the studies according to format, the preponderance of nonsignificant outcome studies under each format suggests that there are relatively minor differences in student achievement based on type of format.

Finally, when these findings are examined across various levels of intensity (e.g., 2 weekends, eight weeks), the research shows no substantial differences in outcomes. Of the ten studies which compared different degrees of intensity, seven reported nonsignificant differences in outcomes (Austin et al., 1988; Blackburn et al., 1977; Brackenbury, 1978; Doyle and Sanders in Doyle, 1978; Kanun et al., 1963; Masat, 1982; and Shapiro, 1988). Of the remaining three studies, one reported findings in favor of the most intensive format studied (Gleason, 1986), one in favor of the least intensive format studied (Boddy, 1985), and the last reported mixed results which varied according to the subject matter (Mazanec, 1972).

However, it is important to note that the methodological and measurement limitations associated with most of these studies, discussed at length in a later section, suggest that it is premature to draw any definitive conclusions. We turn now to a discussion of outcomes research organized by discipline and field of study.

Outcomes by Discipline

Studies of intensive courses have been conducted in a range of disciplines and fields of study. Table 2 provides a summary of major studies organized by discipline and study design (experimental or case study). The table further indicates whether the experimental studies found significant differences in favor of intensive (+ intensive) or traditional (+ traditional) courses.

Table 2 shows (with only one exception) that regardless of discipline, the research finds either no differences between intensive and traditional-length classes or superior outcomes in favor of intensive courses. Of all the disciplines or subdisciplines reported in Table 2, the findings can be summarized as follows: 13 exhibited no significant differences between intensive and traditional formats; 5 disciplines had significant findings in favor of intensive learning; and 6 disciplines exhibited mixed results. All the case studies, which encompassed 10 different disciplines/ subdisciplines, reported positive outcomes in favor of intensive formats.

Table 3 compares results across major fields of study—humanities, social sciences, sciences, and the professions—when the disciplines are grouped according to major field.

Table 3 shows that the social sciences exhibited the largest proportion of significant findings, followed by the humanities. Only one of the studies in the sciences and two of the studies in the professions showed significant outcomes.

TABLE 2. Outcome Studies by Field of Study and Discipline

Field of Study/ Discipline	Experimental Studies			Case Studies*
	Nonsignificant	Significant + Intensive	Significant + Traditional	
HUMANITIES				
English	Allen, 1974 Richey et al., 1965	Mazanec, 1972		
Foreign Languages (general)				Tyler, 1970 Wallace, 1972
French		Gaston, 1974		DuVerlie, 1973 Stephens, 1978
German				Frank, 1973 Richardson, 1973 Keilstrup, 1981
Russian				Solecki, 1971
Spanish				Deveny & Bookout, 1976 Eller, 1983 Troiani, 1986
History	Boddy, 1985			
Philosophy	Brackenbury, 1978			
Speech		Mazanec, 1972		
MATHEMATICS AND SCIENCE				
Mathematics				
Algebra	Mazanec, 1972			
Calculus	Kanun et al., 1963			
Computer Science	Masat, 1982	Boddy, 1985		
Diff. Equations	Kanun et al., 1963			
Statistics				Berk, 1979
Science				
Biology				Pflanzer & East, 1984
Earth Science	Waechter, 1966			
Geography	Doyle & Sanders (in Doyle, 1978) Richey et al., 1965			

(*continued*)

TABLE 2. Outcome Studies by Field of Study and Discipline (*Continued*)

| Field of Study/ Discipline | Experimental Studies | | | Case Studies* |
	Nonsignificant	Significant + Intensive	Significant + Traditional	
Health	Kanun et al., 1963			
Physics				Parlett & King, 1971
Physical Science	Studdard, 1975			
SOCIAL SCIENCES				
Economics	Gleason, 1986 Murphy, 1979	Gleason, 1986		
Human Development				Lasker et al., 1975
Human Sexuality		Ray & Kirkpatrick, 1983		
Political Science		Mazanec, 1972		
Psychology	Kanun et al., 1963 Doyle & Yantis, 1977 Richey et al., 1965	Richey et al., 1965		
Sociology	Kanun et al., 1963	Richey et al., 1965		
PROFESSIONS				
Architecture				Parlett & King, 1971
Business Admin.	Doyle et al., 1980			
Education	Richey et al., 1965 Boddy, 1985		Richey et al., 1965	
Home Economics		Richey et al., 1965		
Library Science	Richey et al., 1965			
Pharmacy	Bester, 1965			
Research Methods	Austin et al., 1988 Knowles, 1972			

+ Intensive—outcomes favor intensive course
+ Traditional—outcomes favor traditional course
*All case studies reported positive outcomes in favor of intensive courses

TABLE 3. Number of Studies Reporting Significant or Nonsignificant Outcomes According to Major Field of Study

	Significant	Nonsignificant	Total
Humanities	3	5	8
Social Sciences	5	6	11
Math and Sciences	1	9	10
Professions	2	8	10

All significant outcomes in the humanities, sciences, and social sciences favored intensive courses while one of the significant studies listed under the professions favored traditional-length courses, and the other favored intensive classes.

It seems remarkable that of all the higher education studies reviewed, only one found intensive courses inferior to traditional-length classes (Richey et al., 1965). This study, as discussed earlier, compared the final course grades between 11 matched courses—one-half of which were semester-length classes and one-half, 13–day intersession courses. The findings revealed that of the 11 pairs of courses studied, only one semester-length course—a graduate class in education—yielded superior outcomes compared with its equivalent in the intersession. All other courses exhibited either nonsignificant or significant outcomes in favor of intensive learning.

In addition to Richey et al.'s study, however, our literature review located one other investigation which found outcomes in favor of longer classes. (Since it studied a noncollege population, it was not included in Appendix A or Tables 2 and 3.) Ilika and Longnion (1977) offered reading classes for two groups of government employees; one group met for 5½ weeks and the other for 11 weeks. Otherwise the "total hours of instruction, instructor, content, tests, and behavioral objectives were the same" (p. 2). The researchers administered the Nelson-Denny Reading Test and the McGraw-Hill Basic Skills System Reading Test as pre- and post-test measures of achievement. The results indicated that the 11-weekgroup's scores on the Nelson-Denny Reading Test increased significantly more than the 5½-week class's. There were no significant differences in outcome on the McGraw-Hill test. Ilika and Longnion concluded that students in adult reading improvement courses learn significantly more under spaced versus massed instructional conditions.

In summary, the vast majority of research on intensive learning indicates equal if not superior short-term results for intensive courses regardless of the discipline or field of study under investigation—although data on the sciences and professions are less convincing. These results also coincide with Eckert's (1972) observation that the great majority of courses can be effectively adapted to a time-compressed format with proper modifications; foreign language and social science courses would be the most successfully adaptable because they often incorporate a considerable amount of class discussion. Our analysis concurs. Although the mechanism for learning is unknown, certain fields of study may benefit from intensive courses more than others.

Long-Term Outcomes

One of the most important questions regarding intensive courses remains: What is the long-term impact on learning? Studies discussed above measured achievement immediately following course completion, but long-term outcomes are equally if not more important—especially in light of spacing effect research. Unfortunately, our literature review located only three studies that compared long-term outcomes between intensive and traditional formats.

Stewart's (1934) study investigated the differences between modular and concurrent scheduling in high school. Stewart compared 180 tenth-year high school students divided into two groups. The control group studied four courses concurrently over a 12 week semester (English, Latin, French, or Spanish, and geometry) with each class period equaling 40 minutes. The experimental group took two courses every six weeks and class periods were extended to 80 minutes. Otherwise, the courses, instructors, content, examinations, and course requirements were identical. Stewart administered standardized achievement tests immediately following the end of the courses, and found that the experimental group's performance exceeded the control group's in every subject. When tested six months later, however, the "concentrated" groups' scores declined significantly more than the "traditional" groups. According to Stewart:

> One might infer from this that the learning of the concentration group "faded out" more rapidly than that of the regular group. In this particular case, however, it should also be pointed out that the mean of the concentration group in November [immediately following the course] was higher than the mean of the regular group in May [six months following completion of the course]. In other words, even with what they had forgotten, the concentration group in November still knew as much as the regular group knew at the close of the experimental period in May (p. 33).

In another study reported earlier, Doyle and his colleagues (1980) studied a business administration class that was offered both in an intensive and a traditional format. While they found that the intensive group earned slightly higher final grades, scores on the cognitive achievement test, administered immediately following the end of the course, were slightly lower. When a post-test was administered nine months later, they found no significant differences across the two groups in terms of their follow-up test scores, but results were slightly higher for the intensive group.

Finally, Waechter (1966) studied two groups of students enrolled in an Elements of Earth Science class that was offered under massed (9–week) and spaced (18–week) conditions. Each class had the same instructors and total amount of instructional time (66 hours). Waechter administered a pre-test and three post-tests: one immediately following course completion, the second after 3 months, and the last 4½ months later. He found no statistical differences in the short-term (pre-test to post-test 1) or long-term (pre-test to post-test 3) gain scores between the two groups and concluded that massed and spaced learning conditions yielded equivalent results.

Although the spacing effect literature discussed earlier suggests that traditional formats may yield superior long-term outcomes over intensive learning conditions, the studies reviewed above suggest otherwise. It seems reasonable to conclude, if future research yields similar findings, that intensive courses are generally not representative examples of massed practice and therefore, one would not likely find significant differences in long-term outcomes between intensive and traditional formats. Clearly more research is needed to provide a more definitive answer.

Course Requirements and Practices

One complaint often lodged against intensive courses concerns academic standards. Many individuals in higher education suggest that intensive courses sacrifice academic standards in the process of adapting to time-compressed formats. For example, Blackburn's et al. (1977) study found that 44 percent of the faculty surveyed at the University of Wisconsin-Oshkosh felt that the 3– and 7–week modular courses negatively affected academic standards. Kirby-Smith's (1987) study noted similar concerns.

Our review did not find any studies that specifically addressed academic standards, but there are several studies that have compared course requirements and practices. For example, Kirby-Smith's (1987) survey of faculty who taught intensive and traditional courses found that one-half of all respondents felt a need to alter the ''mode of presentation'' in order to successfully adapt a traditional course into a time-compressed format (p. 90). Only 45 percent of the respondents strongly agreed or agreed that the two formats could use the same syllabus, readings, and evaluation procedures. Moreover, many faculty respondents said ''projects had to be shortened'' and students were often unable to submit a finished product (p. 91). According to Kirby-Smith, ''many [faculty also] saw a need either to cut the amount of material covered or to cover the material in less depth'' (p. 91).

Allen and his colleagues (1982) surveyed January interim faculty from 36 colleges nationwide and found that they were less likely to lecture, use a standard textbook, cover as much material, assign term papers, and grade on the basis of tests and quizzes than during the regular academic term. However, on a positive note, faculty indicated that they were more likely to utilize in-depth group discussions, "individual and small group projects," experiential learning, and "off-campus activities" (p. 231). Faculty also noted "greater depth of coverage" and "depth of student comprehension" in January interim classes (p. 231).

Similarly, Adelman and Reuben (1984) noted that the Colorado Block Plan, in contrast to traditional formats, utilized more audio-visual presentations, "more computer simulations and fewer labs," journal articles and fewer textbooks, and more quizzes and short essay assignments as opposed to final examinations or term papers (p. 92). Shapiro (1988) also reported differences in course requirements between the two types of formats. He found that his sample of weekend instructors required fewer examinations but valued more class participation and term papers than his sample of instructors in more traditional classes.

Finally, a whole host of case studies indicate that instructors adapt their instructional methods in intensive courses (Deveny and Bookout, 1976; Eller, 1983; Lasker et al., 1975; Parlett and King, 1971; Powell, 1976). Lasker et al. (1975) for example, examined intensive courses at Harvard's Graduate School of Education (HGSE) and compared them with more traditional classes. According to Lasker and his colleagues, HGSE's intensive courses were more process-oriented and encouraged experiential learning. In addition, intensive faculty adopted a more facilitative teaching role and varied class experiences to maintain student interest. Overall, Lasker and his colleagues noted that "intensive courses provide a context for learning that can have enormously high focus and impact" (p. 8).

In summary, the results of these studies suggest that course requirements and practices often differ between intensive and traditional formats but the significance of these findings is unclear. Research is needed to determine if these differences affect academic standards and student achievement. It seems clear, nonetheless, that faculty modify intensive courses in significant ways.

Student Attitudes Toward Intensive Courses

Many researchers have operated on the assumption that courses which heighten student enthusiasm, curiosity, motivation, and enjoyment are more likely to enhance student learning than those that do not. In turn, they have sought to measure students' attitudes regarding their educational experiences. A number of studies have investigated students' viewpoints with regard to intensive courses, and the majority have found that students generally endorse intensive learning—albeit with some reservations. The following section summarizes this research across the five major types of intensive formats: summer, interim, modular, regular term, and weekend. Several representative studies are discussed at length.

Summer

Scholars have surveyed (Patterson, Sedlacek, and Tracey, 1981) or examined (Deveny and Bookout, 1976; Eller, 1983; Keilstrup, 1981; Parlett and King,

1971) students' attitudes towards intensive summer courses and, generally, have found that students typically rate their experiences favorably. The following two studies are representative of the research on summer students' attitudes.

Patterson and his colleagues (1981) surveyed 302 summer students at the University of Maryland-College Park campus and found that students viewed summer courses as much more intense than classes in the regular term and considered their summer courses "stimulating and exciting" (p. 32). The researchers also found significant differences in student satisfaction based on race and gender: non-white females and white males reported significantly greater course satisfaction than white females and non-white males.

Other researchers have measured student satisfaction regarding specific summer courses. Parlett and King (1971), for example, examined student evaluations of an experimental four-week summer physics class offered at the Massachusetts Institute of Technology. At the end of the course, students were asked to rank the aspects of the class they appreciated most. The top three rankings included: a) "get to know an MIT professor well"; b) "have discussion with the instructor"; and c) "work on something continuously rather than having to break off to work on another subject" (p. 18).

In this same study, students were also asked to submit written comments. Parlett and King (1971) analyzed these comments and found that "students perceived the experience as more 'real,' more efficient, more intensive, more integrated, more challenging, and certainly as more enjoyable than their previous physics courses" (p. 27). At the same time, however, students noted "that had it not been for the diversity of activity, the varying schedule, and all the other 'extras' associated with . . . [the course], overstimulation and strain would certainly have been experienced" (p. 19). Overall, the student evaluations overwhelmingly favored the intensive over the traditional format and the researchers concluded that intensive courses were "more conducive to intellectual excitement, effective teaching, and active student participation, than the more conventional arrangement" (p. 28).

Interim

All the literature examining students' attitudes towards interim courses—which included several surveys (Rossman, 1967, 1971; Centra and Sobol, 1974; Lightfield, 1972) and case studies (DuVerlie, 1973; Masat, 1982)—reported positive student evaluations of intensive interim formats. Rossman (1967, 1971) was one of the first researchers to study student attitudes concerning interim sessions. He surveyed 15 to 20 percent of the students at Macalester College for each of four successive years following the inauguration of an interim term. He found that more than three-fourths of the students surveyed, regardless of gender or prior academic record, rated their enjoyment of the interim session higher when compared with other academic terms . Rossman summarized his findings as follows:

During each of the four years, at least three-fourths of the students sampled have seen Interim Term as a successful educational venture and approximately two-thirds have found it to be a personally rewarding educational experience (1967, p. 542).

Centra and Sobol (1974) found strong student support for Rider College's interim term, with some reported preferences. Students rated the social science and science and math courses highest and general liberal arts and business classes lowest. Moreover, among the eight interim study programs offered at Rider College, students evaluated travel and off-campus programs as most effective and lecture and library project programs as the least effective.

DuVerlie (1973) and Masat (1982) also examined student responses to interim courses. DuVerlie described students' responses to an intensive interim course in French offered at the University of Maryland. Students enjoyed the relaxed learning atmosphere and 75 percent indicated they "felt *more* motivated to work and learn [in the interim class] than in their other courses and found learning was not only 'fun' but that more of it took place" (p. 17). Masat recorded several typical student responses to a computer science course offered during a 12–day interim session. One student remarked, "You always had your mind on the subject. Everything was always fresh and you were totally involved with the course" (p. 326). Another student wrote that "in this course you must keep up with the work. If you don't, you may not catch up" (p. 327). Based on the overall positive student response and outcomes, Masat enthusiastically endorsed the intensive format as an efficient and effective alternative to traditional-length courses.

Regular Term

We found three studies which examined student attitudes toward intensive courses offered during the regular semester or quarter (Frank, 1973; Kirby-Smith, 1987; Nahrgang, 1982). Kirby-Smith (1987) administered a 36–item questionnaire to students enrolled in 15 intensive and 12 matched semester-long courses and compared the groups' responses. She identified three questionnaire items that significantly differentiated the groups: students in the intensive group were more critical of the volume of work required, were more likely to report that there was insufficient time to complete assignments, yet were more likely to favor the inclusion of more intensive courses into the university's curriculum.

Kirby-Smith also asked students to identify the advantages and disadvantages of intensive courses. The advantages reported included "scheduling," "over quickly," "less travel time," "concentrated study," "aids in child care," "able to take more courses," "less wasted time," "less expense," and "learn more"—findings which suggest that "intensive" students prefer concentrated formats primarily for their convenience more than their educational merits (p. 106). The disadvantages most often identified were fatigue, excessive workload, "too short a time to process information," "stress," and "could not cover all the material" (p. 126). Significantly, when asked which format they preferred, 86 percent of the intensive students favored the concentrated over the traditional format; only 45 percent of the traditional group indicated the same preference. In addition, 70 percent of the intensive group, as compared with 63 percent of the traditional group, felt that more intensive courses were needed in the curriculum. Yet, after analyzing the total student response, Kirby-Smith concluded that:

> The negative attitudes expressed by faculty and students toward intensive courses being offered concurrently with 15–week courses are cause for alarm and signal a need for further research. . . . Considering the data available regarding problems encountered by faculty and students who are exposed to an intensive and traditional course calendar concurrently, it may be advisable for colleges and universities to limit enrollment in intensive courses to a select group of students who are enrolled in special programs in which all courses are being offered in the intensive mode (pp. 130–131).

Thus, despite the fact that intensive students favored additional intensive courses in the curriculum, Kirby-Smith's analysis of student responses suggested that colleges and universities should scrutinize the practice of scheduling intensive and traditional-length courses concurrently.

Nahrgang (1982) described an intensive German course offered at North Texas State University. The course was the equivalent of four traditional-length German classes and allowed students to complete their foreign language requirement in one semester. According to Nahrgang, students were very satisfied with the intensive experience and rated the course favorably. In fact, on a scale of one ("very successful") to ten ("very unsuccessful"), student evaluations of the course averaged 2.08 (p. 30). Nahrgang attributed the positive student response to the strong collegial relationships formed in the class, the varied instructional methods, and the strong student/faculty commitment to the program.

Weekend
Several studies have surveyed students regarding their attitudes towards weekend courses (Doyle et al., 1980; Doyle and Yantis, 1977; Shapiro, 1988). Doyle and his colleagues, for example, compared student evaluations of a graduate business administration course offered in an intensive and traditional format. Students were asked to evaluate the difficulty and scope of the course, course objectives, required workload, degree of interest stimulated in the subject, amount learned, level of enjoyment, overall value of the course, and the recommendation they would provide to a friend. Doyle and his colleagues found no significant differences between the weekend and traditional students' evaluations on these variables. Intensive students were also asked to evaluate whether concentrated formats "interfered with their ability to complete the course requirements" and whether they "placed *undue* hardships on them with respect to completing the

[course] requirements'' (p. 11). According to Doyle and his colleagues, 40 percent of the intensive students agreed that concentrated formats interfered with assignment completion, but only 25 percent agreed that they caused "*undue* hardships" (p. 11).

In contrast to Doyle's et al. overall findings, Shapiro (1988) found significant differences between students' evaluations of intensive and traditional courses. Shapiro compared graduate student course evaluations submitted in 117 nine-week classes which met one night a week and 204 weekend classes which met over the course of two, three, or four weekends. He found that weekend students, when compared with the nine-week group, reported greater overall satisfaction with their courses, greater interest in the subject matter, and greater course difficulty. They were also more likely to indicate that they learned more, would recommend the course to a friend, and that the instructor's evaluation of the students was fair.

Finally, despite the fact that student response to intensive courses is generally favorable, Doyle and Yantis (1977) offered a summary of common student complaints. According to Doyle and Yantis, students often complain that "far too much work is compressed into too short a time period [and] that the instructor attempted to cover too much material in too short a period of time . . ." (p. B234). They concluded that students are generally enthusiastic about the learning experience but are also keenly conscious of the time constraints and additional pressure.

Modular

There have also been a number of studies concerning student attitudes toward modular courses (Blackburn et al., 1977; Heist and Taylor, 1979; Mazanec, 1972). Blackburn and his colleagues reported that two-thirds of the students who completed intensive courses under the University of Wisconsin-Oshkosh's modular system indicated they were satisfied or very satisfied with the intensive courses. Students also reported "more time to concentrate on the subject," that material was adequately covered, and that such courses were better suited for students holding part-time jobs (Wisconsin, 1978, p. 10). Nevertheless, when a sample of the total student body was asked which time-format they preferred, 70 percent favored 14–week classes.

Colorado College also measured student attitudes after the college converted to a modular system. It surveyed two large samples of graduating seniors in 1977 and 1978 and found that over 90 percent of both samples described their overall experience under the modular plan as moderately to highly favorable and they recommended continuing the Colorado Plan unchanged or with minor modifications (Heist and Taylor, 1979).

Finally, Mazanec (1972) measured students' opinions of four classes (speech, English, political science, and algebra), offered in an intensive (3–week), semi-intensive (6–week), or traditional (15–week) format. When asked which format they preferred, students in the traditional classes demonstrated no significant preference for any particular format; students in the semi-intensive sections favored the semi-intensive time frame over all others; and students in the intensive classes preferred political science and speech in the 3–week format but were "equally divided" between the 3– week or 6–week format for English and mathematics (p. 143). This study indicates that students who experience intensive courses generally prefer them over traditional formats but they favor greater or lesser degrees of intensity depending on the subject matter.

Factors Influencing Variations in Student Attitudes

As the last section illustrated, most studies have found students to be favorably inclined toward intensive learning regardless of type of intensive format. At the same time, however, the research to date shows that different groups of students exhibit more or less support for intensive courses depending on a number of factors: part time enrollment, year in college, achievement level, discipline, and age. To begin, enrollment status has been found to be an influential element. Friedman's (1980) survey of students at a small liberal arts college found that full-time students preferred traditional-length courses which met two or three times per week. Noonan (1977) reported similar results, except his sample of students preferred 90 minute class meetings, twice a week.

Year in college and achievement level also influence student opinion. Rossman (1971) noted that upper division students and students with higher grade point averages rated Macalester College's Interim Term higher vis-a-vis lower division students and students with lower grade point averages.

Student support for intensive study also seems to be influenced by discipline or field of study. Humphrey (in Shapiro, 1988) analyzed student evaluations from 53 master's-level classes in administration and found that course satisfaction was unrelated to its time-format—with one exception: students were more dissatisfied with intensive quantitative courses. Doyle and Yantis (1977) reported similar findings, but Shapiro (1988) found no such association.

Centra and Sobol (1974) reported that students enrolled in social science, science, and math courses evaluated their interim classes higher than students enrolled in other fields of study. Moreover, Mims (1983) surveyed 407 interim art students nationwide and found that they favored intensive schedules over concurrent course formats. According to Mims, students indicated that intensive classes allowed longer periods for concentrated work, stimulated student interest and motivation, and fostered faculty enthusiasm.

Finally, age appears to be another important factor influencing student attitudes. Kirby-Smith (1987) found that significantly more nontraditional students (aged 25 and over) favored additional intensive courses in the institution's curriculum compared with traditional-age students.

In summary, this section reviewed the research related to student attitudes towards intensive courses. Generally, students evaluate intensive courses favorably, particularly those that have experienced concentrated formats. Students especially seem to appreciate their convenience and efficiency, the opportunity they provide for concentrated and uninterrupted study, and the interest and motivation they inspire. Conversely, they dislike the time constraints, stress, and fatigue. Research indicates that certain course formats—such as regular term intensive courses—may heighten stress and fatigue more than others.

Finally, the research suggests that certain student groups support intensive courses more than others. Preliminary research findings indicate that part-time and nontraditional students often prefer intensive courses over traditional formats, as do students in certain disciplines such as social sciences and art.

Despite the fact that these studies consistently find substantial student support of intensive courses, additional research is needed to measure possible variations in student assessments based on student characteristics (e.g., age), course characteristics (e.g., quantitative), course format (e.g., regular term), or degrees of intensity (e.g., two weekend vs. eight weeks).

Studies of Faculty Attitudes Toward Intensive Courses

While surveys have consistently found that students support intensive courses, faculty attitudinal surveys reveal more mixed results. On the one hand, several studies indicate that faculty prefer to teach in traditional time-frames (Friedman, 1980; Kirby-Smith, 1987; Noonan, 1977). On the other hand, a larger number of studies have reported strong faculty endorsements of intensive courses (Allen et al., 1982; Berk, 1979; Centra and Sobol, 1974; Doyle and Yantis, 1977; Eller, 1983; Lasker et. al, 1975; Masat, 1982; Mazanec, 1972; Parlett and King, 1971; Shapiro, 1988; Solecki, 1971). The following discussion reviews the faculty-related research and categorizes the studies according to whether the investigation concerned summer, interim, modular, regular term, or weekend intensive courses. The more representative or illustrative studies are discussed at length.

Summer

Our review uncovered only one survey which measured faculty perceptions of summer school. Tracey, Sedlacek, and Patterson (1980) surveyed summer school faculty at a large state research university. Their findings revealed that summer faculty did not perceive many differences between summer and regular term classes, although advantages and disadvantages were acknowledged. Advantages to teaching in summer school most often identified included supplemental income, small classes, and greater student-faculty interaction; disadvantages included insufficient time to properly cover course material and for students to synthesize information, faculty fatigue, and inadequate faculty compensation. Overall, faculty disapproved of courses shorter than 4½ weeks but were "neutral" about summer courses longer than 5½ weeks (p. 3).

A number of case studies have reported faculty endorsements of intensive summer courses. Deveny and Bookout (1976) found that summer intensive foreign language courses evoke a high degree of "personal satisfaction for the teacher" (p. 63) and Eller (1983) reported that teachers' "efforts are rewarded [in intensive foreign language courses] because student progress is very rapid" (p. 226). Parlett and King (1971) observed that the "the instructor found [the intensive] method of instruction more rewarding, and a more efficient and natural way of communicating his knowledge of physics" (p. 28); and Solecki (1971) reported that "in the instructors' opinion, the [intensive foreign language] course was a great success" (p. 280). Thus, without exception, all the case studies reported positive faculty attitudes toward intensive formats.

Interim

Our review uncovered six surveys which measured faculty attitudes toward interim courses (Allen et al., 1982; Centra and Sobol, 1974; Harris, 1978; Lightfield, 1972; Richey et al., 1965; Rossman, 1967, 1971). Rossman's (1967) study of Macalester College's faculty attitudes toward their Interim Term found that almost one-half of the 130 faculty surveyed reported that they enjoyed the interim session more than the regular term; less than 10 percent rated their interim experience less enjoyable. Moreover, more than one-half of the faculty felt that the interim courses were no more difficult to teach than those in the regular term. Rossman noted that students exhibited higher levels of interim satisfaction than faculty, but nonetheless concluded that faculty were generally satisfied with Macalaster's Interim Term.

Centra and Sobol (1974) also found faculty less supportive of the interim term than students. Their survey of Rider College faculty found that 72 percent of the faculty evaluated the interim session favorably compared with 77 percent of the students. Moreover, 45 percent of the faculty and 69 percent of the students said interim term programs were "very respectable intellectually and academically" (pp. 233–234). Centra and Sobol also noted breakdowns by discipline: Education and liberal arts faculty rated interim term programs highest and business school faculty rated them lowest.

In contrast to the previous two site-specific studies, Allen et al. (1982) conducted a nationwide survey of psychology interim instructors and found a "strong positive overall evaluation of the interim courses when compared with semester courses . . ." (p. 231). Allen and his colleagues inferred that faculty prefer interim courses. According to their data, interim classes more typically resemble seminars, allow for more in-depth discussions, group projects, and experiential activities, and elicit more positive student response.

Finally, Richey et al. (1965) measured faculty attitudes regarding specific courses. They surveyed nine faculty who taught intensive courses during an intersession at Indiana University. Faculty were queried as to whether "course objectives," "course content," "teaching methodology," and "students' accomplishments" were the same, better, much better, worse, or much worse in intersession courses as compared with regular term classes (p. 32). With the exception of course content, at least 75 percent of the faculty indicated that these factors were the same, better, or much better in intersession courses than in regular term classes. However, 56 percent of the instructors reported difficulty covering a semester's worth of material during intersession.

Richey and his colleagues also summarized advantages and disadvantages voiced by faculty. According to Richey et al.:

> The key words lifted from the several favorable comments were "concentration," "integration," "intensity," and "continuity". . . . The words or phrases which appeared most frequently in the list of disadvantages were "less time," "no opportunities for extensive coverage," "decreased occasion for reflective comprehension," and "too rapid assimilation" (pp. 34–35).

Regular Term

Our review uncovered only one survey measuring faculty attitudes toward regular term intensive courses (Kirby-Smith, 1987). Kirby-Smith surveyed and interviewed 20 faculty; 14 intensive course instructors, and 6 who taught traditional-length classes. Kirby-Smith found that intensive course faculty generally equated the academic standards of intensive and traditional courses. For example, she found that almost 79 percent of the "intensive" faculty agreed or strongly agreed that course material could be presented adequately in compressed formats compared with 33 percent of the "traditional" faculty. Moreover, almost 86 percent of the "intensive" faculty agreed or strongly agreed that students could adequately grasp and comprehend course material in time-compressed formats versus 67 percent of the traditional group.

Kirby-Smith also asked faculty to identify the advantages and disadvantages of intensive formats. In terms of advantages, faculty indicated that intensive courses better accommodated the working student and provided enhanced opportunities to combine theory and practice. The major disadvantages identified by faculty included "fatigue," "lack of time for students to digest and apply concepts", and excessive amount of preparation time (p. 95). Moreover, when queried as to which format they preferred, only 45 percent of the faculty surveyed preferred to teach intensive courses; 40 percent favored traditional-length courses; and 15 percent indicated no preference. Interestingly, however, 75 percent of the faculty respondents advocated for more intensive courses in the university's curriculum. Overall, Kirby-Smith concluded that:

> From an analysis of the faculty listing of advantages and disadvantages of intensive courses, the disadvantages are of a much greater magnitude and should lead college

administrators to question whether intensive courses as currently formulated and administered, are appropriate delivery systems for higher education (p. 122).

Kirby-Smith's findings suggest a seeming paradox: faculty tend to prefer to teach in traditional time frames, but they support intensive courses to accommodate students' schedules.

Modular

A number of institutions have surveyed faculty after inaugurating modular scheduling systems. Most of these studies have identified both faculty criticisms and praise regarding this form of intensive instruction. As to criticisms, Taylor and Ware (in Kirby-Smith, 1987) cataloged various faculty criticisms of the Colorado College Block Plan after its implementation. Faculty members, for example, reported that "the constant pressure of reading, discussion, field trips, grading papers, [was] too intense to allow professional scientific work"; and another faculty member added that although students benefitted, intensive instruction was ". . . hard on the teacher" (in Kirby-Smith, p. 38). Blackburn and his colleagues (1977) also noted faculty discontent after the University of Wisconsin-Oshkosh adopted an intensive calendar format. They found that 39 percent of the faculty respondents reported an increase in their workload and 26 percent indicated greater time pressures. Of the faculty who responded to the question, 50 percent negatively evaluated the new intensive format. Blackburn et al. observed that

> most faculty can see how someone else's material can be taught in shorter time-frames or by machines, but they are equally convinced that there is something inherent in the very nature of their own specialty that makes it impossible for it to be taught and learned in less than 14 (and many still insist, 17) weeks (p. 41).

Kuhns (1974) reached similar conclusions when she noted that many faculty teaching under modular systems believe their subjects are incompatible with intensive formats.

However, many of these studies also noted positive faculty responses to intensive instruction. University of Wisconsin-Oshkosh's faculty for example, identified several advantages of the new scheduling format including "schedule or time flexibility for both students and faculty," "professional growth and revitalization," "increased student credit hour production," "increased student options," and "curricular flexibility" (Blackburn et al., 1977, pp. 54–56). In addition to the favorable faculty comments, Blackburn and his colleagues—based on their field observations—also noted several positive effects of intensive scheduling. According to the researchers:

> A fairly complacent and traditional faculty has been tripped into action. Spurred by administrative leaders, faculty are now rethinking curricular and pedagogical matters,

and this is good—for all of the obvious reasons. . . . [T]o take the typical semester offering and package it for a three-week stint required major reflection and creation. What are the aims of this course, really? Who needs to do what to accomplish them? A whole host of basic philosophical and psychological questions had to be asked and answered. . . . [T]hese are important and good activities for faculty to be engaged in at regular intervals (Blackburn et al., pp. 84–85).

Finally, Heist and Taylor (1979) reported that despite faculty discontent, 80 to 94 percent of the Colorado College faculty supported Colorado College's Block Plan, regardless of their field of study. Their data revealed, for example, that 85 percent of the social science faculty, 88 percent of the natural science faculty, and 86 percent of the faculty in the humanities indicated moderate to high support for the Plan.

Weekend

Finally, our review found only one study which measured faculty's views of weekend courses. Shapiro (1988) compared intensive and traditional faculty responses on two different surveys. On one survey, faculty rated students on the quality of written work, motivation level, and quantitative skills among others. The second survey queried instructors as to whether class format interfered with their class preparation, presentation, or students' ability to learn. The analysis revealed that only one item, student motivation, differentiated weekend and traditional faculty's responses to the surveys. According to Shapiro, weekend faculty rated student motivation higher than did faculty teaching traditional courses. Shapiro also noted that weekend faculty more often reported that intensive formats negatively affected student learning—though these findings were not statistically significant.

In summary, the research reviewed above concerning faculty perceptions of intensive instruction reveals mixed results. On the one hand, faculty do not perceive great differences in student performance or ability to meet course objectives. Indeed, faculty seem to appreciate the smaller classes, increased student-faculty interaction, the curricular flexibility, and comradeship often present in intensive courses. On the other hand, it appears that faculty would prefer to teach in traditional time frames but have reconciled themselves to intensive courses to accommodate students' schedules. Moreover, faculty consistently mention fatigue, inability to cover equivalent amounts of material as in traditional-length courses, excessive preparation time, and concerns about student learning as major impediments to intensive courses.

Conclusions

We reach several conclusions based on our examination of the intensive course research. First and foremost, intensive courses have been found to yield equivalent—and sometimes superior—learning outcomes in comparison with traditional-length courses. This finding holds true across all major types of intensive course formats (summer, interim, modular, regular term, weekend). Thus, contrary to conventional wisdom, the literature strongly suggests that intensive formats produce learning outcomes at least equal to traditional designs.

Second, the research results indicate that certain disciplines and fields of study may benefit from intensive formats more than others. As shown in our review, the social sciences and humanities ranked highest in favoring intensive over traditional formats. However, the large number of studies across all fields with no preference between compressed and traditional formats suggest that all courses—regardless of field—can utilize intensive course designs without diminishing educational outcomes.

Third, the surveys and case studies indicate that students are generally supportive of intensive courses and especially appreciate their convenience and efficiency. This raises an important issue. Many in higher education have been reluctant to cater to students' utilitarian needs. But these studies suggest that students' needs can be accommodated without sacrificing educational outcomes. Still, convenience and efficiency may exact a price: student stress and fatigue have been found to be associated with intensive formats. However, additional research is needed to test this supposition.

Fourth, we found that the most significant obstacle to intensive courses is negative faculty attitudes. Intensive courses are highly labor-intensive and can encumber faculty from fulfilling other responsibilities—most notably research. At the same time, however, most faculty seem to want to accommodate student schedules insofar as possible. Thus, faculty often confront two opposing forces: consumer demand for intensive courses, and their own reluctance to commit to intensive experiences.

Fifth, this review examined time and its impact on learning. Consistent with Karweit's (1984) and Walberg's (1988b) reviews of the time and learning literature, a substantial portion of the intensive course research suggests that time is not the principal driving force with regard to learning. Indeed, the preponderance of studies, which have found no differences in outcomes between intensive and tra "tional courses across all formats and degrees of intensity, suggest that time—as it relates to intensity—may have relatively little influence on educa-.ional outcomes when it is considered in isolation. Students can learn effectively under a number of time-compressed circumstances.

Yet, the case studies and many of the quasi-experimental investigations suggest that time—in concert with other factors—may be consequential for student learning. The research suggests several possibilities. If learning is conceived as a process involving a series of inputs and throughputs which in turn influence various educationally-related outputs, there is evidence to suggest that learning experiences are different between many intensive and traditional-length classes. For example, both Blackburn et al. (1977) and Heist and Taylor (1979) found that faculty are forced to scrutinize their course goals and identify the most salient course content in the process of converting traditional classes to intensive formats. Faculty who teach intensive courses are also likely to modify their teaching methods by incorporating more discussion, experiential learning, and facilitation. Studies also suggest that "intensive" students concentrate more on their studies, participate more in class discussions, and are more highly motivated in intensive classes than in traditional-length courses. Intensive courses may heighten student and faculty involvement in the education process which, in turn, could have a significant impact on learning.

Finally, consistent with Csikszentmihalyi's (1982) and Walberg's (1988a) research, the intensive course literature suggests that concentrated, in-depth experiences facilitate student development in ways not yet understood. The case studies, in particular, have consistently reported that students are often motivated, excited, and inspired by intensive course experiences, and that concentrated learning generates a level of satisfaction unlike that experienced in traditional-length classes. Various explanations have been offered for this heightened enthusiasm and satisfaction. Eckert (1972), for example, has argued that concentrated formats foster highly rewarding gestalt experiences which result from a "continued interrelationship among students" and a "coherent view of the subject" (p. 494). Csikszentmihalyi's research suggests that intensive courses may create "optimal experiences" which result from a *"loss of self-consciousness"* (p. 22). Regardless of the explanation, there seems to be considerable intrinsic satisfaction associated with concentrated learning which, in turn, may have untold affects on students' creativity and cognitive development. Clearly this is an important area for further research.

CRITIQUE OF THE LITERATURE

While our discussion of the literature indicates that intensive courses can be effective alternatives to traditional formats, there are serious methodological and conceptual limitations to the research and for this reason, our findings are inconclusive. These limitations can be summarized as follows:

First, most of the experimental studies suffer from design limitations. To begin, only three of the studies reviewed incorporated random assignment, and very few studies attempted to match experimental and control groups or test for homogeneity between groups. Moreover, many of the samples were small and most of the investigations studied course formats in a single institution.

Second, in terms of outcome measures, many of the studies utilized final course grades as the only measure of achievement. There is justifiable concern throughout higher education as to whether course grades are a reliable and valid measure of learning. Since learning is such a complex and multifaceted phenomena, researchers need to use multiple achievement measures to assess learning outcomes (Powell, 1976). Closely related, most of these studies measured the acquisition of factual knowledge and failed to study the impact of intensive learning on "abstract, critical, complex, and reflective" thinking (Pascarella and Terenzini, forthcoming, p. 9). Moreover, value-related, attitudinal, and moral dimensions of learning were largely ignored.

Third, of those studies that used pre- and post-tests, many did so without testing for instrument reliability and validity. Moreover, most of the studies that utilized post-tests, administered them at the end of each course—which introduces another potential source of bias. Post-tests administered at the end of a semester-length class measure longer term retention than a post-test given at the end of a 2– to 3–week intensive course. In turn, achievement outcomes are not necessarily comparable (Gleason, 1986).

Fourth, many of these studies were conducted under different conditions without controlling for extraneous effects. For example, one cannot easily compare the results of an interim course with those of a weekend class offered during the regular semester without taking the two environments into consideration. Furthermore, the degree of course intensity differed between studies. A one-week intensive course differs considerably from an eight-week class. And, many studies failed to control other factors as well—including the total amount of classroom time, the instructor, the instructional method, and the course content and requirements. Future studies need to control for these potentially confounding variables.

In addition to methodological limitations, most of the research has not been anchored in a theoretical or conceptual framework. Out of the 35 studies reviewed, only six investigations tested the relevance of any theory or model to intensive learning (Boddy, 1985; Gleason, 1986; Ilika and Longnion, 1977; Kanun et al., 1963; Waechter, 1966) and only three specific models or theories were examined (massed versus spaced learning, interference theory, and an economic demand model of achievement). No other psychological, sociological, or economic models have been tested. Moreover, there were no inductive attempts to develop a theory of intensive learning.

Finally, the literature provided no interpretive analyses of intensive courses within a broader context of higher education. Intensive courses have significance far beyond the classroom, especially as they begin to challenge traditional notions of time and learning. For example, if one views time as one of many dimensions of curricula (Bergquist et al., 1981), and "curriculum as a temporal, information-processing structure in colleges and universities" (Conrad and Pratt, 1986, p. 249), then the existence and proliferation of intensive courses represent an significant information transformation within higher education—the nature of which is not yet understood. Accordingly, one must wonder what the existence and proliferation of intensive courses suggest about higher education as an evolving social and cultural system. What is the nature of this information transformation, how does this transformation relate to changes in other areas of higher education, and what type of academic and organizational changes can we anticipate in the future (Conrad and Pratt, 1986)? These are important questions, since any attempt to advance intensive courses in the curricula requires a concomitant organizational understanding.

In summary, the literature reviewed in this article contributes to our understanding of intensive learning but the shortcomings of the research also emphasize the need for well designed studies which rigorously compare intensive and traditional formats (Doyle, 1978), conceptual frameworks with which to explicate the findings, and interpretive analyses to understand their meaning and significance.

FUTURE DIRECTIONS FOR RESEARCH

A great deal of research remains to be done. As a guide to future research, we offer the following framework. To begin, we conceive of learning as a process involving a series of inputs and throughputs which in turn influence educational outcomes. To assess the impact of intensive education, researchers clearly need to consider the nature, influence, and interaction of various input variables (e.g., student and faculty characteristics) as well as the environment in which students learn, and relate these to multiple output measures of student achievement. In this context, the following questions might help to guide future research.

Input (Students and Faculty)

1. How do students in intensive courses compare with students in traditional classes? Several researchers have suggested that intensive students differ significantly from the norm. Eckert (1972), for example, suggested that interim students are more motivated and goal-directed. Kirby-Smith (1987) found that her sample of intensive students were older, more often employed full-time, had a higher grade-point-average, and had more children than students in semester-length classes. Kanun et al. (1961) also found intensive summer students to be older and to have earned higher grade-point-averages. To the extent these and other potential differences are common to intensive classes, then preexisting student characteristics may have a significant impact on the learning environment and student achievement.

2. How do faculty who teach intensive courses compare with those in traditional-length classes? Shapiro (1988) found that the faculty who taught intensive weekend courses were more often Ph.D.'s as opposed to Master's recipients and Blackburn et al.'s (1977) study found that intensive course faculty were younger. Future research needs to explore whether there are differences between faculty in intensive and traditional courses and, if so, what consequences—if any—do these have for the classroom environment and student learning.

3. How do students' perceptions and expectations of intensive classes influence course outcomes? For example, do students expect to work harder and consequently perform better? Several studies reported that students in intensive classes were more motivated but student expectations have never been measured.

The Learning Environment

1. How do course requirements and faculty expectations of students compare between intensive and traditional formats and, if different, how does this affect the learning environment and student learning outcomes? The current literature suggests that course requirements are often different between the two formats (Kirby-Smith, 1987; Allen et al., 1982; Adelman and Reuben, 1984), but faculty expectations have yet to be studied.

2. How do student's study patterns compare between intensive and traditional-length courses? Gleason's (1986) study found that students enrolled in two intensive economics courses studied significantly less than students in matched semester-length classes, but they achieved the same or better post-test scores. This study suggests that concentrated formats encourage more efficient methods of learning, but more research is clearly needed.

3. How do pedagogical approaches compare between intensive and traditional-length courses and, if different, how do these variations affect learning? For example, Allen's et al. (1982) survey of interim instructors found that they were less likely to lecture and more likely to utilize group discussions. If this is generally true, it could prove significant. Research on college student achievement indicates that use of discussion over lecture promotes greater long-term retention, transfer of knowledge to new situations, problem solving, attitude change, and motivation for further learning (McKeachie, Pintrich, Lin, and Smith., 1987, p. 70). Pedagogical methods are surely an important consideration.

4. How do course environments compare between intensive and traditional-length courses? There are several studies suggesting that the classroom experience is significantly different between the two formats. For example, Deveny and Bookout (1976) noted increased student-faculty interaction in intensive courses; Lasker et al. (1975) and Nahrgang (1982) reported a stronger bond among students; and Allen et al. (1982) noted more enthusiasm in intensive classes. All of these differences could significantly influence the classroom environment and, in turn, affect student learning outcomes.

5. How does the amount of time-on-task (i.e., productive class time) compare between intensive and traditional-length courses? Doyle and Yantis (1977) speculated that intensive courses may actually incorporate more time-on-task since there is less start-up and wind-down time involved. Moreover, Shapiro (1988) found that students in weekend courses reported more productive use of class time than students in more traditional classes. Since the time and learning liter-

ature indicates that time, particularly productive time, is a factor in learning, time-on-task is an important consideration (Walberg, 1988b).

6. How do stress and fatigue affect learning in intensive courses? The National Institute of Health conducted several studies in which researchers subjected participants to 10–15 hours of foreign language instruction daily. They found that learning was significantly reduced under these conditions and cautioned against utilizing massed teaching techniques in foreign language instruction (Rocklyn and Montague in Hefferlin, 1972). These and other studies indicate that increasing levels of intensity will eventually produce diminishing returns, but the threshold has yet to be determined for various disciplines.

7. Are intensive courses intrinsically rewarding and if so, how does that affect the classroom experience and learning outcomes? Csikszentmihalyi's (1982) research suggests that intense, unfragmented concentration is "autotelic"—or intrinsically rewarding and with time could "become addictive" (pp. 22–23). Several case studies also suggested that there is intrinsic satisfaction associated with concentrated study. If intensive learning inspires greater levels of motivation or intellectual pursuit, then it could be a potent pedagogical tool.

Learning Outcomes

1. How do the immediate (short-term) and long-term learning outcomes compare between intensive and traditional-length courses? This is perhaps the most important question to be answered. Although the short-term outcomes research suggests that intensive courses are effective alternatives to traditional formats, there is much less research on long-term effectiveness. If intensive formats represent forms of massed learning, as many have suggested, their long-term outcomes may be inferior to those in traditional courses.

2. How do different student groups compare in their ability to learn under intensive conditions? For example, do older and younger students learn equally well in intensive courses? Settlemeyer (1973) found no differences in her study of older (over 35) and younger (under 35) nursing students enrolled in an intensive nursing course, but additional research of this type is needed. Other student groups which should be compared include graduate and undergraduate students, high and low achieving students, upper and lower division students, and students with different learning styles.

3. How does the degree of intensity influence student achievement? Do three-week courses yield equivalent results to eight-week courses? As reported earlier, preliminary findings have found little difference in outcomes between various levels of intensity but no study has carefully examined this issue.

4. How does the subject matter influence outcomes in intensive courses? The extant research findings are ambiguous. Most of the studies reviewed here found no difference in outcomes based on subject matter, but a few found that certain

subjects taught in intensive formats yielded superior results to those taught in traditional time-frames (e.g., Mazanec, 1972).

5. Which kinds and levels of learning are appropriate for intensive formats? Bloom (1956) theorized that there are six classes of learning: knowledge, comprehension, application, analysis, synthesis, and evaluation. According to Bloom, each successive level of learning requires increasingly complex and sophisticated thinking on the part of the student, along with greater amounts of time to successfully master. Since higher-order thinking is an important goal throughout postsecondary education, it is important to determine whether "intensive" students can analyze, evaluate, and synthesize course material equally well within the given time structure as students in traditional-length courses. Only one of the studies reviewed addressed this question. Waechter (1966) compared students' acquisition and understanding of science facts in an intensive and semester-length Elements of Earth Science class. He designed a 60–item, multiple choice test to measure factual knowledge and a 20–item, true-false test to measure understanding. Waechter found no statistical evidence to indicate a difference between the two groups' factual knowledge at the end of the course; however, the semester-length class exhibited significantly better understanding of the material. Hence, research may find that higher ordered thinking is best taught in traditional-length courses, but additional research is clearly needed.

6. How do course withdrawals and degree completion rates compare between students who enroll in intensive versus traditional courses? For example, Mazanec (1972) found higher attrition rates for a 15–week mathematics class than either a corresponding 3– or 6–week intensive course. Moreover, Blackburn et al. (1977) noted that the University of Wisconsin-Oshkosh's 14–week classes had greater percentages of incompletes and withdrawals than either the 3– or 7–week classes. Gaston (1974) noted similar results. With regards to graduation, Haney (1985) found no differences in degree completion rates between students who transferred to a senior institution from a modular-based junior college versus a matched group who transferred from a semester based two-year system. This type of research is important. If course withdrawals and degree completion rates differ between the two formats, this could help to inform educational practice in the future.

7. How do intensive courses influence a student's attitude toward learning? Eller (1983), Richardson (1973), Gaston (1974), and Nahrgang (1982) reported that intensive courses increased the number of students continuing into upper-division study in foreign languages. Eckert (1972) reported better class attendance and student motivation in intensive classes. Shapiro found that weekend students reported greater interest in the subject matter than students in more traditional-length courses. Conversely, Allen (1974), Ray and Kirkpatrick (1983), Studdard (1975), and Waechter (1966) all reported no differences in student attitudes toward the subject matter at the end of the course when com-

paring intensive and traditional-length students. Thus, the research findings are unclear and should be investigated more systematically.

Optimizing Factors and Conditions

Research must investigate the optimizing factors to maximize student learning outcomes in intensive courses. Some important questions might include:

1. What disciplines and types of courses are best suited for intensive formats? Although the literature reviewed suggests that a wide variety of courses can be successfully re-organized into intensive formats, no research yet indicates which courses yield the best results.

2. What type of students are best suited for intensive formats? Several case studies have offered opinions. For example, Currall and Kirk (1986) suggested that students with higher grade-point averages will benefit more from intensive instruction; Lasker et al. (1975) asserted that students with an experiential style of learning respond best to intensive formats. However, our review found no experimental studies which have investigated this question.

3. What types of pedagogical styles and instructional practices are best suited for intensive formats? Must teaching strategies change for intensive courses to be effective? Breckon (1989) contends that to be optimally effective, intensive instructors should actively involve students, introduce greater variety into the class structure, utilize greater numbers of "prepared visuals," "pre-course assignments," small group discussions, and in-class projects, give shorter lectures, and emphasize essay over objective exams (p. 65). However, his assertions remain untested.

4. Can certain instructional practices optimize learning? Doyle and Yantis (1977) suggested the use of advance organizers as a pre-instructional strategy to optimize intensive learning. The concept of advanced organizers is based on the work of Ausubel, who argued that information can be learned more effectively if the instructor provides the student with a conceptual structure to anchor new information (Newell, 1984). Homework has also been suggested as an optimizing variable. For example, Weare (1973) investigated the use of nightly homework assignments in intensive courses as a method to optimize learning; he found no differences in outcomes between homework and no-homework groups. Other optimizing strategies might include use of class discussions, small group exercises and projects, or maintenance courses which Richardson (1973) argued was a requisite strategy for long term retention of material learned in intensive courses.

5. Do learning strategies differ between intensive and traditional-length courses and if so, can students effectively "learn how to learn" in time-compressed formats? In other words, can students be taught effective learning strategies for intensive courses that would enhance achievement outcomes?

DISCUSSION

The review of the intensive course literature by Doyle and Yantis (1977) con-cluded that "it is clear from all the available evidence that intensive scheduling works at least as well as, and in some cases better than, traditional scheduling" (p. B-238). But they added that "the mechanisms responsible for the success of this approach have not yet clearly been identified" (p. B-238). Our review of more current literature has led us to similar conclusions. Based on the evidence, intensive courses seem to be effective alternatives to traditional-length classes regardless of format, degree of intensity, or field of study. However, some research suggests that certain disciplines seem to benefit more than others.

The same methodological and conceptual problems that tempered Doyle's and Yantis's conclusions temper ours as well. Our literature analysis also raises two larger issues which universities—as well as researchers—need to address: the relationship between academic time and learning and an epistemological ques-tion concerning intensity and depth vis-a-vis extensiveness and breadth.

Colleges and universities are under heavy pressure to implement outcomes-based assessments. In so doing, postsecondary institutions need to not only investigate the efficacy of intensive courses and other new forms of instructional practices, but they should re-evaluate academic time altogether. As Adelman and Reuben (1984) note, the traditional "credit system substitutes time for perfor-mance as a measure of learning" (p. 91). Consequently, "there is no guarantee . . . that every student has mastered the course material—let alone allied material that may be the stuff of true learning" (p. 92). Conrad (1978) emphasizes that the current system allows no opportunity to match the pace of the instruction to the material presented or the educational goals of the course. Gettinger (1984) argues that the time needed to master subject material has rarely been considered in education. Thus, under the traditional system the relationship between time and learning remains arbitrarily defined and the needs of faculty, students, as well as the subject matter remain subservient to this definition. If learning is truly the essential outcome to education, then time should not remain intractable, inflexible, and uncompromising. Instead, academic time should accommodate—not ignore—educational needs, and colleges and universities should consider a wide variety of course formats which vary according to length, pace, and inten-sity to temporally match course formats with the educational goals of each course and the needs of all students.

Finally, an important epistemological question also emerges from our discus-sion of intensive course research: the relative merits of breadth and extensiveness versus depth and intensity in the pursuit of knowledge. Many colleges and universities adhere to a eclectic tradition where breadth and extensiveness are emphasized over depth and intensiveness. This eclecticism could have a wide range of repercussions for students. For example, some have suggested that this eclectic approach fragments epistemology and prevents students from developing a unified outlook (Glazer, 1987). From a cognitive perspective, eclecticism may impede the development of certain cognitive skills that concentrated, in-depth learning nourishes. The intensive course research suggests that breadth and depth experiences may cultivate different educational perspectives and cognitive skills, and curriculum should incorporate both epistemological assumptions. At this juncture, there seems to be no "right" method to dissiminate knowledge and colleges and universities—as well as researchers—need to investigate many curricular variations. As Toombs (1977–1978) wisely noted, it is not the "formal order" which hinders attempts to improve curriculum, but the tendency to "conceive of a curriculum from a limited frame of reference" (p. 20).

APPENDIX A. Intensive Course Studies by Type of Format

STUDY	COURSE DURATIONS COMPARED	NS	+I	+T	CS
SUMMER					
Austin et al, 1988	1-week; 2½-wknd*; 5–wknd; and 5–week classes	X			
Bester, 1965	6–week and 16–week classes	X			
Boddy, 1985	5–, 8–, and 16–week classes	X	X		
Deveny and Bookout, 1976	8–week class				X
Eller, 1983	8–week class				X
Gaston, 1974	12–week and 2–quarter classes		X		
Gleason, 1986	3– , 5–, and 15–week classes	X	X		
Kanun et al., 1963	5– and 10–week classes	X			
Kanun et al., 1963	2 1/2–, 5–, and 10–week classes	X			
Keilstrup, 1981	6–week class				X
Masat, 1982	3– week, 6–week , and semester-length classes	X			
Murphy, 1979	2–week class	X			
Parlett and King, 1971	4–week and semester-length classes				X
Solecki, 1971	6–week class				X
Stephens, 1978	12–week class				X
Troiani, 1986	10–day class				X
INTERIM					
DuVerlie, 1973	Interim class				X
Masat, 1982	3– week, 6–week , and semester-length classes	X			
Richey et al. 1965	13– day and 17–week classes	X	X	X	
Studdard, 1975	3– and 15–week classes	X			
Tyler, 1970	4–week class				X
Wallace, 1972	3– week class				X

(continued)

APPENDIX A. Intensive Course Studies by Type of Format (*Continued*)

STUDY	COURSE DURATIONS COMPARED	NS	+I	+T	CS
MODULAR					
Blackburn et al., 1977	3– , 7–, and 14–week classes	X			
Haney, 1985	modular and semester classes	X			
Kuhns, 1974	modular and semester classes		X		
Mazanec, 1972	3– , 6–, and 15–week classes	X	X		
Richardson, 1973	8–week class				X
Waechter, 1966	9– and 18–week classes	X			
REGULAR TERM					
Allen, 1974	5– and 15–week classes	X			
Brackenbury, 1978	7–, 8–, 15–week , and 4–wknd classes	X			
Doyle and Sanders (cited in Doyle, 1978)	3– week, 6–week , and semester-length classes	X			
Frank, 1973	one semester class				X
Kirby-Smith, 1987	"intensive" and 15–week classes	X			
Knowles, 1972	7–day and 15–week classes	X			
Ray and Kirkpatrick, 1983	3– and 15–week classes			X	
WEEKEND					
Austin et al., 1988	1-week, 5–week , 2½-wknd, and 5–wknd classes	X			
Berk, 1979	8–day class				X
Brackenbury, 1978	7–, 8–, 14–week , and 4–wknd classes	X			
Doyle, 1978	2-wknd and 4–week classes	X			
Doyle et al., 1980	2-wknd and 16–week classes	X			
Doyle and Yantis, 1977	4–wknd and 9–week classes	X			
Lasker et al., 1975	unspecified				X
Pflanzer and East, 1984	unspecified				X
Shapiro, 1988	2–, 3– , and 9–week and 4–wknd classes	X			

*wknd = weekend
NS = nonsignificant differences in outcome
+I = findings in favor of intensive formats
+T = findings in favor of traditional formats
CS = case study—all case studies favored intensive formats

REFERENCES

Adelman, C. and Reuben, E. (1984). *Starting with Students: Promising Approaches in American Higher Education.* Presented to the Study Group on the Conditions of Excellence in American Higher Education. Washington, DC: National Commission of Excellence in Education; National Institute of Education. (ED 257 411)

Allen, F. A. (1974). A comparison of the effectiveness of the intensive and concurrent scheduling plans for teaching first-semester English composition in the community college. Unpublished doctoral dissertation, North Texas State University.

Allen, J. L. Miller, T. A., Fisher, B., and Moriarty, D. D. (1982). A survey of January interim psychology courses. *Teaching of Psychology* 9(4): 230–231.

Anderson, J. R. (1990). *Cognitive Psychology and Its Implications.* Third Edition. New York: W.H. Freeman and Company.

Austin, T. L., Fennell, R. R., and Yeager, C. R. (1988). Class scheduling and academic achievement in a non-traditional graduate program. *Innovative Higher Education* 12(2): 79–90.

Ausubel, D. P. (1960). The use of advance organizers in the learning and retention of meaningful verbal material. *Journal of Educational Psychology* 51: 267–272.

Bahrick, H. P. and Phelps, E. (1987). Retention of Spanish vocabulary over 8 years. *Journal of Experimental Psychology: Learning, Memory, and Cognition* 13(2): 344–349.

Barnes, B. R. and Clawson, E. U. (1975). Do advance organizers facilitate learning? Recommendations in future research based on an analysis of 32 studies. *Review of Educational Research* 45(4): 637–659.

Belle, Robert L. (1973). The summer sessions rationale in the School of Education, The University of Wisconsin, Madison. Unpublished doctoral dissertation, University of Wisconsin.

Benseler, D. P. and Schulz, R. A. (1979). *Intensive Foreign Language Courses. Language in Education: Theory and Practice, No. 18.* Arlington, VA: ERIC Clearinghouse on Languages and Linguistics. (ED 176 587)

Bergquist, W. H., Gould, R. A., and Greenberg, E. (1981). *Designing Undergraduate Education.* San Francisco: Jossey-Bass Publishers.

Berk, R. A. (1979). Teaching statistics in an intensive semester program. *Improving College and University Teaching* 27(2): 87–88.

Bester, J. F. (1965). Student performance in summer programs. *American Journal of Pharmaceutical Education.* (February): 44–49.

Blackburn, R. T., Armstrong, E. C., and Dykes, M. D. (1977). *Evaluation Report: UW-O FIPSE Project.* Oshkosh, WI: University of Wisconsin-Oshkosh. (ED 150 903).

Bloom, B. S. (1956). *Taxonomy of Educational Objectives, Handbook I: Cognitive Domain.* New York: David McKay Co., Inc.

Boddy, G. W. (1985). Regular vs. compressed semester: a comparison of effectiveness for teaching in higher education. Unpublished doctoral dissertation, University of Nebraska.

Brackenbury, R. L. (1978). What is more elusive than the learning of philosophy. *ERQ.* (Summer): 93–96.

Breckon, D. J. (1989). Teaching college courses in compressed formats. *Lifelong Learning: An Omnibus of Practice and Research* 12(4): 65–66.

Centra, J. A. and Sobol, M. G. (1974). Faculty and student views of the interim term. *Research in Higher Education* 2: 231–238.

Not all references are cited in the text.

Conrad, C. F. (1978). *The Undergraduate Curriculum: A Guide to Innovation and Reform*. Boulder, CO: Westview Press.

Conrad, C. F. and Pratt, A. M. (1986). Research on academic programs: an inquiry into an emerging field. In J. C. Smart (ed.), *Higher Education: A Handbook of Theory and Research*, Vol. 2. New York: Agathon Press, Inc.

Csikszentmihalyi, M. (1982). Toward a psychology of optimal experiences. *Review of Personality and Social Psychology* 3: 13– 36.

Currall, S. C. and Kirk, R. E. (1986). Predicting success in intensive foreign language courses. *The Modern Language Journal* 70: 107–113.

Davis, J. R. (1972). The changing college calendar. *Journal of Higher Education* 43(2): 142–150.

Dempster, F. N. and Farris, R. (1990). The spacing effect: research and practice. *Journal of Research and Development in Education* 23(2): 97–101.

Deveny, J. J. and Bookout, J. C. (1976). The intensive language course: toward a successful approach. *Foreign Language Annals* 9: 58–63.

Doyle, R. J. (1978). Intensive scheduling: the evidence for alternatives in course scheduling patterns. Paper presented at the Eighteenth Annual Forum of the Association for Industrial Research, Houston.

Doyle, R. J., Moursi, M., and Wood, D. (1980). The effects of intensive scheduling: a field experiment. Unpublished manuscript, Central Michigan University, Mt. Pleasant.

Doyle, R. J. and Yantis, J. (1977). *Facilitating Nontraditional Learning: An Update on Research and Evaluation in Intensive Scheduling*. Mount Pleasant, MI: Central Michigan University, Institute for Personal and Career Development. (ED 144 459)

DuVerlie, C. (1973). The disappearance of the academic foreign language program. *American Foreign Language Teacher* 3(3): 16–18, 23, 38.

East, J. R. (1988). *Teaching on Weekends and in Shopping Centers. A Guide for Colleges and Universities*. Indianapolis, IN: Indiana University, Purdue University. (ED 291 328)

Ebbinghaus, H. (1964). *Memory*. (H.A. Ruger and C.E. Bussenius, Trans.). New York: Dover. (Original Work published 1885, trans. 1913).

Eckert, W. H. (1972). The modular calendar of Mount Vernon College. *Liberal Education* 58(4): 492–500.

Eckleberry, R. H. (1958). Editorial comments—the Hiram Study Plan revised. *Journal of Higher Education* 29(4): 225–234.

Eller, K. G. (1983). Developing a summer intensive course at a commuter campus. *Foreign Language Annals* 16(3): 223– 227.

Frank, T. E. (1973). A practical approach to intensive German. *Unterrichtspraxis* 6(1): 5–8.

Frank, T. E. (1971). An intensive program in German. Speech presented at the Annual Meeting of the American Association of Teachers of German, Chicago. (ED 057 701)

Friedman, W. M. (1980). Class scheduling: full-time students and faculty—an exploratory study. *College Student Journal* 14(4): 341–346.

Gaston, W. E. (1974). An analysis of student performance following two contrasting instructional methodologies in a modern foreign language program: a one course intensive strategy versus the traditional two-year sequence for university (lower division) French. Unpublished doctoral dissertation, The University of Tennessee.

Gettinger, M. (1984). Individual differences in time needed for learning: a review of literature. Educational Psychologist 19(1): 15–29.

Giddens, T. R. and Kenny, J. W. (1975). Research models for the evaluation of interim programs. *Research in Higher Education* 3: 393–400.

Glazer, N.Y. (1987). Questioning eclectic practice in curriculum change: a marxist perspective. Signs 12: 293– 304.

Gleason, J. P. (1986). Economic models of time in learning. Unpublished doctoral dissertation, University of Nebraska.

Glover, J. A. and Corkill, A. J. (1987). Influence of paraphrased repetitions on the spacing effect: Journal of Educational Psychology 79(2): 198–199.

Grimes, P. W., Krehbiel, T. L., Nielsen, J. E., and Niss, J. F. (1989). The effectiveness of Economics U$A on learning and attitudes. *Journal of Economic Education.* (Spring): 139–152.

Haney, J. J. (1985). A comparation study of modular and semester schedules. Unpublished doctoral dissertation, Mississippi State University.

Harris, H. L. (1978). *Intersession '78: A Report for the Flexible Calendar Project.* Sacramento, CA: Cosumnes River College. (ED 154 862)

Hefferlin, J. B. (1972). Intensive courses: an old idea whose time for testing has come. *Journal of Research and Development in Education* 6(1): 83– 98.

Heist, P. and Taylor, M. F. (1979). *The Block Plan: A Preliminary Report on a Ten-year Evaluation of the Colorado College Block Plan Format for Intensive Study.* Colorado Springs, CO: Colorado College. (ED 246 739)

Ilika, J. and Longnion, B. (1977). A comparison of a five and one half and an 11 week reading course for governmental employees. Paper presented at the Annual Meeting of the National Reading Conference, New Orleans. (ED 149 311)

Iverson, J. G. (1966). A study of January interim programs with special consideration for secondary teacher education. Unpublished doctoral dissertation, University of North Dakota.

Kalivoda, T. B. (1975). Organization of intensive instruction: dispelling misconceptions and facing realities. *Hispania* 58: 114–121.

Kanun, C., Ziebarth, E. W., and Abrahams, N. (1963). Comparison of student achievement in the summer term and regular quarter. *Journal of Experimental Education* 32(2): 123– 132.

Kanun, C., Ziebarth, E. W. and Abrahams, N. (1962). Comparison of student achievement in the summer term and regular quarter. Unpublished manuscript, University of Minnesota, Minneapolis.

Kanun, C., Ziebarth, E. W., and Abrahams, N. (1961). Comparison of student achievement in the summer term and regular quarter: a pilot study. Unpublished manuscript, University of Minnesota, Minneapolis.

Karweit, N. (1984). Time-on-task reconsidered: synthesis of research on time and learning. Education Leadership 41(8): 32–35.

Karweit, N. (1982). Time on task: A research review. (Report No. 332.) Paper presented at a Meeting of the National Commission on Excellence in Education, Washington, DC. (ED 228 236)

Keilstrup, D. V. (1981). Practical guidelines and activities for an advanced foreign language intensive program. *Modern Language Journal* 65: 377–82.

Kirby-Smith, J. P. (1987). Effects of intensive college courses on student cognitive achievement, academic standards, student attitudes, and faculty attitudes. Unpublished doctoral dissertation, University of Southern California.

Klos, J. J. and Trenton, R. W. (1969). One semester or two. *Journal of Economic Education* 1: 51–55.

Knowles, L. (1972). The intensive semester: an experimental approach to academic achievement. *California Journal of Educational Research* 23: 108–114.

Kuhns, E. (1974). The modular calendar: catalyst for change. *Educational Record* 55(1): 59–64.

Kuhns, E. and Martorana, S. V. (1974). Of time and modules: the organization of instruction. *Journal of Higher Education* 45(6): 430–440.

Lawrenz, F. P. (1984). An evaluation of the effect of two different lengths of inservice training on teacher attitudes. *Journal of Research in Science Teaching* 21(5): 497–506.

Lasker, H., Donnelly, J, and Weathersby, R. (1975). Even on Sunday: an approach to teaching intensive courses for adults. *Harvard Graduate School of Education Association Bulletin* 19: 6–11.

Lightfield, E. T. (1972). An Evaluative Study of the Effects of Adoption of the 4–1–4 Calendar-Curriculum Format. Final Report. St. Petersburg, FL: Eckerd College. (ED 068 039)

Masat, F. E. (1981–82). An immersion course in BASIC. *Journal of Educational Technology Systems* 10(4): 321–329.

Mazanec, J. L. (1972). The effect of course intensity on academic achievement, students attitudes, and mortality rate. Unpublished doctoral dissertation, Michigan State University.

McKeachie, W. J., Pintrich, P. R., Lin, Y. and Smith, D. A. (1987). *Teaching and Learning in the College Classroom. A Review of the Research literature (1986) and November 1987 Supplement*. Ann Arbor, MI: National Center for Research to Improve Postsecondary Teaching and Learning; Washington, DC: Office of Educational Research and Improvement. (ED 314 999).

Mims, S. K. (1983). The impact of time on art learning: intensive vs. concurrent scheduling in higher education. *Studies in Art Education* 24(2): 118–125.

Murphy, D. R. (1979). Learning and intensive instruction. *The Journal of Economic Education*. (Fall): 34–36.

Nahrgang, W. L. (1982). Designing and teaching college-level intensive courses: a pragmatic approach. *Unterrichtspraxis* 15(1): 27–35.

National Center for Education Statistics. (1989a). *Digest of Education Statistics*. Washington, DC: National Center for Education Statistics, Office of Educational Research and Improvement, U.S. Department of Education.

National Center for Education Statistics. (1989b). *Projections of Education Statistics to 2000*. Washington, DC: National Center for Education Statistics, Office of Educational Research and Improvement, U.S. Department of Education.

Newell, J. (1984). Advance organizers: their construction an use in instructional development. In *Instructional Development: The State of the Art, II*. (ED 298 908)

Noonan, R. L. (1977). *Student an Faculty Preferences for Class Scheduling Patterns*, Nova University. (ED 145 886)

Paden, D. W. and Moyer, M. E. (1971). Some evidence on the appropriate length of the Principles of Economics course. *The Journal of Economic Education* 1(2): 131–137.

Parlett, M. R. and King, J. G. (1971). *Concentrated Study: A Pedagogic Innovation Observed*. London: Society for Research into Higher Education.

Pascarella, E. T. and Terenzini, P. T. (forthcoming). College student learning and development.

Patterson, A. M., Sedlacek, W. E., and Tracey, T. J. (1981). Attitudes and characteristics of summer school students. *Southern College Personnel Association Journal* 3(3): 28–34.

Pflanzer, R. G. and East, J. R. (1984). Weekend college: teaching biology on Saturdays. *Journal of College Science Teaching* 14(2): 110–114.

Powell, B. S. (1976). *Intensive Education: The Impact of Time on Learning*. Newton, MA: Education Development Center. (ED 144 195)

Ray, R. E. and Kirkpatrick, D. R. (1983). Two time formats for teaching human sexuality. *Teaching of Psychology* 10(2): 84–88.

Richardson, H. F. (1973). The teaching of college German under a modular system. *Modern Language Journal* 57: 189–194.

Richey, R. W., Sinks, R. W., and Chase, C. I. (1965). A comparison of the academic achievement of students enrolled in the same courses in the spring semester of 1962–1963. Unpublished manuscript, Indiana University, Office of the Summer Sessions, Bloomington.

Rossman, J. E. (1971). The interim term after seven years. *Journal of Higher Education* 42: 603– 609.

Rossman, J. E. (1967). Student and faculty attitudes toward the interim term: an evaluation of curricular innovation. *Liberal Education* 53: 540–547.

Rublee, D. A. and Yarber, W. L. (1983). Instructional units of death education: the impact of amount of classroom time on changes in death attitudes. *JOSH* 53(7): 412–415.

Schoenfeld, C. A. (1967). *The American University in Summer*. Madison, WI: The University of Wisconsin Press.

Settlemeyer, C. A. (1973). Learning and retention by two age group of registered nurses in an intensive course in coronary care nursing. Unpublished doctoral dissertation, University of Pittsburgh.

Shapiro, E. G. (1988). Effects of intensive vs. traditional time formats in IPCD classes. Unpublished manuscript, Central Michigan University, Institute for Personal and Career Development, Mt. Pleasant.

Solecki, J. J. (1971). An intensive method of language teaching. *Foreign Language Annals* 4: 278–282.

Stephens, D. T. (1978). An illustration of "motivating students in the foreign language classroom" in an intensive French course. Foreign Language Annals 11(1): 25–29.

Stewart, H. H. (1934). *A Comparative Study of the Concentration and Regular Plans of Organization in the Senior High School*. New York: Columbia University Press.

Studdard, A. L. (1975). A study comparing a regular semester and an interim term college level physical science course based on changes in student attitudes and understanding of science processes. Unpublished doctoral dissertation, The University of Alabama.

Thompson, H. L. (1985). The ready-for-prime-time players: colleges cater to the adult schedule. *Educational Record* 66(3): 33– 37.

Toombs, W. (1977–78). The application of design-based curriculum analysis to general education. *Review of Higher Education* 1: 18–29.

Tracey, T. J., Sedlacek, W. E., and Patterson, A. M. (1980). *Perceptions of Summer School Faculty at a Large University*. (Counseling Center Research Report No. 7–80). College Park, MD: University of Maryland, Office of Vice Chancellor for Student Affairs. (ED 208 740)

Troiani, E. A. (1986). 10 days or 10 weeks: immersion programs· that work. Paper presented at the Annual Meeting of the Central States Conference on the Teaching of Foreign Languages, Milwaukee. (ED 273 122)

Tyler, D. (1970). 4–1–4 and the audio-lingual skills. *Modern Language Journal* 54: 253– 54.

Underwood, B. J. (1957). Interference and forgetting. *Psychological Review* 64(1): 49–60.

Waechter, R. F. (1966). A comparison of achievement and retention by college junior students in an earth science course after learning under massed and spaced conditions. Unpublished doctoral dissertation, Pennsylvania State University.

Walberg, H. J. (1988a). Creativity and talent as learning. In R. I. Sternberg (ed.), *The Nature of Creativity*, pp. 340–361. Cambridge: Cambridge University Press.

Walberg, H. J. (1988b). Synthesis of research on time and learning. *Educational Leadership* 45(6): 76–85.

Wallace, J. A. (1972). Three weeks equals thirty weeks? A report on an experimental intensive January language course. *Foreign Language Annals* 6: 88–94.

Watkins, B. T. (1989). Many colleges offering intensive weekend programs to give working adults a chance to earn degrees. *The Chronicle of Higher Education.* (November 1): A35, A38.

Weare, W. L. (1973). Homework versus no homework assignments as related to achievement and participation by adults attending short, intensive management courses. Unpublished doctoral dissertation, The University of Iowa.

Wisconsin University-Oshkosh (1978). Evaluation of an Innovative Academic Calendar and its Effectiveness: Final Report. Oshkosh, WI: University of Wisconsin-Oshkosh. (ED 172 648)

Yalden, J. (1978). A comparison of achievement in four intermediate courses in Spanish. System 6(2): 89–97.

Young, R. J. and McDougall, W. P. (1989). Summer session in American colleges and universities: perspectives, practices, problems and prospects. Unpublished manuscript.

Remediation in American Higher Education

Darrel A. Clowes
Virginia Polytechnic Institute and State University

Remediation[1] in higher education is a perennial issue. It is a significant issue today as evidenced by its prominence in the landmark publication of the Carnegie Foundation for the Advancement of Teaching (1977), in regional reports (SREB, 1985), and in national reports (Piland, 1983). It was an issue significant enough for inclusion in Charles Eliot's inaugural address at Harvard (Eliot, 1869); it was a basis for contention at Vassar and Cornell in the late 1800s (Brier, 1984), and it was an element in Finn's recent indictment of American higher education as suffering a "rising tide of mediocrity" (1984). While remediation as an issue has been with us since Civil War days, the characteristics of the students, of the programs, of the program goals, and of the institutions which house them have shifted significantly over time. It is this shifting nature that has presented problems of definition, identification, and measurement that have in turn confounded research and theory building efforts. This review will identify periods within the efforts at remediation in higher education as reflected in its literature, identify lines of inquiry which have proven barren, some which have advanced our understanding in modest ways, and several lines of inquiry that hold promise.

SHIFTING NATURE OF REMEDIATION

The colleges established in America before this century operated with a meager and uneven base in precollegiate education. They were driven to admit inadequately prepared students and developed college preparatory programs for these students. The magnitude of the practice of admitting inadequately prepared stu-

The author wishes to thank Daniel Bock for his assistance in the preparation of this manuscript.

[1]Remediation is one of several terms used in the literature to refer to the effort to assist the underachieving student succeed in higher education. Other related terms are "compensatory" and "developmental" as labels for programs and students. Students are also labeled "underachieving," "high risk," and "at risk" and a variety of other terms. Remedial and remediation will be the primary terms used here. When specific authors or periods are discussed and another term is associated with the author or period, that term will be used.

dents was such that the University of Wisconsin was reported to register 331 students in 1865; 290 were in the college preparatory program and only 41 were enrolled in regular college classes. The practice was so extensive that in 1889 eighty percent of all postsecondary institutions had such programs (Canfield, 1889). This continued until tax-supported secondary schools became common in the early 1900s (Brubacher and Rudy, 1976).

In the first half of the twentieth century American colleges experienced steady growth and gradually were able to raise admissions standards and diminish the emphasis upon college preparatory work. The spread of free secondary education provided the first protection against underprepared students; the emergence of junior colleges from 1900 to the 1940s and the rapid growth of community colleges from the 1940s to the present provided a second level of protection, since these institutions were willing to offer remediation. While colleges and universities were willing to turn remediation over to the emerging junior and community colleges (Richardson, Martens, and Fisk, 1981), they did continue to offer preparatory or remedial work but now under the guise of "college reading programs." Enright and Kerstein (1980) report that in 1942 a significant proportion—between 30 and 60 percent—of the colleges and universities surveyed did or planned to offer a reading or study skills course as a form of remediation.

This pattern continued after the war years. The G.I. Bill brought more and older students to the colleges, and many of these, perhaps two-thirds, lacked the reading and study skills needed for college (Maxwell, 1979). The '60s brought the baby boom era and the continued expansion of higher education in America. Colleges and universities were able to raise admission standards and reduce the number of remedial courses and programs offered. The rapid addition and expansion of community and junior colleges during the '60s also provided relief. Davis (1975) reports that in 1971 less than 50 percent of the colleges had remedial courses, and most of those were community and junior colleges.

The '70s saw the impact of significant social change upon the students entering higher education and upon the goals of many higher education institutions. The civil rights movement and school integration led to increasing numbers of minorities entering higher education. Profound social and economic changes in the society led to increasing numbers of females and students who scored in the lowest third on traditional academic measures entering higher education. Cross (1971) called these the "new students" and documented their presence in first the community and junior colleges and then throughout higher education. Maxwell (1979), writing from the perspective of her program for underprepared students at UCLA, expanded the definition of underprepared to include students with significantly lower academic skills than those of the average student admitted to an institution. A 1982 review of the research on remedial students (Wyatt and Clowes, 1982) reported these new students were increasingly adult and part-time; it went on to speculate that "All this suggests a new type of remedial student, one who is not necessarily financially or culturally disadvantaged but one who has not been taught to read and write at the high school level'' (p. 1). Beckett (1985) added students with central nervous system dysfunctions or severe psychological impairments as a class of remedial students, while Ross and Roe (1986) added international students with language or cultural difficulties, scholarship athletes, and students with handicapping conditions whose deficiencies were not remedied in the secondary school. Fairweather and Shaver (1990) document the presence of handicapped students in two- and four-year institutions while lamenting the low rates of participation and the inadequacy of programs to assist them in their transition to college. It is not surprising that recent studies (Abraham, 1987; Cahalan, 1986) have found programs for remedial students in over 80 percent of the colleges and universities surveyed.

Remediation has been an area of "benign neglect" for most of American higher education's history. Remediation activities have been largely ignored in the literature on higher education and the function has been little studied. Recently, since the movements toward increased access to higher education of the '60s and '70s, remediation has emerged as a significant factor in the curriculum and social agenda of American higher education. However, the kinds of students who are considered remedial have changed significantly over time, and the social agenda undergirding remediation efforts in higher education has also changed. These factors as well as the shifts in program design and assessment criteria over the past decades make comparisons over time difficult and complicate our understanding of the pedagogic and policy issues enmeshed within remediation.

STATE OF THE FIELD

Research on remediation in American higher education has been modest at best. During the periods Cross (1971) labels as the Period of Aristocracy (colonial times to the Civil War) and the Period of Meritocracy (from the Civil War to the Civil Rights movements of the 1950s), little serious research was done. There is trace evidence that programs existed, but little evidence of serious studies of the design or effectiveness of these programs has survived. Rudolph's (1977) history of the undergraduate curriculum does not discuss remediation as a curriculum issue, and Reynolds' (1969) study of the junior college curriculum discusses remediation as a form of skill building he predicts will become important for junior colleges of the future.

The 1960s began the Period of Egalitarianism as numbers of students entered higher education who scored in the bottom third on nationally normed tests of academic ability—Cross's (1971) "new" students. As remediation programs multiplied in higher education, first calls for studies of remediation came and then the studies themselves began to emerge. Roueche (1968) responded to the volume of descriptive material on remediation coming to the ERIC Clearinghouse for Junior Colleges by calling for recognition of remediation as a significant function of higher education and especially the junior college. He also issued a call for basic research in the field. There was little response until Roueche responded to his own call with a series of descriptive studies (Roueche and Kirk, 1973; Roueche and Snow, 1977; Roueche, Baker, and Roueche, 1984).

These studies and others established clearly that remediation programs were increasing in higher education and were a prominent part of the curriculum of higher education. Despite this, remediation was not a respectable or legitimate aspect of the undergraduate curriculum. A publication by the Carnegie Foundation for the Advancement of Teaching (1977) states: "College curricula must be planned on the assumption that all of the new students on campus each year have acquired a certain minimum amount of learning skill and knowledge" (p. 221), but, the report adds: "Once students have been admitted, a college has an obligation to give any support it can to help them succeed in meeting educational goals" (p. 222). The thrust of the Carnegie argument is that secondary schools have responsibility for basic skills preparation, and colleges and universities have a supportive but secondary role in that endeavor. Recent content analyses of the professional literature underscore the marginal nature of remediation in higher education. Kuh et al. (1986) analyzed the research literature on college students between 1969 and 1983. Eleven hundred and eighty-nine articles were reviewed and the primary and secondary topics covered were identified. Of a possible incidence of coverage of just under 2,400 articles (1,189 $\times$ 2), there were only 215 instances of topics being covered that might possibly be related to remediation. Of the 215 articles (11 percent of the total), 91 were instances of coverage of "minority" students, 49 covered "learning styles," 42 focused on "study skills," 22 on "educationally disadvantaged," and 11 on "handicapped" students. No topic related to remediation received "considerable" attention (100 or more incidents of coverage) as defined by the authors. Clowes and Towles (1985) analyzed the contents of the journal published by the American Association of Community and Junior Colleges (currently the *Community, Technical and Junior College Journal*) from 1930 to 1980. They found remediation the least addressed of all curriculum areas and even detected a decline in coverage during the last 20 years. With scant attention from major journals covering research on college students or the major issues of the community colleges, remediation must be considered a marginal enterprise.

Legitimation
The legitimation of remediation, a movement away from benign neglect and marginality toward acknowledgment as an accepted activity and object of research in higher education, has been underway for some time and may be close to attainment. In 1977 the National Association for Remedial/Developmental

Studies in Postsecondary Education held its first national conference. The Association, now the National Association for Developmental Education, has remained active and continues to sponsor a national conference and a variety of state and regional organizations and conferences on developmental education in higher education. A Center for Developmental Education was established at Appalachian State University with assistance from the Kellogg Foundation. The Center has sponsored a journal since 1977, now the *Journal of Developmental Education*, and sponsors training institutes and graduate study for practitioners of remedial education in higher education. Jossey-Bass has established a *New Directions for Learning Assistance Centers*. These activities provide an academic legitimacy for remedial education. Recent surveys have again documented the strong presence of learning assistance centers, remedial programs, and remedial courses in higher education (Abraham, 1987; Lederman, Ryzewic, and Ribaudo, 1983; Sullivan, 1980; Wright and Cahalan, 1985). This continued documentation of the presence of remedial activities has gone a long way to establish the fact of remediation activities in higher education. It has not made them desirable or truly respectable.

Respectability may be a function of the role remediation can play in supporting the open admissions policies of community colleges and many four-year institutions. Open access is a cornerstone of the community and junior college mission. It is also a cornerstone for a significant number of four-year institutions' missions since the promise of equal opportunity finds expression at the state level in public policy supporting access to higher education for all our citizens.

The need for remediation has perhaps been best documented in New Jersey through the continuing activities of the New Jersey Basic Skills Council. In a series of reports beginning in the late 1970s, assessments of the skill levels of first-time students entering New Jersey's public colleges are reported (see Morante, Faskow, and Menditti, 1984a, 1984b). Carefully developed measures are a strong point of the Basic Skills Council's work, and the levels of remediation needed by students at all levels of the higher education system are eye-opening. Among full-time students entering all levels of public higher education in New Jersey, 30 percent needed remediation in writing, 30 percent in basic computation, another 31 percent in elementary algebra, and 34 percent in reading; the authors believe the rates for part-time students would be even higher (Morante, Faskow and Menditti, 1984b). Martin Trow (1982–83) summed up the situation well:

> American colleges are no strangers to underprepared students or remedial instruction. And today our problems, and indeed many of our responses, are remarkably similar to those of the 19th century college. We share with our academic forebears a powerful democratic ethos, weak secondary education, the pressure of the market felt through enrollment-driven budgets, and the absence of any central agency for setting or enforcing high school curricula or standards for college entry. Today, as in the past, all

of these and other forces are bringing to our public colleges and universities many students who are not, on entry, prepared to do work at a standard which those institutions define as "college level". (p. 17)

Concern for the competing demands for providing access to higher education while also maintaining appropriate levels of quality within higher education has moved remediation activities out of the shadows and into the mainstream of academic life. The emergence of community colleges as a potential institutional base for remediation within higher education has also made remediation more acceptable to higher education practitioners and to public policy makers. The formation of professional associations, institutes housed in academic institutions, and the emergence of journals specific to the field have all contributed to the legitimation of remediation in higher education.

Program Design
The period after World War II saw modest growth in the college-age population but major growth in both enrollments in higher education and in the proportion of the college-age population entering higher education. A portion of the surge in enrollment was represented by the increased entry of women, minorities, and part-time students (Cohen and Brawer, 1982); another portion of the increase was represented by increasing rates of college enrollment among cohorts of graduating high school seniors (Clowes, Hinkle, and Smart, 1986). Many of these students enrolling in higher education, perhaps as many as a third, were candidates for remediation. Therefore attention shifted away from the existing isolated reading and study skill courses towards programs designed specifically to assist these students in coping with college. Attention also was directed to identifying programs and practices that were effective. Community colleges were the institutions most impacted by these "new" students and the first to be looked at in an effort to rationalize the practice of remediation.

Search for Effective Programs and Practices.
As community colleges attempted to cope with remediation for increasing numbers of students, it gradually became clear that there were few agreed-upon principles or practices on which to fall back. Institutions developed programs in isolation and with very little information about how other institutions coped. The professional literature had not given prominence or even recognition to remediation as a topic of concern for higher education; the ERIC system was in its infancy, and state and national associations concerned with remediation in higher education did not develop until the mid '70s. Roueche (1968) and Moore (1970) questioned the effectiveness of remediation efforts in community colleges and called for research in the field. Losak (1972) reported a study which concluded that remediation programs at a leading institution, Miami-Dade Junior College,

did not contribute to student success. It was in this context that the primary researchers of the '70s focused upon the identification of successful programs and practices. The institution first considered was the community college, the institution perceived to be at the forefront of remediation efforts. Attention then gradually shifted to include all colleges and universities.

In a review of the literature on remediation programs, Bock (1990) reached two broad conclusions. First, "there is little consensus with regard to the structure, management, or efficacy of these programs," and "a piecemeal approach to helping high-risk students succeed has been used, for the complete range of responses needed is not found within a single program model" (p. 31). Second, he stated the emphasis on remedial programs shifted from academic skills prior to the 1950s to an emphasis in the 1950s and '60s upon academic skills addressed through programmed instruction complemented by attention to the personal and social needs of students.

In the 1970s and '80s Bock identified a movement toward a more unified approach to remediation which attempted to bring together the cognitive dimension represented by the subject matter specialist and the affective dimension represented by student services professionals. This unified or developmental approach took the form either of a special instructional unit of the college designed to deliver services to the remedial student or of a learning support center or learning laboratory as a special facility with tutors and support staff. These efforts were often in combination with curriculum innovations such as writing across the curriculum or an integrated critical thinking program. Bock's conclusions are reasonable, although he accepts the logic of connecting programmed learning techniques based upon the systems model and the positivist world view inherent in it with the affective elements and more subjective world view associated with student development. Apple (1979), Aronowitz and Giroux (1985), and others believe these are incompatible philosophic positions and question their happy coexistence within a single program using a common set of pedagogic practices and principles.

The search for effective programs and practices continued through the '70s and '80s. Morrison and Ferrante (1973) studied compensatory programs in the community college as an institutional response to contest mobility[2] working within the American society and impacting negatively on the lower socioeconomic classes. In 1971 they surveyed the 53 public and private two-year institutions that participated in the annual research on "National Norms for Entering College Freshman" conducted by the American Council on Education and the

---

[2]Contest mobility is a system in which elite status is the prize in an open contest and is taken by the aspirants' own efforts. While the "contest" is governed by some rules of fair play, the contestants have wide latitude in the strategies they may employ. Since the "prize" of successful upward mobility is not in the hands of an established elite to give out, the latter cannot determine who shall attain it and who shall not (Turner, 1960, p. 856).

Higher Education Research Institute at the University of California at Berkeley. The result was a profile of the instructional and curricular practices and the support services (e.g., financial aid, counseling) provided for remedial students at these institutions. Morrison and Ferrante noted the wide array of services and practices but made no effort to identify effective practices. This study served as a benchmark for those to follow.

In 1972 Roueche and Kirk (1973) chose a reputational sample of five effective remedial programs and did a descriptive study of the programs. They concluded that remediation programs can be effective in assisting students to succeed in college. They endorsed no single organizational or instructional practice, but they did find dedicated faculty, personalized instruction, and counseling support essential ingredients of successful programs. A major problem recognized was the poor success students experienced moving from remedial courses or programs into the mainstream curriculum and its courses. This study was flawed by its limited sample and imprecise measure of effectiveness; however, it was influential in the emerging remedial education field.

Cross (1976) reported on a 1974 survey of 20 percent of the membership of the American Association of Community and Junior Colleges. She was able to present a profile of program characteristics representative of practices in the community colleges in 1970 and in 1974. From the survey and an excellent analysis of the research on remediation, she was able to identify and to encourage a shift from skills training to an emphasis on a unified or pluralistic approach to supporting student success. She called this approach developmental education. She also anticipated an "instructional revolution" based on mastery learning. This study was grounded solidly in the research on learning and student development and set the framework against which most future research was designed. She did not identify existing "effective" practices but rather pointed toward promising directions for future work.

The search for effective programs continued and expanded to include four-year institutions. Grant and Hoeber (1978) looked to programs in both two- and four-year institutions and found no conclusive evidence of effectiveness and no model programs in which they were confident. Roueche and Snow (1977) made an ambitious attempt to identify effective programs and practices. In 1976 they surveyed a sample of 150 public two-year and 150 four-year institutions. They asked institutions to declare whether they were successful and to describe their programs. Six two-year and six four-year institutions were identified as "exemplary" and described as models. A strength of this study was its identification of three configurations within remedial programs: those which operate with isolated remedial courses housed in academic departments and taught by academic faculty, those which offer special courses for remedial students outside the academic departments but taught by faculty from the disciplines, and those with separate courses and faculty in an instructional unit committed to remedial education. Based upon their observations, Roueche and Snow argue for the separate department as the most effective model, especially for two-year colleges. The weakness of this study is the failure to establish clear criteria for excellence or for the "exemplary" programs identified.

This effort by Roueche and Snow (1977) marks the apex of the movement to identify the "one best way" or the "exemplary" program. Subsequent studies have had more modest goals and a narrower perspective. Maxwell (1979) addressed the question of effective program design from her perspective as a former teacher, counselor, and director of the Learning Assistance Program at the University of California at Berkeley. The program design she worked from was the learning assistance center, a separate instructional unit designed to bring the academic and student support efforts of the institution to bear upon the underprepared student. This design was presented as a vehicle for unifying the services needed by the student, but her real attention was to the management and political concerns of an instructional function on the fringes of the curriculum of a research university. Maxwell discussed effective practice in each of several specific academic areas (e.g., math, English composition) but departed from Roueche and others in concentrating on the parts—but not the whole—of the remediation program. This work represents a shift toward a subject matter emphasis within the context of remediation.

Trillin (1980) continued this perspective. She reported on the activities at the City University of New York during the period of open admissions and the tenure of Mina Shaughnessy as director of the Instructional Resource Center. Again the emphasis was upon the academic areas and the teaching of skills, and like Maxwell she emphasized the role of counseling and support services. Maxwell (1979), Trillin (1980), and Sullivan (1980) all support the learning assistance center as an appropriate separate center to coordinate an institution's efforts to assist the remedial student, but none attempts to defend the approach as the ideal. Sullivan's contribution is his documentation of the widespread use of learning assistance centers; he gives little information about the design, organization, or effectiveness of the programs.

A focus upon the components of remediation programs was again demonstrated in the 1987 Southern Regional Education Board (SREB) study (Abraham, 1987). This study was a survey of institutions in the SREB states to find if there was agreement on a most basic program design element—the criteria for placement of a student in a remedial program or course. There was none. Roueche and Baker (1987) again used a reputational survey to identify the "most effective community colleges" in the United States, but the definition of most effective was left to the individual panelist's judgment. This survey produced one exemplary institution, Miami-Dade Community College, whose programs and management are characterized as a model. The authors describe the remediation program at the institution but are careful to point out it is successful in the specific context of that one institution and is not the model for other programs. In a similar manner Tomlinson (1989), in a synoptic monograph about the field, concluded that "From a global perspective, successful programs are found to have two characteristics in common: comprehensiveness in their support services and institutionalization within the academic mainstream" (p. 41). She reports on programs in two institutions that represent these characteristics but presents no evidence to support their designation as "successful" programs and does not make a strong case for adopting these program designs over others. It appears that the search for the ideal program is over. Acceptance that there is no "one best way" to design remediation programs represents a tacit acknowledgment in the field that the delivery of remediation is a complex and multifaceted enterprise. Successful remediation is not directly related to program design. The program purposes, students, institutions, curriculum and the faculty are each too diverse to allow for easy solutions.

Search for Theory—Program Characteristics.
While the Period of Aristocracy in American higher education (Cross, 1971) was a time when remediation was addressed through college preparatory departments, in the Period of Meritocracy remediation efforts became distributed over the college curriculum. Specialized courses in reading, study skills, and "bonehead" math and English offered by academic departments were the vehicles. The Period of Egalitarianism can be characterized as a period of gradual movement away from isolated course-based remediation efforts toward a unified or comprehensive approach to remediation. Programs were designed around counseling centers and counselors, around subject matter specialists assembled in learning assistance centers or academic divisions, or occasionally as loose federations of "remedial" faculty housed in separate academic departments but united by their shared work with remedial students. There was considerable debate during the 1960s and 1970s about the proper form of remedial activities, and three different conceptual bases were promulgated—one based on student characteristics, one based on developmental theory, and one based on organizational principles. However, there was little evidence of programing designed from a theoretical or conceptual base.

Student characteristics were used by Losak, Jefferson, and Sutton (1969) to distinguish among types of underprepared student. Their central argument was that not all underprepared students were underprepared because they lacked academic ability, but most were treated as if that were their problem. They make the point that underachieving students have in common their failure to achieve in an academic setting but may not have any other characteristics in common. Moore (1970) made the same point a year later and Maxwell (1979) a decade later. Losak, Jefferson, and Sutton proposed a four-way distinction among students: students with low achievement but high academic potential, students with low achievement and psychopathology, those with low achievement and mild central nervous system dysfunction, and finally those with low achievement and low intelligence. The authors implied different approaches and program designs would be appropriate for each category of student. There does not appear to have been any specific follow-up of this conceptualization except for the later recognition that students with central nervous system disorders are a separate category of student with special needs.

The desirability of addressing both the cognitive and the affective dimensions of remedial students was articulated by Cross (1976). She identified various learner needs and described programmatic responses to meet these needs. Remedial education was distinguished from developmental based upon purpose.

> If the purpose of the program is to overcome academic deficiencies, I would term the program remedial, in the standard dictionary sense in which remediation is concerned with correcting weaknesses. If, however, the purpose of the program is to develop the diverse talents of students, whether academic or not, I would term the program developmental. (p. 31)

This conceptualization of remedial education as skills development and as one component of something larger, developmental education, has had a long-lasting effect. This conceptualization was consistent with the emergence, especially in the community college, of instructional units designed to bring together affective and cognitive approaches to better serve remedial students.

Roueche and Snow (1977) used the term "developmental" and urged an integrated approach to remediation involving teachers, counselors, peer helpers, and learning centers all working out of an academic unit committed to the developmental student. Clowes (1979) drew a similar distinction between remedial and developmental education and proposed program characteristics logically associated with each. Clowes (1980) also proposed a clear distinction be made between the three primary terms in the field—remedial, compensatory, and developmental—and proposed definitions for each. The term "developmental" has become the preferred term in remediation. Despite a modest movement toward unified programs in community colleges and some four-year institutions throughout the '70s and into the '80s (McGrath and Spear, 1987), the emphasis of most programs still appears to be upon academic skill building. It appears the adoption of these conceptualizations of remedial as distinct from developmental is only cosmetic.

Lombardi (1979) proposed a four-phase organization of remediation based on the client groups served. He proposed a pre-transfer program track that remedies deficiencies in grades or courses needed for transfer to a senior institution, a skill-based remedial track, an Adult Basic Education track for adults needing basic literacy training for the GED, and a track for the handicapped. This design has been partially used as institutions set up separate Adult Basic Education programs as a continuing education component and develop special programs for the handicapped. However, there is no evidence that this conceptualization, or that of Losak, Jefferson, and Sutton, or that of Cross was the source of program revisions or designs. Program changes and designs can as logically be explained as organizational adaptations to diverse client groups.

No concept or theory has emerged to guide program design. Developmental education has emerged as a term frequently used, but developmental education is so broadly applied it is difficult to gain guidance from the multiple interpretations and practices with which it is associated.

Search for Theory—Demographics and Social Characteristics.
Fundamental questions for researchers and practitioners of remediation in higher education are "Who are the remedial students?" and "Are they different from other students?" Cross (1971) provided a pragmatic and useful definition: "New students to higher education . . . are operationally defined as those scoring in the lowest third among national samples of young people on national tests of academic ability" (p. 13). Cross was writing about the students entering postsecondary education in the Period of Egalitarianism and particularly during the 1960s as higher education was opened to students who had previously not aspired to college or had been unable to attend. She developed a synthesis of the existing research and especially data from four major studies conducted in the 1960s— Project Talent and three studies conducted by E.T.S.: the Growth Study, SCOPE (School to College: Opportunities for Postsecondary Education) and CGP (Comprehensive Guidance and Placement Program).

Factors such as socioeconomic class as shown through father's occupation and education and student's aptitude, race, and gender were used to distinguished the new students from the traditional and the remedial student from the non-remedial. Low SES, low measured aptitude, membership in a minority race, and being female were disproportionately associated with being a new student and a remedial student. However, the majority of remedial students remained white males with low aptitude and SES. This study provided evidence that the new students to higher education were different from the traditional student in terms of SES, aptitude, race, and gender. It also established differences in attitudes toward self and education that were rooted in family background and served to distinguish these students from the traditional students. Cross suggested that remedial students, as predominantly new students, were different from traditional students on both demographic and attitudinal measures. She recommended that efforts be made to change student attitudes and to change the ways colleges interface with their students to increase the probability of remedial students surviving in the institutions.

Cross suggested the Period of Egalitarianism in higher education began during the 1960s and possibly would extend beyond. A recent study of enrollment rates utilizing data from Project Talent, the National Longitudinal Study of the High School Class of 1972, and High School and Beyond supports that proposal (Clowes, Hinkle, and Smart, 1986). A modest expansion of enrollment in higher education was reported for low SES, for low aptitude, and for minority high school graduates; a major gain was reported for female high school graduates. These findings support the argument for an egalitarian function in higher education, since students usually described as marginal are entering higher education in increasing numbers and are approaching, but not matching, the enrollment rates of students from the dominant culture. However, a marked difference in enrollment rates by type of institution was also reported. Community colleges and other open access institutions absorb disproportionate numbers of these new students. Olivas (1979) identified the concentration of minorities in community colleges, especially urban community colleges, as a potential barrier to their involvement in all sectors of higher education. Here transfer from community colleges is seen as a barrier since transfer rates from two- to four-year institutions have been so low compared with the progress of comparable students who begin at four-year institutions. Thus students entering higher education through the community college are placed at a disadvantage (Astin,1977; Grubb, 1991). Richardson and Bender (1985) document the continuing uneven distribution of minorities in higher education. They find minorities concentrated in open access institutions in urban areas. Since open access universities and community colleges are lower status institutions in higher education, this also presents a limitation upon the egalitarian function of higher education.

These and other studies inform us about the shifts in student demographics in higher education, but they are not helpful in identifying an underlying theory for remediation. The new students entering higher education have now distributed themselves across the range of higher education institutions. Some of them are remedial students, but many are not. Some traditional students are remedial students. Remedial students are as likely to vary as much on demographic variables within an institution as they do between institutions. Perhaps the primary gain from this line of inquiry is an increased awareness of the concentration of minorities in urban institutions and the need to consider the special needs of minority students.

Search for Theory—Psychological Traits.
Aside from their poor academic performance, do remedial students differ systematically from other students? This question has intrigued researchers and practitioners because a clear cause for poor performance would make possible a clear solution. That clear cause has, however, been elusive. The search is complicated by the lack of a common definition for the remedial student. Personal, situational, and institutional variables confound the issue since the term remedial and its variants serve primarily to label a student who is a poor achiever rather

than to designate a type of individual with specific and common characteristics. The characteristics of students labeled remedial appear to vary over time, with the type of institution, and even with the specific institution the student enters. All of these factors have contributed to the difficulty of identifying psychological factors (or other types of factors) associated with poor academic performance for broad categories of students.

Several general characteristics or traits such as intelligence, motivation, and cognitive style have been investigated; narrower constructs such as self-concept, locus of control, field dependence/independence, anxiety and coping behaviors, and even right and left brain dominance have also been considered. None of these has yielded easily as the culprit associated with the underachieving student. Maxwell (1979) relates this effort to identify causes for students' underachievement or even poor achievement in college to an increased pressure for solutions to the problems presented by underachievement. She asserts that

> . . . at about the same time that college counselors concluded there was little they could do to help underachieving, failing students, colleges and universities were forced to recruit and accept large numbers of educationally disadvantaged students and favor students with the poorest chances for success, those who would be least responsive to traditional educational programs and counseling. (p. 204)

The Period of Egalitarianism was representative of an ideology which dictated that access to higher education, at least to some aspects of higher education, was a right of all Americans and that participation in higher education was the preferred path to success in the society. To support this ideology, it was desirable to identify specific characteristics of remedial students which would allow them to be "fixed" and brought into the mainstream of the society. In this spirit, a variety of attempts were made to identify psychological traits associated with remedial students to account for their poor academic performance.

Intelligence measurement has not been a reliable indicator of a student needing remediation. Evans and Dubois (1972) are representative of the researchers who find intelligence measures unreliable indicators of those needing remediation. They identified two types of remedial or high-risk student: the slow learner and the inadequately prepared student. Low intelligence may be associated with the former; it is not directly associated with the latter. Motivation has been considered by several investigators, but its effect and the precise meaning of motivation have not been clear. Klingelhofer and Hollander (1973) reviewed the literature and concluded that high-risk students had limited ability at analytic problem solving, difficulty with abstract goals, and a strong preference for applied studies over more scholarly studies. Cross (1971) found a similar vocational rather than an academic orientation among the high-risk students. A sense of powerlessness and inability to control their destiny were identified as characteristics of high-risk students by Maxwell (1979). Griffin (1980) identified delay and avoidance of academic challenges and poor work and study habits as characteristics of low-achieving students. All of these characteristics can be grouped under the general heading of motivation, but they provide little basis for a systematic approach to the remedial student except to underscore the need for counseling support and attention to the affective dimension of students. That these qualities separate the remedial student from non-remedial students is unclear.

Cognitive style was a variable of considerable interest in the 1970s. Blanton and Bullock (1973) and Messick and Associates (1976) contributed major reviews of the research on cognitive style. A cautious note was sounded by Cronbach and Snow (1977), who reviewed the field and concluded that the literature on cognitive style was too inconsistent to support generalizations or to provide a basis for curriculum designs. Although references to cognitive or learning styles appear in the literature on remediation (see Boylan, 1985; Posey, 1984; Rabianski-Carriuolo, 1989), a cautious note is usually struck about the concept and few implications for practice are drawn. In related developments Cross (1976) associated a particular learning characteristic, field dependence, with the ''new students'' in higher education. Poor or negative self-concept has also been associated with the underachieving student by several writers (Cross, 1976; Maxwell, 1979; Roueche and Snow, 1977) as has external locus of control (Maxwell, 1979). There is no solid evidence to support a direct causal link between any one of these concepts and underachievement or poor achievement in higher education. Nor is there clear evidence to suggest that remedial students differ systematically from non-remedial students in the possession of these traits. The broad field of college student learning has not integrated the concepts of intelligence, motivation, or cognitive style into the curriculum and instructional practices of higher education (Fincher, 1985); neither has the sub-field of remedial education.

Perhaps Moore (1983) has summarized the situation best. He warns that

. . . spending an inordinate amount of time linking academic skill deficiencies in adults to self-worth, cultural factors, race, economics, family dysfunction and disorganization, and past performance has not proved to be a useful exercise in terms of information that will help . . . improve the teaching and learning process. (p. 33).

In the Period of Egalitarianism there may have been a desire on the part of practitioners and researchers in remediation to find an explanation for poor academic achievement that would allow redressing. This would be consistent with the ideology of the period which argued that all individuals were inherently equal despite differences in performance. Explanations for poor academic performance based on fundamental differences among classes of people, such as Jensen's theory of racial differences (1969), ran counter to the ideology of the time and were ignored or rejected. Efforts were made to find traits or theories that explained the differences among people and would allow remediation to provide meaningful equality of opportunity. Although these efforts to find psychological traits associated with underachieving students were understandable and laudable, they ultimately fell before the realities of research findings and the complexity of the issues involved.

Search for Theory—Learning Theory.
Learning theory offered yet another opportunity to provide a theoretical foundation for an instructional design that would allow remediation to succeed and become a vehicle to ensure equality of opportunity. The behaviorist tradition provided systematic instructional designs like individualized instruction, programmed instruction, computer-assisted instruction, and mastery learning. Cross (1976) was a leading spokesperson for this view as she discussed the "instructional revolution" to come. Cognitive psychology provided approaches to teaching and learning using cognitive style, with Messick (1976) the lead spokesperson. Developmental psychology provided endorsement for attention to the affective domain of students, but student development was not typically seen as a primary curricular concern. Student development as a concern for student services specialists has a well-developed literature and theory base (Creamer, 1980; Miller and Prince, 1978; Parker, 1978), but there have been no comparable movements in academic program or curriculum design generally or for remediation specifically. Cross (1976) and Brown (1982) provided a linkage of principles of developmental theory and practice in remediation, and Boylan (1986a, 1986b, 1986c) explored the implications of developmental theory for practice. Despite their efforts, little evidence exists for the successful integration of developmental theory into the practice of remediation. This is true despite the widespread use of the term "developmental" as the preferred label for remediation efforts. In similar fashion neither theory drawn from the behaviorist camp nor theory from the cognitivist camp has provided a sustaining basis for program design.

Conclusions on Program Design.
No theoretical or conceptual basis has been established as an undergirding for program design in remediation. The field appears dominated by an eclectic approach in which promising ideas and practices are identified, modified, adopted, and occasionally assessed. Theory is used after the fact to justify practice as often as it is used to plan practice; there is no way to distinguish the two possibilities. It appears the field is driven by neither theory nor research; rather, it is grounded in practical experience and is eclectic.

There appear to be two related explanations for this. First, remediation is a function of higher education that carries a heavy ideological weight. The ideology of equality mandates treating all students the same within the institution and assuming they are basically the same coming to the institution. This ideology conflicts with the honoring of differences, which also has high value in the

American culture. These ideological burdens complicate the effort to develop theory or employ research findings. Second, the complexities of the research problems involved have exceeded the resources brought to the issues of remediation. Single-institution studies using a limited number of variables and modest statistical methods do not yield the results that large-scale studies conducted over time and with more powerful statistical treatments would yield. In the same way, case studies and other qualitative studies following a systematic research design have rarely been conducted[3]. The resources available have severely limited the scale of research and the quality of the findings.

The Period of Egalitarianism carried with it an ideology that all students could succeed; their failure to succeed was seen as the failure of the institutions of higher education, their faculty, and their programs. Fincher (1985) identified this situation in the context of a discussion of learning theory.

> The arrival of pluralism and diversity in education has meant too frequently that any explanation of achievement or accomplishment in terms of individual capabilities is suspect. Differences in interests, motives, and cognitive styles are permissible, but differences in aptitude, readiness, or predispositions are suspected of genetical or hereditarian biases that are unacceptable in an egalitarian society. (p. 84)

Students would not be held culpable; considerations outside the student would be held responsible. This situation, I believe, has predisposed program designers and curriculum specialists to concentrate on instructional designs and social and psychological theories consistent with a view that student motivations, learning styles, etc. can be identified, addressed, and accommodated by the institution.

The complexity of the research questions appropriate to remedial education has been indicated in the preceding material. Most research to date has been survey research on practices. More specific studies have usually been restricted to single institutions and to a limited set of variables (see Grant and Hoebner, 1978; Kulik, Kulik, and Shwalb, 1983). A further complication has been the failure of most research to utilize control groups of non-remedial students or to control for a wide variety of variables like institutional type, student age and status as full or part-time students, SES, and a host of other potentially confounding variables which represent indicators of differences among students and institutions. There have been only tentative efforts to address remediation as a "multisource phenomena." Unlike areas with sustained research traditions such as learning theory, research on remediation in higher education is in an early stage. The wide range of variables associated with remediation have not yet been fully identified. Remediation as a research area could benefit from multivariate

---

[3]The Richardson, Fisk, and Okum (1983) study is an exception to this observation. This study was conducted with federal funds. The work of the New Jersey Basic Skills Council has a narrow descriptive focus but is an example of the results obtained through sustained state funding in the area of remediation.

research to develop insight into the relationships that exist among the variables in the field. A related step would be work to generate theory appropriate to the field which could then be used to guide future research.

Program Effects

Beyond the simple but central questions "Who are the remedial students?" and "Are they different from non-remedial students?" is another question—"Do remediation programs work?" The first two questions dominated interest during the Period of Egalitarianism; the third has dominated the decade of the '80s. This shift needs to be understood in context. While Cross (1971) set forth the three periods used in this paper to mark stages in the evolution of American higher education, she never meant them to be more than helpful conceptualizations for complex issues and forces operating within the society. There was clear concern that the last period identified, the Period of Egalitarianism, might be a short-lived or even ephemeral phenomena. That appears to have been the case. While the '60s and '70s did see a converging of public opinion, legislation, and institutional policy around an ideology favorable to egalitarian actions in the society and therefore in higher education, that ideology weakened in the '80s. Presidents Reagan and then Bush became our national figureheads, a strongly conservative social agenda was advocated for the country (Aronowitz and Giroux, 1985; Shor, 1986), and major reports critical of public education and of higher education were written and released. These reports and their effects may, in retrospect, represent the end of Cross's Period of Egalitarianism and signal a subsequent "Period of Reconsideration" or "Retrenchment." They may also represent a return to the ideology of the Period of Meritocracy and signal that the flirtation with an egalitarian stance was only a brief aberration in higher education's history. The long-term effects of these reports and the values they represent are conjecture; the content of the reports is clear.

All five reports emphasize the need for quality in undergraduate education. The National Endowment for the Humanities (Bennett, 1984) and the Association of American Colleges (1985) reports do not discuss access or remediation; the National Institute of Education report (Study Group on the Conditions of Excellence in American Higher Education, 1984) supports open access to higher education and urges colleges to provide remediation to ensure success in college course work. The Southern Regional Educational Board reports (1985a, 1985b) are supportive of open access, urge skill-based remediation geared to success in college course work, and emphasize statewide efforts and cooperation with secondary schools. In none of these reports is development seen as a specific goal of remediation; the emphasis is completely upon remediation as the improvement of needed academic skills. Assessment is urged with a clear emphasis on success in college courses and persistence in college as the criteria of interest.

Emphasis upon assessment of student outcomes has been a characteristic of public debate and policy in the '80s. The Southern Association of Colleges and Schools has made student outcomes assessment mandatory for accreditation; Florida, Georgia, and Texas have established statewide tests for competence for entry to or advancement within higher education. This debate and the actions taken to date represent pressure for demonstrable academic success on the open access policies and remediation programs associated with the Period of Egalitarianism. Collectively they add urgency to the longstanding question in remediation "Do remediation programs work?" and may signal a reopening of questioning about the role and legitimacy of remediation in higher education.

General Effects.
Recent efforts to assess the effectiveness of remedial programs can be dated from Roueche's 1968 publication which surveyed the field and found no significant research existent on the rapidly emerging remedial programs in community colleges. Losak (1972) reported on the results of a well-designed single institution study employing a comparison of remediated and non-remediated matched samples of students on retention, grade point average and number of credit hours completed in the mainstream curriculum. He reported no meaningful differences between the remediated and non-remediated students. Roueche and Kirk (1973) studied remedial students in several institutions and reported significant positive effects for remediation. The research was flawed by the failure to employ control groups or to consider outcomes after leaving the remedial program and entering the mainstream curriculum. Later, Grant and Hoeber (1978) reviewed the literature and found no evidence of success for remedial programs.They challenged claims of having identified programatic factors as "most successful" because

> The faultiness of the logic in these cases is only superseded by the faultiness of the data to support such assumptions. The inability of most researchers to adequately isolate and test individual variables would alone refute such statements. (p. 17)

Kulik, Kulik, and Shwalb (1983) did a meta-analysis of the research literature that represented the most rigorous analysis to that point. They faulted most research to that time as ". . . unsystematic in their selection of studies and subjective and idiosyncratic in their interpretations" (p. 398). The studies used in the meta-analysis were restricted to studies of high-risk students identified by low test scores, low grades in school or college, or membership in a disadvantaged group. Measured outcomes and control groups were required for inclusion in the analysis as well as avoidance of "crippling methodological flaws." These requirements reduced the pool of studies from 504 to 60. The results of the meta-analysis were mixed. The effects of special programs for high-risk students when assessed on grade point average or persistence were significant. The strength of the effects was modest, however, and unevenly distributed.

Effects were greatest when programs began in the high school years, were somewhat less when programs began in the freshman year of college, and were lowest when programs began after the freshman year. In addition, program effects were negligible in community colleges, somewhat greater in 4-year colleges, and greatest in doctoral universities. Finally, effects on persistence were greater in recent studies than they were in earlier studies. (406)

New Jersey has developed a notable program for assessing entering college students' basic skills; that program has been expanded to provide measures of the effectiveness of remedial programs in the state. The strengths of this program are its focus upon the specific skill areas needing remediation, its longitudinal design, and its separation of programs in the county colleges (community colleges), state colleges, and Rutgers University. The results of that assessment effort have been generally favorable across all institutional types.

> Data included in the Basic Skills Council report to the Board of Higher Education on the character and effectiveness of remedial programs in Fall, 1981, confirmed the council's belief that remediation can and does help students. In comparison to those students who needed remediation but did not complete it or did not enroll in it, students completing remediation were much less likely to drop out of college after one semester and much more likely to complete college-level courses for credit and receive higher grade point averages. (Morante, Fashow, and Menditto, 1984a, p. 8)

These findings were confirmed in subsequent studies (New Jersey Basic Skills Council, 1986). Although the question of program effects on a broad scale is not clearly answered, there appears to be an emerging consensus that remediation does have positive effects. The specific correlates of success, the specific criteria for success, and the financial and social costs associated with remediation have not been well addressed.

Program Assessment.

The efforts to determine if remedial programs were effective have now merged with the accountability movement. Assessment has become a mandated activity in many states and has focused on learner outcomes. Remediation programs are shaped by these broader influences, and practitioners and institutional researchers have been gradually developing evaluation strategies tailored to their own needs and interests.

Early efforts were not well received. Cross (1976) disparaged evaluations done in the 1960s and before because ". . . the criteria for the success of the programs were poorly formulated, the research designs were naive, and the data interpretations and implications for improvement were weak" (p. 32). Basic design flaws like not using control groups or tests for statistical significance combined with questionable measures were cited as general weaknesses by Anderson (1973). The research of the next decade was not received much better. Ross and Roe (1986) believe evaluation has improved since the 1970s. The failure to synthesize the existing research has been criticized (Akst and Hecht, 1980) while Richardson, Martens, and Fisk (1981) have assailed the unsystematic treatment of student characteristics, program and instructional design, and criteria for success. Roueche, Baker, and Roueche (1984) surveyed postsecondary institutions and reported few institutions using sound evaluation practices. Roueche (1984) was especially critical of the continuing practice of collecting data only while students are in remediation rather than tracking them into the mainstream curriculum.

The 1980s have seen significant progress in the development of models and measures for the assessment of remedial programs. Achievement and persistence have become generally accepted as measures of success or program worth (Basonic, 1982). An emphasis on achievement and persistence in the mainstream courses after remediation has also become accepted as an important measure (Fadale and Winter, 1985; Kulik, Kulik, and Shwalb, 1983; New Jersey Basic Skills Council, 1986).

A number of alternative success measures (e.g., completion of 12 credit hours, of individual goals, and transfer) have been proposed for non-traditional students and especially for the community college where degree attainment may not be a student goal (Morris and Losak, 1986). The multiplicity of variables that impact on remediation programs have made evaluation difficult. Institutional type is a critical but little considered variable. Research universities have different environments and expectations than community colleges. Commuter institutions have different environments and expectations than residential institutions. Admissions policies, curriculum, and support services all impact on the remediation program. Student variables abound. Demographic and background variables are important but so are time of entry into higher education, choice of major, and student status. It is increasingly important to recognize the variables that impact on specific remedial programs. Clearly, there is no ''one size fits all'' selection of variables to use when considering the effectiveness of a particular program on particular students in a particular institution.

Evaluation designs also need to be flexible to accommodate each context. While early evaluation efforts in education relied on quantitative measures and clearly established goals in the Tyler model, later efforts have acknowledged the importance of goal-free evaluation and of process-oriented evaluation.

> Increasingly the assumption that we can anticipate the outcomes of programs and design measurements for those outcomes is being challenged, and alternative models are being proposed that allow the activities of the program itself to influence (Stufflebeam) or determine (Scriven) the characteristics and effects of the programs that are considered in evaluation. (Clowes, 1981, p. 19)

There are a number of general evaluation schemes currently in use in education. Dressel (1976) has put forth one with four phases—planning, input, process, and product—each of which may be the object of formative, summative, or both forms of evaluation. House (1978) developed an eight-model taxonomy of evaluation methods while Guba and Lincoln (1981) have reduced the eight models to two types of evaluation: countenance and response. Apparently, there is no best model. Remediation and assessment are both developing fields. It seems logical that the more useful approaches to assessment of remedial programs or practices would be the most flexible and adaptive approaches. Definitions of remediation are unclear or unstated in most institutions and in most states (Piland, 1983), but without clear definitions to guide a program, clear goals are difficult to establish and to evaluate. Little attention is given to differentiating types of remedial students. Goals for handicapped students, foreign students, and low-aptitude students probably are not the same. The measures most useful to indicate the success of a particular program are still unsettled, although grade point average and retention after entry into the mainstream curriculum have emerged as basic measures. With the uncertainty existent in the field, it seems inappropriate to use a Tyler type of approach, with set measures and goals and a prescribed level of attainment established as criteria for success. An emphasis on formative as well as summative approaches would seem best suited for remediation.

Two models have been derived from the general evaluation literature and practices specifically for the assessment of remediation programs at the institutional level. Somers (1987a) presents and reviews Boylan's four-tiered program evaluation model and Clowes's stage model for program evaluation. Boylan's model (see Somers, 1987b) moves from first gathering descriptive data to then asking formative questions about student outcomes as a measure of program effectiveness and as a guide to improvement of practice. A third level consists of summative questions based on measures with a longer perspective (up to five years). The final level is the recognition that unanticipated outcomes do occur and must be acknowledged and considered.

The Clowes model (Clowes, 1984) identifies different audiences, purposes, and forms of qualitative and quantitative data which can be considered through four stages of evaluation. The first stage considers activities within the remediation program; the second stage addresses the transition from the remedial to the mainstream curriculum. The third stage is normative; it calls for reassessing the goals established initially to guide the program, while the fourth stage is a feedback loop that calls for reassessment of the measures to be used based upon the reassessment of goals in stage three. Somers (1987a) regards the models as complementary and assesses them as follows:

> The comparative simplicity of the Boylan design provides an exquisitely ready and easy formula for both the novice and the experienced evaluator. A further advantage is that it may be executed more expeditiously. However, the Boylan model lacks the continuity supplied by the interfaces among the stages of the Clowes design. Similarly,

Boylan's design also lacks an indigenous feedback loop that, in Clowes's model, makes provision for 'evaluating the evaluation.' Finally, tied tightly as it is to internal program goals, Boylan's model fails to capitalize on opportunities for incorporating potentially useful data as might be externally derived, e.g., by the professional judgement approach.

Because of its comparative sophistication and initial independence from internal program goals, the Clowes model takes longer to execute—indeed, it theoretically could be run indefinitely. It demands vigorous execution, and its potential for the redundant could render it hopelessly cumbersome. Nevertheless, it is this writer's contention that the greatest strength of the Clowes design derives from its realistic approach. Compensating for the ambiguity of the educational process, Clowes eloquently and correctly advocates measuring program effectiveness against evolving, consensual goals rather than against the a priori goals of some heuristic model that is assumed to be both shared and understood by all concerned parties. (p. 4)

Institutions are often faced with the difficulty of determining where a remediation program actually exists. There is some evidence that the emphasis even in community colleges is shifting from identifiable programs functioning as discrete instructional units to remediation through assignment of students to designated courses and laboratory activities (Fidale and Winter, 1985). This development makes data gathering difficult and compromises the ability of an institution to use most evaluation models. A promising recent development has been the development of computer software to track students through sequences of designated courses (Hamilton, 1989). This offers the potential for automating an evaluation system using student transcript records as the basic data source.

The accountability movement in education generally has led to increased state attention to assessment and to the assessment of remediation programs. Piland (1983) conducted a nationwide study of state level assessment activities surveying state directors of community/junior colleges as they represented the institutional type most associated with remediation. There was little evidence of agreement among states on the definitions, funding, or location of remediation efforts. There was no indication of common assessment plans or procedures. New Jersey is unique among the states in developing a series of subject area tests, requiring they be administered to all students entering state institutions, and then using the data for assessment of remediation efforts (New Jersey Basic Skills Council, 1986). Texas established the Texas Academic Skills Program (TSAP) in 1988 mandating testing of all students entering public colleges and universities, placement in remedial programs for students with skill deficiencies, and institutional reporting of the results of the remediation programs. Other states have indirect measures of remediation. Florida has employed the College Level Academic Skills Test (CLAST) for entering freshmen and rising college juniors while The Georgia University System uses the Regent's Testing Program in the sophomore year as a "competency" measure.

Cost is a major barrier to establishing statewide assessment programs (Potter, 1986), as are higher education's traditions of autonomous operation in curricular areas and the politics of most states. While states may require some assurance of student progress at the institutional level, there is little evidence of a widespread movement to impose specific assessment models on higher education. Until institutional measures of student success are in place, it will be very difficult for states to require a separate assessment of a function as diffused as remediation. All the problems inherent in statewide institution-based assessment exist and are compounded by efforts to find common measures and criteria for remediation across multiple institutions. That is a formidable task.

Effects Upon Institutions.
There is a slowly emerging awareness that remediation programs have an effect upon the institutions in which they function. The generalization that bringing significant numbers of new kinds of students into an institution will gradually change the nature of the student body and eventually the institution is one most can accept at face value. However, more subtle influences have been identified. Richardson, Fisk, and Okun (1983) conducted an in-depth observation of instructional practices at an open-access institution. They identified accommodation of the students who lacked basic skills as a major force changing the curriculum. Instruction became a process of reducing material to manageable "bites" of information communicated with a minimum of reading or writing required. Learning became a process of information gathering and then regurgitation. The authors described a gradual "dumbing down" of the curriculum and the emergence of "functional literacy" as the norm at the institution rather than "academic literacy." They went further and described the impact upon support services and administrative practices of an institution so enrollment driven that it recruits and admits students unable to function at reasonable levels of literacy and numeracy. At one level this is a description of what could occur at an institution without a remedial program to protect the institution and its curriculum from the impact of underprepared students. At another level this study is a warning of the impact a critical mass of underprepared students can have upon the core functions, the curriculum and academic support systems, of an institution if they are ignored or poorly addressed. At the least, the Richardson, Fisk, and Okun study validates the belief that students can affect their institutions just as much as institutions can affect their students.

This concern for the effect of significant numbers of students who must undergo remediation before they enter the mainstream curriculum is echoed by McGrath and Spear (1987), who argue that differing uses of literacy caused by large numbers of underprepared students are changing the nature of community colleges and making them distinct from other forms of higher education. They argue that remediation efforts are themselves part of the problem, since they reduce literacy within the institution.

> Put crudely, the appearance of large numbers of underprepared students in the class-rooms of traditional academic disciplines has led traditional academics more and more frequently to mimic the practices and vocabulary of remedial/developmental programs which suggests either a mechanical ''skills'' orientation or a social service mission aimed at individual affective development. (p. 17)

> The consequences for the institution are that the norms of literate activity are rene-gotiated downward, ultimately altering the entire intellectual climate of the school. (p. 19)

This represents an extension of the argument developed by Richardson, Fisk, and Okun (1983) and is a warning of the negative effects open-access and remediation programs can have upon an institution if they come to be a dominant characteristic of the institution and of its culture. The culture of an institution has itself become a legitimate object of study (Kuh, 1988; London, 1978; Tierney, 1989). Questions about the culture of a remedial program and its effects upon the culture of the institution, however, have only begun to be raised and have not been investigated in any depth. If remedial programs are to be with us, these become significant projects.

A different perspective on the effects of remediation programs upon institu-tions is offered by Brint and Karabel (1989). They argue that the community college, in the ideal if not always in fact, serves to break down the segmentation of higher education into a hierarchy of types of institutions, provides opportunity for student movement or ''permeability'' across institutional types, and allows multiple opportunities for entry to higher education. They argue this ''classless-ness'' in higher education is essential to maintaining an ideology of an open and democratic society. This argument can be extended beyond the community col-lege to encompass all open-access institutions. Unmentioned in the article but essential to its conclusions is the existence of remediation programs that are successful. In this perspective remediation efforts and the students they support impact not only on the institution but on the society beyond the institution. Extremely little research has been done in these areas. Significant issues are involved and need to be addressed, including the effects of participating in remediation programs on student aspirations and attitudes, and the curricular and career patterns available to and followed by remedial students.

Effects Upon Students.
There has been little research on the effect of remedial programs on their stu-dents. There are anecdotal stories about student successes, but systematic study is scant. How do students react to being involved in remedial programs? What

attitudes and beliefs are reinforced? How do these students experience the culture of the institution and is it a different culture than the non-remedial student experiences? To some extent these questions require the use of qualitative research methods for reasonable answers. However, they also represent a shift in attention away from programmatic and instructional issues toward issues involving the impact of the programs upon individual students or categories of students.

Weil (1986) has modeled an interesting approach. One type of learner, the delayed entry adult, was studied in depth to understand the constructs that might be useful in better understanding how these learners experience higher education. This grounded theory approach generated questions for further study and provided new ways to understand higher education and its effects. In another study by Vandett (1985) a particular category of remedial student in a community college—white females over 25 who had dropped out—were studied through life histories, and hypotheses were generated. Weis (1985) has studied institutional culture and demonstrated the stresses created for the student and the institution when the match is poor. Recently Kempner (1990) used a case study based on interviews with "critical cases" to develop an understanding of the culture of an institution. While the research focused on identifying the faculty culture, the method could be useful in developing insight into the culture of remediation programs and into the world of the students and faculty involved. Rose (1989) provides a moving example of the power of autobiographic work; he provides insight into the world of both the student and the faculty member in remediation programs. This work illustrates the potential of both autobiography and biography as tools to understand the special worlds within remediation.

Public Policy

The national education agenda stresses quality in elementary, secondary, and higher education. Federal student loan programs support access to higher education for the economically disadvantaged, and federal legislation in support of the handicapped may soon bring significant numbers of the handicapped through secondary school and into higher education. Most support continues for programs for special populations. However, there is no clear federal level imperative for remediation. States are also concerned with academic quality and are more conscious of the other side of the coin—remediation. Whether remediation will exist in a state's higher education system is not an issue. Given the quality of public schooling and the needs of students entering higher education, remediation is needed. There are, however, some efforts to shift responsibility for remediation in higher education from the colleges and universities to the community colleges (Piland, 1983). This appears to be a matter of economics and status rather than a research-informed issue. Kulik, Kulik, and Shwalb (1983) found more success for remediation in four-year over two-year colleges. A study by Bock (1990) found no difference by institutional type. It would appear the issue of where remediation ought take place is one which deserves further study before policy is set.

If remediation is to be successful, adequate funding is needed. Piland (1983) surveyed the states and found wide variation in financial support for remediation. If small classes and individualized instruction and support are to be employed, remediation must be funded at a rate in excess of standard academic courses. That is not now the case. Before decisions are made about the level of funding for remediation, studies of the investment necessary to bring students to levels of success in higher education ought be done. These studies would be dependent upon the development of assessment models that could yield quantifiable measures of student success against which cost analyses could be run. This is yet to be done. For an institution, perhaps the starting point ought be institutional research focused on specific remediation programs and specific categories of remedial students. From a statewide perspective, the issue of whether remediation is most effective or efficient delivered at the elementary, middle, secondary, or postsecondary level is a logical starting place.

CONCLUSIONS

Remediation has been an issue in American higher education since Colonial days, but the nature and the object of the activity has continuously evolved. Remediation in the Period of Aristocracy was a pre-collegiate activity devoted to skill building. The Period of Meritocracy maintained the skill-building emphasis but also saw remediation serve to support expanded access to higher education. The Period of Egalitarianism carried both these functions forward and added a concern for the full development of the student and an expanded access function. It is unclear whether the ideology of the Period of Egalitarianism has continued. Skill building seems the primary purpose of remediation currently, and the hoped for changes in the institutions to better accommodate non-traditional students have not happened on the scale anticipated. There appears to be a stratification occurring among institutions of higher education with the community colleges assuming higher education's primary responsibility for providing access and remediation. Remediation is recognized as an important function, but it has not achieved full legitimation. It still exists on the margins of the higher education enterprise. It is further marginalized by attempts to consign it to the community college.

Research on remediation has been hampered by a lack of serious attention from higher education scholars. Most of the research has been done by researchers associated primarily with the community college. That research has been descriptive and defensive in nature. Descriptive research was needed to build a base of knowledge; defensive research was done to support remediation as a function and to defend its place in higher education. Defensive research did help maintain and support the place of remediation in higher education; it did little to advance our understanding of the programs and their effects. The larger research agendas in higher education have not been applied consistently to remediation or to the community colleges and open-access four-year institutions in which it is primarily located. Conversely, neither remediation programs nor open-access institutions have been included in most research on higher education. Studies of environmental press, student development, enrollment models, and of attrition have been developed in large, usually selective, residential universities and seldom applied to the open-access institutions and to remediation.

There are signs of change, and that bodes well for our understanding of remediation. Cross (1976) began the process of defining the remedial student. We now are able to identify a number of sub-groups with the remedial label that need to be studied separately. Specific minorities, older students, foreign students, low aptitude and low achievement students, high or average aptitude and low achievement students, physically handicapped students and those with learning disabilities all warrant independent consideration. Our failure to disaggregate these students in studies has confounded our findings for some time. Institutional and program variables must be controlled for in a similar fashion. These steps will allow us to employ multivariate designs. Wolfle (1985) cautions against the inherent limitations of multivariate research designs—particularly about the need for theory to guide causal modeling. This is where theories developed from general higher education research need to be applied to open-access institutions and to remediation programs. Nora (1990) represents an example of this approach; he used multivariate analysis to apply theory from the retention research in higher education to Hispanics in a community college setting. Additional work of this sort will contribute greatly to our knowledge of the factors which influence success in remediation and the relationships among them.

Our understanding of the effects of remediation programs upon the students and faculty within them and upon the institutions that house them is limited. More needs to be known. Naturalistic inquiry offers hope for the beginnings of understanding. Several studies have been done; more need to be done. Case studies and ethnographies can provide the hypotheses to fuel additional research about program effects. Remediation is a complex area within the curriculum of higher education. It is multifaceted and warrants careful research from both the qualitative and quantitative perspective.

Stage (1990) credits Kenneth Feldman (1989) with the observation that dissatisfaction and persistence are the essential characteristics of the research enterprise. As students of remediation in higher education we must be dissatisfied with the state of the field, its research models, and its assessment techniques. More than that, however, we must be persistent. We must persist in connecting research on remediation to research in the balance of higher education. We must persist in developing and testing better hypotheses to explain the phenomena we observe, and we must persist in being dissatisfied with remediation as practiced so we may continue to improve upon what we do and know.

REFERENCES

Abraham, A.A., Jr. (1987). *Readiness for college: Should there be statewide placement standards?* (A Report on College-Level Remedial/Developmental Programs in SREB States.) Atlanta, GA: Southern Regional Education Board. (ERIC Document Reproduction Service No. ED 280 369).

Akst, G., and Hecht, M. (1980). Program evaluation. In A.S. Trillin (ed.), *Teaching Basic Skills in College.* San Francisco: Jossey-Bass.

Anderson, W.W. (1973, November). *Evaluation of college reading and study skills programs.* Paper presented at the annual meeting of the College Reading Association, Silver Springs, MD. (ERIC Document Reproduction Service No. ED 084 514)

Apple, M. (1979). *Ideology and Curriculum.* Boston: Routledge and Kegan Paul.

Aronowitz, S., and Giroux, H. (1985). *Education Under Siege: The Conservative, Liberal and Radical Debate Over Schooling.* South Hadley, MA: Bergin and Garvey.

Association of American Colleges. (1985). *Integrity in the College Curriculum.* Washington, DC: Association of American Colleges.

Astin, A.W. (1977). *Four Critical Years.* San Francisco: Jossey-Bass.

Basonic, N. (1982). The academic performance and persistence pattern of a selected group of developmental students at Harrisburg Area Community College. (Doctoral dissertation, University of Pennsylvania). Dissertation Abstracts International, 43, 640-A.

Beckett, G. (1985). Developmental education: A definition. Portsmouth, OH: Shawnee State Community College. (ERIC Document Reproduction Service No. ED 258 635)

Bennett, W.J. (1984). *To Reclaim a Legacy: A Report on the Humanities in Higher Education.* Washington, DC: National Endowment for the Humanities.

Blanton, W.E., and Bullock, T. (1973). Cognitive style and reading behavior. *Reading World* 12: 276–287.

Bock, D. (1990). An assessment of how selected two- and four-year sectors of higher education are contributing to the progress of high risk students. (Doctoral dissertation, Virginia Polytechnic Institute and State University, 1989). Dissertation Abstracts International, 50, 1908A.

Boylan, H.R. (1985). Reviewing learning styles inventories: The Canfield and Kolb LSIs. *Research in Developmental Education* 3: 1–6.

Boylan, H.R. (1986a). Models of student development: Part I. *Research in Developmental Education* 3(4): 1–3.

Boylan, H.R. (1986b). Models of student development: Part II. *Research in Developmental Education.* 3(5): 1–3.

Boylan, H.R. (1986c). Theoretical foundations of developmental education. *Research in Developmental Education.* 3(3): 1–6.

Brier, E. (1984). Controversy of the underprepared student at Vassar College and Cornell University, 1965–90. Paper presented at the meeting of the Association for the Study of Higher Education in Chicago, Illinois, 1984. (ERIC Document Reproduction Service No. ED 245 600)

Brint, S., and Karabel, J. (1989). American education, meritocratic ideology, and the legitimation of inequality: The community college and the problem of American exceptionalism. *Higher Education, 18:* 725–735.

Brown, W.C. (1982). College learning assistance: A developmental concept. *Journal of College Student Personnel*. 23: 395–401.

Brubacher, J.S., and Rudy, W. (1976). *Higher Education in Transition: A History of American Colleges and Universities 1636–1976*. Third Edition. New York: Harper and Row.

Cahalan, M., and Others. (1986). College Level Remediation. Fast Response Survey System Report No. 19. (Report No. CS-86–218) Washington, DC: Center for Statistics (OERI/ED). (ERIC Document Reproduction Service No. ED 274 290).

Canfield, J.H. (1889). *The Opportunities of the Rural Population for Higher Education*. Nashville, TN: National Council on Education.

Carnegie Foundation for the Advancement of Teaching. (1977). *Missions of the College Curriculum*. San Francisco: Jossey-Bass.

Cohen, A.M., and Brawer, F.B. (1982). *The American Community College*. San Francisco: Jossey-Bass.

Clowes, D.A. (1979). Form and function. *Journal of Developmental and Remedial Education*. 3(2–3): 13.

Clowes, D.A. (1980). More than a definitional problem: Remedial, compensatory, and developmental education. *Journal of Developmental and Remedial Education*. 4: 8–10.

Clowes, D.A. (1981). Evaluation methodologies for Learning Assistance Programs. In C.C. Walvekar (ed.), New Directions for College Learning Assistance Centers: *Assessment of Learning Assistance Services*. (No. 5). San Francisco: Jossey-Bass.

Clowes, D.A. (1984). The evaluation of remedial/developmental programs: A stage model of program evaluation. *Journal of Developmental Education* 8(14–15): 27–30.

Clowes, D.A., Hinkle, D.E., and Smart, J.C. (1986). Enrollment patterns in postsecondary education, 1960–1982. *Journal of Higher Education* 57: 121–133.

Clowes, D.A., and Towles, D. (1985). Community and junior college journal: Lessons from fifty years. *Community, Technical, and Junior College Journal* 56: 28–32.

Creamer, D.G. (ed.) (1980). *Student Development in Higher Education: Theories, Practices and Future Directions*. (ACPA Media Publication Number 27). Cincinnati, OH: American College Personnel Association.

Cronbach, L.J., and Snow, R.E. (1977). *Aptitude and Instructional Methods: A Handbook for Research on Interactions*. New York: Irvington.

Cross, K.P. (1971). *Beyond the Open Door: New Students in Higher Education*. San Francisco: Jossey-Bass.

Cross, K.P. (1976). *Accent on Learning*. San Francisco: Jossey-Bass.

Davis J.A. (1975). *The Impact of Special Services programs for Disadvantaged Students*. Princeton, NJ: Educational Testing Service.

Dressel, P.L. (1976). *Handbook of Educational Evaluation*. San Francisco: Jossey-Bass.

Dunbar, W. (1935). Public versus private control of higher education in Michigan, 1817–1855. *Mississippi Valley Historical Review* 22: 390–392.

Eliot, C.W. (1869). *A Turning Point in Higher Education: The Inaugural Address of Charles William Eliot as President of Harvard College, October 19, 1869*. Cambridge: Harvard University Press.

Enright, G., and Kerstiens, G. (1980). The learning center: Towards an expanded role. In O. Lennings and R. Nayman (eds.), *New Roles for Learning Assistance*. San Francisco: Jossey-Bass.

Evans, H.M., and Dubois, E.E. (1972). Community/junior college remedial programs—reflections. *Journal of Reading* 16: 38–45.

Fairweather, J.S., and Shaver D.M. (1990). A troubled future? Participation in postsecondary education by youths with disabilities. *Journal of Higher Education* 61: 332–348.

Feldman, K. (1989, November). College students: Choice and success. Remarks for research paper session at the annual meeting of the Association for the Study of Higher Education, Atlanta, GA.

Fidale, L.M., and Winter, G.H. (1985, April). Summary paper: Assessing the effectiveness of developmental/remedial programs in two year colleges. Paper presented at the annual conference of the American Educational Research Association, Chicago, IL.

Fincher, C. (1985). Learning theory and research. In J.C. Smart (ed.), *Higher Education: Handbook of Theory and Research.* Vol 1. New York: Agathon Press.

Finn, C.E. (1984). Trying American higher education: An eight count indictment. *Change* 16: 28–33, 47–51.

Grant, M.K., and Hoeber, D. (1978). *Basic Skills Programs: Are They Working?* Washington, DC: ERIC Clearinghouse on Higher Education.

Griffin, J.M. (1980). Underprepared students in community colleges: Common personality and biographical characteristics. *Community College Review* 8: 15–19.

Grubb, W.N. (1991). The decline of community college transfer rates. *Journal of Higher Education* 62, 194–222.

Guba, E.G., and Lincoln, Y.S. (1981). *Effective Evaluation: Improving the Usefulness of Evaluation Results Through Responsive and Naturalistic Approaches.* San Francisco: Jossey-Bass.

Hamilton, J.M. (1989). *Assessing Academic Progress in Sequenced Courses.* Gainesville, GA: Gainesville College, Office of Institutional Research.

House, E.R. (1978). Assumptions underlying evaluation models. *Educational Researcher* 7: 4–12.

Irn-Nejad, A., McKeachie, W.J., and Berliner, D.C. (eds.) (1990). Toward a unified approach to learning as a multisource phenomena [Special issue]. *Review of Educational Research* 60: 4.

Jensen A. (1969). How much can we boost I.Q.? *Harvard Educational Review* 39: 1–124.

Kempner, K. (1990). Faculty culture in the community college: Facilitating or hindering learning? *Review of Higher Education* 13: 215–236.

Klingelhofer, E.L., and Hollander, L. (1973). *Educational Characteristics and Needs of New Students: A Review of the Literature.* Berkeley, CA: Center for Research and Development in Higher Education, University of California.

Kuh, G. (1988). *Invisible Tapestry: Culture in American Colleges and Universities* (ASHE-ERIC Higher Education Report No. 1.) Washington, DC: Association for the Study of Higher Education.

Kuh, G.D., Bean, J.P, Bradley, R.K., Coomes, M.D., and Hunter, D.E. (1986). Changes in research on college students published in selected journals between 1969 and 1983. *Review of Higher Education* 9: 177–192.

Kulik, C.L., Kulik, J.A., and Shwalb, B.J. (1983). College programs for high- risk and disadvantaged students: A meta-analysis of findings. *Review of Educational Research* 53: 397–414.

Lederman, M.J., Ryzewic, S.R., and Ribaudo, M. (1983 September). *Assessment and Improvement of the Academic Skills of Entering Freshmen: A National Survey.* (Research Monograph Series, report No. 5). New York: City University of New York. (ERIC Document Reproduction Service No. ED 238 973).

Lombardi, J. (1979). Four phases of developmental education. (ERIC Junior College Resource Review). Los Angeles: ERIC Clearinghouse for Junior Colleges. (ERIC Document Reproduction Service No. 165858)

London, H.B. (1978). *The Culture of a Community College*. New York: Praeger.

Losak, J.G. (1972). Do remedial programs really work? *The Personnel and Guidance Journal* 50: 383– 386.

Losak, J.G., Jefferson, T, and Sutton, C. (1969). Psychological characteristics of the academically underprepared student. Miami, FL: Miami-Dade Junior College. (ERIC Document Reproduction Service No. ED 041 577)

Maxwell, M. (1979). *Improving Student Learning Skills: A Comprehensive Guide to Successful Practices and Programs for Increasing the Performance of Underprepared Students*. San Francisco: Jossey-Bass.

McGrath, D., and Spear, M.B. (1987). The politics of remediation. In K.M. Ahrendt (ed.), New Directions for Community Colleges: *Teaching the Developmental Student* (No. 57). San Francisco: Jossey-Bass.

Messick, S., and Associates. (1976). *Individuality in Learning: Implications of Cognitive Styles and Creativity for Human Development*. San Francisco:Jossey-Bass.

Miller, T.K., and Prince, J.S. (1978). *The Future of Student Affairs: A Guide to Student Development for Tomorrow's Higher Education*. San Francisco: Jossey-Bass.

Moore, W., Jr. (1983). Special roles with special students. In A. S. Thurston and W. A. Robbins (eds.), New Directions for Community Colleges: *Counseling: A Critical Function for the 1980s* (No. 43). San Francisco: Jossey-Bass.

Moore, W., Jr. (1970). *Against the Odds: The High-Risk Student in the Community College*. San Francisco: Jossey-Bass.

Morante, E.A., Faskow, S., and Menditti, I.N. (1984a). The New Jersey basic skills assessment program, Part I. *Journal of Developmental and Remedial Education* 7(2): 2–4, 32.

Morante, E.A., Faskow, S., and Menditti, I.N. (1984b). The New Jersey basic skills assessment program, Part II. *Journal of Developmental and Remedial Education* 7(3): 6–9, 32.

Morris, C., and Losak, J. (1986). *Student Success at Miami-Dade Community College: Issues and Data*. (Research Report No. 86–22). Miami, FL: Miami-Dade Community College, Office of Institutional Research.

Morrison, J.L., and Ferrente, R. (1973). *Compensatory Education in the Two-Year College*. University Park, PA: Center for the Study of Higher Education.

New Jersey Basic Skills Council. (1986). *Effectiveness of Remedial Programs in New Jersey Public Colleges and Universities*. Trenton, NJ: New Jersey Department of Higher Education.

Nora, A. (1990). Campus-based aid programs as determinants of retention among Hispanic community college students. *Journal of Higher Education* 61: 312–331.

Olivas, M.A. (1979). *The Dilemma of Access: Minorities in Two Year Colleges*. Washington, DC: Howard University Press.

Parker, C.A. (ed.) (1978). *Encouraging Development in College Students*. Minneapolis: University of Minnesota Press.

Piland, W. (1983). *Remedial Education in the States*. Normal, IL: National Council of State Directors of Community/Junior Colleges. (ERIC Document Reproduction Service No. ED 251 160)

Posey, E.J. (1984). Learning styles inventory: Implementation research. *Journal of Developmental Education* 7: 16–18.

Potter, D.L. (1986). *The Measurement of Student Achievement and the Assurance of Quality in Virginia Higher Education*. Richmond, VA: State Council of Higher Education for Virginia.

Rabianski-Carriuolo, R. (1989). Learning styles: An interview with Edmond W. Gordon. *Journal of Developmental Education* 13: 18–20, 22.

Reynolds, J. (1969). *The Comprehensive Junior College Curriculum*. Berkeley, CA: McCutchan Publishing Corporation.

Richardson, R.C., Jr., and Bender, L.W. (1985). *Students in Urban Settings: Achieving the Baccalaureate Degree*. (ASHE-ERIC Research Report No. 6) Washington, DC: Association for the Study of Higher Education.

Richardson, R.C., Jr., Fisk, E.C, and Okun, M.A. (1983). *Literacy in the Open-Access College*. San Francisco: Jossey-Bass.

Richardson, R., Martens, K., and Fisk, E. (1981). *Functional Literacy in the College Setting*. (ASHE-ERIC Research Report No. 3.) Washington, DC: Association for the Study of Higher Education.

Rose, M. (1989). *Lives on the Boundary: The Struggles and Achievements of America's Underprepared*. New York: The Free Press.

Ross, E.P., and Roe, B.D. (1986). *The Case for Basic Skills Programs in Higher Education*. (Fastback 238.) Bloomington, IN: Phi Delta Kappa. (ERIC Document Reproduction Service No. ED 273 166)

Roueche, J. E. (1968). *Salvage, Redirection or Custody? Remedial Education in the Community and Junior College*. Washington, DC: American Association of Junior Colleges.

Roueche, J.E. (1984). *Literacy Needs and Development in American Community Colleges*. Washington, DC: National Institute of Education. (ERIC Document reproduction Service No. 240 291)

Roueche, J.E., and Baker, G.A. (1987). *Access and Excellence: The Open-Door College*. Washington, DC: The Community College Press.

Roueche, J.E., Baker, G.A., and Roueche, S.D. (1984). *College Responses to Low-Achieving Students: A National Study*. Orlando, FL: Media Systems Corporation.

Roueche, J. E., and Kirk, R. W. (1973). *Catching Up: Remedial Education*. San Francisco: Jossey-Bass.

Roueche, J. E., and Snow, J.J. (1977). *Overcoming Learning Problems: A Guide to Developmental Education in College*. San Francisco: Jossey-Bass.

Rudolph, F. (1977). *Curriculum: A History of the American Undergraduate Course of Study Since 1636*. San Francisco: Jossey-Bass.

Shor, I. (1986). *Culture Wars: School and Society in the Conservative Restoration 1969–1984*. New York: Routledge and Kegan Paul.

Somers, R.L. (1987a). Evaluation of developmental education programs: Issues, problems, and techniques. *Research in Developmental Education* 4: 1–6.

Somers, R.L. (1987b). *Issues, Problems, and Techniques in Program Evaluation*. Boone, NC: The Telementoring Project, Reich College of Education, Appalachian State University.

Southern Regional Education Board. (1985a). *Access to Quality Undergraduate Education, A Report to the Southern Regional Education Board by Its Commission for Educational Quality*. Atlanta, GA: Southern Regional Education Board.

Southern Regional Education Board. Commission for Educational Quality. (1985b). *Improving Teacher Education: An Agenda for Higher Education*. (A Report). Atlanta, GA: Southern Regional Education Board.

Stage, F.K. (1990). Research on college students: Commonality, difference, and direction. *Review of Higher Education* 13: 249–258.

Study Group on the Conditions of Excellence in American Higher Education. (1984).

Involvement in Learning: Realizing the Potential of American Higher Education. Washington, DC: National Institute of Education.

Sullivan, L.L. (1980). Growth and influence of the learning center movement. In K.V. Lauridsen (ed.), New Directions for College Learning Assistance: *Examining the Scope of Learning Centers.* (No. 1). San Francisco: Jossey-Bass.

Tierney W.G. (1989). *Curricular Landscapes, Democratic Vistas: Transformative Leadership in Higher Education.* New York: Praeger.

Tomlinson, L.M. (1989). *Postsecondary Developmental Programs: A Traditional Agenda with New Imperatives.* (ASHE-ERIC Higher Education Report No. 3.) Washington, DC: Association for the Study of Higher Education.

Trillin, A.S., and Associates. (1980). *Teaching Basic Skills in College: A Guide to Objectives, Skills Assessment, Course Content, Teaching Methods, Support Services, and Administration.* San Francisco: Jossey-Bass.

Trow, M. A. (1982–83). Underprepared students at public research universities. In Cross, K.P. (ed.), Current Issues in Higher Education: No. 1. *Underprepared Learners* (pp.16–26). Washington, DC: American Association for Higher Education.

Turner, R. (1960). Sponsored and contest mobility and the school system. *The American Sociological Review* 25, 855–867.

Vandett, N. (1985). A naturalistic investigation of women's decisions to leave school: applications of three theories to community college attrition. (Doctoral dissertation, Virginia Polytechnic Institute and State University, 1985). Dissertation Abstracts International, 46, 2172–A.

Weil, S.W. (1986). Non-traditional learners within traditional higher education institutions: discovery and disappointments. *Studies in Higher Education* 11: 219–235.

Weis, L. (1985). *Between Two Worlds: Black Students in an Urban Community College.* Boston: Routledge and Kegan Paul.

Wolfle, L.M. (1985). Applications of causal models in higher education. In Smart, J.C. (ed.). *Higher Education: Handbook of Theory and Research*, Vol. 1. New York: Agathon Press.

Wright, D.A., and Cahalan, M.W. (1985, April). Remedial/developmental studies in institutions of higher education: Policies and practices 1984. Paper presented at the annual conference of the American Educational Research Association, Chicago, IL. (ERIC Document Reproduction Service No. ED 263 828).

Wyatt, P., and Clowes, D. (1982, December). Report from research and evaluation committee: Characteristics of the 'New Student' in higher education. National Association for Remedial/Developmental Studies in Post-Secondary Education Newsletter. pp. 1, 4.

Author Index

Abraham, A.A., 76, 462, 464, 468
Abrahams, N. (Kanun),* 418, 419, 426-428,
    445, 446, 452
Abrami, P.C., 146, 149, 169, 170, 172,
    174, 175, 177, 178, 187, 190, 194,
    200, 209, 210, 212, 218-220
Adelman, C., 61, 70, 432, 447, 451
Agresti, A., 383, 399
Ahlgren, A., 379
Ahumada, M.M., 103
Aitkin, M., 397
Akst, G., 480
Aldrich, J.H., 382, 383, 386
Aleamoni, L.M., 144, 182, 191, 203, 212
Alexander, J.C., 89, 124
Allaire, Y., 6
Allen, J.L., 423, 427, 431, 438, 447, 449,
    452
Allport, F., 45, 241
Alperstein, G.S., 277
Alpert, D., 55
Altbach, P.G., 95
Althusser, L., 126
Amemiya, T., 383, 393
Andersen, C.J., 39, 236, 248, 251-255, 257,
    262-264, 266, 268, 269, 275, 276,
    279, 282, 283, 285, 286, 288, 289,
    291, 293
Anderson, D., 382, 383, 397
Anderson, R.C. (McAllister), 369, 370, 415
Anderson, S., 382, 383, 394
Angelo, T., 60, 479
Anker, A.L. (Griffith), 369
Anthony, R., 38
Apple, M., 466
Argyris, C., 5, 21
Armstrong, E.C. (Blackburn), 421, 422,
    426, 431, 436, 441-443, 446, 449,
    450, 453

Armstrong, J.
Aronowitz, S., 466, 477
Astin, A.W., 37, 40, 43, 51, 53, 60-62,
    71-73, 236, 265, 266, 279-282, 312,
    314, 316, 472
Athos, A.G., 6
Attinasi, Jr., L.C., 305
Aubrect, J.D., 190, 199
Auquier, A. (Anderson), 382, 383, 394
Austin, J.T., 258, 382, 418, 423, 424, 426,
    428, 452
Austin, L., 44
Austin, T.L., 423, 424, 426, 453
Ausubel, D.P., 450
Averch, H.A., 94

Bacharach, S.B., 11
Bahrick, H.P., 415
Bailey, M., 165
Baird, L.L., 282-284
Baker, J.A.W., 277, 279
Baldridge, J.V., 11, 14
Ball, D.A., 275
Banning, C.S., 352
Banta, T., 53
Bare, A., 72
Barker, L.L., 275, 278, 280
Barnard, C.I., 7
Barnes, J., 162, 163
Barrett, W., 3
Barrow, C.W., 86, 132-134, 305
Basonic, N., 480
Basow, S.A., 204, 205
Bateman, G., 69
Batista, E.E., 193, 203, 204
Batson, C.D., 9
Bauer, B., 270
Baughman, G.W., 290
Baughman, J.C., 354
Bayer, A.E., 351, 356, 368, 370, 371
Bean, J.P., 67 (Hossler), 463 (Kuh)
Beatty, W.W., 147
Becher, T., 48, 55, 59

Subject Index

A

Academia, and the state, 85–86
Academic culture, 7
Academic discipline
  and effectiveness ratings, 205–207
  intensive course research by, 426–30
Academic freedom
  effect of collegiality, 8
  and government, 91
  and organizational control, 55–56
  and the state, 93
  students, 101
Academic program design, 68–69
Academic quality, 37–39. *See also* Outcomes
  analysis methods, 62, 64–66
  costs, 74
  definition, 39
  fundamental conflicts, 55–59
  in intensive courses, 431–32
  intensive courses and, 440–41
  management framework, 60–67
  measurement systems, 71–72
  rankings, 39
  and remedial education 485
  research agenda, 72
  variations in, 68
Academic senate, 22
Academic tenure. *See* Tenure
Academic variance, history of, 47–54
Accountability
  by academic institutions, 59
  and remedial education, 479, 482
Accounting, reputational rankings, 275
Accreditation, development, 51
Achievement tests, reliability, 175–76
Administrators, authority sharing, 19
Adult education, 411
  learning theories in, 154
  remedial, 470–71, 485
Affirmative action, 91
  case law and, 100
Agricultural rankings, reputational, 274

Agriculture, U.S. Department of, 131
Alienation, of ethnic minority students, 320–26
Allocated time, 417
Allport, Gordon, 241
Alumni
  research on, 69–70
  teaching evaluation by, 158–59
Ambiguity, zones of, 29
American Association of Collegiate Schools of Business, 274
American Association of Community and Junior Colleges, 463, 467
American Council on Education
  graduate school rankings, 239–40
  reputational rankings, 251
American Journal of Sociology, 128–30
American Political Science Association, 246
American Psychology Association, 254
American Sociological Review, 130–32
American Sociologist, 266
America's Best Colleges, 271
Andersen, Charles J., 251–55
Anti-positivism, 309
Appalachian State University, 464
Applicability paradigm, 152
Arizona Department of Corrections, 120–22
Art education, reputational rankings, 276
Artists-in-residence programs, 237
Assessment. *See also* Student outcomes;
      Reputational rankings
  Astin program, 61–62
  basic skills, 464, 479
  current practices, 61
  outcome-based, 451
  performance-based, 71
  and quality improvement, 43
  remedial education, 479
  statewide programs, 483
Association of American Colleges
  member rankings, 235
  remedial education, 477
  reputational rankings, 238

507

Contents of Previous Volumes

VOLUME III

Order from:
Agathon Press, c/o Maxway
225 West 34th Street, New York, NY 10001
(212) 947-6100
$54 each volume.